Payroll Accounting 2022

Eighth Edition

Jeanette M. Landin, Ed.D., M.B.A.
Landmark College

Paulette Schirmer, D.B.A., M.B.A.
University of Alaska Southeast

Mc
Graw
Hill

PAYROLL ACCOUNTING 2022, EIGHTH EDITION

Published by McGraw Hill LLC, 1325 Avenue of the Americas, New York, NY 10121. Copyright © 2022 by McGraw Hill LLC. All rights reserved. Printed in the United States of America. Previous editions © 2021, 2020, and 2019. No part of this publication may be reproduced or distributed in any form or by any means, or stored in a database or retrieval system, without the prior written consent of McGraw Hill LLC, including, but not limited to, in any network or other electronic storage or transmission, or broadcast for distance learning.

Some ancillaries, including electronic and print components, may not be available to customers outside the United States.

This book is printed on acid-free paper.

1 2 3 4 5 6 7 8 9 LWI 24 23 22 21

ISBN 978-1-260-72879-8
MHID 1-260-72879-X
ISBN 978-1-264-11211-1 (loose-leaf edition)
MHID 1-264-11211-4 (loose-leaf edition)

Executive Portfolio Manager: *Steve Schuetz*
Product Developers: *Sarah Sacco*
Marketing Manager: *Claire McLemore*
Content Project Managers: *Harvey Yep; Brian Nacik*
Buyer: *Laura Fuller*
Designer: *Beth Blech*
Content Licensing Specialists: *Gina Oberbroeckling*
Cover Image: *Andrew Krasovitckii/Shutterstock*
In-chapter design image credit: *Ralf Hiemisch/Getty Images*
Compositor: *Straive*

All credits appearing on page or at the end of the book are considered to be an extension of the copyright page.

Library of Congress Control Number: 2021913783

About the Authors

©Tom Raffelt

Jeanette Landin

Landmark College
Jeanette Landin is an associate professor of business and accounting at Landmark College in Putney, Vermont, where she teaches undergraduate accounting and business courses to an at-risk student population. She is a baccalaureate student advisor and works with students to prepare them for employment. Dr. Landin earned her BA degree from the University of California at Irvine before receiving her M.B.A and Ed.D. from the University of Phoenix, where she researched college success strategies for at-risk students. She has earned master's certificates in accounting and autism spectrum disorders.

Dr. Landin is an active member of the Institute for Management Accountants (IMA), the American Accounting Association, Teachers of Accounting Curriculum at Two-Year Colleges (TACTYC), the Association of Certified Fraud Examiners (ACFE), and Vermont Women in Higher Education (VWHE). She previously served as an active member of the California Business Educators Association and the Western Business Educators Association. Dr. Landin has served as the IMA's Committee for Academic Relations chair and as a peer reviewer for the American Accounting Association. She is a peer reviewer for the *Transnational Journal of Business* and the Associate Editor for Accounting with the Multimedia Educational Resource for Learning and Online Teaching (MERLOT).

©Ryan Kauzlarich

Paulette Schirmer

University of Alaska Southeast
Paulette Schirmer is an assistant professor of accounting with the University of Alaska Southeast for its accounting courses. She received her BS in accounting from Metropolitan State College of Denver (now Metropolitan State University of Denver), her M.B.A. from Regis University, and her D.B.A. from the University of Phoenix, where she researched globalization strategies for small businesses.

Dr. Schirmer was also recently an accountant with the Division of Finance for the State of Alaska. She worked as the statewide training coordinator and assisted with developing and troubleshooting the accounting program's reporting system. Dr. Schirmer was active in preparing Alaska's Comprehensive Annual Financial Report and assisted with the budgetary implementation, departmental accounting, and structure training.

Dedications

The authors dedicate this book to the following individuals:

For Chris, Kierstan, and Meaghan, who are the center of my universe, and for Dad, who believed in me until the very end.

—Jeanette Landin

For Royce and Elizabeth, who kept me grounded and reminded me to have fun. For Christina, who reminds me to stop and breathe.

—Paulette Schirmer

A Note from the Authors

We are excited to share the new edition of *Payroll Accounting 2022* with you. Payroll accounting is detailed, deadline-driven, and of utmost importance for the successful functioning of a business. The changing, detailed nature of payroll accounting involves legal challenges, economic changes, technological advances, and—above all—governmental obligations. Our text takes a modern approach to payroll accounting, incorporating coverage of real-world issues that many students will face in their careers, such as cybersecurity, payroll fraud, labor planning, and labor costs. We believe that this textbook's information and ancillary materials contribute to a comprehensive understanding of payroll accounting in the 21st century and will make accounting students more valuable to the organizations they work for in their careers.

But as educators, we understand that providing the content is not enough, so we provide multiple opportunities for students to practice in Connect. Whether you are teaching face-to-face, hybrid, or online, *Payroll Accounting 2022* is flexible enough to be used in courses as short as 3 weeks and as long as 15 weeks. We are proud of what we have accomplished with this text, and we thank the faculty and students who have provided feedback to refine the content in this edition. We strongly believe that we have taken payroll accounting education to a higher level of rigor.

Our payroll accounting approach is different from other existing texts because of our perspective about payroll's role in business. To us, payroll is more than pressing buttons, writing checks, and submitting forms—payroll is the story of **people.** These people include the ones within the business who make decisions about the company's directions and the people who work for the business and depend on their paychecks to support their livelihoods. We wrote this text because we wanted students to develop a sense of how business directly affects employees' lives and vice versa.

In light of the COVID-19 pandemic and changes to payroll practices that have emerged in 2020 and 2021, we have included information specific to employees and employers' governmental provisions. We did not wish to overload this edition with what we hope will be temporary changes to payroll practices during the pandemic. However, we wanted to make the information available for students who may encounter workplace issues related to the pandemic in the future.

To foster the connection between business and people, each chapter's introductory story contains recent events involving payroll accounting that highlight the connections among payroll, legislation, business decisions, and people affected by all the decisions made. In Chapter 1 and Chapter 2, we highlighted specific challenges stemming from the shift from employees working in a central location to working from home regarding payroll law and practice on both employees and employers. In Chapter 3, we explored the debate about increasing the minimum wage at the federal level. Chapter 4 explored the effects of the legislative guidance and temporary changes to fringe benefits to both employers and employees, such as the changes to Flexible Spending Accounts. In Chapter 5, we focused on the use of the 2021 Form W-4 and the effects of the employee Social Security tax deferral that occurred in late 2020. We removed the use of the IRS Income Tax Withholding Assistant spreadsheet because the 2021 tax tables were not updated into the tool at the time of publication. In Chapter 6, we explored the CARES Act's effects on employer tax reporting, especially as it pertains to Form 941, which was changed in June 2021 to reflect COVID-related tax reporting needed as of the second quarter of 2021. Finally, our Chapter 7 introduction considers how the shift to cloud-based accounting may affect future accounting practice despite a future return to centralized offices.

What makes this text a modern approach is that we believe that payroll is the connection between financial and managerial accounting. It has everyday connections to businesses, people, and the greater economy in a myriad of ways. Our approach is to encourage students to know the **how** of computing payroll and the **why** because we believe strongly that the future of the accounting profession involves knowledge of both the process and the purpose within the broader scheme of business. We have included materials to demonstrate the integration of payroll in other aspects of both managerial and financial accounting and business operations. Within Appendixes D and E, we have provided information that allows readers to connect their learning about payroll within the context of their own state's legal framework and links to each state's revenue department to facilitate specific learning. We are passionate about college education because we are both accounting faculty, and we bring a wealth of experience in accounting, education, industry, and governmental settings that informs our writing.

Our text features many interesting real-world connections. We've drawn examples from many different disciplines to help make payroll accounting come alive for teachers and students alike. We want to call specific attention to two discussions that are unique to our text: (1) the content in Chapter 6 that explores labor planning for employers (Learning Objectives 6-5 and 6-6) and (2) the discussion in Chapter 7 about the function of labor costs in business and employee benefit reports as strategic tools

(Learning Objectives 7-5 and 7-6). We believe that this information contributes to a comprehensive understanding of payroll accounting in the 21st century. It will make accounting students more valuable as emerging accountants embarking upon their careers.

We strongly believe that payroll accounting needs to be applied, so we provide both a continuing problem, located at the end of each chapter, and a comprehensive problem, located in Appendix A, that may be presented in either three-month or one-month versions. Technological integration of the continuing problem and Appendix A within Connect provides an excellent tool for student learning and faculty assessment of course learning objectives. SmartBook 2.0, LearnSmart, and guided example videos of tax-form completion lead to reinforcement of both concepts and key terminology. We are excited to produce this work through McGraw-Hill because of its top-quality teaching and learning resources available through Connect. Teaching traditional payroll accounting and Internet-based financial accounting via McGraw-Hill's Connect platform for several years has been a wonderful experience for both our students and ourselves.

The AACSB guidelines encourage the achievement of the highest possible standards in business education. We believe that students should understand both how payroll should be completed and how it can be manipulated for personal gain. Payroll fraud continues to be a major source of loss for companies, and it is surprising to find how common it is. We've included examples of the frauds that employees have perpetrated in recent years. According to the Government Accounting Office, payroll fraud of all types, including misclassification of workers, costs the federal government $16 billion annually. We hope that these stories enliven and enrich your class discussions. We've also updated the payroll processing options in Chapter 1 to reflect an accurate representation of the current state of the available technology used by businesses of any size (Learning Objective 1-5). In Chapter 2, we explored situations in which an individual may have multiple employers and changes implemented by the USCIS and the U.S. Department of Health and Human Services for Multistate employers (Learning Objective 2-2). We believe that this information about multiple employers and multistate employees is a growing issue that will challenge employers, especially as payroll employees have been working from remote locations.

Another new piece in this edition is the updated Employee Earnings Register to capture employees' data on Form W-4 and apply it to federal income tax computations. (Learning Objective 5-1). We have updated our section about cryptocurrency as a means of transmitting payroll amounts due. It is important to understand that cryptocurrency as a means of paying employees, while being considered, is a complicated issue because of its connection to the stock market, as opposed to a central bank, as a basis for its value. This topic is evolving. We are certain that we will witness the evolution of payment methods that will involve cryptocurrency in the future as far as regulating its use and protecting employee pay and employer tax remittance.

We continue to rely on our colleagues' guidance, instructor feedback, and student suggestions to keep us grounded and push us to deliver the best possible content. We hope you enjoy reading this book as much as we enjoy writing it!

Jeanette Landin
Paulette Schirmer

Changes to the Eighth Edition

Based on our reviewers' and users' feedback, we have included additional content in this eighth edition of *Payroll Accounting*. During the process of updating the eighth edition content, we clarified the payroll register as to marital status and types of dependents in both Chapter 3 and Chapter 5. We examined the CARES Act and the Payroll Protection Program in Chapter 1. We included a visual tool to assist the students with payroll register understanding in Chapter 3. We added clarification of Social Security taxes computation as the employee approaches the wage base in Chapter 5. We refined garnishment specifics and added a table regarding it to Chapter 5.

We have maintained our content about the available payroll certification exams. A correlation guide is included in Appendix F that aligns the learning objectives in the text with the topics included on payroll certification examinations offered by the National Association of Certified Professional Bookkeepers (NACPB), the American Institute of Professional Bookkeepers (AIPB), and the American Payroll Association (APA).

We appreciate all feedback and user recommendations we have received because they have helped us create a stronger, more complete text. The changes we have made have added clarity, updated information, and additional opportunities for students to demonstrate their understanding of the presented concepts.

The following are specific changes to each chapter.

Chapter 1

In Chapter 1, we updated payroll-related legislation to reflect as many changes as possible before publication. We clarified the differences between the Equal Pay Act of 1963 and the Lilly Ledbetter Act of 2009, including a current example of how the Lilly Ledbetter Act has occurred recently. We added information about the CARES Act and the Payroll Protection Program (PPP), which are still evolving issues, as well as COVID updates from OSHA, especially COBRA coverage as it relates to COVID-related job loss. We clarified the difference between Enterprise and Individual coverage under FLSA to foster student understanding of the law's fine details. We clarified the Affordable Care Act's current status since it was challenged in the courts during 2020. Finally, we extended our ethics discussion to include international laws and ethics.

Chapter 2

Chapter 2 now contains a completed example of a state's new hire reporting form. We clarified the difference between the 20-day state-based new hire reporting requirements and the three-day requirement associated with reporting information on the I-9. We updated the Independent Contractor final rule from 2020 and the working hours per month as reported by the Department of Labor. We updated data about paycard use and the rationale for the expansion of its use. We discussed the trend toward working from home as an outgrowth of COVID and the potential paradigm shift toward hybrid working arrangements.

Chapter 3

Chapter 3 contains two new visuals: One to help students understand the payroll register and the location of the required information, and one to assist with the understanding of the total, prove, and rule process. We updated the Department of Labor ruling about gig economy workers. We adjusted our payroll register format to segregate the employee's marital status and dependents for easier tax computations. We updated the 8 and 80 rule for nurses during the COVID pandemic. We have clarified pay practices for on-call and deceased workers and have added holiday and vacation pay examples using the payroll register.

Chapter 4

We continue to expand the discussion of fringe benefits in Chapter 4. We explored specific fringe benefits that employers have offered during the COVID pandemic. We clarified specific benefits that have recently been offered and may continue after the conclusion of the pandemic.

Chapter 5

Chapter 5 expanded our explanation about using pages three and four of the 2020 (and later) Form W-4 in conjunction with the Federal Income Tax Withholding Assistant spreadsheet. We added clarification to the computation of Social Security tax for employees whose wages approach the annual wage base. We discussed how employees who work from home might be subject to different state and local taxes than they would otherwise have been before

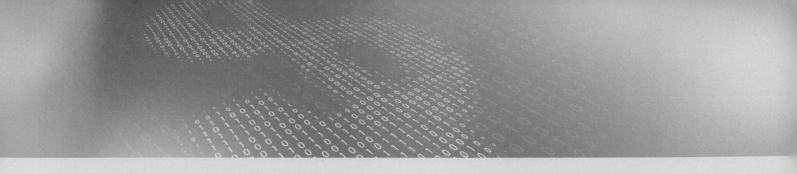

the pandemic because of the change in their primary work location. We added tables to explain garnishment maximums by category.

Chapter 6

In Chapter 6, we explained how the CARES Act provisions affect employer tax due dates in 2021 and 2022. We discussed the changes to tax forms in 2021 and the optional Social Security tax deferral that affected employees in late 2020. We explored the PPP program changes in early 2021 to provide additional relief targeted for small employers.

Chapter 7

Chapter 7 explores the effects of the COVID pandemic on payroll accounting practices. We highlighted how payroll costs could rise despite decreased employment.

Appendix A: Comprehensive Payroll Project

In Appendix A, we continued emphasizing the completion of the payroll register and the transfer of data to both employees' earnings records and accounting entries.

We included the New Hire Report form for Nevada and updated the payroll register to reflect current practices.

Appendix C: Federal Income Tax Tables

We updated both the percentage and the wage-bracket methods of determining federal income tax withholding to reflect the most current tax rates available. We have included both Publication 15 and Publication 15-T in this appendix.

Appendix D: State Income Tax Information

We updated the tax rates for each state in Appendix D.

Appendix F: Payroll Certification Information

We continued correlating the learning objectives in this text with the topics included on payroll certification examinations offered by the National Association of Certified Professional Bookkeepers (NACPB), the American Institute of Professional Bookkeepers (AIPB), and the American Payroll Association (APA). We included the certification exam requirements and contact information for each certification organization.

Text Features

Chapter Opener

Each chapter opens by focusing on a payroll accounting topic related to a real-world company to set the stage for the topic of the chapter.

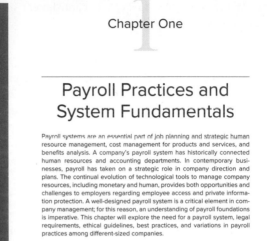

Chapter One

1

Payroll Practices and System Fundamentals

Payroll systems are an essential part of job planning and strategic human resource management, cost management for products and services, and benefits analysis. A company's payroll system has historically connected human resources and accounting departments. In contemporary businesses, payroll has taken on a strategic role in company direction and plans. The continual evolution of technological tools to manage company resources, including monetary and human, provides both opportunities and challenges to employers regarding employee access and private information protection. A well-designed payroll system is a critical element in company management; for this reason, an understanding of payroll foundations is imperative. This chapter will explore the need for a payroll system, legal requirements, ethical guidelines, best practices, and variations in payroll practices among different-sized companies.

LEARNING OBJECTIVES

After studying Chapter 1, you should be able to:

LO 1-1   Identify Legislation That Pertains to Payroll and Business

LO 1-2   Discuss the Legal Framework Specific to Payroll Accounting

Which Law?

Stop & Check

1. Requires employers to verify the employee's legal right to work in the United States?	a. COBRA
2. Protects the rights of disabled workers?	b. ERISA
3. Governs the management of retirement plans?	c. Civil Rights Act of 1991
4. Protects discrimination of workers older than age 40?	d. PRWOR
5. Creates safe work environments for employees?	e. SOX
6. Mandates equal pay for equal work?	f. ADEA
7. Extends medical benefits for terminated employees?	g. HIPAA
8. Ensures that child support obligations will be paid?	h. ADA
9. Protects workers and families with preexisting medical conditions?	i. OSHA
10. Enforces payment of monetary damages because of discrimination?	j. Equal Pay Act of 1963
11. Requires internal controls on payroll practices of public companies?	k. IRCA
	l. SECURE

Stop & Check

The Stop & Check feature allows students to review their understanding of the content just read. It also enables instructors to conduct formative assessments at multiple points throughout each chapter, testing the students' understanding informally as well as offering opportunities to expand on the material.

Trends to Watch

Each chapter contains a feature box that connects payroll-related recent events with industry trends that shape the future of the profession. These trends offer instructors more opportunities to expand upon chapter topics, fostering discussion and application.

Trends to Watch

LEGAL ENVIRONMENT

To say that the legal environment of payroll is continually evolving is an understatement. Since 2017, we have witnessed the following legal challenges:

- Increasing numbers of private employers and localities raise the minimum wage significantly to close the minimum wage gap and the living wage.
- Challenges to the Affordable Care Act related to the overturn of the individual mandate for health care coverage.
- Supplemental wage rate changes for payments of bonuses.
- State enforcement of predictive scheduling, fair/flexible scheduling laws on changing employee's schedules.
- Reframing the federal income tax structure, treatment for nonresident aliens, supplemental wage withholding rates, and inflation adjustments.

Some trends to watch include

- A shift to complete digitalization of payroll processes, including partial or complete remote work options.
- Increased guidance about payroll tax impacts of COVID-19 as it affects employees, both part- and full-time.
- An increase in the need for centralized and fully communicated company policies to meet remote workers' needs.
- Payroll data will increase in importance for business decisions.

End-of-Chapter Assessments

Students can demonstrate their understanding through assessments designed to complement the chapter's learning objectives. Each chapter has review questions, exercises, and problems, with the exercises and problems having two sets each chapter (Set A and Set B). Each type of assessment is designed to measure student learning as follows:

- Questions for review are designed to check for students' remembrance of concepts.
- Exercises check for understanding and application of chapter concepts.
- Problems allow students to apply and analyze payroll accounting principles.

Exercises Set A

E1-1A.
LO 1-1, 1-2
Lupore Fabrics obtained a contract in Watts Mills, South Carolina, that involves the production of materials for military uniforms, a project contracted with the federal government for $2,800,000. What laws govern the wages Lupore Fabrics pays to its workers for this project? (Select all that may apply.)
1. Davis–Bacon Act
2. Sarbanes–Oxley Act
3. Walsh–Healey Act
4. FLSA

E1-2A.
LO 1-1, 1-2
Martine Piccirillo works as the payroll clerk for Centinix, a security company that hires many part-time and temporary workers who are paid hourly. What law governs the hiring or documenting of these workers?
1. ADEA
2. FLSA
3. IRCA
4. USERRA

Critical Thinking Exercises

Want to challenge your students further? The Critical Thinking Exercises require students to consider complex real-world situations that build confidence and turn learning into mastery. These exercises offer possibilities for team presentations or class debate.

Critical Thinking

CT1-1. You have been hired as a Dynozz Medical Software consultant, which is facin[g] IRS audit of its accounting records. During your review, you notice anomali[es] the payroll system involving overpayments of labor and payments to termin[ated] employees. What should you do?

CT1-2. Liliya Milic is the accountant for Syiva, a local nonprofit organization. She [has] been tasked with managing the payroll costs so that staffing levels may re[main] the same even if funding levels change. She considers outsourcing the payr[oll to] a payroll processing company. What are some factors that Liliya should con[sider] in her decision? Why are these factors important?

In the Real World: Scenarios for Discussion

Each chapter contains a discussion scenario that is drawn from real-world events. These scenarios encourage the expansion of chapter content and allow students to apply their learning to real situations.

In the Real World: Scenario for Discussion

Domino's Pizza franchises in New York were sued by the state of New York in 20[ ] wage theft at 10 stores. Under New York law, a corporation and a franchiser ar[e] employers if they meet certain employee control criteria. The state found that Do[mino's] met the criteria for being a joint employer because it mandates a significant number [of pol]icies with which franchisers must comply. The problem arose when Domino's man[dated] the use of PULSE payroll software, which the pizza company knew to be flawed a[nd did] not attempt to remedy. The flawed software led to employees being paid at rates [below] the legal minimum wage, failed to pay overtime, did not reimburse employees for v[ehicle] use, and abused tip credit guidelines.

Internet Activities

The Internet Activities at the end of each chapter offer students the chance to use their web navigation skills to expand on their learning. These exercises attract tech-savvy learners, allowing them to form their own understanding of payroll concepts on their own terms.

Continuing Payroll Project: Prevosti Farms and Sugarhouse

Toni Prevosti is opening a new business, Prevosti Farms and Sugarhouse, a small company that will harvest, refine, and sell maple syrup products. In subsequent chapters, students will have the opportunity to establish payroll records and complete payroll information for Prevosti Farms and Sugarhouse.

sianc/Shutterstock

Toni has decided that she needs to hire employees for the business to grow. Complete the application for Prevosti Farms and Sugarhouse's Employer Identification Number (Form SS-4) with the following information:

Prevosti Farms and Sugarhouse is located at 820 Westminster Road, Bridgewater Vermont, 05520 (which is also Ms. Prevosti's home address), phone number 802-555-3456. Bridgewater is in Windsor County, Vermont. Toni, the responsible party for a Limited Liability Corporation created in the United States with one member (disregarded entity) has decided that Prevosti Farms and Sugarhouse will pay its employees on a biweekly basis. To... Social Security... 055-22-0443. The begin... of the...

Continuing Payroll Project: Prevosti Farms and Sugarhouse

Starting with Chapter 1, each chapter has an integrated, continuing payroll project—about a fictional company Prevosti Farms and Sugarhouse—that matches the chapter content and affords students a macro-level understanding of how each piece of payroll fits together.

Comprehensive Payroll Project: Wayland Custom Woodworking

The Comprehensive Payroll Project (Appendix A) allows students to track a quarter's worth of payroll transactions for a company. This Comprehensive Payroll Project offers instructors increased flexibility in teaching and assessment by offering a simulation equivalent to a full quarter of a fictitious company's payroll activities, including payroll transactions, pay processing, and tax form completion. The Comprehensive Payroll Project may be presented in different lengths—as short as one month or in its three-month entirety—to meet curricular needs. Instructors may assign this in connection with many chapters of the book or use it as a final project for their courses.

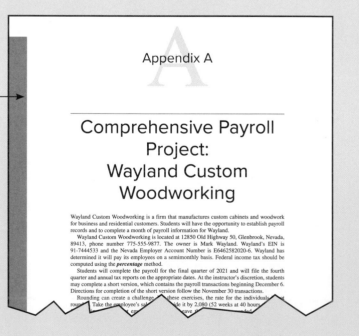

Appendix A

Comprehensive Payroll Project: Wayland Custom Woodworking

Wayland Custom Woodworking is a firm that manufactures custom cabinets and woodwork for business and residential customers. Students will have the opportunity to establish payroll records and to complete a month of payroll information for Wayland.

Wayland Custom Woodworking is located at 12850 Old Highway 50, Glenbrook, Nevada, 89413, phone number 775-555-9877. The owner is Mark Wayland. Wayland's EIN is 91-7444533 and the Nevada Employer Account Number is E6462582020-6. Wayland has determined it will pay its employees on a semimonthly basis. Federal income tax should be computed using the *percentage* method.

Students will complete the payroll for the final quarter of 2021 and will file the fourth quarter and annual tax reports on the appropriate dates. At the instructor's discretion, students may complete a short version, which contains the payroll transactions beginning December 6. Directions for completion of the short version follow the November 30 transactions.

Rounding can create a challenge... these exercises, the rate for the individual... Take the employee's sal... ide it by 2,080 (52 weeks at 40 hours...

Connect for *Payroll Accounting 2022*

- **SmartBook 2.0®** A personalized and adaptive learning tool used to maximize the learning experience by helping students study more efficiently and effectively. SmartBook 2.0 highlights where in the chapter to focus, asks review questions on the materials covered and tracks the most challenging content for later review. SmartBook 2.0 is available both online and offline.

- **End-of-chapter content** is a robust offering of review and question material designed to aid and assess the student's retention of chapter content. The end-of-chapter content is composed of both static and algorithmic exercises, problems, critical thinking exercises, and continuing payroll projects, which are designed to challenge students using McGraw-Hill Education's state-of-the-art online homework technology. Guided example videos are also provided with select end-of-chapter problems, which help walk students through complex payroll processes. Instructors can also assign test bank questions to students in both static and algorithmic versions.

- **Auto-graded payroll and tax forms** are integrated into Connect and are assignable. Students can complete the forms in these problems to gain a better understanding of how payroll forms are prepared in today's digital world.

- **Guided example videos** are also provided with select end-of-chapter problems, which help walk students through complex payroll processes. Instructors can also assign test bank questions to students in both static and algorithmic versions.

- **The comprehensive payroll project** from Appendix A is available on Connect in an auto-graded format. Students will apply skills, such as preparing tax forms and payroll registers, to complete the payroll process for a company from start to finish. Instructors can choose from the full three-month version or the shorter one-month version for their Connect assignment.

- **The test bank** for each chapter has been updated for the seventh edition to stay current with new and revised chapter material, with all questions available for assignment through Connect. Newly available within Connect, Test Builder is a cloud-based tool that enables instructors to format tests that can be printed or administered within a LMS. Test Builder offers a modern, streamlined interface for easy content configuration that matches course needs, without requiring a download. Test Builder provides a secure interface for better protection of content and allows for just-in-time updates to flow directly into assessments.

Auto-Graded Forms

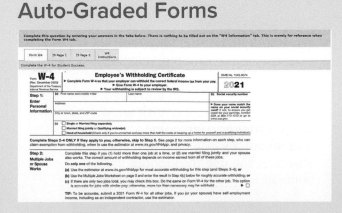

Comprehensive Payroll Project

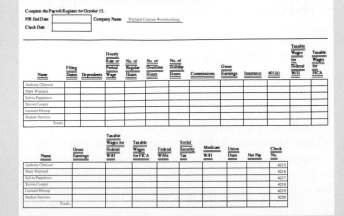

Instructors: Student Success Starts with You

Tools to enhance your unique voice

Want to build your own course? No problem. Prefer to use an OLC-aligned, prebuilt course? Easy. Want to make changes throughout the semester? Sure. And you'll save time with Connect's auto-grading too.

65% Less Time Grading

Study made personal

Incorporate adaptive study resources like SmartBook® 2.0 into your course and help your students be better prepared in less time. Learn more about the powerful personalized learning experience available in SmartBook 2.0 at **www.mheducation.com/highered/connect/smartbook**

Laptop: McGraw Hill; Woman/dog: George Doyle/Getty Images

Affordable solutions, added value

Make technology work for you with LMS integration for single sign-on access, mobile access to the digital textbook, and reports to quickly show you how each of your students is doing. And with our Inclusive Access program you can provide all these tools at a discount to your students. Ask your McGraw Hill representative for more information.

Padlock: Jobalou/Getty Images

Solutions for your challenges

A product isn't a solution. Real solutions are affordable, reliable, and come with training and ongoing support when you need it and how you want it. Visit **www.supportateverystep.com** for videos and resources both you and your students can use throughout the semester.

Checkmark: Jobalou/Getty Images

Students: Get Learning that Fits You

Effective tools for efficient studying

Connect is designed to help you be more productive with simple, flexible, intuitive tools that maximize your study time and meet your individual learning needs. Get learning that works for you with Connect.

Study anytime, anywhere

Download the free ReadAnywhere app and access your online eBook, SmartBook 2.0, or Adaptive Learning Assignments when it's convenient, even if you're offline. And since the app automatically syncs with your Connect account, all of your work is available every time you open it. Find out more at **www.mheducation.com/readanywhere**

> *"I really liked this app—it made it easy to study when you don't have your textbook in front of you."*
>
> - Jordan Cunningham,
> Eastern Washington University

Everything you need in one place

Your Connect course has everything you need—whether reading on your digital eBook or completing assignments for class, Connect makes it easy to get your work done.

Calendar: owattaphotos/Getty Images

Learning for everyone

McGraw Hill works directly with Accessibility Services Departments and faculty to meet the learning needs of all students. Please contact your Accessibility Services Office and ask them to email accessibility@mheducation.com, or visit **www.mheducation.com/about/accessibility** for more information.

Acknowledgments

This eighth edition of *Payroll Accounting* would not have been possible without the patience, guidance, and encouragement of Steve Schuetz, executive portfolio manager; the diligence and commitment of Sarah Sacco, product developer; the support and leadership of Harvey Yep and Brian Nacik, content project managers; the incredible form templates designed by Kitty O'Donnell; and the amazing artwork of Beth Blech, designer. We further want to thank Claire McLemore, marketing manager; Beth Cray, content licensing specialist; Kevin Moran, director of digital content; Xin Lin, lead product manager; and the composition team at SPi Global. Thanks go to our project development team who handled every formatting request with professionalism. Special thanks to M. Jeff Quinlan, Madison Area Technical College, for his contributions to verify the accuracy of our content.

Countless other colleagues have offered their feedback, insights, and inspiration during various stages of this project. We want to extend sincere thanks to the reviewers who helped us shape the eighth edition:

April Mohr
Jefferson Community and Technical College

Beth Vaughn
Zane State College

Cammy Wayne
William Raney Harper College

Chad Nichols
Rowan-Cabarrus Community College

Christy Lefevers
Catawba Valley Community College

Corinne Fraud
Muscatine College

Dawn Wright
Ozarks Technical Community College

Debbie Trumbo
Gwinnett Technical College

Gerald Childs
Waukesha County Technical College

Joseph Nicassio
Westmoreland County Community College

Karen Mozingo
Pitt Community College

Kelley Butler
Ivy Tech Community College

Marina Grau
Houston Community College

Mark Reddick
Chattahoochee Technical College

Nicole Johnson
Wake Technical Community College

Pamela Watkins
Durham Technical Community College

Samuel Welchel
Greenville Technical College

Sherilyn Reynolds
San Jacinto College

Theresa Meza
James Sprunt Community College

Victoria Badura
Metropolitan Community College

Wil Harri
Pima Community College
Our heartfelt thanks to all who have helped us continue to improve this text.

Jeanette Landin

Paulette Schirmer

Brief Contents

Contents

Payroll Accounting 2022

Chapter One

Payroll Practices and System Fundamentals

Payroll systems are an essential part of job planning and strategic human resource management, cost management for products and services, and benefits analysis. A company's payroll system has historically connected human resources and accounting departments. In contemporary businesses, payroll has taken on a strategic role in company direction and plans. The continual evolution of technological tools to manage company resources, including monetary and human, provides both opportunities and challenges to employers regarding employee access and private information protection. A well-designed payroll system is a critical element in company management; for this reason, an understanding of payroll foundations is imperative. This chapter will explore the need for a payroll system, legal requirements, ethical guidelines, best practices, and variations in payroll practices among different-sized companies.

LEARNING OBJECTIVES

After studying Chapter 1, you should be able to:

LO 1-1   Identify Legislation That Pertains to Payroll and Business

LO 1-2   Discuss the Legal Framework Specific to Payroll Accounting

LO 1-3   Discuss the Ethical Guidelines for Payroll Accounting

LO 1-4   Identify Contemporary Payroll Practices

LO 1-5   Compare Payroll Processing Options for Different Businesses

Drazen_/Getty Images

Payroll Accounting Goes Remote

Amid the wide variety of changes employers and employees experienced during 2020, one aspect is here to stay: Remote payroll accounting.

Although online payroll services have been evolving for several years, the practice of completing payroll-related duties became entirely remote out of necessity during 2020. The transition from in-house payroll processing to a hybrid or fully remote model was challenging yet necessary. Employers and employees adapted to a new payroll accounting model and reporting that transpired alongside the development of robust professional communication systems such as Zoom. A challenge was to ensure the security and accuracy of the payroll process, and software was developed to meet that need.

Top CPA firms such as Friedman, located in Pennsylvania, and Prager Metis, located in New Jersey, adapted to the fully remote model by ensuring that their computer-based hardware and software at the corporate offices could withstand the computerized traffic. Additionally, payroll employees ensured their home-based WiFi connections were robust and that they had the necessary forms, software, instructions, and other documentation to complete their work remotely.

The question for the future is if the remote payroll processing will continue as a fully remote, hybrid, or office-based practice. Each company will have to make the appropriate choice.

(Source: Accounting Today)

Employment legislation is highly complex and dynamic. Large or small, employers must abide by the law and be aware when it changes. In Chapter 1, we will explore the basics of payroll systems, including legal and ethical issues involved with employee pay.

LO 1-1   Identify Legislation That Pertains to Payroll and Business

Photographs in the Carol M. Highsmith Archive, Library of Congress, Prints and Photographs Division.

Unlike many other accounting types, payroll affects most (if not all) members of an organization. Payroll errors can lead to serious internal and external problems. Internal errors may cause a company to pay excessive wages for unneeded overtime, underpay employees, forego profits, or employ the wrong number or type of workers during seasonal or other workflow changes. Managers use internal reports about labor usage, staffing levels, and employee compensation trends to ensure operational effectiveness. Organizational decision-makers use these reports to control labor costs, hire additional employees to meet surge demands, and manage the cost of goods sold. Payroll errors can result in governmental fines, taxes, or legal charges related to labor law violations. Employers provide external reports to the Internal Revenue Service (IRS), state government tax departments, and many more agencies, depending upon the company's nature.

2020 was an extraordinary year for payroll accountants. Paychex® recommended that the following items must be clearly articulated and verified for year-end reporting:

- All in-house payroll records, including voided checks.
- All employee pension and retirement-related items.
- Any fringe benefits.
- Healthcare and dependent-related items.
- All insurance-related items.

(Source: Accounting Today)

According to the **United States Bureau of Labor Statistics**, as of 2019, employment in accounting jobs is expected to increase 4 percent through 2029, which is the average growth for business professions. Salaries average $45,800 for payroll clerks, $80,538 for payroll supervisors, and $101,857 for payroll managers, according to the 2021 salary guides available via www.salary.com.

The legislative framework governing employers' payroll systems is complex. Although several fundamental laws still exist, payroll and human resource laws reflect societal evolution over time. Note how some of these laws have been challenged or changed since their inception.

The *Equal Pay Act of 1963*, which extended the provisions of the *Fair Labor Standards Act (FLSA)*, mandated that males and females be paid equally for equal work. As of 2020, 48 states have enacted legislation that clarifies and/or extends the original 1963 act. Any employees who feel they have been paid unequally based upon gender have legal options to rectify the situation:

- First, they should gather documentation regarding the differential and determine if other employees in question are willing to substantiate the difference.
- Second, they should speak with their supervisor to question the pay differential.
- Should the supervisor be unwilling to discuss or adjust the pay discrepancy, an attorney may become a necessary third step.

This act was modified by the *Lilly Ledbetter Fair Pay Act of 2009*, which removed the 180-day statute of limitations on unequal treatment claims.

In 1979, Lilly Ledbetter, an employee of Goodyear Tire and Rubber Company, started at the same pay rate as males in the same position. Over time, management declined her raises based on negative reviews that Ms. Ledbetter later claimed were discriminatory. Under the provisions of the 1963 Equal Pay Act, the claimant had 180 days to file a complaint. Although the U.S. Supreme Court agreed with her discrimination claims, it ruled in favor of Goodyear because of the lack of timeliness of Ms. Ledbetter's filing. This ruling ultimately led to the Lilly Ledbetter Fair Pay Act of 2009.

In January 2021, the Federal Appeals Court for the 7th Circuit in Chicago upheld a case brought by Dr. Cheryl Kellogg in which she alleged wage discrimination. In *Kellogg v. Ball State University,* Dr. Kellog's employer told her that she did not warrant a wage consistent with her education because her husband worked for the same institution, and she was not in need of the money. The appeals court overruled any concerns regarding the case's timing because of the Lilly Ledbetter Fair Pay Act.

(Source: U.S. EEOC, Education Week)

The *Civil Rights Act of 1964* prohibited discrimination based on race, creed, color, gender, and national origin. Since 1964, this act has been extended by Executive Order 11478 to protect people with AIDS, pregnant workers, people with different sexual orientations, and people with disabilities. In June 2015, the U.S. Supreme Court ruled in *Obergefell v. Hodges* (U.S. Supreme Court No. 14-556) that same-sex marriage was legal and could not be banned in any state. This extension of the 1964 Civil Rights Act represented another step toward the legal protection of worker dignity.

CREATISTA/Getty Images

The *Age Discrimination in Employment Act of 1967 (ADEA)* prevents mandatory retirement of older employees (older than age 40) and prohibits age-based discrimination in hiring.

An AARP survey conducted in Oregon found that 62 percent of workers over the age of 40 who have applied for employment have been discriminated against due to their age. Approximately 35 percent of job applicants over the age of 40 have been asked age-related questions during job interviews, which is a violation of ADEA. As of 2021, ORS 659A.009 mandated that the individual's ability to perform a job, not the person's age, is the standard for employment.

(Source: AARP, Oregon Laws)

The *Occupational Safety and Health Act of 1970 (OSHA)* defined and enforced healthy and safe working environments for employees. Employee safety programs and personal protective equipment represent an additional cost to the employer. Still, fines for non-compliance and payments made following workplace injuries are often far more costly: fines range from $13,494 per serious violation to $134,937 (2021 figures) for willful or repeated violations.

The COVID-19 pandemic required additional strengthening and clarity in the OSHA standards for Personal Protective Equipment (PPE) and the General Duty of employers for employee safety.

Summary of changes

1. OSHA required employers to provide appropriate PPE for employees, including protection for eyes, hands, and the face. Special provisions of this requirement included a respiratory protection plan when respirators were required.

2. OSHA amended the general duty clause to require that employers provide a safe workplace that protected employees from physical harm to the greatest possible extent.

(Source: OSHA)

The *Employee Retirement Income Security Act of 1974 (ERISA)* regulates retirement and pension plans. ERISA has been extended by the *Consolidated Omnibus Budget Reformation Act of 1985 (COBRA)*. During 2007–2009, some employee retirement funds' value decreased, causing employees to postpone retirement. The Internal Revenue Service imposes limitations on retirement plan contributions, and those limits have shifted to reflect the need for employees to recoup losses sustained during the recession. Since that time, employee retirement benefits have shifted from being a financial burden to becoming an employee hiring and retention strategy. Retirement researchers are contemplating proposing a mandatory retirement savings law.

COBRA extended medical benefits for terminated employees at the employee's expense for up to 18 months post-employment by qualified employers. It should be noted that not all companies are subject to COBRA provisions and that states may offer "mini-COBRA" plans for employees of companies with fewer than 20 employees. The repeal of the Defense of Marriage Act (DOMA) in 2013 forced employers to offer COBRA coverage to same-sex spouses. As of 2020, terminated employees who opt not to enroll in COBRA plans may enroll

Donenko Oleksii/Shutterstock

in *Marketplace* plans or Medicaid for up to 60 days post-termination. If the employee chooses not to use the COBRA plan immediately, they may enroll in it at the company's next enrollment period.

COBRA benefits currently extend to beneficiaries, including employees, dependent spouses, and children. Benefits are paid to beneficiaries in the event of reduced hours or separation of employment for any reason excluding gross misconduct and upon the death of the employee. If the company offers retiree benefits, COBRA coverage also extends to beneficiaries in Chapter 11 bankruptcy.

In 2020, the *Setting Every Community Up for Retirement Enhancement (SECURE) Act* granted small employers tax incentives to implement an automatic retirement plan enrollment for their employees. Alternatively, the act allows small employers to form a group that would allow each business's employees to have better access to retirement plans than the employer could offer by itself.

A development in 2019 involved the IRS approval of an employer connecting employee 401(k) contributions toward payment of their student loans. In one instance, the guidelines for an employer's contribution to the employee's student loan were that the employees were paying at least 2 percent of their salary toward their student loans during a given period. Other companies, such as Abbott, offer an expanded 401(k) employer match for employees who meet similar guidelines regarding their student loan repayment.

(Source: Employee Benefit News)

The *Immigration Reform and Control Act of 1986 (IRCA)* requires employers to verify that employees are legally able to work in the United States. Form I-9 is the most common payroll-related application of this law. Immigration and citizenship laws require collecting information within an I-9, and retention is three years from the date of hire or one year from the date of termination (whichever is longer).

Information collected on Form I-9 is monitored closely to ensure that the employee is legally authorized to work in the United States. Employers may also use the *E-verify* system to confirm legal employment eligibility. Note that the E-verify system does not replace the completion of the I-9 but does offer employers the opportunity to check legal employment eligibility rapidly via the Internet.

The ***Americans with Disabilities Act of 1990 (ADA)*** extended the provisions of the Civil Rights Act of 1964 by ensuring that people with disabilities have the same opportunities as those without mental or physical impairment. This law applies to employers with 15 or more employees on the payroll, including full-time and part-time workers. The enactment of the ***Americans with Disabilities Act Amendments Act (ADAAA)*** in 2008 extended the definition of disability to include many disabilities. Final Regulations on the ADAAA in 2011 clarified the definitions of disability and the required accommodations to include the following:

Westend61/Getty Images

- The expansion of the definition of disability includes a lower standard of the definition of impairment.
- The determination of impairments requires the employee to be assessed individually.
- Except for corrective lenses, the determination of disability does not include devices that provide relief or mitigation of the condition, such as hearing aids.
- Impairments that occur periodically or episodically or that are in remission are still considered impairments.
- Any disability determination must not require extensive analysis.

The ***Civil Rights Act of 1991*** granted employees who have been discriminated against the chance to be paid monetary damages through legal proceedings. This act applies to American employers and American-controlled employers with internationally based operations.

Workplace diversity and inclusion have become an increasing priority at workplaces during the last decade. As of 2020, *Forbes* posted its listing of the best workplaces for diversity and inclusion, sourced from polls of 60,000 Americans who worked for companies with a minimum of 1,000 employees. The top three employers included

1. SAP Software

2. Henry Ford Health System

3. Procter & Gamble

(Source: *Forbes*)

The ***Family and Medical Leave Act of 1993 (FMLA)*** granted employees the right to take medical leave under reasonable circumstances without fear of job loss. The employee may have to take unpaid leave, but medical benefits must continue under FMLA provisions. Upon returning from family leave, the employer must provide an equivalent position with equivalent pay, benefits, and employment terms. The employer has many responsibilities under the FMLA that involve employee notification of benefits and processes while on leave.

Pixtal/AGE Fotostock

As of 2020, several states have enacted higher-paid family leaves legislation: California, Connecticut, New Jersey, New York, Oregon, Rhode Island, Washington D.C. (July 2020), and Massachusetts (January 2021). More states consider paid family leave, which will lead to further clarification about paid family leaves, limits, and specific provisions.

In 2017, legislators passed the Tax Cuts and Jobs Act (Public Law 115-97) in Washington. This provided a tax credit to employers who offer their employees paid leave under the FMLA. Employers may be eligible for a credit of 12.5 percent up to 25 percent, whereas the employee's rate of payment is 50 percent or more of what the employee would normally be paid during the normal course of work for the company. Eligibility limits of the type of employer and employee exist under regulations (see **Sec. §13403**).

The Tax Cuts and Jobs Act (TCJA) has led to specific areas of focus for employers. These areas of focus include

- Controversy: When the TCJA provisions expire at the end of 2025, companies may need to re-file tax returns, making record-keeping and changes made due to the TCJA enactment a critical function in payroll.
- International tax: For companies with an international presence, including employees, the TCJA may result in new tax liabilities.
- Compensation for executives: TCJA affected highly compensated employees' tax treatment and fringe benefits offered to workers. This has led to scrutiny of compensation plans and their legal compliance.
- State taxes: Because of TCJA provisions, some states have witnessed tax increases for employees. Since each state has different tax laws, and not all states have chosen to comply with TCJA provisions, state taxation has become increasingly complex.

(Source: AICPA)

The *Uniformed Services Employment and Reemployment Rights Act of 1994 (USERRA)* governs military service members' rights in terms of length of military service, return to work, and accommodations for injured veterans. USERRA was amended as to service members' rights in 2005. In 2011, USERRA was further amended by the Veterans Opportunity to Work Act, which allowed USERRA to recognize claims of a hostile work environment resulting from an individual's military status.

The U.S. Department of Labor investigates many cases involving service members' rights. Army veteran Lisa Slater returned to her job as a security officer, which she held for 13 years with her company, after deployment on active duty. However, upon her return to her employment, she found that she was classified as a new employee, which was a violation of USERRA. She received approximately $20,000 in back wages, and her seniority was restored following arbitration.

(Source: U.S. DOL)

The *Personal Responsibility and Work Opportunity Reconciliation Act of 1996 (PRWOR)* mandated that employers file a new hire reporting form within 20 days after an employee initially commences work. This act protects children and needy families by enforcing child support obligations. The child support provisions of PRWOR were strengthened by the passage of the *Personal Responsibility, Work and Family Promotion Act of 2002*, which reauthorized PRWOR when it expired.

According to the Office of Child Support Enforcement (OSCE), employers assisted in collecting over $24 billion during 2018 through their timely reporting of new hires. Additionally, the Temporary Assistance for Needy Families (TANF) for child support in arrears decreased by 11 percent between 2008 and 2018.

(Source: Office of Child Support Enforcement)

The ***Health Insurance Portability and Accountability Act of 1996 (HIPAA)*** protects workers and their families who have preexisting medical conditions from discrimination based on those conditions. The Ebola outbreak in 2014 led to additional guidance about HIPAA rights and notifications to interested parties, including employers, during emergencies.

Jeanette Landin

> HIPAA protections continue even after a business ceases operations. Filefax Inc. of Illinois was ordered to pay approximately $100,000 in fines because of HIPAA violations, although the company is no longer in business. The issue leading to the fines involved a lack of secure storage of employee health records following an investigation by the Office of Civil Rights.
>
> (Source: U.S. HHS)

The ***Defense of Marriage Act of 1996 (DOMA)*** restricted payroll-related taxes and benefits to include only traditionally married couples, denying married status to people in same-sex unions. The U.S. Supreme Court overturned DOMA in its ruling in *U.S. v. Windsor* on September 6, 2013. The Internal Revenue Service subsequently mandated that all married same-sex couples must be treated as married for all tax purposes. The repeal of DOMA had a ripple effect throughout all payroll phases because of the need to amend business and personal tax return filings back to 2011, owing to the three-year amendment rule. The effects of DOMA's repeal also have had a ripple effect on employee rights, highlighting the need for additional legislative clarification.

The repeal of DOMA provoked the need to clarify the term "family member." Following the U.S. Supreme Court decision in *Obergefell v. Hodges (2015)*, the U.S. Department of Labor updated the definition of spouse to include same-sex marriages, regardless of where they live.

Maskot/Getty Images

> In *U.S. v. Windsor,* Ms. Windsor and her wife were recognized as a married couple by the state of New York, and her compensation was taxed accordingly. However, the IRS sued Windsor for unpaid taxes because her same-sex marriage violated DOMA. The U.S. Supreme Court found that DOMA violated Windsor's Fifth Amendment right to liberty and overturned DOMA. The IRS subsequently dropped its lawsuit.
>
> (Source: U.S. Supreme Court)

The ***Sarbanes–Oxley Act of 2002 (SOX)*** provided criminal penalties for violations of ERISA. SOX provides protections for whistleblowers (Sec. § 806) and mandates auditors' rotation among publicly owned companies (Sec. § 203). SOX Section 302 mandates that corporate officers must attest to the accuracy and completeness of the financial statements' contents. An additional consideration for SOX public companies regarding payroll is that the internal controls of a payroll system must be reported under the law's guidelines (Sec. § 404). Costs of SOX compliance have sparked discussion about the act's effectiveness.

> In 2020, SOX and the Dodd–Frank Act, which involved consumer protection and oversight of trading via the New York Stock Exchange, intersected to strengthen consumer protections (known as *qui tam* rewards). The intersection led to a bill introduced in
>
> *(continued)*

> *(concluded)*
>
> Congress to create an independent board to oversee auditor conduct in publicly held companies, thus limiting conflicts of interest and protecting individuals who invest in companies traded on the stock market.
>
> (Source: National Law Review)

The *American Recovery and Reinvestment Act of 2009 (ARRA)* provided tax credits for employers and employees through the Making Work Pay provisions. Although ARRA's provisions have expired, parts of it were reinstated through the *American Taxpayer Relief Act of 2012 (ATRA)*. Many of the ATRA provisions were extended through 2015 by extending the Work Opportunity Tax Credit and extended through 2021. The *Protecting Americans from Tax Hikes (PATH) Act* of 2015, which also prevented certain types of tax fraud, extended the ATRA provisions by offering employers tax credits for hiring qualified veterans and individuals who have endured long-term unemployment.

As times change, new legislation will be enacted, and existing laws are sometimes repealed and amended. An example of evolving legislation includes new local laws regarding fairness in scheduling employees' shift work schedules. Right-to-work laws are another example of employment-related legislation. As of 2020, 27 U.S. states and Guam have enacted right-to-work legislation that promotes an employee's right to opt-out of union membership. West Virginia's law has been deemed unconstitutional, and the case will likely go to the state's Supreme Court of Appeals. At the time of this writing, the notion of the right to work without forcing union participation is being considered by the U.S. Congress.

The payroll accountant's job is consistent and continual learning and research to ensure that the company is complying with all current regulations and reporting requirements. Many states, but not all, have additional payroll tax laws. Federally mandated payroll laws will be addressed in the next section.

(Source: WagePoint)

Which Law?

Stop & Check

1. Requires employers to verify the employee's legal right to work in the United States?
2. Protects the rights of disabled workers?
3. Governs the management of retirement plans?
4. Protects discrimination of workers older than age 40?
5. Creates safe work environments for employees?
6. Mandates equal pay for equal work?
7. Extends medical benefits for terminated employees?
8. Ensures that child support obligations will be paid?
9. Protects workers and families with preexisting medical conditions?
10. Enforces payment of monetary damages because of discrimination?
11. Requires internal controls on payroll practices of public companies?
12. Gives small employers incentives to establish retirement plans?

a. COBRA
b. ERISA
c. Civil Rights Act of 1991
d. PRWOR
e. SOX
f. ADEA
g. HIPAA
h. ADA
i. OSHA
j. Equal Pay Act of 1963
k. IRCA
l. SECURE

LO 1-2 Discuss the Legal Framework Specific to Payroll Accounting

Why did businesses start withholding taxes from employees' paychecks? Federal income tax withholding was temporarily instituted in 1861 to recover from the Civil War's high costs; however, this tax was repealed in 1872. Throughout the 19th century, cities were growing in the wake of the Industrial Revolution, as factories and companies increased automation and institutionalized mass production. People moved from rural to urban areas in unprecedented numbers, and the need for infrastructure and civil services grew. Roads needed to be built, law enforcement personnel needed to be increased, and disease outbreaks prompted sanitation systems.

stoatphoto/Shutterstock

Therefore, the U.S. Congress formalized the permanent continuation of the federal income tax instituted during the Civil War as a means to fund the infrastructure improvements of the booming cities. After many failed attempts to reinstate a federal income tax, Congress passed the *Sixteenth Amendment to the U.S. Constitution* in 1909, ratified by states in 1913. This version incorporated a tiered income tax, including exemptions and deductions, to limit the tax imposed on wages earned; it was the harbinger of many employment-related laws (see Figure 1-1).

During the Great Depression of the 1930s, the stock market collapsed, financial institutions went bankrupt, and companies released workers or ceased business operations. The government needed money to fund programs that would stimulate economic recovery. Additionally, the need for a social welfare system emerged as the number of displaced workers increased. The 1930s became a decade of landmark employment legislation that defined the legal environment for employers and employees, most of which remains enforced in 2020.

In 1931, Congress passed the *Davis–Bacon Act*, creating a standard of wages for governmental contracts totaling more than $2,000. The increased standard wages created under the Davis–Bacon Act brought additional revenue to small businesses and the communities where the contract workers lived, bought groceries, and purchased other services or goods. The Davis–Bacon Act comprised more than 60 different federal statutes, providing a prevailing wage and wage classification strategy to guide employers and contractors. As of 2021, the minimum wage for all employees affected by the Davis–Bacon Act is $10.95 per hour, unless the local prevailing minimum wage rate is higher.

FIGURE 1-1
Timeline of Payroll Legislation

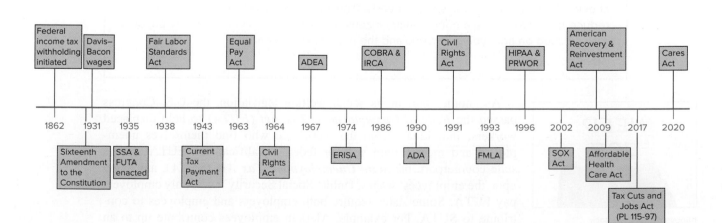

Payroll Regulations Timeline

The determination of wages to be paid to workers affected by the Davis–Bacon Act varies by geographic area, contract, and type of work performed. To facilitate wage determination, the U.S. Department of Labor maintains a website (https://beta.sam.gov/). Employers may access their specific contract in question and research the contract provisions to ensure that employees are paid appropriately.

The *Walsh–Healey Public Contracts Act* of 1936 affected governmental contractors providing goods or services exceeding $10,000. The act required companies to pay workers a minimum wage for all hours worked under 40 per week and a half (regular pay times 1.5) per hour for any hours over 40 per week. The Walsh–Healey Public Contracts Act also prohibited the employment of individuals younger than 16 years of age. Compliance with this act is enforced through the Employment Standards Administration Wage and Hour Division of the Department of Labor. These standards also apply to workers within the District of Columbia.

In 1935, the *Social Security Act (SSA)*, also known as the *Federal Insurance Contributions Act (FICA)*, established a contribution-driven fund to help the average U.S. worker respond to the social and financial distress caused by the Great Depression. Originally, the Social Security tax was designed such that younger workers supported retired, disabled workers and surviving families of deceased workers. It is important to note that the worker does not need to die or become disabled to receive Social Security benefits; the truth is that age and disability are components in the decision but are not the only factors considered when awarding Social Security benefits. A contribution-driven fund's employees and employers pay a percentage of gross earnings into the Social Security fund. Originally, the fund was designed to be earmarked for a specific individual upon retirement. Still, the fund currently assists families who experience diminished wages and working situations because of the worker's infirmity, or the illness of a family member that prevents their entry into the workforce, and monetary benefits to dependents of retired or deceased workers. Social Security is synonymous with *Old-Age, Survivors, and Disability Insurance (OASDI)*. *Medicare tax,* a government-mandated health insurance program for individuals, was also included in the SSA legislation. As of 2021, the age at which individuals may receive full retirement benefits is 67 years for people born after 1960. The full retirement age will increase from 65 years by two months each year for people born prior to 1960 until it reaches the full retirement age of 67. Individuals may begin receiving permanently reduced benefits as early as age 62, but their Social Security payments will be reduced incrementally.

(Source: Social Security Administration)

As of 2021, Social Security paid 9.7 million disabled workers a monthly benefit. This figure represented a milestone for the Social Security Administration because that number was the highest that had ever been paid. Furthermore, SSA estimated that approximately 62 percent of American retirees depended on their Social Security checks for basic food and shelter needs. The funds received from Social Security reduce the poverty rate among senior citizens. The amount of Social Security payouts varies based on age, years of work, and the highest wages earned.

(Source: Motley Fool)

happystock/Shutterstock

As another part of its social welfare legislation, the U.S. Congress passed the *Federal Unemployment Tax Act (FUTA)* to help displaced workers, individuals from the workforce who find themselves unemployed and meet certain state or federal qualifications. FUTA and its state counterpart, the *State Unemployment Tax Act (SUTA)*, are based upon the employees' wages. Unlike Social Security taxes, only employers pay FUTA. Some states require both employers and employees to contribute to SUTA. For example, Alaskan employees contribute up to an annual amount of $218 (2021 figure) to SUTA, which is collected at a rate of 0.50 percent of wages; employers contribute up to 2.57 percent of employee wages until they reach $43,600 in annual gross earnings (2021 figure). Should an employee have more than one employer, the employee can request a return for the amounts over the annual earnings maximum in the following year. The COVID-19 pandemic strained states' unemployment funds in 2020, and increases to SUTA rates and policies may be significant in future years.

The *Fair Labor Standards Act (FLSA)* of 1938 required more detailed record keeping and worker protection. This act regulates the minimum wage, which most workers are familiar with, stated as the lowest an individual under certain classifications can be paid. Less commonly known, the minimum wage applies only to workers at businesses that meet certain conditions, which is defined by either enterprise or individual coverage. Additionally, tipped employees, such as restaurant servers, are exempt from minimum wage standards under FLSA. In the contemporary business world, a business that does not conduct interstate commerce is rare, but the provision in FLSA remains in effect.

FLSA: Enterprise vs. Individual Coverage

Under FLSA, two types of coverage prevail: Enterprise coverage and Individual coverage.

Enterprise Coverage:
- The company must have a minimum of two employees.
- The volume of sales or business performed annually must exceed $500,000.
- Firms such as hospitals, schools, government agencies, and residential care facilities are always considered under enterprise coverage.

Individual Coverage:
- Firms that regularly conduct interstate business, such as companies that produce goods for shipment to a different state, have employees who travel to other states, or otherwise conduct business with firms or people in other states.

(Source: DOL)

An important fact about FLSA wage guidelines is that no maximum wage cap exists. Securities and Exchanges Commission (SEC) regulations stipulate that high-ranking public companies' employees' compensation packages must be published with the company's mandatory annual report.

The Department of Health and Human Services determined in 2020 that the poverty level for a family of four was $26,200, which translates to a wage of approximately $12.60 per hour. In other words, the minimum wage for a family to live comfortably (referred to as a *living wage*) would need to exceed $12.60 to maintain a "normal" standard of living. As of this publication date, the federal *minimum wage* is $7.25 per hour, although some states and locales may mandate a higher minimum wage.

(Source: The Balance)

FLSA guidelines define maximum hours, minimum age, pay rates, and mandatory break times. This part of the FLSA was an outgrowth of the early 20th century's industrial environment when no such guidelines existed. Horror stories about working conditions and children working 12- to 14-hour days abounded during the 1930s. The FLSA created the classifications of exempt and nonexempt workers. Exempt workers are salaried workers who are not subject to certain wage and overtime provisions of FLSA. Nonexempt workers are protected by the provisions of the FLSA and are therefore subject to wage and overtime provisions.

Additionally, FLSA regulation does not apply to pay periods or to the amount of paid time off given to employees. Those two items are at the discretion of the employer. Paid time off has become a topic of discussion since 2010. McDonald's began offering it to nonexempt employees in 2015 as a regular part of employee benefit packages in response to pressure from labor leaders. Eleven states and more than 30 municipalities have instituted paid sick leave for employees as of 2020. The paid sick leave laws vary widely among the states.

The third class of workers, independent contractors, is not subject to the payment provisions of the FLSA. *Independent contractors* are typically treated as vendors of a business. Independent contractors are not employees of the business and are not reflected in payroll records. The IRS uses *Form SS-8* to help determine employee or independent contractor status. The Department of Labor ruled that improper classification of workers diminished workers' legal protections under the FLSA and declared that the following items must be considered when classifying a worker as an employee or an independent contractor:

1. The extent to which a worker is an integral element of the employer's business.
2. Whether the worker's managerial skills affect his or her opportunity for profit or loss.
3. Relative investments in facilities and equipment by *both* the employee and the employer.
4. The extent to which the worker exercises independent business judgment.
5. The permanent nature of the working relationship between the employer and employee.
6. The type and extent of the control that the employer has over the employee.

(Source: U.S. Department of Labor)

Penalties for misclassification of employees as independent contractors can be high. If the misclassification is intentional on the employer's part, the monetary amount of the penalty is higher. In the case of *Fair v. Communications Unlimited Inc.*, the U.S. District in Missouri found that the employer had deliberately miscategorized workers in 10 states as independent contractors to avoid paying overtime wages required under the FLSA. The employer was ordered to provide the names and other contact information to the court to determine appropriate overtime compensation awards.

(Source: Google Scholar)

To obtain the remittance of employers' withholding taxes, the federal government needed a way to standardize the collection of taxes from employers. Before the *Current Tax Payment Act (CTPA) of 1943*, no formalized guidelines for remittance of taxes existed. Before the CTPA, employers' remittance was inconsistent and unreliable as a funding source for governmental projects. The CTPA was passed during World War II to guarantee funds to support the country's involvement in the war. The CTPA created the requirement for the submission of estimated taxes on wages earned during the year of earning instead of after the end of the year as previously required.

Another employer obligation is *workers' compensation*, commonly known as *workers' comp.* Unlike other payroll-specific laws, state laws govern workers' compensation laws. Employer requirements for providing workers' comp coverage vary from state to state. They are not required in certain states if the employer has fewer than a certain minimum number of employees. Because workers' compensation is an insurance program, it is not considered a tax; however, it is a state-mandated employer payroll expense.

Workers' compensation is an insurance policy carried by employers to provide wage continuation and pay for medical services for workers injured while doing business. The amounts assigned to the policy vary by work being performed and associated risks for various professions. For example, heavy equipment operators would have a higher workers' comp rate than office workers because their injury exposure is deemed higher by the insurance industry. The COVID-19 pandemic impact on

wavebreakmedia/Shutterstock

certain businesses, such as meat-packing plants, may lead to changes in workers' compensation insurance procedures in future years.

Workers' compensation plans are subject to annual audits and are based upon payroll wages less any employees exempted from the coverage, typically working owners. Employers must report all employee wages; however, only one-third of overtime hours are reported to the workers' compensation auditor. Each state has different requirements for coverage and eligibility. The number of employees over which workers' compensation insurance is required varies per state, as shown in Table 1-1.

The *Affordable Care Act (ACA)* of 2010 was one of the most significant payroll accounting changes in recent years. Although the act's primary focus was to ensure health care coverage for all Americans, employers have several reporting responsibilities related to the act. One of the responsibilities included in Section 1003 is the disclosure and justification for rates of plans and any increases in premiums. Another reporting requirement is the number of full-time equivalents (FTE) employees, the cost of insurance coverage provided to employees, and the elimination of a waiting period for health insurance coverage. The Affordable Care Act legislation covers 974 pages and contains many provisions and contingencies, including a requirement for continuing premium review. In 2017, the Affordable Care Act mandated financial penalty on individuals who elected not to have medical insurance was overturned by Executive Order 13765. In 2018, a judge in Texas ruled that Executive Order 13765 caused the ACA to be unconstitutional. In 2021, the U.S. Supreme Court vacated the lower court's ruling in Texas, which means the ACA is consistent with the U.S. Constitution and remains a current law.

According to the Internal Revenue Service, employers must report whether they provide Minimum Essential Coverage part of their company-sponsored benefits, including any group health plans, COBRA plans, or preexisting insurance coverage. Health insurance coverage is reported on IRS Form 1095 A, B, or C as follows:

- Form 1095-A is for individuals who have purchased insurance from the Healthcare Marketplace, not through an employer. The Marketplace issues this form.

- Form 1095-B reports information to the IRS for individuals with minimum essential coverage through group insurance plans provided by governmental employers and qualified private-sector employers. Additionally, employers who are not applicable large employers but who sponsor self-insured group health plans must report information about employees (and their spouse and dependents) who enroll in the coverage to their employees, even though the employers are not subject to the employer shared-responsibility provisions or the information reporting requirements for applicable large employers.

- Form 1095-C is for applicable large employers who provide health insurance where the employer is responsible for the act's shared responsibility provision. This form is issued by employers who offer coverage but are not self-insured and have 50 or more full-time and/or full-time equivalent employees.

The employer must file IRS form 1095-B or 1095-C and furnish a copy to the insured if the insured received medical insurance benefits for as few as one day of one month during a calendar year. The transmittal form, which contains a summary of all Form 1095 issued, required the IRS is Form 1094-A, B, or C, depending on the type of 1095 issued.

(Source: IRS)

The 2017 *Tax Cuts and Jobs Act* and represented sweeping changes to the tax code. This law profoundly affected payroll taxes, especially employee federal income tax liability, and required a comprehensive reframing of employee income tax computation. Specific changes to payroll included a change to the Social Security wage base, adjustments to nonresident alien withholding, adjustments for inflation, and decreases in supplemental wage withholding

TABLE 1-1
Workers' Compensation Laws by State

STATE	MINIMUM NUMBER OF EMPLOYEES
Alaska	1 (may be self-insured)
Alabama	5
Arizona	1
Arkansas	3
California	1
Colorado	1
Connecticut	1 (including uninsured subcontractors)
Delaware	1
D.C.	1
Florida	4 (except noted industries), 1 (construction), 6 (agricultural), 12 (seasonal)
Georgia	3
Hawaii	1
Idaho	1 (including part-time workers)
Illinois	1 (including part-time workers)
Indiana	1
Iowa	1 (excluding very low salary employers)
Kansas	1 (exempt if annual gross payroll is less than $20,000 or agricultural employer. Sole proprietors and LLC members are exempt from coverage)
Kentucky	1
Louisiana	1 (including part-time, either employees or subcontractors, exceptions for agriculture only employers)
Maine	1 (subcontractors must also be covered)
Maryland	1 (agricultural employers must have at least 3 employees or a payroll of less than $15,000 annually)
Massachusetts	1 (domestic workers must be covered if they work more than 16 hours per week)
Michigan	1 (certain family members who are employees may be exempt, certain very small employers are exempt), 3 (private employers)
Minnesota	1
Mississippi	5 (certain subcontractors' employees are covered, excludes domestic, farm, non-profit fraternal, charitable, religious, or cultural organizations)
Missouri	5 (includes full and part-time, seasonal, temporary), 1 (construction), except farm laborers, domestic servants, certain real estate agents, direct sales, commercial motor-carrier owner-operators
Montana	1
Nebraska	1
Nevada	1 (excluding independent enterprises)
New Hampshire	1 (including part-time workers)
New Jersey	1
New Mexico	3 (construction employers must cover any employees)
New York	1
North Carolina	3 (only 1 employee for businesses that involve radiation exposure)
North Dakota	1 (including part-time, seasonal, temporary workers)
Ohio	1
Oklahoma	1 (when a business has 5 or fewer family members as employees, the family members are exempt from coverage)
Oregon	1
Pennsylvania	1
Rhode Island	4
South Carolina	4 (some occupations exempt if <$3,000 in annual payroll), (including part-time workers)
South Dakota	1
Tennessee	5 (construction, subcontractors, and coal businesses must always have it)
Texas	No mandatory coverage except government contractors
Utah	1
Vermont	1 (agricultural/farming employers with annual payroll <$10,000 are exempt) (including part-time workers)
Virginia	3 (including part-time workers)
Washington	1
West Virginia	1 (independent contractors, agricultural employers with <3 employees, and casual employers are exempt)
Wisconsin	3 (including part-time workers, compliance time requirement varies by industry)
Wyoming	1

(Sources: NFIB and WCC)

rates. The Internal Revenue Service issued new mid-year tax withholding tables and forms in response to the changes mandated in this act. It introduced a new Employee's Withholding Certificate (Form W-4) and tax guide in 2020.

The *Consolidated Appropriations Act of 2018* increased the E-Verify program's funding, an Internet-based system that offers employers instant verification of an employee's eligibility to work in the United States. It is important to note that the E-Verify program does not replace the need to complete Form I-9 upon employee hire because it is a voluntary service. The following table from the USCIS compares the E-Verify program against the I-9 requirement.

Form I-9	E-Verify
Mandatory	Voluntary for most businesses
Requires a Social Security number	Requires a Social Security number
No photo required on identity documents	Photo is required on identity documents.
MUST be used to re-verify expired employment authorization	MAY NOT be used to re-verify employment authorization

(Source: USCIS)

Another important part of the Consolidated Appropriations Act included monetary penalties of $1,000 per instance (plus damages) for employers who withhold employee tip earnings inappropriately. This section of the act repealed a 2017 Department of Labor regulation that prevented employers from requiring that all tips be placed into a pool for tipped and nontipped employees. Although the act did not remove tip pools, it prevented managers and supervisors from participating in the tip pools.

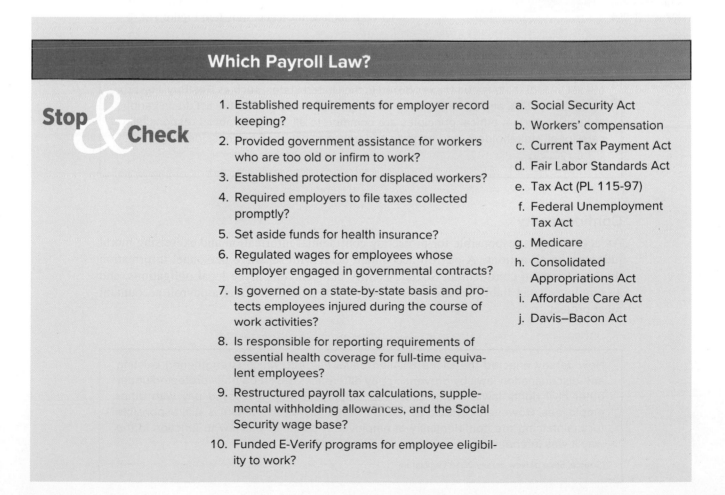

Which Payroll Law?

Stop & Check

1. Established requirements for employer record keeping?
2. Provided government assistance for workers who are too old or infirm to work?
3. Established protection for displaced workers?
4. Required employers to file taxes collected promptly?
5. Set aside funds for health insurance?
6. Regulated wages for employees whose employer engaged in governmental contracts?
7. Is governed on a state-by-state basis and protects employees injured during the course of work activities?
8. Is responsible for reporting requirements of essential health coverage for full-time equivalent employees?
9. Restructured payroll tax calculations, supplemental withholding allowances, and the Social Security wage base?
10. Funded E-Verify programs for employee eligibility to work?

a. Social Security Act
b. Workers' compensation
c. Current Tax Payment Act
d. Fair Labor Standards Act
e. Tax Act (PL 115-97)
f. Federal Unemployment Tax Act
g. Medicare
h. Consolidated Appropriations Act
i. Affordable Care Act
j. Davis–Bacon Act

The ***Coronavirus Aid, Relief and Economic Stimulus (CARES) Act of 2020*** was enacted to provide economic relief for individuals and businesses. It included an individual economic stimulus and encouragement for businesses to keep their employees. A tax credit of 50 percent of employees' wages (up to $10,000 in wages per employee) promoted employee retention for firms that sustained economic hardship during the pandemic and offered loans, funded by the Small Business Administration, to employers.

3D_creation/Shutterstock

LO 1-3 Discuss the Ethical Guidelines for Payroll Accounting

Professional *ethics* is critical in any accounting context, and especially so in payroll accounting. After the Enron accounting scandal and the passage of the Sarbanes–Oxley Act of 2002 (SOX), ethics became a focus of the accounting profession as a whole. Even with the SOX framework, the payroll industry is rife with ethical violations, including fraud and theft. The payroll accountant is entrusted to handle money belonging to the firm and rightfully owed to the government and company employees. Payment of these monies becomes a moral contract between the company and the recipients; therefore, ethics are vital in payroll accounting. Several accounting organizations, including the American Institute of Certified Public Accountants (AICPA), Institute of Management Accountants (IMA), and International Federation of Accountants (IFAC), have delineated codes of ethics that are applied in the accounting profession. The basic guidelines of an ethics code include the tenets shown in Figure 1-2.

FIGURE 1-2
Basic Guidelines for a Code of Ethics

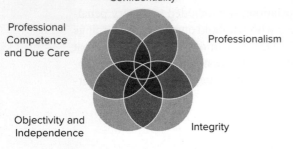

Confidentiality

Professional Competence and Due Care

Professionalism

Objectivity and Independence

Integrity

Ethisphere maintains an annual list of the most ethical companies in the world. In 2021, the list included many companies based in the United States, such as BestBuy, Hasbro, Salesforce, TIAA, and several others. Although the companies on the list are in various industries, certain ethical principles are common to all: integrity, social responsibility, care for all stakeholders, and honesty and transparency in all business dealings.

(Source: Ethisphere)

Confidentiality

An accountant is responsible for protecting confidential information and exercising moral judgment in all actions. A payroll accountant deals with sensitive personnel information that must remain confidential. Social Security numbers, employee legal obligations, and an employer's tax liabilities are a few examples of information that a payroll accountant must protect.

New Jersey enacted the Diane B. Allen Equal Pay Act, which strengthened existing anti-discrimination laws by preventing pay differences based on traits protected under other civil rights laws. It also protected employees who discussed pay with other employees. However, it should be noted that the payroll accountant is still responsible for maintaining the confidentiality of employee records for this law to function in the way it was intended.

(Source: State of New Jersey 2018 Legislature)

Professionalism

Accountants must uphold *professionalism* by maintaining confidentiality, maintaining the public's trust, and upholding professionalism in their practice. In terms of payroll accounting, professionalism includes honoring the firm's needs, its employees, and associated governmental entities. A payroll accountant must complete all tasks and adhere to deadlines despite any personal issues. Personal honesty and transparency of transactions are the core of acting professionally.

stockfour/Shutterstock

> Bechtel, a company that focuses on sustainable energy, company planning, and other location-based issues, has a code of conduct that has evolved over 100 years and multiple countries. Their ethical code requires employees to become educated and aware of potential ethical and legal conflicts in the United States and any of the countries in which they operate.
>
> (Source: Bechtel)

Integrity

In the workplace; integrity is the most important asset a professional can possess. *Integrity* involves doing the right thing despite any external pressure, personal temptations, or conflicts of interest. When weighing the integrity of a decision, the main question is: Am I doing what is right and just for everyone concerned? Any course of action that lacks integrity potentially restricts the rights of interested parties and compromises the company's best interests. The AICPA's code of ethics includes explicit direction about not covering up mistakes as part of an accountant's integrity.

> Payroll fraud can happen anywhere that pressures, opportunities, and rationalizations exist. A payroll specialist for a District of Columbia consulting firm was indicted on embezzlement charges involving fictitious employees. The payroll specialist stole over $250,000, including amounts deposited for payroll taxes, by changing the pay disbursement details of terminated employees. Instead of leaving the employees' files in a "terminated" status, the altered detail allowed automatic salary payments to continue but deposited to the payroll specialist's personal account. The payroll specialist, who plead guilty to wire fraud, was ordered to repay the employer $250,000 and was sentenced to 21 months in prison.
>
> (Source: U.S. Department of Justice)

Objectivity and Independence

Accountants must take care to be independent of any pressures that would compromise the integrity of their work. These pressures can come from business or personal relationships that may affect a payroll accountant's judgment concerning the best interests of all concerned in a given situation. *Objectivity* in accounting means that the accountant considers only facts relevant to the task at hand, independent of all other pressures. The Public Company Accounting Oversight Board (PCAOB) specifies that *independence* may be compromised if any of the following situations occur:

- Commitment to a future purchase of financial interest in a client's business.
- Personal or family ownership over 5 percent of a client's business.
- Professional engagement with a client's firm in which the payroll professional had a personal interest such as partial ownership.

> Social obligations may compromise a payroll accountant's objectivity. The AICPA Code of Ethics Section 17 specifically addresses social club membership as a factor in losing an accountant's independence or objectivity. Such club membership could create a social debt that may cause an accountant to commit payroll fraud.
>
> (Source: AICPA)

fizkes/Shutterstock

Professional Competence and Due Care

Professional competence and *due care* revolve around an accountant's competence and assume that the accounting professional is equally competent as other people in a similar role. In payroll accounting, due care is an ongoing process that involves education, training, and experience. According to the AICPA, an accountant must remain current with accounting practices and legal developments to comply with due care requirements. Payroll laws and tax guidelines change regularly. As a payroll accountant, it is essential to remain aware of annual changes that the IRS and other accounting bodies publish through participation in professional accounting organizations, subscriptions to accounting industry publications, and participation in discussions at accounting conferences.

Staying current with payroll changes is an ongoing task. Some of the sources for this information include

- IRS (www.irs.gov).
- AICPA (www.aicpa.org).
- Financial Accounting Standards Board (FASB) (www.fasb.org).
- American Payroll Association (www.americanpayroll.org).
- U.S. Department of Labor (www.dol.gov).
- Compliance Tools for HR Professionals (www.hr.blr.com).

What's Ethical?

Stop & Check

1. Giles Montragon is the payroll accountant for his company. His boss informs him that the company is considering switching payroll systems and asks for his input. What are some ethical concerns involved in changing accounting software?

2. Liza Beals, the payroll manager, is in a sorority. At a social event, she discovers that one of her sorority sisters works for the same company. Her sorority sister asks Liza for confidential information about one of her department employees, claiming that the sorority oath requires Liza's compliance. What should Liza do?

Blue Planet Studio/Shutterstock

LO 1-4   Identify Contemporary Payroll Practices

Contemporary accounting practices reflect the effects of technology and electronic communications on business. Payroll practices have adapted to include modern tools that facilitate data transmission, and new challenges such as the following have emerged:

- Direct deposit regulations for employee pay and tax remittances.
- Electronic filing requirements.
- New timekeeping methods.
- The availability of paycards as a method of wage and salary disbursement.
- Government contract influences on the payroll.
- International employees.

- Simultaneous in-house and outsourced payroll personnel.
- Integration of payroll into other company functions.
- Security of confidential, electronic personnel information.
- Cloud-based software designed for security, accessibility, and portability of data.

Payroll is not a stand-alone department. Integrated software packages offered by mainstream accounting software providers, such as QuickBooks and Sage 100, allow business owners to view data across departments and synthesize the information to make large-scale decisions. Contemporary payroll systems serve as a tool for strategic planning, performance measurement, and customer/vendor relations using mobile, cloud-based platforms that may be accessed through Internet-connected devices. Payroll accountants are a key element in the decision-making process. They must remain educated about legal and compliance issues and remain current in their understanding of software applications and relevant technological concerns.

The payroll accountant plays a vital role in a company's structure, no matter how large or small. Payroll and other employee benefits often represent the largest category of a company's expenses. Chipotle Mexican Grill Inc. (CMG) originally started as a subsidiary of McDonald's. CMG is now a separate entity and currently reported nearly $1.5 billion in payroll expenses in its stores during the fiscal year 2019, which represented an 11 percent increase over 2018. As an innovative company in the fast-food market, CMG has integrated technology and sustainability measures to engage customers and promote locally sourced ingredients to support local farmers. Notice in the following table how, despite technology integration, CMG's labor expenses are nearly as large as its product-related expenses.

CHIPOTLE MEXICAN GRILL INC.			
OPERATING COSTS AND EXPENSES (in millions, selected data)			
Company-operated restaurant expenses	2020	2019	2018
Food, beverage, and packaging	1,932.8	1,847.9	1,600.8
Labor	1,593.0	1,472.1	1,326.1
Occupancy	387.8	363.1	347.1
Other operating costs	1,030.0	760.8	680.0
General & administrative expenses	466.3	451.6	375.5
Total operating expenses	5,694.5	5,142.4	4,606.6
Operating income	290.2	444.0	258.4

(Source: SEC)

Payroll Preparation Options

Several options exist for payroll preparation. The most frequently used methods for contemporary payroll preparation are electronic accounting programs. Other options available are the manual calculation of payroll using spreadsheets and charts prepared by the Internal Revenue Service and payroll preparation by outsourcing the process to a third party such as **ADP**, **Paychex®**, and **myPay Solutions**. A hybrid solution that allows the company to outsource certain payroll functions to an external provider exists with online accounting software provided by companies such as Intuit and Sage, creators of **QuickBooks** and **Sage 100**, respectively.

Online banks are starting to enter the payroll industry as a means to facilitate payroll access via smartphones. **Chime Bank** advertises access to directly deposited funds up to two days before the employer's payment date, based on the employer's funds availability. Another option targeted for small employers includes **Amboy Bank**, which offers payroll processing, reporting, and banking services that simplify the payroll process for both employers and their employees.

Regardless of the payroll preparation method, the payroll accountant needs to understand how the process should work. In the event of hardware failure, legislative actions, or tax changes, the accountant must ensure accurate payroll preparation. Companies can lose credibility as the result of flawed payroll and be subject to substantial fines, IRS audits, and civil litigation. Cases in which companies have paid fines for improper payroll practices abound.

Chuy's Mesquite Broiler in Arizona was fined over $20,000 in late-payment penalties and had to pay employees nearly $115,000 in unpaid overtime pay. The employer chose to pay its employees the first 40 hours of work via check and overtime in a separate check or cash. The problem was that the separate check for the overtime was paid at regular pay rates that did not include the overtime premium required by FLSA.

(Source: *KOLD*)

Some companies have seriously shortchanged employees' paychecks, paying fines in addition to the standard payroll expenditures. Other tales of employee overpayment highlight payroll systems problems, such as computer glitches that have delayed payment of the company's wages. Because the computer glitches are ultimately the responsibility of a company's president or CEO and represent a potential for ethical breaches, the volume of legislation and stories of problems involving payroll administration point to the need for a well-established payroll system. Despite the numerous federal and state legislative actions concerning payroll practices, none delineate the format and design of a payroll system.

The information contained in the personnel records is highly sensitive and must be protected against intrusion from unnecessary parties. The *Privacy Act of 1974* guarantees the safeguarding of information in private personnel records and mandates information safekeeping and due process rights to individuals. Consider the implications of the legal requirements of information safekeeping:

- Personnel records contain information about an individual's marital status, children, other dependents, and legal residence—sensitive information that must be protected under the Privacy Act of 1974.
- Payroll records generally have information about the hourly rate and salary information for each employee. Access to these records is protected by provisions of the *Equal Employment Opportunity Commission (EEOC)* and could provoke or inhibit discrimination lawsuits.
- The information contained in payroll records influences the accuracy and integrity of a company's accounting records. The recording of payroll expenses and liabilities affects a company's profitability, which influences investor and customer relations.
- Companies engaging in business with the federal government must comply with the Davis–Bacon Act (for federal contracts) and potentially the *Copeland Anti-Kickback Act* of 1934 (or construction projects, protecting taxpayers from unethical pay practices).
- The number of hours worked by an employee must comply with the Fair Labor Standards Act provisions.
- Deductions for payroll, especially for retirement plans, must be documented and verified per the Sarbanes–Oxley Act of 2002.

Employers must file tax deposits for employee withholding, Social Security, Medicare, FUTA, and SUTA taxes according to an identified timeline depending upon the size of the company's payroll. Taxes may be remitted via telephone, Internet, mail, or the company's payroll software program. Additional reports are required from the employer on either a quarterly or an annual basis. A company has many responsibilities within its payroll system:

- Tax withholding must be done consistently, reflecting the requirements of federal, state, and local authorities.
- Employers must match amounts withheld from employee paychecks for certain payroll taxes.

- Withholding of deductions that the employee voluntarily elects, such as health care, insurance, and investments, must be correctly recorded and reported.
- Timely and accurate payment must be made to the employee, government agencies, and companies for which the employee has designated the voluntary deductions.
- Tax and other liabilities must be reported to governmental agencies per established deadlines.

An accurate payroll system allows managers to focus on the firm's business, not payroll administration. As such, a well-designed system benefits the employees and governmental agencies, and thus the firm. The timely forwarding of any monies withheld from employees, either by governmental regulation or voluntary election, is critical to a firm's success.

Besides administrating employee pay, a well-designed and accurately maintained payroll system is necessary during inevitable governmental audits or potential business operation interruptions, as seen during the COVID-19 pandemic during 2020. An audit is a process by which a third-party organization, either a public accounting firm or a government agency, inspects the accounting records for accuracy, integrity, and compliance with federal rules and regulations. During a payroll audit, the auditor inspects the company's records of employee pay, tax remittance, and voluntary deduction maintenance. The thought of audits instills fear into the hearts of even the most seasoned accounting professionals. Their salvation, however, is to establish and maintain an accurate payroll system.

Consider the growth of selected companies:

rh2010/123RF

- Tom's of Maine started in 1968 as a local organic personal care product company and is now a nationally recognized leader in environmental stewardship and sustainability. (Source: www.tomsofmaine.com)
- Ben and Jerry's, which started with a $5 correspondence course in ice-cream making and a $12,000 investment in 1978, has become an icon of premium ice cream and environmental causes. Ben and Jerry's has since been purchased by the Unilever Corporation and maintains an independent board of directors. (Source: www.benjerry.com)
- McDonald's Corporation was started in 1955 by the McDonald brothers when selling their hamburger business to Ray Kroc. The brand is now an international icon for fast food, serving approximately 68 million customers in 120 countries each day.

These companies share similar beginnings: one location, a few employees, and a relatively simple payroll. As each company has grown, so has the payroll complexity, including multiple departments and facilities in many states and countries. At the heart of each company are a well-run business model and a sound payroll system that has evolved with it.

Tracking and monitoring employee hours, locations, and applicable governmental requirements within various nations require knowledgeable payroll staff, willing to remain current with accounting trends and international regulations. Sophisticated payroll systems enable companies to create, populate, and file many documents using current software and Internet technology.

Privacy Protection

A company must make every reasonable effort to protect personnel information contained in payroll records. This is a critical part of any payroll accountant's job. Several federal privacy acts exist to protect the information contained in payroll and personnel records. Additionally, many states have enacted or expanded specific data privacy legislation. Each state's privacy law refers to "reasonable" steps that companies must take to protect customers' information.

greenbutterfly/Shutterstock

Privacy acts include (but are certainly not limited to)

- U.S. Department of Health and Human Services **Privacy Act 09-40-0006** pertains to public employees' eligibility for pay, entitlements, raises, and benefits.

- Common-Law Privacy Act, which pertains to freedom from misuse or abuse of one's private affairs.
- Privacy Act of 1974, about the use of information about private citizens.
- Computer Fraud and Abuse Act (CFAA) of 1986 addresses cybercrime, an issue that has grown in importance in recent years.

The General Accounting Office of the federal government has been working on revising guidelines about the privacy of records and releasing information as the Internet and e-business evolve. The U.S. Congress has sought ways to address contemporary computer-based cyber threats but has not passed legislation at the federal level. States have enacted privacy laws, especially as they pertain to social media, to protect employees against cyber hacks.

> Online privacy is a growing concern, and it affects the security of payroll data. Employees at New-York-based Barney's went unpaid in early 2020 when a hacker group gained control of the payroll system on one of its servers. Employees were unpaid for over a week, and some employees terminated their employment in protest.
>
> (Source: *Page Six*)

Tero Vesalainen/Shutterstock

The common element among these laws is protecting sensitive employee information such as addresses, dependents, compensation amounts, and payroll deductions. The payroll accountant is also responsible for discretion in discussing pay rates, bonuses, or other compensation-related topics with employees and management. Sensitive topics should never be discussed with anyone other than the employee or appropriate managers. All employment-related items may be viewed during an audit of payroll records, and auditors must treat the information with absolute confidentiality.

One way that the federal government keeps track of employers is with *Employer Identification Numbers (EINs)*. The EIN allows the IRS to know which companies may have employees, generating employment tax revenue for the government, and creating tax liabilities for employers. Form SS-4 (see Figure 1-3) is used to apply for an EIN by providing the personal Social Security number, type of business, and the existence of any prior EINs for a business owner. The EIN is required for all tax deposits, tax returns, and informational returns. It will appear on the company's Form W-2s, 940s, 941s, state tax forms, and the company's annual tax return. Form SS-4 may be completed either on paper or through an IRS online request portal that contains the same information as the paper form.

Confidential Records

Stop & Check

You are the payroll clerk of a company. A group of students approaches you to work on a class project and asks to see confidential personnel and payroll records. What would you do? What are the laws regarding the situation?

FIGURE 1-3
Example of Form SS-4

Form **SS-4** (Rev. December 2019) Department of the Treasury Internal Revenue Service	**Application for Employer Identification Number** (For use by employers, corporations, partnerships, trusts, estates, churches, government agencies, Indian tribal entities, certain individuals, and others.) ▶ Go to *www.irs.gov/FormSS4* for instructions and the latest information. ▶ See separate instructions for each line. ▶ Keep a copy for your records.	OMB No. 1545-0003 EIN

Type or print clearly.

1	Legal name of entity (or individual) for whom the EIN is being requested		
	Thomas Braden			

2	Trade name of business (if different from name on line 1)	3	Executor, administrator, trustee, "care of" name
	Braden Fisheries		

4a	Mailing address (room, apt., suite no. and street, or P.O. box)	5a	Street address (if different) (Don't enter a P.O. box.)
	1234 Coastal Highway		
4b	City, state, and ZIP code (if foreign, see instructions)	5b	City, state, and ZIP code (if foreign, see instructions)
	Anchorage, AK 99509		

6	County and state where principal business is located
	Anchorage, Alaska

7a	Name of responsible party	7b	SSN, ITIN, or EIN
	Thomas Braden		445-54-4554

8a	Is this application for a limited liability company (LLC) (or a foreign equivalent)? ☑ Yes ☐ No	8b	If 8a is "Yes," enter the number of LLC members ▶ 3

8c	If 8a is "Yes," was the LLC organized in the United States? . . . . ☑ Yes ☐ No

9a Type of entity (check only one box). **Caution:** If 8a is "Yes," see the instructions for the correct box to check.

☐ Sole proprietor (SSN) _____
☐ Partnership
☐ Corporation (enter form number to be filed) ▶ _____
☐ Personal service corporation
☐ Church or church-controlled organization
☐ Other nonprofit organization (specify) ▶ _____
☑ Other (specify) ▶ **Disregarded Entity**

☐ Estate (SSN of decedent) _____
☐ Plan administrator (TIN) _____
☐ Trust (TIN of grantor) _____
☐ Military/National Guard ☐ State/local government
☐ Farmers' cooperative ☐ Federal government
☐ REMIC ☐ Indian tribal governments/enterprises
Group Exemption Number (GEN) if any ▶

9b	If a corporation, name the state or foreign country (if applicable) where incorporated	State	Foreign country

10 **Reason for applying** (check only one box)
☑ Started new business (specify type) ▶ **Commercial Fishing**
☐ Hired employees (Check the box and see line 13.)
☐ Compliance with IRS withholding regulations
☐ Other (specify) ▶

☐ Banking purpose (specify purpose) ▶ _____
☐ Changed type of organization (specify new type) ▶ _____
☐ Purchased going business
☐ Created a trust (specify type) ▶ _____
☐ Created a pension plan (specify type) ▶ _____

11	Date business started or acquired (month, day, year). See instructions. 05/01/2021	12	Closing month of accounting year December

13	Highest number of employees expected in the next 12 months (enter -0- if none). If no employees expected, skip line 14.	14	If you expect your employment tax liability to be $1,000 or less in a full calendar year **and** want to file Form 944 annually instead of Forms 941 quarterly, check here. (Your employment tax liability generally will be $1,000 or less if you expect to pay $5,000 or less in total wages.) If you don't check this box, you must file Form 941 for every quarter. ☐

Agricultural	Household	Other
15		

15	First date wages or annuities were paid (month, day, year). **Note:** If applicant is a withholding agent, enter date income will first be paid to nonresident alien (month, day, year) . . . . ▶ 05/15/2021

16 Check **one** box that best describes the principal activity of your business.
☐ Construction ☐ Rental & leasing ☐ Transportation & warehousing
☐ Real estate ☐ Manufacturing ☐ Finance & insurance
☐ Health care & social assistance ☐ Wholesale-agent/broker
☐ Accommodation & food service ☐ Wholesale-other ☐ Retail
☑ Other (specify) ▶ **Commercial Fishing**

17	Indicate principal line of merchandise sold, specific construction work done, products produced, or services provided. Fish and Seafood

18	Has the applicant entity shown on line 1 ever applied for and received an EIN? ☐ Yes ☑ No If "Yes," write previous EIN here ▶

Third Party Designee	Complete this section **only** if you want to authorize the named individual to receive the entity's EIN and answer questions about the completion of this form.		
	Designee's name		Designee's telephone number (include area code)
	Address and ZIP code		Designee's fax number (include area code)

Under penalties of perjury, I declare that I have examined this application, and to the best of my knowledge and belief, it is true, correct, and complete.

Name and title (type or print clearly) ▶ Thomas Braden, President

	Applicant's telephone number (include area code)
	907-555-1346

Signature ▶ *Thomas Braden*   Date ▶ 05/01/2021

	Applicant's fax number (include area code)
	907-555-9876

For Privacy Act and Paperwork Reduction Act Notice, see separate instructions.   Cat. No. 16055N   Form **SS-4** (Rev. 12-2019)

Source: Internal Revenue Service.

LO 1-5 Compare Payroll Processing Options for Different Businesses

Companies have several options for payroll processing. The option a company chooses depends on the business's size, the business's complexity in terms of geographic placement and business

Jeanette Landin

model, the capital available for payroll processing, and the availability of trained personnel.

During the middle of the 20th century, employers measured workers' time using punch clocks and handwritten timesheets. Contemporary time collection devices serve as more than simple time clocks. Although the old-fashioned punch clocks still exist, companies have integrated different time-collection systems as part of their office security and computer access procedures. Time clocks are used as part of a security system to log in people as they enter a building for work, yield analysis of simple on-site versus working-hour time.

Many companies now use biometric devices such as fingerprint readers to collect time for their hourly employees. Systems such as **Kronos** offer biometric badges and time-collection devices that connect with office telephones. Using computer access as another type of collection device serves a similar function and can offer specific task tracking and precise timekeeping functionality. With mobile connectivity growth, companies now have many smartphone apps, such as **WhenIWork** and **ExakTime,** to track employee attendance and productivity. Practices relating to time collection are a vital element in payroll accuracy.

The basic elements of a payroll system are similar for all companies, but this is when size does matter. However, it is the company's size and the complexity of the laws that affect payroll procedures. Let's look at the differences between large and small company payrolls and then explore certified payroll issues.

Large Businesses

Large companies present intricate problems for payroll accountants. Companies such as Apple, Alphabet (Google), and Microsoft have multiple divisions, many of which exist in different geographical locations. General Electric (GE) has different companies that operate as separate entities within GE's framework. Payroll procedures reflect the intricacy of the company's structure and may take many forms.

Elnur Amikishiyev/123RF

One of the major challenges in larger organizations is the existence of multiple departments in which an individual employee may work on any given day. Some companies can have shared employees who will have allocable time to more than one department; for example, one employee may work for both the marketing and the production departments. When this occurs, the payroll accountant will have to record the time worked for each department, and pay rates may differ based on the tasks that the employee performs for each department.

A common payroll procedure with large companies involves employee portals on company websites. On the company's payroll website, employees may enter vacation time, overtime, and other issues that pertain to the employee's payroll data. Through the same website, employees may change withholding allowances and voluntary deductions and maintain certain aspects of their employees' files. Such web-based portals contain highly sensitive information, and the security of the information is an obvious concern for the companies who use them. Multiple identity checks and security measures are in place to ensure employee data privacy, such as SSL (secure sockets layer) encryption, *VPN* (a virtual private network), and CAPTCHA programs designed to differentiate between humans and other computer programs.

Providing employees with Internet-based access to their personnel files is a challenging issue. Federal laws do not grant employees the right to access their personnel files, and companies must be aware of state laws before providing access. Questions of assigning access to other parties (such as union representatives), access to file artifacts, and the employee's right to challenge items in their file are issues that a firm should address when creating a web portal through which employees may access payroll records. Also, issues of cybersecurity and online privacy must be addressed.

(Source: SHRM)

To overcome some of the issues with payroll processing; large companies may rely heavily on payroll service vendors to assist with payroll preparation and human resources integration. Providers such as MyPaySolutions and ADP work with the company's security needs to offer websites that are secure and integrate multiple personnel functions seamlessly. Some larger firms will work with software engineers to develop independent systems, specifically meeting unique company needs.

Large companies face other issues related to accurate timekeeping, such as the volume of employee records. Companies with computerized time-measurement systems may link employees' computer logins, telephone logins, or building access with the payroll system. Companies working with radio frequency time cards and electronic payroll monitoring can properly allocate employee time to specific machines or production lines. With the currently available computer software and services, large companies have many options to maintain their payroll systems' accuracy and integrity.

Small Businesses

One apparent difference between large and small businesses is the volume and handling of payroll records. A small number of employees generally leads to fewer payroll-related transactions. Manual payroll systems may be maintained in very small businesses, including the use of handwritten time cards. Outsourcing of payroll activities may not be as prominent. With a small company, the amount of time to complete payroll-related tasks may be less than in a large company. For a small company, the task can be performed without disrupting the revenue-producing tasks of the business.

mavo/Shutterstock

Small companies have the option of processing payroll in-house with a minimum of difficulty. However, small companies may lack specifically trained payroll personnel, which may place employee pay and benefits on other personnel and increase the risk of pay or tax inaccuracies. The human resource director, office manager, and payroll professional may perform the same person's roles. Using payroll software and a properly designed payroll system, the task of payroll for a small company is generally manageable by minimal company staff. Small companies may choose to explore outsourcing as the company grows. Outsourcing payroll may be a viable option if the task becomes unwieldy or legal obligations become unmanageable.

Small companies have an option to use hosting services as a way to access cloud-storage, subscription-based services that possess security comparable to on-site accounting software. Hosted payroll accounting software can change in scale without the need for additional software licensing, update issues, or specific hardware.

For more information about hosted payroll, check out these top-rated services:

- Paychex
- Intuit Payroll
- Gusto
- OnPay
- SurePayroll

(Source: Business News Daily)

Depending on the size of the company, number of employees, and complexity of the payroll process, the company may choose to purchase a computer-based accounting system, it may continue to prepare worksheets and manual payroll checks, or it can decide to use an *outsourced vendor* for payroll preparation and associated tasks to an external vendor. Contemporary best practices often include cloud-based software due to the frequency and necessity of software updates and the file size. Whichever decisions the company makes as it grows, the importance of understanding the mechanics of the payroll process is paramount. Whether a company performs the payroll process in-house or outsources it, it is liable for payroll filing compliance. The next section provides an overview of the various computer-based systems available.

Common payroll mistakes made by small firms include

- Misclassifying employees as independent contractors.
- Paying payroll late.
- Omitting the value of gift cards awarded to employees as part of their taxable income.
- Failure to make timely and/or accurate payroll tax deposits.
- Improper treatment of expense reimbursements made to employees.
- Incorrect treatment of taxable fringe benefits.

(Source: *Accounting Today*)

Large vs. Small

Stop & Check

1. What are three potential payroll processing issues faced by large companies?
2. How does payroll processing differ between large and small companies?

Computer-Based Systems

Various accounting software packages exist to facilitate payroll-related accounting tasks, including QuickBooks, Sage 100, and Microsoft Dynamics GP. The use of computerized payroll systems eliminates approximately 80 percent of payroll processing time and errors. Computerized accounting systems foster the integration of payroll data with other company financial functions through Enterprise Resource Planning (ERP), allowing decision-makers to develop a comprehensive understanding of the company's operational needs. Although payroll professionals must verify employee data and update the software at regular intervals, computerized systems reduce the burdens of manual pay calculations, pay disbursement, and report compilation from the payroll accountant.

When used properly, small companies may benefit from a computerized payroll system. Although concerns about the confidentiality of personnel records exist, electronic access to records may streamline certain tasks, such as employee information updates and overtime reporting. Additionally, as the year-end approaches, companies can deliver the employees' W-2 (see Figure 1-4) tax forms electronically, ensuring employees' rapid access to their tax documents.

A trend in payroll processing involves the issuance of electronic paycards, much like preloaded credit cards, instead of paper checks. Paycards offer the employees the flexibility to wait for their paycheck to be deposited at a bank. Companies that offer direct deposit as a payment option must offer paycards to employees who do not have bank accounts. However, a paycard can be lost or stolen, and with it, the employee's paycheck. Additionally, employers may be charged fees for

FIGURE 1-4
Form W-2 Wage and Tax Statement

22222	**a** Employee's social security number **444-44-4444**	OMB No. 1545-0008		
b Employer identification number (EIN) 12-1234567			**1** Wages, tips, other compensation 21689.20	**2** Federal income tax withheld 1858.00
c Employer's name, address, and ZIP code Some Company 123 Main Street Anywhere, Anystate 00000			**3** Social security wages 22369.20	**4** Social security tax withheld 1386.89
			5 Medicare wages and tips 22369.20	**6** Medicare tax withheld 324.74
			7 Social security tips	**8** Allocated tips
d Control number			**9**	**10** Dependent care benefits
e Employee's first name and initial Last name Suff. Connie L. Baines P.O. Box 11211 Sioux City, IA 73217			**11** Nonqualified plans	**12a** DD 707.00
			13 Statutory employee ☐ Retirement plan ☒ Third-party sick pay ☐	**12b**
			14 Other	**12c**
f Employee's address and ZIP code				**12d**
15 State Employer's state ID number IA 1866748	**16** State wages, tips, etc. 21689.20	**17** State income tax 976.01	**18** Local wages, tips, etc.	**19** Local income tax **20** Localityname

Form **W-2** Wage and Tax Statement   2021   Department of the Treasury—Internal Revenue Service
Copy 1—For State, City, or Local Tax Department

Source: Internal Revenue Service.

loading a paycard. When companies consider paycards as an option, it is important to communicate to employees an understanding that there may be costs assessed by the card issuer.

Internet-Based Systems

Internet-based accounting software is an option for a company that does not need, or have the resources to purchase, a computer-based accounting system. Computer-based accounting systems such as QuickBooks, Microsoft Dynamics GP, and Sage 100 Standard offer both desktop and Internet-based services for businesses. Companies such as such as Xero and Wave have developed Internet-only accounting packages accessible for a monthly fee. The advantages of using Internet-based services include the ease of access for accounting personnel and managers and automatic software updates. A potential disadvantage of relying on Internet-based software for a company's accounting is information security issues.

Accounting Today conducted case studies with firms that had used Internet-based accounting software and highlighted the following:

Positive Aspects	Challenges
Timely identification of financial issues because of the ease of access to company records	Users cannot usually customize certain information layouts to suit specific company needs
Low price for software access and "real-time" knowledge of business information	Not suitable for highly complex businesses such as large manufacturing operations
Increased opportunity for collaboration in the business planning and monitoring process	Employee resistance to learning about new software and company accounting process
Continual software updates for changes in tax rates or other related practices	More options available than company personnel knew how to use

It is estimated that advances in predictive software and Artificial Intelligence-based systems will make accounting software more useful for small businesses, enabling companies to engage in real-time business analysis that had been previously out of their reach. Additionally, software advances will enable business owners to be more flexible in conducting business regarding the work location, information demands, and data transmittal.

(Source: *Accounting Today*)

Manual Systems

With manual payroll systems, the payroll employee relies on deduction percentages presented in publications from the Internal Revenue Service. *Publication 15* (also known as *Circular E*) and *Publication 15-T* are the manual payroll accountant's best friends, along with periodic updates and supplemental publications.

namtipStudio/Shutterstock

The largest challenges the manual payroll preparer faces are time constraints and updated tax tables. Companies can determine the length of time between the end of the payroll period and the employee payments to a certain extent. However, employers must make every reasonable effort to pay their employees in a timely and accurate manner to avoid ethical breaches and potentially costly litigation.

Manual payroll accountants may use spreadsheet programs, such as Microsoft Excel. The accountant can create lookup formulas or other connecting formulas to facilitate the payroll process's accurate completion. Spreadsheets with formulas or macros should be used only if the accountant understands the formulas and can verify the linkage before finalizing payroll to ensure that calculations are correct.

> According to the IRS, approximately 40 percent of all small businesses make payroll errors, averaging $845 in fines per year. The most common errors include mathematical computations, missed payments, or late payments.
>
> (Source: *Journal of Accountancy, IRS*)

Outsourced Payroll Systems

Outsourced payroll processing has become rather popular to ensure compliance with the changing legal structure and withholding requirements. When a company chooses to use an outsourcing firm to complete the payroll processes, there are several considerations: records retention, confidentiality, compliance, timeliness, and thoroughness. Managers should review the cost/benefits of outsourcing a firm's payroll processes before committing.

External payroll providers offer flexibility and advanced data analysis that might be challenging for smaller internal departments. During a survey of more than 2,000 accounting professionals, an overwhelming margin stated they would prefer to outsource payroll functions because of the process's time. External payroll management providers such as ADP and Paychex® assist company owners and managers with strategic planning and related human resources issues. However, outsourcing is not a wise decision for all companies. For a small company, outsourcing may not be cost-effective. For large or international companies, outsourcing may be the only option to manage payroll complexity.

A recent trend in payroll accounting involves cloud-based computing, meaning that the data is housed on a server external to the firm and accessible via an Internet connection. Companies such as ADP offer cloud-based payroll and human resource functions for businesses. These services reduce costs by allowing a company to avoid hardware and software costs associated with payroll. However, issues have arisen with payroll vendor stability and information security.

> In late 2019, payroll provider MyPayrollHR terminated business operations abruptly, leaving hundreds of thousands of employees without the pay they were due from the thousands of employers that relied on the service. FBI investigators have warned companies to complete thorough background and reliability checks on outsourced payroll vendors before entrusting employee payroll to them.
>
> (Source: American Payroll Association)

Certified Payroll

Companies who do business with the federal government under the Davis–Bacon Act must file a report (see Figure 1-5 for Form WH-347) delineating the payroll paid as part of the government

FIGURE 1-5

Form WH-347 Certified Payroll

U.S. Department of Labor
Wage and Hour Division

PAYROLL
(For Contractor's Optional Use; See Instructions at www.dol.gov/whd/forms/wh347instr.htm)
Persons are not required to respond to the collection of information unless it displays a currently valid OMB control number.

WHD
U.S. Wage and Hour Division
Rev. Dec. 2008

NAME OF CONTRACTOR ☐ OR SUBCONTRACTOR ☐	ADDRESS	OMB No.:1235-0008 Expires: 04/30/2021

PAYROLL NO.	FOR WEEK ENDING	PROJECT AND LOCATION	PROJECT OR CONTRACT NO.

(1) NAME AND INDIVIDUAL IDENTIFYING NUMBER (e.g. LAST FOUR DIGITS OF SOCIAL SECURITY NUMBER) OF WORKER	(2) NO. OF WITHHOLDING EXEMPTIONS	(3) WORK CLASSIFICATION	OT. OR ST.	(4) DAY AND DATE — HOURS WORKED EACH DAY	(5) TOTAL HOURS	(6) RATE OF PAY	(7) GROSS AMOUNT EARNED	(8) DEDUCTIONS — FICA	WITH-HOLDING TAX			OTHER	TOTAL DEDUCTIONS	(9) NET WAGES PAID FOR WEEK
			O											
			S											
			O											
			S											

Source: U.S. Department of Labor.

contract with each payroll. ***Certified payroll*** is how the federal government keeps track of the money spent as part of government contracts. Davis–Bacon Act–related wages and the state versions of those regulations require special handling and knowledge. Certified payroll facilitates governmental internal accountability and verifies that Davis–Bacon Act requirements are met.

Information needed to complete a Certified Payroll report includes

✓ Company-specific identifying information.
✓ The job being worked on and its duration.
✓ Employee information that includes a social security number and address.
✓ Hours worked on each job and the pay rate associated with it.
✓ Gross pay earned for the week.
✓ Taxes, withholdings, and fringe benefits.
✓ Net pay earned per employee.

Choosing payroll technology can be a complex task for employees charged with finding appropriate technological solutions. Some of the considerations include

- Flexibility in pay options.
- Time collection procedures.
- Tax reporting.
- Geotagging of employee work locations.
- Software affordability.
- Software update schedules.

What Is the Difference?

Stop & Check

In a few words, compare the following:

a. Manual payroll systems
b. Computerized payroll systems
c. Outsourced payroll systems
d. Certified payroll

LEGAL ENVIRONMENT

To say that the legal environment of payroll is continually evolving is an understatement. Since 2017, we have witnessed the following legal challenges:

- Increasing numbers of private employers and localities raise the minimum wage significantly to close the minimum wage gap and the living wage.
- Challenges to the Affordable Care Act related to the overturn of the individual mandate for health care coverage.
- Supplemental wage rate changes for payments of bonuses.
- State enforcement of predictive scheduling, fair/flexible scheduling laws on changing employee's schedules.
- Reframing the federal income tax structure, treatment for nonresident aliens, supplemental wage withholding rates, and inflation adjustments.

Some trends to watch include

- A shift to complete digitalization of payroll processes, including partial or complete remote work options.
- Increased guidance about payroll tax impacts of COVID-19 as it affects employees, both part- and full-time.
- An increase in the need for centralized and fully communicated company policies to meet remote workers' needs.
- Payroll data will increase in importance for business decisions.

Summary of Payroll Practices and System Fundamentals

Accounting practices have existed for centuries, and a need continually exists for employers to compensate employees for the work they have performed. Once the United States began taxing personal income, payroll processing became increasingly complex. During the 20th century, payroll practices evolved to include withholding taxes from employees, remitting payroll taxes to government agencies, maintaining accurate and confidential records, and incorporating civil rights-related legislation. Payroll accounting is a field that requires precision and attention to minute details due to its changing nature. Additionally, payroll accountants must adhere to ethical guidelines, including due care, objectivity, and independence, professional competence, integrity, and confidentiality because of the nature of their work.

The establishment of a 21st-century payroll system involves careful, deliberate planning. The framework used for the payroll system must have ample room for company growth, structure to ensure system stability, and trained payroll personnel to ensure that company and government deadlines are met. Using the best practices outlined in this chapter may help a company implement a robust payroll system, whether the system is maintained by company personnel, outsourced, completed manually, or accomplished using specifically designed software. Robust payroll system design may reduce or prevent problems with employees and governmental entities.

Key Points

- Legislation that has affected employees' working conditions has mandated many aspects of the workplace, including civil rights, retirement and health benefits, and reinvestment in American workers.

- Payroll-specific legislation has influenced working hours and employee wages and was updated in 2020 to address contemporary employer concerns.

- Employer and employee tax laws have been enacted, and the remittance of tax obligations has been mandated.

- Payroll accountants must adhere to ethical guidelines because of the nature of the work performed.

- The ethical principles of confidentiality, integrity, objectivity, independence, and professional competence and due care guide the payroll accounting profession.

- Payroll practices include the electronic transmission of employee pay and tax obligations.

- The security of employee information is an ongoing concern for companies, especially with the electronic transmission of sensitive data.

- Payroll may be processed at a central corporate site or through an outsourced payroll processing company.

- Many companies use payroll accounting software, such as QuickBooks and Sage 100.

- Cloud-based payroll processing has offered many resources for companies, including partial or total payroll preparation services.

- Payroll security and privacy are critical to ensure employer legal compliance and to protect employees.

Vocabulary

ACA	EEOC	OSHA
ADA	Employer Identification	Personal Responsibility,
ADAAA	Number (EIN)	Work and Family
ADEA	Enterprise Coverage	Promotion Act of 2002
ARRA	Equal Pay Act of 1963	Privacy Act of 1974
ATRA	ERISA	Protecting Americans from
Certified payroll	Ethics	Tax Hikes (PATH) Act
Circular E	FICA	Professional competence
Civil Rights Act of 1964	FLSA	Professionalism
Civil Rights Act of 1991	FMLA	PRWOR
COBRA	FUTA	Publication 15
Consolidated	HIPAA	Publication 15-T
Appropriations Act of	Independence	SECURE
2018	Independent contractor	Sixteenth Amendment to
Copeland Anti-Kickback	Individual Coverage	the U.S. Constitution
Act	Integrity	Social Security Act (SSA)
Coronavirus Aid, Relief	IRCA	SOX
and Economic Stimulus	Lilly Ledbetter Fair Pay Act	SUTA
(CARES) Act of 2020	of 2009	Tax Cuts and Jobs Act
Current Tax Payment Act	Living Wage	USERRA
(CTPA) of 1943	Medicare	VPN
Davis–Bacon Act of 1931	Minimum Wage	Walsh–Healey Public
DOMA	OASDI	Contracts Act
Due care	Objectivity	Workers' compensation

Review Questions

1. What is the purpose of a payroll system?

2. What are two of the differences between large- and small-company payroll practices?

3. What is certified payroll? Which companies must use it?

4. Why might it be a good idea to let employees manage their payroll records? What are some of the pitfalls?

5. What are two ways a payroll system may protect a company in the event of a visit from a government auditor?

6. What is payroll outsourcing? When might a company consider outsourcing its payroll?

7. What are three examples of federal laws that are essential to ensure legal, fair hiring practices?

8. What are the major types of payroll processing methods?

9. What are two laws governing the taxes that employers must withhold from employees?

10. What are the guidelines for FLSA in terms of overtime and pay rate?

11. Why was the Social Security Act of 1935 created? What were its provisions?

12. What are two of the advantages of a computerized payroll system over a manual system?

13. Which act created the term "Full-Time Equivalents"?

14. How has cloud-based payroll processing affected contemporary payroll practices?

15. What are two of the differences between the completion of the I-9 and the use of E-Verify systems?

16. What was the purpose of the SECURE Act?

17. What are two of the challenges that arise from the use of outsourced payroll systems?

18. What distinguishes a "living wage" from the minimum wage?

19. How does the Equal Pay Act of 1963 differ from the Lilly Ledbetter Fair Pay Act of 2009?

Exercises Set A

E1-1A.
LO 1-1, 1-2

Lupore Fabrics obtained a contract in Watts Mills, South Carolina, that involves the production of materials for military uniforms, a project contracted with the federal government for $2,800,000. What laws govern the wages Lupore Fabrics pays to its workers for this project? (Select all that may apply.)
1. Davis–Bacon Act
2. Sarbanes–Oxley Act
3. Walsh–Healey Act
4. FLSA

E1-2A.
LO 1-1, 1-2

Martine Piccirillo works as the payroll clerk for Centinix, a security company that hires many part-time and temporary workers who are paid hourly. What law governs the hiring or documenting of these workers?
1. ADEA
2. FLSA
3. IRCA
4. USERRA

E1-3A.
LO 1-1, 1-2

Jackson Wyman was dismissed from his employment at Precision Dynamics because of an incident regarding his race. Mr. Wyman sued Precision Dynamics for $150,000 because of the discrimination. Which of the following laws provides for monetary awards during discrimination lawsuits?
1. FLSA
2. ADEA
3. ADA
4. Civil Rights Act of 1991

E1-4A.
LO 1-1, 1-2

Ovenet Inc. is a qualified private-sector company that provides health insurance to its employees. The company is self-insured. Which of the following forms should the company provide its employees to comply with the Affordable Care Act?
1. 1095-A
2. 1095-B
3. 1095-C

E1-5A.
LO 1-3

Rubin Schaub is a payroll accountant who works for a private firm. He completed his most recent professional development course in 2005. Which of the following ethical issues has he violated?
1. Confidentiality
2. Objectivity and independence
3. Professional competence and due care
4. Integrity

E1-6A.
LO 1-4, LO 1-5

Merlin Anson owns Uninix Computers, a company with five employees. As a small business owner, he has several options for payroll processing. What factors should he consider when deciding on which payroll processing option is best for Uninix Computers? (Select all that apply.)
1. The number of independent contractors.
2. The physical size of the office facility.
3. The amount of money he has to spend on payroll processing.
4. The computer technology used by the business.

Match the following terms with their definitions:

E1-7A.	Manual payroll	a. A preloaded credit card is used to pay employees.
E1-8A.	Timecard	b. The process of gathering information about hours worked for one or more employees.
E1-9A.	Paycard	c. A web-based application wherein employees can modify certain payroll-related information.
E1-10A.	Employee Internet portal	d. Governs accounting for firms with federal government contracts in excess of $2,000.
E1-11A.	Certified payroll	e. A record of the time worked during a period for an individual employee.
E1-12A.	Outsourced payroll	f. Examples of companies used for outsourcing payroll processing.
E1-13A.	Auditor	g. Provided funding for the E-Verify program.
E1-14A.	ADP and Paychex®	h. Payroll administration using a paper payroll register.
E1-15A.	Time collection	i. The use of an external company to track time and benefits and pay employees.
E1-16A.	Davis–Bacon Act	j. A person or group who examines a company's accounting records for accuracy.
E1-17A.	Consolidated Appropriations Act	k. A way for governmental agencies to track the payroll associated with a government contract.

Problems Set A

P1-1A.
LO 1-2

Hayim Accardi is the accounting manager for a small, local firm with full- and part-time staff. How do FLSA guidelines regarding working hours apply to Hayim's employees?

P1-2A.
LO 1-4, 1-5

Micah Sherman works in the payroll department at Radiance Windows. The employer has determined that the payroll functions should be moved to a cloud-based platform that can support its 500 employees, be used remotely, and have requested recommendations. What options could Micah propose?

P1-3A.
LO 1-1, 1-2

Elias Motta is the office manager and payroll clerk for his company, composed of 12 employees. An employee, Sylvia Gladwin, stops by Elias's office and wants to view her payroll record. What privacy regulations must Elias consider before granting his co-worker access?

P1-4A.
LO 1-3

A group of employees, who read on a website that income tax collection is illegal, approach Hawa Furst, the controller for a large company. They request that he stop withholding income taxes from their pay unless he can explain what laws govern income tax collection. What should Hawa tell them?

P1-5A.
LO 1-1, 1-2

Kalea Germain is a warehouse worker for a small grocery market. As she was moving some merchandise, the loading dock door unexpectedly fell and injured her. How does OSHA apply to Kalea for this type of injury?

P1-6A.
LO 1-4

Kevin Magnus is a payroll accountant for Mama Bear Trading Co.. A coworker from the packaging department contacts Kevin via electronic communication and requests to see all employees' payroll records for a specific payroll date. How should Kevin respond?

P1-7A.
LO 1-3

Libbi Alberighi and Flavia van Peij are friends who work for the same company. Libbi manages a manufacturing department, and Flavia supervises the payroll clerks. Which ethical guidelines or rules would these friends need to remember when discussing work?

P1-8A.
LO 1-1, 1-2

At Denniston Industries, employees have the option of choosing employer-sponsored health insurance. What responsibilities does the employer have according to COBRA upon the termination of an employee?

P1-9A.
LO 1-3

Katelijn Preston is a new manager at Resterra Inc. She is looking at using the E-Verify process for new hires. What recommendations can you give her about the differences between having an employee complete the I-9 and the E-Verify process?

P1-10A.
LO 1-4

Cahya Russell is a new employee in the payroll department for Winhook Industries. She has had several employees approach her with questions but is unsure how privacy regulations could affect her response. What advice would you give her about privacy laws and payroll?

Exercises Set B

E1-1B.
LO 1-1, 1-2

Emmett Colquhoun is a military veteran who requires many absences for medical reasons. His boss at Betri Farms has demanded that he reduce the number of sick days unless he provides his medical history. Which law(s) protect Emmett? (Select all that apply.)
1. ADA
2. FLSA
3. USERRA
4. HIPAA

E1-2B.
LO 1-1, 1-2

Gale Rana is a production worker at Gexo Manufacturing, which produces air conditioning systems. After working there for 10 years, she discovers through conversations with a colleague with the same title and similar seniority that her wage is 20 percent lower than his wage. She feels that she has been a victim of discrimination. Which law(s) govern her situation?
1. FLSA
2. Civil Rights Act of 1964
3. ADEA
4. Lilly Ledbetter Fair Pay Act of 2009

E1-3B.
LO 1-4, 1-5

Mathias Acker is the new bookkeeper for Meganyx Enterprises, a small business consulting firm, and was hired to replace a long-time employee who retired. Upon starting the position, Mathias notices that the prior bookkeeper used a purely manual system. The company owner has said that Mathias may update the payroll system. What options are available?

E1-4B.
LO 1-2

Gina Harris is a payroll accountant at Sucre Foods. She works remotely from her home office, communicates with colleagues via Zoom, and has a VPN to prevent her computer data from hackers. Which privacy law(s) require her to protect the information on her computer, even from her family members? (Select all that apply.)
1. HHS Privacy Act 09-40-0006
2. Common-Law Privacy Act
3. Privacy Act of 1974
4. CFAA of 1986

E1-5B.
LO 1-3

Michael Marrioni is in the payroll department at Seven Wonders International Foods. He is part of a social organization, along with several of his coworkers. Which of the following ethical standards could become compromised in social situations?
1. Integrity
2. Professionalism
3. Professional competence and due care
4. Confidentiality

E1-6B.
LO 1-5

Khaled Watson is the payroll accountant for Antizio Electronics, a company that engages in federal contracts. He wants to ensure that the company is compliant with the provisions of the Davis–Bacon Act. What is the name of the process used to monitor payroll compliance in this situation?
1. Contracted payroll
2. Davis–Bacon verification
3. Certified payroll
4. Outsourced payroll

Match the following items with their definitions:

E1-7B.	USERRA	a.	A provision of the Sarbanes–Oxley Act.
E1-8B.	*U.S. v. Windsor*	b.	Instituted a tiered income tax on workers.
E1-9B.	Internal controls documentation	c.	Prohibited employment of individuals younger than 16 years of age.
E1-10B.	HIPAA	d.	Strengthened the child support provisions of PRWOR.
E1-11B.	Lilly Ledbetter Fair Pay Act	e.	Legislation that governs the treatment of military service personnel.
E1-12B.	Sixteenth Amendment	f.	A worker who is not subject to a company's direction or its payroll laws.
E1-13B.	Walsh–Healey Public Contracts Act	g.	Repealed the 180-day statute of limitations on equal pay complaints.
E1-14B.	Independent contractor	h.	Reframing federal employee income tax computations.
E1-15B.	Personal Responsibility, Work and Family Promotion Act of 2002	i.	The case responsible for the U.S. Supreme Court's repeal of DOMA.
E1-16B.	IRCA	j.	Protects the confidentiality of employee medical records.
E1-17B.	Tax Cuts and Jobs Act	k.	Mandates completion of Form I-9.

Problems Set B

P1-1B.
LO 1-4, 1-5

Maura Hatton is a payroll accountant with Scottish Traders Inc. One of her colleagues poses a question about the legality of the deduction for Social Security tax from her pay. What should Maura tell her colleague?

P1-2B.
LO 1-1, 1-2

Jolana Thomas is the payroll clerk for Telemba Communications. One of the company's employees, Darijo Boon, informs Jolana that he feels that he was the victim of unequal pay three years prior. What law(s) guide Darijo's complaint?

P1-3B.
LO 1-3

Clara Hudnall is Conosis Incorporated's payroll accountant. During a casual conversation with co-workers, she learns that Thorben Vinkovic, a co-worker, is deliberately overstating the number of hours worked during each pay period because of a personal economic situation. Which ethical guidelines pertain to this situation? What should Clara do with this knowledge?

P1-4B.
LO 1-4

Alene Meyers works in the payroll department for Racine Traders. The company has experienced a decline in revenue over the past six months. The company president asks her to delay the remittance of payroll taxes to make more cash available to the company. Which act would be violated if Alene complies with the company president's request?

P1-5B.
LO 1-1, 1-2, 1-3

During a review of payroll records, Osvaldo Morena notices that a female employee in Department A receives a significantly lower salary than similarly skilled male employees in the same department. What actions should Osvaldo take in this situation?

P1-6B.   Samuel Alescio is an accountant for Diado, a large, multinational
LO 1-3   firm. He notices that the new state payroll tax updates have not been
          installed in the firm's software during payroll processing. What ethical
          guidelines govern his behavior in this situation?

P1-7B.   Nitza Croce is an employee of Autonder, a contractor that provides gov-
LO 1-2   ernmental construction services in Washington, DC. The current con-
          tract is for $250,000. Nitza is 22 and is paid $9.50 per hour. How does
          the Walsh–Healey Public Contracts Act affect her?

P1-8B.   Eugene Robertson works as a payroll clerk at Hyperend Inc. He shares
LO 1-4   an office with three other co-workers and must examine documents
          containing personal information as a regular part of his duties. Based
          on the provisions of the Privacy Act of 1974, what responsibilities does
          Eugene have regarding the payroll records he handles?

P1-9B.   Larissa Abiodun is a senior payroll administrator for Falcive Landscape
LO 1-5   Design. The company has 15 employees and annual revenues of
          $10 million. She has been using and maintaining manual payroll records
          for the last 20 years of her career. The president of Falcive Landscape
          Design wants to explore options for computerized payroll processing.
          Which payroll option is the most suitable for both Larissa and Falcive
          Landscape Design? Why?

P1-10B.   Alfredo Bellini is the payroll accountant for Pyrondo Fireworks, and he
LO 1-2   has been asked for information about employees and independent con-
          tractors. What are three of the key differences between employees and
          independent contractors?

Critical Thinking

CT1-1. You have been hired as a Dynozz Medical Software consultant, which is facing an
        IRS audit of its accounting records. During your review, you notice anomalies in
        the payroll system involving overpayments of labor and payments to terminated
        employees. What should you do?

CT1-2. Liliya Milic is the accountant for Syiva, a local nonprofit organization. She has
        been tasked with managing the payroll costs so that staffing levels may remain
        the same even if funding levels change. She considers outsourcing the payroll to
        a payroll processing company. What are some factors that Liliya should consider
        in her decision? Why are these factors important?

In the Real World: Scenario for Discussion

Domino's Pizza franchises in New York were sued by the state of New York in 2016 for
wage theft at 10 stores. Under New York law, a corporation and a franchiser are joint
employers if they meet certain employee control criteria. The state found that Domino's
met the criteria for being a joint employer because it mandates a significant number of policies with which franchisers must comply. The problem arose when Domino's mandated
the use of PULSE payroll software, which the pizza company knew to be flawed and did
not attempt to remedy. The flawed software led to employees being paid at rates below
the legal minimum wage, failed to pay overtime, did not reimburse employees for vehicle
use, and abused tip credit guidelines.

Food for thought:

1. Should the franchisers be held liable as joint employers with Domino's? Why or
    why not?

2. Which laws pertain to employee wages? How would they apply in this situation?

3. What could be done to ensure future legal compliance?

Internet Activities

1-1. Using the website www.jstor.org, search for articles about payroll-related laws or relevant employment legislation. Once you find an article, summarize the article and explain how the legislation influenced contemporary payroll practices.

1-2. Visit the website of the American Payroll Association at www.americanpayroll.org. On the right side of the Home page, you will find articles about recent developments in payroll practices and legislation. Choose an article and create a presentation to your class about how its content affects payroll practice.

1-3. Want to know more about the specifics of some of the concepts in this chapter? Check out these websites:

www.dol.gov/whd/

www.taxhistory.com/1943.html

www.workerscompensationinsurance.com

connecteam.com/employee-time-clock-app/

www.adp.com

www.paychex.com

1-4. Would it help to see a video explanation of FLSA coverage? Go to the link below and select Topic 1: Coverage. https://www.dol.gov/whd/flsa/videos.htm

1-5. Check out www.employer.gov to see the Department of Labor's Office of Compliance site. This site contains guidelines for employers about their specific responsibilities to employees, compliance deadlines, posters, and other resources. Its employee-focused website, www.worker.gov, contains worker-focused resources geared to foster understanding of employee rights under the law.

1-6. Using the website www.ncsea.org search for research about child support statistics, collections per year, and payroll professionals' role in the process.

sianc/Shutterstock

Continuing Payroll Project: Prevosti Farms and Sugarhouse

Toni Prevosti is opening a new business, Prevosti Farms and Sugarhouse, a small company that will harvest, refine, and sell maple syrup products. In subsequent chapters, students will have the opportunity to establish payroll records and complete payroll information for Prevosti Farms and Sugarhouse.

Toni has decided that she needs to hire employees for the business to grow. Complete the application for Prevosti Farms and Sugarhouse's Employer Identification Number (Form SS-4) with the following information:

Prevosti Farms and Sugarhouse is located at 820 Westminster Road, Bridgewater, Vermont, 05520 (which is also Ms. Prevosti's home address), phone number 802-555-3456. Bridgewater is in Windsor County, Vermont. Toni, the responsible party for a Limited Liability Corporation created in the United States with one member (disregarded entity), has decided that Prevosti Farms and Sugarhouse will pay its employees on a biweekly basis. Toni's Social Security number is 055-22-0443. The beginning date of the business is February 1, 2021. Prevosti Farms and Sugarhouse will use a calendar year as its accounting year. Toni anticipates that she will need to hire six employees initially for the business, three of whom will be agricultural and three who will be office workers. The first date of wage disbursement will be February 10, 2021. Toni has not had a prior EIN.

Form **SS-4** (Rev. December 2019) Department of the Treasury Internal Revenue Service	**Application for Employer Identification Number** (For use by employers, corporations, partnerships, trusts, estates, churches, government agencies, Indian tribal entities, certain individuals, and others.) ▶ Go to *www.irs.gov/FormSS4* for instructions and the latest information. ▶ See separate instructions for each line. ▶ Keep a copy for your records.	OMB No. 1545-0003 EIN

Type or print clearly.

1 Legal name of entity (or individual) for whom the EIN is being requested

2 Trade name of business (if different from name on line 1)	**3** Executor, administrator, trustee, "care of" name

4a Mailing address (room, apt., suite no. and street, or P.O. box)	**5a** Street address (if different) (Don't enter a P.O. box.)
4b City, state, and ZIP code (if foreign, see instructions)	**5b** City, state, and ZIP code (if foreign, see instructions)

6 County and state where principal business is located

7a Name of responsible party	**7b** SSN, ITIN, or EIN

8a Is this application for a limited liability company (LLC) (or a foreign equivalent)? . . . . ☐ Yes ☐ No	**8b** If 8a is "Yes," enter the number of LLC members . . . . ▶

8c If 8a is "Yes," was the LLC organized in the United States? . . . . ☐ Yes ☐ No

9a **Type of entity** (check only one box). **Caution:** If 8a is "Yes," see the instructions for the correct box to check.

☐ Sole proprietor (SSN) _____ ☐ Estate (SSN of decedent) _____
☐ Partnership ☐ Plan administrator (TIN) _____
☐ Corporation (enter form number to be filed) ▶ _____ ☐ Trust (TIN of grantor) _____
☐ Personal service corporation ☐ Military/National Guard ☐ State/local government
☐ Church or church-controlled organization ☐ Farmers' cooperative ☐ Federal government
☐ Other nonprofit organization (specify) ▶ _____ ☐ REMIC ☐ Indian tribal governments/enterprises
☐ Other (specify) ▶ Group Exemption Number (GEN) If any ▶

9b If a corporation, name the state or foreign country (if applicable) where incorporated	State	Foreign country

10 **Reason for applying** (check only one box)

☐ Started new business (specify type) ▶ _____ ☐ Banking purpose (specify purpose) ▶ _____
  ☐ Changed type of organization (specify new type) ▶ _____
  ☐ Purchased going business
☐ Hired employees (Check the box and see line 13.) ☐ Created a trust (specify type) ▶ _____
☐ Compliance with IRS withholding regulations ☐ Created a pension plan (specify type) ▶ _____
☐ Other (specify) ▶

11 Date business started or acquired (month, day, year). See instructions.	**12** Closing month of accounting year
13 Highest number of employees expected in the next 12 months (enter -0- if none). If no employees expected, skip line 14.	**14** If you expect your employment tax liability to be $1,000 or less in a full calendar year **and** want to file Form 944 annually instead of Forms 941 quarterly, check here. (Your employment tax liability generally will be $1,000 or less if you expect to pay $5,000 or less in total wages.) If you don't check this box, you must file Form 941 for every quarter. ☐

Agricultural	Household	Other

15 First date wages or annuities were paid (month, day, year). **Note:** If applicant is a withholding agent, enter date income will first be paid to nonresident alien (month, day, year) . . . . ▶

16 Check **one** box that best describes the principal activity of your business. ☐ Health care & social assistance ☐ Wholesale-agent/broker
☐ Construction ☐ Rental & leasing ☐ Transportation & warehousing ☐ Accommodation & food service ☐ Wholesale-other ☐ Retail
☐ Real estate ☐ Manufacturing ☐ Finance & insurance ☐ Other (specify) ▶

17 Indicate principal line of merchandise sold, specific construction work done, products produced, or services provided.

18 Has the applicant entity shown on line 1 ever applied for and received an EIN? ☐ Yes ☐ No
If "Yes," write previous EIN here ▶

Third Party Designee	Complete this section **only** if you want to authorize the named individual to receive the entity's EIN and answer questions about the completion of this form.	
	Designee's name	Designee's telephone number (include area code)
	Address and ZIP code	Designee's fax number (include area code)

Under penalties of perjury, I declare that I have examined this application, and to the best of my knowledge and belief, it is true, correct, and complete.

Name and title (type or print clearly) ▶

Applicant's telephone number (include area code)

Signature ▶ Date ▶

Applicant's fax number (include area code)

For Privacy Act and Paperwork Reduction Act Notice, see separate instructions. Cat. No. 16055N Form **SS-4** (Rev. 12-2019)

Source: Internal Revenue Service.

Answers to Stop & Check Exercises

Which Law?	Which Payroll Law?
1. k	1. d
2. h	2. a
3. b	3. f
4. f	4. c
5. i	5. g
6. j	6. j
7. a	7. b
8. d	8. i
9. g	9. e
10. c	10. h
11. e	
12. l	

What's Ethical?

1. Answers will vary. Some concerns include data privacy and integrity in the software switchover, tax and employee pay integrity on the new software, and employee pay methods.
2. Answers will vary. Liza could choose to ignore her sorority sister's request, claiming confidentiality. She could also discontinue active participation in the sorority. In any case, Liza must not consent to her sorority sister's request for confidential information.

Confidential Records

As a payroll clerk, your task is to protect the privacy and confidentiality of the information you maintain for the company. If a student group—or any personnel aside from the company's payroll employees and officers—wishes to review confidential records, you should deny their request. If needed, you should refer the group to your department's manager to discuss the matter in more depth. The laws that apply to this situation are the Privacy Act of 1974, U.S. Department of Labor OCFO-1, and potentially HIPAA.

Large vs. Small

1. Large companies face issues with multiple departments, employee access to online personnel portals, employee data security, and timekeeping accuracy.
2. For small companies, the cost of outsourcing the payroll function needs to be considered. On one hand, a small company may not have personnel who are proficient with payroll regulations and tax reporting requirements, which leaves a company vulnerable to legal actions and stringent fines. However, engaging a payroll service company may be cost prohibitive. The decision to outsource the payroll for a small company should take into account the number of personnel, locations, and types of operations in which the company engages.

What Is the Difference?

a. Manual payroll systems involve the use of paper-and-pencil record keeping or a spreadsheet program, such as Microsoft Excel. This is most appropriate for very small firms.
b. Computerized payroll systems can be used by any company, regardless of size. Examples of computerized systems include QuickBooks, Sage 100, and Microsoft Dynamics GP. These computer packages range in price, depending on the company size and operational scope.
c. Outsourced payroll involves the engagement of a third party to manage a company's payroll data, issue employee compensation, and prepare tax forms.
d. Certified payroll pertains to companies with employees who work on federal government contracts. Certified payroll ensures that a company reports payroll expenditures of contractually allocated money.

Chapter Two

Payroll System Procedures

Payroll procedures have a dual focus: (1) governmental rules and (2) the company's needs. The company must abide by the applicable governmental and industrial regulations or face potential fines, sanctions, or closure. To comply with regulations, a company must make several decisions: pay frequency, pay types (e.g., direct deposit, paycards, or paper checks), employee benefits, and handling of pay advances. The payroll accountant must prepare for the integration of new hires, transfer of employees among departments, and terminations that occur during the normal course of business. Employee benefits and government-required payroll deductions complicate the employee payment process.

Accountants handle documents that have varying levels of confidentiality. Some items include receipts for expenses, invoices from vendors, and other business-related documents that are not confidential. Employee-related documents that payroll accountants handle are usually private and often contain highly sensitive personal information. Various regulations regarding the length of retention and storage procedures apply to payroll documents. An important note about financial or personnel documentation is that any documents connected with fraudulent activity have no time limit for retention purposes. In the event of suspected fraud, investigators may request relevant fraud-related documents at any time.

LEARNING OBJECTIVES

After studying Chapter 2, you should be able to:

LO 2-1 Identify Important Payroll Procedures and Pay Cycles

LO 2-2 Prepare Required Employee Documentation

LO 2-3 Differentiate between Exempt and Nonexempt Workers

LO 2-4 Explain Pay Records and Employee File Maintenance

LO 2-5 Describe Internal Controls and Record Retention for a Payroll System

LO 2-6 Discuss Employee Termination and Document Destruction Procedures

RichLegg/Getty Images

Payroll: Going to and from the Physical Office

The pandemic during 2020 forced a paradigm shift in payroll processing. Since many businesses shifted their operations from a centralized location to home-based offices, key procedures required examination and careful consideration. Payroll accountants who shifted to working from home had to consider cybersecurity measures to prevent hacking of confidential information on their personal networks. The cultural norms of working hours and office locations shifted profoundly, resulting in a new work model that could continue indefinitely.

Companies might not revert to previous working norms. Many employees prefer to work from home and are reluctant to engage in the old model of commuting between their home and office. Workplace efficiency has increased for some workers, but others have encountered challenges with internet connections and the costs of necessary office equipment and security measures. A shift away from paper-based payroll records to cloud-based software and a hybrid workplace, in which job duties may be completed from virtually any location, is the future of the payroll accounting profession.

(Source: Paytech, Infosecurity)

> **Personnel and payroll files are closely related. In Chapter 2, we will explore payroll system procedures, including information about file security, legally required documents, and internal controls.**

LO 2-1   Identify Important Payroll Procedures and Pay Cycles

Sam Edwards/age fotostock

The documentation required for paying employees starts before the first employee is hired. The Employer Identification Number (EIN), obtained online from the IRS, is the first step in employer documentation, closely followed by the employee information files. Under the Fair Labor Standards Act (FLSA), certain information is required in every employee file. According to the U.S. Department of Labor, the required information to be maintained in the employee file includes:

1. Employee's full name as used for Social Security purposes, and the employee's identifying symbol or number, if used in place of the employee's name on any time, work, or payroll records.
2. Address, including zip code.
3. Birthdate, if younger than 19.
4. Sex and occupation.
5. Time and day of the week when employee's workweek begins.
6. Hours worked each day and total hours worked each workweek.
7. The basis on which employee's wages are paid.
8. Regular hourly pay rate.
9. Total daily or weekly straight-time earnings.
10. Total overtime earnings for the workweek.
11. All additions to or deductions from the employee's wages.
12. Total wages paid each *pay period*.
13. Date of payment and the pay period covered by the payment.

Payroll documentation regulations protect employees by ensuring that they receive accurate paychecks. These regulations also keep employers in compliance with tax regulations and provide an audit trail for government bodies. *New hire reporting* requirements ensure that employees pay legal obligations such as child support and garnishments.

Figure 2-1 shows a sample Employee Information Form, which contains elements of the employee file's information. Note that the firm's human resources department maintains the employee file. The payroll department maintains the employee information form shown in Figure 2-1, so some FLSA elements may not appear on the form.

FIGURE 2-1
Sample Employee Information Form

EMPLOYEE EARNING RECORD

NAME	Jonathan A. Doe	Hire Date	1/1/2021		Dependent child<17	1
ADDRESS	100 Main Street	Date of Birth	4/16/2002		Dependent other	1
CITY/STATE/ZIP	Anytown, MD 21220	Position	Sales	PT /(FT)	Step 4a W-4 Info	none
TELEPHONE	202-555-4009	Filing Status	Married/Joint		Step 4b W-4 Info	none-standard
SOCIAL SECURITY					Step 4c W-4 Info	none
NUMBER	987-65-4321	Pay Rate	$15 (HR)/ WK/ MO		HR/Wk/Mo	

Period Ended	Hrs Worked	Reg Pay	OT Pay	Gross Pay	401(k)	Fed Inc. Tax	Social Sec. Tax	Medicare	State Inc. Tax	Total Deduct	Net Pay	YTD
1/15/2021	80.00	1,200.00	-	1,200.00	25.00	-	74.40	17.40	49.94	166.74	1,033.26	1,033.26

The Equal Employment Opportunity Commission's protection of employee rights, especially when it leads to a lawsuit, involves the firm's personnel documentation. Accurate and correctly maintained payroll records are vital because they reflect its employees' treatment. In certain states, such as Illinois, employees can inspect their personnel files and issue rebuttals for incorrect items.

When a company develops or reviews its payroll system, the payroll accountant faces a myriad of tasks. The employer must answer several questions, including:

- How will the company handle new hires?
- What information will be maintained in employee personnel files?
- Where will files be stored, and who is responsible for file security?
- What will the procedure be when an employee transfers from one department to another?
- What is the procedure to follow upon employee termination?
- What processes should the company establish to ensure government compliance?
- How will employee time and attendance be tracked?
- How long do employee files need to be retained after an employee leaves the company?
- Do employees have the legal right to inspect their files, and what procedures should be in place when employees request to see their files?
- Where will the mandatory FLSA Minimum Wage Poster (Figure 2-2) be displayed?

Pay Cycles

Let's start with a basic question: How often should the company pay its employees? Regardless of which accounting system the company uses, the determination of the pay cycle, or *pay periods*, is the first thing a new company needs to establish. Options for payroll cycles include the following:

Daily payroll is typically paid at the end of the day or by the next business day. This payroll processing method is typical in day labor situations; however, it should be noted that day labor could be treated as independent contractor work and thus not be subject to payroll, payroll taxes, or a W-2. Daily payroll could potentially have 365 or 366 pay periods, due to leap year.

Weekly payroll is typically used in a five-day workweek. The employees receive their paychecks the following Friday. Several types of companies use a weekly payroll system, including grocery stores, construction, and professional offices. This pay frequency may lead to 52 pay periods per year.

Biweekly payroll is typically processed based on a two-week period, and employees receive their paychecks approximately a week after the end of the pay period. Pay dates may be any weekday. This pay frequency generally has 26 pay periods per year. There may be 27 pay periods in a biweekly payroll; however, this is rare, and typical calculations will use 26.

Semimonthly payroll is paid twice a month. Examples of semimonthly payroll pay dates include (1) the 1st and 15th of the month and (2) the 15th and last day of the month. This is not the same as biweekly payroll, and taxation and hours paid are different. Employees receive 24 pay disbursements per year when using a semimonthly payroll system.

Monthly payroll is less frequently used than other methods. Some companies process payroll once per month and may allow a semimonthly draw to the employees. When employees are allowed to draw their wages at mid-month, the employer may or may not take payroll taxes out of the draw. If the mid-month draw does not have payroll taxes withheld, the month-end payroll will need to recover all taxes and withholdings for the month from the employee.

Figure 2-3 shows the different types of pay cycles a company can offer its employees.

FIGURE 2-2
FLSA Minimum Wage Poster

EMPLOYEE RIGHTS
UNDER THE FAIR LABOR STANDARDS ACT

FEDERAL MINIMUM WAGE
$7.25 PER HOUR
BEGINNING JULY 24, 2009

The law requires employers to display this poster where employees can readily see it.

OVERTIME PAY   At least 1½ times the regular rate of pay for all hours worked over 40 in a workweek.

CHILD LABOR   An employee must be at least 16 years old to work in most non-farm jobs and at least 18 to work in non-farm jobs declared hazardous by the Secretary of Labor. Youths 14 and 15 years old may work outside school hours in various non-manufacturing, non-mining, non-hazardous jobs with certain work hours restrictions. Different rules apply in agricultural employment.

TIP CREDIT   Employers of "tipped employees" who meet certain conditions may claim a partial wage credit based on tips received by their employees. Employers must pay tipped employees a cash wage of at least $2.13 per hour if they claim a tip credit against their minimum wage obligation. If an employee's tips combined with the employer's cash wage of at least $2.13 per hour do not equal the minimum hourly wage, the employer must make up the difference.

NURSING MOTHERS   The FLSA requires employers to provide reasonable break time for a nursing mother employee who is subject to the FLSA's overtime requirements in order for the employee to express breast milk for her nursing child for one year after the child's birth each time such employee has a need to express breast milk. Employers are also required to provide a place, other than a bathroom, that is shielded from view and free from intrusion from coworkers and the public, which may be used by the employee to express breast milk.

ENFORCEMENT   The Department has authority to recover back wages and an equal amount in liquidated damages in instances of minimum wage, overtime, and other violations. The Department may litigate and/or recommend criminal prosecution. Employers may be assessed civil money penalties for each willful or repeated violation of the minimum wage or overtime pay provisions of the law. Civil money penalties may also be assessed for violations of the FLSA's child labor provisions. Heightened civil money penalties may be assessed for each child labor violation that results in the death or serious injury of any minor employee, and such assessments may be doubled when the violations are determined to be willful or repeated. The law also prohibits retaliating against or discharging workers who file a complaint or participate in any proceeding under the FLSA.

ADDITIONAL INFORMATION
- Certain occupations and establishments are exempt from the minimum wage, and/or overtime pay provisions.
- Special provisions apply to workers in American Samoa, the Commonwealth of the Northern Mariana Islands, and the Commonwealth of Puerto Rico.
- Some state laws provide greater employee protections; employers must comply with both.
- Some employers incorrectly classify workers as "independent contractors" when they are actually employees under the FLSA. It is important to know the difference between the two because employees (unless exempt) are entitled to the FLSA's minimum wage and overtime pay protections and correctly classified independent contractors are not.
- Certain full-time students, student learners, apprentices, and workers with disabilities may be paid less than the minimum wage under special certificates issued by the Department of Labor.

≡WHD   **WAGE AND HOUR DIVISION**
UNITED STATES DEPARTMENT OF LABOR

1-866-487-9243
TTY: 1-877-889-5627
www.dol.gov/whd

WH1088   REV 07/16

Source: U.S. Department of Labor.

FIGURE 2-3
Pay Periods

Daily	• 365 or 366 periods
Weekly	• 52 periods
Biweekly	• 26 periods
Semimonthly	• 24 periods
Monthly	• 12 periods

What's in the File?

Stop & Check

1. Which of the following artifacts must be included in the employee file?
    a. Full name and address.
    b. Occupation.
    c. Mother's maiden name.
    d. Pay rate.
    e. Date of payment.
    f. Spouse's name.

Match the pay frequencies:	The number of pay periods:
2. Monthly	a. 26 or 27
3. Semimonthly	b. 12
4. Biweekly	c. 52
5. Weekly	d. 24

LO 2-2   Prepare Required Employee Documentation

Employees versus Independent Contractors

People who work for a company may be classified as either employees or independent contractors, depending on the nature of the work and withholding payroll-related taxes from the worker's compensation. According to the Internal Revenue Service (IRS), millions of workers have been misclassified, which has led to employers not depositing the full amount of taxes. Employees miss out on benefits. The use of IRS Form SS-8, the Determination of Worker Status for Purposes of Employment Taxes and Income Tax Withholding, is a way that employers may receive official guidance about worker classification. This form is available from the IRS and elicits information about the behavioral control, financial control, and the worker's relationship to the firm as ways to determine the correct status of the worker as an employee or an independent contractor. When the employer submits this form, the IRS makes the final determination of employee status.

Purestock/Superstock

Rawpixel.com/Shutterstock

Employees

The determination of a worker as an employee has two primary criteria according to labor laws. The first is the *work direction,* which means that the employer substantially directs the worker's performance. The employer provides the primary tools that an employee uses; for example, the employee may be given a desk, computer, company car, or other items needed to complete the assigned work. The other criterion is the *material contribution,* which means that the work that the employee completes must involve substantial effort. An employer withholds payroll taxes from an employee's compensation, provides company-specific benefits, and includes the worker on governmental reports.

Independent Contractors

Classification of a worker as an independent contractor (IC) means that the employer does not direct the worker's specific actions and does not provide the tools needed to complete the work. For example, if a worker performed accounting services for a company but used a privately owned computer and printer and determined the number and timing of the hours worked for the company, the worker could be classified as an independent contractor. An independent contractor may or may not perform work that constitutes a material contribution to the employer.

10'000 Hours/DigitalVision/Getty Images

Another identifier of an independent contractor is the duration of the relationship with the employer. Independent contractors tend to have shorter-term relationships with the business than employees do. Furthermore, an independent contractor will not share in profits or losses of the company in the same manner as employees. Finally, independent contractors are not subject to FLSA provisions for minimum wage and overtime pay.

Payment records for independent contractors, although maintained separately from payroll records, are instances in which payroll accountants must be aware of employee classification and record-keeping requirements to avoid fraudulent activity. The independent contractor generally works for specified fees that they bill to the company, which typically pay them through their accounts payable department, not payroll. Independent contractors are also responsible for their own payroll taxes. The topic of worker classification as an employee or independent contractor has become increasingly important in the past decade. Many employers have sought to reduce governmental fines and other liabilities stemming from the incorrect classification of workers.

The IRS uses three common-law tests to clarify whether a worker is an employee or an independent contractor:

1. **Behavioral Control:** To what extent does the employer have the right to control and direct the worker's actions?
2. **Financial Control:** This guideline pertains to the worker's unreimbursed expenses, investment in job-related tools, availability of worker's services to other entities outside the company, and how the worker is paid.
3. **Relationship of the Parties:** This includes details related to any work-related contracts between the employer and the worker, benefits offered, permanency of the relationship, and the relationship between the worker's services and the firm's normal business operations.

As of 2020, the U.S. Department of Labor issued a final rule to clarify independent contractor status determination. Three specific factors, included in the final rule, guide the employer's justification of the worker's classification as either an employee or an independent contractor:

1. The skill needed for the individual to complete the work
2. The permanence of the working relationship between the individual and the business
3. The importance of the individual's work within the scope of the firm's operations

For additional clarification, the employer should review the new Independent Contractor Status final rule, which may be obtained via the Department of Labor.

The gig economy, in which individuals engage in part-time, self-directed work, has evolved since its introduction over the last decade. One part of this evolution is governmental regulation, which has lacked clarity because of the independent nature of workers' duties and needs. Another issue is the power of workers engaged in the gig economy. These workers have not formed unions, which would cloud an employee's distinction versus an independent contractor. Furthermore, individuals who rely on gig work to meet financial needs do not have long-term benefits such as company-sponsored medical and retirement assistance, leading to economic issues in the years to come.

(Source: The HR Digest)

Further clarification about determining employment status may be located in IRS Publication 1779. Upon request, the firm may request official guidance from the IRS by submitting Form SS-8. Penalties are levied on employers who deliberately misclassify employees to cut payroll costs; in addition to penalties, the employers may have to provide unpaid wages to misclassified employees. As of 2021, the Wage and Hour Division of the Department of Labor had recovered more than $1.4 billion in back wages due to misclassified workers. Starting with tax year 2020, the IRS has switched from using form 1099-MISC to 1099-NEC for reporting independent contractor earnings over $600 when they have performed a service in line with the business.

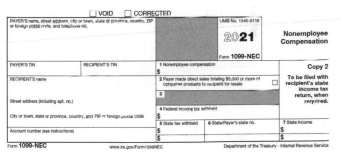

Reporting New Employees

Reporting newly hired employees is considered important by governmental bodies. Why is this so?

- First, reporting employees creates a registry to monitor people who owe child support or other court-ordered garnishments.
- Second, it helps immigration agencies track immigrants to ensure that they are still legally able to work in the United States.
- Third, for certain professions such as teaching, the new-hire reporting system can be used to communicate issues such as ethical violations for which governmental or accrediting bodies have censured the professional.
- Finally, the new hire reporting system assists with the administration of COBRA medical benefits.

All newly hired employees must provide specific documentation. For legal purposes, the minimum amount of documentation allowed is Form *W-4* (see Figure 2-4) and the *I-9* (see Figure 2-5). Form W-4 is a publication of the Internal Revenue Service. The main purpose behind the W-4 is to help the employer determine the correct amount of federal income taxes to withhold from the employee's payroll. Employees may make changes to the information on Form W-4 at any time during the year. A best practice concerning Form W-4 is to request that employees file a new form each January. States may have similar withholding forms, which should similarly be completed. Since Form W-4 was significantly changed in 2020, it is worth noting that employees hired before 2020 do not need to complete a new Form W-4, but those hired after January 1, 2020, must complete the new form.

Notice that the 2020 Form W-4 is significantly different from prior years:

- Step 1: Personal information, including full name, address, social security number, and marital status.
- Steps 2-4: These are used only for employees with additional income through a spouse's job, deductions for dependents, and additional income tax adjustments based on worksheets contained in the full form.
- Step 5: Employee and employer's signature and date.

In the following example, Jonathan W. Doe was born on 5/17/1991 and lives at 123 Main Street, Anytown, Kansas 54932. He is single and claims one withholding allowance. His Social Security number is 987-65-4321. His employer is Homestead Retreat at 9010 Old Manhattan Highway, Olathe, Kansas 59384, with an Employer Identification Number of 92-1117654. His email address is jonathandoe@anymail.com, and his phone number is (620)555-2299. When he filled out his new hire paperwork on May 1, 2021, Jessica Stolpp in Human Resources for Homestead Retreat verified his identity with both his Social Security card and his driver's license (G93847562), which expires on his birthday in 2024.

Additional Withholding

If an employee has more than one job or a spouse who works, an option to avoid having to owe taxes at the end of the year is to withhold additional federal income taxes out of each check. Additional withholdings are requested within the employee's Form W-4. This can be either a straight dollar value or an additional percentage. These amounts are withheld from the employee and submitted with the employer's normal federal payroll tax deposits. Employees may elect to include backup withholding amounts in Step 4 of Form W-4, which directs the employer to withhold additional tax amounts. Backup withholding may occur in situations where the employee received additional, nontaxable income (such as dividends, royalties, or interest payments) or when the IRS notified the employee of underreported income issues.

The I-9 form is published by the Department of Homeland Security, which stipulates that this form must be completed within three business days of the employee's start date. Registration of employees using the I-9 form minimizes negative implications associated with monitoring legally authorized workers in the United States and tracking people with legal obligations such as child support and other garnishments.

The final page of the I-9 form contains the documents the employee provides to verify identity and eligibility to work in the United States. Employees must provide either one item from List A *or* one item from both List B *and* List C.

FIGURE 2-4

Form W-4 Employee Withholding Certificate (Completed Example)

Form **W-4**	**Employee's Withholding Certificate**	OMB No. 1545-0074
(Rev. December 2020) Department of the Treasury Internal Revenue Service	▶ Complete Form W-4 so that your employer can withhold the correct federal income tax from your pay. ▶ Give Form W-4 to your employer. ▶ Your withholding is subject to review by the IRS.	2021

Step 1: **Enter Personal Information**	**(a)** First name and middle initial Jonathan W	Last name Doe	**(b)** Social security number 987-65-4321

Address
123 Main Street

City or town, state, and ZIP code
Anytown, KS 54932

▶ Does your name match the name on your social security card? If not, to ensure you get credit for your earnings, contact SSA at 800-772-1213 or go to *www.ssa.gov*.

(c) ☑ **Single** or **Married filing separately**

☐ **Married filing jointly** or **Qualifying widow(er)**

☐ **Head of household** (Check only if you're unmarried and pay more than half the costs of keeping up a home for yourself and a qualifying individual.)

Complete Steps 2–4 ONLY if they apply to you; otherwise, skip to Step 5. See page 2 for more information on each step, who can claim exemption from withholding, when to use the estimator at *www.irs.gov/W4App*, and privacy.

Step 2: **Multiple Jobs or Spouse Works**	Complete this step if you (1) hold more than one job at a time, or (2) are married filing jointly and your spouse also works. The correct amount of withholding depends on income earned from all of these jobs. Do **only one** of the following. **(a)** Use the estimator at *www.irs.gov/W4App* for most accurate withholding for this step (and Steps 3–4); **or** **(b)** Use the Multiple Jobs Worksheet on page 3 and enter the result in Step 4(c) below for roughly accurate withholding; **or** **(c)** If there are only two jobs total, you may check this box. Do the same on Form W-4 for the other job. This option is accurate for jobs with similar pay; otherwise, more tax than necessary may be withheld . . . . . ▶ ☐ **TIP:** To be accurate, submit a 2021 Form W-4 for all other jobs. If you (or your spouse) have self-employment income, including as an independent contractor, use the estimator.

Complete Steps 3–4(b) on Form W-4 for only ONE of these jobs. Leave those steps blank for the other jobs. (Your withholding will be most accurate if you complete Steps 3–4(b) on the Form W-4 for the highest paying job.)

Step 3: **Claim Dependents**	If your total income will be $200,000 or less ($400,000 or less if married filing jointly):		
	Multiply the number of qualifying children under age 17 by $2,000 ▶ $		0
	Multiply the number of other dependents by $500 . . . . ▶ $		0
	Add the amounts above and enter the total here	**3**	$ 0

Step 4 (optional): **Other Adjustments**	**(a) Other income (not from jobs).** If you want tax withheld for other income you expect this year that won't have withholding, enter the amount of other income here. This may include interest, dividends, and retirement income	**4(a)**	$ 0
	(b) Deductions. If you expect to claim deductions other than the standard deduction and want to reduce your withholding, use the Deductions Worksheet on page 3 and enter the result here	**4(b)**	$ 0
	(c) Extra withholding. Enter any additional tax you want withheld each **pay period** .	**4(c)**	$ 0

Step 5: **Sign Here**	Under penalties of perjury, I declare that this certificate, to the best of my knowledge and belief, is true, correct, and complete. ▶ *Jonathan W. Doe* **Employee's signature** (This form is not valid unless you sign it.)	▶ 5/1/2021 **Date**

Employers Only	Employer's name and address Homestead Retreat, 9010 Old Manhattan Highway, Olathe, KS 59384	First date of employment 5/1/2021	Employer identification number (EIN) 92-1117654

For Privacy Act and Paperwork Reduction Act Notice, see page 3.   Cat. No. 10220Q   Form **W-4** (2021)

Source: irs.gov.

FIGURE 2-5
I-9 Employment Eligibility Verification Form

	Employment Eligibility Verification	**USCIS**
	Department of Homeland Security	**Form I-9**
	U.S. Citizenship and Immigration Services	OMB No. 1615-0047
		Expires 10/31/2022

▶ **START HERE: Read instructions carefully before completing this form. The instructions must be available, either in paper or electronically, during completion of this form. Employers are liable for errors in the completion of this form.**

ANTI-DISCRIMINATION NOTICE: It is illegal to discriminate against work-authorized individuals. Employers **CANNOT** specify which document(s) an employee may present to establish employment authorization and identity. The refusal to hire or continue to employ an individual because the documentation presented has a future expiration date may also constitute illegal discrimination.

Section 1. Employee Information and Attestation *(Employees must complete and sign Section 1 of Form I-9 no later than the **first day of employment**, but not before accepting a job offer.)*

Last Name *(Family Name)*	First Name *(Given Name)*	Middle Initial	Other Last Names Used *(if any)*
Doe	Jonathan	W	

Address *(Street Number and Name)*	Apt. Number	City or Town	State	ZIP Code
123 Main Street		Anytown	KS	54932

Date of Birth *(mm/dd/yyyy)*	U.S. Social Security Number	Employee's E-mail Address	Employee's Telephone Number
05/17/1991	9 8 7 - 6 5 - 4 3 2 1	jonathandoe@anymail.com	(620) 555-2299

I am aware that federal law provides for imprisonment and/or fines for false statements or use of false documents in connection with the completion of this form.

I attest, under penalty of perjury, that I am (check one of the following boxes):

☒ 1. A citizen of the United States

☐ 2. A noncitizen national of the United States *(See instructions)*

☐ 3. A lawful permanent resident (Alien Registration Number/USCIS Number): N/A

☐ 4. An alien authorized to work until (expiration date, if applicable, mm/dd/yyyy): N/A
Some aliens may write "N/A" in the expiration date field. *(See instructions)*

Aliens authorized to work must provide only one of the following document numbers to complete Form I-9:
An Alien Registration Number/USCIS Number OR Form I-94 Admission Number OR Foreign Passport Number.

QR Code - Section 1
Do Not Write In This Space

1. Alien Registration Number/USCIS Number: N/A
OR
2. Form I-94 Admission Number: N/A
OR
3. Foreign Passport Number: N/A
Country of Issuance: N/A

Signature of Employee *Jonathan W. Doe*	Today's Date *(mm/dd/yyyy)* 5/1/2021

Preparer and/or Translator Certification (check one):

☒ I did not use a preparer or translator.   ☐ A preparer(s) and/or translator(s) assisted the employee in completing Section 1.
(Fields below must be completed and signed when preparers and/or translators assist an employee in completing Section 1.)

I attest, under penalty of perjury, that I have assisted in the completion of Section 1 of this form and that to the best of my knowledge the information is true and correct.

Signature of Preparer or Translator	Today's Date *(mm/dd/yyyy)*

Last Name *(Family Name)*	First Name *(Given Name)*

Address *(Street Number and Name)*	City or Town	State	ZIP Code

🛑 *Employer Completes Next Page* 🛑

Employment Eligibility Verification

Department of Homeland Security

U.S. Citizenship and Immigration Services

USCIS
Form I-9
OMB No. 1615-0047
Expires 10/31/2022

Section 2. Employer or Authorized Representative Review and Verification

(Employers or their authorized representative must complete and sign Section 2 within 3 business days of the employee's first day of employment. You must physically examine one document from List A OR a combination of one document from List B and one document from List C as listed on the "Lists of Acceptable Documents.")

Employee Info from Section 1	Last Name *(Family Name)* Doe	First Name *(Given Name)* Jonathan	M.I. W	Citizenship/Immigration Status 1

List A Identity and Employment Authorization	OR	List B Identity	AND	List C Employment Authorization

List A	List B	List C
Document Title N/A	Document Title Driver's license issued by state/territory	Document Title Social Security card (unrestricted)
Issuing Authority N/A	Issuing Authority Kansas	Issuing Authority Social Security Administration
Document Number N/A	Document Number G93847562	Document Number 987654321
Expiration Date *(if any) (mm/dd/yyyy)* N/A	Expiration Date *(if any) (mm/dd/yyyy)* 05/17/2024	Expiration Date *(if any) (mm/dd/yyyy)* N/A
Document Title N/A		
Issuing Authority N/A	**Additional Information**	QR Code - Section 2 Do Not Write In This Space
Document Number N/A		
Expiration Date *(if any) (mm/dd/yyyy)* N/A		
Document Title N/A		
Issuing Authority N/A		
Document Number N/A		
Expiration Date *(if any) (mm/dd/yyyy)* N/A		

Certification I attest, under penalty of perjury, that (1) I have examined the document(s) presented by the above-named employee, (2) the above-listed document(s) appear to be genuine and to relate to the employee named, and (3) to the best of my knowledge the employee is authorized to work in the United States.

The employee's first day of employment *(mm/dd/yyyy)*: 05/01/2021 *(See instructions for exemptions)*

Signature of Employer or Authorized Representative *Jessica Stolpp*	Today's Date *(mm/dd/yyyy)* 5/1/2021	Title of Employer or Authorized Representative Human Resources
Last Name of Employer or Authorized Representative Stolpp	First Name of Employer or Authorized Representative Jessica	Employer's Business or Organization Name Homestead Retreat

Employer's Business or Organization Address *(Street Number and Name)* 9010 Old Manhattan Highway	City or Town Olathe	State KS	ZIP Code 59384

Section 3. Reverification and Rehires *(To be completed and signed by employer or authorized representative.)*

A. New Name *(if applicable)*			B. Date of Rehire *(if applicable)*
Last Name *(Family Name)*	First Name *(Given Name)*	Middle Initial	Date *(mm/dd/yyyy)*

C. If the employee's previous grant of employment authorization has expired, provide the information for the document or receipt that establishes continuing employment authorization in the space provided below.

Document Title	Document Number	Expiration Date *(if any) (mm/dd/yyyy)*

I attest, under penalty of perjury, that to the best of my knowledge, this employee is authorized to work in the United States, and if the employee presented document(s), the document(s) I have examined appear to be genuine and to relate to the individual.

Signature of Employer or Authorized Representative	Today's Date *(mm/dd/yyyy)*	Name of Employer or Authorized Representative

LISTS OF ACCEPTABLE DOCUMENTS
All documents must be UNEXPIRED

Employees may present one selection from List A
or a combination of one selection from List B and one selection from List C.

LIST A		LIST B		LIST C
Documents that Establish Both Identity and Employment Authorization	OR	**Documents that Establish Identity** AND		**Documents that Establish Employment Authorization**
1. U.S. Passport or U.S. Passport Card		1. Driver's license or ID card issued by a State or outlying possession of the United States provided it contains a photograph or information such as name, date of birth, gender, height, eye color, and address		1. A Social Security Account Number card, unless the card includes one of the following restrictions:
2. Permanent Resident Card or Alien Registration Receipt Card (Form I-551)				(1) NOT VALID FOR EMPLOYMENT
				(2) VALID FOR WORK ONLY WITH INS AUTHORIZATION
3. Foreign passport that contains a temporary I-551 stamp or temporary I-551 printed notation on a machine-readable immigrant visa		2. ID card issued by federal, state or local government agencies or entities, provided it contains a photograph or information such as name, date of birth, gender, height, eye color, and address		(3) VALID FOR WORK ONLY WITH DHS AUTHORIZATION
4. Employment Authorization Document that contains a photograph (Form I-766)				2. Certification of report of birth issued by the Department of State (Forms DS-1350, FS-545, FS-240)
5. For a nonimmigrant alien authorized to work for a specific employer because of his or her status:		3. School ID card with a photograph		3. Original or certified copy of birth certificate issued by a State, county, municipal authority, or territory of the United States bearing an official seal
a. Foreign passport; and		4. Voter's registration card		
		5. U.S. Military card or draft record		
b. Form I-94 or Form I-94A that has the following:		6. Military dependent's ID card		
(1) The same name as the passport; and		7. U.S. Coast Guard Merchant Mariner Card		4. Native American tribal document
				5. U.S. Citizen ID Card (Form I-197)
(2) An endorsement of the alien's nonimmigrant status as long as that period of endorsement has not yet expired and the proposed employment is not in conflict with any restrictions or limitations identified on the form.		8. Native American tribal document		6. Identification Card for Use of Resident Citizen in the United States (Form I-179)
		9. Driver's license issued by a Canadian government authority		
		For persons under age 18 who are unable to present a document listed above:		7. Employment authorization document issued by the Department of Homeland Security
6. Passport from the Federated States of Micronesia (FSM) or the Republic of the Marshall Islands (RMI) with Form I-94 or Form I-94A indicating nonimmigrant admission under the Compact of Free Association Between the United States and the FSM or RMI		10. School record or report card		
		11. Clinic, doctor, or hospital record		
		12. Day-care or nursery school record		

Examples of many of these documents appear in the Handbook for Employers (M-274).

Refer to the instructions for more information about acceptable receipts.

The US Citizen and Immigration Service (USCIS) implemented new changes in 2020:

- A fillable PDF version of the form with drop-downs for dates and prefilled lists.
- A new citizenship/immigration status section.
- Form availability in Spanish.

The E-Verify system was implemented in 2017 to provide employers with a fast, free way to verify an employee's legal eligibility to work in the United States. It should be noted that participation in E-Verify is *voluntary,* and that completion of the I-9 is *mandatory.*

(Source: USCIS)

The payroll accountant should retain a copy of the Employment Eligibility Verification Form (I-9) and a current Employee Withholding Allowance Certificate (W-4) in every employee's permanent file, although no legislation mandates that practice. The employer should request a new Form W-4 from employees annually in January to ensure that all addresses, life situations, and other information remain current. Because of the timing constraints on releasing annual tax documents such as Forms W-2 and W-3, employers should verify employees' Form W-4 information as close as possible to January 1 each year.

Hiring Packet Contents

Many companies' *hiring packets* may be as basic as completing the Forms W-4 and I-9 or could be incredibly complex if foreign workers and multiple types of voluntary or mandated deductions are involved. Common items in a hiring packet are the aforementioned federal forms, state and local withholding allowance forms, elections for voluntary deductions, insurance paperwork, and an offer letter that specifies the pay rate and start date. Not all companies have the same items in

Photographee eu/Shutterstock

the hiring packet, and no federal legislative guidelines exist. After reviewing the company's needs and the legal requirements for the position, the firm's management determines the hiring packet contents. Many companies also include diversity self-declaration paperwork to ensure compliance with equal opportunity legislation, requirements under federal contracts, and other special requirements in the event of a payroll audit.

Notification of New Hires to State Offices

The Immigration Reform and Control Act mandates that employers notify state offices within 20 days of an employee's start date. State forms for fulfilling this requirement vary, and states offer online registration for new hires. One purpose of registering new hires with states is to maintain databases for child support enforcement. Fines for nonreporting of new hires vary, both on the number of unreported new hires and incomplete information. The penalty for noncompliance is strictly enforced and ranges from $25 per unreported employee to $500 for intentional nonreporting. An example of a new hire reporting form is in Figure 2-6.

Reporting new hires is a complex task with high potential for companies' errors with employees in multiple states. The Office of Management and Budget (OMB) has designed a form (see excerpt in Figure 2-7) for multistate employers to register and designate one state as the primary place to which they will send new hire reports. They can designate on the form the other states in which they have employees. The use of the multistate registry helps employers ensure they remain in compliance with the law.

Another issue to consider is the multiple employer rule. For individuals with multiple, and sometimes joint, employers, the issue of withholding appropriate taxes arises. According to the U.S. Department of Labor, the joint employer test involves four factors:

1. Who hires/fires the employee.
2. Which employer substantially controls the employee's work.
3. Which employer determines the employee's pay rate and method.
4. Who maintains the employee's employment records.

FIGURE 2-6
Sample New Hire Reporting Form

Michigan Department of Treasury
3281(Rev. 9-12)

State of Michigan New Hire Reporting Form

Federal law requires public (State and local) and private employers to report all newly hired or rehired employees who are working in Michigan to the State of Michigan.[1] This form is recommended for use by all employers who do not report electronically.

Michigan New Hire Operations Center
P.O. Box 85010
Lansing, MI 48908-5010
Phone: (800) 524-9846
Fax: (877) 318-1659

- A newly hired employee is an individual not previously employed by you, and a rehired employee is an individual who was previously employed by you but separated from employment for at least 60 consecutive days.

- Reports must be submitted within 20 days of hire date (i.e., the date services are first performed for pay).

- This form may be photocopied as necessary. Many employers preprint employer information on the form and have the employee complete the necessary information during the hiring process.

- When reporting new hires with special exemptions, please use the MI-W4 form.

- Online and other electronic reporting options are available at: www.mi-newhire.com.

- Employers who report electronically and have employees working in two or more states may register as a multi-state employer and designate a single state to which new hire reports will be transmitted. Information regarding multi-state registration is available online at: http://www.acf.hhs.gov/programs/cse/newhire/employer/private/newhire.htm#multi or call (410) 277-9470.

- Reports will not be processed if mandatory information is missing. Such reports willl be rejected and you must correct and resubmit them.

- For optimum accuracy, please print neatly in all capital letters and avoid contact with the edge of the box. See sample below.

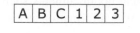

EMPLOYEE Information *(Mandatory)*

Social Security Number: 987 65 4321

First Name: Isabelle
Middle Initial: I

Last Name: Libertie

Address: 2022 Watson Way

City: Charlevoix
State: MI

Zip Code: 49720
Hire Date: 03 01 2021

OPTIONAL

Date of Birth: 08 28 1999

Driver's License No: J 2 5 3 6 4 7 8 9 6 8 6 4

EMPLOYER Information *(Mandatory)*

Federal Employer Identification Number (FEIN): 12 3456789

Employer Name: Charlevoix Ski and Sports

Address: 5632 State Street

City: Charlevoix
State: MI

Zip Code: 49720

OPTIONAL

Contact Name: Gerald Morris

Contact Phone: 231 555 6445

Contact Fax: 231 555 6488

Contact Email:

---

[1] Ref: Social Security Act section 453A and the Personal Responsibility and Work Opportunity Reconciliation Act (PRWORA) of 1996 (P.L. 104-193), effective October 1, 1997.

FIGURE 2-7
Multistate Employer Registration Form

OMB Control No: 0970-0166
Expiration Date: 07-31-2022

MULTISTATE EMPLOYER REGISTRATION FORM FOR NEW HIRE REPORTING

Employers who have employees working in two or more states may use this form to register to submit their new hire reports to one state or make changes to a previous registration. Multistate employers may also visit https://ocsp.acf.hhs.gov/OCSE/ to register or make changes electronically.

Federal law (42 USC 653A(b)(1)(A)) requires employers to supply the following information about newly hired employees to the State Directory of New Hires in the state where the employee works:

- Employee's name, address, Social Security number, and the date of hire (the date services for remuneration were first performed by the employee)
- Employer's name, address, and Federal Employer Identification Number (FEIN)

   If you are an employer with employees working in two or more states, AND you will transmit the required information or reports magnetically or electronically, you may use this form to designate one state where any employee works to transmit ALL new hire reports to the State Directory of New Hires.

If you are no longer a multistate employer OR you are a multistate employer but no longer report to a single state, check "No Longer a Multistate Employer" in the box below.

☐ **No Longer a Multistate Employer (If checked, complete items 1-4 and 6-7 and return the form via email (preferred), fax, or mail (see last page for return information).**

If you need help completing this form, call the Multistate Employer Help Desk at 1-800-258-2736, Option #1 (8:00 a.m - 5:00 p.m. ET).

Please note that all fields are required unless otherwise noted as optional.

1. **Enter your company's Federal Employer Identification Number (FEIN) without hyphen. This is the nine-digit number used by the IRS to identify your company.**

   FEIN:

2. **Enter today's date in MM/DD/YYYY format.**

   Date:

3. **Enter your company's name. This is the name associated with the FEIN in item 1.**

   Employer Name:

   Enter your company's address, including city, state, and ZIP code. This is the address associated with the FEIN in item 1. If your company's FEIN address is a foreign address, print the country's name and Postal code.

   Employer Address:

   City: State:

   ZIP code:

   (For foreign addresses only) Country Name: _____   Country Postal Code: _____

<u>Subsidiary Information:</u> Please go to **www.acf.hhs.gov/css/resource/multiple-fein-spreadsheet** to access the **Multiple FEIN Spreadsheet, enter information about all your company's subsidiaries, and submit it with this form. Subsidiaries are companies wholly controlled by your company.**

We need the below information about your company's subsidiaries.

FEIN	Organization Name	Address Line1	Address Line2	Address Line3	City	State	Province	Country	ZIP/ Postal Code	Address Delivery Type (Optional)
										■ **Payroll/Income Withholding Order** ■ **National Medical Support Notice** ■ **Verification of Employment** ■ **Workers Compensation**

4. **Enter the name of the state or U.S. territory your company designated to report new hire information to.**

    NOTE: The state you choose must be a state in which you have one or more employees. Refer to the state listing shown in item 5.

5. **Check the box next to the additional states or U.S. territories where your company has employees working. Do not put a check next to the state or territory you selected in item 4. You must select at least one state or territory in this list to register as a multistate employer.**

☐ Alabama ☐ Alaska ☐ Arizona ☐ Arkansas ☐ California ☐ Colorado
☐ Connecticut ☐ Delaware ☐ Dist. of Col ☐ Florida ☐ Georgia ☐ Guam
☐ Hawaii ☐ Idaho ☐ Illinois ☐ Indiana ☐ Iowa ☐ Kansas
☐ Kentucky ☐ Louisiana ☐ Maine ☐ Maryland ☐ Massachusetts ☐ Michigan
☐ Minnesota ☐ Mississippi ☐ Missouri ☐ Montana ☐ Nebraska ☐ Nevada
☐ New Hampshire ☐ New Jersey ☐ New Mexico ☐ New York ☐ North Carolina ☐ North Dakota
☐ Ohio ☐ Oklahoma ☐ Oregon ☐ Pennsylvania ☐ Puerto Rico ☐ Rhode Island
☐ South Carolina ☐ South Dakota ☐ Tennessee ☐ Texas ☐ Utah ☐ Vermont
☐ Virgin Islands ☐ Virginia ☐ Washington ☐ West Virginia ☐ Wisconsin ☐ Wyoming
☐ All States and Territories

6. **Enter your name, title, work phone number, work email address (do not use Gmail, Yahoo, MSN, or Hotmail email addresses), and work fax number.**

    Company's Business Contact Name:

    Phone: Fax (optional):

    Email:

7. **BE SURE TO SIGN THIS FORM. By completing this form, I certify that the information provided is accurate and that I am authorized to complete this form on my company's behalf.**

    Signature of the person completing this form:

Source: U.S. Department of Health and Human Services.

Foreign Workers

Employers who hire foreign citizens face additional challenges. The employer must verify that the employee is legally allowed to work in the United States. Generally, the I-9 form serves this purpose, but there may be occasions when the prospective employee does not have an appropriate government-issued visa for working in the United States. If no visa exists, the employer may file a petition with the U.S. Citizenship and Immigration Services office to gain permission for the foreign employee to work in the United States through an *H-1B visa*. The **H-1B** visa is authorized for employers to hire foreign workers who have specialized university-level expertise to benefit the company. As of 2020, the maximum number of regular H-1B visas permitted by USCIS was 65,000 employees. An additional 20,000 H-1B visas were available for foreign workers with advanced degrees. The fees for permanent workers not in the protected classes range from $500 to $5,000, depending on the classification of the worker's preference, the size of the employer, and the employee's nonimmigrant status. In the case of foreign workers, the employer must file Form 1042 for any payments made. For information about the Permanent Worker Visa Preference Categories, please visit the U.S. Citizenship and Immigration Services website (www.uscis.gov).

An H-1B visa's purpose is to facilitate the employment of foreign workers who possess specialized skills, as defined by U.S. statute 20 CFR § 655.700. "Specialty occupation" is defined as possessing specialized knowledge, with the minimum educational requirement being a bachelor's degree or commensurate experience, or a distinguished fashion model.

(Source: Cornell Law School)

U.S. Workers in Foreign Subsidiaries

Many companies have foreign subsidiaries and divisions that employ U.S. expatriate workers. The *Foreign Account Tax Compliance Act (FATCA)* of 2010 requires employers to report to the IRS the wages of permanent U.S. citizens working in foreign locations to facilitate the appropriate taxation of such workers. Under the IRS Foreign Earned Income Exclusion, expatriate workers must file Form 673 with their employer to exclude the first $108,700 of annual wages (2021 figure) from U.S. taxation. Still, they must pay income tax on income over that amount and declare foreign assets.

Payroll for companies who operate in multiple countries requires additional considerations in the payroll process. After establishing a legal business presence in another country, the firm must consider the country's payroll laws. For example, some countries require employers to issue meal vouchers to employees, and employment contracts' legal content varies.

Another significant area of difference between the United States and other countries is data privacy. While many privacy laws exist in the United States, the General Data Protection Regulation (GDPR) in the European Union delineates stringent guidelines regarding personal information handling. Under GDPR, even Microsoft Excel spreadsheets must have privacy protection to meet regulatory guidelines.

Other significant issues involve continual awareness of currency exchange rates and money transfers to ensure accurate and timely pay for employees. Finally, global companies should maintain consistent calendars to remain consistent in payments among the countries in which the firm operates and issue receipts for amounts paid to employees.

(Source: Global Payroll Management Institute)

Statutory Employees

Some personnel, normally classified as independent contractors, must be treated as employees for tax purposes. The IRS classifies *statutory employees* as workers who meet any of the following guidelines:

- A driver who distributes beverages (other than milk) or meat, vegetable, fruit, or bakery products or picks up and delivers laundry or dry cleaning, if the driver is a single company's agent or is paid on commission.

- A full-time life insurance sales agent whose principal business activity is selling life insurance or annuity contracts, or both, primarily for one life insurance company.
- An individual who works at home on materials or goods that a company supplies and that must be returned to that company or a designated agent in accordance with furnished specifications for the work to be done.
- A full-time traveling or city salesperson who works on a single company's behalf and turns in orders from wholesalers, retailers, contractors, or operators of hotels, restaurants, or other similar establishments. The goods sold must be merchandise for resale or supplies for use in the buyer's business operation. The work performed for that single company must be the salesperson's principal business activity.

scyther5/Getty Images

Recall that the primary differences between an employee and an independent contractor are that the independent contractor sets his or her own hours and provides the tools necessary to complete the task. Statutory employees are a hybrid of an employee and an independent contractor. To ensure proper and timely remittance of employment taxes, the IRS has mandated that the employer withhold FICA taxes from statutory employees in the same manner as other company personnel; however, federal income taxes are not withheld from statutory employees' pay.

The term *statutory employee* may be applied to other types of workers on occasions. In 2019, Slawomir Fiedziuszko, an aerospace engineer who was semi-retired at the time, performed consulting work for a contractor of Space Systems Loral (now called Maxam). He contested the withholding of employment taxes, claiming that he was a consultant, not an employee. In the case, the judge upheld the decision to classify Mr. Fiedziuszko as an employee because he worked from home doing work designed specifically to meet Maxam's specifications. Under the definition of a statutory employee, Mr. Fiedziuszko met the third criteria to be considered a statutory employee because his work was completed using Maxam's proprietary software in accordance with established specifications.

(Source: *Forbes*)

Entering New Employees into the Database

The method of entering a new employee into the payroll system depends on the employer's system. A manual system would require tasks such as adding the employee to the federal, state, and local lists for taxes withheld and adding the new hire to the list of employees to pay. Manual systems should have a checklist of all employees to ensure that no one is missed in the process.

Setting up a new employee in an automated system involves many more steps. The payroll employee enters in the pertinent data (see Figure 2-8). Employee number, name, address,

FIGURE 2-8

Employee Database Information Sample

Employee Details   **Bibitor LLC**

PERSONAL INFO	PAY INFO		TAX INFO	
	Regular Pay:	$14.00/hr	SSN:	122-13-1231
	Pay By:		Fed:	Single / 1
Jackson L. Mann	Deductions:	Vanguard 3.0%	VT:	Single/ 0
19 River Road South	Contributions:	Vanguard 1.0%		
Putney VT 05346				
Hired: 01/01/2021		Vacation: 40 hours/year (accrued at start of year)		
Born: 08/24/1996	Time Off	Paid time off: 40 hours/year (accrued at start of year)		
		Sick: 40 hours/year (accrued at start of year)		

Social Security number, wage, pay frequency, withholding information from W-4, department, and contact information are typically included. The payroll employee must designate a worker's compensation classification, state of employment, and local jurisdiction (when local taxes are applicable). Depending on state requirements and employer preferences, additional location codes, job classification codes, and other identifying characteristics may also be required.

Who Are You?

Stop & Check

1. Go to the U.S. Citizenship and Immigration Services website, located at www.uscis.gov, and type I-9 into the search box on the website. Click on the link for the PDF version of the I-9 form to obtain a digital copy. What are two different ways that you would be able to prove your eligibility for work in the United States?

2. Go to the IRS website, located at www.irs.gov, and type W-4 into the website's search box. Click on the link for the PDF version of the W-4 to obtain a digital copy. Assume you have more than one job and estimate the amount to include as income from other jobs. Complete the multiple job worksheet. Was your estimate close? Explain.

3. What are three examples of statutory employees?

LO 2-3 Differentiate between Exempt and Nonexempt Workers

Company employees may be classified as either exempt or nonexempt workers. The distinction between the two terms is how the wage and hour provisions of FLSA apply to the worker. *Exempt* workers are not subject to (i.e., are exempt from) the FLSA wage and hour provisions; wage and hour laws usually apply to *nonexempt* workers. The details of the worker's classification as exempt or nonexempt are always maintained in payroll records. Still, the inclusion of this information in other personnel records is at the employer's discretion.

Drazen Zigic/Getty Images

Many different types of employees are classified as exempt from FLSA provisions, including certain computer professionals and outside salespersons. Companies will typically classify highly skilled workers such as accountants, general managers, human resource managers, and upper management as exempt, salaried employees. Because job titles alone are not a basis for the classification of employees as exempt from FLSA provisions, the U.S. Department of Labor has issued guidelines for the most common types of employees. Note that for workers to be classified as exempt, they must meet *all* elements in the following tests to achieve exempt status.

- Executive Exemption
  - Salary compensation must be no less than $684 per week.
  - Managing the firm must be a primary duty of the employee.
  - The employee must supervise and otherwise direct at least two other full-time employees (or an equivalent).
  - The employee must have the authority to hire and fire other employees.
- Administrative Exemption
  - Salary compensation must be no less than $684 per week.
  - The primary duty must include office performance or other nonmanual labor-related directly to the management of the firm's operations.
  - The employee must exercise independent judgment in the performance of normal duties.

- Professional Exemption
  - Learned Professional
    - Salary compensation must be no less than $684 per week.
    - This employee must perform work characterized by advanced learning, primarily academic in nature, and requires consistent discretion and judgment.
    - The employee's advanced knowledge must be in a field that involves science or learning.
    - The employee must have acquired that knowledge through specialized intellectual education.
  - Creative Professional
    - Salary compensation must be no less than $684 per week.
    - This employee's primary work duty must involve invention, imagination, or originality, requiring judgment and discretion.

(Source: DOL)

When workers are employed on a salary basis, they are paid to perform a specific job regardless of the number of hours worked to accomplish that job. A primary difference is that nonexempt salaried individuals receive overtime pay for any hours exceeding 40 per week. The difference between salaried and hourly workers about overtime calculation is that salaried workers will receive their normal shift hours of pay, even when not working the full shift, and do not receive overtime when they work more than 40 hours per week.

Hourly nonexempt employees receive a predetermined amount per hour of work performed (or fraction thereof). Some employers may make an election that permits four 10-hour shifts; should the election be made, the employee would be subject to overtime rates only after the 40 hours have been performed. It should be noted that some employers have a company policy stating that they pay overtime for employees who work more than 8 hours per day (or 10 hours, if that is the normal work shift); however, paid overtime is only mandated by the FLSA weekly. According to the Bureau of Labor Statistics (BLS), the average number of hours worked per week was 34.8 hours in 2020 (see Figure 2-9) and fluctuated monthly. The BLS noted the numbers of hours worked per week varied by industry and that U.S. workers spent approximately 3.9 billion hours in any given month.

Classifying employee wages as to salary versus hourly is a basic determination linked to the type of work performed and its position. Salaried *exempt* employees are not subject to overtime, are paid to do a specific job, and fulfill the FLSA requirement of self-direction; however, not all salaried employees are classified as exempt. Certain jobs such as nurses, police officers, and upper-level administrators may earn a fixed salary but are classified as *nonexempt* because of the nature of management direction in their function. Nonexempt workers do not generally supervise other employees and generally work under the direction of a supervisor.

Leased and Temporary Employees

Employers occasionally experience a need to have an additional employee but do not have the time to use a traditional hiring process. In this event, employers may either lease an employee or contact a temporary employment agency. Although these terms may sound similar, the difference between the leased and temporary employees involves determining employer intent and liability for worker injuries and errors.

Under IRS code section 414(n), an employee is classified as a *leased employee* if all the following conditions exist:

1. A formal agreement exists between the employer and the employee leasing organization.
2. The employee works on a full-time basis.
3. Employee actions are directed by the recipient company (i.e., the lessee).

Leased employees are considered common-law employees and are eligible for the same benefits as regular employees, including compensation practices, employer contributions, and so forth. The IRS stipulates that no more than 20 percent of a company's workers may be leased.

FIGURE 2-9

Average Working Hours of All Employees

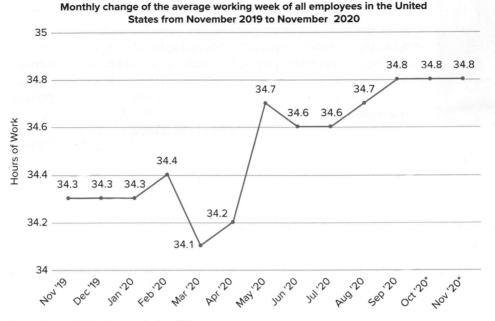

Monthly change of the average working week of all employees in the United States from November 2019 to November 2020

Source: Bureau of Labor Statistics, Statista, 2021.

The Tax Cuts and Jobs Act of 2017 included a provision in which employers who leased employees from Professional Employer Organizations (PEOs) could qualify for a 20 percent profit deduction under section 199A of the Act. PEOs serve companies by acting as the hiring body and human resource managers for workers. In January 2019, the IRS clarified under §1.199A-2(b)(2)(ii) that employers who use third-party employees through a PEO could consider those leased employees as common-law employees and would qualify for the profit deduction and subsequent decrease in tax liability.

(Source: JDSupra)

A temporary employee differs from a leased employee in the direction of the employee's actions. The *temporary employee* is an employee of the employment agency, which directs them to fill specific short-term needs of various employers. Temporary employees may work either full-time or part-time, depending on the employer's needs, and are only eligible for the benefits made available by the temporary agency.

Who Are You?

Stop & Check

1. What is the difference between exempt and nonexempt workers?
2. What is the threshold after which an employee must be paid overtime, according to FLSA?
   a. 30 hours
   b. 35 hours
   c. 40 hours
   d. 45 hours
3. What is the difference between a leased employee and a temporary employee?

SDI Productions/Getty Images

LO 2-4 Explain Pay Records and Employee File Maintenance

One of the most important parts of any payroll system is maintaining employee pay records, especially considering the classification of exempt versus nonexempt employees and the legislation that pertains to overtime pay. The maintenance of accurate and detailed records that reflect the pay period, pay date, pay rate, and deductions are critical not only because it is a legal requirement in delivering accurate pay but also for positive employee relations. Employers retain physical copies of employees' time records, pay advice, and any other documentation processed with the paycheck. Other types of documentation include:

- Request for a day off.
- Reports of tardiness or absenteeism.
- Detailed records of work completed during that day's shift.
- Records of overtime worked.

Technological advances allow employers to scan and save this information digitally, such as using a digital file within the payroll accounting system. The trend toward remote work implies that employee records could become increasingly digital.

Many payroll apps allow for multiple payment methods and payment of employees, independent contractors, and part-time workers by scanning images directly into the software. These apps often include Human Resources integration. The following apps are examples of the increasing digitization of payroll functions:

- Payable
- Square Payroll
- eFileCabinet
- Trinet

The availability of digital copies facilitates managerial, auditor, or authorized executives' review, approval, or commentary on the documentation attached to payroll documents. Digital copies also permit transparency of records between the employer and employee, reducing miscommunication and payroll discrepancies, and facilitating Internet employee record portals.

Pay Records

Employee wages involve far more than simple hourly rates or periodic salary payments. The first payroll decision should be the company's pay frequency (daily, weekly, biweekly, semimonthly, monthly). The choice of payment frequency affects the applicable amounts for employee income tax withholding. Separate schedules for federal income taxes are provided in IRS Publication 15-T (available at www.irs.gov), which is released in November for the following year (i.e., 2021 tax information would normally be released during November 2020). Once the employer determines the pay frequency, the payroll accountant can establish the payroll record submission and pay disbursement schedule for company employees.

Pay Rate

The pay rate is the amount per hour per pay period. The company determines the employee should be compensated. The determination of pay rate depends upon many employee variables: experience, education, certifications, governmental regulations (minimum wage, Davis–Bacon wages, etc.), hours worked, or a combination of all of the above. Employers

Department of the Treasury
Internal Revenue Service

Publication 15-T
Cat. No. 32112B

Federal Income Tax Withholding Methods

For use in **2021**

Contents

Source: Department of the Treasury Internal Revenue Services.

may also pay specific rates for jobs performed. For example, employees working in a manufacturing environment may be subject to a different pay scale when cross-trained and working in a sales capacity. Minimum wage rates vary per state, and different parts of the same state may have different wages and may increase minimum wage amounts at various times during the year.

> The idea of paying a living wage continues to be a prominent issue. A living wage is defined as the amount of money needed to sustain the desired lifestyle. In Virginia, the Richmond Living Wage Program is a certificate program co-sponsored by state and local leaders to encourage businesses to focus more on employees' needs than on the business's profitability. This program encourages consumers to patronize businesses that have demonstrated their dedication to delivering a living wage to their employees.
>
> The Massachusetts Institute of Technology (MIT) created a living wage calculator to facilitate awareness of the cost of living in different communities in the United States. This calculator is located at http://livingwage.mit.edu/
>
> (Source: Virginia Business)

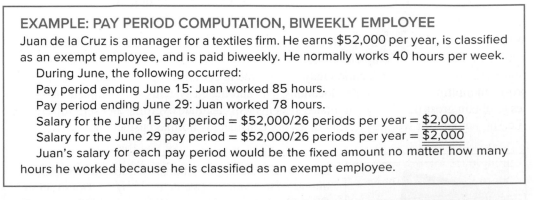

EXAMPLE: PAY PERIOD COMPUTATION, BIWEEKLY EMPLOYEE

Juan de la Cruz is a manager for a textiles firm. He earns $52,000 per year, is classified as an exempt employee, and is paid biweekly. He normally works 40 hours per week.

During June, the following occurred:

Pay period ending June 15: Juan worked 85 hours.

Pay period ending June 29: Juan worked 78 hours.

Salary for the June 15 pay period = $52,000/26 periods per year = $2,000

Salary for the June 29 pay period = $52,000/26 periods per year = $2,000

Juan's salary for each pay period would be the fixed amount no matter how many hours he worked because he is classified as an exempt employee.

Hourly employees are protected by the FLSA and eligible for overtime pay. When overtime pay is applied, hourly employees may earn more than their salaried counterparts. FLSA determines overtime rules and rates; however, some states may have additional requirements for overtime pay. Overtime is calculated at one-and-a-half times the employee's hourly rate. For FLSA, overtime applies only to hours worked exceeding 40 in a week (with some exceptions). Some states, such as California, may also require that employees receive overtime pay for any hours worked exceeding 8 per day in addition to the 40 hours per week, making it possible for an hourly employee to earn overtime pay without reaching the 40 hours in the week.

NOTE: In this textbook, nonexempt employees receive overtime pay for hours worked more than 40 hours per week, unless otherwise noted.

> The concept of a fluctuating workweek for salaried nonexempt employees has been a source of confusion for employers. Some salaried nonexempt employees work in industries that require them to be available at different times based on company needs. Employees who are nonexempt and salaried but have hours that are changeable due to the nature of the job may receive overtime during periods when they work more than 40 hours in a given week.

Commissions and piece-rate compensation offer employees incentives for specific jobs. A *commission* is a percentage of sales or services performed by an individual. An example of a commission would be a sales representative receiving 1 percent of all sales he or she initiates. *Piece rate* connects employee compensation with the production of a good or service. Piece rate compensation was widely used in the United States before industrialization and automated manufacturing. For example, when a shoe was being made, the person preparing the sole would receive a set rate per item.

> The California state legislature passed Assembly Bill (AB) 1513, which established guidelines about productive time and rest time for piece-rate employees. This bill also established a specified time period for employers to pay employees back pay because of the legal change. AB 1513 affected employees in various industries, including spas and salons, in which workers' compensation was connected to the number of treatments completed.
>
> (Source: California DIR)

Compensation structures can become complex if the employee is compensated using multiple payment types. A sales representative may receive a salary and commissions while working on the sales floor but receive hourly and piece rate if filling in on the manufacturing floor. Proper classification of the employee's workday's various aspects becomes exceptionally important for the correct processing of the payroll.

Entering Hours

When it is time to prepare the payroll, an automated system will provide the payroll employee with a simple form to complete, typically including wage type and hours worked. An additional classification of job location may be required in complex organizations if the employee works in multiple departments or locations. The automated systems will complete mathematics to obtain gross pay. Most automated systems will calculate overtime and shift differentials (i.e., higher pay for working during times not considered "normal business hours").

fizkes/iStock/Getty Images

Many web-based applications exist to track employee attendance and calculate pay. **TimeStation, ClockShark,** and **TimeDock** use Quick-Read (QR) codes, employee PINs, and GPS location tagging to verify employee work. These apps may be useful tools for companies with employees at remote locations. Apps such as **CalculateHours** allow employees to calculate their hours worked and email the timesheet to a supervisor. Other apps, such as the **iTookOff** paid leave tracker, allow employees to manage their paid time off through a synchronized app.

Calculations of Weekly Regular Time and Overtime

Even with automated systems, the payroll accountant must determine the breakdown of each employee's regular and overtime hours. Recall the discussion regarding the FLSA standard of 40 hours in a week. This is where the calculation of overtime becomes important. The employee's hours are added up. The pay period's total is computed to determine if the employee worked more than 40 hours total for any given week, and overtime is separated from regular hours worked for wage calculations. If the employee did not work more than 40 hours, the total regular hours are noted on the time card. If the employee did work more than 40 hours, the hours worked will be divided between the 40 regular hours and the overtime pay computation.

Depending upon company policy, the existence of paid holidays or sick days may alter payroll calculations. However, holiday hours, sick time taken, and vacation days are not usually included in the worked hours to determine overtime. Figure 2-10 shows a few examples of states and locations that offer mandatory paid sick leave.

According to the FLSA, employers are not required to pay for employee sick time; however, many states have either passed legislation or have pending bills that would mandate employer-paid sick time. Since 2008, more than 30 separate locations, including cities and entire states, have passed paid sick time legislation. This is a partial list of areas that have legislated paid sick leave.

FIGURE 2-10
Locations with Mandatory Paid Sick Leave

States/Districts	Counties	Cities
Washington, DC	Orange County, FL	Pittsburgh, PA
Arizona	Montgomery County, MD	Milwaukee, WI
California	Cook County, IL	Seattle, WA
Connecticut	Westchester County, NY	Plainfield, NJ
Massachusetts		Elizabeth, NJ
Maryland		New Brunswick, NJ
Michigan		Jersey City, NJ
New Jersey		Tacoma, WA
Oregon		Newark, NJ
Rhode Island		New York City, NY
Vermont		Passaic, NJ
Washington		East Orange, NJ
		Paterson, NJ
		Irvington, NJ
		Montclair, NJ
		Trenton, NJ
		Minneapolis, MN
		Philadelphia, PA
		Bloomfield, NJ
		Chicago, IL

(Source: Rocket Lawyer)
Note: States that have passed mandatory sick-time laws may have cities whose sick-time laws differ.

Worker Facts

Stop & Check

1. Which classification of workers is subject to the wage and hour provisions for overtime in the Fair Labor Standards Act?
2. What is the difference between exempt and nonexempt employees in overtime pay requirements?
3. What is the difference between commission and piece-rate pay as far as the basis for the compensation?
4. What is the difference between the minimum wage and a "living wage"?

LO 2-5 Describe Internal Controls and Record Retention for a Payroll System

The confidentiality of payroll information is one of the most important controls in establishing a payroll system, and internal controls are critical. Pay records such as timesheets are considered confidential documents, and personnel who handle or maintain such files, either paper or computerized, must ensure the privacy of the information they contain. Small firms may maintain the confidentiality of handwritten time sheets; however, multifacility companies may need to use more secure time-collection methods to ensure information privacy.

Henrik5000/iStock/Getty Images

Strategic planning of the payroll system prior to implementation can prevent data errors and losses related to inadequate *internal controls*. Most importantly, the payroll system design should be reviewed regularly to determine its effectiveness and appropriateness for the company size and correct errors before they become magnified.

Internal controls are a necessity, especially for small companies. The median loss to companies where fraud has occurred is $108,000. Examples of easily implemented internal controls include:

- Transparency in the flow of money in and out of the organization.
- Involvement in cost management and expense disbursal.
- Engagement of multiple employees in the record-keeping process.
- Attentiveness to employee behavior.
- Recognition that any organization may become a fraud victim.

The need for internal controls increases as a company engages more fully with internet portals such as time-tracking and payroll processing sites. Technological changes introduce a new level of vulnerability into a company's data, so robust internal control practices are vital. The shift to remote work during 2020 highlighted unexpected risks in the payroll audit process, including:

- Increased opportunity for fraud.
- Compromised internal controls.
- Increased potential for legal noncompliance, especially about the CARES Act.

(Source: *Strategic Finance*; AccountingWeb)

A company with many departments and many employees will generally have a more complex *review process* than a small company. In an organization with one office and a dozen or fewer employees, certain steps of the verification process may be omitted, and fewer people are required to conduct it. Conversely, a large organization with several departments and many employees could have several verification levels in the ***payroll review*** process. Even outsourced payroll requires levels of the review process. The payroll executed by an external company is only as accurate as the data provided. For instance, a company could have a payroll review process, such as the one shown in Figure 2-11.

A critical issue within internal controls is the determination of authorized signers. A best practice within a company is to have more than one designated signatory for payroll checks. Often, these signers are different people than those involved in the review process. The extra time it takes to review and obtain the necessary signatures is time well spent, as long as it prevents costly errors.

Documentation of the payroll process is vital. As should be clear by now, the execution of payroll is not merely writing checks to employees. Proper documentation of payroll entails a well-delineated procedure and properly trained personnel. Table 2-1 contains examples of different documentation controls, the activities involved in each, and the employees required to participate in internal controls.

FIGURE 2-11
Payroll Review Process: Steps to Ensure Accurate Payroll

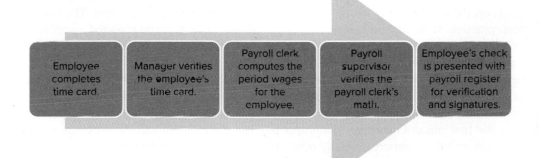

TABLE 2-1
Documentation Controls

Procedure	Example of Internal Control Activities	Could Be Performed by
Review and approval of time data from time cards or other time collection devices	Completion of the time collection procedure Review of time collection for accuracy and approval	Employee's supervisor
Overtime approval	Approve the amount and type of overtime to be paid	Employee's supervisor
Approval for leave of absence or other unpaid time off	Obtain all prior approvals for unpaid time away due to FMLA or other reasons	Employee's supervisor
Timely entering of payroll data	Enter the payroll data into the payroll system on time, and check for data integrity and accuracy	Payroll clerk
Payroll system security	Make sure that only designated employees or payroll vendors have access to payroll data	Payroll supervisor
Approval of the payroll before issuance	Obtain the approval from the signatory before issuing checks	An authorized signer(s)
Maintenance of paid time off (e.g., vacation, sick, etc.)	Ensure that employees receive the exact amount agreed upon	Payroll clerk; employee; supervisor; other designees
Access to payroll data	Ensure that payroll data is confidential and secure	Payroll supervisor
Separation of duties	Make sure that different people verify data, enter data, verify checks	Payroll supervisor
Training of payroll staff	Ensure that payroll department employees and other department supervisors are aware of and follow company payroll policies	Payroll supervisor

Review of Time Collected

All workers' hours reported manually on time cards or electronically through other methods must be verified for accuracy before completing any payroll. Simple issues in employee underpayment (which can cause federal penalties) or overpayment (which can erode the company's available cash) can occur even with sophisticated systems. Time collection and employee payment errors can lead to reduced employee morale, lawsuits, and fines.

> One of the largest payroll fraud schemes involved $70 million in payroll deposits made to MyPayrollHR, a New York-based company engaged in cloud-based payroll processing. Although the clients had done everything correctly, the owner of MyPayrollHR abruptly stopped operating after collecting employer funds and not disbursing payroll amounts due to employees for two consecutive pay periods.
>
> (Source: KrebsonSecurity)

Overtime Approval

Hourly employees are subject to federal overtime provisions, commonly known as time-and-a-half, but may include other pay bases such as double-time and so forth. FLSA guarantees nonexempt employees' rights to appropriate pay for the hours worked; however, employees can misreport the overtime they work, costing the company money in the process. Therefore, the best practice is to obtain supervisor approval on all employee-reported overtime. Computerized systems can also affect the reported overtime. The data is only as accurate as of the person who entered it.

One of the authors worked at a company that once paid her for 75 hours of overtime in one pay period—when she should have had only 7.5. This kind of error can cause chaos for both the employee, who must return the money, and the employer, who should not have paid it in the first place. Once again, improper pay can erode the morale of the employees. Overpayment on hours can create many other overpayments, including (but not limited to) federal withholding taxes, Medicare, Social Security taxes, and pension or 401(k) contributions that are driven by gross wages.

> A significant percentage of corporate fraud involves payroll tampering or embezzlement. In Atlanta, Georgia, a payroll and accounting manager pled guilty to wire fraud after investigators discovered that she had embezzled $1.5 million over a six-year period through improper payroll deposits. The employee had created a fake employee and instructed the outsourced payroll company to direct deposit that employee's pay into her own personal bank account. The employee had a file for the fictitious worker. A multiperson payroll verification process could have shortened the duration and reduced the amount of the embezzlement.
>
> (Source: *Accounting Today*)

Approval for Leave of Absence or Other Unpaid Time Off

The employee's supervisor is one level of oversight to ensure that the payroll data reaches the payroll department accurately and quickly. Supervisors work closely with their employees and should approve overtime and paid time off. Supervisors review individual timesheets for accuracy before delivery to the payroll department. Control of time away from work is the responsibility of the employee's supervisor, at the very minimum. The department supervisor should approve the time off. This approval must be tracked and maintained by the payroll department to ensure integrity in the payroll records. A suggested best practice is to keep requests for time away attached to the payroll stub for the affected pay period. The use of leave forms provides companies with a paper trail used to clarify perceived discrepancies in pay.

Web-based services facilitate requests, approvals, and tracking for paid time off. Apps such as Zenefits allow managers to adjust paid time off, approve and track employee requests, synchronize calendars, and download reports detailing employee time away from work.

(Source: Zenefits)

File Security

Based on the amount of legislation regarding the privacy and security of personnel information, it is important to understand that all files about payroll, whether paper or electronic, must be kept secure from tampering. Another reason for *file security*, or restriction of personnel file access, is the firm's governmental payroll obligations. The tax information contained in the payroll records is required to prepare timely and accurate payment of payroll taxes, which is nearly as important as paying the employees. Examples of secure payroll records include multiple passwords for system access, locking of file cabinets with controlled key disbursement, and encryption programs.

Because payroll data contains highly personal and private information, the security of the data is important. To maintain file security, access to payroll records is restricted to a relatively small number of people. Paper-based payroll data is stored in a secure location; similarly, electronic payroll data is securely backed up and encrypted.

Data privacy and fund protection are a high priority for companies and legislators. Preventing breaches of payroll record security is a high priority and an evolving issue. The Electronic Fund Transfer Act of 1978, created to prevent problems with newly created ATM cards, has been expanded to address fraud and theft issues with *paycards*, a preloaded credit card that allows an employee to access funds without needing a bank account. Paycard use for payroll disbursement was estimated to be nearly $57 billion in 2015 and continues to be the fastest-growing payroll method in the United States, with 5.9 million active paycards being used as of 2017 and is expected to grow annually as paycard regulation and protections expand. With the gig economy's growth and the number of unbanked employees, paycards are a relatively secure method of disbursing immediately accessible pay.

In *Jessie Chavez v. PVH Corporation* (2013), the defendant had to pay $1.85 million to Chavez because of fees deducted from the plaintiff's payroll card, which meant that the full amount of the wages was reduced; additionally, the plaintiff had not agreed to paycard use in advance. State laws vary regarding employment authorization for disbursing pay in the form of a paycard. As of 2021, at least 10 percent of all employees are unbanked, meaning that they do not have a bank account and rely on paycards to receive their earnings.

The Consumer Financial Protection Bureau (CFPB) proposed legislation in 2014 to include specific language on paycards, informing employees of their right to request another form of payroll disbursement. As of October 2016, the CFPB issued a rule that regulated the posting of accounting, disclosures, and overdraft credit that became effective as of October 2017. This rule was updated and finalized in 2019.

The Electronic Funds Transfer Act, of which Regulation E is the most pertinent to payroll cards, implemented specific protections for employees who use paycards to receive their pay. This ruling that was effective in 2019 added Regulation Z that mandated disclosure of all paycard-related fees and other paycard-related information to employees.

(Source: American Payroll Association; Law360)

Alternating Duties and Cross-Training

The cross-training of payroll professionals can act as a safeguard of payroll information. One of the goals of the Sarbanes–Oxley Act of 2002 was to protect the integrity of accounting data by legislating document retention requirements, corporate officer responsibility for financial accuracy, and the rotation of duties by auditors. The same principle applies to payroll system workers. Cross-training and alternating the people's duties in the payroll process may avoid or minimize errors and potential issues stemming from corruption. Furthermore, cross-training and rotation of duties foster professional development and proficiency with multiple tasks. This rotation of payroll duties refers only to personnel within the payroll department, not opening the payroll processing to non-accounting departments.

> Cross-training employees has more benefits than fraud deterrence. Offering employees the chance to learn other duties empowers them in their professional development, fostering a sense of fulfillment among employees. Cross-training also grants employees the opportunity to consider different perspectives and gain a broader understanding of its operations. Finally, cross-training is linked to better problem-solving ability because employees understand diverse tasks.
>
> (Source: *Forbes*)

Who Does Which Job?

Imagine that you have been approached to assist a business owner concerned about the security of his or her company's payroll. In a team of three or four people, decide how you would distribute payroll responsibilities to implement excellent internal control procedures. How did you divide the responsibilities? Explain.

Best Practices Involved in Employee File Maintenance

Maintenance of employee files is as important as the protection of employee information. IRS Regulation 26 CFR 1.6001 clearly states that the method of *file maintenance* is the employer's responsibility. The Internal Revenue Code recommends record labeling, the creation of backup copies, and secure record storage. An important note is that despite the choice of record maintenance, the employer retains all liability for auditor access to the information upon demand. Items such as time and work records, including time cards and electronic work records, must be maintained to be available for auditors because these items are vital components of a payroll system audit.

> **26 CFR 1.6001–1 Records.**
>
> (a) *In general.* Except as provided in paragraph (b) of this section, any person subject to tax under subtitle A of the Code (including a qualified State individual income tax which is treated according to section 6361(a) as if it was imposed by chapter 1 of subtitle A), or any person required to file a return of information concerning income, shall keep such permanent books of account or records, including inventories, as are sufficient to establish the amount of gross income, deductions, credits, or other matters required to be shown by such person in any return of such tax or information.
>
> (Source: GPO)

Payroll record maintenance is important for employees at all levels of the organization. IRS Revenue Procedure 98-25, 1998-1 CB 689, was enacted in 1998 to govern the maintenance procedures and duration of record-keeping for companies with employees. Provisions of the law include payroll transaction details such as time worked, pay dates, employee status, record reconciliation, and correlation of IRS reports and employee records. Concerning executive-level pay, the company must keep records of how the executive's pay was derived, including bench-

Andrey_Popov/Shutterstock

marks from similar companies, payout period, and scheduled increases. All pay disbursed must be justified according to the amount and type of work performed, regardless of employee level or classification. A company's payroll and legal department should work closely to determine and implement a maintenance and record destruction program that complies with IRS requirements but avoids the inaccessibility of data that occurs with information overload.

Electronic Records

Many companies have moved to electronic scanned copies of payroll records that allow immediate access to employee files from a password-protected format. In remote locations, payroll accountants can send the managers and employees Adobe Acrobat files requiring a password to access pay records. Several data encryption programs are currently on the market, allowing payroll managers to select the best fit for their individual company. All hard copies (i.e., paper versions) of payroll information must be in a locked file cabinet with limited access.

Computers have become a necessary part of a business and offer significant benefits to the accounting department. Most accounting software for the preparation of payroll includes password requirements that the company can control, limiting access to electronic information about employees, pay, and personal information. Many regulatory agencies have addressed record security and safeguarding procedures; for example, the Food and Drug Administration enacted 21 CFR Part 11 that delineates electronic record security and safeguarding procedures.

Payroll accounting, according to the definition by the Internal Revenue Code, is a closed system because only certain employees are granted access to the information contained in the electronic records. All aspects of information security are the employer's responsibility, including access to, creating, and maintaining electronic personnel and pay records. Record identifiers would log who had accessed an electronic file, when, and from what location. Record logging provides an additional measure of security and protection against unauthorized access (also called *hacking*), as well as tracking whether unauthorized changes occur on records.

Andrey_Popov/Shutterstock

According to the FBI, more than $1 billion per year has been lost to hackers using ransomware. Ransomware is malicious code placed into a computer system by hackers to obtain a monetary fee to release access to a company's computerized information. The city of Atlanta, Georgia, encountered ransomware that was downloaded onto the city's computer system during a city-related Internet search. As a result of the attack, the city's daily operations were halted because workers could not access their computers.

(Source: ArsTechnica, TrendMicro)

Like other payroll records, electronic records, especially those accessible over the Internet, must be safeguarded to prevent fraudulent activity and data corruption. Employers can access information via a company's intranet (inside the organization) or the Internet using encryption programs, passwords, and secured website locations. It is important to note that once a company has allowed Internet access to its payroll files, it is opening itself up to additional risks from hacking or wrongful use of the payroll information. It is the payroll accountant's responsibility to report any suspicious activity to company managers or the company's information security department.

Payroll as a Non-Solo Effort

One best practice is to have more than one person involved in the generation and maintenance of payroll records. Many errors can occur when the total payroll responsibility rests with one person. Errors that occur may result from a complex hacking effort or a simple failure to remove the system access from a former employee.

- Nonexistent or "ghost" employees could be created and paid via the payroll system. The person committing the fraud could circumvent the payroll system and divert the funds to himself or an accomplice.
- Terminated employees could continue to be paid via the payroll system, or the funds could be subverted to someone else perpetrating the fraud.
- Sales commission plans, employee bonus plans, incentive programs, and other arrangements intended to induce particular behaviors are subject to the employee's and management's manipulation.
- The payroll checks distributed to employees could be stolen individually or *en masse* before their distribution. Also, check fraud could be perpetrated using actual checks or just the account information.
- The company's payroll system or payroll service provider could suffer a breach of the security protocols protecting the computer systems, allowing any combination of fraud or theft to be perpetrated.

Other instances of payroll fraud could have been avoided with a *separation of duties*, which involves the division of related tasks to prevent fraud. Internal controls promote improved accuracy when more than one person is involved in payroll preparation and disbursement. A division of record maintenance, employee verification, and the spread of pay disbursement responsibilities among different employees, depending upon the company's size, would prevent many of the preceding problems. This protects the employer from complaints and potential legal issues stemming from payroll anomalies and provides a level of protection and verification to employees. Auditors look for well-defined internal controls within organizations to ensure legal compliance and file integrity.

- A payroll worker, disgruntled with his job, stole almost $300,000 from different companies by transferring the organizations' money into different bank accounts that he owned.
- A former bookkeeper forged $80,000 in payroll checks before the company owner discovered the discrepancy.
- In the Los Angeles Unified School District, internal inspectors found that the pay system was issuing paychecks to deceased employees.
- In an audit of the Department of Transportation records in Florida, the auditors found that the paper files supporting the payroll system had been discarded to make room in the office. The audit revealed overpayments to employees caused by an incorrect calculation and a lack of payroll verification. Of the employees who were overpaid, only one returned the money.

In the event of a data breach, the company must act quickly to contain the damage and prevent additional issues. The American Payroll Association offered the following action steps that companies should take when they experience a breach in their accounting data software:

Step 1   Prevent the spread of the data breach by taking payroll systems to an offline state and restrict access to records.

Step 2   Determine the scale of the threat or breach. Gather all related data and facts involving the breach and assess any vulnerabilities in the system.

Step 3   Contact the appropriate law enforcement officials to notify them of the crime and to open an investigation. Notify the Federation of Tax Administrators at www.taxadmin.org to engage their service in the investigation.

Step 4   Review the company's data storage, retention, and authorization policies to identify ways to prevent future occurrences.

Document Retention Requirements

According to IRS Regulation 26 CFR 1.6001, records about any financial transaction must remain available for *payroll audit*, the inspection by regulating bodies, at all times. The purpose of the tax code is to maintain records for legal purposes in the suspicion of fraudulent activity. IRS Regulation 26 CFR 1.6001 pertains to manual and computerized records, including payroll records prepared by third-party sources. Both manual and electronic documents must be maintained so that they maintain accessibility for the duration, similar to tax record retention.

When a company institutes a retention schedule, the requirements of legislation and the IRS must be considered. The retention period does not begin until the disbursement of pay occurs, or the employee terminates employment, whichever occurs last. Remember: In the event of fraudulent activity, retention requirements no longer apply, and the courts can request all company records.

Companies must abide by both state and federal law regarding document retention. Employee payroll records, consisting of all forms and payroll compensation statements, must be retained following *termination* or separation. Although no regulations exist for the retention and archiving of internal payroll documents (e.g., a *payroll register*), a general guideline is that the internal documents should be stored with the other payroll accounting records and destroyed per accounting record guidelines.

According to the FLSA, the following records must be maintained for a minimum of **three** years:

- Payroll and other related records
- Union Contracts
- Contacts involving exclusions from the regular pay rate
- Any agreements about overtime rates
- Any certificates about workers who would receive sub-minimum wages
- Records referring to sales that would form the basis for employee commissions

Similarly, the following records must be retained for a minimum of **two** years under FLSA:

- Employment and earnings records.
- Any tables used to compute company wage rates.
- Worker schedules to support time worked.
- Any other records that contain information about wage additions or deductions.

Note that no guidelines exist for any particular order of these documents, but any copies of these records must be clear if copied or otherwise transmitted.

When an employee is terminated, records for the employee and reason for termination must be retained for a period of one year. If an employee qualifies under ADEA, all payroll records must be retained for a period of three years. The Lilly Ledbetter, Fair Pay Act, created a record retention requirement of an additional three years for primary records (pay records or bargaining agreements) and two years for supplementary data (time cards, wage rate tables, piece-rate records).

Note: As a suggested practice to meet the various requirements, many businesses will set document retention at three years for all files.

In 2018, the state of Massachusetts discovered that the state comptroller's website had not listed the Massachusetts State Police salaries in its reports since 2010. Because most of the State Police earn more than $150,000 annually, the omitted amount was substantial. The governor requested an overtime audit to detect potential abuses that could leave the state vulnerable to legal proceedings.

(Source: WBUR News)

Agencies that have the right to audit payroll records include

- The Internal Revenue Service (IRS).
- Federal and state Departments of Labor.
- Department of Homeland Security.
- Other state and local agencies.
- Labor unions.

The following is a chart that explains federal record retention requirements, including relevant laws and types of documents:

Payroll Records (time sheets, electronic records, etc.)	• Three-year retention period • An additional five-year post-termination retention is recommended due to Lilly Ledbetter Act • Includes employee data, any pay records, and all compensation, financial and nonfinancial
Employee Federal, State, and Local Tax Records	• Four years from date the tax is due or paid • Includes all W-4s, state and local tax withholding forms, requests for additional tax withholding, and tax remittances
Form I-9 and Accompanying Employment Eligibility Documents	• Three years after hire OR • One year after termination, whichever is longer
Employee Benefits and Contributions	• Six years • All retirement plan contributions, plan changes, records pertaining to any other employee voluntary deductions
Health Plan Documentation	• No written guidelines, but a minimum of six years is recommended • All written notices about changes in health coverage, especially for health coverage after termination of employment

Even if your company outsources payroll activities, it is still accountable for all records and the information transmitted to the payroll service companies. The third-party payroll service provider attends only to the processing of company payroll but is not responsible for payroll tax payments. Tax remittance remains the liability of the company. Instances in which companies have diverted payroll tax liabilities for personal purposes have resulted in sizable fines and companies' sanctions.

In 2017, the IRS levied a $1 million lien against the property of CCH Oncology of Buffalo, New York. The company failed to remit or file returns for income, Social Security, and Medicare taxes for both the employees' and the employer's shares starting approximately July 2016. The lien amount included failure to pay and failure to file penalties as well as interest.

(Source: *The Buffalo News*)

Internal Controls and Audits

1. Which of these is *not* a payroll internal control procedure?
    a. Overtime approval.
    b. Removal of payroll oversight.
    c. Cross-training.
    d. File security.
2. Which of these records should be retained in the event of a payroll audit?
    a. Employee medical records.
    b. Employee reviews.
    c. Employee time and work records.
    d. Employee nonpayroll correspondence.

LO 2-6 Discuss Employee Termination and Document Destruction Procedures

When employees are terminated, either voluntarily (i.e., resignation) or involuntarily (i.e., termination), the employer has payroll issues unique to the situation. The common element to each termination is the paperwork needed. When an employer terminates a worker's employment involuntarily, the burden of proof for the termination is on the employer, should the case ever require legal scrutiny.

In *Graziadio v. Culinary Institute of America* (2016), the plaintiff was terminated involuntarily after taking two consecutive three-week leaves to care for her children. The Culinary Institute of America claimed that Graziadio had not filed the required paperwork for leave under the FMLA. At first, the court ruled in favor of the Culinary Institute of America because the proper paperwork was not on file. However, further investigation found that the Culinary Institute of America's human resources director, who refused to allow Graziadio to return to work, had not responded to Graziadio's numerous email requests for FMLA paperwork to justify her absence and to return to work.

(Source: FindLaw)

Employee Termination

There are two different methods of separation of an employee from the company: **termination** and **resignation**. Termination is generally initiated by the employer; resignation is usually requested by the employee. When an employee leaves a company, the payroll accountant must complete several steps concerning the employee's and the firm's records. The employee's final paycheck will reflect a culmination of hours worked, and depending on company policies, vacation earned and not taken and

Steve Debenport/Getty Images

sick time earned and not taken. Depending on the company's policies, if the employee's compensation is commission-based, there should be an agreement between management and the employee regarding their sales and the final paycheck's timing to ensure the payment of all earned commissions.

Final hours are calculated the same as for any normal pay period. The employee's daily hours are calculated to determine regular and overtime, and the worked hours are added together to determine weekly hours and weekly overtime. If the employee earned any vacation or sick time, those hours might also need to be paid out on the final paycheck. Vacation and sick time are not included in the worked hours for the determination of overtime.

A limited amount of legislation exists about the payment of a severance package upon termination. In general, two situations exist in which severance packages may be required by legislation: The closure of a company facility and many employee layoffs. If a large number of employees are laid off, a severance package may be required if any promise, written or oral, of a severance package exists or if the company has a history of paying severance packages to laid-off employees. For specific guidelines, the state's employment department would be the primary resource for official guidance (see Appendix E for state contact information).

In terms of payroll accounting, a major difference between the termination and the resignation of an employee, besides the circumstances surrounding the employee's separation from the company (layoff, termination for cause, resignation, etc.), is the timing of the delivery of the final pay disbursement. When an employee quits, any compensation due will be processed and disbursed on the company's next scheduled pay date. However, when the employee is terminated, the company may be mandated to immediately issue the final paycheck or within a short time frame to comply with state labor laws. There is no federal regulation for the timing of the issuance of the employee's final pay, although the Department of Labor explicitly mandates back pay owed to former employees. Table 2-2 contains information about states' employee termination pay guidelines.

Document Destruction

Although many state and federal laws delineate the time requirement for document retention; there are also several methods for regulated *document destruction* of sensitive payroll data. How must confidential payroll-related documents be destroyed? It is not as simple as throwing old payroll documents in the trash. Preferred destruction methods of confidential payroll documents include incineration, confidential shredding services, or paper records pulping. Electronic records must be purged from the server. Although specific destruction procedures and regulations vary among states and localities, the basic guidelines of confidential destruction after the required retention period are common to most areas. From small-

scale record destruction using in-office paper shredders to large-scale operations such as ProShred, Iron Mountain, and many other companies, destruction of confidential business documents is a serious concern because of the federal privacy laws governing payroll documents.

A best practice in document destruction is creating a policy regarding document retention and destruction schedules. An employee in charge of these schedules would be tasked with ensuring that all paper records are stored appropriately and retained for the proper legal time. Another best practice is to separate payroll-related documentation into the following categories:

Steve Cole/Getty Images

- Private personnel information such as Forms W-4 and I-9, court-ordered garnishments, wage information, and direct deposit instructions.
- Employee benefits paperwork, including benefit elections, FMLA documentation, workers' compensation evidence, and flexible spending account information.
- Any investigative information is maintained separately because of the absence of a statute of limitations on employee fraud.

By separating the employee paper files into these categories, document retention and destruction guidelines may be observed more efficiently.

TABLE 2-2
States' Termination and Resignation Pay Guidelines

State	Guideline	State	Guideline
AL	No termination pay guidelines.	MT	Immediately upon termination unless the employer's written policy extends the time to the next regular payday; next regular pay date, or 15 days, whichever is earlier, for resignation.
AK	Within three working days upon termination; at the next regular pay date that is at least more than three days upon resignation.	NE	Next regular payday or within two weeks, whichever is sooner for both termination and resignation.
AZ	Within seven working days or the end of the next pay period, whichever is sooner.	NV	Immediately upon termination; next scheduled pay date or seven days, whichever is sooner upon resignation.
AR	Within seven days of discharge (railroad employees only), no law exists for resignation.	NH	Within 72 hours upon termination; the next pay date in the event of a layoff.
CA	Immediately upon discharge for termination; within 72 hours upon resignation.	NJ	Next regularly scheduled payday for both termination and resignation.
CO	Immediately upon discharge (i.e., within 6 hours of the next business day or 24 hours if payroll is processed off-site) for termination; next scheduled pay date upon resignation.	NM	Within five days upon termination; next scheduled pay date upon resignation.
CT	No later than the next business day upon termination; next scheduled pay date upon resignation.	NY	Next regularly scheduled payday for both termination and resignation.
DE	Next regularly scheduled payday for termination and resignation.	NC	Next regularly scheduled payday for both termination and resignation.
DC	No later than the next business day following termination; next scheduled pay date or within seven days upon resignation.	ND	Next regularly scheduled payday or within 15 days whichever occurs first; next regularly scheduled payday.
FL	No termination or resignation pay guidelines.	OH	No termination pay legislation; within 15 days upon resignation.
GA	No termination or resignation pay guidelines.	OK	Next regularly scheduled payday for both termination and resignation.
HI	At the time of termination unless conditions render pay impossible, next business day. Next business day if resignation with notice.	OR	By the end of the next business day upon termination, within 48 hours days upon resignation with notice or next scheduled payday without notice.
ID	Next regular payday or within 10 days, excluding weekends and holidays, whichever occurs first; within 48 hours upon employee written request for both termination and resignation.	PA	Next regularly scheduled payday for both termination and resignation.
IL	Next regularly scheduled payday for both termination and resignation.	RI	Next regularly scheduled payday for both termination and resignation.
IN	Next regularly scheduled payday for both termination and resignation.	SC	No law exists for resignation within 48 hours or the next scheduled payday, not to exceed 30 days upon termination.
IA	Next regularly scheduled payday for both termination and resignation.	SD	Next regularly scheduled payday or whenever the terminated employee returns all the employer's property for both termination and resignation.
KS	Next regularly scheduled payday for both termination and resignation.	TN	Next regularly scheduled payday or 21 days, whichever comes later for both termination and resignation.
KY	Next regular payday or 14 days, whichever is later for both termination and resignation.	TX	No later than six days after termination; by the next scheduled pay date upon resignation.
LA	Next regular payday or 15 days, whichever is sooner for both termination and resignation.	UT	Within 24 hours upon termination; next scheduled pay date upon resignation.
ME	Next scheduled payday or within two weeks after a demand from the employee, whichever is sooner for both termination and resignation.	VT	Within 72 hours upon termination; next scheduled pay date or the following Friday (if not pay date) upon resignation.
MD	Next, regularly scheduled payday for both termination and resignation.	VA	Next, regularly scheduled payday for both termination and resignation.
MA	Immediately upon termination; next scheduled pay date or the following Saturday upon resignation.	WA	Next, regularly scheduled payday.
MI	Next, regularly scheduled payday for both termination and resignation.	WV	On or before the next scheduled payday upon termination; next scheduled pay date upon resignation.
MN	Immediately upon termination; next regular pay date upon resignation unless there are less than five days until payday, then 20 days after the last day of work under resignation.	WI	Next regularly scheduled payday or within one month, whichever is sooner upon termination; within 24 hours if layoff; next scheduled pay date upon resignation.
MS	No termination or resignation pay guidelines.	WY	Within five business days for both termination and resignation.
MO	Immediately upon termination; no law for resignation.		

(Source: FindLaw.)

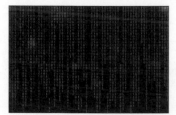
SVshot/Shutterstock

Electronic Records

As the use of electronic payroll records has grown, the need to define appropriate destruction procedures has become increasingly apparent. Simply deleting a website or a portion of the data does not guarantee the security of confidential information. Details of the website's design and system change documentation must be maintained to facilitate record disposal. Guidelines for electronic records disposition include:

- Data disposition instructions, including dates and authorized administrators.
- Record destruction schedules involving security encryption.
- Technical documentation for each record system.
- Identifying information for file indexes and unique records.
- If a website is involved, technical documentation of the site architecture should be maintained.

> The proliferation of electronic accounting records, especially payroll-related data, has led to the Department of Defense Data Wipe Method's adoption, commonly referred to as DoD 5220.22-M, which sanitizes electronic records. Various data wiping tools have this software tool, including DBAN, CBL Data Shredder, and ErAse.
>
> (Source: Lifewire)

Destroy and Terminate

Stop & Check

1. How should paper payroll records be destroyed? How about electronic records?

2. Charlie, a resident of Hawaii, is terminated without cause from his job on October 11. He is terminated at the end of the day after the payroll manager has left. When must he receive his final pay? Is the employer required to pay him a severance package? Explain.

Summary of Payroll System Procedures

The establishment of a payroll system involves careful planning and deliberation. The framework used for the payroll system needs to have enough room for company growth and enough structure to make sure that company and governmental deadlines are met. Using the best practices outlined in this chapter can help a company implement a robust payroll system, whether the system is maintained by company personnel or outsourced, completed manually or electronically using specifically designed software. Adequate payroll system design can save a company from problems with employees and governmental entities and prevent data breaches and fraud.

Although pay processes and methods vary among companies, the framework of internal review and the necessity for accuracy remains the fundamental aspects of any payroll system. Documentation of an employee's eligibility to work in the United States and the compensation method, rates, tax liabilities, and voluntary withholdings are critical elements of employee files that the payroll accountant needs to produce accurate payroll disbursements. The process of entering items into a payroll system varies depending on the type of work done and the compensation rates, for which the payroll accountant must have documentation. Depending on the company's preferences, anything from manual records to computerized

PAYROLL PROCEDURES

As we move further into the digital age, payroll procedures are changing to meet employer needs, technological availability, and employee accessibility. Some procedures that have changed since 2017 include:

- Affordable Care Act employer reporting requirement clarification.
- An increase in the use of Internet-based employee files, which requires increasingly sophisticated security software and company protocols.
- Changes to limitations on the number of and fees related to visas for foreign workers.
- More mobile-friendly workplaces and payroll management.
- An increase in the "virtual marketplace," in which employers and employees will telecommute or otherwise perform work from geographically dispersed locations.
- Dual-factor authentication to enhance cybersecurity and restrict access to electronic personnel records.
- An increase in flexible working hours as employees work from home.
- Changes to paid time off regulation and management.
- Increases in requests for accurate timekeeping for remote workers, possibly including geotagging through cell phone data.
- A shift toward precise data capture and digitIzation of all human resource and payroll records.

records to external payroll vendors may be used to track the payroll. At employee termination, final payment must be issued, but the final pay's timing depends on state legislation.

Payroll record-keeping and maintenance are complex issues and subject to several federal and state regulations. Employee personal information must be safeguarded at all times, and information privacy is paramount. Now that many companies are resorting to electronic pay records, information safeguarding is essential, and encryption efforts are multidimensional, involving the accounting, legal, and information systems departments of an organization. Destruction of payroll-related documents after the required retention period is a serious concern, and an entire industry focuses on document retention and destruction.

Key Points

- Communication protocol varies among companies and departments within companies.
- Upon employment, company personnel must ensure Form W-4 and the I-9 to determine accurate taxes and legal eligibility to work in the United States.
- Ethical payroll practices require the protection of information and dissemination only to the employee or specifically relevant supervisory staff.
- Employees are classified as either exempt or nonexempt from FLSA provisions.
- To be classified as an exempt employee requires an examination of job duties.
- Control of the payroll system involves regular system design review and delineation of specific tasks.
- Whether completed internally or by an outsourced vendor, payroll is only as accurate as the information provided.
- Pay periods are at the discretion of the company. The IRS has developed tax tables (i.e., tax withholding amounts) for each pay interval that are contained in Publication 15-T, an annual IRS guide to payroll that was updated in 2021.

- File security is of utmost importance, especially when files are stored electronically and accessed via an Internet portal.
- Documentation for payroll exceptions such as time away from work should be maintained separately from regular work time documentation.
- Calculations of pay can involve many variables and require reviewing each employee's information before pay issuance.
- Final pay needs to reflect all earned compensation, paid time off, and deductions up to the termination date.
- The timing of final pay disbursement when an employee is terminated depends on state law.
- Document retention and destruction procedures are important for data security and audit purposes.

Vocabulary

Biweekly payroll	I-9	Piece rate
Commission	Internal control	Resignation
Daily payroll	Leased employee	Review process
Document destruction	Monthly payroll	Semimonthly payroll
Exempt	New hire reporting	Separation of duties
File maintenance	Nonexempt	Statutory employee
File security	Pay period	Temporary employee
Foreign Account Tax	Paycard	Termination
Compliance Act (FATCA)	Payroll audit	W-4
H-1B visa	Payroll register	Weekly payroll
Hiring packet	Payroll review	

Review Questions

1. What are the necessary elements of internal control for a payroll department?
2. Why should more than one person prepare/verify payroll processing?
3. What documents should be included in all new-hire packets?
4. Why are new hires required to be reported to the state's employment department?
5. When must a terminated employee be paid his or her final paycheck for the state in which you live?
6. What are the five main payroll frequencies?
7. What are two of the best practices in establishing a payroll system?
8. What are the important considerations in setting up a payroll system?
9. What are two different tasks involved in payroll accounting?
10. What agencies or organizations can audit a company's payroll records?
11. How long should employee records be retained?
12. Why are independent contractors not paid through a company's payroll system?
13. What is the difference between termination and resignation?
14. What are the differences among daily, weekly, biweekly, semimonthly, and monthly pay periods?
15. What differentiates exempt and nonexempt employees?
16. What challenges does a company face when using cloud-based payroll and personnel records?
17. What two regulations pertain to employee paycard use?

Exercises Set A

E2-1A.
LO 2-1, 2-4

Kira Tran, a nonexempt employee at Winslow Woods, works a standard 7:00–4:00 schedule with an hour for lunch each day. Kira received overtime pay for hours in excess of 40 per week. During the week, she worked the following schedule:

- Monday: 9.25 hours
- Tuesday: 7.5 hours
- Wednesday: 8.75 hours
- Thursday: 6.75 hours
- Friday: 8.25 hours

How many hours of overtime did Kira work this week?

1. 0 hours
2. 0.50 hours
3. 2 hours
4. 2.25 hours

E2-2A.
LO 2-1

Lillian Weatherby receives her pay every other week while working for the federal government. Which of the following choices describes her pay frequency?

1. Biweekly
2. Semimonthly
3. Weekly
4. Monthly

E2-3A.
LO 2-2

Lila Rivera is a new employee for Divera Glass. Which federal forms must she complete as part of the hiring process? (Select all that apply.)

1. W-4
2. W-2
3. SS-8
4. I-9

E2-4A.
LO 2-5, 2-6

Wilbur Matthews, a resident of Texas, resigned from his employment with Grand Lake Cattle Farms on October 7, 2021. The next pay date for the company is October 11. By what date should he receive his final pay?

1. October 7
2. October 11
3. October 13
4. October 31

E2-5A.
LO 2-5

Charlene Kelley is a new nonexempt sales associate for Oyondo Retail Stores. She completes her timecard for the pay period. To ensure proper internal control, what is the next step in the payroll review process?

1. Submit the time card to the payroll clerk.
2. Have a friend check her math for accuracy.
3. Submit the timecard to her manager for review.
4. Enter the time card data directly into the payroll system.

E2-6A.
LO 2-6

Alfonso Silva needs additional filing space at the end of the year in the company's off-site, secured storage. He sees several boxes of payroll records marked for the current year's destruction. What methods can Alfonso use to dispose of the payroll records? (Select all that apply.)

1. Contact an offsite record destruction service.
2. Place the boxes containing the records in the company trash disposal.
3. Shred the records, and then dispose of the shredded paper.
4. Incinerate the payroll records marked for destruction.

E2-7A.
LO 2-1

Jacqueline Blue is a payroll clerk at Quaking Aspens Antiques. As she reviews employee files, what information should be present for each employee? (Select all that apply.)

1. Spouse's name
2. Pay rate
3. Occupation
4. Supervisor name

E2-8A.
LO 2-2

Ginger Klein is the payroll clerk for Neolane Transportation. A colleague who is classified as an independent contractor requests to be classified as an employee. What factors should Ginger consider? (Select all that apply.)
1. Relationship of the parties
2. Behavioral control
3. Method of compensation
4. Financial control

E2-9A.
LO 2-2

What are the forms of identification that establish *employment authorization* for the I-9? (Select all that apply.)
1. Driver's license
2. Native American tribal document
3. Voter registration card
4. Social Security card

E2-10A.
LO 2-2

What are the forms of identification that establish *identity* for the I-9? (Select all that apply.)
1. State-issued driver's license
2. U.S. passport
3. School record
4. Certified copy of the birth certificate

E2-11A.
LO 2-3

Jamie Patil is a candidate for the position of a sales manager with Retrozz Furniture. She is going to be required to supervise several employees and can determine the direction in which she will complete the assignments given to her. What guidelines should she follow when classifying workers as exempt or nonexempt? (Select all that apply.)
1. OSHA
2. FLSA
3. Department of Labor
4. IRS

E2-12A.
LO 2-3

Susana Robledo is the office manager for Wardley and Sons Auto Detailing. Because it is a small office, she is required to keep track of all employee records and pay both employees and contractors. Which of the following are legal factors that will differentiate exempt from nonexempt employees? (Select all that apply.)
1. Number of hours worked
2. Type of work performed
3. Employee age and education
4. Amount of supervisor-given direction

Problems Set A

P2-1A.
LO 2-1

Louis Trivaldi is a vice president of sales at Fields Brothers Autos and earns an annual salary of $59,000. What is Louis's period pay for each of the following pay frequencies?
1. Biweekly
2. Semimonthly
3. Weekly
4. Monthly

P2-2A.
LO 2-2, 2-3

Reuben Walker is a part-time worker for Senior Solvers who uses company equipment in the performance of his job duties. He asks the payroll supervisor, Gina Turner, to grant him independent contractor status. What should Gina tell him?

P2-3A.
LO 2-5

You are the new payroll supervisor for your company. Which payroll documentation control procedures are now your responsibility?

P2-4A.
LO 2-2

Leona Figueroa is a new employee in the payroll department of Octolium Computers. After working at the company for one week, she asks you why it is so important to submit new hire documentation. What guidance will you offer her?

P2-5A.
LO 2-4

You are the payroll accounting clerk for your company, Conose Advertising, which has 50 employees. The controller has recently switched the firm from an in-house payroll system to an outsourced payroll provider. What are your responsibilities within the company for payroll records and employee file issues?

P2-6A.
LO 2-2

Aaron Tallchief is a citizen of the Northern Pomo Indian Nation. In completing his I-9, he provides an official Northern Pomo Indian Nation birth certificate to establish identification and employment eligibility. Is this sufficient documentation? Why or why not?

P2-7A.
LO 2-3

Maria Rupert is the payroll supervisor at All Family Investments. Management is requesting to have the investment salespeople, who are paid on an hourly basis, be classified as exempt employees because their job duties occasionally require evening and weekend work. What tests should the investment salespeople meet to achieve exempt status?

P2-8A.
LO 2-6

Twinte Cars, a California corporation, has internal corporate requirements that stipulate a three-year payroll document retention period. It enters into a contract with an international company that mandates a six-year payroll document retention requirement. How should Twinte Cars balance these requirements?

P2-9A.
LO 2-2

Ted McCormick is a full-time life insurance agent with Centixo Insurance, a small insurance company. The company has classified him as an employee, and he feels that he should be classified as an independent contractor because he receives no company benefits and sets his own office hours. Should he be reclassified as an independent contractor? Why or why not?

P2-10A.
LO 2-2

Evelyn Hardy is an employee of Polyent Plastics, a company with headquarters in Rock Island, Illinois. She lives and works in Doha, Qatar, and earns an annual salary of $97,300. The company has been withholding U.S. federal income taxes from her pay, but Evelyn believes that she should be exempt because she is an expatriate. What course of action should Evelyn take?

P2-11A.
LO 2-2, 2-4

Complete the W-4 for employment at Plexivent Plastics starting 9/6/2021. The employer's address is 1 Plastics Way, Lincoln Valley, ND 58430, and EIN is 56-4658631.
Henry Walker Pierce
2024 Denhoff Highway, Apartment 12
Lincoln Valley, ND 58430
SSN: 687-55-4658
Marital status: Married filing jointly with 2 Dependents under 17
One job and spouse does not work
Does not require any additional amount to be withheld

P2-12A.
LO 2-2, 2-4

Complete the I-9 for employment at Plexivent Plastics starting 9/6/2021. The employer's address is 1 Plastics Way, Lincoln Valley, ND 58430, and the EIN is 56-4658631. Henry is starting work on 9/6/2021. Be sure to complete Section 2 of Form I-9.
Henry Walker Pierce
2024 Denhoff Highway, Apartment 12
Lincoln Valley, ND 58430
SSN: 687-55-4658
Marital status: Married
Date of Birth: 8/15/1999
U.S. Citizen
Henry's North Dakota driver's license number is MKJ-462856 and expires on his birthday in 2024.
Office Manager James MacMillan verified the information for the company.

Form **W-4**	**Employee's Withholding Certificate**	OMB No. 1545-0074

Form **W-4**
(Rev. December 2020)
Department of the Treasury
Internal Revenue Service

Employee's Withholding Certificate

▶ Complete Form W-4 so that your employer can withhold the correct federal income tax from your pay.
▶ Give Form W-4 to your employer.
▶ Your withholding is subject to review by the IRS.

OMB No. 1545-0074

2021

Step 1: **Enter Personal Information**	**(a)** First name and middle initial	Last name	**(b)** Social security number

Address

City or town, state, and ZIP code

▶ **Does your name match the name on your social security card?** If not, to ensure you get credit for your earnings, contact SSA at 800-772-1213 or go to *www.ssa.gov*.

(c) ☑ **Single** or **Married filing separately**

☐ **Married filing jointly** or **Qualifying widow(er)**

☐ **Head of household** (Check only if you're unmarried and pay more than half the costs of keeping up a home for yourself and a qualifying individual.)

Complete Steps 2–4 ONLY if they apply to you; otherwise, skip to Step 5. See page 2 for more information on each step, who can claim exemption from withholding, when to use the estimator at *www.irs.gov/W4App*, and privacy.

Step 2: **Multiple Jobs or Spouse Works**	Complete this step if you (1) hold more than one job at a time, or (2) are married filing jointly and your spouse also works. The correct amount of withholding depends on income earned from all of these jobs.

Do **only one** of the following.

(a) Use the estimator at *www.irs.gov/W4App* for most accurate withholding for this step (and Steps 3–4); **or**

(b) Use the Multiple Jobs Worksheet on page 3 and enter the result in Step 4(c) below for roughly accurate withholding; **or**

(c) If there are only two jobs total, you may check this box. Do the same on Form W-4 for the other job. This option is accurate for jobs with similar pay; otherwise, more tax than necessary may be withheld . . . . . ▶ ☐

TIP: To be accurate, submit a 2021 Form W-4 for all other jobs. If you (or your spouse) have self-employment income, including as an independent contractor, use the estimator.

Complete Steps 3–4(b) on Form W-4 for only ONE of these jobs. Leave those steps blank for the other jobs. (Your withholding will be most accurate if you complete Steps 3–4(b) on the Form W-4 for the highest paying job.)

Step 3: **Claim Dependents**	If your total income will be $200,000 or less ($400,000 or less if married filing jointly):		

Multiply the number of qualifying children under age 17 by $2,000 ▶ $ _____

Multiply the number of other dependents by $500 . . . . . ▶ $ _____

Add the amounts above and enter the total here . . . .   **3** $ _____

Step 4 (optional): **Other Adjustments**	**(a) Other income (not from jobs).** If you want tax withheld for other income you expect this year that won't have withholding, enter the amount of other income here. This may include interest, dividends, and retirement income	**4(a)**	$
	(b) Deductions. If you expect to claim deductions other than the standard deduction and want to reduce your withholding, use the Deductions Worksheet on page 3 and enter the result here	**4(b)**	$
	(c) Extra withholding. Enter any additional tax you want withheld each **pay period** .	**4(c)**	$

Step 5: **Sign Here**	Under penalties of perjury, I declare that this certificate, to the best of my knowledge and belief, is true, correct, and complete.

▶ _____
Employee's signature (This form is not valid unless you sign it.)

▶ _____
Date

Employers Only	Employer's name and address	First date of employment	Employer identification number (EIN)

For Privacy Act and Paperwork Reduction Act Notice, see page 3.   Cat. No. 10220Q   Form **W-4** (2021)

Source: Internal Revenue Service.

Employment Eligibility Verification
Department of Homeland Security
U.S. Citizenship and Immigration Services

USCIS
Form I-9
OMB No. 1615-0047
Expires 10/31/2022

▶**START HERE:** Read instructions carefully before completing this form. The instructions must be available, either in paper or electronically, during completion of this form. Employers are liable for errors in the completion of this form.

ANTI-DISCRIMINATION NOTICE: It is illegal to discriminate against work-authorized individuals. Employers **CANNOT** specify which document(s) an employee may present to establish employment authorization and identity. The refusal to hire or continue to employ an individual because the documentation presented has a future expiration date may also constitute illegal discrimination.

Section 1. Employee Information and Attestation *(Employees must complete and sign Section 1 of Form I-9 no later than the **first day of employment**, but not before accepting a job offer.)*

Last Name *(Family Name)*	First Name *(Given Name)*	Middle Initial	Other Last Names Used *(if any)*

Address *(Street Number and Name)*	Apt. Number	City or Town	State	ZIP Code

Date of Birth *(mm/dd/yyyy)*	U.S. Social Security Number	Employee's E-mail Address	Employee's Telephone Number
	☐☐☐ - ☐☐ - ☐☐☐☐		

I am aware that federal law provides for imprisonment and/or fines for false statements or use of false documents in connection with the completion of this form.

I attest, under penalty of perjury, that I am (check one of the following boxes):

☐ 1. A citizen of the United States

☐ 2. A noncitizen national of the United States *(See instructions)*

☐ 3. A lawful permanent resident   (Alien Registration Number/USCIS Number): _____

☐ 4. An alien authorized to work   until (expiration date, if applicable, mm/dd/yyyy): _____
      Some aliens may write "N/A" in the expiration date field. *(See instructions)*

Aliens authorized to work must provide only one of the following document numbers to complete Form I-9:
An Alien Registration Number/USCIS Number OR Form I-94 Admission Number OR Foreign Passport Number.

QR Code - Section 1
Do Not Write In This Space

1. Alien Registration Number/USCIS Number: _____

OR

2. Form I-94 Admission Number: _____

OR

3. Foreign Passport Number: _____

   Country of Issuance: _____

Signature of Employee	Today's Date *(mm/dd/yyyy)*

Preparer and/or Translator Certification (check one):

☐ I did not use a preparer or translator.   ☐ A preparer(s) and/or translator(s) assisted the employee in completing Section 1.
(Fields below must be completed and signed when preparers and/or translators assist an employee in completing Section 1.)

I attest, under penalty of perjury, that I have assisted in the completion of Section 1 of this form and that to the best of my knowledge the information is true and correct.

Signature of Preparer or Translator	Today's Date *(mm/dd/yyyy)*

Last Name *(Family Name)*	First Name *(Given Name)*		

Address *(Street Number and Name)*	City or Town	State	ZIP Code

STOP *Employer Completes Next Page* **STOP**

Employment Eligibility Verification
Department of Homeland Security
U.S. Citizenship and Immigration Services

USCIS
Form I-9
OMB No. 1615-0047
Expires 10/31/2022

Section 2. Employer or Authorized Representative Review and Verification

(Employers or their authorized representative must complete and sign Section 2 within 3 business days of the employee's first day of employment. You must physically examine one document from List A OR a combination of one document from List B and one document from List C as listed on the "Lists of Acceptable Documents.")

Employee Info from Section 1	Last Name (Family Name)	First Name (Given Name)	M.I.	Citizenship/Immigration Status

List A Identity and Employment Authorization	OR	List B Identity	AND	List C Employment Authorization

List A — Identity and Employment Authorization

Document Title

Issuing Authority

Document Number

Expiration Date (if any) (mm/dd/yyyy)

Document Title

Issuing Authority

Document Number

Expiration Date (if any) (mm/dd/yyyy)

Document Title

Issuing Authority

Document Number

Expiration Date (if any) (mm/dd/yyyy)

List B — Identity

Document Title

Issuing Authority

Document Number

Expiration Date (if any) (mm/dd/yyyy)

List C — Employment Authorization

Document Title

Issuing Authority

Document Number

Expiration Date (if any) (mm/dd/yyyy)

Additional Information

QR Code - Sections 2 & 3
Do Not Write In This Space

Certification: I attest, under penalty of perjury, that (1) I have examined the document(s) presented by the above-named employee, (2) the above-listed document(s) appear to be genuine and to relate to the employee named, and (3) to the best of my knowledge the employee is authorized to work in the United States.

The employee's first day of employment *(mm/dd/yyyy)*: _____ *(See instructions for exemptions)*

Signature of Employer or Authorized Representative	Today's Date (mm/dd/yyyy)	Title of Employer or Authorized Representative

Last Name of Employer or Authorized Representative	First Name of Employer or Authorized Representative	Employer's Business or Organization Name

Employer's Business or Organization Address (Street Number and Name)	City or Town	State	ZIP Code

Section 3. Reverification and Rehires *(To be completed and signed by employer or authorized representative.)*

A. New Name (if applicable)			B. Date of Rehire (if applicable)
Last Name (Family Name)	First Name (Given Name)	Middle Initial	Date (mm/dd/yyyy)

C. If the employee's previous grant of employment authorization has expired, provide the information for the document or receipt that establishes continuing employment authorization in the space provided below.

Document Title	Document Number	Expiration Date (if any) (mm/dd/yyyy)

I attest, under penalty of perjury, that to the best of my knowledge, this employee is authorized to work in the United States, and if the employee presented document(s), the document(s) I have examined appear to be genuine and to relate to the individual.

Signature of Employer or Authorized Representative	Today's Date (mm/dd/yyyy)	Name of Employer or Authorized Representative

Form I-9 10/21/2019

Page 2 of 3

LISTS OF ACCEPTABLE DOCUMENTS
All documents must be UNEXPIRED

Employees may present one selection from List A
or a combination of one selection from List B and one selection from List C.

LIST A	LIST B	LIST C
Documents that Establish Both Identity and Employment Authorization	**Documents that Establish Identity**	**Documents that Establish Employment Authorization**
OR	**AND**	
1. U.S. Passport or U.S. Passport Card	1. Driver's license or ID card issued by a State or outlying possession of the United States provided it contains a photograph or information such as name, date of birth, gender, height, eye color, and address	1. A Social Security Account Number card, unless the card includes one of the following restrictions:
2. Permanent Resident Card or Alien Registration Receipt Card (Form I-551)		(1) NOT VALID FOR EMPLOYMENT
		(2) VALID FOR WORK ONLY WITH INS AUTHORIZATION
3. Foreign passport that contains a temporary I-551 stamp or temporary I-551 printed notation on a machine-readable immigrant visa	2. ID card issued by federal, state or local government agencies or entities, provided it contains a photograph or information such as name, date of birth, gender, height, eye color, and address	(3) VALID FOR WORK ONLY WITH DHS AUTHORIZATION
4. Employment Authorization Document that contains a photograph (Form I-766)		2. Certification of report of birth issued by the Department of State (Forms DS-1350, FS-545, FS-240)
	3. School ID card with a photograph	
5. For a nonimmigrant alien authorized to work for a specific employer because of his or her status:	4. Voter's registration card	3. Original or certified copy of birth certificate issued by a State, county, municipal authority, or territory of the United States bearing an official seal
a. Foreign passport; and	5. U.S. Military card or draft record	
b. Form I-94 or Form I-94A that has the following:	6. Military dependent's ID card	
(1) The same name as the passport; and	7. U.S. Coast Guard Merchant Mariner Card	4. Native American tribal document
(2) An endorsement of the alien's nonimmigrant status as long as that period of endorsement has not yet expired and the proposed employment is not in conflict with any restrictions or limitations identified on the form.	8. Native American tribal document	5. U.S. Citizen ID Card (Form I-197)
	9. Driver's license issued by a Canadian government authority	6. Identification Card for Use of Resident Citizen in the United States (Form I-179)
	For persons under age 18 who are unable to present a document listed above:	7. Employment authorization document issued by the Department of Homeland Security
6. Passport from the Federated States of Micronesia (FSM) or the Republic of the Marshall Islands (RMI) with Form I-94 or Form I-94A indicating nonimmigrant admission under the Compact of Free Association Between the United States and the FSM or RMI	10. School record or report card	
	11. Clinic, doctor, or hospital record	
	12. Day-care or nursery school record	

Examples of many of these documents appear in the Handbook for Employers (M-274).

Refer to the instructions for more information about acceptable receipts.

Source: U.S. Citizenship and Immigration Services.

Exercises Set B

E2-1B.
LO 2-1, 2-4

Howard Walters, a nonexempt employee of Consolidated Utilities, works a standard 10:00 a.m. to 7:00 p.m. schedule with an hour for lunch. Howard works in California, a state that requires overtime pay for hours exceeding 8 per day and for those exceeding 40 in a week. During the week, he worked the following schedule:

- Monday: 8.75 hours
- Tuesday: 7.75 hours
- Wednesday: 8.50 hours
- Thursday: 8.00 hours
- Friday: 8.25 hours

Based on the state's requirements, how much overtime has Howard worked during the period?

1. 2 hours
2. 1.25 hour
3. 1 hour
4. 2.75 hours

E2-2B.
LO 2-1

Michael Hatton is a salaried employee earning $49,850 annually. He receives his payroll twice per month. Which of the following best describes the pay frequency?

1. Biweekly
2. Semimonthly
3. Weekly
4. Monthly

E2-3B.
LO 2-4, 2-6

On June 21, 2021, Dolores Goodman was terminated from her job at Black Diamond Sports in New Hampshire. Black Diamond Sports pays its employees biweekly on Fridays, and the next payday is 7/2/2021. When must she receive her final paycheck?

1. On the next pay date
2. Within seven days
3. Immediately upon discharge
4. Within 72 hours

E2-4B.
LO 2-4, 2-6

Leonard Andrews ended his employment with Atlas Inks on March 20, 2021. When is the earliest that Atlas Inks may destroy his payroll records?

1. March 21, 2022
2. March 21, 2023
3. March 21, 2024
4. March 21, 2025

E2-5B.
LO 2-5

Elijah Brown is a new payroll clerk at Zata Imports, a company with 250 employees. He has completed entering all timecard data for the pay period. What should Elijah's next step in the payroll review process be?

1. Ask employees to verify that the time Elijah entered is accurate.
2. Generate paychecks and prepare them for signature.
3. Ask his supervisor to verify the accuracy of the payroll data.
4. Have another payroll clerk verify the data accuracy.

E2-6B.
LO 2-6

Elaine Wheeler needs additional filing space at the end of the year in the company's office and chooses to use off-site, secured storage. Upon arriving at the storage facility, she discovers that the unit is nearly full and sees several boxes marked for destruction at the end of the calendar year. What are Elaine's options regarding the destruction of the payroll records marked for destruction? (Select all that apply.)

1. She should take the oldest year's boxes to the closest recycling facility.
2. She should make arrangements to pulp or burn the paper payroll records marked for destruction.
3. She should arrange to have a document destruction service pick up the boxes marked for destruction.
4. She should bring a shredding machine to the storage facility and prepare to shred the records marked for destruction.

E2-7B.
LO 2-1

Gerardo Rogers is conducting a review of the payroll files for each employee at Meejo Games. Which of the following items must be present in the file? (Select all that apply.)

1. Basis upon which compensation is paid.
2. Overtime pay earned during each pay period.
3. Hours worked during each pay period.
4. Break times taken each day.

E2-8B.
LO 2-2

Jane McCarthy is preparing to compute employee pay and needs to determine the amount of employee federal income taxes to be withheld. Which of the following should she consult?

1. USCIS I-9
2. IRS Publication 15-t
3. DHS Schedule F
4. SSA Schedule 8

E2-9B.
LO 2-2

Judy Baker is a new employee of Farnsdel and Brothers, LLP. Which of the following will provide proof of *employment authorization* for the completion of the I-9? (Select all that apply.)

1. U.S. passport
2. U.S. military identification card
3. U.S. citizen identification card
4. State-issued driver's license

E2-10B.
LO 2-2

Rupert Pelliere is completing the I-9 for his new employment with the state of New Mexico. Which of the following provides proof of his *identity*? (Select all that apply.)

1. Social Security card
2. Certificate of birth abroad, issued by the U.S. Department of State
3. New Mexico driver's license
4. U.S. passport

E2-11B.
LO 2-3

Laverne Watkins is a candidate for the position of marketing clerk with the promotions department of Paramba Productions, earning $10.25 per hour. She will work occasional overtime in her new position and will not have managerial or supervisory duties as a regular part of her job description. Why should Laverne be classified as a nonexempt employee? (Select all that apply.)

1. Her annual wages are lower than the minimum exempt salary.
2. She has no supervisory or managerial duties.
3. She has the term *clerk* in her job title.
4. She will work occasional overtime.

E2-12B.
LO 2-3

Rex Marshall manages a ski resort with year-round and seasonal employees. Assuming that the ski resort engages in interstate commerce, which are the FLSA requirement(s) that Rex should consider? (Select all that apply.)

1. Hourly wages paid to employees.
2. Safety of the working conditions.
3. Number of hours worked per week.
4. Employee age and weekly work schedule.

Problems Set B

P2-1B.
LO 2-2

Tasha Webb is an independent contractor for Antimbu Exports, where you are the payroll accountant. She feels that she should receive employee benefits because of the number of hours that she dedicates to the company. What guidance could you offer Tasha?

P2-2B.
LO 2-6

Roland Wexler was terminated for cause from Santel Auto Parts in North Carolina on July 20, 2021. As of the date of his termination, he had worked 22 hours of regular time. Employees at Santel Auto Parts are paid semi-monthly on the 15th and last day of the month. Roland would like to know when he will be paid for the accrued hours. What will you tell him?

P2-3B.
LO 2-2

Sara Northman is a member of the Algonquin Indian Nation and is a new employee at Predeo Game Designs. During the process of completing her I-9, she claims that the only way to prove her identity is the Algonquin Indian Nation official birth certificate. Is this document sufficient to prove employment authorization for the purposes of the I-9? Why or why not?

P2-4B.
LO 2-2

Abraham Manning is a new employee of Symity Batteries. He is curious about the purpose of the requirements for new hire documentation to be forwarded to government agencies. What should you tell him?

P2-5B.
LO 2-3

Pedro Arturo wants to start his own company and hire employees. Because you are a seasoned payroll professional, he approaches you for guidance about the differences between exempt and nonexempt employees. What would you tell him?

P2-6B.
LO 2-5

Katrina Wilkins is a new payroll clerk for Remm Plumbing. She is curious about the purpose of the different steps in the payroll review process and asks you, her supervisor, for guidance. What would you tell her?

P2-7B.
LO 2-4

Francesca Aldri started as a payroll accountant at Sticktoit Adhesives, a company with 100 employees. She soon notices that the former payroll accountant had been processing payroll manually and suggests that the company immediately switch to cloud-based payroll. What types of documentation must be maintained in employee records?

P2-8B.
LO 2-5

Tara Morris, a payroll clerk, has received a promotion and is now the payroll supervisor for Fligen Enterprises. What document control items could now become her responsibility?

P2-9B.
LO 2-2

Herman Watkins is in the payroll department of Neombee Plastics, a multistate company. The company has historically been filing employee information with each state. What alternative exists for multistate employers?

P2-10B.
LO 2-1

Derek Allen is the payroll supervisor for Caposis Freight. His company is preparing to merge with another distribution company that has a different pay cycle. The president of the company wants to know the difference between biweekly and semimonthly pay cycles as far as to pay dates and payment amounts are concerned. What should Derek tell him?

P2-11B.
LO 2-2, 2-4

Complete the W-4 for employment starting 5/21/2021 at Martel Semiconductors, located at 2445 Manchester Road, Lakehurst, NJ 08733, EIN of 26-4684136.
Terence A. Noren
221 First Street
Lakehurst, NJ 08733
SSN: 785-56-4321
Single with no dependents
No additional tax withholding

P2-12B.
LO 2-2, 2-4

Complete the I-9 for employment starting 5/21/2021 at Martel Semiconductors, located at 2445 Manchester Road, Lakehurst, NJ 08733, EIN of 26-4684136. Be sure to complete Section 2 of Form I-9.
Terence A. Noren
221 First Street
Lakehurst, NJ 08733
SSN: 785-56-4321
Birthdate: 6/5/1998
Terence presented his driver's license and Social Security card to the Human Resources Manager, Bree Andrews, to review.
New Jersey Driver's License #N15368497531246, Expires on his birthday in 2023

Form W-4
(Rev. December 2020)
Department of the Treasury
Internal Revenue Service

Employee's Withholding Certificate

▶ Complete Form W-4 so that your employer can withhold the correct federal income tax from your pay.
▶ Give Form W-4 to your employer.
▶ Your withholding is subject to review by the IRS.

OMB No. 1545-0074

2021

Step 1: Enter Personal Information	(a) First name and middle initial	Last name	(b) Social security number
	Address		▶ **Does your name match the name on your social security card?** If not, to ensure you get credit for your earnings, contact SSA at 800-772-1213 or go to *www.ssa.gov.*
	City or town, state, and ZIP code		

(c) ☑ **Single** or **Married filing separately**
☐ **Married filing jointly** or **Qualifying widow(er)**
☐ **Head of household** (Check only if you're unmarried and pay more than half the costs of keeping up a home for yourself and a qualifying individual.)

Complete Steps 2–4 ONLY if they apply to you; otherwise, skip to Step 5. See page 2 for more information on each step, who can claim exemption from withholding, when to use the estimator at *www.irs.gov/W4App*, and privacy.

Step 2:
Multiple Jobs or Spouse Works

Complete this step if you (1) hold more than one job at a time, or (2) are married filing jointly and your spouse also works. The correct amount of withholding depends on income earned from all of these jobs.

Do **only one** of the following.

(a) Use the estimator at *www.irs.gov/W4App* for most accurate withholding for this step (and Steps 3–4); **or**

(b) Use the Multiple Jobs Worksheet on page 3 and enter the result in Step 4(c) below for roughly accurate withholding; **or**

(c) If there are only two jobs total, you may check this box. Do the same on Form W-4 for the other job. This option is accurate for jobs with similar pay; otherwise, more tax than necessary may be withheld . . . . . ▶ ☐

TIP: To be accurate, submit a 2021 Form W-4 for all other jobs. If you (or your spouse) have self-employment income, including as an independent contractor, use the estimator.

Complete Steps 3–4(b) on Form W-4 for only ONE of these jobs. Leave those steps blank for the other jobs. (Your withholding will be most accurate if you complete Steps 3–4(b) on the Form W-4 for the highest paying job.)

Step 3:
Claim Dependents

If your total income will be $200,000 or less ($400,000 or less if married filing jointly):

Multiply the number of qualifying children under age 17 by $2,000 ▶ $ _____

Multiply the number of other dependents by $500 . . . . ▶ $ _____

Add the amounts above and enter the total here . . . .   **3** $

Step 4 (optional):
Other Adjustments

(a) **Other income (not from jobs).** If you want tax withheld for other income you expect this year that won't have withholding, enter the amount of other income here. This may include interest, dividends, and retirement income . . . .   **4(a)** $

(b) **Deductions.** If you expect to claim deductions other than the standard deduction and want to reduce your withholding, use the Deductions Worksheet on page 3 and enter the result here . . . .   **4(b)** $

(c) **Extra withholding.** Enter any additional tax you want withheld each **pay period** .   **4(c)** $

Step 5:
Sign Here

Under penalties of perjury, I declare that this certificate, to the best of my knowledge and belief, is true, correct, and complete.

▶ _____
Employee's signature (This form is not valid unless you sign it.)

▶ _____
Date

Employers Only	Employer's name and address	First date of employment	Employer identification number (EIN)

For Privacy Act and Paperwork Reduction Act Notice, see page 3.   Cat. No. 10220Q   Form **W-4** (2021)

Employment Eligibility Verification
Department of Homeland Security
U.S. Citizenship and Immigration Services

USCIS
Form I-9
OMB No. 1615-0047
Expires 10/31/2022

▶**START HERE:** Read instructions carefully before completing this form. The instructions must be available, either in paper or electronically, during completion of this form. Employers are liable for errors in the completion of this form.

ANTI-DISCRIMINATION NOTICE: It is illegal to discriminate against work-authorized individuals. Employers **CANNOT** specify which document(s) an employee may present to establish employment authorization and identity. The refusal to hire or continue to employ an individual because the documentation presented has a future expiration date may also constitute illegal discrimination.

Section 1. Employee Information and Attestation *(Employees must complete and sign Section 1 of Form I-9 no later than the **first day of employment**, but not before accepting a job offer.)*

Last Name *(Family Name)*	First Name *(Given Name)*	Middle Initial	Other Last Names Used *(if any)*

Address *(Street Number and Name)*	Apt. Number	City or Town	State	ZIP Code

Date of Birth *(mm/dd/yyyy)*	U.S. Social Security Number	Employee's E-mail Address	Employee's Telephone Number
	☐☐☐ - ☐☐ - ☐☐☐☐		

I am aware that federal law provides for imprisonment and/or fines for false statements or use of false documents in connection with the completion of this form.

I attest, under penalty of perjury, that I am (check one of the following boxes):

☐ 1. A citizen of the United States

☐ 2. A noncitizen national of the United States *(See instructions)*

☐ 3. A lawful permanent resident   (Alien Registration Number/USCIS Number): _____

☐ 4. An alien authorized to work   until (expiration date, if applicable, mm/dd/yyyy): _____
Some aliens may write "N/A" in the expiration date field. *(See instructions)*

Aliens authorized to work must provide only one of the following document numbers to complete Form I-9:
An Alien Registration Number/USCIS Number OR Form I-94 Admission Number OR Foreign Passport Number.

QR Code - Section 1
Do Not Write In This Space

1. Alien Registration Number/USCIS Number: _____

OR

2. Form I-94 Admission Number: _____

OR

3. Foreign Passport Number: _____

Country of Issuance: _____

Signature of Employee	Today's Date *(mm/dd/yyyy)*

Preparer and/or Translator Certification (check one):

☐ I did not use a preparer or translator.   ☐ A preparer(s) and/or translator(s) assisted the employee in completing Section 1.

(Fields below must be completed and signed when preparers and/or translators assist an employee in completing Section 1.)

I attest, under penalty of perjury, that I have assisted in the completion of Section 1 of this form and that to the best of my knowledge the information is true and correct.

Signature of Preparer or Translator	Today's Date *(mm/dd/yyyy)*

Last Name *(Family Name)*	First Name *(Given Name)*

Address *(Street Number and Name)*	City or Town	State	ZIP Code

🛑 *Employer Completes Next Page* 🛑

Employment Eligibility Verification
Department of Homeland Security
U.S. Citizenship and Immigration Services

USCIS
Form I-9
OMB No. 1615-0047
Expires 10/31/2022

Section 2. Employer or Authorized Representative Review and Verification

(Employers or their authorized representative must complete and sign Section 2 within 3 business days of the employee's first day of employment. You must physically examine one document from List A OR a combination of one document from List B and one document from List C as listed on the "Lists of Acceptable Documents.")

Employee Info from Section 1	Last Name *(Family Name)*	First Name *(Given Name)*	M.I.	Citizenship/Immigration Status

List A Identity and Employment Authorization	OR	List B Identity	AND	List C Employment Authorization

List A	List B	List C
Document Title	Document Title	Document Title
Issuing Authority	Issuing Authority	Issuing Authority
Document Number	Document Number	Document Number
Expiration Date *(if any) (mm/dd/yyyy)*	Expiration Date *(if any) (mm/dd/yyyy)*	Expiration Date *(if any) (mm/dd/yyyy)*
Document Title		
Issuing Authority	Additional Information	QR Code - Sections 2 & 3 Do Not Write In This Space
Document Number		
Expiration Date *(if any) (mm/dd/yyyy)*		
Document Title		
Issuing Authority		
Document Number		
Expiration Date *(if any) (mm/dd/yyyy)*		

Certification: I attest, under penalty of perjury, that (1) I have examined the document(s) presented by the above-named employee, (2) the above-listed document(s) appear to be genuine and to relate to the employee named, and (3) to the best of my knowledge the employee is authorized to work in the United States.

The employee's first day of employment *(mm/dd/yyyy)*: _____   *(See instructions for exemptions)*

Signature of Employer or Authorized Representative	Today's Date *(mm/dd/yyyy)*	Title of Employer or Authorized Representative
Last Name of Employer or Authorized Representative	First Name of Employer or Authorized Representative	Employer's Business or Organization Name

Employer's Business or Organization Address *(Street Number and Name)*	City or Town	State	ZIP Code

Section 3. Reverification and Rehires *(To be completed and signed by employer or authorized representative.)*

A. New Name *(if applicable)*			B. Date of Rehire *(if applicable)*
Last Name *(Family Name)*	First Name *(Given Name)*	Middle Initial	Date *(mm/dd/yyyy)*

C. If the employee's previous grant of employment authorization has expired, provide the information for the document or receipt that establishes continuing employment authorization in the space provided below.

Document Title	Document Number	Expiration Date *(if any) (mm/dd/yyyy)*

I attest, under penalty of perjury, that to the best of my knowledge, this employee is authorized to work in the United States, and if the employee presented document(s), the document(s) I have examined appear to be genuine and to relate to the individual.

Signature of Employer or Authorized Representative	Today's Date *(mm/dd/yyyy)*	Name of Employer or Authorized Representative

Form I-9 10/21/2019

Page 2 of 3

LISTS OF ACCEPTABLE DOCUMENTS
All documents must be UNEXPIRED

Employees may present one selection from List A
or a combination of one selection from List B and one selection from List C.

LIST A Documents that Establish Both Identity and Employment Authorization	OR	LIST B Documents that Establish Identity	AND	LIST C Documents that Establish Employment Authorization

1. U.S. Passport or U.S. Passport Card
 	
2. Permanent Resident Card or Alien Registration Receipt Card (Form I-551)
 	
3. Foreign passport that contains a temporary I-551 stamp or temporary I-551 printed notation on a machine-readable immigrant visa
 	
4. Employment Authorization Document that contains a photograph (Form I-766)
 	
5. For a nonimmigrant alien authorized to work for a specific employer because of his or her status:
  a. Foreign passport; and
  b. Form I-94 or Form I-94A that has the following:
    (1) The same name as the passport; and
    (2) An endorsement of the alien's nonimmigrant status as long as that period of endorsement has not yet expired and the proposed employment is not in conflict with any restrictions or limitations identified on the form.
 	
6. Passport from the Federated States of Micronesia (FSM) or the Republic of the Marshall Islands (RMI) with Form I-94 or Form I-94A indicating nonimmigrant admission under the Compact of Free Association Between the United States and the FSM or RMI
		1. Driver's license or ID card issued by a State or outlying possession of the United States provided it contains a photograph or information such as name, date of birth, gender, height, eye color, and address
		
		2. ID card issued by federal, state or local government agencies or entities, provided it contains a photograph or information such as name, date of birth, gender, height, eye color, and address
		
		3. School ID card with a photograph
		
		4. Voter's registration card
		
		5. U.S. Military card or draft record
		
		6. Military dependent's ID card
		
		7. U.S. Coast Guard Merchant Mariner Card
		
		8. Native American tribal document
		
		9. Driver's license issued by a Canadian government authority
		
		For persons under age 18 who are unable to present a document listed above:
		
		10. School record or report card
		
		11. Clinic, doctor, or hospital record
		
		12. Day-care or nursery school record
				1. A Social Security Account Number card, unless the card includes one of the following restrictions:
				  (1) NOT VALID FOR EMPLOYMENT
				  (2) VALID FOR WORK ONLY WITH INS AUTHORIZATION
				  (3) VALID FOR WORK ONLY WITH DHS AUTHORIZATION
				
				2. Certification of report of birth issued by the Department of State (Forms DS-1350, FS-545, FS-240)
				
				3. Original or certified copy of birth certificate issued by a State, county, municipal authority, or territory of the United States bearing an official seal
				
				4. Native American tribal document
				
				5. U.S. Citizen ID Card (Form I-197)
				
				6. Identification Card for Use of Resident Citizen in the United States (Form I-179)
				
				7. Employment authorization document issued by the Department of Homeland Security

Examples of many of these documents appear in the Handbook for Employers (M-274).

Refer to the instructions for more information about acceptable receipts.

Source: U.S. Citizenship and Immigration Services.

Critical Thinking

2-1. When Omnimia Graphics was looking to implement a payroll accounting system, the manufacturing firm had several options. With only 40 employees, the manual preparation of payroll through spreadsheets and handwritten timecards was a comfortable option for the firm. Another option was to convince the senior management of Omnimia Graphics to implement a software program for payroll processing. How should the company handle the maintenance of the current payroll records? What internal control issues should be addressed?

2-2. You have been hired as a consultant for Semiva Productions, a company facing an IRS audit of its accounting records. During your review, you notice anomalies in the payroll system involving overpayments of labor and payments to terminated employees. What would you do?

In the Real World: Scenario for Discussion

The Lilly Ledbetter Fair Pay Act of 2009 centered on a case in which Ms. Ledbetter discovered documents that revealed discrimination against her that resulted in unequal pay practices. The company argued that the documents were confidential and scheduled for destruction and that Ms. Ledbetter should not have had access to the information. What are the issues in this case in terms of document privacy and retention? How could the situation have been prevented in the first place?

Internet Activities

2-1. Using a search engine such as Google, Yahoo, or Bing, search the Internet for the term "new hire packet contents." Compile a list of the different new hire packet items that you find in at least three companies. What are some unique items that you found on the companies' lists? Check out the IRS's video about determining the correct amount of withholding allowances for your Form W-4, https://www.youtube.com/watch?v–BBuAzW43K1A&feature=youtu.be.

2-2. Go to www.irs.gov and search for IRS e-file security. List the facts that the IRS cites about why e-filing is secure. What about these practices makes the customer's information secure? How could the IRS improve e-filing security?

2-3. Want to know more about some of the concepts discussed in this chapter? Check out

    www.uscis.gov

    www.irs.gov/businesses

    www.archives.gov/federal-register/cfr/subject-title-26.html

    www.proshred.com

    www.ironmountain.com

2-4. The Massachusetts Institute of Technology (MIT) has created a website with a living wage calculator. This tool is designed to help people compute the wages they need to earn in order to achieve their desired lifestyle. Check it out at Living Wage Calculator, http://livingwage.mit.edu.

Continuing Payroll Project: Prevosti Farms and Sugarhouse

Prevosti Farms and Sugarhouse pays its employees according to their job classification. The following employees make up Sugarhouse's staff:

Employee Number	Name and Address	Payroll Information
A-Mille	Thomas Millen	Hire Date: 2-1-2021
	1022 Forest School Rd	DOB: 12-16-1992
	Woodstock, VT 05001	Position: Production Manager
	802-478-5055	PT/FT: FT, exempt
	SSN: 031-11-3456	M/S: Married/Joint
	401(k) deduction: 3%	Pay Rate: $35,000/year
	Section 125 deduction: $155	Dependents under 17: 3
		Dependents over 17: 1
		Step 4 information: none

Employee Number	Name and Address	Payroll Information
A-Towle	Avery Towle 4011 Route 100 Plymouth, VT 05102 802 967-5873 SSN: 089-74-0974 401(k) deduction: 5% Section 125 deduction: $100	Hire Date: 2-1-2021 DOB: 7-14-2001 Position: Production Worker PT/FT: FT, nonexempt M/S: Single Pay Rate: $12.00/hour Dependents under 17: 0 Dependents over 17: 0 Step 4 information: none
A-Long	Charlie Long 242 Benedict Road S. Woodstock, VT 05002 802-429-3846 SSN: 056-23-4593 401(k) deduction: 2% Section 125 deduction: $155	Hire Date: 2-1-2021 DOB: 3-16-1997 Position: Production Worker PT/FT: FT, nonexempt M/S: Married/Joint Pay Rate: $12.50/hour Dependents under 17: 2 Dependents over 17: 0 Step 4 information: none
B-Shang	Mary Shangraw 1901 Main Street #2 Bridgewater, VT 05520 802-575-5423 SSN: 075-28-8945 401(k) deduction: 3% Section 125 deduction: $100	Hire Date: 2-1-2021 DOB: 8-20-1999 Position: Administrative Assistant PT/FT: PT, nonexempt M/S: Single Pay Rate: $11.00/hour Dependents under 17: 0 Dependents over 17: 1 Step 4 information: none
B-Lewis	Kristen Lewis 840 Daily Hollow Road Bridgewater, VT 05523 802-390-5572 SSN: 076-39-5673 401(k) deduction: 4% Section 125 deduction: $155	Hire Date: 2-1-2021 DOB: 4-6-1985 Position: Office Manager PT/FT: FT, exempt M/S: Married/Joint Pay Rate: $32,000/year Dependents under 17: 2 Dependents over 17: 1 Step 4 information: none
B-Schwa	Joel Schwartz 55 Maple Farm Way Woodstock, VT 05534 802-463-9985 SSN: 021-34-9876 401(k) deduction: 5% Section 125 deduction: $100	Hire Date: 2-1-2021 DOB: 5-23-1993 Position: Sales PT/FT: FT, exempt M/S: Married/Joint Pay Rate: $24,000/year base plus 3% commission per case sold Dependents under 17: 2 Dependents over 17: 0 Step 4 information: none
B-Prevo	Toni Prevosti 820 Westminster Road Bridgewater, VT 05520 802-555-3456 SSN: 055-22-0443 401(k) deduction: 6% Section 125 deduction: $155	Hire Date: 2-1-2021 DOB: 9-18-1987 Position: Owner/President PT/FT: FT, exempt M/S: Married/Joint Pay Rate: $45,000/year Dependents under 17: 3 Dependents over 17: 2 Step 4 information: none

The company has the following departments:

Department A: Agricultural Workers

Department B: Office Workers

1. You have been hired to start on February 1, 2021, as the new accounting clerk. Your employee number is B-STUDE, where "B" denotes that you are an office worker. Your

---

Form W-4
(Rev. December 2020)
Department of the Treasury
Internal Revenue Service

Employee's Withholding Certificate

▶ Complete Form W-4 so that your employer can withhold the correct federal income tax from your pay.
▶ Give Form W-4 to your employer.
▶ Your withholding is subject to review by the IRS.

OMB No. 1545-0074

2021

Step 1:

Enter Personal Information

(a) First name and middle initial   Last name

(b) Social security number

Address

City or town, state, and ZIP code

▶ **Does your name match the name on your social security card?** If not, to ensure you get credit for your earnings, contact SSA at 800-772-1213 or go to *www.ssa.gov*.

(c) ☑ Single or Married filing separately
☐ Married filing jointly or Qualifying widow(er)
☐ Head of household (Check only if you're unmarried and pay more than half the costs of keeping up a home for yourself and a qualifying individual.)

Complete Steps 2–4 ONLY if they apply to you; otherwise, skip to Step 5. See page 2 for more information on each step, who can claim exemption from withholding, when to use the estimator at *www.irs.gov/W4App*, and privacy.

Step 2:

Multiple Jobs or Spouse Works

Complete this step if you (1) hold more than one job at a time, or (2) are married filing jointly and your spouse also works. The correct amount of withholding depends on income earned from all of these jobs.

Do **only one** of the following.

(a) Use the estimator at *www.irs.gov/W4App* for most accurate withholding for this step (and Steps 3–4); **or**

(b) Use the Multiple Jobs Worksheet on page 3 and enter the result in Step 4(c) below for roughly accurate withholding; **or**

(c) If there are only two jobs total, you may check this box. Do the same on Form W-4 for the other job. This option is accurate for jobs with similar pay; otherwise, more tax than necessary may be withheld . . . . . ▶ ☐

TIP: To be accurate, submit a 2021 Form W-4 for all other jobs. If you (or your spouse) have self-employment income, including as an independent contractor, use the estimator.

Complete Steps 3–4(b) on Form W-4 for only ONE of these jobs. Leave those steps blank for the other jobs. (Your withholding will be most accurate if you complete Steps 3–4(b) on the Form W-4 for the highest paying job.)

Step 3:

Claim Dependents

If your total income will be $200,000 or less ($400,000 or less if married filing jointly):

Multiply the number of qualifying children under age 17 by $2,000 ▶ $ _____

Multiply the number of other dependents by $500 . . . . ▶ $ _____

Add the amounts above and enter the total here . . . .

3 $

Step 4 (optional):

Other Adjustments

(a) **Other income (not from jobs).** If you want tax withheld for other income you expect this year that won't have withholding, enter the amount of other income here. This may include interest, dividends, and retirement income . . . .

4(a) $

(b) **Deductions.** If you expect to claim deductions other than the standard deduction and want to reduce your withholding, use the Deductions Worksheet on page 3 and enter the result here . . . .

4(b) $

(c) **Extra withholding.** Enter any additional tax you want withheld each **pay period** .

4(c) $

Step 5:

Sign Here

Under penalties of perjury, I declare that this certificate, to the best of my knowledge and belief, is true, correct, and complete.

▶ _____
Employee's signature (This form is not valid unless you sign it.)

▶ _____
Date

Employers Only

Employer's name and address

First date of employment

Employer identification number (EIN)

For Privacy Act and Paperwork Reduction Act Notice, see page 3.   Cat. No. 10220Q   Form **W-4** (2021)

Source: Internal Revenue Service.

Employment Eligibility Verification
Department of Homeland Security
U.S. Citizenship and Immigration Services

USCIS
Form I-9
OMB No. 1615-0047
Expires 10/31/2022

▶**START HERE:** Read instructions carefully before completing this form. The instructions must be available, either in paper or electronically, during completion of this form. Employers are liable for errors in the completion of this form.

ANTI-DISCRIMINATION NOTICE: It is illegal to discriminate against work-authorized individuals. Employers **CANNOT** specify which document(s) an employee may present to establish employment authorization and identity. The refusal to hire or continue to employ an individual because the documentation presented has a future expiration date may also constitute illegal discrimination.

Section 1. Employee Information and Attestation *(Employees must complete and sign Section 1 of Form I-9 no later than the **first day of employment**, but not before accepting a job offer.)*

Last Name *(Family Name)*	First Name *(Given Name)*	Middle Initial	Other Last Names Used *(if any)*

Address *(Street Number and Name)*	Apt. Number	City or Town	State	ZIP Code

Date of Birth *(mm/dd/yyyy)*	U.S. Social Security Number	Employee's E-mail Address	Employee's Telephone Number
	☐☐☐ - ☐☐ - ☐☐☐☐		

I am aware that federal law provides for imprisonment and/or fines for false statements or use of false documents in connection with the completion of this form.

I attest, under penalty of perjury, that I am (check one of the following boxes):

☐ 1. A citizen of the United States

☐ 2. A noncitizen national of the United States *(See instructions)*

☐ 3. A lawful permanent resident   (Alien Registration Number/USCIS Number): _____

☐ 4. An alien authorized to work   until (expiration date, if applicable, mm/dd/yyyy): _____
Some aliens may write "N/A" in the expiration date field. *(See instructions)*

Aliens authorized to work must provide only one of the following document numbers to complete Form I-9:
An Alien Registration Number/USCIS Number OR Form I-94 Admission Number OR Foreign Passport Number.

QR Code - Section 1
Do Not Write In This Space

1. Alien Registration Number/USCIS Number: _____
OR
2. Form I-94 Admission Number: _____
OR
3. Foreign Passport Number: _____
Country of Issuance: _____

Signature of Employee	Today's Date *(mm/dd/yyyy)*

Preparer and/or Translator Certification (check one):

☐ I did not use a preparer or translator.   ☐ A preparer(s) and/or translator(s) assisted the employee in completing Section 1.
(Fields below must be completed and signed when preparers and/or translators assist an employee in completing Section 1.)

I attest, under penalty of perjury, that I have assisted in the completion of Section 1 of this form and that to the best of my knowledge the information is true and correct.

Signature of Preparer or Translator	Today's Date *(mm/dd/yyyy)*

Last Name *(Family Name)*	First Name *(Given Name)*

Address *(Street Number and Name)*	City or Town	State	ZIP Code

STOP *Employer Completes Next Page* STOP

Employment Eligibility Verification
Department of Homeland Security
U.S. Citizenship and Immigration Services

USCIS
Form I-9
OMB No. 1615-0047
Expires 10/31/2022

Section 2. Employer or Authorized Representative Review and Verification

(Employers or their authorized representative must complete and sign Section 2 within 3 business days of the employee's first day of employment. You must physically examine one document from List A OR a combination of one document from List B and one document from List C as listed on the "Lists of Acceptable Documents.")

Employee Info from Section 1	Last Name *(Family Name)*	First Name *(Given Name)*	M.I.	Citizenship/Immigration Status

List A	OR	List B	AND	List C
Identity and Employment Authorization		**Identity**		**Employment Authorization**

List A	List B	List C
Document Title	Document Title	Document Title
Issuing Authority	Issuing Authority	Issuing Authority
Document Number	Document Number	Document Number
Expiration Date *(if any) (mm/dd/yyyy)*	Expiration Date *(if any) (mm/dd/yyyy)*	Expiration Date *(if any) (mm/dd/yyyy)*
Document Title		
Issuing Authority	Additional Information	QR Code - Sections 2 & 3 Do Not Write In This Space
Document Number		
Expiration Date *(if any) (mm/dd/yyyy)*		
Document Title		
Issuing Authority		
Document Number		
Expiration Date *(if any) (mm/dd/yyyy)*		

Certification: I attest, under penalty of perjury, that (1) I have examined the document(s) presented by the above-named employee, (2) the above-listed document(s) appear to be genuine and to relate to the employee named, and (3) to the best of my knowledge the employee is authorized to work in the United States.

The employee's first day of employment *(mm/dd/yyyy)*: _____ **(See instructions for exemptions)**

Signature of Employer or Authorized Representative	Today's Date *(mm/dd/yyyy)*	Title of Employer or Authorized Representative
Last Name of Employer or Authorized Representative	First Name of Employer or Authorized Representative	Employer's Business or Organization Name

Employer's Business or Organization Address *(Street Number and Name)*	City or Town	State	ZIP Code

Section 3. Reverification and Rehires *(To be completed and signed by employer or authorized representative.)*

A. New Name *(if applicable)*			B. Date of Rehire *(if applicable)*
Last Name *(Family Name)*	First Name *(Given Name)*	Middle Initial	Date *(mm/dd/yyyy)*

C. If the employee's previous grant of employment authorization has expired, provide the information for the document or receipt that establishes continuing employment authorization in the space provided below.

Document Title	Document Number	Expiration Date *(if any) (mm/dd/yyyy)*

I attest, under penalty of perjury, that to the best of my knowledge, this employee is authorized to work in the United States, and if the employee presented document(s), the document(s) I have examined appear to be genuine and to relate to the individual.

Signature of Employer or Authorized Representative	Today's Date *(mm/dd/yyyy)*	Name of Employer or Authorized Representative

LISTS OF ACCEPTABLE DOCUMENTS
All documents must be UNEXPIRED

Employees may present one selection from List A
or a combination of one selection from List B and one selection from List C.

LIST A		LIST B		LIST C
Documents that Establish Both Identity and Employment Authorization	**OR**	**Documents that Establish Identity**	**AND**	**Documents that Establish Employment Authorization**
1. U.S. Passport or U.S. Passport Card		1. Driver's license or ID card issued by a State or outlying possession of the United States provided it contains a photograph or information such as name, date of birth, gender, height, eye color, and address		1. A Social Security Account Number card, unless the card includes one of the following restrictions: (1) NOT VALID FOR EMPLOYMENT (2) VALID FOR WORK ONLY WITH INS AUTHORIZATION (3) VALID FOR WORK ONLY WITH DHS AUTHORIZATION
2. Permanent Resident Card or Alien Registration Receipt Card (Form I-551)				
3. Foreign passport that contains a temporary I-551 stamp or temporary I-551 printed notation on a machine-readable immigrant visa		2. ID card issued by federal, state or local government agencies or entities, provided it contains a photograph or information such as name, date of birth, gender, height, eye color, and address		2. Certification of report of birth issued by the Department of State (Forms DS-1350, FS-545, FS-240)
4. Employment Authorization Document that contains a photograph (Form I-766)		3. School ID card with a photograph		3. Original or certified copy of birth certificate issued by a State, county, municipal authority, or territory of the United States bearing an official seal

5. For a nonimmigrant alien authorized to work for a specific employer because of his or her status:
  a. Foreign passport; and
  b. Form I-94 or Form I-94A that has the following:
    (1) The same name as the passport; and
    (2) An endorsement of the alien's nonimmigrant status as long as that period of endorsement has not yet expired and the proposed employment is not in conflict with any restrictions or limitations identified on the form.
		4. Voter's registration card		

		5. U.S. Military card or draft record		4. Native American tribal document
		6. Military dependent's ID card		5. U.S. Citizen ID Card (Form I-197)
		7. U.S. Coast Guard Merchant Mariner Card		6. Identification Card for Use of Resident Citizen in the United States (Form I-179)
		8. Native American tribal document		
		9. Driver's license issued by a Canadian government authority		7. Employment authorization document issued by the Department of Homeland Security
		For persons under age 18 who are unable to present a document listed above:		
6. Passport from the Federated States of Micronesia (FSM) or the Republic of the Marshall Islands (RMI) with Form I-94 or Form I-94A indicating nonimmigrant admission under the Compact of Free Association Between the United States and the FSM or RMI		10. School record or report card		
		11. Clinic, doctor, or hospital record		
		12. Day-care or nursery school record		

Examples of many of these documents appear in the Handbook for Employers (M-274).

Refer to the instructions for more information about acceptable receipts.

Form I-9 10/21/2019

Source: U.S. Citizenship and Immigration Services.

Social Security number is 555-55-5555, you are full-time, nonexempt, and paid at a rate of $34,000 per year. You have elected to contribute 2 percent of your gross pay to your 401(k) and will have $100 per pay period for Section 125. Complete the W-4 and the I-9 to start your own employee file. You are single with only one job. You live at 1644 Smitten Road, Woodstock, VT 05001. You will not be claiming anything for section 4 of the W-4. Your phone number is (555) 555-5555. Your date of birth is 01/01/2001. You are a citizen of the United States and provide a Vermont driver's license #88110009 expiring 01/01/23 in addition to your Social Security card for verification of your identity. Mary Shangraw verified the information for the company. Prevosti Farms and Sugarhouse is located at 820 Westminster Road, Bridgewater, VT, 05520. Prevosti has an EIN of 22-6654454.

2. Complete the employee information form for each employee. Enter the pay rate earnings for each employee.

Employee Earnings Register

NAME _____ Hire Date _____ Dependent child <17 _____

ADDRESS _____ Date of Birth _____ Dependent other _____

CITY/STATE/ZIP _____ Position _____ PT / FT Step 4a W-4 Info _____

TELEPHONE _____ Filing Status _____ Step 4b W-4 Info _____

SOCIAL SECURITY NUMBER _____ Exempt/Nonexempt _____ Step 4c W-4 Info _____

Pay Rate _____ Hr / Wk / Mo / Yr

Period Ended	Hrs Worked	Reg Pay	OT Pay	Comm	Gross Pay	Social Sec Tax	Medicare	Fed Inc Tax	State W/H Tax	Sect 125	401(k)	Total Deduc	Net Pay	YTD

Source: U.S. Citizenship and Immigration Services.

EMPLOYEE EARNING RECORD

NAME _____ Hire Date _____

ADDRESS _____ Date of Birth _____

CITY/STATE/ZIP _____ Position _____

TELEPHONE _____ Filing Status _____

SOCIAL SECURITY NUMBER _____ Exempt/Nonexempt _____

POSITION _____ Pay Rate _____

Period Ended	Hrs Worked	Reg Pay	OT Pay	Holiday	Comm	Gross Pay	Ins	401(k)	Taxable Pay for Federal	Taxable Pay for FICA

Taxable Wages for Federal	Taxable Wages for FICA	Federal W/H	Social Sec. Tax	Medicare Tax	State Inc. Tax	Total Deduc	Net Pay	YTD Net Pay	YTD Gross Pay

EMPLOYEE EARNING RECORD

NAME		Hire Date	
ADDRESS		Date of Birth	
CITY/STATE/ZIP		Exempt/Nonexempt	
TELEPHONE		Married/Single	
SOCIAL SECURITY NUMBER		Pay Rate	
POSITION			

Period Ended	Hrs Worked	Reg Pay	OT Pay	Holiday	Comm	Gross Pay	Ins	401(k)	Taxable Pay for Federal	Taxable Wages for FICA

Taxable Wages for Federal	Taxable Wages for FICA	Federal W/H	Social Sec. Tax	Medicare Tax	State Inc. Tax	Total Deduc	Net Pay	YTD Net Pay	YTD Gross Pay

EMPLOYEE EARNING RECORD

NAME		Hire Date	
ADDRESS		Date of Birth	
CITY/STATE/ZIP		Exempt/Nonexempt	
TELEPHONE		Married/Single	
SOCIAL SECURITY NUMBER		Pay Rate	
POSITION			

Period Ended	Hrs Worked	Reg Pay	OT Pay	Holiday	Comm	Gross Pay	Ins	401(k)	Taxable Pay for FICA	Taxable Pay for Federal

Taxable Wages for Federal	Taxable Wages for FICA	Federal W/H	Social Sec. Tax	Medicare Tax	State Inc. Tax	Total Deduc	Net Pay	YTD Net Pay	YTD Gross Pay

EMPLOYEE EARNING RECORD

NAME _____   Hire Date _____

ADDRESS _____   Date of Birth _____

CITY/STATE/ZIP _____   Exempt/Nonexempt _____

TELEPHONE _____   Married/Single _____

SOCIAL SECURITY NUMBER _____   Pay Rate _____

POSITION _____

Period Ended	Hrs Worked	Reg Pay	OT Pay	Holiday	Comm	Gross Pay	Ins	401(k)	Taxable Pay for Federal	Taxable Pay for FICA

Taxable Wages for Federal	Taxable Wages for FICA	Federal W/H	Social Sec. Tax	Medicare Tax	State Inc. Tax	Total Deduc	Net Pay	YTD Net Pay	YTD Gross Pay

EMPLOYEE EARNING RECORD

NAME _____   Hire Date _____

ADDRESS _____   Date of Birth _____

CITY/STATE/ZIP _____   Exempt/Nonexempt _____

TELEPHONE _____   Married/Single _____

SOCIAL SECURITY NUMBER _____   Pay Rate _____

POSITION _____

Period Ended	Hrs Worked	Reg Pay	OT Pay	Holiday	Comm	Gross Pay	Ins	401(k)	Taxable Pay for Federal	Taxable Pay for FICA

Taxable Wages for Federal	Taxable Wages for FICA	Federal W/H	Social Sec. Tax	Medicare Tax	State Inc. Tax	Total Deduc	Net Pay	YTD Net Pay	YTD Gross Pay

EMPLOYEE EARNING RECORD

NAME _____   Hire Date _____

ADDRESS _____   Date of Birth _____

CITY/STATE/ZIP _____   Exempt/Nonexempt _____

TELEPHONE _____   Married/Single _____

SOCIAL SECURITY NUMBER _____   Pay Rate _____

POSITION _____   _____

Period Ended	Hrs Worked	Reg Pay	OT Pay	Holiday	Comm	Gross Pay	Ins	401(k)	Taxable Pay for Federal	Taxable Pay for FICA

Taxable Wages for Federal	Taxable Wages for FICA	Federal W/H	Social Sec. Tax	Medicare Tax	State Inc. Tax	Total Deduc	Net Pay	YTD Net Pay	YTD Gross Pay

EMPLOYEE EARNING RECORD

NAME _____   Hire Date _____

ADDRESS _____   Date of Birth _____

CITY/STATE/ZIP _____   Exempt/Nonexempt _____

TELEPHONE _____   Married/Single _____

SOCIAL SECURITY NUMBER _____   Pay Rate _____

POSITION _____   _____

Period Ended	Hrs Worked	Reg Pay	OT Pay	Holiday	Comm	Gross Pay	Ins	401(k)	Taxable Pay for Federal	Taxable Pay for FICA

Taxable Wages for Federal	Taxable Wages for FICA	Federal W/H	Social Sec. Tax	Medicare Tax	State Inc. Tax	Total Deduc	Net Pay	YTD Net Pay	YTD Gross Pay

EMPLOYEE EARNING RECORD

NAME	_____	Hire Date	_____
ADDRESS	_____	Date of Birth	_____
CITY/STATE/ZIP	_____	Exempt/Nonexempt	_____
TELEPHONE	_____	Married/Single	_____
SOCIAL SECURITY NUMBER	_____	Pay Rate	_____
POSITION	_____		

Period Ended	Hrs Worked	Reg Pay	OT Pay	Holiday	Comm	Gross Pay	Ins	401(k)	Taxable Pay for Federal	Taxable Pay for FICA

Taxable Wages for Federal	Taxable Wages for FICA	Federal W/H	Social Sec. Tax	Medicare	State W/H	Total Deduc	Net Pay	YTD Net Pay	YTD Gross Pay

Answers to Stop & Check Exercises

What's in the File?

1. a, b, d, e
2. b
3. d
4. a
5. c

Who Are You?

1. Student answers will vary. One possible way to prove both identity and employment is a current U.S. passport. Alternatively, a current state-issued driver's license and a Social Security card will work for the purposes of the I-9.
2. Student answers will vary. When evaluating the earnings of more than one job, the breakdown of includable amount by pay period is often overlooked.
3. Student answers will vary. Examples of statutory employees include the following: A driver who distributes beverages (other than milk) or meat, vegetable, fruit, or bakery products or who picks up and delivers laundry or dry cleaning if the driver is a single company's agent or is paid on commission. A full-time life insurance sales agent whose principal business activity is selling life insurance or annuity contracts, or both, primarily for one life insurance company. An individual who works at home on materials or goods that a company supplies and that must be returned to that company or a designated agent in accordance with furnished specifications for the work to be done. A full-time traveling or city salesperson who works on a single company's behalf and turns in orders from wholesalers, retailers, contractors, or operators of hotels, restaurants, or other similar establishments. The goods sold must be merchandise for resale or supplies for use in the buyer's business operation. The work performed for that single company must be the salesperson's principal business activity.

Exempt vs. Nonexempt

1. Exempt workers are exempt from the overtime provisions of FLSA. Exempt workers tend to be employees in a company's managerial or other leadership functions, in which they may need to work more than 40 hours per week to complete their tasks. Exempt workers usually receive a fixed salary per period that is not based on the number of hours worked. Nonexempt workers tend to be compensated on an hourly basis and often do not have managerial or leadership responsibilities. It should be noted that some nonexempt workers do have managerial or leadership responsibilities and may receive a fixed salary; however, these particular employees are covered by the overtime provisions of FLSA.
2. c (40 hours)
3. The leased employee is a common-law employee of the firm, whereas the temporary employee is an employee of the temporary agency.

Worker Facts

1. Hourly workers and nonexempt workers are protected by FLSA.
2. Exempt workers receive a fixed amount of money and generally direct the actions of other employees; nonexempt workers are eligible for overtime and generally have their work directed by a manager.
3. Commission workers are typically tied to sales completed by the individual; piece-rate pay is determined by the number of pieces the employee completes during a shift or period.
4. Student answers may vary but should include: minimum hourly rate is set by the U.S. Federal government. Minimum wage rates can and do vary per state, and different parts of the same state may have different minimum wages. The minimum wage may differ from a "living wage," which is an amount needed to meet basic subsistence needs. A calculating tool was provided in the chapter for discussion on living wages in various locations.

Who Does Which Job?

Student answers will vary. The answer should reflect a clear separation of duties, cross-training, rotation of tasks, and security protocols.

Internal Controls and Audits

1. b
2. c

Destroy and Terminate

1. Paper payroll records should be shredded or burned. Computer records should be purged from the server and all other storage devices.
2. Charlie should receive his final pay on October 11, and no later than October 12. His employer is not required to provide him with a severance package, although he may be eligible for his accrued vacation pay.

Chapter Three

Gross Pay Computation

Two important terms in payroll accounting are gross pay and net pay. *Gross pay* is the total amount of wages earned before deducting amounts for taxes or other deductions. *Net pay* is the amount of money the employee actually receives in a paycheck after all taxes and other deductions have been subtracted. In this chapter, we will focus on computing gross pay.

The calculation of an employee's gross pay is the first step for payroll processing. Employee pay may be calculated in different ways. *Hourly* employees are paid for each hour, or fraction thereof, that they work on a given day. Salaried employees are broken into two classifications based on FLSA legislation: *exempt* and *nonexempt*. Salaried exempt employees receive pay based on the job they perform, regardless of the number of hours it takes to perform the job. Salaried nonexempt employees may receive both *salary* and *overtime*. Another class of employees works on a *commission* basis, which means that some of their wages are based on sales revenue. The final classification is *piece-rate* employees. Typically found in manufacturing environments, employees are paid based upon the number of pieces completed during a work shift.

LEARNING OBJECTIVES

After studying Chapter 3, you should be able to:

LO 3-1   Analyze Minimum Wage Pay for Nonexempt Workers

LO 3-2   Compute Gross Pay for Different Pay Bases

LO 3-3   Calculate Pay Based on Hours and Fractions of Hours

LO 3-4   Calculate Overtime in Various Situations

LO 3-5   Create a Payroll Register

LO 3-6   Apply Combination Pay Methods

LO 3-7   Explain Special Pay Situations

Alex Segre/Alamy Stock Photo

Minimum Wage: Should It Be Increased?

The Fair Labor Standards Act (FLSA) established a minimum wage and standard weekly working hours to protect workers. The federal standard for regular weekly working hours is 40, and the act states that employees who work more than 40 hours per week must receive overtime wages of at least one and a half times their regular hourly wage. The Federal minimum wage has been $7.25 per hour since 2009.

The debate about increasing the minimum wage has continued for over a decade. As of 2021, 21 states use the federal minimum, have a minimum wage lower than the federal level, or do not state a minimum wage. In many cases, adjacent states have a wildly different minimum wage. Economists and business leaders have debated the minimum wage. Those supporting an increase to the federal minimum wage note that the current minimum wage has not kept pace with the Consumer Price Index. Employees are actually earning less in 2021 than in previous years in terms of consumer items' affordability. People not supporting a change to the federal minimum wage claim that small businesses would be adversely affected by labor costs.

The quandary about federal, state, and living wages is one that employers face in many parts of the country. The conundrum occurs when the employer must choose between profits and employee well-being. This issue of increasing the minimum wage has gained importance during the COVID pandemic and the challenges businesses have encountered in their continuing operations.

(Sources: The San Diego Union-Tribune, NBC News)

Employee pay is the focus of Chapter 3. We will examine different bases for gross pay computations, discuss how these compensation bases differ and introduce the payroll register as a tool in pay calculation.

LO 3-1   Analyze Minimum Wage Pay for Nonexempt Workers

Joos Mind/Getty Images

Two primary classifications of employees exist: exempt and nonexempt. These classifications refer to the provisions of the Fair Labor Standards Act (FLSA). The FLSA provisions protect nonexempt employees, including clerical, factory, and other nonmanagerial employees. Nonexempt employees are operative workers whose workdays may vary in duration, whose tasks do not meet the U.S. Department of Labor guidelines for exempt employees, and do not generally have supervisory or managerial duties. Exempt employees include employees who meet the U.S. Department of Labor guidelines for exempt classification, including job titles such as Department Supervisor or Warehouse Manager.

For hourly workers, FLSA contains wage provisions that stipulate the *minimum wage* an employer may pay an employee. However, the law exempts some employers from the minimum wage requirements. According to the U.S. Department of Labor, the following conditions exempt an employer from paying the federal minimum wage:

- Firms that do not engage in interstate commerce as part of their business production.
- Firms with less than $500,000 of annual business volume.

Note that certain firms are always covered by the FLSA provisions, regardless of their interstate commerce or annual business volume participation. These businesses include hospitals, schools for mentally or physically disabled or gifted children, preschools, schools of any level, and governmental agencies. Under FLSA section 3(y), law enforcement and fire protection employees may have specified work periods ranging from 7 to 28 days. Employees would be paid for overtime only after a predefined number of working hours.

FLSA was modified in 1974 to include explicit provisions about domestic workers. Since 1974, minimum wage provisions cover domestic service workers, such as nannies and chauffeurs. Note that the 1974 modification specifically excluded occasional babysitters and employees who provide domestic companion services for the elderly. In 2015, the U.S. Congress further amended FLSA to include caregivers and other direct care employees who provide in-home companionship services as being subject to the federal or state minimum wage, whichever is higher. It should be noted that domestic workers who reside on the employer's premises permanently or for an extended time period are exempt from FLSA provisions.

> For live-in domestic service workers who are essentially on duty 24 hours per day, the U.S. Department of Labor has issued a sleep-time requirement of 8 hours per day, of which 5 hours must be consecutive, and adequate sleeping facilities must be provided. According to **Fact Sheet 79D**, if the employee's sleep time is interrupted for any reason, the employee must be compensated for that time.
>
> (Source: DOL)

Minimum Wage

An important consideration with the minimum wage provision of the FLSA is the existence of separate tiers of the minimum wage. Wages for *tipped employees* are lower than those of non-tipped employees. Federal wage and hour laws as of 2021 stipulate a federal minimum wage of $7.25 and a minimum hourly wage of $2.13 for tipped employees. States may enact additional minimum wage laws to address the specific economic needs of their population. This minimizes federal legislative needs to revisit the minimum wage annually.

Many American nonexempt employees receive a wage higher than the federal minimum wage. Since the federal minimum wage has not changed since 2009, states and municipalities have made legislative changes that increase the minimum wage. Among the states that have enacted minimum wages higher than the federal guidelines, most have enacted guidelines that automatically increase the minimum wage annually, reducing the need for recurring legislative action in this regard.

(Source: Pew Research Center)

As of 2021, 29 states and the District of Columbia have minimum wage rates higher than the federal minimum wage. Note that seven states have a minimum wage less than the FLSA minimum wage or is not specified. When the minimum wage is not specified, the federal minimum wage applies. These lower minimum wages may be paid by employers who are not subject to FLSA provisions because they do not conduct interstate commerce. A map depicting minimum wages for 2021 is shown in Figure 3-1, and the details of specific minimum wage rates are shown in Table 3-1. Examples involving employee pay with different minimum wages follow.

EXAMPLE 1: STATE MINIMUM WAGE LOWER THAN THE FEDERAL MINIMUM WAGE

Don Mayer works for a Georgia employer that conducts no interstate commerce and whose annual business volume is less than $300,000. He is a field worker on a family-owned farm and earns the minimum wage for Georgia. How much would he earn for a 40-hour pay period?

Georgia minimum wage: $5.15 per hour

40 hours × $5.15/hour = $206

Because the employer does not meet the requirements that would force it to pay Don the federal minimum wage, it may pay the state's minimum wage.

FIGURE 3-1
Minimum Wage Hourly Rates for 2021

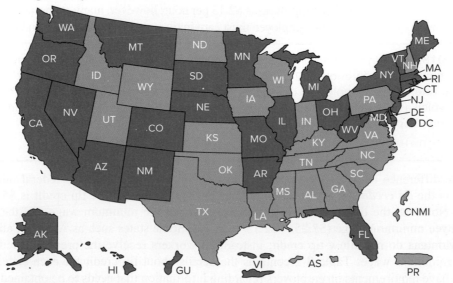

Source: U.S. Department of Labor, 2021.

Legend: The states highlighted in dark blue have minimum wage amounts higher than the federal minimum wage of $7.25 per hour.

TABLE 3-1

2021 Minimum Wage Hourly Rates by State

AK	$10.34	IA	$7.25	MS	None†	PA	$7.25
AL	None†	ID	7.25	MT	$8.75*	RI	11.50
AR	11.00	IL	11.00	NC	7.25	SC	None†
AZ	12.15	IN	7.25	ND	7.25	SD	9.45
CA	13.00*	KS	7.25	NE	9.00	TN	None†
CO	12.32	KY	7.25	NH	7.25	TX	7.25
CT	12.00	LA	None†	NJ	12.00	UT	7.25
D.C.	15.00	MA	13.50	NM	10.50	VA	7.25
DE	9.25	MD	11.75	NV	9.00*	VT	11.75
FL	8.65	ME	12.15	NY	12.50*	WA	13.69*
GA	5.15†	MI	9.65	OH	8.80*	WI	7.25
HI	10.10	MN	10.08*	OK	7.25*	WV	8.75
		MO	10.30	OR	12.00	WY	5.15†

Source: U.S. Department of Labor, 2021.

* These states have stipulations that change the minimum wage based on different variables. Consult the state's revenue office for specific details.

† In states with no minimum wage or one lower than the federal minimum wage, the federal minimum wage prevails as long as they meet FLSA revenue and interstate commerce thresholds.

EXAMPLE 2: STATE MINIMUM WAGE HIGHER THAN THE FEDERAL MINIMUM WAGE

Wendy Roberts is a minimum wage worker in the state of Washington. She works for a national restaurant chain and has a standard 37.5-hour workweek. How much would she earn during a 75-hour, two-week pay period?

Washington minimum wage: $13.69 per hour

75 hours × $13.69/hour = <u>$1,026.75</u>

Because Wendy works for a national chain restaurant, it is safe to assume that it conducts interstate commerce and earns more than $500,000 in revenues per year. She would be compensated at the state minimum wage in any case.

Tipped Employees

Workers in professions such as waiters, waitresses, bartenders, food service workers, and some hotel service personnel may receive an hourly wage less than the minimum wage rates listed in Table 3-1. The rationale for the decreased minimum wage is that these employees can earn tips (*tipped wages*) from patrons of the establishments as a regular part of their employment. The federal minimum wage for tipped employees is $2.13 per hour; however, many states have different regulations about how much the employee must earn in tips to meet federal wage and hour laws.

> In 2018, voters in Washington, DC, approved Initiative 77, which will gradually increase the tipped wage through 2026 until it meets the minimum wage area. As of 2021, a final rule allowed employers to require tipped employees to pool their tips with staff for which a tip is not expected. This rule was designed to offer an incentive to traditionally non-tipped restaurant employees.
>
> (Source: The Hill)

The difference between the tipped employee minimum wage and the federal minimum wage is the *tip credit*. Federal wage and hour laws mandate that the tip credit is $5.12 per hour. Note that the tip credit is the difference between the minimum wage and the tipped employee minimum wage ($7.25 − $2.13 = $5.12). Some states such as Alaska, California, and Montana do not allow tip credit; instead, all workers receive the prevailing federal or local minimum wage. Table 3-2 contains the details about tip credit for each state. Some states have requirements on employers regarding information that needs to be obtained before applying for a tip credit. For example, North Carolina requires a monthly or per pay period affidavit from employees of the total amount of tips.

TABLE 3-2
Table of 2021 Minimum Hourly Wages for Tipped Employees by State

Jurisdiction	Basic Combined Cash and Tip Minimum Wage Rate	Maximum Tip Credit Against Minimum Wage	Minimum Cash Wage	Definition of Tipped Employee by Minimum Tips Received (monthly unless otherwise specified)
Federal: Fair Labor Standards Act (FLSA)	$7.25	$5.12	$2.13	More than $30
State Law Does Not Allow Tip Credit				
Note: The minimum rate is the same for tipped and non-tipped employees				
Alaska			10.34	
California 25 or fewer employees			13.00	
26 or more employees			14.00	
Minnesota:				
Large employer Annual receipts > $500,000 per year			10.08	
Small employer Annual receipts < $500,000 per year			8.21	
Montana:				
Business with gross annual sales exceeding $110,000			8.75	
Business with gross annual sales of $110,000 or less			4.00	
Nevada			8.25	With no health insurance benefits provided by the employer and received by the employee
			7.25	With health insurance benefits provided by the employer and received by the employee
Oregon			11.25	
Washington			13.69	
State Law Allows Tip Credit				
Arizona	12.15	3.00	9.15	Not specified
Arkansas	11.00	7.37	2.63	More than $20
Colorado	12.32	3.02	9.30	More than $30
Connecticut:	12.00			At least $10 weekly for full-time employees or $2.00 daily for part-time in hotels and restaurants. Not specified for other industries
Hotel, restaurant		5.62	6.38	
Bartenders who customarily receive tips		3.77	8.23	
Delaware	9.25	7.02	2.23	More than $30
District of Columbia (D.C.)[2]	15.00	10.00	5.00	Not specified
Florida	8.65	3.02	5.63	
Hawaii	10.10	0.75	9.35	More than $20
Idaho	7.25	3.90	3.35	More than $30
Illinois	11.00	40% of applicable minimum wage (4.40)	6.60	$20
Indiana	7.25	5.12	2.13	Not specified
Iowa	7.25	2.90	4.35	More than $30
Kansas	7.25	5.12	2.13	More than $20
Kentucky	7.25	5.12	2.13	More than $30

(continued)

Jurisdiction	Basic Combined Cash and Tip Minimum Wage Rate	Maximum Tip Credit Against Minimum Wage	Minimum Cash Wage	Definition of Tipped Employee by Minimum Tips Received (monthly unless otherwise specified)
Maine	12.15	6.07	6.08	More than $30
Maryland	11.75	7.37	3.63	More than $30
Massachusetts	13.50	7.95	5.55	More than $20
Michigan	9.65	5.98	3.67	Not specified
Missouri	10.30	50% (5.15)	5.15	Not specified
Nebraska	9.00	6.87	2.13	Not specified
New Hampshire	7.25	55% of applicable minimum wage (3.99)	45% of the applicable minimum wage (3.26)	More than $30
New Jersey	12.00	7.87	4.13	Not specified
New Mexico	10.50	7.95	2.55	More than $30
New York	See website[3]			Not specified
North Carolina	7.25	5.12	2.13	More than $20
North Dakota	7.25	33% of applicable minimum wage (2.39)	4.86	More than $30
Ohio: *Applies to employees of businesses with annual gross receipts of greater than $305,000 per year*	8.80	4.40	4.40	More than $30
Oklahoma	7.25	5.12	2.13	Not specified
Pennsylvania	7.25	4.42	2.83	More than $30
Rhode Island	11.50	7.61	3.89	Not specified
South Carolina			2.13	Not specified
South Dakota	9.45	50% (4.725)	4.725	More than $35
Tennessee			2.13	
Texas	7.25	5.12	2.13	More than $20
Utah	7.25	5.12	2.13	More than $30
Vermont: *Employees in hotels, motels, tourist places, and restaurants who customarily and regularly receive >$120/ month in tips for direct and personal customer service*	11.75	5.875	5.875	More than $120
Virginia	7.25	5.12	2.13	Not specified
West Virginia	8.75	70% (6.13)	2.62	Not specified
Wisconsin	7.25	4.92	2.33	Not specified
Wyoming	7.25	5.12	2.13	More than $30

(Source: U.S. Department of Labor, 2021)

EXAMPLE: TIPPED EMPLOYEE IN OKLAHOMA, MINIMUM WAGE MET

Abigail Hansford is a tipped employee in Stillwater, Oklahoma. During a 40-hour work-week and pay period, she earned $220 in tips.

> Hourly tipped minimum wage: $2.13 per hour.
> $2.13 per hour × 40 hours = $85.20 in wages
> Tips earned: $220
> Total wages and tips earned during the pay period:
> $220 + $85.20 = <u>$305.20</u>

The federal and state minimum wage is $7.25 per hour. The minimum wage for a 40-hour workweek:

$7.25 per hours × 40 hours = $290

Therefore, Abigail has earned more than the federal and state minimum wage. The employer does not need to contribute to Abigail's pay during the pay period.

In 2021, the U.S. Department of Labor declared gig economy workers (e.g., working for Uber, DoorDash, etc.) as independent contractors because they met the definitions of work control, skills required, and tool ownership established under FLSA. This final rule increased efficiency for the worker, boosted job satisfaction, and prevented the companies' misclassification.

(Source: The Verge, U.S. Department of Labor)

EXAMPLE: TIPPED EMPLOYEE IN RHODE ISLAND, MINIMUM WAGE *NOT* MET

Grayson Jeffries is a tipped waiter in Warwick, Rhode Island. During a 40-hour work and pay period, he earned $75 in tips.

Hourly tipped minimum wage: $3.89 per hour.

$3.89 per hour × 40 hours = $155.60 in wages

Tips earned: $75

Total wages and tips earned during the pay period:
$155.60 + 75 = $230.60

The state minimum wage for Rhode Island is $11.50 per hour. During a 40-hour workweek and pay period, the minimum pay for an employee is:

$11.50 per hour × 40 hours = $460.00

Because Grayson has not earned the minimum wage, the employer must pay the difference between the earned wages and tips and the minimum wage:

$460.00 − $230.60 = $229.40 to be added to Grayson's pay by the employer to bring his pay to the minimum wage.

Pay Your Employees Correctly

Stop & Check

1. Heather Pai works as a clerk receiving minimum wage for a pharmaceutical company in North Carolina that pays its employees biweekly. She is classified as nonexempt, and her standard workweek is 40 hours. During a two-week period, she worked 88 hours and received $638.00. Was Heather's pay correct? Explain.

2. Tony Dupuis works as a publisher's representative receiving minimum wage in Maryland. He works 39.5 hours during a one-week period. How much should he receive?

3. Mary Lindquist is a temporary worker for a popular radio station, a large employer in Minnesota. She receives the minimum wage and works 32 hours per week. How much should she receive for two weeks of work?

4. Tony Hardwick is a tipped minimum wage worker for a Minnesota restaurant with $615,000 in annual revenues. He worked 75 hours during a biweekly pay period, in which he earned $1,000 in tips. What is his gross pay (excluding tips)?

Goodboy Picture Company/Getty
Images

LO 3-2   Compute Gross Pay for Different Pay Bases

Salaried Workers

Employees in highly technical, qualification-driven positions within a company are generally classified as exempt from FLSA regulations. Accountants, engineers, lawyers, managers, and supervisors are included in this classification. **Section 13(a)(1)** of the FLSA defines the eligible exempt employees in the following job descriptions: executives, administrative personnel, professionals, and outside sales representatives. **Section 13(a)(17)** of the FLSA also allows specific computer-related employees to be included in salaried workers' classification. The FLSA provides a minimum wage for salaried workers of not less than $684 per week, per the Final Rule that went into effect as of January 2020. Also, the Final Rule, according to **29 CFR 778.114**, stipulates an employer may use the fluctuating workweek method if the employee works hours that vary from week to week and receives a fixed salary as straight time compensation. The hourly rate is then computed by dividing the salary amount by the number of hours actually worked.

Companies often use a technique called "job leveling" to determine salaries for exempt employees. This technique uses job analysis to define common types of responsibilities to generate pay grades. Although this technique intends to determine objective pay criteria, this practice has led to staffing imbalances, multiple titles for similar jobs, and employee morale issues.

Since job leveling was clarified in 2015, firms have experienced mixed results regarding employee morale and engagement. Changes in work location, flexible schedules, and certain job duties have prompted additional classification to the idea of job leveling. The driving question has changed from "what the employee does" to "why is this job necessary." The focus of job leveling has become a discussion of the job's purpose within its operations' broader context.

(Source: SHRM, Lattice)

For nonexempt salaried workers, the employment contract entered into between the employee and the employer determines at what level of hourly work they would receive overtime pay. Many salaried nonexempt worker contracts, when specified, are for 45 hours per week. If the contract stipulates that 45 hours per week is the standard workweek for a salaried, nonexempt employee, then the employee is still subject to FLSA overtime rules for hours worked past 40. For this textbook, the standard workweek is five days out of a seven-day week.

EXAMPLE: SALARIED, NONEXEMPT EMPLOYEE

Brad Hammond, a salaried, nonexempt employee, earns $1,000 per week and has a standard 45-hour workweek.

Hourly compensation: $1,000/45 hours = $22.22 per hour
Overtime rate = $22.22 × 1.5 = $33.33 per hour

Because this employee is classified as nonexempt according to FLSA guidelines, the employee is subject to overtime compensation, and the hourly rate is needed to compute overtime pay.

For the same salaried, nonexempt employee, if the contract between employee and employer stated that all hours *exceeding* 45 were covered, the individual would need to work 45.25 hours or more in the week to qualify for overtime. These are typically non-FLSA companies.

However, *if* the contract stated that only 40 hours were required before the overtime rates are applied, then the 5 hours would be paid at overtime rates.

Note: A salaried *exempt* worker would be paid $1,000 per week regardless of the number of hours worked.

Employers may not prorate a salaried worker's pay when the number of hours worked is fewer than the contractual hour requirement. An exception to this would be time away from work per the employer's sick or vacation policy. The company would allow employees to take paid time off under either of these programs to supplement their missed wages. Companies may also offer salaried employees the option of leave without pay for missed days; however, contractual hours covered under leave without pay must be documented and signed by both a manager and the employee.

Salary Translation to Hourly Rates

The calculation of gross pay for salaried employees depends on the firm's choice of pay periods. An employee's gross pay is determined by dividing the annual pay by the number of pay periods in a year. For instance, if a firm paid employees every month, then the salary calculation would be $\frac{1}{12}$ of the yearly amount. It is occasionally necessary to determine the hourly rate for salaried employees. To get the hourly rate, you would use the following equation:

$$\text{Hourly rate} = \frac{\text{Annual amount}}{\text{Total hours worked per year}}$$

To arrive at the total number of hours worked per year, multiply the number of weeks in a year (52) by the number of hours worked in a standard workweek without overtime.

$$\text{Hourly rate} = \frac{\text{Annual salary}}{\text{Number of hours in a standard workweek} \times 52 \text{ weeks per year}}$$

Because the calculation of overtime, holiday, or vacation time for salaried workers could be based upon the individual's job duties, knowing how to calculate that amount will enable accurate pay.

EXAMPLE

Jackie Ainsley earns a salary of $60,000 per year for ABD Industries. ABD Industries pays its employees every month.

Gross pay = $60,000 per year/12 months = <u>$5,000 per month</u>

If she were a nonexempt employee, it would become necessary to calculate her hourly rate. When calculating the hourly rate, using the correct number of hours in a regular workweek is critical in determining the overtime pay rate. Note the following examples computing the hourly rate using different regular workweeks.

Number of Hours in the Regular Workweek	$\dfrac{\text{Annual salary}}{\text{Number of hours} \times 52 \text{ weeks}}$	Hourly Rate
40	$\dfrac{60{,}000}{(40 \times 52)}$	$28.85
37.5	$\dfrac{60{,}000}{(37.5 \times 52)}$	$30.77
35	$\dfrac{60{,}000}{(35 \times 52)}$	$32.97

What happens if the salaried employee decides to take unpaid leave during a pay period? That amount must be deducted from the gross pay amount. With unpaid leave, the amount of time taken and the number of regular hours in the pay period are the major factors.

EXAMPLE: UNPAID LEAVE

Michelle Barre wants to take two extra days off around a holiday but has no paid time remaining for the year. ABD Industries pays Michelle $60,000 annually on a biweekly basis, and there are 80 hours in a pay period. At 8 hours per day, she will be taking 16 hours of unpaid leave (8 hours × 2 days).

Using the example of Michelle's work with ABD Industries with her regular working hours as 40 hours per week, her normal salary is

80 hours × $28.85/hour = $2,308 per pay period

To calculate her pay, including the unpaid leave, we need the proportion of her paycheck that will be unpaid. We calculate the proportion of the total paycheck she will be taken as unpaid leave.

Unpaid portion: 16 hours

Normal hours per pay period: 80

Unpaid portion = 16/80 = 0.20

That means she will receive 100 − 0.20 = 0.80 (or 80 percent) of her normal gross pay.

Gross pay per period with 16 hours unpaid time:

$2,308 × 0.80 = $1,846.40

Note: Using a rounded hourly rate (shown in this example) to compute period pay will differ from results using nonrounded hourly rates. We have also not separated the holiday pay intentionally for this example.

In many instances, nonexempt employees are paid on a salary basis to avoid paperwork such as *time cards* or pay sheets if they consistently work a fixed number of hours per week. According to **29 CFR 778.113(a)**, the employer and employee must agree on the standard number of hours to be worked each week for which the employee shall receive pay. However, if the employee is classified as a nonexempt, the FLSA requires that these salaried workers are eligible for overtime. A nonexempt hourly rate is necessary to compute pay beyond the agreed-upon weekly hours per **29 CFR 778.113(a)**.

If the employee works less than the agreed-upon number of hours during the week, some states have provisions by which the employee's salary is adjusted to match the actual hours worked. In this case, the hourly rate is again necessary to make sure the gross pay is correctly calculated.

Salaried Workers and Minimum Wage Comparisons

If a salaried nonexempt worker for whom FLSA provisions apply, the fixed weekly salary must adhere to minimum wage guidelines. The minimum wage applies to salaried non-exempt employees whose wages do not exceed $684 per week. The U.S. Department of Labor has established this salary level as one of the exemption tests from FLSA provisions.

EXAMPLE: SALARIED NONEXEMPT EMPLOYEE PAY

Sally Albritton is a receptionist for KTC Incorporated, located in California. She is salaried and works 40 hours per week, but she is nonexempt because her job classification is nonmanagerial.

If she were paid $275 per week

Hourly wage = $275/40 hours per week = $6.88/hour

This amount is below the federal minimum wage test for exempt employees. Sally would need to be paid a minimum of $290 per week for her work to meet FLSA minimum wage requirements because of her weekly 40-hour work agreement with her employer. Considering that California has a much higher minimum wage than the federal minimum wage, it would be necessary to determine the appropriate minimum wage for her location and company size. The employer must contribute additional money to meet the minimum wage requirement.

Hourly Workers

Hourly workers are paid for any hours or fraction of the hours they work. These employees may be either skilled or unskilled. Hourly employees must receive overtime for hours worked more than 40 per week, according to FLSA. Overtime is the same for hourly workers as it is for salaried nonexempt workers. Hourly workers may be paid for each minute worked, and the computation of those minutes depends upon company policy. Companies may offer different work shifts and workday lengths, such as four 10-hour shifts or five 8-hour shifts, to reach the 40 hours needed. State regulations may require the company to file an election to pay no overtime for the two additional hours per day. The reason stated should not be overtime avoidance, but a deemed economic benefit for the longer schedules. For example, setup time in a manufacturing environment can eliminate anywhere from half an hour to an hour of productive time. By working the longer schedules, manufacturing efficiency can be improved.

> In Asheville, North Carolina, the city changed the working hours for employees in the public works department to be 10-hour shifts. The change in working hours has led to increased employee satisfaction. Additionally, the department consumed less electricity and natural gas by closing the office one day per week. Although a four-day workweek is not appropriate for all departments and job functions, it is an option that employers may consider.
>
> In 2020, research into the idea of longer workdays and shorter workweeks revealed that the flexibility to have shorter workweeks would be a progression for traditional U.S. companies. The possibility for increased flexibility, especially when working from home or having a hybrid work schedule grew in its appeal for most employees.
>
> (Source: WLOS; SHRM)

Hourly Workers in More Than One Job Classification

An employee working for an hourly wage may work in more than one job classification. When this occurs, the employee's pay per classification may vary. For example, a manufacturing employee may work on the sales counter, where the pay differential provides an additional $1.50 per hour. When situations like this occur, the payroll accountant must be informed of hours performed for each job classification to provide accurate pay, classification, and reporting. Methods used to communicate this include notes on the time card, and schedules provided to the payroll clerk, or job duty notification forms.

> **EXAMPLE: HOURLY PAY WITH DIFFERENT RATES**
> Merrill Cabral is an hourly worker for a fast-food establishment in Louisiana and earns $7.25 per hour. He occasionally is the crew chief, during which he receives a $2 per hour differential. During a 40-hour workweek, he worked 16 hours as a crew chief and 24 hours as a regular employee. His pay would be calculated as follows:
>
> Regular pay: 24 hours × $7.25/hour = $174
>
> Crew chief pay: $7.25/hour + $2.00/hour differential = $9.25/hour
>
> 16 hours × $9.25/hour = $148
>
> Gross pay = $174 + $148 = $322

Commission Work

Commissions are compensation based on a set percentage of the sales revenue for a product or service that the company provides. Commission-based compensation is appropriate in the following types of situations:

- Retail sales personnel.
- Automotive sales personnel.

- Media databases or monitoring that pertains to media relations.
- Marketing sales agents.

EXAMPLE: COMMISSION WORKER PAY

An ice machine company may have sales representatives earning a 5 percent commission on all sales made. If sales representative A sells $100,000 worth of ice machines during July, the commission due is computed as follows:

Sales price × Commission rate = $100,000 × 5% = $5,000

Note: Commissions may be contingent upon the company's commission return/warranty policy.

If sales representative A had returns of $7,500 during August, the commission for that month could be reduced:

Returns × Commission rate = deduction from commissions $7,500 returns × 5% commission rate = $375 deducted from commissions during August.

Note that the commission deduction policy varies among employers and is not mandated by any legislation.

An important classification of a sales representative's job is the difference between inside and outside sales. An inside sales representative conducts business via telephone, email, or other electronic means and may not travel to customer sites. An outside sales representative meets with customers either at the customer's facility or another agreed-upon location. Some inside sales representatives are covered under the FLSA and must receive at least minimum wage for their labors. Outside sales representatives are excluded from minimum wage requirements under FLSA. In a 2010 circuit court decision, the judge ruled that inside sales representatives are nonexempt from FLSA wage and hour provisions, whereas outside sales and retail sales representatives are exempt.

EXAMPLE: INSIDE SALES REPRESENTATIVE, LESS THAN MINIMUM WAGE

Helen Steinel works as an inside sales representative in the company store and receives a 5 percent commission for all her sales during her shift. During the week, she made 15 sales via telephone with a total dollar value of $1,500.

Commissions = Dollar value of sales × Commission rate.

Commissions = $1,500 × 5% = $75

Based upon a 40-hour workweek, she would have effectively earned **$1.88** per hour; thus, the employer would be responsible for meeting the minimum wage requirements under FLSA. The employer would have to adjust Helen's compensation to meet the minimum wage requirements for the specific location and local laws.

EXAMPLE: OUTSIDE SALES REPRESENTATIVE, LESS THAN MINIMUM WAGE

Samantha Durant works as an outside sales representative for the same company. She made sales this week of $2,000 and has an agreed-upon commission percentage of 10 percent of her total sales revenue. Commission = 2,000 × 10% = $200; $200 per week/40 hours = $5.00 hour. Because she is an outside sales representative, she is exempt from minimum wage regulations under FLSA.

Gross Pay for Commission-Based Employees

In situations where the employee is principally engaged in the sale of a product or service but in no way engaged in the item's manufacturing, a commission pay basis is appropriate. In some states, the commission-based employee may receive commissions for work, even after termination, if the sale was completed before termination. In many ways, commission-based pay is a contract between the employer and the employee to sell a product. The payment for such a contract may not be reneged upon, even after termination of employment. It should be noted that many states prohibit deductions about the cost of doing business from an employee's commission. In other words, if a customer received a product that was damaged, lost, or otherwise destroyed, the employee's commission would not be affected.

EXAMPLE

Sonja Hinton works as an outside salesperson with Bayfront Watercraft in California. Her whole function with Bayfront is to sell the company's products to customers at the customer's facility or other agreed-upon locations. She receives a commission of 5 percent based on the retail price of all sales she makes. During May, she sold $20,000 of products during one week.

Commission = $20,000 × 0.05 = <u>$1,000</u>

Commission pay can vary by employer, the client, sales volume, and employee based on their seniority or experience with the company. Different products may also have varying commission rates, and changes in sales volume can alter commission rates. A sample of a commission-tracking sheet follows.

skynesher/Getty Images

EXAMPLE: COMMISSION TRACKING SHEET

Salesperson	Client	Product or Service	Total Sales Price	Rate	Commission
Anthony Bauer	Thompson Milbourne	RR-223	$1,245	2%	$24.90
Anthony Bauer	Kockran Heights	RS-447	$2,016	5%	$100.80
Anthony Bauer	Hoptop Ranges	RT-11	$892	3.5%	$31.22

Commissions earned must be tracked closely for a variety of reasons:

- Employees' pay accuracy.
- Sales employee performance.
- Sales tracking.
- Job order tracking.
- Returns/reductions of commissions paid accuracy.

Commission pay must still meet FLSA minimum wage standards unless the employee is classified as an exempt worker. Like salaried nonexempt employees, commission-based employees are subject to the 40-hour workweek as a basis for FLSA minimum wage computations.

EXAMPLE: EFFECTIVE PAY RATE, EXCEED MINIMUM WAGE

In the example concerning Sonja Hinton at Bayfront, Sonja's pay was $1,000 for 40 hours of work.

Sonja's effective wage = $1,000/40 hours = <u>$25/hour</u>

EXAMPLE: EFFECTIVE PAY RATE, LOWER THAN THE MINIMUM WAGE

Anita Edward, another inside sales commission-based employee at Bayfront Watercraft, made only $250 in commission for the week she worked 40 hours.

Effective hourly rate = $250/40 hours = <u>$6.25/hour</u>

(continued)

(concluded)

This amount is below the minimum wage in California. The employer's responsibility is to compensate the employee at the appropriate minimum wage, so Bayfront would have to adjust Anita's compensation to meet FLSA requirements.

Piece-Rate Work

Piece-rate work involves paying employees for each unit they manufacture or each action they complete. Compensation based on task completion is one of the oldest forms of performance-based pay. Dating back to the 16th century, piece-rate pay is thought to have evolved from journeyman artisans whose masters paid them per unit they completed. Before computations of hourly wages, piece-rate was an accurate measure of how productive an employee was. Frederick Taylor wrote about a piece-rate system in 1896, citing that it emphasized efficiency and production. However, a criticism of Taylor's writing is that the piece-rate system overemphasizes production and may create an adversarial relationship between workers and managers.

California's AB 1513, passed in 2016, amended California Labor Code 226.2 and mandated that piece-rate workers be paid for nonproductive time during the workday. Pay during the nonproductive time would be at a different rate than the normal piece-rate work. This nonproductive time includes the employee's time under the employer's control but not on a rest or recovery break. The argument for paid nonproductive time for piece-rate workers is that the employee remains under the employer's control despite the lack of productivity.

(Source: California Department of Industrial Relations)

FLSA requirements subjected the piece-rate system to minimum wage requirements. Piece-rate workers must be paid no less than the minimum wage for their location, forcing employers to accurately track their work. In many ways, piece-rate pay is more difficult to track and administer than other payment types. Not only must the employees be compensated for the work they complete, but they are also subject to FLSA minimum and daily break provisions, including lunch and other breaks. Piece-rate work has also fallen under some suspicion regarding the quality of work being performed. This can add a review to the completed work.

EXAMPLE: PIECE-RATE PAY, EXCEED THE MINIMUM WAGE

John Samuelson is a piece-rate worker in Tennessee who receives $15 per completed piece of work. During a week, he completes 30 pieces and works 40 hours.

John's pay = $15/per piece completed × 30 pieces completed = $450

Hourly rate equivalent = $450/40 hours = $11.25/hour

John's pay exceeds the FLSA minimum wage for his location, so the employer does not have to adjust John's compensation.

EXAMPLE: PIECE-RATE WORKER, BELOW MINIMUM WAGE

Sarah McDowell works for the same employer as John and receives the same rate of pay. She completes 15 pieces during the week.

Sarah's pay = $15/piece × 15 = $225

Hourly rate equivalent = $225/40 = $5.63/hour

Sarah's pay does not meet the minimum wage requirement, so the employer would have to examine Sarah's work and pay rates to ensure that she meets the FLSA minimum wage requirements.

A wide variety of occupations benefit from piece-rate pay systems. Some of these occupations are:

Vineyard workers	Inspectors
Carpenters	Property Assessors
Machinists/fabricators	Production workers
Sheep shearers	Forest workers

The common thread is that each position has an output quantifiable and linked to some aspect of a manufacturing or service industry. The important part of piece-rate work is that a quantifiable base must be linked with a specified standard rate per amount of work.

Vineyard workers: Tons of grapes harvested
Inspectors: Number of items inspected
Installers: Number of items installed
Customer service agents: Number of customers assisted
Machinists/fabricators: Number of items produced
Sheep shearers: Pounds of wool gathered
Forest workers: Amount of wood chopped and/or processed

At Bayfront Watercraft, the manufacturing department has different types of fabricators, installers, and other production workers in addition to Pat (the hull maker). Let us assume that Joanna works in the upholstery department, where she constructs vinyl covers for seats. Rick is in the assembly department and assembles steering mechanisms for the boats.

EXAMPLE: PIECE-RATE COMPUTATION, DIFFERENT EMPLOYEES

Worker	Number of Items	Rate per Item	Gross Pay
Pat Wu	30 hulls	$100	$3,000
Joanna Yoder	100 seat covers	25	2,500
Rick Karmaran	25 steering mechanisms	40	1,000

Each worker is compensated based on the work he or she completes. In some companies, workers may work on multiple items for which different rates exist. In cases where one worker completes multiple pieces at different rates, each piece's rates must be computed.

EXAMPLE: TOTAL PAY, ONE PIECE-RATE EMPLOYEE

Worker	Item	Number of Items	Pay per Item	Total Pay
John Brichacek	Motor installation	10 motors	$50 per motor	$500
	Rudder installation	15 rudders	20 per rudder	300
			Total pay for John:	$800

A separate record for each employee is important in piece-rate pay, especially when the employee works with multiple production items at different rates. Overtime rates for piece-rate workers are computed differently than for hourly workers. Once the standard number of pieces per hour is determined, the amount per hour per piece can be computed. Since the hourly rate now includes the overtime hours worked, the specific overtime hours would only be multiplied by 1/2 instead of the 1-1/2 of other workers.

EXAMPLE: PIECE RATE WITH OVERTIME PAY

Bayfront determines that 50 ignition assemblies can reasonably be completed in a 40-hour workweek by one worker. Ignition assemblies are paid at a rate of $25 per assembly.

(continued)

(concluded)

Standard amount paid per 40-hour workweek: $1,250

50 assemblies × $25/assembly = $1,250

Hourly amount = $1,250/40 hours = $31.25/hour

If the employee worked overtime, the rate would be computed as follows:

Overtime wages = Hourly rate + (0.5 × Hourly rate × Overtime hours)

If an employee worked a 45-hour workweek, the pay would be computed as

Standard amount per week + Overtime pay

= $1,250 + ($31.25/hour × 5 hours overtime) + ($15.625 × 5 hours overtime)

= $1,484.375, which would be <u>$1,484.38</u> (rounded)

According to FLSA provisions, piece-rate workers must have a standard number of items that can be reasonably completed each day that allows for breaks and rest periods. To increase compensation, it could be straightforward for an employee to overwork to complete more items. According to 29 CFR 525.12(h)(2)(ii), piece-rate employees must have a standard number of items per period, and most are subject to minimum wage provisions. However, if an employee is paid a different rate for nonproductive time, the regular rate is the regular rate and the nonproductive rate.

Computations for Different Bases

Stop & Check

1. Natasha Uttrecht is a marketing representative who earns a 3 percent commission based on the revenue earned from the marketing campaigns she completes. During the current pay period, she completed a marketing campaign with $224,800 in revenue. How much commission will she receive from this campaign?

2. Jeremy Wikander is a specialty artisan for a luxury car maker based in South Carolina. He makes handcrafted dashboards and receives $550 per completed assembly. During a semimonthly pay period, he completes two dashboard assemblies and works 90 hours. How much does he receive for the completion of the assemblies? Does this amount comply with minimum wage requirements? Explain.

3. Lanea Kiehn is a salaried worker making $57,000 per year for a company using biweekly payroll. Her standard schedule is 40 hours over five days per week. She has used all of her vacation time before this pay period and fell ill for three days. What effect does this have on the current pay period? Will her gross pay be the same as if she had vacation time available? (**Note:** Only round final calculations.)

LO 3-3   Calculate Pay Based on Hours and Fractions of Hours

Both salaried nonexempt and hourly employees are paid based upon the number of hours (or fractions thereof) worked. The payroll accountant must learn how to convert a fraction of a 60-minute clock into a fraction of 100. While accounting software packages can convert minutes into payable units, the payroll accountant typically does this math. Fortunately, the math for this calculation is fairly straightforward.

EXAMPLE: CONVERSION OF MINUTES TO DECIMALS AND FRACTIONS

If an employee works 30 minutes, then the computation for pay purposes is

30 minutes ÷ 60 minutes/hour = 0.5 hour or 50/100

If an employee works 33 minutes, the payroll computation is

33 minutes ÷ 60 minutes/hour = <u>0.55</u> hour or <u>55/100</u>

Note: This calculation is necessary when the employer pays using the hundredth-hour method instead of the quarter-hour method. If this had been a quarter-hour computation, the number of minutes would have been rounded to the closest 15-minute increment, which is 0.50 hours.

Calculations of employee wages are broken down by the hour or fraction thereof. Regardless of the employee's classification, a determination of pay per pay period causes the payroll accountant to break down all wages. Salaries are determined based upon a yearly salary and therefore need to be broken down per pay period (monthly, semimonthly, weekly, or biweekly). Companies may pay employees by fractions of an hour (hundredth-hour basis) or by the quarter-hour (rounded to the nearest 15-minute interval), depending upon company policy. The next section will walk you through the calculations of both the hundredth and quarterly processes.

Hourly Calculations

Depending on the company's policy, time payments can be paid either by the individual minute or rounded to the nearest designated interval. Hourly calculations are a combination of minutes and hours. Hours are broken into two categories: regular and overtime. When determining the hourly wage for a salaried individual, the number of average hours required under the salary must be known.

EXAMPLE: HOURLY WAGE COMPUTATION, SALARIED EMPLOYEE

If a manager is expected to work 45 hours per week at $75,000 per year, the effective hourly wage would be

$75,000/(45 × 52 weeks) = $75,000/2,340 = <u>$32.05 per hour</u>

EXAMPLE: WEEKLY PAY INCLUDING PAID SICK TIME

Jason Taylor worked four days during the payroll week. He worked 7.5 hours the first day, 8.75 hours the second day, 7 hours the third day, and 9.5 hours the fourth day. He used 8 hours of his paid sick time on one day during the week. He is paid overtime for any hours worked more than 40 per week.

Regular hours: 7.5 + 8.75 + 7 + 9.5 = <u>32.75 hours</u>

He will also receive 8 hours of sick time.

Jason's gross pay = 32.75 regular hours + 8 sick = <u>40.75 hours</u>

Even though Jason has more than 40 hours on his payroll, 8 are not considered "worked" and would therefore not be included in the calculation to determine overtime.

EXAMPLE: WEEKLY PAY INCLUDING PAID HOLIDAY TIME

Karen Golliff worked four days during the week with a holiday on Monday. Her hours worked were 8.25 hours the first day, 9 hours the second day, 7.75 hours the third day, and 8.5 hours the fourth day. The company pays 8 hours for a holiday. She is paid for any hours worked more than 40 hours per week.

Regular hours: 8.25 + 9 + 7.75 + 8.5 = <u>33.5 hours</u>

She will also be paid 8 hours of regular pay for the holiday.

(continued)

(concluded)

Karen's gross pay will contain 41.5 hours of regular pay, including 8 hours of holiday pay. Karen has not worked more than 40 hours because the holiday is not included in *worked* hours, so she will not receive overtime.

niroworld/123RF

Quarter-Hour System

Some employers compensate employees based on rounding working hours to the nearest 15 minutes, a system widely known as the *quarter-hour system*. The payroll accountant becomes responsible for rounding the time either up or down consistently across all individuals and pay periods. If an individual worked 8 hours and 6 minutes, he would be paid for 8 hours. However, if that same individual were to work for 8 hours and 8 minutes, he would be paid for 8 hours plus 15 minutes of overtime if the company pays for overtime on any hours worked over 8 in a day.

EXAMPLE: ROUNDING MINUTES FOR THE QUARTER-HOUR SYSTEM

- 0–7 minutes past the previous 15-minute interval rounds *down* to the previous 15-minute interval.
Example: 10:06 a.m. would count as 10:00 a.m. in the quarter-hour system.

- 8–15 minutes past the previous 15-minute interval rounds *up* to the next 15-minute interval.
Example: 10:09 a.m. would count as 10:15 a.m. in the quarter-hour system.

EXAMPLE: QUARTER-HOUR SYSTEM COMPUTATION, ROUNDING TO THE PREVIOUS QUARTER-HOUR

Amanda Leong worked from 8 a.m. until noon. She took 1 hour for lunch and returned to work at 1 p.m. At the end of the day, Amanda ended up leaving work at 4:20 p.m. Using the quarter-hour system

- From 8 a.m. to noon: 4 hours

- From 1 p.m. to 4:20 p.m.: 3.25 hours, because 4:20 p.m. rounds down to 4:15 p.m. under the quarter-hour system.
- Total time: 4 + 3.25 = <u>7.25 hours</u>

EXAMPLE: QUARTER-HOUR SYSTEM COMPUTATION, ROUNDING TO THE NEXT QUARTER-HOUR

Justin Fretwell worked from 8 a.m. until 12:30 p.m. before taking a half-hour lunch. He returned at 1 p.m. and worked until 4:10 p.m. His employer pays on the quarter-hour system, so Justin would be paid as follows:

- From 8 a.m. to 12:30 p.m.: 4 hours, 30 minutes = 4.5 hours
- From 1 p.m. to 4:10 p.m.: 3.25 hours, because 4:10 p.m. rounds up to 4:15 p.m. under the quarter-hour system.
- Total time for the day: <u>7.75 hours</u>

Hundredth-Hour System

The *hundredth-hour system* is similar to the quarter-hour system in that it calculates partial hours of work performed. Instead of rounding the employee's time to 15-minute intervals, the hundredth-hour system divides the hour into increments. The calculation of partial minutes is simple:

$$\text{Conversion of minutes to hundredth hour} = \frac{\text{Number of minutes in partial hour}}{60 \text{ minutes per hour}}$$

EXAMPLE: CONVERSION FROM MINUTES TO HUNDREDTH-HOUR

If an employee worked 4 hours and 16 minutes,

4 hours + 16 minutes/60 minutes per hour = <u>4.27 hours</u>

EXAMPLE: HUNDREDTH-HOUR TIME COMPUTATION

Leslie Mellor works an 8-hour shift that had 15 minutes of additional overtime. Her normal hourly rate is $10/hour. Her pay would be computed as follows:

- 8 hours × $10 per hour = $80 regular pay
- 15 minutes overtime = 15/60 = 0.25 hour
- Overtime = 0.25 hours × $10/hour × 1.5 = $3.75
- Total pay for the day = $80 + $3.75 = <u>$83.75</u>

Following is an example of how the time may appear on an individual's time card. Note that an employer should choose only one method of computing partial hours—quarter-hours or hundredth-hours—and apply it to all situations and all employees.

EXAMPLE: QUARTER-HOUR COMPUTATION, WEEKLY PAY DETAILS

Amanda Parker: Employee Number 1776M				
Clock In	Clock Out	Clock In	Clock Out	Hours Worked
08:00	11:00 rounds up	12:00	16:54	7 hours 54 minutes = 8.00 hours
08:00	11:30 rounds down	12:30	17:05	8 hours 5 minutes = 8.00 hours
07:00	12:09 rounds up	13:15	17:30	9 hours 24 minutes = 9.5 hours
07:30	12:21 rounds down	13:24 rounds up	17:30	8 hours 57 minutes = 8.75 hours
			Total	34.25 hours

In the next example, notice how the same employee with the same amount of time worked would have different hourly computations based on hundredth-hour computations. The difference in the hourly computations leads to a difference in compensation for the period.

EXAMPLE: HUNDREDTH-HOUR COMPUTATION, WEEKLY PAY DETAILS

Amanda Parker: Employee Number 1776M				
Clock In	Clock Out	Clock In	Clock Out	Hours Worked
08:00	11:00	12:00	16:54	7 hours 54 minutes = 7.9 hours
08:00	11:30	12:30	17:05	8 hours 5 minutes = 8.08 hours
07:00	12:09	13:15	17:30	9 hours 24 minutes = 9.4 hours
07:30	12:21	13:24	17:30	8 hours 57 minutes = 8.95 hours
			Total	34.33 hours

BEST PRACTICE: QUARTER-HOUR OR HUNDREDTH-HOUR?
Debate exists around the question of which timekeeping system is better, quarter-hour or hundredth-hour. The best practices in this regard focus on consistency and accuracy. If the company feels that the hundredth-hour timekeeping system is more appropriate for their needs, they need to create that policy and implement it through their payroll and timekeeping systems. The FLSA guidance is that quarter-hour is the federal requirement.

Which is the best practice? It depends on decisions made by the company.

Quarter-Hour vs. Hundredth-Hour

1. Blue Sky Manufacturing has historically paid its employees according to the quarter-hour system. Software changes have caused them to change to the hundredth-hour system. What is the number of hours worked under the quarter-hour system? What is the time worked under the hundredth-hour system? (Hint: convert to 24-hour clock to make calculations easier.)

Employee	Time In	Time Out	Time In	Time Out	Total
Ann Gottlieb	8:06 a.m.	12:25 p.m.	1:20 p.m.	4:57 p.m.	Quarter-hour: Hundredth:
Nevada Lofkin	7:58 a.m.	12:02 p.m.	1:02 p.m.	5:05 p.m.	Quarter-hour: Hundredth:
Pat Blackburn	8:32 a.m.	11:54 a.m.	1:05 p.m.	5:32 p.m.	Quarter-hour: Hundredth:

2. Why do discrepancies exist between the quarter-hour time and the hundredth-hour time totals?

3. Why would it be worthwhile for Blue Sky Manufacturing to switch to the hundredth-hour system?

Elnur/Shutterstock

LO 3-4 Calculate Overtime in Various Situations

Nonexempt employee overtime may occur in a variety of situations. When an employee works past the FLSA maximum hours per week, the employee must be compensated at a rate of 1.5 times the regular hourly rate. However, situations exist when employees must be compensated at more than the standard overtime premium, and others exist when exempt employees may receive overtime pay. We will explore examples of overtime compensation in a variety of situations.

Standard Overtime Pay

In general, FLSA-stipulated overtime includes hours worked more than 40 during a 7-day, 168-hour week. No limit on the number of hours an employee may work per week exists for employees over 16 years of age. No legislation stipulates that employees must be paid at overtime rates on Saturdays and Sundays as long as the total number of hours worked is less than 40 during a period of seven consecutive days. An important fact to note is that the regular pay rate may not be below the FLSA or state-based minimum wage, especially in the case when overtime pay has been earned.

According to the Bureau of Labor Statistics, the average number of weekly overtime hours as of 2021 was 3.3 per employee. Although this may seem to be a relatively low number, employee overtime can become a significant amount for a large employer. For example, the city of Las Cruces, New Mexico, failed to pay overtime for employees who worked at local events, citing a flex-time agreement. The city was forced to pay over $8,500 in overtime pay for a single event in early 2020.

(Sources: Bureau of Labor Statistics, *Las Cruces Sun News*)

The first example explains basic overtime pay computation for a nonexempt employee with a 40-hour workweek. The second part of the example reflects the bonus payment as a normal part of the employee's pay.

Overtime on retail or service salaries with the commission has two rules that must be met for the commissions to be included in the wage base for the overtime calculations: (1) the employee's regular payments must be more than 1½ times the statutory minimum wage and (2) more than one-half of the employee's compensation must be from the commissions.

EXAMPLE: NONEXEMPT PAY CALCULATION

Monique Martin works as a maintenance worker at a busy office building. She earns $52,000 annually, is paid weekly, and is classified as nonexempt. Her standard work-week is 40 hours. Since Monique is classified as a nonexempt worker, she can receive overtime for any hours worked more than 40 per week per her employment contract.

During the pay period ending April 22, Monique worked 50 hours. As a result, Monique would receive her weekly pay *plus* overtime calculated to include the non-discretionary bonus. To determine her hourly wage, divide her annual pay by the total hours worked during the year. Her gross earnings for the April 22 pay period would be as follows:

Name	M/S	#Dep	Hourly Rate	No. of Regular Hours	No. of Overtime Hours	Regular Earnings	Overtime Earnings	Gross Earnings	401(k)	Insurance	Taxable Wages for Federal W/H	Taxable Wages for FICA
Monique Martin	S	1	25.00	40	10	1,000.00	375.00	1,375.00				

Note that Monique's regular pay and overtime pay are calculated separately and then added together to determine the gross pay.

Hourly rate plus bonus

If Monique were eligible for a bonus as part of her employment agreement, her bonus would be added to her regular pay to determine the hourly rate on which the overtime is based. In this example, if Monique received a $120 bonus for her work, the overtime computation would be as follows:

Name	M/S	#Dep	Hourly Rate	No. of Regular Hours	No. of Overtime Hours	Bonus	Regular Earning	Overtime Earning	Gross Earning	401(k)	Insurance	Taxable Wages for Federal W/H	Taxable Wages for FICA
Monique Martin	S	1	25.00	40	10	120.00	1,000.00	420.00*	1,540.00				

* Calculation: $40 * 25 = $1,000 + 120 = $1,120 / 40 = $28 * 1.5 = $42 * 10 = $420

Overtime for Employees of Hospitals and Residential Care Facilities

Overtime computation differs from the standard rate for employees who work at hospitals and residential care facilities. FLSA section **7(j)** applies a rule to these workers known as the *Eight and Eighty (8 and 80)* rule. According to the 8 and 80 rule, the number of consecutive days is 14 instead of 7. Similarly, the threshold for overtime is 80 hours during the work period instead of 40. An example reflecting the 8 and 80 rule follows.

EXAMPLE: 8 AND 80 OVERTIME CALCULATION

Victor Garner is a Licensed Professional Nurse (LPN) at Fountainside Hospital. During the period starting June 5 and ending June 18, he worked 95 hours. Victor is classified as nonexempt and earns an hourly wage of $31.50. Victor's pay for the two-week period would be as follows:

Name	M/S	#W/H	Hourly Rate	No. of Regular Hours	No. of Overtime Hours	Regular Earning	Overtime Earning	Gross Earning	401(k)	Insurance	Taxable Wages for Federal W/H	Taxable Wages for FICA
Victor Garner	S	1	31.50	80	15	2,520.00	708.75	3,228.75				

Note that the first 80 hours are paid at the regular hourly rate. The 15 additional hours are paid at the overtime premium rate.

Overtime for nurses took on a different aspect during the COVID pandemic. Most nurses worked overtime as of mid-2020 to respond to the critical needs of the hospitals. Nurses in Milford, Massachusetts, involved the National Labor Relations Board in their drive to have reasonable hours and safe working conditions.

(Source: Patch)

Tipped Employee Overtime

Another overtime situation involves tipped employees. According to the FLSA, employers may consider tips earned by the employee when computing overtime pay. A best practice when the employer chooses to use the tips earned as part of the overtime computation is to notify the employee in advance that their tips will be included in the overtime pay calculation. An example of both situations will show how the wage computations differ with and without tips included.

EXAMPLE: TIPPED EMPLOYEE OVERTIME

Elsie Morales is a nonexempt tipped employee at the Love House Bar and Grill in Arvada, Colorado. The minimum cash wage in Colorado is $8.98 per hour, and the tip credit is $3.02 per hour (i.e., the minimum wage for Colorado is $12.00 per hour). During the pay period beginning January 31, 2021, and ending February 6, 2021, Elsie worked 48 hours and earned $300 in tips.

Without the consideration of tips, and based on the state minimum wage, Elsie must be paid $624.00 for the 48 hours worked, as follows:

Name	M/S	#W/H	Hourly Rate	No. of Regular Hours	No. of Over-time Hours	Tips	Regular Earning	Overtime Earning	Gross Earning	401(k)	Insurance	Taxable Wages for Federal W/H	Taxable Wages for FICA
Elsie Morales	S	1	12.00	40	8		480.00	144.00	624.00				

Overtime pay with tips included as part of the hourly wage

If the employer counted the $300 in tips earned toward the minimum cash overtime wage, Elsie would not be eligible for any further compensation because the gross earnings exceeded the minimum due.

Name	M/S	#W/H	Hourly Rate	No. of Regular Hours	No. of Over-time Hours	Tips	Regular Earning	Overtime Earning	Gross Earning	401(k)	Insurance	Taxable Wages for Federal W/H	Taxable Wages for FICA
Elsie Morales	S	1	8.98	40	8	300.00	659.20	197.76	856.96				

Earnings calculation

Regular earnings: $300 + (8.98 \times 40) = \$300 + 359.20 = 659.20$

Overtime earnings: $\$659.20/40 = \$16.48/hour \times 1.5 = \$24.72 \times 8 = \$197.76$

Overtime pay excluding tips as part of the hourly wage

If the employer did not count Elsie's tips toward the hourly wage, her pay would be computed as follows:

Name	M/S	#W/H	Hourly Rate	No. of Regular Hours	No. of Over-time Hours	Tips	Regular Earning	Overtime Earning	Gross Earning	401(k)	Insurance	Taxable Wages for Federal W/H	Taxable Wages for FICA
Elsie Morales	S	1	8.98	40	8		359.20	107.76	466.96				

In this case, the employer would need to pay Elsie the difference between the minimum wage and the minimum tipped wage:

$\$466.96/40 = 11.674/hour$

40 hours $\times$ \$12.00 per hour = \$480.00

$\$480.00 - \$466.96 = \$13.04$

Note that state laws vary as to the inclusion of tips in tipped employee overtime calculations.

Piece-Rate Employee Overtime

Piece-rate workers are eligible for overtime on a similar basis to hourly nonexempt employees. However, because they are paid on a piece-rate basis, the overtime computation is based on the number of pieces completed and the total number of productive hours worked during the consecutive seven-day period.

EXAMPLE: PIECE-RATE EMPLOYEE OVERTIME

Edmund Dennis is a piece-rate employee at Snowy Day Sculptures in Terrace Lake, New Mexico. He earns $75 per finished sculpture. During the week of February 27, he worked 48.5 hours and completed 12 sculptures. He is paid minimum wage (i.e., $7.50 per hour) for nonproductive time; during the week of February 27, he had four nonproductive time hours. His overtime would be calculated based on the productive time of 44.5 hours as follows:

Name	M/S	#W/H	Piece Rate	# of Pieces Completed	No. of Regular Hours	No. of Over-time Hours	Piece Rate Earnings	Regular Earning	Over-time Earning	Gross Earning	401(k)	Insurance	Taxable Wages for Federal W/H	Taxable Wages for FICA
Edmund Dennis	S	1	75	12	40	4.5	900.00	30.00	45.51	975.51				

Earnings calculation

Piece-rate earnings: $12 \times \$75 = \$900$

Regular earnings = $4 \times \$7.50 = \$30$

Overtime = $\$900/44.5 \times 0.5 = \$10.11 \times 4.5 = \$45.51$

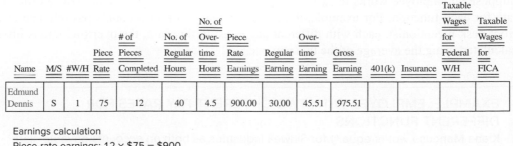

(continued)

(concluded)

Note that the overtime earnings are computed based on the piece-rate earnings divided by the total number of productive hours, which yields an effective hourly rate. That hourly rate is multiplied by 1.5 and the number of overtime productive hours to determine the overtime pay.

Salaried Nonexempt Overtime

When the employee is a salaried nonexempt worker, the standard number of working hours per week depends on the hiring agreement. If the number of hours agreed upon is 40 per week, then the standard overtime examples should be followed. However, if the number of agreed-upon hours is 45 per week, the overtime is calculated using 45 hours to determine the hourly rate, and time worked more than 40 hours is subject to overtime premiums. The same principle applies to employees who work four 10-hour shifts, shifts with differential rates, or other similar arrangements.

EXAMPLE: SALARIED NONEXEMPT POSITION WITH A NORMAL 45-HOUR WORK SCHEDULE

Clay Curtis is an administrator for Strickland Farms and earns $52,000 annually, paid biweekly. He is a salaried nonexempt employee with a standard 45-hour workweek. During the two-week pay period ending September 25, Clay worked 99 hours. His overtime would be computed as follows:

Name	M/S	#W/H	Salary	No. of Regular Hours	No. of Overtime Hours*	Regular Earning	Overtime Earning	Gross Earning	401(k)	Insurance	Taxable Wages for Federal W/H	Taxable Wages for FICA
Clay Curtis	S	1	2,000.00	90	9	2,000.00	633.27	2,633.27				

Earnings calculation

* Although Clay has a 45-hour standard workweek, per FLSA he must be paid overtime for all hours worked in excess of 40. The number of overtime hours is 99 − (2 weeks × 40 hours/week), or 19.

Overtime rate = $52,000/(45 × 52) = $22.22 × 1.5 = $33.33 × 19 = $633.27

The U.S. Department of Labor forced the owners of an Evansville, Indiana, business to pay approximately $300,000 in overtime and back wages. The restaurant was a repeat offender of FLSA minimum wage violations and was fined to pay hourly kitchen employees as exempt workers and violate tipped minimum wage laws for servers.

(Source: Courier & Press)

Overtime for Employees Who Work in Two or More Separate Functions

Suppose an employee works in two separate functions in the company and earns a different rate for each function. For example, the employee may work in accounts payable and as a front desk receptionist, each with different pay rates. In this case, the overtime rate is often calculated using the average of the two pay rates.

EXAMPLE: EMPLOYEE WITH TWO DIFFERENT PAY RATES FOR DIFFERENT FUNCTIONS

Kiana Mancuso works equally for Sidwell Industries as both an accounts payable clerk and a front desk receptionist. She earns $18.50 per hour for accounts payable and $15 per hour for reception work. During the week ending October 27, Kiana worked

50 hours; 26 hours were in accounts payable, and the rest were at the front desk. Her pay would be computed as follows:

Name	M/S	#W/H	Hourly Rate	No. of Regular Hours	No. of Overtime Hours	Regular Earning	Overtime Earning	Gross Earning	401(k)	Insurance	Taxable Wages for Federal W/H	Taxable Wages for FICA
Kiana Mancuso—accounts payable	S	1	18.50	20	6	370.00	166.50	536.50				
Kiana Mancuso—front desk	S	1	15.00	20	4	300.00	90.00	390.00				
Total Earnings								926.50				

Note that company policies on overtime pay may vary from the situations described. When in doubt, the payroll accountant should refer to the FLSA overtime calculator advisor published by the U.S. Department of Labor.

How Does Overtime Affect Gross Pay?

Stop & Check

1. Tommy Grubb is a hospital worker in the city of Keene, New Hampshire. Which rule governs his overtime pay?

2. Michaele Gerald is a salaried nonexempt employee who earns $39,000 per year, paid biweekly, and commission is based on sales of service contracts representing less than half her pay. How does her commission income affect any overtime compensation?

3. Ralph Scott is a waiter at Good Eats Diner. What are the two ways that his employer might compute his overtime earnings about his tip income?

Rawpixel.com/Shutterstock

LO 3-5   Create a Payroll Register

The *payroll register* is the payroll accountant's internal tool that helps ensure the accuracy of employee compensation. A payroll register can be completed manually, in a spreadsheet program such as Microsoft Excel, in accounting software programs such as QuickBooks, or by payroll outsourcing companies such as ADP or Paychex. Like other worksheets that accountants use, the payroll register is a company's confidential document subject to document retention and destruction rules.

Payroll Register Data

The payroll register is annotated at the top with the beginning and ending dates of the payroll period. Each employee has a separate row in the register. The register contains columns to reflect each employee's specific payroll information, such as:

1. Employee name.
2. Filing status.
3. Number and type of dependents.
4. Hourly rate or period salary.
5. The number of regular hours worked.
6. The number of overtime hours worked.

7. Regular pay.

8. Overtime pay.

9. Gross pay.

10. Federal income tax withheld.

11. Social Security tax withheld.

12. Medicare tax withheld.

13. State income tax withheld (where applicable).

14. Other state taxes.

15. Local taxes (if applicable).

16. 401(k) or other retirement plan deductions.

17. Insurance deductions.

18. Garnishments or levies.

19. Union dues.

20. Any other deductions.

21. Net pay.

22. Check or payment ID number.

It may seem tedious to complete a register each payroll period, but the register offers more information than just the employee compensation. The register also contains information about employer liabilities for taxes and the employees' voluntary deductions that the employer must remit to the appropriate places at a future date. A sample payroll register with annotations to correlate with the above list of items is shown in Figure 3-2.

Note that other columns may be added to meet the company's needs. Other columns that may appear on a payroll register include commission, piece rate, standby hours, and sleep time. The purpose of the payroll register is to document the employees' time and hours worked and provide totals of the compensation for each category. Employers use these categorizations as part of labor analysis and planning tasks.

FIGURE 3-2
Sample Payroll Register with Annotations

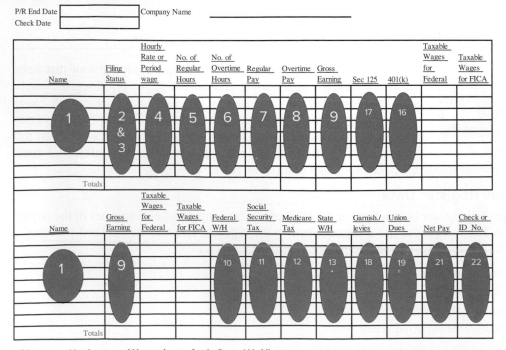

* Other state and local taxes would have columns after the State withholding tax.
† Other voluntary or mandated deductions would be in this location.

A separate payroll register is maintained for each pay period. To ensure accuracy, the accountant totals, proves, and rules the register.

WHAT DO *TOTAL, PROVE,* AND *RULE* MEAN?

Total: Each column and row are totaled.

Prove: The column totals are added horizontally, *and* row totals are totaled vertically. The aggregate column and row totals must be equal.

Rule: Column totals are double underlined to show that they have been totaled.

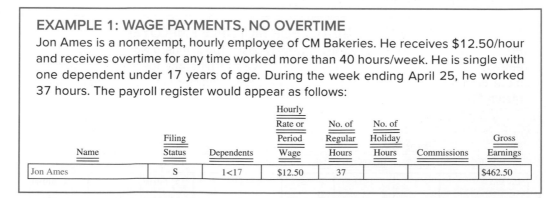

Track Employee Compensation Using a Payroll Register

A payroll register is a tool used by payroll accountants to ensure accurate tracking of employee compensation. The following examples will demonstrate different scenarios using a payroll register.

EXAMPLE 1: WAGE PAYMENTS, NO OVERTIME

Jon Ames is a nonexempt, hourly employee of CM Bakeries. He receives $12.50/hour and receives overtime for any time worked more than 40 hours/week. He is single with one dependent under 17 years of age. During the week ending April 25, he worked 37 hours. The payroll register would appear as follows:

Name	Filing Status	Dependents	Hourly Rate or Period Wage	No. of Regular Hours	No. of Holiday Hours	Commissions	Gross Earnings
Jon Ames	S	1<17	$12.50	37			$462.50

In Example 1, the employee's hourly rate is multiplied by the number of hours worked to obtain the period's gross pay. The use of the Regular Earnings column is introduced here, although no overtime exists. Example 2 will show how overtime is included in a payroll register.

EXAMPLE 2: WAGE PAYMENT WITH OVERTIME

Mike Brown is a nonexempt, hourly employee of Strong Coffee Company and earns $18.50/hour. He is married, filing jointly with two dependents under 17 years of age.

(continued)

(concluded)

He receives overtime for any hours worked more than 40 during a weekly period. During the period ended September 20, he worked 45.75 hours. The payroll register would appear as follows:

Name	Filing Status	Dependents	Hourly Rate or Period Wage	No. of Regular Hours	No. of Overtime Hours	Reg. Earnings	Overtime Earnings	Gross Earnings
Mike Brown	MJ	2<17	$18.50	40	5.75	$740.00	$159.56*	$899.56

* Overtime earning = $18.50/hour × 5.75 hours × 1.5 (overtime premium) = $159.56.

Notice that the payroll register in Example 2 is expanded to include a breakdown of regular earnings and overtime earnings. This practice aims to facilitate computations, ensure accuracy, and allow for future analysis of overtime worked during a given period.

Example 3 contains a payroll register for a salaried, exempt employee. Notice the difference in the columns used to record the period salary.

EXAMPLE 3: SALARY PAYMENT

Rae Smith is a manager at Hartshorn Industries. She is a salaried, exempt employee and is married, filing jointly with three dependents under 17 and 1 other dependent. She earns a salary of $2,000 per pay period. For the period ending July 31, the payroll register would appear as follows:

Name	Filing Status	Dependents	Hourly Rate or Period Wage	No. of Regular Hours	No. of Overtime Hours	No. of Holiday Hours	Commissions	Gross Earnings
Rae Smith	MJ	3<17; 1 Other	$2,000.00					$2,000.00

It is common in a company to have both salaried and hourly employees, and all employees must be represented on a payroll register. Example 4 contains employees with pay variations that commonly exist in business.

EXAMPLE 4: PAYROLL REGISTER FOR MULTIPLE EMPLOYEES

PBL Freight pays its employees on a biweekly basis. The standard workweek for hourly employees is 40 hours, and employees receive overtime pay for any hours worked more than 40 during a week. The following payroll register is for the period ending March 19:

Name	Filing Status	Dependents	Hourly Rate or Period Wage	No. of Regular Hours	No. of Overtime Hours	Reg. Earnings	Overtime Earnings	Gross Earnings
Mary Jahn	S	1<17	$ 15.25	40		$ 610.00		$ 610.00
John Charles	MJ	3<17	$2,750.00			$2.750.00		$ 2.750.00
Ranea Hu	MJ	4<17 1 Other	$ 21.50	40	6	$ 860.00	$193.50	$ 1,053.50
						$4,220.00	$193.50	$ 4,413.50

Notice how the columns are totaled in Example 4. Each earnings column is totaled vertically, and the double underline (i.e., ruling) denotes that the computations are concluded. The total in the bottom-right corner proves that the sum of the rows in the Gross Earnings column equals the Regular Earnings and Overtime Earnings columns. Once the payroll register is totaled, proved, and ruled, it is ready for the next step in the payroll process.

The Payroll Register

Stop & Check

1. What is the purpose of the payroll register?
2. What are five of the columns that usually appear in a payroll register?
3. Why are computations for regular hours and overtime hours entered in different columns?

LO 3-6   Apply Combination Pay Methods

Hello Lovely/Getty Images

Employers often offer *combination pay* methods. Sometimes the employee performs two different jobs for the same employer, and those two tasks have different compensation bases. Other situations involve payroll-based incentives that link to company productivity. Note how the payroll register reflects these combination pay methods in the following examples.

Base Salary Plus Commission

A common method includes a base salary plus a commission or piece rate, depending on the nature of the work performed. Another method is salary plus hourly compensation that reflects a standard set of work hours plus additional hours that are paid only when worked. The combination pay method aims to meet minimum wage requirements and encourage employees to achieve sales or production goals. The base salary offers both the employer and the employee a level of stability in pay amounts because they will know the minimum amount of compensation for each pay period. Whatever the employees earn above the base salary may vary from pay period to pay period, depending on their capabilities, production needs, and customer needs.

EXAMPLE: BASE SALARY PLUS COMMISSION

Henri Jay is a salaried, exempt employee of Night Lights Security. He is single with two dependents under the age of 17. His compensation package includes a commission based on sales of security system packages to customers. During the pay period ending January 15, he earned $1,500 in salary and 4 percent commission on $10,000 of sales.

Commission = $10,000 × 0.04 = $400

Name	Filing Status	Dependents	Hourly Rate or Period Wage	Commissions	Gross Earnings
Henri Jay	S	2<17	$1,500.00	$ 400.00	$1,900.00

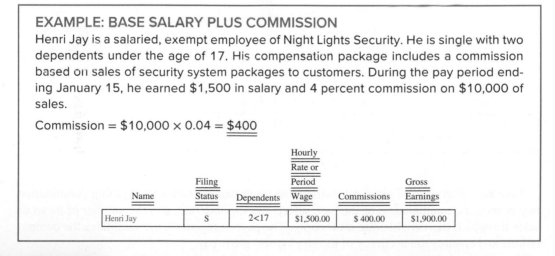

bikeriderlondon/Shutterstock

Many types of jobs have a combination pay method because it has been found to boost employee productivity and maintain FLSA compliance. Some jobs that use combination pay methods are

District managers	Account executives
Recruiters	Retail sales workers
Farmworkers	Real estate salespersons

To compute combination pay methods, knowledge of the employee's base salary plus variable rate is essential.

EXAMPLE: DIFFERENT COMBINATION METHODS, THE SAME COMPANY

Todd Jones is an account executive for Bayfront Watercraft. He earns a base salary of $36,000 plus a commission of 0.5 percent on each sale he makes. He is married with six dependents: Four under the age of 17 and two other dependents. Suppose that Todd sold $100,000 of boats during a biweekly pay period ending June 15.

Base salary = $36,000/26 = $1,384.62.

Commission = $100,000 × 0.5% = $500.

Total pay for Todd: $1,884.62

The payroll register for Todd's June 15 pay would appear as

Name	Filing Status	Dependents	Hourly Rate or Period Wage	Commissions	Gross Earnings
Todd Jones	MJ	4<17; 2 other	$1,384.62	$500.00	$1,884.62

Maria Dee installs the seating in the boats for Bayfront Watercraft. She is single with one dependent under the age of 17. In her position, she earns a base salary of $26,000 per year plus a piece rate of $100 for each boat completed during the pay period. During the pay period, Maria installed the seating for eight boats.

Salary = $26,000/26 = $1,000

Piece-rate pay = $100 × 8 = $800

Total Pay for Maria: $1,800

The payroll register, including both employees for the June 15 pay period would appear as follows:

Name	Filing Status	Dependents	Hourly Rate or Period Wage	Piece Rate Pay	Commissions	Gross Earnings
Todd Jones	MJ	4<17; 2 other	$1,384.62		$500.00	$1,884.62
Maria Dee	S	1<17	$1,000.00	$800.00		$1.800.00
Totals			$2,384.62	$800.00	$500.00	$3,684.62

Like any other type of payment method, the important element in computing combination pay is accurate maintenance of the base salary, the variable rate, and the number of items or sales for which the variable rate must apply. The payroll register's use facilitates the computations and ensures the accuracy of the employees' gross pay.

Payroll Draw

A special situation in commission-based pay is a situation called a *draw*. A draw generally involves an employee whose regular compensation is little more than the minimum wage, such as a retail sales position. Employees have sales goals they must meet and receive compensation on a commission basis once they meet or exceed those sales goals. If the sales goal is not met, the employee may draw a salary against future commissions. The expectation with a draw is that the employee will eventually generate enough sales to cover any draws during pay periods when sales revenues were lower than expected.

A draw is generally associated with a commission-only job in which the employer allows new employees to receive money for expected future commissions. With a draw, it is implied that the draw may occur regularly. However, paying employees solely based on commission and draw has been challenged because it does not recognize employee rest breaks and nonproductive time. In *Bermudez Vaquero v. Stoneledge Furniture LLC,* the court upheld the FLSA rules regarding mandatory rest breaks.

(Source: MorganLewis)

Salary Plus Commission and Draw

Salaried employees who receive commission may be eligible to draw against that commission at the company's discretion. This pay combination could be for external salespeople who have commissions as a relatively large portion of their regular income.

EXAMPLE: SALARY PLUS COMMISSION AND DRAW

Kari Lee is an employee in the sales department of Fastball Sports. She is single with one dependent under the age of 17, and her annual base salary is $12,000, paid monthly. She is expected to earn between $1,000 and $3,000 in sales commissions each month and may draw up to $3,000 per month against future earnings.

During October, she earned $1,000 in commissions in addition to her salary. She decided to take an additional $1,000 draw against her future earnings. The payroll register would reflect this compensation as follows.

Name	Filing Status	Dependents	Hourly Rate or Period Wage	Reg. Earnings	Draw	Commissions	Gross Earnings
Kari Lee	S	1<17	$1,000.00	$1,000.00	$1,000.00	$1,000.00	$3,000.00

In this case, Kari could have withdrawn up to $3,000 against future earnings. If her employment is terminated before she earns enough sales commission to repay the draw, she will have to repay the company for that money. It is important to keep track of employee draws to ensure that the employee repays the draw.

Another example where the company may allow individuals to draw on their payroll exists when the pay period is monthly. In this situation, many employers allow their employees to draw up to 30–40 percent of their wages at mid-month. Some organizations may not withhold taxes from the draw, and the employee will have the full amount of taxes withdrawn upon the next payroll.

Employers must be careful when allowing employees to draw against future wages. A written and signed authorization must be obtained from the employee that specifies when the draw will be deducted from the employee's future wages to avoid legal issues with deductions, such as wage garnishments, that could be affected by the draw.

EXAMPLE: SALARY PLUS DRAW, EMPLOYEE INELIGIBLE FOR COMMISSION

Scott Fay is a new salesperson with Bayfront Watercraft, hired on September 24. He has no dependents. He receives a base salary of $19,500 per year, paid biweekly, plus

(continued)

(concluded)

a 5 percent commission on sales once he achieves his sales quota of $20,000 during a pay period. During the pay period ending September 30, Scott closed $10,000 in sales, making him ineligible for a September commission. He is eligible to draw up to the minimum commission for the pay period, $20,000 × 5%, or $1,000. The payroll register would reflect his pay as follows:

Name	Filing Status	Dependents	Hourly Rate or Period Wage	Reg. Earnings	Draw	Commissions	Gross Earnings
Scott Fay	S	0	$750.00	$750.00	$1,000.00		$1,750.00

Period salary = $19,500/26 pay periods = $750.00
Commission draw = $20,000 × 0.05 = $1,000.00.

Incentive Stock Options (ISOs)

tupungato/Getty Images

Other employee compensation plans, known as *incentive stock options (ISOs)*, allow an employee to report a small base salary for tax purposes and be issued company stock that must be held for a certain period before being sold. In some instances, the stock option may be exercised after three months of employment, and in other cases, it may be after one year of employment. The purpose of ISO stock option plans is a deferral of taxes and salary liabilities for the employer and employee. This type of compensation is often found in executive pay packages.

In the class-action lawsuit *McElrath v. Uber Technologies,* the plaintiff stated that employees were offered an ISO as a significant part of the compensation package. The issue arose because Uber had accelerated the exercisability of its ISOs to make the compensation attractive. However, when employees exercised their options, the company refused to allow employees to receive the promised compensation on a tax-deferred basis consistent with an ISO. Instead, Uber changed the ISOs to nonqualified stock options (NSOs), which changed the taxation on employee compensation.

(Source: Classaction.org)

EXAMPLE: EXECUTIVE SALARY WITH ISO

Leo Wilde was hired as a regional manager with Amificat International. Amificat International's stock had a market price of $25 per share when Leo was hired. He was offered an annual salary of $78,000 paid biweekly and an ISO of 1,000 shares at $25 per share that could be exercised one year after his hire date.

Biweekly salary = $78,000/26 = $3,000

Note that the ISO, valued at $25,000 at the time of hire, may not be exercised for one year. The stock option's value would depend on the market price on the date that Leo exercised the stock option by selling his shares. In any case, the ISO does not appear on the payroll register but would be included in the employee's total compensation.

Combination Pay Methods

Stop & Check

1. Shelly Penzo, a service administrator, receives a base salary of $42,000 per year paid semimonthly, plus $100 commission for each service contract she sells to her customers. During a pay period, she sells five contracts. What is her gross pay for the period?

2. Adam Reininger is a new salesperson with S&D Music. He receives a base salary of $36,000 paid monthly. Company policy allows him to draw 35 percent of his salary on the 15th of each month. How much will Adam receive at mid-month if he elects to take a draw? How much will he receive at the end of the month if he takes the 35 percent draw?

3. Joy Mrowicki, an executive for Adarma Chemicals, receives an annual salary of $75,000 plus an additional 3 percent in an ISO. What is the amount of stock she receives annually? What is her total annual compensation?

BassittART/F+/Getty Images

LO 3-7   Explain Special Pay Situations

Compensation laws have many exceptions. According to the FLSA, every aspect of labor legislation, including minimum wage and overtime provisions, has its less common applications. The introduction of new types of knowledge-based employment during the 21st century and the continuance of more traditional agricultural tasks necessitate examining these special pay situations.

Compensatory Time

The FLSA allows public employees to receive *compensatory (comp) time*, often called "comp time," in place of overtime. According to section 3(s)(1)(c) of the FLSA, exempt public employees must receive comp time equal to 1.5 times the overtime hours worked. Therefore, if a public employee worked 5 hours of overtime, the comp time awarded must be 7.5 hours.

The private sector often misconstrues comp time. FLSA provisions for comp time are only for public-sector employees, such as government workers, law enforcement, and seasonally hired laborers. Unless specifically designated by a firm's policies, a private-sector employer is not required to offer comp time. Additionally, many private-sector employers offer comp time on a straight-line basis, meaning that they offer the same number of compensatory hours as the number of overtime hours worked. Firefighters, police, and other emergency workers may receive a maximum of 480 comp hours annually; other public-sector employees are eligible for up to 240 hours of comp time based upon union-negotiated contracts. Certain union comp time contracts will only cover specific peak periods for the work being performed.

When calculating an employee's gross pay, it is prudent to know any effects that a comp time award may have on overtime pay to ensure that the employee's compensation is accurate.

EXAMPLE: PUBLIC EMPLOYEE COMPENSATORY TIME

David Donahue works as an exempt employee of the federal government. In his work, he accrues 8 hours of overtime during a pay period when he completes additional work for an absent co-worker. According to FLSA regulations, David must receive 12 hours of comp time because he is not eligible for paid overtime as an exempt government employee.

On-Call Time

Some professions require employees to be available for work outside of normal working hours. This availability is known as *on-call time*, and two classes of on-call time exist On-call at the employer's premises and on-call away from the employer's premises.

- If the employee is required to remain at the employer's premises, the employee's freedom is restricted, and he or she **must** be compensated for the on-call time.

- If the employee is not restricted to the employer's premises for the on-call time, compensation is **not required.**

The town of Jay, Maine, began a pilot program in June 2020 during which firefighters received on-call pay to be available 10 hours per day. The purpose of the program was to provide fire department support during daytime hours. Each firefighter receives a stipend of $40 for being on-call in addition to regular pay. Despite the payroll cost, the response time improved, and services became more available for the surrounding towns.

(Source: Sun Journal)

In either case, company policy must be specific regarding the conditions of the on-call time. The number of hours specified for on-call compensation must be added to the employee's gross pay. Company policy should also be specific about the pay rate for the on-call time, especially if the pay rate differs from the employee's regular pay rate.

EXAMPLE: ON-CALL TIME

Kevin Gee works as a service representative for Built Strong, an equipment manufacturer. He earns $19.25/hour for a standard 40-hour workweek and is married, filing separately with two dependents under the age of 17. Built Strong requires that each service representative rotate on-call duties in one-week increments, during which they remain available for service calls outside of working hours but may otherwise engage in personal activities. During this on-call time, company policy stipulates that on-call service representatives receive 2 hours of regular pay for each on-call day. Kevin was on-call during the biweekly pay period ending February 25 and would receive 14 hours of additional straight-time pay for his on-call time. The payroll register would reflect the on-call pay as follows:

Name	Filing Status	Dependents	Hourly Rate or Period Wage	No. of Regular Hours	No. of On-Call Hours	Reg. Earnings	On-Call Earnings	Gross Earnings
Kevin Gee	MS	2<17	$19.25	80	14	$1,540.00	$269.50	$1,809.50

Robert Kneschke/Shutterstock

Sleep Time, Travel Time, and Wait Time

Although a growing trend toward telecommuting exists in the 21st century, employees have traditionally commuted to and from work. Travel to and from an office is not a compensable time; however, many employees do not work at a single location. Additionally, many employees travel for their employer's benefit for training or other business requirements. Similarly, employees may be required to wait by their employer, as in the case of a chauffeur or a bus driver. Other employees, such as firefighters or medical personnel, may be required to work 24-hour shifts and be given at least 5 hours of paid *sleep time* during that 24-hour period. An agreement between the employer and employee may exclude up to 8 hours if the employer provides furnished facilities for uninterrupted sleep.

According to FLSA, the guideline that assists in determining compensable activity in these three situations is if the activity is for the employer's benefit. Travel among customer- or business-related sites are compensable as *travel time* because it directly benefits the employer. Requiring a driver to wait as part of the job description also benefits the employer and is compensated as *wait time*. Travel from the employee's home to the office or the first customer site in the morning and returning home in the evening benefits the employee and is not compensable.

EXAMPLE: SLEEP TIME

Dan Morli is a first-year surgical resident at Mercy Hospital and is classified as a non-exempt employee who earns $124,000 per year, paid semimonthly. The standard workweek is 40 hours. He is single with no dependents. He works two 24-hour shifts per week in the regular course of his employment. His employer provides him a quiet sleeping area, per FLSA requirements. During a single 24-hour shift in the November 15 pay period, he sleeps 7 hours. According to FLSA guidelines, his pay may not be reduced for the first 5 hours that he sleeps. Dan's gross pay will reflect a 2-hour reduction for the additional sleep over the 5-hour requirement.

The hourly rate needs to be computed to determine the deduction for the excess sleep time: $124,000/(40 × 52) = $59.62

The payroll register would appear as follows:

Name	Filing Status	Dependents	Hourly Rate or Period Wage	Hourly Rate	Sleep Hours >5	Reg. Earnings	Less Excess Sleep Time	Gross Earnings
Dan Morli	S	0	$5,166.67	$59.62	2	$5,166.67	$(119.24)	$5,047.43

Note the inclusion of the sleep hours over five and the deduction. The purpose of tracking this information is to highlight specific issues with employee performance and related costs, which leads to stronger managerial control.

Image Source

Jury Duty

Employees may be summoned to serve on a jury for court cases. If an employee is required to serve jury duty, the pay given to employees for the time spent away from work in this capacity is at the employer's discretion. Some employers pay their employees their full compensation, while others pay a predetermined alternate amount. If an employee receives full compensation while on jury duty, the company may require the employee to return or reject the jury duty pay.

Vacation and Holiday Hours

Employees commonly have paid time off in the form of holiday or vacation time. Although no legislation exists for the number of holidays observed by a company or the number of vacation hours per employee, the time for these situations should be classified using the payroll register to ensure its annotation in the employees' files. The following examples show how vacation and holiday pay should be annotated.

EXAMPLE: HOLIDAY HOURS

Terri Granahan is an hourly employee at Purplemouse Company, earning $15.60 per hour, paid biweekly on a 40 hour per week basis. She has no dependents. She is eligible for two weeks of vacation per year. During one pay period, she took three days

(continued)

(concluded)

of vacation. The payroll register would appear as follows. Notice how the regular hours and the vacation hours are recorded in different columns.

Name	Filing Status	Dependents	Hourly Rate or Period Salary	No. of Regular Hours	No. of Vacation Hours	Gross Earnings
T. Granahan	S	0	$15.60	56	24	$1,248.00

A similar approach is taken with holiday pay.

In November 2021, Purplemouse Company has holidays on Thanksgiving and the Friday after Thanksgiving. A different employee, Sam Jarvis, is a nonexempt salaried employee earning $39,000 annually, paid biweekly. Same is married filing jointly and has two dependents under the age of 17. Sam works 5 hours overtime during this holiday period. In this case, the annual salary must be converted to hourly pay to determine the amount of overtime pay, although the regular hours and holiday hours remain at the period salary.

Annual Salary = $39,000/ (52 weeks × 40 hours) = $18.75 per hour

Overtime pay = $18.75/hour × 1.5 = $28.13 (rounded) × 5 hours = $140.63

Name	Filing Status	Dependents	Hourly Rate or Period Salary	No. of Regular Hours	No. of Overtime Hours	No. of Holiday Hours	Gross Earnings
S. Jarvis	MJ	2	$1,500.00	64	5	16	$1,640.63

Subminimum Wage Situations

wavebreakmedia/Shutterstock

Tipped employees are not the only workers who may legally receive compensation lower than the minimum wage. Other specific classes of employees may receive an hourly wage that is less than the FLSA minimum wage.

A 1996 amendment to the FLSA, described in **Section 6(g)**, allows workers younger than the age of 20 to be paid a minimum wage of $4.25 per hour, but only for the first 90 calendar days of employment.

Note that overtime worked by employees who are paid at subminimum wage rates may not be less than the federal minimum wage.

EXAMPLE: YOUNG EMPLOYEE

Cady Horn is a new employee of The Big Chicken, a fast-food restaurant in Glendale, Arizona, where new employees are paid minimum wage. Cady is 18 years of age and is single with no dependents. During the weekly pay period ending July 18, she worked 37 hours. The payroll register would appear as follows:

Name	Filing Status	Hourly Rate or Period Wage	No. of Regular Hours	Reg. Earnings	Gross Earnings
Cady Horn	S-0	$4.25	37	$157.25	$157.25

An employer may obtain a certificate to pay a worker with disabilities related to the work performed an amount less than the minimum wage. According to **Section 14(c)** of the FLSA, employers must obtain a certificate to pay less than the minimum wage.

EXAMPLE: DISABLED WORKER

Christi Snow is employed as a call-center representative with OEC Dispatch in Bend, Oregon. She is disabled due to a hearing impairment, and OEC Dispatch has obtained a certificate under section 14(c) of the FLSA to pay Christi $10.75/hour, which is less than the Oregon minimum wage of $12/hour. During the weekly pay period ending March 10, Christi worked 44 hours, 4 hours of overtime. She is single with two dependents. The payroll register for the period would appear as follows:

Name	Filing Status	Hourly Rate or Period Wage	No. of Regular Hours	No. of Overtime Hours	Reg. Earning	Overtime Earnings	Gross Earnings
Christi Snow	S-2	$10.75	40	4	$430.00	$64.50	$494.50

Full-time students in the employ of retail establishments, agriculture, colleges, and universities may receive a wage that is 85 percent of the federal minimum wage under FLSA Section 14(c). Like disabled employees, the employer must obtain a certificate authorizing the sub-minimum wage.

EXAMPLE: FULL-TIME STUDENT WAGE

Kay Stone works in the café at Valparaiso University in Valparaiso, Indiana. She is a full-time student at the university and is 20 years old. According to the FLSA, she may receive 85 percent of the minimum wage.

Indiana minimum wage: $7.25/hour

Full-time student wage = $7.25/hour × 0.85 = $6.16/hour

In her employment at the café, Katie may legally be paid $6.16 per hour while she is a full-time student. During the week of May 4, she worked 35 hours. She is single with no dependents. The payroll register would appear as follows:

Name	Filing Status	Hourly Rate or Period Wage	No. of Regular Hours	Reg. Earning	Gross Earnings
Kay Stone	S-0	$6.16	35	$215.60	$215.60

According to Section 14(a) of the FLSA, student learners in vocational education programs may be paid at a rate of 75 percent of the federal minimum wage. Similar to situations involving disabled employees, the employer must obtain a certificate authorizing the sub-minimum wage.

EXAMPLE: STUDENT WORKER IN VOCATIONAL EDUCATION PROGRAM

Ben Yoo is enrolled at Middlebury High School in Maine and is taking a shop class as part of his program. Ben is 16 and is single with no dependents. He works for Vining's Cabinets as an apprentice woodworker. After obtaining a certificate from the U.S. Department of Labor's Wage and Hour National Certification Team, Vining's Cabinets pays Ben an hourly wage of $9 because of his enrollment in the shop class his high

(continued)

(concluded)

school. During the weekly pay period ending December 18, Ben worked 36 hours. The payroll register would reflect his pay as follows:

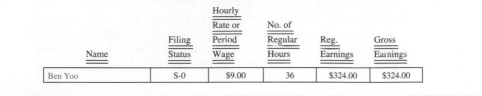

Name	Filing Status	Hourly Rate or Period Wage	No. of Regular Hours	Reg. Earnings	Gross Earnings
Ben Yoo	S-0	$9.00	36	$324.00	$324.00

Olena Yakobchuk/Shutterstock

Nonqualified Deferred Compensation

Certain employees may be subject to the nonqualified deferred compensation provisions of IRS Code section 409(a). Nonqualified deferred compensation pertains to employees who earn compensation in one period but elect to receive it later. A common example of this practice involves teachers who work during the nine-month academic year but elect to receive compensation for 12 months. Under section 409(a), this type of compensation is taxed like any other employee pay.

Pension Payments

Employers occasionally offer pension plans to their employees. The percent of employees who participate in employer-sponsored pensions has decreased due to the availability of alternate retirement plans (401(k), 403(b), etc.), and pension funding has experienced shortfalls among both private and governmental employers. When the pension enters the payout period, the retired employee receives their pension less any federal tax due. FICA taxes do not apply to pension plan payments.

Retroactive Pay

If an employee is due retroactive pay ("back pay") because of compensation increases or labor union negotiations, the wages must be issued at the earliest time, and all applicable taxes are due. To receive back pay, the FLSA has three methods available:

1. The Department of Labor's Wage and Hour Division may provide supervision for the payment.
2. The Secretary of Labor may bring a lawsuit for back pay plus an equal amount of damages.
3. The employee may initiate a lawsuit for the back pay *plus* an equal amount of damages *plus* attorney's fees and court costs.

It is important to note that the statute of limitations for back pay lawsuits is two years. However, if willful nonpayment can be proven, the statute of limitations is three years.

In early 2019, the Gilroy (California) Federation of Paraeducators agreed to grant pay raises to the educational support staff retroactive to July 1, 2017. This pay raise was spread incrementally over two fiscal years to spread the impact on the school district's budget.

(Source: *Gilroy Dispatch*)

Wages for Deceased Employees

If an employee dies while a current employee of a firm, it is important to understand the payroll implications associated with gross pay. IRS guidelines stipulate that wages earned before the employee's death must be paid as accurately as possible to reflect the amount of work performed. A special note about deceased employee pay is that the employee's pay if issued specifically in a check form may need to be reissued to the deceased employee's estate. In many states, the pay for a deceased employee goes to the surviving spouse or children (if no surviving spouse exists) as long as the pay is below state-mandated thresholds.

What Is the Correct Pay?

Stop & Check

1. Alex Longwith is a nonexempt employee of The Silver Club. He works 10 hours of overtime during a pay period and requests that he receive compensatory time instead of overtime pay. The Silver Club's overtime policy states that compensatory time may be offered at 1.5 times the number of hours worked more than 40. His employer grants his request and offers him 10 hours of compensatory time. How much comp time should Alex receive? Explain.

2. Stacy Albom is a student in a vocational program at a cosmetology school. She accepts employment as a shampooer at Cuts & Styles Hair Salon in Alabama. The agreement between the school and the salon is that students receive the student-learner minimum wage. How much should Stacy be paid per hour?

Trends to Watch

EMPLOYEE COMPENSATION

Employee compensation tends to be a hot topic because it affects people on a personal level. Some developments since 2019 in employee compensation include the following:

- Increased diligence in overtime tracking and compensation following a lawsuit involving large companies.
- New types of incentive pay increase employee engagement, including merchandise rewards, additional company benefits, and other nonmonetary awards.
- Discussions of the legality of differential pay levels for travel time by nonexempt employees.
- Discussions about gaps in wages between people with and without a college education.
- Increased minimum wage for exempt employees.
- Employee pay affects from work from home agreements.
- Expansion of racial and gender pay equality initiatives.
- The widespread use of digital wallets to transfer payment directly to employees from employers via smartphone.
- Variable pay situations that award incentives for workgroups and team performance.
- A federal minimum wage increase to $15/hour by 2026.

Summary of Gross Pay Computation

Gross pay is the employee's compensation before taxes and other withholdings are deducted; net pay is the amount of money an employee receives after taxes and other deductions are subtracted. We discussed the different types of pay computation methods, including salary, hourly, commission, and piece-rate pay. Gross pay is complex, and various combinations exist to meet the needs of the traditional and the gig economies.

We looked at the effect of FLSA provisions and the applicability of different compensation methods and offered examples of some job classifications that could be compensated using different methods. We discussed using a payroll register in computing gross pay and explored the concepts of the total, prove, and rule to ensure accurate computation of gross pay.

We explored a variety of situations involving overtime pay and discussed the computations for different pay bases. We concluded with a discussion of special compensation situations, including on-call time, time spent unoccupied for the employer's benefit, and situations in which an employee may receive less than the FLSA minimum wage. The conclusion had an explanation of retroactive pay and other less-common pay situations.

Key Points

- Gross pay is the total amount earned by an employee before the deductions for taxes or other withholdings.
- Employees may be subject to the wage and hour provisions of the FLSA (nonexempt), or they may not (exempt), depending on the type of job and employee duties.
- Nonexempt hourly employees are compensated on the basis that recognizes an economic connection between work performed and wages paid.
- Nonexempt salaried employees work a fixed number of working hours per week and receive overtime compensation.
- Exempt employees receive a fixed salary and may work more hours than their nonexempt colleagues.
- Commission-based pay connects employee compensation with sales revenue.
- Piece-rate pay compensates employees based on the manufacturing or completion of goods or services.
- The payroll register is an integral tool to ensure the accuracy of payroll computations, especially in combination pay situations.
- Employees who work on a commission basis may have the option to draw against future earnings.
- ISOs are a means of offering compensation on a tax-deferred basis connected to the market price of the company's stock.
- Compensatory time is legally required for public-sector exempt employees and may be offered to private-sector employees at the employer's discretion.
- Overtime pay is computed according to the IRS guidelines, as appropriate to the employee's pay base.
- Employees may be compensated when they are unoccupied if they are required to be available for the employer's benefit.
- Retroactive "back pay" and pension pay are situations requiring additional care in processing to avoid lawsuits.
- In certain circumstances, employees may receive less than the FLSA minimum wage.

Vocabulary

Combination pay
Commission
Compensatory (comp)
 time
Draw
Eight and Eighty
 (8 and 80)
Exempt
Gross pay
Hourly
Hundredth-hour system

Incentive stock options
 (ISOs)
Minimum wage
Net pay
Nonexempt
On-call time
Overtime
Payroll register
Piece rate
Prove
Quarter-hour system

Rule
Salary
Sleep time
Time cards
Tip credit
Tipped employee
Tipped wages
Total
Travel time
Wait time

Review Questions

1. How is overtime pay computed for nonexempt, salaried workers?

2. When do overtime rates apply?

3. How does minimum wage affect commission employees?

4. How does the tipped minimum wage differ from the FLSA minimum wage?

5. What types of occupations are typically salaried?

6. What is an ISO, and how does it affect employee pay?

7. What is the difference between a salary and a draw?

8. How is overtime computed for piece-rate employees?

9. In what situations could a salaried employee receive overtime pay?

10. What is the primary difference between commission work and piece-rate work?

11. In what situations might an employee draw money against his or her future pay?

12. What is the difference between quarter-hour and hundredth-hour pay?

13. Why are companies moving toward the hundredth-hour system?

14. What is comp time?

15. Under what circumstances may an employee receives compensation for on-call time?

16. When are wait time, travel time, and sleep time compensable?

17. Aside from tipped employees, under what circumstances may an employee receive less than the FLSA minimum wage?

18. What is one of the three methods for employees to receive retroactive pay?

19. What amount did the Final Rule stipulate as to the minimum wage for salaried workers?

Exercises Set A

E3-1A.
LO 3-1

Thomas Wilson is a minimum wage worker in Nevada. He is contemplating a move to another state. Which of the following states would be the most favorable in terms of the highest minimum wage?
1. Idaho
2. California
3. Utah
4. Arizona

E3-2A.

LO 3-1

FLSA provisions always cover certain types of businesses. Which of the following businesses are always covered by FLSA? (Select all that apply.)

1. Fruit stands selling only locally obtained goods that conduct no interstate business.
2. A school for children with learning disabilities.
3. A privately run hospital.
4. A Social Security Administration branch office.

E3-3A.

LO 3-1

Ashley Woods is a tipped employee in Washington, DC. What is the minimum tipped wage for her location?

1. $2.13/hour
2. $3.25/hour
3. $4.75/hour
4. $5.00/hour

E3-4A.

LO 3-1

Alfredo Gonzalez, a waiter at the Seven Wonders Restaurant in Honolulu, Hawaii, receives the tipped minimum wage. During a 40-hour workweek, how much must he earn in tips to meet the minimum wage requirement?

1. $30.00
2. $54.00
3. $95.20
4. $125.30

E3-5A.

LO 3-2

Marty Burgess works for Hyrolated Sports. His compensation is based on sales of store products to customers. Which type of pay basis represents Marty's pay?

1. Piece rate
2. Hourly
3. Commission
4. Salary

E3-6A.

LO 3-3

Lana Reid is an accounting clerk at Tenity Enterprises who is paid $18.15 per hour. During a week's pay period, she worked 39 hours and 41 minutes. Based on a hundredth-hour pay method, what is her gross pay for the period? (Round the final answer to two decimal places.)

1. $726.00
2. $721.46
3. $716.93
4. $720.25

E3-7A.

LO 3-4

According to the FLSA, what is the basis used to determine overtime worked for standard nonexempt workers?

1. The 8 and 80 rule.
2. The excess over 40 hours during any pay period.
3. The excess over 40 hours in seven consecutive days.
4. The excess over 8 hours in a 24-hour period.

E3-8A.

LO 3-4

Eugene Torres works in a shared role for Multiglass Computers. He works in both the programming and the research departments for the company and splits his time equally in both roles. Eugene is paid $20 per hour in the programming department and $28 per hour in the research department. When he works overtime in the research department, what is his pay rate?

1. $30 per hour
2. $36 per hour
3. $42 per hour
4. $48 per hour

E3-9A.

LO 3-5

Of the items in the following list, which one(s) should appear in a payroll register? (Select all that apply.)

1. Name
2. Home address
3. Shifts worked
4. Hours worked

E3-10A.

LO 3-5

Jeremiah Watson is a salaried, exempt employee with Megadepartment Stores. He is single with one dependent under 17 and earns $35,500 per year. Complete the payroll register for the biweekly pay period ending March 8, 2021, with a pay date of March 12, 2021.

P/R End Date:									
Check Date:						Company Name:			
Name	Filing Status	Dependents	Hourly Rate or Period Wage	No. of Regular Hours	No. of Overtime Hours	Reg. Earnings	Overtime Earnings	Gross Earnings	

E3-11A.

LO 3-6

Latanya Brown is an employee of Giant Computers, where her job responsibilities include selling computers and software to customers. Latanya is married filing jointly with two dependents under 17. She receives an annual salary of $42,000 and receives a 3 percent commission on all sales. During the semimonthly pay period ending September 30, 2021, Latanya sold $20,000 of computers and software. Complete the payroll register for the September 30 pay period with a pay date of October 5.

P/R End Date:									
Check Date:						Company Name:			
Name	Filing Status	Dependents	Hourly Rate or Period Wage	No. of Regular Hours	No. of Overtime Hours	Commissions	Reg. Earnings	Overtime Earnings	Gross Earnings

E3-12A.

LO 3-7

Jude Sizemore Is a full-time student at Sioux City College in Sioux City, Iowa, where he works in the library. What is the minimum hourly wage that he may receive?

1. $7.25 per hour
2. $6.50 per hour
3. $6.16 per hour
4. $5.44 per hour

Problems Set A

P3-1A.

LO 3-3

Brian Packer worked the following schedule: Monday, 9 hours; Tuesday, 7 hours 30 minutes; Wednesday, 8 hours 48 minutes; Thursday, 8 hours 25 minutes; Friday, 8 hours. The employer pays overtime for all time worked in excess of 40 hours per week. Complete the following table. Determine Brian's total time worked according to the (a) quarter-hour method and (b) the hundredth-hour method. Which is the more favorable method for Brian, quarter-hour or hundredth-hour?

	Quarter-Hour Time	Hundredth-Hour Time	More Favorable Method
B. Packer			

P3-2A.

LO 3-2

Bobby Howard is a salaried exempt employee at Coric Industries. He is married filing jointly with two dependents under 17. His contract stipulates a 40-hour workweek at $47,500 per year. During the week ending November 27, there was a company-paid holiday for one day. Calculate Bobby's weekly pay. Round period wages to five decimal points.

Name	Filing Status	Dependents	Hourly Rate or Period Wage	No. of Regular Hours	No. of Holiday Hours	Reg. Earnings	Holiday Earnings	Gross Earnings

P3-3A.
LO 3-2

Cheryl Bryant completed designing 22 custom cakes on her 18-cake contract as an employee of Frontier Wedding Planners. There is a bonus earned if the individual exceeds 145 percent of her piece contract. How many cakes must Cheryl complete in the remainder of the week to receive the bonus?

P3-4A.
LO 3-5

Morris Lann works for Talbert Electronics. He is a shared employee; he works in the manufacturing department and has been trained to work the sales counter when needed. He was asked to work the sales counter for two days, 5 hours each day during other employees' vacations. When he works in the manufacturing department, he earns $17.75 per hour. Morris earns a $1.50 pay differential for working the sales counter. He worked a total of 38 hours and 38 minutes during the week. Morris is married filing joint with no dependents. Compute Morris's pay for the week ending August 20 using the hundredth-hour system. (Use a separate line for each job classification.)

Name	Filing Status	Dependents	Hourly Rate or Period Salary	No. of Regular Hours	Reg. Earnings
Total Pay					

P3-5A.
LO 3-3

Marcell Teague submitted a pay card reflecting the following hours worked at Kicy Inc. He earns $16.02 per hour. The company pays overtime only on hours worked exceeding 40 per week. The company is considering changing from quarter-hour to hundredth-hour time collection. Under the current quarter-hour system, each time the employee clocks in or out, the time is rounded to the nearest quarter-hour. Calculate Marcell's time for both the quarter-hour and hundredth-hour systems. (Round your intermediate calculations and final answers to two decimal places.)

In	Out	In	Out	Total Hours with Quarter-Hour	Total Hours with Hundredth-Hour
8:00	11:22	12:17	5:22		
7:29	12:30	1:45	4:10		
9:12	11:45	12:28	3:36		
8:00	11:00	12:02	5:00		

What is Marcell's total pay in a quarter-hour system?_____
What is Marcell's total pay in a hundredth-hour system? _____

P3-6A.
LO 3-4

Gail Schneeweis is a nurse at Central City Hospital. She is paid $32.50 per hour and has a 40-hour standard workweek. During the biweekly pay period from January 11-24, she worked a total of 87 hours. What is her gross pay?

P3-7A.

LO 3-5

Terry McNutt, a single employee with two dependents under the age of 17, is paid $12 per hour and receives a commission on net sales. He does not receive a commission until his net sales exceed $150,000. Once the minimum net sales are reached, he receives a 4 percent commission on his sales at Skidoo Sports. During the week of January 24, he sold $87,000 of ski equipment; however, he had $2,250 of returns from the prior week's sales. Company policy requires that commissions on sales returns are deducted from the employee's pay, regardless of current commission earnings. Compute Terry's gross pay for the 40-hour weekly pay period.

Name	Filing Status	Dependents	Hourly Rate	No. of Regular Hours	Reg. Earnings	Commissions	Gross Earnings

P3-8A.

LO 3-1, 3-2

Geoffrey Young, an outside sales representative for Marshall Communications, receives a 20 percent commission on all new marketing packages he sells in his sales territory. During the week of April 5, he sold $9,700 of new subscriptions and worked 40 hours.

What is his gross pay?_____

Is he subject to minimum wage laws?_____

Why or why not?_____

P3-9A.

LO 3-1, 3-2

Telemarketers receive $15 commission on all new customers that sign up for cell phone service through Movill Networks. Each telemarketer works 40 hours. The company ran a competition this week to see who could sign up the largest number of new customers, and the winner would get a bonus of $75. Because these employees are paid solely on commission, the employer must ensure that they earn the federal minimum wage for 40 hours each week. Compute the gross pay for each of the following outbound sales representatives.

Employee	Number of New Customers Signed	Total Commission	Difference between Commission and Minimum Pay (if the minimum is not met)	Total Gross Pay
S. McCulloch	25			
F. Odell	18			
S. Heller	23			
V. Caro	15			

P3-10A.

LO 3-1, 3-2

Each of the following workers is piece-rate workers at Golden Boats in Connecticut. If the employees have a standard 40-hour workweek, what is their effective hourly wage? Based on the state's minimum wage in Connecticut, calculate each employee's minimum weekly pay. What is the difference the employer must pay between the calculated gross pay and the calculated state's minimum pay, if any? (Reminder: Divide gross pay by 40 hours to determine the hourly wage.)

Worker	Number of Items	Rate per Item	Gross Pay	Gross Pay/ 40 Hours	Minimum Pay	Difference to Be Paid by the Employer
J. Crocker	25 boat hulls	$25				
B. McMurtrie	150 seat covers	$10				
H. Jacoby	15 steering mechanisms	$24				

P3-11A.
LO 3-4

Damien Carranza is a nonexempt employee of Verent Enterprises where he is a salesperson, earning a base annual salary of $30,000 with a standard 40-hour workweek. He earns a 3 percent commission on all sales during the pay period. During the weekly pay period ending August 21, Damien closed $25,000 in sales and worked 4 hours overtime. What is his gross pay for the period?

P3-12A.
LO 3-1, 3-2, 3-4

Nigel McCloskey is a waiter at Albicious Foods in South Carolina. He is single with one other dependent. He receives the standard tipped hourly wage. During the week ending October 22, 20XX, he worked 44 hours and received $210 in tips. Calculate his gross pay, assuming his tips are included in the overtime rate determination.

Name	Filing Status	Dependents	Reg. Hourly Rate	Overtime Rate	No. of Regular Hours	No. of Overtime Hours	Reg. Earnings	Tips	Overtime Earnings	Gross Earnings

Does Albicious Foods need to contribute to Nigel's wages to meet FLSA requirements? _____

If so, how much should be contributed? _____

P3-13A.
LO 3-5

Stephanie Parker is a salaried, nonexempt administrator for Forise Industries and is paid biweekly. Her annual salary is $63,000, and her standard workweek is 45 hours. During the pay period ending February 5, 2021, she worked 8 hours overtime. She is married filing jointly with two dependents under the age of 17. Complete the following payroll register for Stephanie's pay. (Round intermediate calculations to two decimal points.)

Name	Filing Status	Dependents	Period Salary	Hourly Rate	Overtime Rate	No. of Regular Hours	No. of Overtime Hours	Reg. Earnings	Overtime Earnings	Gross Earnings

P3-14A.
LO 3-7

Rico Musgrove is an 18-year-old worker in the receiving department of Trynix Inc. in St. Paul, Minnesota. He notices that he received $170.00 gross pay for 40 hours of work on his first paycheck. Did his employer pay him correctly? Explain.

Exercises Set B

E3-1B.
LO 3-1

Lynne Everton is a minimum wage worker in Oklahoma. She is contemplating moving to a state with a more favorable minimum wage. Which of the following states should she choose?
1. Texas
2. Arkansas
3. Louisiana
4. New Mexico

E3-2B.

LO 3-1

Which one of the following workers are covered by FLSA provisions? (Select all that apply.)
1. Factory manager for an international company.
2. Part-time babysitter earning $1,000 annually.
3. Professional chauffeur earning $25,000 annually.
4. Assistant fire chief for a small town.

E3-3B.

LO 3-1

Adrienne Soeur is a tipped employee at Wild Waves in Maine. What is the minimum tipped wage for her area, assuming she receives in excess of $30 in tips per pay period?
1. $9.35/hour
2. $2.13/hour
3. $6.08/hour
4. $8.25/hour

E3-4B.

LO 3-1

Dan Busby is a waiter at the Snowtop Diner in Vermont. He earns the tipped minimum wage. During a 40-hour work-week in February 2021, how much must he earn in tips to satisfy the minimum wage requirement (without consideration of the tip credit)?
1. $85.20
2. $235.00
3. $190.00
4. $349.20

E3-5B.

LO 3-2

Austin Sherman is an employee of Divacee Designs. He is an interior designer paid based on the number and complexity of the customer designs he generates. What pay basis most accurately describes his compensation?
1. Hourly
2. Commission
3. Piece-rate
4. Salary

E3-6B.

LO 3-3

Doreen George, a stocker at Dender Factory Outlet, is paid hourly and earns $12.45 per hour. During a one-week period, she worked 39 hours and 19 minutes. How much would her gross pay be under the quarter-hour system? (Round your final answer to two decimal places.)
1. $485.55
2. $488.66
3. $489.49
4. $491.78

E3-7B.

LO 3-4

Johnny Clark is a tipped employee at Pyrolia Pizza. What are the two methods his employer may use to determine his overtime compensation?
1. Compute gross pay based on the minimum cash wage plus tips.
2. Compute gross pay based on an average of the minimum cash wage and the maximum tip credit.
3. Compute gross pay based on the minimum cash wage, excluding tips.
4. Compute gross pay based on the minimum cash wage multiplied by the overtime rate (i.e., 1.5).

E3-8B.

LO 3-4

Jacques Beasley is a salaried nonexempt accounting clerk for Supplies Enterprises contracted to work 40 hours per week. How should his overtime be determined, according to FLSA?
1. Any hours worked in excess of 40 during a consecutive 7-day period.
2. Any hours worked in excess of 45 during a consecutive 7-day period.
3. Any hours worked in excess of 80 during a consecutive 14-day period.
4. Any hours worked in excess of 45 during a consecutive 14-day period.

E3-9B.
LO 3-5

Of the following items listed, which ones should appear in a payroll register? (Select all that apply.)
1. Gross pay
2. Hourly rate
3. Period ending date
4. Office number

E3-10B.
LO 3-4, 3-5

Eric Moser is an hourly employee working for Plains Poultry. He is single with no dependents and earns $16.25 per hour. During a biweekly pay period ending February 20, 2021, he worked 88.5 hours. Complete the payroll register with the period's information assuming a 40-hour week. (Note: round overtime rate computation to three decimal places. All earnings should be rounded to two decimal places.)

Name	Filing Status	Hourly Rate	Overtime Rate	No. of Regular Hours	No. of Overtime Hours	Regular Earnings	Overtime Earnings	Gross Earnings

E3-11B.
LO 3-6

Paula Warren is an Arctic Outdoor Gear employee, where she earns a base salary of $27,200 plus an 8 percent commission on all sales. She is married filing joint with four dependents, three under 17 years of age and one other. During the biweekly pay period ended June 16, 2021, Paula made $15,000 in sales. Complete the payroll register for the pay period.

Name	Filing Status	Period Salary	Sales	Reg. Earnings	Commission Earnings	Gross Earnings

E3-12B.
LO 3-7

Sherrill Pullman is 18 years of age and is a new employee of Camicero Bank in Hendersonville, Tennessee. What is the minimum hourly wage that she may receive during the first 90 days of employment?
1. $9.47 per hour
2. $2.13 per hour
3. $7.25 per hour
4. $4.25 per hour

Problems Set B

P3-1B.
LO 3-3

Gail Richter worked the following schedule: Monday, 7 hours 42 minutes; Tuesday, 8 hours 23 minutes; Wednesday, 9 hours 28 minutes; Thursday, 8 hours 12 minutes; Friday, 8 hours 6 minutes. The employer pays overtime in accordance with FLSA regulations. Determine Gail's total time worked according to the (a) quarter-hour method and (b) the hundredth-hour method. Which is the more favorable method for Gail, quarter-hour or hundredth-hour?

	Quarter-Hour Time	Hundredth-Hour Time	More Favorable Method
R. Trout			

P3-2B.
LO 3-2

Solvegi Jameson is a salaried exempt employee at Big State College with a contract that stipulates 35 hours per week at $57,000 per year. She is married filing joint with two dependents under 17. The pay period ending November 26 contained two company-paid holidays. Calculate Solvegi's biweekly pay based on a standard five-day workweek. Round wages to five decimal points. (Hint: Determine Solvegi's hourly wage to determine holiday pay.)

Name	Filing Status	Dependents	Period Salary	Hourly Rate	No. of Regular Hours	No. of Holiday Hours	Reg. Earnings	Holiday Earnings	Gross Earnings

P3-3B.
LO 3-2

Doris Black completed 1,750 pieces on her 2,000-piece contract for Make It Work. There is a bonus earned if the individual exceeds 115 percent of the piece contract. How many more pieces must Doris complete in the remainder of the pay period to receive the bonus?

P3-4B.
LO 3-4, 3-5

Katrina Hughes is a shared employee; she works in the accounting department and has been trained to work at the front desk in times of need. During one weekly pay period, she was asked to work at the front desk on four days for 5 hours each day. When she works in the accounting department, she earns $17.26 per hour and earns $13.75 per hour for working at the front desk. She worked a total of 45 hours during the week. Complete the payroll register using separate lines for each job classification, and place the overtime on her accounting department hours.

Name	Filing Status	Hourly Rate	No. of Regular Hours	No. of Overtime Hours	Reg. Earnings	Overtime Earnings	Gross Earnings

P3-5B.
LO 3-3

Kirk McAllister earns $15.30 per hour at Jolly Creamery. Compute his pay under both the hundredth-hour and quarter-hour systems. The company is considering switching from a quarter-hour method to a hundredth-hour method. Kirk submitted the following time card (Hint: convert times to a 24-hour clock for ease of computation):

In	Out	In	Out	Total Hours with Quarter-Hour	Total Hours with Hundredth-Hour
8:08	11:54	12:47	4:52		
9:04	12:23	1:11	5:07		
7:45	11:48	12:52	4:21		
7:57	12:18	1:06	5:17		

Kirk's total pay in the hundredth-hour system: _____
Kirk's total pay in a quarter-hour system: _____
Which is the most beneficial for Kirk?: _____

P3-6B.
LO 3-4

Shelli Quintanilla is the concierge at Hotel Amize where she is a non-exempt employee earning $18 per hour plus a $250 biweekly bonus based on customer reviews. During the pay period of November 27–December 10, she worked 85 hours and earned the entire bonus. What is her gross pay for the pay period, assuming a 40-hour standard workweek?

P3-7B.
LO 3-4, 3-5

Dan Nicholes is a commission-based employee who is married filing jointly with two other dependents. He is paid $17.25/hour and receives a 7 percent commission on net sales. He does not receive commissions until his net sales exceed $60,000 during a weekly period at KC Medical Marketing. For the week ending June 4, 2021, he worked 48 hours and sold $75,000 of medicinal supplies. Compute his gross pay for the week.

Name	Filing Status	Dependents	Hourly Rate or Period Wage	No. of Regular Hours	No. of Overtime Hours	Commissions	Reg. Earnings	Overtime Earnings	Gross Earnings

P3-8B.

LO 3-1, 3-2

Lacie Bingham, an outside sales representative for Redoo Insurance, receives 4 percent commission on all new policies she receives in her sales territory. During the pay period ending April 16, she sold $150,000 of new policies and worked 40 hours.

What is her gross pay? _____

Is she subject to minimum wage laws? _____

Why or why not?_____

P3-9B.

LO 3-1, 3-2

Outbound sales representatives at Alindu Magazines in Arizona receive a $20 commission on all new customers they sign up for new magazine subscriptions. Each Outbound sales representative works 40 hours. During a weekly competition, the Outbound sales representative who sold the most subscriptions was awarded a $125 bonus. Because these employees are paid solely on commission, the employer must ensure that they earn the federal minimum wage for 40 hours each week. Compute the gross pay for each of the following Outbound sales representatives and the difference when the commission pay is less than the gross pay at minimum wage.

Employee	New Customers Signed	Total Commission	Gross Pay at Minimum Wage	Difference between Commission and Minimum Pay (if the minimum is not met)
H. Meyers	35			
M. Jansen	19			
K. Bartels	42			
T. Macklin	29			

P3-10B.

LO 3-1, 3-2

For each of the piece-rate workers at Perigen Snowsports, determine gross pay. If the employees have a standard 37.5-hour workweek, determine their effective hourly rate. Based on the minimum wage for New Hampshire, what is the minimum wage they must receive each week? If they are not receiving the FLSA minimum wage for the pay period, what is the difference that must be paid by the employer? (Remember: Effective hourly rate equals the gross pay divided by 37.5 hours.)

Worker	Number of Items	Rate per Item	Gross Pay	Gross Pay/ 37.5 Hours	Minimum Pay	Difference to Be Paid by the Employer
S. Jackson	25 snowboards	$9.00				
A. Foster	30 helmets	$7.75				
L. Howard	80 bindings	$4.50				

P3-11B.

LO 3-4

Latoyia Judge is a piece-rate employee at Anible Computers. She receives $30 for each desktop computer that she assembles and has a standard 40-hour workweek. During the weekly pay period ending December 15, she completed the assembly of 48 computers and worked 44 hours, all of which are productive hours. What is her gross pay for the period?

P3-12B.

LO 3-1, 3-2

Parker Thomas is the concierge at the Trans-Canada Resort in Michigan. He is single with one other dependent. He receives the standard tipped hourly wage for the state. During the week ending June 4, 2021, he worked 40 hours and received $105 in tips. Compute Parker's pay for the period.

Name	Filing Status	Dependents	Hourly Rate or Period Wage	No. of Regular Hours	Reg. Earnings	Tips	Gross Earnings

Does the Trans-Canada Resort need to contribute to Parker's wages to meet FLSA minimum wage requirements?_____
If so, how much must the employer contribute?_____

P3-13B.
LO 3-5

Dennis Murphy is a salaried, nonexempt administrative assistant for Dionti Investments and is paid semimonthly. He is married filing joint with five dependents under 17. His annual salary is $65,000, and his standard work-week is 37.5 hours. During the pay period, he worked 10 hours overtime. Compute Dennis's gross pay for the period ending August 20, 2021.

Name	Filing Status	Period Salary	Hourly Rate	Overtime Rate	No.of Overtime Hours	Reg. Earnings	Overtime Earnings	Gross Earnings

P3-14B.
LO 3-7

Annie Adams is a 19-year-old accounting clerk with Quijen Accounting Solutions. During the first month of her employment at Quijen, she noticed that she received $369.75 for her first biweekly pay covering 87 regular hours. Did the employer pay her correctly? Explain.

Critical Thinking

3-1. West Virginia State University has a policy of hiring students to work in its bookstores and cafeterias. Assuming that 138 students work for the university at minimum wage rates, what is the total amount of pay they will receive for a biweekly pay period, assuming each work 30 hours per week?

3-2. Thomas Campbell owns Veiled Wonders, a firm that makes window treatments. Some merchandise is custom-made to customer specifications, and some are mass-produced in standardized measurements. He has production workers who work primarily on standardized blinds and some employees who work on custom products on an as-needed basis. How should he structure his pay methods for his production workers?

In the Real World: Scenario for Discussion

Many states offer incentives to hire disabled individuals. When doing so, the employer must receive a specific waiver allowing them to pay sub-minimum wage. This can be a great outreach for the employer in assisting the disabled community to obtain independence and a sense of self-worth.

Review two state agencies, determine the wages that may be paid to the disabled workers, and what benefits two different states have. What federal incentives are there for hiring disabled workers?

Internet Activities

3-1. Using a search engine such as Google, Yahoo, or Bing, search "commission-based pay." Sites such as the Society for Human Resource Management (www.shrm.com) have many articles about commission-based pay and workplace cases. Choose a case and find out as much as you can about the company involved. Why do you think that commission-based pay is such a popular topic among human resource professionals?

3-2. Go to www.accountingtools.com/podcasts and look for payroll-related podcasts. Once you have listened to one or more podcasts, what do you feel was the most interesting information you learned?

3-3. Want to learn more about the concepts in this chapter? Check out

www.dol.gov/whd/minwage/america.htm

www.flsa.com/coverage.html

http://webapps.dol.gov/elaws/otcalculator.htm

3-4. Would you like to watch a video to learn more about FLSA treatment of minimum wage, hours worked, and overtime? Check out the following links:

Topic 2: Minimum Wage

Topic 4: Hours Worked

Topic 5: Overtime

Continuing Payroll Project: Prevosti Farms and Sugarhouse

The first day of work for Prevosti Farms and Sugarhouse for all employees is February 1, 2021. February 5 is the end of the first pay period and includes work completed during the week of February 1–5. Compute the employee gross pay using 35 hours as the standard workweek for all employees except Mary Shangraw, who works 20 hours per week and receives overtime for any time worked past that point per company policy. The other hourly employees receive overtime pay when they work more than 35 hours in one week. Joel Schwartz has made $5,000 in case sales at a 3 percent commission rate during this pay period. Remember that the employees are paid biweekly. Note that the first pay period comprises only one week of work, but the pay frequency for federal income tax purposes is biweekly.

Exempt employee pay information is as follows:

Name	Annual Salary	Notes
Millen	$35,000	
Lewis	$32,000	
Schwartz	$24,000	plus 3% commission on sales
Prevosti	$45,000	

The hours for the nonexempt employees are as follows:

Name	Hourly Rate	Hours Worked 2/1–2/5	Regular Time Pay	Overtime Pay	Commission Pay	Gross Pay
Towle	$12.00	35 hours				
Long	$12.50	40 hours				
Shangraw	$11.00	21 hours				
Success (You)	$18.68	35 hours				

Complete the payroll register for the period's gross pay. Pay will be disbursed on February 10, 2021, starting with check number 6628.

February 19, 2021, is the end of the final pay period for the month. Schwartz has sold $7,500 of products during this pay period at a 3 percent commission. Complete the payroll register for the period's gross pay. Pay will be disbursed on February 24, 2021, and check numbers will continue from prior payroll.

The hours for the nonexempt employees are as follows:

Name	Hourly Rate	Hours Worked 2/6–2/19	Regular Time Pay	Overtime Pay	Commission Pay	Gross Pay
Towle	$12.00	80 hours				
Long	$12.50	70 hours				
Shangraw	$11.00	42 hours				
Success (You)	$18.68	70 hours				

P/R End Date _____

Check Date _____

Company Name: _____

Name	Filing Status	Type and Number of Dependents	Hourly Rate or Period Wage	No. of Regular Hours	No. of Overtime Hours	No. of Holiday Hours	Commissions	Gross Earnings	Sec 125	401(k)	Taxable Wages for Federal W/H
Totals											

Name	Gross Earnings	Taxable Wages for Federal W/H	Taxable Wages for FICA	Federal W/H	Social Security Tax	Medicare W/H	State W/H Tax	Garnishment	United Way	Net Pay
Totals										

Answers to Stop & Check Exercises

Pay Your Employees Correctly

1. No. Heather should have received time-and-a-half for the additional 8 hours. Her pay should have been $667.00 [(80 × 7.25) + (8 × 1.5 × 7.25)]
2. $464.13 (39.5 × 11.75)
3. $645.12 (32 × 2 × 10.08)
4. $756.00 (75 × 10.08)

Pay Computations for Different Basis

1. $6,744.00 ($224,800 × 3%)
2. $1,100.00. Yes, because $1,100.00/90 hours = $12.22 per hour. South Carolina has no dictated minimum wage so federal minimum wage would apply.
3. With unpaid time, her current pay will be less; if she had vacation time, there would be no difference.

Standard salary per biweekly payroll: $57,000/26 = $2,192.310769

($57,000/(40 × 26 × 2)) = $27.40384 per hour × (8 × 3) for unpaid leave of $657.69216

Current pay $2,192.30769 − 657.69216 = $1,534.62 (rounded)

Quarter-Hour vs. Hundredth-Hour

1. Ann:
   Quarter-hour: 8.25 hours
   Hundredth-hour: 7.93 hours
   Nevada:
   Quarter-hour: 8 hours
   Hundredth-hour: 8.12 hours
   Pat:
   Quarter-hour: 8 hours
   Hundredth-hour: 7.82 hours
2. The difference exists because the time worked during a quarter-hour system is rounded to the nearest quarter hour. In a hundredth-hour system, the worker is paid for the exact number of minutes worked.
3. It would be beneficial to adopt a hundredth-hour system to reduce payroll inaccuracies that may affect both employees and company profits.

How Does Overtime Affect Gross Pay?

1. FLSA Section 7(j) covers the overtime rules for hospital and residential care facilities and would fall under the 8 and 80 rule.
2. Since the commissions do not represent more than half her pay, they have no effect on overtime earnings.
3. His employer could include Ralph's tips by adding them to his gross pay based on the cash wage. This total with tips becomes the hourly rate used to determine overtime earnings. The other method would be to exclude the tip income, using the cash wage only as the basis for overtime computations.

The Payroll Register

1. To document the employees' time and hours worked as well as to provide totals of the compensation by each category.
2. Name, marital status, number of withholdings, hourly rate, number of regular hours, number of overtime hours, commission, piece rate, regular earnings, overtime earnings, gross earnings.
3. To facilitate calculations of regular and overtime, help ensure accuracy, and allow for analysis of overtime worked.

Combination Pay Methods

1. Base pay = $42,000 ÷ 24 = $1,750
   Commission = $100 × 5 = $500
   Gross pay = $2,250
2. $36,000 ÷ 12 = $3,000 per month
   $3,000 × 0.35 = $1,050 mid-month draw
   $3,000 − $1,050 draw = $1,950 received at the end of the month
3. $75,000 × 0.03 = $2,250 received in stock
   Annual compensation = $75,000 + $2,250 = $77,250

What Is the Correct Pay?

1. 15 hours because compensatory time must be awarded at 1.5 times regular hours.
2. $5.44 per hour ($7.25 × 75%)

Chapter Four

Fringe Benefits and Voluntary Deductions

Fringe benefits are noncash forms of compensation that employers use to reward an employee for company service. Examples of fringe benefits include the use of a company car, health and life insurance, dependent care, gym memberships, and many other perks offered as a privilege of working for a particular employer. Employers are not required to offer fringe benefits, and the presence of certain benefits serves as an incentive for potential employees to join the company. By offering fringe benefits, an employer can avoid the need to rely on high salary and wage amounts to attract employees and build morale. However, the cost of offering fringe benefits can impede the company's cash flow. The challenge is to provide a salary and fringe benefit package that attracts the desired employees at a manageable cost.

The IRS classifies fringe benefits as deductible from an employee's pay on either a pre-tax or a post-tax basis, depending on the type of benefit. Pre-tax deductions reduce the employee's current taxable income and may be taxed at a later time; for example, contributions to a qualifying retirement program would be a pre-tax deduction. Other fringe benefits are deducted from an employee's compensation after computing taxes, making the perk a post-tax benefit. The IRS clearly differentiates between taxable and non-taxable fringe benefits in *Publication 15-B*.

LEARNING OBJECTIVES

After studying Chapter 4, you should be able to:

LO 4-1   Define Fringe Benefits within the Context of Payroll

LO 4-2   Interpret Cafeteria Plan Types

LO 4-3   Describe Fringe Benefit Exclusion Rules

LO 4-4   Explain Fringe Benefit Valuation Rules

LO 4-5   Differentiate between Pre-Tax and Post-Tax Deductions

LO 4-6   Apply Rules for Withholding, Depositing, and Reporting Benefits

Marcos Castillo/Shutterstock

2021: An Unexpected Turn in Fringe Benefits

Broad societal changes commenced in 2020 that have changed the course of traditional fringe benefits. A fringe benefit plan often included medical insurance, paid time off, vacation time, and other offerings in previous years. Google was famous for offering laundry services, on-site cafeterias, and other less-common perks. The COVID-19 pandemic and the need for many employees to work from home and be conscious of personal safety changed the benefits landscape profoundly.

Expanded health insurance coverage was one of the first changes. The need for social distancing and other self-isolation techniques highlighted a growing need for mental health resources. Income reduction or loss led to a need for the intentional inclusion of financial education as a vital resource, and some employers created emergency savings accounts as an employee benefit. Flexible work schedules, which had been available on an as-requested basis for many firms, became part of the "new normal." In recognition of pets' role in mental health, pet insurance became a new fringe benefit.

Will the U.S. workforce resume pre-pandemic work norms and benefits? That is a pervasive question and not easy to answer. Since available technology has proven sufficient to continue many business practices, the need to return to old norms may become impractical in certain industries. The evolution of video technologies has removed much of the need for in-person meetings. However, certain industries in which customer involvement is vital may indeed return to traditional practices. In any case, the old way of viewing fringe benefits may be gone.

(Sources: Dice, Employee Benefits News)

> Despite the additional cost involved, fringe benefits are an important part of attracting and retaining high-quality employees. We will explore different types of fringe benefits and their treatment for payroll purposes in Chapter 4.

LO 4.1   Define Fringe Benefits within the Context of Payroll

Rawpixel.com/Shutterstock

Payroll has been said to be the intersection of human resources and accounting because of the need to include employee information and record all financial transactions involving work performed. Fringe benefits are an extension of that notion because these benefits are rewards given to employees in return for their service to the company. The correlation between employee satisfaction and retention is often a result of the employer's fringe benefits.

The term *fringe* was applied to these noncash benefits because they were an insignificant part of employee *compensation*. Over time, the Bureau of Labor Statistics has found that fringe benefits actually constitute an additional 25–33 percent of an employee's annual compensation. Despite the inherent monetary value, the importance of fringe benefits is best seen in terms of employee satisfaction, and long-term increases in revenue and net income. This section will examine the purpose of fringe benefits and the treatment of this form of noncash compensation as it pertains to pay and taxation.

Purpose of Fringe Benefits

Employees have often been considered one of the costs of conducting business. The employer's obligation to pay employment taxes and supply additional benefits to entice employee engagement was viewed as a necessary, albeit expensive, part of its financial structure. Research conducted during the past decade has found that the advantages gained from providing fringe benefits far outweigh the related costs in terms of employee productivity, creativity, and revenue production.

Employers continually introduce new or expanded benefit plans to attract, develop, and keep good employees, especially during and after COVID. Examples of companies offering such benefits include:

- PricewaterhouseCoopers and Fidelity Investments have benefits packages that include mental health and child care to support employees who work from home.

- Noodles & Company offered a program called LifeAtNoodles that included a wide range of benefits, including expanded, flexible time off, wellness initiatives, family planning, and other incentives.

- Prudential included education and support to teach coping methods during the pandemic.

- Domino's offered employees an option to receive their pay on demand at the end of daily work shifts.

(Source: Employee Benefits News)

Hallmarks of fringe benefits include the following indicators:

- All employees have access to the benefit because of their working relationship with the employer.
- Employees enjoy improved living conditions as a result of the benefit.
- The ability to receive the benefit is not related to employee performance.

- Fringe benefits supplement employees' cash compensation.
- These benefits may be either deducted pre- or post-tax.
- Fringe benefits promote the welfare of all employees.
- Legislative treatment of fringe benefits involves certain mandatory tax deductions from employee pay.

Fringe benefits may be included in employee pay, although they are not part of the cash compensation package. It is important to note fringe benefits are taxable unless they are specifically excluded per *Publication 15-B*. In the next section, we will explore how fringe benefits appear on an employee's pay advice.

Including Benefits in Pay

In Chapter 3, we discussed the computation of employee gross pay. Some fringe benefits may increase employee pay and could be taxable. Examples of this include but are not limited to employer-provided vehicles, mileage, leasing, and commuting. The items to be included in gross pay are valued at the level as if they were purchased through a third party, often referred to as an arms-length transaction.

State laws regarding fringe benefits, while based on IRS regulations, may vary regarding paid sick time and paid time off. Furthermore, employees must receive an annual notice that contains details about balances accrued in sick time and paid time off categories. Employers are not required to disburse cash compensation for the accrued time at termination and can decide if the unused time may be rolled over to the next year.

During the COVID pandemic, the landscape of fringe benefits changed to support differences in employee needs. Health plans were redesigned to address employees' mental and financial health needs. Diversity and inclusion programs were recognized as vital elements of employee benefits programs.

(Source: BenefitsPro)

Fringe Benefits and Payroll Taxes

Certain fringe benefits change tax calculations, such as Federal Withholding, Medicare, or Social Security taxes. Others do not affect the calculation for taxes and are considered post-tax benefits. The IRS requires that all fringe benefits that involve deductions from pay or for which the employee contributes part of regular compensation must be listed explicitly on the employee's *pay advice*. A sample pay advice is contained in Figure 4-1. The affected deductions include Federal withholding (W/H), SSI, Medicare, and State withholding (W/H), and the fringe benefits include pre-tax insurance and 401(k) voluntary deductions.

An exception to this requirement involves *de minimis* benefits. *De minimis* benefits include items with a value that is so minimal that accounting for it would be unnecessary. These items include an occasional coffee or an isolated postage stamp, both relatively small in value. However, it should be noted that when *de minimis* items become a regular benefit, such as a cup of coffee every day, instead of an occasional one, then the value aggregates to become a sum that could be treated as taxable income.

De minimis benefits, according to IRS Publication 15-B, have such minimal accounting value that the accounting for it is deemed impractical. Examples of de minimis benefits include (but are not limited to):

- Employee use of a company copier, as long as personal use does not exceed 15 percent of the employee's total usage of that equipment for business purposes.
- Noncash, low-value holiday or birthday gifts.
- Similar gifts for family illnesses or birth celebrations.

FIGURE 4-1
Sample Pay Advice

Hazlitt Industries
2210 Secours Way
Springfield, MA 02312

199203

Stephen Torrisi   Date   11/05/20XX

One-thousand one-hundred twenty-two and 77/100   dollars   1,122.77

Payee: Stephen Torrisi
Address: 3230 Longview Drive
City/State Zip: Agawam, MA 02249   Signed: *Mitchell North*

Payroll End Date 10/31/20XX   Payroll Pay Date 11/05/20XX   Check: 199203

Employee Name Stephen Torrisi   Employee Number 42850   Rate 21.50

Description	Earnings	YTD Gross	Description	Deductions	YTD Deductions
Regular	1,720.00	32,680.00	Federal W/H	275.47	5,233.93
Holiday			SSI	106.64	2,026.16
Commissions			Medicare	24.94	473.86
			State W/H	88.58	1,683.02
			Pretax Insurance	50.00	950.00
Total Earnings	1,720.00	32,680.00	401(k)	51.60	980.40
			Total Deductions	597.23	11,347.37

- Group–term life insurance for the death of a dependent if the life insurance face value does not exceed $2,000.
- Certain meals, occasional picnics, and parties for employees and their guests.
- Occasional tickets to sporting or theater events.
- Personal use of an employer-provided cell phone is provided primarily for noncompensatory business purposes.

Notice that *de minimis* benefits are generally classified as occasional use. If the use of a fringe benefit becomes more than occasional, such as season tickets to sporting or arts events or club memberships, the benefits are not considered *de minimis*.

(Source: IRS)

Dollar General offered its employees an incentive to ensure their safety: Four hours of additional pay for receiving the COVID vaccine. They offered this benefit to avoid situations in which an employee would have to choose between their health and arriving for scheduled work shifts. Although the incentive was a one-time opportunity for additional pay, it would still be subject to taxes.

(Sources: Human Resource Executive)

Voluntary fringe benefits have two basic types of treatments regarding payroll taxes: They may be deducted either before or after *mandatory deductions* (i.e., taxes) have been calculated.

FIGURE 4-2
Fringe Benefits and Payroll Tax Treatment (IRS Publication 15-B)

Fringe Benefits and Payroll Tax Treatment			
Type of Fringe Benefit	Income Tax Exempt	FICA Taxes Exempt	FUTA Tax Exempt
Accident and health benefits*	XX	XX	XX
Achievement awards (up to $1,600 for qualified plan awards, $400 for nonqualified)	XX	XX	XX
Adoption assistance	XX		
Athletic facilities owned or leased by the employer†	XX	XX	XX
De minimis benefits	XX	XX	XX
Dependent care assistance (up to $5,000 annually)	XX	XX	XX
Education (i.e., tuition) assistance (up to $5,250 annually)	XX	XX	XX
Employee discounts (various limits apply)	XX	XX	XX
Employee stock options (depending on the type of option)	XX	XX	XX
Employer-provided cell phone (if not otherwise compensated)	XX	XX	XX
Group–term life insurance	XX	XX‡	XX
Health savings accounts (HSAs) for qualified individuals	XX	XX	XX
Lodging on the employer premise (for the employer convenience as a condition of employment)	XX	XX	XX
Meals (exempt if *de minimis* or for employer convenience on employer premises)	XX	XX	XX
No-additional-cost services	XX	XX	XX
Retirement planning services	XX	XX	XX
Transportation benefits (commuting and rail passes up to $270, exempt if *de minimis*)	XX	XX	XX
Tuition reduction for undergraduate education (graduate if the employee engages in teaching or research)	XX	XX	XX
Working condition benefits	XX	XX	XX

*Does not include long-term care benefits if they are included in flexible spending accounts.
†Exempt if substantially all use during the calendar is by employees, their spouses, and their dependent children. The facility is on the employer's premises or a location owned or leased by the employer.
‡Up to cost of $50,000 of coverage. The excess over $50,000 must appear on the employee's Form W-2.
(Source: IRS)

The IRS specifies which fringe benefits may be deducted on a pre-tax basis and which must be treated as post-tax deductions in Publication 15-B, which is updated annually. Employers are responsible for remitting amounts withheld for fringe benefits promptly and reporting annual totals to employees on Form W-2. Figure 4-2 details the type of fringe benefit and payroll tax treatment follows.

Freeograph/Shutterstock

EXAMPLE: FRINGE BENEFIT
Phil Cahill is an employee of Cohen Corporation, a company that offers undergraduate educational assistance as a fringe benefit. According to the IRS, the first $5,250 of Phil's tuition assistance is not subject to payroll taxes. In 2021, Phil received reimbursement from his employer of $7,250 in education assistance. The additional $2,000 is taxable income for Phil.

Fringe Benefits 101

Stop & Check

1. What are the two main categories of fringe benefits?
2. Which of the following benefits is not considered a fringe benefit? (Use Figure 4-2 as a reference.)
    a. Educational assistance for undergraduate students.
    b. Group—term life insurance over $250,000.
    c. Overtime hours worked during the year.
    d. Cell phones for business purposes.
    e. Retirement planning services.
3. Which of the following fringe benefits would also be exempt from Social Security and Medicare taxes?
    a. Working condition benefits.
    b. Adoption Assistance.
    c. Qualified Health Savings Accounts
    d. Qualified Achievement Awards.

LO 4-2   Interpret Cafeteria Plan Types

Andrei_R/Shutterstock

The Internal Revenue Code has a special program to assist workers with necessary health care expenses. Section 125 of the IRS code was initially enacted in 1978 and has been revised several times. It permits employers to offer employees a choice between two or more cash and qualified benefits. The employer must explicitly describe the plan benefit, rules governing the benefit, and ways that the employee may both pay for and obtain the benefits. Employee-elected deductions for qualified cafeteria plan benefits are withheld on a pre-tax basis.

Examples of qualified insurance benefits include:

*   Accident and health benefits.
*   Long-term care benefits.
*   Group—term life insurance (including costs not excluded from wages).
*   Health Savings Accounts (HSAs).

Cafeteria plans, also known as Section 125 plans, are offered by the employer and are usually deducted on a pre-tax basis to make employer-sponsored benefits more affordable for employees. In essence, a cafeteria plan allows employees to convert fringe (i.e., non-cash) benefits into tax savings. Although they often pertain to health coverage, cafeteria plans may also include dependent care and other expenses. Participation in cafeteria plans potentially saves employees upwards of 7.65 percent (the FICA taxes) and may save more money, depending on their income tax bracket. If an employee chooses to receive benefits under the cafeteria plan, this does not convert a fringe benefit to a taxable one.

Premium Only Plan (POP)

A *premium only plan (POP)* is a type of cafeteria plan that allows employees to deduct premiums for employer-sponsored group insurance on a pre-tax basis. Deducting the premium on a

TABLE 4-1
Types of Insurance that May Be Included in a Premium Only Plan

Health	Dental	Vision
Prescription	Cancer	Medicare Supplement
Accident	Disability	Hospital Indemnity
Employee Group Term Life*		

*Employee Group Term Life insurance premiums are subject to a limit of $50,000 per employee and may be subject to a 10-employee minimum.

pre-tax basis allows the employee to have a lower tax liability. A list of POPs that employers may provide and are subject to Section 125 pre-tax provisions is provided in Table 4-1. Note that not all employers offer all types of insurance coverage.

Employers benefit by offering POPs because employee premiums deducted on a pre-tax basis reduce the employer's FICA tax liability. Offering pre-tax deductions for group insurance coverage as part of their employee benefits package is also beneficial to employers because participation in health plans has been correlated with reductions in employee sick time and related health care costs. POPs allow employees to offset the cost of rising health care premiums by allowing employees to deduct the premiums on a pre-tax basis.

EXAMPLE: PRE-TAX DEDUCTION OF HEALTH INSURANCE PREMIUM

Cathie Hollins, an employee of Wolfe & Associates, has the option to deduct her health insurance premium on a pre-tax basis. She consulted her payroll accountant about the difference between pre-tax and post-tax premium deduction and received this analysis:

	Pre-Tax vs. Post-Tax Premium Deduction	
	Pre-Tax	Post-Tax
Period gross pay	$2,500	$2,500
Health insurance premium	250	250
Taxable income	$2,250	$2,500

The pre-tax deduction would lower taxable income, resulting in less federal, state, and local income tax deducted from Cathie's pay.

Flexible Spending Arrangement (FSA)

Another benefit that can be included in the cafeteria plan is a ***flexible spending arrangement (FSA)***. FSAs are available to assist in the payment of medical expenses, including certain co-payments and prescriptions, transportation, and certain child care expenses. According to IRS Publication 502, examples of includible medical expenses are:

- Acupuncture.
- Ambulance service.
- Automobile expenses when traveling for medical purposes.
- Braille books and magazines.
- Chiropractor.
- Hearing aids.
- Lead-based paint removal.
- Wheelchair.

It should be noted that any employee contributions to an FSA over $2,750 annually (2021 amount) are treated as taxable income. The FSA's purpose is not to defer taxable income or to avoid paying taxes but to reduce the financial burden of health care costs.

Cafeteria plan–based FSAs generally have a "use it or lose it" provision, meaning that any unused funds at the end of the plan year may not be accessed afterward. However, the IRS permits employers to roll over up to $500 annually per employee at the employer's discretion.

EXAMPLE: FSA EFFECT ON ANNUAL GROSS SALARY

For plans that have a year starting after December 31, 2020, the maximum annual amount an employee may contribute to an FSA offered under Section 125 is $2,750 per person. As an example, Faith Goldman is an employee of Kuzmeckis Doors. She earns $50,000 annually and elects to contribute $2,700 of her annual pay to an employer-sponsored FSA. Her taxable pay would be reduced as follows:

Annual pay − FSA election = $50,000 − $2,750 = $47,250

Faith has $500 remaining out of her annual FSA election at the end of the calendar year. Her employer allows her to carry over the balance to next year and requires that it be spent by March 15. She would need to spend the remaining balance on qualified medical expenses and provide documentation as required to support the expenditures. The employee would forfeit any amount remaining from the prior year after March 15.

One benefit of cafeteria plans is that employees may choose two or more benefits that consist of cash and noncash elements. For example, they may elect to have health insurance premiums *and* a flexible spending arrangement deducted on a pre-tax basis.

EXAMPLE: PRE-TAX VS. POST-TAX WITH A FLEXIBLE SPENDING ARRANGEMENT (FSA)

Cathie Hollins also can contribute to an FSA for her annual out-of-pocket medical expenses and decides to use that to meet cafeteria plan requirements. She is paid semimonthly and decides to contribute $2,400 to a qualified FSA. Her taxable income would be as follows:

	Pre-Tax vs. Post-Tax	Premium Deduction
	Pre-Tax	Post-Tax
Period gross pay	$2,500	$2,500
Health insurance premium	250	250
FSA	100	-0-
Taxable income	$2,150	$2,500

Note the difference between her taxable income in both situations. The use of pre-tax deductions can significantly reduce Cathie's tax liability.

In response to unanticipated dependent care and medical needs related to the COVID-19 pandemic, the IRS introduced flexibility into FSA rules in 2021. In

Notice 2021-15, the IRS changed two significant provisions of FSAs: (1) It allowed employees to contribute additional funds to their FSA during 2021 outside of benefits election times, and (2) it allowed employees to roll over unused FSA amounts, which would have expired in March 2021, until December 31, 2021. Both of these actions allowed employees to access pre-tax dollars for medical or dependent care that may not otherwise have been available to respond to needs during the pandemic.

(Source: IRS)

Health Savings Account (HSA)

Another type of cafeteria plan is a *health savings account (HSA)* that can pay for qualified medical expenses. It is important to note that HSAs may only be used in conjunction with a cafeteria plan by employees with a ***high-deductible health plan (HDHP)***. The 2021 definition of a high-deductible health plan includes the following deductible limits:

- $1,400 annual deductible (self-coverage).
- $2,800 annual deductible (family).
- $7,000 out-of-pocket expenses maximum (self-coverage).
- $14,000 out-of-pocket expenses maximum (family).

FSA vs. HSA

FSA	HSA
Must be offered by an employer.	Only permitted for employees with an HDHP (see deductible rules).
Independent contractors do not qualify.	Independent contractors do not qualify.
Employees may elect to contribute up to $2,750.	Employees may contribute to HSAs as follows: • $3,600 (single) • $7,200 (married) • $1,000 (additional catch-up amount for employees over age 55)
Employees may use any amount of the annual contribution at any time, regardless of how much they have contributed for the year.	Functions like a bank account in that the employee owns the funds contributed, although employers may also contribute funds.
The employer owns the plan and unused annual the employer may retain contributions.	All funds contributed are the property of the employee.
The employer decides if they want to give employees a grace period (up to March 15 in most cases) to use annual elections.	Unused funds rollover each year and continue to grow with the account. Unused funds do not affect the yearly contribution limits.
Employees must provide receipts or provider evidence to support used funds.	Employees may not access more funds than they have contributed to the HSA.
FSA contributions are reported on the W-2.	Employees must report all used funds with their personal income tax returns.
Annual contributions must be elected each year.	Employees may change their annual contribution at any time.

Dragon Images/Shutterstock

One aspect of HSAs that differentiates them from FSAs is that the amounts employees contribute to an HSA may remain in the account for use later in life. These funds may be reserved for medical costs and long-term care and are not taxable when used for medical expenses. Money withdrawn for nonmedical expenses is subject to income taxes. Another difference is that anyone with an HDHP may establish an HSA with a trustee, even if their employer does not offer the benefit. However, not all HSAs can be considered tax-exempt. Only HSAs included as part of the company's qualifying Section 125 cafeteria plan are deemed exempt from Social Security, Medicare, and federal income taxes.

HDHPs are a way for employers to offer affordable insurance premiums for their employees. However, many employees have delayed care or have reported increased out-of-pocket costs while using an HDHP. Other employees with an HDHP reported that their employer offered no other healthcare option. Employees with an HSA as part of their HDHP noted an increase in their appreciation for the plan and its flexibility for future use.

(Source: PRNewswire)

A note about HSAs is the money contributed to the account may roll over from year to year as long as the employee is part of an HDHP. Certain HSA plans allow participants to invest money into mutual funds or other investments. It should also be noted HSAs do not have the same restrictions for spending as FSAs.

Employers may make tax-exempt contributions to their employees' HSAs as long as they make comparable contributions to all company employee accounts according to the category or coverage and the employment category (e.g., full-time, part-time). Employer contributions to HSAs are tax-exempt from federal income tax, FICA, and FUTA because sums contributed are not considered employee wages.

An issue with cafeteria plans is the exclusion of sole proprietors, partners, shareholders in an S-corporation who have greater than a 2 percent share in the company, and members of limited liability companies (LLCs) who elect to be taxed as partnerships. According to Section 125, these individuals may not participate in a cafeteria plan. The problem is that 73 percent of business owners fall into one of these exclusions, which means that many people cannot participate in qualified cafeteria plans, missing out on the tax benefits.

(Source: *Financial Regulation News*)

What is served in the cafeteria plan?

Stop & Check

1. Which of the following types of insurance may be included in a POP?
   a. Cancer
   b. Vision
   c. Auto
   d. Dental
2. What are two of the differences between FSAs and HSAs?
3. What constitutes an HDHP?

LO 4-3   Describe Fringe Benefit Exclusion Rules

Remember that fringe benefits are noncash compensation. We have discussed the tax treatment of benefits deducted from employee income on a pre-tax basis using a cafeteria plan. Other fringe benefits may not be included in a cafeteria plan and are generally not reported as compensation. Employers routinely offer these excluded fringe benefits, and payroll accountants need to understand specific tax rules to represent them accurately on employee W-2s.

Excluded fringe benefits exist that are not part of a cafeteria plan and, despite the cash value, do not generally constitute a taxable portion of employee pay. The value of these fringe benefits is exempt from federal income tax, FICA taxes, and FUTA tax and is not reported on the employee's W-2. The table in Figure 4-2 contains specific details of fringe benefit exclusions and limitations of the exclusions. This section will examine fringe benefits not specifically addressed in *Publication 15-B* that are commonly offered by companies.

ColorBlind Images/Blend Images LLC

Prizes and Awards

Workplace prizes and awards are ways for employers to influence employee morale by offering noncash rewards for winning competitions and achieving milestones such as company tenure. In Publication 15-B, the cash-value limit on achievement awards is $1,600 annually for those given in accordance with a qualified plan; the limit for nonqualified awards is $400. A *qualified plan* is one that considers all employees equally, not favoring highly compensated employees. According to IRS Publication 535, these types of achievement awards are for improvements to safety programs and the longevity of service to the employer. The following example contains some context for achievement awards.

Simon Hawkins is a sales employee at Austin Trailers and Motorsports. The company offers achievement awards regularly to reward sales employees for achieving safety goals and longevity of service. All sales staff members are eligible for these awards, including the company officers.

NONTAXABLE ACHIEVEMENT AWARD
On June 5, 2021, Simon won an award of $500 for achieving the highest safety record during May. According to Publication 15-B, this achievement award would not be reported on Simon's W-2 as taxable income.

TAXABLE PORTION OF ACHIEVEMENT AWARD: CASH AWARD
As of December 31, 2021, Simon had won the award for compiling a comprehensive safety plan on four separate occasions during the calendar year. The total of his achievement awards is $500 × 4, or $2,000. Because the achievement awards received exceeded $1,600, the additional $400 ($2,000 − $1,600) would be reflected as taxable income on his W-2.

TAXABLE PORTION OF ACHIEVEMENT AWARD: NONCASH AWARD
In addition to winning the cash prizes for safety achievement, Simon received a new smartphone with a value of $1,000 for 10 years of service to the company. As his awards' value is now $3,000, the excess of value over $1,600 will be reflected as taxable income.

Erik Isakson/Getty Images

Gym Memberships

Employee discounts for gym memberships are a common fringe benefit that employers use to promote wellness initiatives. If the employer has on-site athletic facilities (either on the employer's premises or other premises owned or leased by the employer) that are restricted to use by employees, their spouses, and their dependents, the benefit would be nontaxable. However, if an employer provides gym memberships to off-site clubs at no additional cost to employees, even on a qualified plan, the gym membership cost is taxable. Likewise, if the athletic facility is open to the public and employees and their dependents, the value of the membership would be taxable.

Mark Dierker/McGraw Hill

EXAMPLE: OFF-SITE GYM MEMBERSHIP
Claire Warner is an employee of Althea Productions. Her employer offers memberships at a local gym as an optional benefit for employees. These memberships are at no additional cost to the employee and have a $75 per month cash value. Because the gym membership has an annual value of $900 and is not an on-site athletic facility, it must be counted as income and reported on Claire's Form W-2.

Personal Use of Company Vehicle

Company cars are a common fringe benefit given to employees who regularly drive as part of their job. Business use of these company cars is considered a nontaxable fringe benefit because it is an asset provided to the employee for use that specifically benefits the company, much like a computer or office equipment. The taxable portion occurs when the employee uses the company-provided vehicle for personal business. Employers often request that employees document personal use of the business vehicle at the end of the calendar year to identify taxable income associated with the company car properly.

> In the case of *Scott v. Scott,* an issue that arose was the value of fringe benefits used to determine the defendant's income for use in divorce proceedings. The plaintiff contended that the use of a company truck was not calculated into the value of the defendant's income that was used as the basis of calculating child support. Upon reviewing the defendant's total compensation, including all fringe benefits, the Supreme Court of Georgia found that the defendant's actual monthly income was substantially more than previously stated and increased the monthly child support obligation.
>
> (Source: *Justia*)

Gift Cards

If an employee received gift cards as a fringe benefit, the gift cards' cash value must be included as compensation on the employee's Form W-2. For example, if an employee entered a company-sponsored raffle at company functions during the year and won a $100 gift card to a local restaurant, the $100 must be added as compensation to the employee's Form W-2. There is no minimum amount of cash or cash equivalent gift cards that would be excluded under *de minimis* fringe benefits.

Eugenio Marongiu/Image Source

Employer-Provided Snacks and Meals

Employers often have coffeemakers and kitchen facilities available for employees. If the employer *occasionally* provides food or beverage as an employee perk, the benefit's cash value is considered *de minimis* and is not taxable. However, if the employer routinely provides food or beverages for employee consumption at no additional charge to the employees, then the cash value of those items must be reported as compensation on the employee's Form W-2.

> ### EXAMPLE: PIZZA FRIDAYS
> Laurie Ortega works for Excellent Embroidery and Screen Printing. On Fridays, the company provides a pizza lunch for all employees. The pizza intends to promote employee morale on Fridays and to celebrate weekly accomplishments. Although the weekly value of Friday pizza per employee of Excellent Embroidery is small, it aggregates to an additional $100 per employee over a year. Laurie would see an additional $100 in compensation added to her Form W-2 for this noncash fringe benefit.

Keep in mind that fringe benefits may appear in many different forms. The payroll accountant needs to be aware of the perks offered to employees and Publication 15-B guidelines. This publication fosters awareness of potential additions to employee compensation and provides accurate reports to employees and governmental authorities.

> For a fringe benefit to be excluded, the employer must be prepared to prove that providing the benefit, not simply adding it to employee gross pay, substantially improves conditions at the firm. For example, the addition of an on-site gym must provide significant benefits above what it would cost employers to add the amount associated with a gym membership to employee pay. Proving that the benefit is substantial could include tracking the number of employees who use the on-site facility versus those who request and use an external gym membership.
>
> (Source: Mondaq)

Excluded Fringe Benefits

Stop & Check

1. Clayton Clark is an employee at Glazier Foods Inc., where he is in the shipping and receiving department. His employer provides an athletic facility on the premises for employees to use. Would this benefit be taxable on Clayton's W-2? Why or why not?

2. Marcia Zimmerman is an employee of the Moeller Gallery, and she has a company-issued vehicle to use to conduct business. Does this vehicle represent a fringe benefit? Why or why not?

LO 4.4 Explain Fringe Benefit Valuation Rules

Hill Street Studios/Getty Images

Now that we have an idea about what fringe benefits are and how they fit into a payroll context, it is time to address specific rules about fringe benefits valuation. As noted in the case of *Scott v. Scott,* the value of fringe benefits potentially increases the total value of an employee's income without directly affecting the cash they receive. Note that the details for fringe-benefit valuation rules appear in Publication 15-B and are updated annually.

Proper valuation of vehicles is essential for benefits evaluation. Employers must know the value of the benefits they provide to ensure that they withhold appropriate amounts of tax for the use of company property such as vehicles.

General Valuation Rule

The *general valuation rule (GVR)* is the most common way to determine the value of fringe benefits. The GVR uses *fair market value (FMV)* as the cornerstone of valuation. Fair market value is defined as the price a person would need to pay to obtain a good or service from a third party in an arms-length transaction. In other words, if an employee needed to obtain a gym membership, the price paid for that individual membership would constitute the fair market value. In this section, we will explore different applications of the GVR with explanations of the method used to determine the value for payroll reporting purposes.

Personal Use of Company Vehicle: Lease Value Rule

Alex Varlakov/Hemera/Getty Images

Access to a company car can present a challenge in evaluating the specific amount associated with the personal use of the asset. To compute the value of the employee's personal use of the asset, the IRS uses a complex method that involves the car's age, the fair market value of the asset, and miles driven. Three primary methods exist for determining value: the *lease value rule*, the *commuting rule*, and the *cents-per-mile rule*. Figure 4-3 contains an example of how a company could derive the valuation using the lease value method. Publication 15-B does provide an annual lease amount for vehicles. After the annual amount of the lease has been determined, the amount is then multiplied by the percentage of personal use of the vehicle. This amount is considered taxable income to the employee. When the employer provides the vehicle's fuel, this must also be included in the previous calculations. Employer-paid fuel is calculated at FMV or 5.5 cents per mile of personal use. If the employer does not provide fuel, then there is no addition to the calculation for fuel.

In the form provided in Figure 4-3, the employee, Nina Falco, claims that she uses the company car for personal use 25 percent of the calendar year. By obtaining the data requested in the form and computing the fringe benefit's value, Nina has received $892.21 in noncash

FIGURE 4-3

Value of the Personal Use of a Company Car: Lease-Value Rule

Kascka Incorporated

Worksheet to Calculate Personal Use of Company Vehicle

(Lease Value Rule)

Employee Name:_____Nina Falco_____

Vehicle Make:_____Ford_____   Vehicle Year: _2021_____

Vehicle Model:_____Fusion_____

Odometer Mileage on the First Day of Use During the Year:_____790_____

Odometer Mileage on the Last Day of Use During the Year:_____15,990_____

Annual Lease Method

Fair Market Value of Vehicle:_____$25,000_____

Annual Lease Value:_____$6,850_____ *(Use Table 3-1 in Publication 15b)*

Enter Number of Days Available for Use During the Year:_____190_____

Divide by the Number of Days in the Tax Year:____365_____

Prorated Annual Lease Percentage:____52.1%_____

Prorated Annual Lease Value: _____$3,568.85 ($6,850 x 52.1%)_____

Percent of Personal Use During the Year (from employee statement):____25%_____

Personal Annual Lease Value:_____$892.21_____(Prorated Annual Lease Value x % Personal Use)

If fuel is provided by the employer, enter personal miles: 3,800 x $0.055/mile[1] = **$209.00**

Total Personal Use Taxable Income:_____$892.21 + 236.50 = $1,101.21_____

[1]Fuel provided by the company is valued at $0.055 per mile per personal use purposes.

Note: The number of personal miles is computed by determining the total miles driven during the year (15,990 - 790 = 15,200 miles), then multiplying that total by the percentage of personal use (15,200 × 25% = 3,800 miles).

compensation for this fringe benefit. The company has also provided fuel for the vehicle (at 5.5 cents per mile), and the number of personal miles is used to compute the personal value of fuel consumption. The total value of this benefit for Nina is $1,101.21 and must be added to her Form W-2 as compensation.

Personal Use of a Company Vehicle: Commuting Rule

Like the situation in the lease value rule, the employee has a company vehicle for use. However, the commuting rule applies to employees strictly forbidden from using the vehicle outside of work hours and for personal purposes. The vehicle is only available for transport to and from work and during the workday. Under the commuting rule, the employee computes the number of miles driven for commuting to and from work and multiplies that by $1.50 to determine the valuation for this fringe benefit. Figure 4-4 contains an example of how this rule is applied, assuming a 38-mile round-trip commute done each day of the week.

In Figure 4-4, we see that providing a company car and charging an employee based on the number of miles in the commute can lead to a higher fringe benefit valuation than seen in the lease value rule.

Personal Use of a Company Vehicle: Cents-per-Mile Rule

Another way to determine a company car's value as a fringe benefit is to use the IRS standard mileage rate. This rate is updated each year. For 2021 the rate is $0.56 per Publication 15-B.

FIGURE 4-4

Value of the Personal Use of a Company Car: Commuting Rule

Kascka Incorporated

Worksheet to Calculate Personal Use of Company Vehicle

(Commuting Rule)

Employee Name: ___NinaFalco___

Vehicle Make: ___Ford___ Vehicle Year: _2021_

Vehicle Model: ___Fusion___

Odometer Mileage on the First Day of Use During the Year: ___790___

Odometer Mileage on the Last Day of Use During the Year: ___15,990___

Commuter Rule

Number of miles driven for daily commute to and from work: ___38___

Number of Days worked during the year: ___350___

Total number of commute miles driven during the year (38 x 350): 13,300

Value of company vehicle for commuting: (13,300 x $1.50/mile): $19,950

FIGURE 4-5

Value of the Personal Use of a Company Car: Cents-per-Mile Rule

Kascka Incorporated

Worksheet to Calculate Personal Use of Company Vehicle

(Cents-per-Mile Rule)

Employee Name: ___Nina Falco___

Vehicle Make: ___Ford___ Vehicle Year: _2021_

Vehicle Model: ___Fusion___

Odometer Mileage on the First Day of Use During the Year: ___790___

Odometer Mileage on the Last Day of Use During the Year: ___15,990___

Cents-per-Mile Rule

Number of miles driven during the year: ___15,200___

Number of miles OR percent driven for personal use: _25%_

Total number of commute miles driven during the year (15,200 x 0.25): 3,800

Value of company vehicle for commuting: (3,800 x $0.56/mile): $2,128.00

The cents-per-mile rule uses the number of personal miles driven and multiplies it by the standard mileage rate to determine the fringe benefit's value. The purpose of the cents-per-mile rule is to consider costs of maintenance and insurance for the vehicle, both of which may increase for the company when the vehicle is driven for personal purposes. Figure 4-5 contains an example of applying the cents-per-mile rule.

The choice of company car valuation method rule determines the company's policy and the vehicle's actual use in terms of total miles driven for business, the value of the asset, and the primary user of the vehicle. Publication 15-B contains specific details for the payroll accountant to determine which method is the most appropriate. No matter which method is chosen, it is important to be consistent in the application of personal vehicle use valuations.

Unsafe Conditions

A special rule applies if a company vehicle is provided to an employee only because of unsafe conditions. This rule's foundation is that the employee would walk, bicycle, or use public transportation under normal conditions. An example of an unsafe condition in which this rule may apply would be in the event of a sudden snowstorm that makes the employee's normal travel mode unsafe. In this case, the IRS rule is that the employee is charged $1.50 for a one-way commute (i.e., to or from home), and this charge should be either subtracted from the employee's wages or reimbursed to the company by the employee.

Scherbinator/Shutterstock

Other Transportation Benefits

Another transportation benefit that employers can offer is a transit pass. These provide employees access to commuter vehicles (six or more passengers required) through the pass. Employers in larger cities, where parking is a premium, may provide parking subsidies to their employees. When there are toll roads present, an employer may provide prepaid commuter passes to their employees to meet the toll roads' cost. Employers may exclude up to $270 (2021 value) from the employee's wages for these benefits. Any amount paid by the employer more than $270 for a commuter pass would be taxable income for the employee.

> Employers in Seattle with more than 20 employees must offer pre-tax monthly deductions to employees for transit or vanpool expenses. These monies will then be used to reimburse employees for the costs of qualifying expenses.
>
> (Source: APA)

Fringe Benefit Valuations

Stop & Check

1. Oliver Robertson is a field service representative whose primary job function is to visit customer sites. His primary base for computing mileage is his home. During 2021, he drove a total of 30,250 miles, 15 percent of which was for personal use. Using the IRS standard mileage rate of 56 cents per mile, what is the value of this fringe benefit using the cents-per-mile rule?

2. Katie Turner is a sales representative for a large pharmaceuticals company. She drives a 2020 Lexus ES, which has a fair market value of $47,000 and a lease value of $12,250. Katie has had the use of the vehicle for 180 days during 2020. She drives the vehicle 20 percent for personal use, and her employer does not provide fuel. Using the lease value rule, what is the value of the fringe benefit? (Round final figure to two decimal places.)

GET FIT GYM
startup fee $145
$45 monthly fee

LO 4.5   Differentiate between Pre-Tax and Post-Tax Deductions

Two classes of deductions exist: pre-tax and post-tax. Pre-tax deductions are those deductions withheld from an employee's *gross pay*, which is the amount of compensation before computing tax liability or applying deductions. The effect of pre-tax deductions is that they reduce the taxable income of the employee. Pre-tax deductions are *voluntary deductions* that have been legislated by the federal government as eligible for pre-tax withholding status, including certain types of insurance, retirement plans, and cafeteria plans.

Post-tax deductions are deducted from employee pay after federal, state, and local income taxes and FICA taxes have been deducted. Amounts deducted on a post-tax basis include both voluntary and court-mandated deductions. The voluntary deductions taken on a post-tax basis involve fringe benefits such as gym memberships, charitable contributions, repayment of company loans, optional insurance (e.g., auto, home), and union dues. Court-mandated deductions deducted on a post-tax basis may include child support garnishments, tax liens, credit card garnishments, and other legally directed items.

Insurance

Employers may provide subsidized health insurance coverage for their employees. The employees pay a portion of these health insurance expenses out of their paycheck, and the company makes up the difference. How much a company pays is determined by the company and could vary greatly, depending on the costs of health insurance and the employee's policy. For health insurance plans to qualify for pre-tax status, they must meet the guidelines stated in the IRS Code.

According to the IRS, the following guidelines are used to determine if a health insurance plan qualifies for pre-tax status:

- Health plans offered through the state's small or large group market.
- An employer's self-insured health plan.
- The Department of Defense's Non-Appropriated Fund Health Benefits Program.
- A governmental plan.
- COBRA health coverage.
- Retiree health coverage.

(Source: IRS)

The IRS specifies these items as pre-tax because it reflects the belief that health insurance is necessary, allowing employees to reduce their tax liability and ultimately reduce the financial burden on families and employers by proactively supporting medical care.

EXAMPLE: PRE-TAX MEDICAL PREMIUM

Kelli Dennis works for Gunderson Associates. Her employer offers medical insurance for which the premiums may be taken on a pre-tax basis. Kelli is a salaried employee who earns $48,000 annually and is paid on a semimonthly basis. Her premium for medical insurance is $125 per pay period. Consider the following difference in taxable income:

	Medical Insurance Deducted on a Pre-Tax Basis	Medical Insurance NOT Deduced on a Pre-Tax Basis
Annual salary	$48,000	$48,000
Period salary	$48,000/24 = $2,000	$48,000/24 = $2,000
Medical insurance deduction	$125	$0
Taxable income	$1,875	$2,000

In 2010, the Affordable Care Act was passed, providing small businesses a tax credit for providing health insurance coverage when their employees are at low- and moderate-income levels.

The act extended coverage of children until the age of 26 to be included as an option to employees on a pre-tax basis. This is only for employees covered under a qualifying cafeteria plan.

In response to the Affordable Care Act, IRS Code 6056 changed the reporting requirements for employees' health insurance programs. Employers with more than 50 employees are required to file an information return with the IRS and must provide a detailed summary of health coverage to employees. The value of the insurance coverage contributed by the employer must be reported on the employee's W-2 year-end tax statement within box 12 using code DD. It should reflect the amounts contributed by both the employee and the employer. It is important to remember that the amounts reported on the W-2 for the employer's contribution to health insurance do not add to the employee's taxable wages.

According to the Internal Revenue Service, the Affordable Care Act mandates that individuals have "minimum essential coverage."

Examples of minimum essential coverage include:

- Employer-provided health insurance.
- Health insurance purchased through an approved health insurance exchange.
- Coverage provided under federal auspices such as Medicare and Medicaid.
- Privately purchased health insurance.

Minimum essential coverage does not include the following limited benefit or limited-term coverage plans:

- Vision and dental insurance issued on a stand-alone basis (i.e., not grouped with a medical insurance policy).
- Workers' compensation insurance.
- Accidental death and disability plans maintained by the employer.

(Source: Tax Cuts and Job Act, IRS)

Supplemental Health and Disability Insurance

Another option many employers are offering is a flow-through (i.e., the company does not cover any of the costs) of supplemental health and disability insurance. One of the largest insurance providers is the American Family Life Assurance Company of Columbus (AFLAC). AFLAC comprises a variety of policies with separate treatment for taxation purposes (whether pre- or post-tax). The IRS Revision Ruling 2004-55 deals specifically with the tax treatment of short- and long-term disability, and IRS Code Sections 104(a)(3) and 105(a) deal with the exclusion of short- and long-term disability benefits from employees' gross wages. Long-term disability insurance is excluded from taxable income under the ruling. If an employer pays for long-term disability insurance, these amounts may be excluded from or included in gross pay, depending upon the company's election. When determining the tax treatment for the supplemental health insurance, the IRS guidance provides the following: If the income derived will be estimated to be tax-free, then the cost associated will also be tax-exempt.

Note: Supplemental health and disability plan premiums are not tax-exempt from Social Security and Medicare taxes.

EXAMPLE: SUPPLEMENTAL HEALTH INSURANCE DEDUCTION
Paul Nichols is a salaried exempt employee of Mark One Restoration Services. He earns $78,000 annually and is paid biweekly. The employer offers him medical insurance

and supplemental health insurance with premiums of $150 and $75, respectively. Paul elects to have both premiums withheld on a pre-tax basis.

Salary per period ($78,000/26)	$3,000.00
Less: Medical insurance premium	150.00
Less: Supplemental medical insurance premium	75.00
Taxable income*	$2,775.00

*Note: Taxable income computed here pertains to computations of federal income tax. The taxable income for Social Security and Medicare taxes would be $2,850 because supplemental medical insurance premiums are not exempt from FICA taxes.

Retirement Plans

Shutterstock

Retirement plans were covered under the Employee Retirement Income Security Act (ERISA) of 1974 in conjunction with the Internal Revenue Code. There are two basic types of retirement plans: *defined benefit* and *defined contribution*. In a defined benefit plan, the employer guarantees the employee a specific income level once retirement has been reached. For example, under a defined benefit plan, the employer may guarantee 10 percent of the average salary earned in the final five years of employment.

In a defined contribution plan, the individual places money from his or her payroll, pre-tax, into a retirement plan, and the company may or may not match to a percentage. There are several different types of defined contribution plans, such as *401(k)*, *SIMPLE 401(k)*, *403(b)*, *457*, *IRA*, *SIMPLE*, *SEP*, *ESOP*, and profit-sharing.

Note: Although some qualified 401(k) plans may be considered cafeteria plans and may be excluded from FICA tax liability, the IRS states in Publication 15-B that most 401(k) plans are subject to Social Security and Medicare taxes. For this text's purposes, we will assume that the 401(k) plans are not included in federal or state tax calculations but are included in Social Security and Medicare tax calculations. See Table 4-2 for an explanation of the different retirement plan types.

TABLE 4-2
Retirement Plan Types

Type of Plan	Description
401(k)	A group of investments, typically invested in stock market-based or mutual fund-based plans.
403(b)	Similar to a 401(k) but offered by nonprofit employers such as governmental agencies, hospitals, and schools.
457	Similar to 401(k) and 403(b) but has no penalty for fund withdrawal before age 59-1/2. Generally offered to governmental and certain nongovernmental employees.
Savings Incentive Match Plan for Employees (SIMPLE)	The major limitation is employers may not have more than 100 employees. Funds are specifically set aside for the individual employee in a bank, mutual fund account, or stock market SIMPLE 401(k).
Individual Retirement Account (IRA)	Funds are specifically set aside for the individual employee in a bank or mutual fund account.
Employee Stock Ownership Plan (ESOP)	The company offers employees the ability to earn company stock for the duration of their employment.
Simplified Employee Pension (SEP)	A tax-favorable IRA is set up by or for the employee, and the employer contributes the funds into the account. The SEP is tax-favorable because it reduces the employee's income tax liability.

EXAMPLE: RETIREMENT PLAN EMPLOYEE CONTRIBUTION

Whitney Robinson is a salaried, exempt employee of Hovey Heating and Cooling. She is single with one dependent under 17 years of age and receives an annual salary of $60,000, paid semimonthly. She elects to contribute 6 percent of her period pay to the company-sponsored 401(k) plan on a pre-tax basis. Her taxable income would be computed as follows:

Salary per period ($60,000/24)	$2,500.00
Less: 6% contribution to 401(k)*	150.00
Taxable income	$2,350.00

*Note: The 401(k) deduction is *not* exempt from Social Security and Medicare taxes.

Each year, the IRS imposes a cap on pre-tax retirement plan contributions. For 2021, the limit on 401(k) contributions is $26,000. People over 50 years of age may contribute a pre-tax "catch-up" amount up to $6,500.

Post-Tax Deductions

After the employer withholds the pre-tax and mandatory amounts from an employee's pay, other withholdings may apply. These other withholdings, known as post-tax deductions, comprise both voluntary and **mandated deductions**. An example of a voluntary post-tax deduction is a charitable contribution elected by the employee. Mandated post-tax deductions include **garnishments** and **union dues**. Post-tax deductions are amounts that the IRS has declared that cannot reduce the employee's tax liability. A general guide to garnishments is in Table 4-3.

Charitable Contributions

Many companies offer to deduct funds for approved charitable organizations directly from the employee's pay. This **charitable contribution** is typically withheld *after* taxes have been calculated. The individual will report the charitable contribution on his or her itemized tax return. There are separate requirements for meeting the deductible percentage outside the scope of this text.

TABLE 4-3
Garnishment Rules

Type of Garnishment	Maximum Percentage of DISPOSABLE Income
Child Support or Alimony	50% if the employee is supporting another spouse or child. 60% if the employee is not supporting another spouse or child. NOTE: If child support is >12 weeks in arrears, an additional 5% may be added to the garnishment.
U.S. Government debts	15% of earnings over federal minimum wage weekly earnings.
Student Loans	15% of earnings over federal minimum wage weekly earnings.
Consumer Credit	25% of earnings over federal minimum wage weekly earnings.
Tax Levies	See IRS Publication 1494.
Personal Bankruptcy	Lower of 25% or 30 times the amount of weekly income over federal minimum wage.

EXAMPLE: NET PAY WITH A CHARITABLE CONTRIBUTION

Perry Wallace is an employee at Working Environments in Winchester, New Hampshire. He earns $29,000 annually and is paid weekly. He is single with one withholding allowance.

He has pre-tax health insurance of $25 and a charitable contribution to the United Way of $10 per pay period. His taxable income would be as follows:

Period pay	$557.69
Less: Health insurance	25.00
Taxable income	$532.69

Note that Perry's taxable income does *not* reflect his United Way contribution. Because that contribution is computed on a post-tax basis, it does not affect taxable income.

Court-Ordered Garnishments

There are several reasons that a court may order an employer to withhold amounts from an employee's pay and redirect those funds to a regulatory agency. The most common garnishments are for child support, alimony, and student loans. Garnishments apply to ***disposable income:*** the amount of employee pay after legally required deductions such as income taxes have been withheld. If an employee has one garnishment order for 10 percent and receives a second for 15 percent, any further garnishment requests will be deferred until the disposable income is at a level that is available for garnishments.

Consumer credit:

According to Title III of the ***Consumer Credit Protection Act (CCPA)***, garnishments may not be more than (a) 25 percent of the employee's disposable earnings OR (b) the amount by which an employee's disposable earnings are greater than 30 times the federal minimum wage, or $217.50.

Child support:

Garnishments for child support or alimony may be up to 50 percent of disposable income, with an additional 5 percent for any child support that is more than 12 weeks in arrears.

Nontax debts owed to federal agencies:

Garnishments for nontax amounts to federal agencies may not total more than 15 percent of disposable income.

Ken Cavanagh/McGraw Hill

Union Dues

When employees are part of a union that requires regular dues, the employer must withhold those dues from the employee as a post-tax payroll deduction. The union uses dues to fund its activities, which include representation in employee-employer negotiations and political activism. Some employers may pay the union dues for their employees as part of their noncash compensation, but there is no requirement for them to do so.

Employees of the American Civil Liberties Union (ACLU) chose to form a labor union in 2021. What distinguished the ACLU union from other labor unions is the ACLU's nonprofit status. Comprising over 300 employees in multiple cities, one purpose is to prevent staff turnover and implement robust investment strategies. Other purposes include support for employees' wages and benefits.

(Source: *The Washington Post*)

Pre-tax vs. post-tax deductions

1. Which act offered a small-business tax credit for employees' health insurance premiums?

2. What are examples of different retirement plans that may qualify as pre-tax withdrawals?

3. Otis Singleton has disposable pay of $1,790.00 for his biweekly pay period. He receives a court-ordered garnishment for credit card debt of $15,000. What is the maximum amount that may be withheld from Otis's pay?

4. Otis questioned the amount of the garnishment in question 3, claiming that he has health insurance of $125 and union dues of $45 that must also be withheld from his pay. How much should be withheld for the garnishment? Explain.

LO 4.6 Apply Rules for Withholding, Depositing, and Reporting Benefits

Providing benefits as a condition of employment is an important part of employee compensation. In many cases, amounts of money associated with benefits are quantifiable, such as insurance premiums, employee contributions, or specific mandatory deductions. In other cases, the fringe benefit valuation rules are needed. The next piece of the puzzle is actually withholding, depositing, and reporting the organizations' benefits.

Rules for Withholding Amounts Related to Benefits

As a general rule, the money associated with employee benefits should be withheld when the benefit is made available. It is up to the employer's discretion if the money should be withheld during a pay period, monthly, annually, and so forth. Therefore, any employee contributions to cafeteria plans, FSAs, HSAs, or other benefits should be deducted from regular pay. A best practice is to document the amounts of voluntary deductions in writing for the employee to acknowledge and sign.

Comstock/PunchStock

Sums of money related to benefits should be deducted from employee pay promptly. The IRS stipulates that the value of all noncash benefits must be determined no later than January 31 of the following year. This deadline facilitates reporting of the fringe benefits on the employees' W-2s. It additionally allows the employer time to deposit any necessary amounts on time.

The IRS reported that the number of employer audits increased because of the reporting of fringe benefits and taxes due. According to the IRS, when an audit is triggered because of red flags in the computer selection program, one of the first areas checked is employer valuation and fringe benefits reporting. Other items considered include the employer's internal control system and workers' classification as employees or independent contractors.

(Source: *Accounting Today*)

An exception to the general rule is the IRS's *special accounting rule* for noncash benefits provided only in the last two months of the calendar year. Benefits given during this period may be treated as paid during the following calendar year; however, only the benefits' value may be treated as such. Although employers may opt to use the special accounting period for specific benefits, all employees who receive that benefit must also have it reported in accordance with the special accounting rule.

EXAMPLE: SPECIAL ACCOUNTING RULE

Marion Morrison is an employee of Connections Inc. and drives a company car. According to the special accounting rule, the company deferred the taxable amount of Marion's personal use of the company car during November and December 2021 until January 2022. This practice would reduce Marion's taxable income for 2021, but she would still be liable for her 2022 taxes. Connections Inc. would be required to notify Marion of its use of the special accounting rule for her personal company car use no later than January 31, 2022.

Treatment of Taxable Benefit Withholdings

No matter how the employee receives specific benefits; the employer must treat the benefit as though it was paid annually. The rationale for this treatment is to guarantee that taxable benefits are reflected appropriately on employee W-2s. The employer may change the timing of any amounts withheld for benefits as necessary for the entire company and individual employees.

One caveat to the rules for withholding involves the transfer of property associated with benefits. For example, if the benefit involved is an investment, any amount withheld from the employee must coincide with the investment transfer.

Regarding the valuation of taxable fringe benefits, employers may choose to add the periodic value of the fringe benefit to period pay and tax it at the employee's regular tax rate. Alternatively, the employer may report the total value and withhold federal income tax at the 25 percent rate. An example of this practice would involve the valuation of personal company car use if reported annually. In that case, the employer may add the full amount of the benefit valuation to a single pay period and deduct the taxes at that time.

Employees have found that their "free" fringe benefits may be subject to taxes. Wellness programs involving gym memberships, nutritional counseling, and other services provided at no cost to employees may be added to an employee's gross income and subject to income and FICA taxes.

(Source: *Forbes*)

Rules for Depositing Amounts Related to Benefits

Employer deposit rules related to benefits are nearly as diverse as the benefits themselves. Like the withholdings, the deposit frequency depends on the timing of deductions from employee pay and recipient requirements (when applicable). A general rule for taxes withheld is that the deposit of these amounts must follow employer deposit rules, covered in Chapter 6. The employer should estimate the amount of the benefit transmitted on a specific date, remit taxes, and transmit any other monies as necessary.

EXAMPLE: DEPOSIT OF EMPLOYEE 401(K) CONTRIBUTIONS

Theresa Bowen, an employee of TMS Physical Therapy, contributes 4 percent of her gross pay to her employer-sponsored employee stock option benefit. Theresa is paid biweekly and earns $52,000 annually. The employer makes quarterly deposits to the stockbroker. In this example, Theresa's contribution is $2,000 × 0.04, or $80, per pay period. The employer would deduct the amounts from Theresa's pay and retain it in a liability account, which they would deposit with the stockbroker at the appropriate time each quarter.

Depositing taxes for noncash fringe benefits will occasionally require an estimate of the taxes due. An example of when such an estimate may occur would be employee meals. The employer would estimate the value of the meals and deposit the appropriate amount of tax because it would be a taxable fringe benefit. It is important to note that the estimate needs to be as accurate as possible. The underpayment of taxes associated with noncash fringe benefits will result in IRS penalties.

Rules for Reporting Benefits

Benefit reports occur in two different places: the employee's Form W-2 and the total compensation report. Each report serves a different purpose.

- Form W-2 serves as a report of all wages and associated taxes for a calendar year. All taxable benefits are reported as wages on the employee's Form W-2. This reporting method ensures that the employer calculates the correct amount of income taxes and that the employee's annual tax return reflects the proper amounts of income.
- The total compensation report is a report given to the employee from the company that details all benefits in monetary terms. This report allows employees to have an accurate statement of their service's cash and noncash value to the employer.

Gorodenkoff/Shutterstock

Custom benefits software Is becoming more popular among employers. Companies specializing in employee benefits provide integrated custom platforms that address employer withholding, depositing, and reporting needs.

Examples of benefits management software platforms include the following companies:

- BambooHR
- Ceridian
- Workday

These platforms sometimes cost more than $100,000, making them too expensive for many small- and some medium-sized employers. Innovations in technology may ultimately make these platforms more affordable. Changes in reporting laws certainly make them necessary.

(Source: *Employee Benefit Adviser*)

According to the IRS and the Department of Labor, some of the most common benefits errors are:

- Incorrectly defined compensation.
- Delays in the remittance of employees' contributions for benefits.
- Improper definition of employee eligibility and enrollment in benefit plans.
- Incorrect employee vesting in plans.
- Benefit forfeitures.
- Improper use of loans made to participants.
- Incorrect use of hardship distributions.
- Incorrectly recorded plan expenses.

The best way to avoid errors is to involve both the payroll and the human resources departments in benefits determinations to ensure proper implementation and internal classification of related monies. Benefit plans should be reviewed annually to ensure accuracy in legal compliance, remittance procedures, and reconciliation of employee contributions with payroll records.

Employee Benefits reporting

Stop & Check

1. When should employers withhold amounts of money associated with benefits from employee pay?

2. Brandon McLaughlin is an employee of Creighton Steel and receives several fringe benefits due to his employment. He wants to know the value of his employment, both cash and noncash. What report should he request from his employer?

3. Vivian King is an employee of Nabors Drilling. She receives her Form W-2 in January and notices that her gross pay exceeds her annual salary. As the payroll accountant, you are aware of all fringe benefits available to and used by employees. What would you tell Vivian to help her understand the difference?

Summary of Fringe Benefits and Voluntary Deductions

Fringe benefits are an integral part of employee compensation and often significantly influence an employee's cost. Common forms of fringe benefits are health insurance and retirement but can encompass an endless variety of employee perks. Certain noncash fringe benefits are subject to employment taxes, which requires an employer to be aware of the taxes associated with offering certain types of benefits.

Trends to Watch

EMPLOYEE BENEFITS

Employers' attitudes toward employee benefits have changed since 2018. Benefits have become important negotiating tools for employees, which has resulted in the following:

- Large companies such as Google, Facebook, and Costco have developed a reputation for offering generous benefits.
- Employees are using sites such as Glassdoor and Salary.com to rate prospective employers' total compensation packages.
- Values associated with fringe benefits have risen in proportion to employee salaries.
- Employers are starting to offer financial wellness planning—apart from retirement planning.
- The legislation is being introduced to encourage employers and employees in student loan reduction payments.
- Innovative healthcare plan designs that focus on benefits provision instead of simply managing costs.
- Student loan repayment assistance, extended through 2026.
- Telehealth benefits that allow flexibility in receiving needed care.
- Additional mental health resource availability.
- An expansion of nonmedical health plans that can be tailored to individual needs.

A primary category of fringe benefits involves employer-sponsored medical insurance plans. Most medical insurance plans may be deducted from an employee's pay on a pre-tax basis, which reduces the employee's tax liability. Employee medical insurance premiums are deducted on a pre-tax basis; this fringe benefit is often part of a cafeteria plan. Other pre-tax benefits, such as flexible spending arrangements (FSA), may be included.

Certain types of noncash fringe benefits are excluded from taxation. Commonly excluded fringe benefits are *de minimis* benefits that have a small value that accounting for the cost would be unrealistic. Other noncash fringe benefits not subject to taxes involve the employer's items for their own conveniences, such as on-site meals and company cars. However, company cars' personal use is subject to tax, based on the employer's valuation method.

Many voluntary benefits are deducted from employee pay on a post-tax basis. Other post-tax deductions include court-mandated deductions and garnishments. It is important to note the legal limits of garnishing employee pay to ensure that an appropriate amount is deducted. Employers are responsible for withholding, depositing, and reporting all deductions from an employee's pay, especially when those deductions are taxes. The total amount of annual compensation, including pay, taxes, and benefits, may be reported on Form W-2 and the total compensation report.

Key Points

- Fringe benefits are an important part of an employee's compensation package because they help attract and retain high-quality employees.
- Fringe benefits have been correlated with increases in employee productivity and company revenue.
- Fringe benefits may be statutory or voluntary in nature.
- Pre-tax deductions are used for qualified deductions and to reduce the taxable wage base.
- Cafeteria plans allow employees to exclude medical premiums and qualified medical expenses from income tax and FICA taxes.
- Certain pre-tax deductions are subject to FICA taxes.
- Excluded fringe benefits are subject to specific IRS rules that govern amounts and taxation.
- Personal use of company vehicles is evaluated to determine the amount of income the employee is taxed on their Form W-2.
- Post-tax deductions include garnishments, union dues, and charitable contributions.
- Garnishments are subject to maximum percentages of disposable income, depending on the type of garnishment.
- Employer withholding of amounts associated with providing employee benefits varies depending on the benefit and subject to taxes.
- Taxes associated with taxable noncash fringe benefits must be deposited when the benefit is transmitted to the employee.
- Employers report the valuation of noncash fringe benefits as part of the employee's Form W-2 and the total compensation report.

Vocabulary

401(k)
403(b)
457
Cafeteria plan
Cents-per-mile rule
Charitable contribution
Commuting rule
Compensation
Consumer Credit Protection
 Act (CCPA)
De minimis
Defined benefit
Defined contribution
Disposable income

ESOP
Fair market value (FMV)
Flexible spending
 arrangement (FSA)
Fringe benefit
Garnishments
General valuation rule
 (GVR)
Gross pay
Health savings account
 (HSA)
High-deductible health plan
 (HDHP)
IRA

Lease value rule
Mandated deductions
Mandatory deductions
Pay advice
Post-tax deductions
Premium only plan (POP)
Publication 15-B
Qualified plan
SEP
SIMPLE
SIMPLE 401(k)
Special accounting rule
Union dues
Voluntary deductions

Review Questions

1. Why do companies offer fringe benefits to their employees?

2. Approximately what percentage of employee compensation includes fringe benefits?

3. What are three examples of voluntary fringe benefits?

4. What are the two reports associated with fringe benefits?

5. What are two examples of voluntary deductions?

6. What are two examples of pre-tax deductions?

7. What are two types of insurance that may be deducted pre-tax under a cafeteria plan?

8. What are the four categories of cafeteria plans?

9. How does an FSA affect an employee's taxable wages?

10. What are three examples of excluded fringe benefits?

11. What are the ways that the value of a company vehicle as a fringe benefit is determined?

12. What are garnishments, and how must they be handled?

13. How do post-tax deductions differ from pre-tax deductions?

14. How does the special accounting rule affect the withholding of benefits?

15. How often must employers deposit taxes associated with taxable fringe benefits?

Exercises Set A

E4-1A.
LO 4-1, 4-4

Ruth Garcia is a children's photographer for Midlands Photography Studios. She would like advice about using an FSA for miscellaneous prescriptions and other medical expenses. What reason(s) would you give her for having an FSA account? (Select all that apply.)

a. The monthly amount is deducted on a pre-tax basis.

b. The employee's income that is subject to income tax(es) is reduced.

c. The income subject to Social Security and Medicare taxes is reduced.

d. The FSA will continue from year to year if she does not use it.

E4-2A.
LO 4-1

Dev Holmes is a metalworker at Bartleby's Metal Shop. Which of the following would likely be fringe benefits that his employer would provide because they would be needed as part of his job? (Select all that apply.)

a. Heat-resistant gloves
b. On-site cafeteria
c. Welding mask
d. Personal accounting services

E4-3A.
LO 4-2

Lori Garrett is wondering what elements are in a qualified health plan. Which of the following would be included? (Select all that apply.)

a. Mental health benefits
b. Prescription drugs
c. Pet Insurance premiums
d. Preventive and wellness services

E4-4A.
LO 4-2

What is a significant difference between flexible spending arrangements (FSAs) and health savings accounts (HSAs)?

a. Only FSAs may be included as part of a cafeteria plan.
b. HSAs may accompany any type of employer-sponsored health insurance.
c. Amounts contributed to HSAs may remain in the account for use later in life.
d. No annual pre-tax contribution limit exists for FSAs.

E4-5A.
LO 4-1

Jeannie Velshi is an employee who receives educational assistance from her employer in the amount of $15,000 per year. How is this amount treated for tax purposes?

a. None of it is taxable
b. All of it is taxable
c. $5,250 is taxable
d. $9,750 is taxable

E4-6A.
LO 4-4

Ana Cole is an employee of Wilson In-Home Healthcare Services. She is issued a company vehicle so that she may drive to customer sites. Which of the general valuation rules would be appropriate to compute the value of the asset for any personal use? (Select all that apply.)

a. Cents-per-mile rule
b. Commuting rule
c. Unsafe conditions rule
d. Lease value rule

E4-7A.
LO 4-5

Which of the following describes the primary difference between a 401(k) and a 403(b) retirement plan?

a. The 401(k) is a defined benefit only plan.
b. The 403(b) is a defined contribution only plan.
c. The 401(k) is restricted to investments in stocks only.
d. The 403(b) is restricted to use by nonprofit companies.

E4-8A
LO 4-5

Which of the following is true about fringe benefits?

a. They represent additional cash paid directly to employees.
b. They are only available for employees and their families.
c. They represent additional compensation given for services performed.
d. The amount of the fringe benefit is never subject to income tax.

E4-9A.
LO 4-5

How is disposable income computed?

a. Gross pay less pre-tax deductions.
b. Gross pay less pre-tax deductions and income taxes.
c. Gross pay less mandatory deductions.
d. Gross pay less Social Security and Medicare taxes.

E4-10A.
LO 4-6
By what date must a company declare the value of noncash benefits used in 2021?
a. January 1, 2022
b. December 31, 2022
c. February 1, 2022
d. January 31, 2022

Problems Set A

P4-1A.
LO 4-1, 4-2
George Sargent is a new employee at Asbury Park Entertainment. He is debating if he should enroll in a POP with the opportunity for an FSA or an HDHP with an opportunity for an HSA. The POP premium is $350 per month and the annual deductible is $500. For the HDHP, the monthly premium is $200 and the annual deductible is $1,200. Explain the options of each to George?

P4-2A.
LO 4-1
Joe Ramsey is a computer programmer at Biosphere Communications. He approaches you, the payroll accountant, about his garnishment for child support, claiming that he wishes to remit it personally because he needs to increase his net pay. What advice should you offer him?

P4-3A.
LO 4-1, 4-2
Alisha Thomas is a graphic designer at a large marketing firm. She earns $56,000 annually, paid biweekly. She contributes 5 percent of her gross pay to her qualified 401(k) plan on a pre-tax basis and has a pre-tax medical premium of $350. What is her taxable income per pay period?

P4-4A.
LO 4-3
Keren Wiseman is an employee of Dimensionworks Designs in New Mexico. She received the following achievement awards from her employer during 2021:
- Best safety plan, Santa Fe County: $1,200
- Top emergency plan layout, New Mexico: $1,600
- Ten-year employee award: $750

The achievement awards are eligible under qualified plan.
How much of her achievement award income is taxable?

P4-5A.
LO 4-1, 4-3
John Cotton is an employee at Radiance Senior Living. He received the following benefits from his employer during 2021 on the company's location for company purposes:
- Personal protective equipment: $50 per month
- Employer-provided cell phone: $50 per month
- Meals: $100 per month

What amount of these benefits is taxable for 2021?

P4-6A.
LO 4-4
Judi Pendergrass is an account representative at Ever Pharmaceuticals. She has a company car for customer visits, which she uses to commute from work to home on Friday nights and from home to work on Monday mornings, 50 weeks per year. Her commute is 25 miles in each direction. Using the commuting rule, what is the valuation of the fringe benefit?

P4-7A.
LO 4-4
Brent Bishop is the vice president of operations for Southern Sweets Bakery. He drives a 2021 Toyota Prius as his company car, and it has a fair market value of $41,500. The prorated annual lease value per Publication 15-B for the vehicle is $10,750. He reported driving 34,750 miles during 2021, of which 20 percent were for personal reasons. The company pays his fuel and charges him five cents per mile for fuel charges. Using the lease value rule, what is the valuation of Brent's company car benefit?

P4-8A.
LO 4-5

Geraldine Wolfe is a supervisor at Fantastigifts. She has an annual salary of $45,000, paid biweekly, and a garnishment for consumer credit of $375. Assuming that her disposable income is 80 percent of her gross pay per period, does the garnishment follow the CCPA? If not, what is the maximum garnishment allowed for Geraldine's consumer credit garnishment?

P4-9A.
LO 4-1,
4-2, 4-5

Joy Warren is an employee at Jankoski Cycles. She earns a salary of $37,765 annually, paid semimonthly. She contributes to the following fringe benefits and other deductions:

- Medical insurance: $220 per pay period
- Dental insurance: $15 per pay period
- 401(k): 6 percent of gross pay
- Additional withholding: $125 per month

What is the total annual amount of Joy's fringe benefits and other deductions?

P4-10A.
LO 4-6

Gavin Range is the payroll accountant for Comptech Industries. His employer decided to use the special accounting rule for 2021. Which months may be included in the special accounting rule?

P4-11A.
LO 4-1,
4-2, 4-3, 4-5

Elijah Hamilton is the payroll accountant at White Box Builders. He is preparing an information package about voluntary and fringe benefits. Using the following list of fringe benefits, classify each benefit as pre-tax or post-tax *and* as taxable or tax-exempt for federal income taxes.

Employee Benefits				
Benefit	Pre-tax	Post-tax	Taxable	Tax-exempt
401(k)				
Medical insurance				
Off-site gym membership				
United Way contributions				
AFLAC				
Tuition assistance up to $5,250 annually				
Commuter passes up to $270 monthly				

Exercises Set B

E4-1B.
LO 4-1

Which of the following fringe benefits is exempt from federal income tax but subject to FICA tax?
a. Moving expense reimbursements
b. Tuition reduction for undergraduate education
c. Pet insurance
d. Working condition benefits

E4-2B.
LO 4-1

Taylor Struyk is an employee of New York Boutiques, Inc. She is a traveling salesperson who routinely meets with customers at their places of business. Which of the following fringe benefits would be appropriate for her employer to provide for Taylor to conduct business? (Select all that apply.)
a. Personal stylist
b. Tuition assistance
c. Clothing allowance
d. Cell phone

E4-3B.
LO 4-2

Which of the following is a co-requisite of a health savings account (HSA)?
a. No employer-provided insurance
b. A high deductible health plan
c. Multiple health insurance plans held by the same employee
d. A flexible spending arrangement

E4-4B.
LO 4-2

What is the annual maximum amount that an employee may contribute to a flexible savings arrangement before it becomes taxable income?
a. $2,250
b. $2,450
c. $2,750
d. $2,850

E4-5B.
LO 4-3

Mike Mallin is an employee of All-Adventure Tours. All-Adventure Tours offers tuition reimbursement as a fringe benefit. What is the maximum amount that may be excluded from his taxes as a fringe benefit?
a. $4,000
b. $4,750
c. $5,000
d. $5,250

E4-6B.
LO 4-4

Juan Potter is an employee of Convergent Technologies whose job is strictly based in the company's office. His employer has authorized his use of a company vehicle for commuting purposes, as necessary. Which of the general valuation rules would be appropriate to evaluate the value of this fringe benefit?
a. Lease value rule
b. Unsafe conditions rule
c. Commuting rule
d. Cents-per-mile rule

E4-7B.
LO 4-2

Cameron Levitt is the payroll accountant for Glowing Yoga. He is preparing a presentation about Section 125 cafeteria plans. Which of the following items may qualify for inclusion in a cafeteria plan?
a. Health benefits
b. Adoption assistance
c. Childcare expenses
d. Education assistance

E4-8B.
LO 4-5

Eric Rubin is the payroll accountant of Central Communications. He is researching retirement plan options for his employer. Central Communications has 135 employees and is a for-profit company. Which of the following plans should he consider? (Select all that apply.)
a. IRA
b. 457
c. 403(b)
d. 401(k)

E4-9B.
LO 4-1

Which of the following is/are examples of fringe benefits? (Select all that apply.)
a. Education assistance (up to $5,250 annually)
b. Dependent care assistance (up to $5,000 annually)
c. Vacation packages
d. Retirement planning services

E4-10B.
LO 4-5

Which of the following are always post-tax deductions? (Select all that apply.)
a. Garnishments
b. Qualified health insurance
c. Charitable contributions
d. Retirement plan contributions

E4-11B.
LO 4-6

To which two months does the special accounting rule pertain?
a. January and February
b. November and December
c. The last two months of the company's fiscal year
d. December and January of the following year

Problems Set B

P4-1B.
LO 4-1, 4-2

Richard Cox is a new employee at Big Tech Computers. He is debating whether he should enroll in a POP with the opportunity for an FSA or an HDHP with an opportunity for an HSA. The POP premium is $550 per month and the annual deductible is $400. For the HDHP, the monthly premium is $175 and the annual deductible is $1,400. Explain the options of each to Richard.

P4-2B.
LO 4-1

Orlando Collier is employed as a concierge at Strawberry Lodge, an upscale resort in the Adirondack Mountains. He asks you, the payroll accountant, which deductions from his pay are considered voluntary fringe benefits. Where would you tell him to look on his pay stub?

P4-3B.
LO 4-1, 4-2

Teri Benson is a manager at Complex Ventures, Inc. Teri contributes $2,750 annually to an FSA and has medical insurance with a $500 monthly premium. Teri earns a salary of $72,200 and is paid biweekly. What is the taxable income per period?

P4-4B.
LO 4-3

Jordy Richman is employed at Rockstar Music. Jordy is receiving education assistance of $5,750 per year from Rockstar Music to complete a bachelor's degree from an accredited college. How much of that assistance is taxable?

P4-5B.
LO 4-1, 4-3

Jewel Lyman is an employee in the office of Salvaggio & Wheelers, Attorneys at Law. She received the following benefits during 2021:
- Medical insurance: $250 per month
- Commuter pass: $500 per month
- Employer-paid membership to Anytime Gym: $75 per year
- Dependent care assistance: $3,600 per year

What is the total taxable amount for Jewel's 2021 benefits?

P4-6B.
LO 4-4

Rodney Atwater is a sales representative for American Silk Mills. Because he visits customer sites, he has a company car. He drove 25,500 miles during 2021, of which he reported 15 percent was personal miles. Using the cents-per-mile rule, what is the valuation of this benefit for 2021?

P4-7B.
LO 4-4

Janice Lucas is the president of Miller Custom Coffee Roasters. She drives a 2020 Mercedes E300 with a fair market value of $57,500. The lease value is $14,750. The odometer started at 655 and was reported at 32,855 at the end of the year. The car was available all of 2021. Janice reported that she drove 32,200 miles during 2021, of which 9,800 were for personal reasons. The company pays all her fuel and charges her five cents per personal mile for fuel costs. What is her 2021 valuation using the lease value rule?

P4-8B.
LO 4-5

Haley Price is an employee at Finesong Jewelry. She earns a salary of $38,850 per year, paid biweekly, and has a credit card garnishment. Assuming that Haley's disposable income is 85 percent of her gross pay, what is the maximum amount per period that may be deducted for the garnishment?

P4-9B.

Ari Friedman is an employee at Ruby Investments, with an annual salary of $92,500, paid biweekly. Ari has the following fringe and voluntary benefits:
- Medical insurance: $400 per month
- 401(k): 3 percent of gross pay
- Flexible spending arrangement: $2,550 annually
- Charitable contribution: $65 per pay period

What is the total amount Ari contributes to fringe benefits and voluntary deductions annually?

P4-10B.
LO 4-6

Arla Dodson is the payroll accountant for Penn & Associates Investments. The company owner decided on December 15, 2021, that he would invoke the special accounting rule. By what date does Arla need to notify affected employees that the rule is being used?

P4-11B.
LO 4-1, 4-2,
4-3, 4-5

Kerry Palmer is reviewing benefits with you, the payroll accountant for Silly Lemon Films. Classify the following benefits in which she is interested as pre-tax or post-tax deductions *and* as taxable or tax exempt for federal income tax.

K. Palmer Benefits				
Benefit	Pre-Tax	Post-Tax	Taxable	Tax Exempt
Medical insurance				
FSA				
AFLAC				
Graduate school tuition at $11,000 annually				
On-site meals				

Critical Thinking

4-1. Malcolm Figueroa is a sales employee of Carefree Pools and Spas Inc. In 2021, he was issued a company car with a fair market value of $35,000. He drove a total of 22,000 miles; used the car for 2,000 miles for personal use; and his employer paid for fuel, charging Malcolm 5.5 cents per mile. Under the lease-value rule, what is the amount that must be added to Malcolm's gross pay for 2021? (Use the following table for lease values.)

4-2. Malcolm's employer offers him the option to use the cents-per-mile rule instead of the lease-value rule for 2021. Which method will yield the lower gross income for Malcolm? (Use 56 cents per mile in your calculations.)

(1) Automobile FMV	(2) Annual Lease
$ 0 to 999	$ 600
1,000 to 1,999	850
2,000 to 2,999	1,100
3,000 to 3,999	1,350
4,000 to 4,999	1,600
5,000 to 5,999	1,850
6,000 to 6,999	2,100
7,000 to 7,999	2,350
8,000 to 8,999	2,600
9,000 to 9,999	2,850
10,000 to 10,999	3,100
11,000 to 11,999	3,350
12,000 to 12,999	3,600
13,000 to 13,999	3,850
14,000 to 14,999	4,100
15,000 to 15,999	4,350
16,000 to 16,999	4,600
17,000 to 17,999	4,850
18,000 to 18,999	5,100
19,000 to 19,999	5,350
20,000 to 20,999	5,600

(1) Automobile FMV	(2) Annual Lease
21,000 to 21,999	5,850
22,000 to 22,999	6,100
23,000 to 23,999	6,350
24,000 to 24,999	6,600
25,000 to 25,999	6,850
26,000 to 27,999	7,250
28,000 to 29,999	7,750
30,000 to 31,999	8,250
32,000 to 33,999	8,750
34,000 to 35,999	9,250
36,000 to 37,999	9,750
38,000 to 39,999	10,250
40,000 to 41,999	10,750
42,000 to 43,999	11,250
44,000 to 45,999	11,750
46,000 to 47,999	12,250
48,000 to 49,999	12,750
50,000 to 51,999	13,250
52,000 to 53,999	13,750
54,000 to 55,999	14,250
56,000 to 57,999	14,750
58,000 to 59,999	15,250

In the Real World: Scenario for Discussion

Project labor agreements (PLAs) are used in certain states to promote pay and benefit equity for construction workers. Specifically, PLAs ensure that construction workers who choose not to join a union have access to the same pay and benefits as their union-affiliated colleagues. PLAs ensure that the presence or absence of a labor union is not a factor in the contract bidding process, therefore encouraging more contractors to bid on construction projects. Proponents of PLAs contend that they expand employment opportunities. Opponents claim that the PLA cannot exist in at-will employment states.

Which side is more correct? How can at-will employment laws exist where PLAs are allowed?

Internet Activities

4-1. Health insurance is a rapidly changing and evolving field. Employers have many options and concerns to consider. Check out www.npr.org/sections/health-care/ to listen to podcasts about health insurance and employer issues. What issues do employers currently face?

4-2. Using a site such as Google, Yahoo, or Safari, search for the term "fringe benefits." Sites such as HR360 and Employee Benefit Adviser contain insights into fringe benefits and guidance about the tax treatment for benefits. Why do you think that fringe benefits are important enough to influence an employee's choice of employer?

4-3. Go to www.benefitspro.com and search for benefits-related podcasts. Once you have listened to one or more podcasts, describe the insights you gained from the information presented?

4-4. Want to know more about the topics discussed in this chapter? Go to the following links:

www.healthcare.gov/law/index.html

www.aflac.com

www.investopedia.com

www.irs.gov/pub/irs-pdf/p15b.pdf

www.dol.gov/general/topic/wages/garnishments

4-5. Can employers charge employees for their uniforms? Check out the U.S. Department of Labor video at https://www.youtube.com/watch?v=PoZCux0rTN8&feature=youtu.be

Continuing Payroll Project: Prevosti Farms and Sugarhouse

Although the company has already established medical and retirement plan benefits, Toni Prevosti wants to consider other benefits to attract employees. As the company's accountant, you have been tasked with annotating employee earnings records with benefit elections for each employee. The following sheet contains details of employee choices. These costs are employer-paid and will take effect on the first pay period of March.

To calculate the life insurance benefit, multiply the employee's annual salary by 1 percent. For example, if an employee earned $50,000 per year, the life insurance would be $50,000 × 0.01 = $500.

Employee	Flex-Time	Childcare Assistance (under $5,000 annually)	FSA (annual)	Education Assistance ($4,000 annually)	Life Insurance (at 1% of annual salary value)	Long-Term Care Insurance $15 per period	Gym Membership $15 per month
Millen	Yes	Yes	$500.00	No	Yes	No	Yes
Towle	No	No	1,200.00	Yes	No	No	Yes
Long	Yes	Yes	700.00	Yes	Yes	No	Yes
Shangraw	Yes	No	200.00	No	Yes	No	No
Lewis	No	No	1,600.00	No	Yes	Yes	No
Schwartz	No	No	450.00	Yes	Yes	No	Yes
Prevosti	Yes	No	900.00	No	Yes	No	Yes
Student	No	No	300.00	Yes	No	No	Yes

Annotate the Employee Earning Records with payroll-related benefit elections. The amount per period should be included in the record. As an example, if an employee elected to contribute $1,300 to his or her FSA, the period payroll deduction would be $1,300/26, or $50. The estimated yearly earnings used for insurance purposes for the hourly employees are computed as follows: (hourly wages times number of hours worked per week × 52) then divide by 26 pay periods to get an amount per pay period. For example: If Shangraw worked 20 hours per week, the computation is $11/hour × 52 weeks = $11,440 per year. Insurance is computed as $11,440 × 1% = $114.40/26 = $4.40 per pay period.

EMPLOYEE EARNING RECORD

NAME	Thomas Millen	Hire Date 2/1/2021	Dependent child < 17 3
ADDRESS	1022 Forest School Road	Date of Birth 12/16/1992	Dependent other 1
CITY/STATE/ZIP	Woodstock, VT 05001	Position Production Manager PT/(FT)	Step 4a W-4 Info none
TELEPHONE	802-478-5055	Filing Status Married/Joint	Step 4b W-4 Info none
SOCIAL SECURITY NUMBER	031-11-3456	Exempt/Nonexempt Exempt	Step 4c W-4 Info none
		Pay Rate $35,000.00 Hr / Wk / Mo/(Yr)	

Flex-Time	Child Care	FSA Amount	Educational Assistance	Life Ins.	Long-Term Care	Gym Membership	Total Benefit

EMPLOYEE EARNING RECORD

NAME	Avery Towle	Hire Date	2/1/2021	Dependent child < 17	0
ADDRESS	4011 Route 100	Date of Birth	7/14/1991	Dependent other	0
CITY/STATE/ZIP	Plymouth, VT 05102	Position	Production Worker PT/(FT)	Step 4a W-4 Info	none
TELEPHONE	802-967-5873	Filing Status	Single	Step 4b W-4 Info	none
SOCIAL SECURITY NUMBER	089-74-0974	Exempt/Nonexempt	Non-exempt	Step 4c W-4 Info	none
		Pay Rate	$12.00 (Hr) / Wk / Mo / Yr		

Flex-Time	Child Care	FSA Amount	Educational Assistance	Life Ins.	Long-Term Care	Gym Membership	Total Benefit

EMPLOYEE EARNING RECORD

NAME	Charlie Long	Hire Date	2/1/2021	Dependent child < 17	2
ADDRESS	242 Benedict Road S.	Date of Birth	3/16/1997	Dependent other	0
CITY/STATE/ZIP	Woodstock, VT 05002	Position	Production Worker PT/(FT)	Step 4a W-4 Info	none
TELEPHONE	802-429-3846	Filing Status	Married/Joint	Step 4b W-4 Info	none
SOCIAL SECURITY NUMBER	056-23-4593	Exempt/Nonexempt	Non-exempt	Step 4c W-4 Info	none
		Pay Rate	$12.50 (Hr) / Wk / Mo / Yr		

Flex-Time	Child Care	FSA Amount	Educational Assistance	Life Ins.	Long-Term Care	Gym Membership	Total Benefit

EMPLOYEE EARNING RECORD

NAME	Mary Shangraw	Hire Date	2/1/2021	Dependent child < 17	0
ADDRESS	1901 Main Street #2	Date of Birth	8/20/1999	Dependent other	1
CITY/STATE/ZIP	Bridgewater, VT 05520	Position	Administrative Assistant (PT)/FT	Step 4a W-4 Info	none
TELEPHONE	802-575-5423	Filing Status	Single	Step 4b W-4 Info	none
SOCIAL SECURITY NUMBER	075-28-8945	Exempt/Nonexempt	Non-exempt	Step 4c W-4 Info	none
		Pay Rate	$11.00 (Hr) / Wk / Mo / Yr		

Flex-Time	Child Care	FSA Amount	Educational Assistance	Life Ins.	Long-Term Care	Gym Membership	Total Benefit

EMPLOYEE EARNING RECORD

NAME	Kristen Lewis	Hire Date	2/1/2021	Dependent child < 17	2
ADDRESS	840 Daily Hollow Road	Date of Birth	4/6/1985	Dependent other	1
CITY/STATE/ZIP	Bridgewater, VT 05523	Position	Office Manager PT/(FT)	Step 4a W-4 Info	none
TELEPHONE	802-390-5572	Filing Status	Married/Joint	Step 4b W-4 Info	none
SOCIAL SECURITY NUMBER	076-39-5673	Exempt/Nonexempt	Exempt	Step 4c W-4 Info	none
		Pay Rate	$32,000.00 Hr / Wk / Mo/(Yr)		

Flex-Time	Child Care	FSA Amount	Educational Assistance	Life Ins.	Long-Term Care	Gym Membership	Total Benefit

EMPLOYEE EARNING RECORD

NAME	Joel Schwartz	Hire Date	2/1/2021	Dependent child < 17	2
ADDRESS	55 Maple Farm Way	Date of Birth	5/23/1985	Dependent other	0
CITY/STATE/ZIP	Woodstock, VT 05534	Position	Sales PT/(FT)	Step 4a W-4 Info	none
TELEPHONE	802-463-9985	Filing Status	Married/Joint	Step 4b W-4 Info	none
SOCIAL SECURITY NUMBER	021-34-9876	Exempt/Nonexempt	Exempt	Step 4c W-4 Info	none
		Pay Rate	$24,000 + Commiss Hr / Wk / Mo/(Yr)		

Flex-Time	Child Care	FSA Amount	Educational Assistance	Life Ins.	Long-Term Care	Gym Membership	Total Benefit

EMPLOYEE EARNING RECORD

NAME	Toni Prevosti	Hire Date	2/1/2021	Dependent child < 17	3
ADDRESS	820 Westminster Road	Date of Birth	9/19/1987	Dependent other	2
CITY/STATE/ZIP	Bridgewater, VT 05521	Position	Owner/President PT/(FT)	Step 4a W-4 Info	none
TELEPHONE	802-555-3456	Filing Status	Married/Joint	Step 4b W-4 Info	none
SOCIAL SECURITY NUMBER	055-22-0443	Exempt/Nonexempt	Exempt	Step 4c W-4 Info	none
		Pay Rate	$45,000.00 Hr / Wk / Mo/(Yr)		

Flex-Time	Child Care	FSA Amount	Educational Assistance	Life Ins.	Long-Term Care	Gym Membership	Total Benefit

EMPLOYEE EARNING RECORD

NAME	Student Success	Hire Date	2/1/2021
ADDRESS	1644 Smitten Road	Date of Birth	1/1/1991
CITY/STATE/ZIP	Woodstock, VT 05001	Position	Accounting Clerk
TELEPHONE	555-555-5555	Filing Status	Single
SOCIAL SECURITY NUMBER	555-55-5555	Exempt/Nonexempt	Non-exempt
		Pay Rate	$34,000.00

Dependent child < 17	0
Dependent other	0
PT/(FT) Step 4a W-4 Info	none
Step 4b W-4 Info	none
Step 4c W-4 Info	none
Hr / Wk / Mo/(Yr)	

Flex-Time	Child Care	FSA Amount	Educational Assistance	Life Ins.	Long-Term Care	Gym Membership	Total Benefit

Answers to Stop & Check Exercises

Fringe Benefits 101

1. Fringe benefits will fall under the pre-tax or post-tax categories.
2. b and c.
3. a, c, and d.

What Is Served in the Cafeteria Plan?

1. a, b, and d
2. A flexible spending account (FSA) can be taxable when contributions are over $2,750 annually by the employee. The purpose is to defer, not avoid, paying taxes, and there is typically a "use it or lose it" policy where the funds expire at a point in time when not used. Health savings accounts (HSAs) may only be used in conjunction with a cafeteria plan where there is a high deductible, and the funds may be available longer for related medical care.
3. An HDHP has the following limits: $1,400 annual deductible (single), $2,800 annual deductible (family), $7,000 out-of-pocket expenses maximum (single), and $14,000 out-of-pocket expenses maximum (family).

Excluded Fringe Benefits

1. No, because it is provided on the employer's premises and is operated by the company and restricted to use by its employees, their spouses, and dependents.
2. A portion of the cost of the car that would represent the personal use portion of mileage will be included in Marcia's gross income. However, any amount that is directly related to the job would be excluded under the Working Conditions Benefits.

Fringe Benefit Valuations

1. $2,541 (30,250 miles × 15% × 0.56).
2. The value of the fringe benefit is $1,208.22, computed as follows (round final figure to two decimals):

Fair market value of the vehicle:	$ 47,000
Annual lease value:	12,250
Prorated annual lease value:	49.315%
Percent of personal use during the year:	20%
Personal annual lease value:	$1,208.22

Pre-Tax vs. Post-Tax Deductions

1. Affordable Care Act.
2. 401(k); 403(b); Savings Incentive Match Plan for Employees (SIMPLE); Individual Retirement Account (IRA); Employee Stock Ownership Plan (ESOP); Simplified Employee Pension (SEP).
3. $447.50 calculated as: $1,790 disposable income × 25%.
4. Union dues and health insurance are not legally required and thus would not affect the amount of the disposable income available for garnishments.

Employee Benefits Reporting

1. Monies should be withheld from the employee when the benefit is made available; normal practice is to deduct these as the employees receive their pay (daily, weekly, biweekly, semimonthly, monthly, annually).
2. The total compensation report can be given to Brandon to explain the total cost of benefits and compensation received.
3. There are several fringe benefits that must be included in taxable income to the employees. These include personal use of a company-provided vehicle, commuting paid by the employer, or lease of a vehicle.

Chapter Five

Employee Net Pay and Pay Methods

Death and taxes are two certainties in life. Taxes are withheld from employees' earnings and remitted to the governing body. Companies operate as the collector and depositor of income taxes, garnishments, and other deductions on behalf of the employee. The tax code permits certain qualifying deductions to be taken out of an employee's pay before calculating income taxes. These deductions are called pre-tax deductions. Other deductions are removed from the employee's pay after income taxes have been calculated; these are called post-tax deductions. Circular E, also known as *Publication 15* (and all supplemental materials), from the Internal Revenue Service provides a comprehensive list of employee taxes, employer responsibilities, and guidance for special situations. *Publication 15-T* was introduced in 2020 and is focused on wage-bracket tables and percentage method computation amounts.

Taxes and both voluntary and mandated deductions all reduce the gross pay that we computed in Chapter 3. This chapter will explore the effects of these deductions and any other fringe benefits on employee take-home pay, also called *net pay*.

LEARNING OBJECTIVES

After studying Chapter 5, you should be able to:

LO 5-1   Compute Employee Net Pay

LO 5-2   Determine Federal Income Tax Withholding Amounts

LO 5-3   Compute Social Security and Medicare Tax Withholding

LO 5-4   Calculate State and Local Income Taxes

LO 5-5   Apply Post-Tax Deductions

LO 5-6   Discuss Employee Pay Methods

Photo by Supoj Buranaprapapong/Moment/Getty Images

Payroll Disbursal: "Real-Time Payments" and "On-Demand"

In the payroll accounting world, pay periods allow for the regular distribution of employees' wages and salaries according to a predefined schedule. It also allows for the appropriate computation of taxes and other deductions. Most employees are accustomed to the practice of waiting for a payday, cashing payroll checks, and experiencing delays between the end of the pay period and receipt of net pay. According to various sources, such as CNBC, Forbes, and NPR, most Americans live paycheck to paycheck, meaning that they spend all of their net pay before the arrival of the next payroll disbursement.

In 2021, payroll vendors Paychex and DailyPay received acclaim for their introduction of technology to access their earnings more quickly. Paychex debuted its "Real-Time Payments" (RTP) disbursement technology that allows people to access their pay outside of banking hours. Using RTP, employees have access to their net pay instantly instead of waiting to receive a paycheck or direct deposit. DailyPay launched a similar service called "OnDemand" that allows employers to disburse employee earnings outside of the payroll schedule. OnDemand allows employers to make off-cycle payroll disbursements in the event of layoffs, emergencies, or other payroll-related actions that would prompt the need for pay outside of the usual payroll cycle. Although these technologies have different purposes, they have one element in common: Paying employees quickly.

(Sources: Paychex via PR Newswire, Daily Pay via PR Newswire)

Net pay computations and payment methods affect employee take-home pay and accessibility to earned income. Chapter 5 will explore the computations of employee net pay and the methods used to transmit that pay to the employees.

pattarawat/Shutterstock

LO 5-1   Compute Employee Net Pay

Now that we have discussed the computation of gross income, it is time to focus on the various taxes and miscellaneous voluntary or court-ordered deductions withheld and to determine the employee's *net pay*, which is the amount of cash an employee receives in a physical check, cash, direct deposit, or a paycard. The process of computing gross pay involves several steps, each of which must be completed accurately. We will explore the details of pre-tax deductions, tax computations, and post-tax deductions in the following sections of this chapter.

In 2020, the Tax Cuts and Jobs Act of 2017 led to a new Form W-4 and different tax tables. An employee's federal income tax, for those who filed the 2020 Form W-4, is computed based on the employee's tax filing status, pay frequency, taxable earnings, and spouse's employment status—a vast difference from prior years. We will be using the current year's Form W-4 exclusively.

Once the employer has computed the employee's gross pay, the next step is to deduct mandatory (i.e., legislated), voluntary, and mandated (i.e., court-ordered or union-regulated) amounts. These deductions include federal income tax, Medicare, and Social Security taxes, which are the primary mandatory deductions. Other mandatory deductions that the employee may be subject to include *state income taxes*, city or county income taxes, and regional taxes. For example, Denver has a "head tax" for those employees working within the city and county; Mountain View, California, instituted a similar tax because of Google's presence in the city. Federal Unemployment Tax is the sole employer-only tax. Some states require employees to contribute to the State Unemployment Tax, whereas other states consider it an employer-only tax.

Pay Computation Steps

The following steps show the process for computing each employee's pay:

1. Start with the employee's gross pay.
2. Subtract the pre-tax deductions to get the total taxable earnings.
3. Compute the taxes to be withheld from the total taxable earnings.
4. Deduct the taxes.
5. Deduct any other voluntary or mandated deductions.
6. The result is the employee's net pay.

The easiest way to keep track of all deductions and ensure pay accuracy is to use a payroll register. In the following examples, we will show the computations and a sample of the payroll register representation.

EXAMPLE: NET PAY COMPUTATION

Marco Myles receives a salary of $2,000 paid biweekly and has earned $46,000 year-to-date. He is married, filing jointly with one dependent under 17. The checkbox in Step 4(c) is not checked. Marco works for KOR Inc. in Charleston, West Virginia, where his state income tax is 6 percent. His pre-tax deductions include medical insurance of $50, a cafeteria plan of $75, and a 401(k) of 3 percent of his gross salary per pay period. He has charitable contributions of $10, union dues of $62, and a court-ordered garnishment of $120. Taxable income computation is the same for both federal and state income tax purposes. Let us compute Marco's net pay step-by-step:

Gross pay	$2,000.00
Less: Pre-tax medical insurance deduction	−50.00
Less: Cafeteria plan	−75.00
Less: 401(k) contribution	−60.00
Total taxable earnings	$1,815.00
Less: Federal income tax*	−9.08
Less: Social Security tax[†]	−116.25
Less: Medicare tax[‡]	−27.19
Less: West Virginia state income tax[§]	−108.90
Less: Charitable contribution	−10.00
Less: Union dues	−62.00
Less: Garnishment	−120.00
Net pay	$1,361.58

*$1,815 has a tax bracket of $86.00 and the $2,000 credit for a dependent under 17 is divided by 26 for a per pay period credit amount of $76.92, leaving $9.08 federal income tax.
[†]$2,000 − 50 − 75 = 1,875 × 0.062 = 116.25$
[‡]$2,000 − 50 − 75 = 1,875 × 0.0145 = 27.19$
[§]$1,815 × 0.06 = 108.90$

The payroll register for Marco Myles's pay would appear as follows:

Name	Filing Status	Dependents	Hourly Rate or Period Wage	No. of Regular Hours	No. of Overtime Hours	No. of Holiday Hours	Gross Earnings	401(k)	Insurance	Cafeteria Plan	Taxable Wages for Federal W/H	Taxable Wages for FICA
Marco Myles	MJ	1 < 17	2,000.00				2,000.00	60.00	50.00	75.00	1,815.00	1,875.00

Name	Gross Earning	Taxable Wages for Federal W/H	Taxable Wages for FICA	Federal W/H	Social Security Tax	Medicare W/H	State W/H Tax	Charitable Contribution	Union Dues	Garnishment	Net Pay
Marco Myles	2,000.00	1,815.00	1,875.00	76.08	116.25	27.19	108.90	10.00	62.00	120.00	1,361.58

Grossed-Up Pay

An employer will occasionally want to pay an employee a specific net amount, perhaps as a bonus. However, all federal, state, and local taxes must be applied. The employee's pay must be "grossed up" to satisfy tax liabilities and achieve the net pay desired.

EXAMPLE: "GROSSING UP" AN EMPLOYEE'S PAY

Caitlyn Lanneker is an employee of Pacifica Enterprises, located in the state of Washington. The firm's president wants to award Caitlyn a $150 bonus at the end of the year to reward her. Use the following steps to compute the gross-up amount:

1. Compute the tax rate for federal income tax and FICA. The tax rate on bonuses is 22 percent, per Publication 15-T. The Social Security (6.2 percent) and Medicare taxes (1.45 percent) must be added to this rate. For bonuses, the total tax rate equals 22% + 6.2% + 1.45%, or 29.65%. (For nonbonus gross-up, compute the tax rate using amounts from Appendix C.) Add any state or local income tax rates to this computation as necessary.

2. To calculate the net tax rate, subtract the tax rate percentage from 100 percent (i.e., 100% − tax rate) to get the net tax rate. This bonus is 100% − 29.65%, or 70.35% because no state or local income tax rates apply.

3. The gross-up amount equals the net pay divided by the net tax rate.

For example, for Caitlyn to receive a $150 bonus, the equation to calculate the gross pay is $150/70.35% = <u>$213.22.</u>

Note: Typically, voluntary pre-tax or post-tax deductions are not withheld from bonus checks.

In Ada County, Idaho, the highway district examined its commissioner's compensation package. When he was hired in 2020, he was given a three-year contract. If the commissioner were released from the contract early or resigned, he would receive a grossed-up lump sum for his health coverage in addition to the annual $169,750 salary and other payments.

(Source: Idaho Statesman)

Differentiating Between Gross and Net Pay

Stop & Check

1. What is the difference between gross pay and net pay?
2. What are three items that may be deducted from gross pay?
3. What does it mean to "gross-up" an amount paid to an employee?

LO 5-2 Determine Federal Income Tax Withholding Amounts

Now let us shift our focus to *mandatory deductions* that must be withheld from employee pay. The first class of mandatory deductions is the federal income tax. This is an employee-only tax, meaning that the employer does not contribute a matching amount for the federal income tax withheld from an employee's pay.

Federal Income Taxes

Andrii Yalanskyi/Shutterstock

The first tax we will cover is the *federal income tax*. The federal income tax represents amounts to be withheld from employed persons, calculated using the information reported by the employee on Form W-4. The withheld tax is the employee's deposit against income taxes. The employer acts as a collector and depositor for these funds. When an individual files the income tax return, the amount withheld from his or her pay during the year reduces the amount he or she may have to pay with the return. Federal taxable income is reduced by pre-tax deductions discussed previously.

There are two commonly used methods to calculate the employee's federal income tax in manual systems: Wage bracket and percentage. In 2020, the IRS issued Publication 15-T for the sole purpose of income tax calculations, given that two types of Forms W-4 were in use at that time. We will explain the federal income tax computation methods using the 2021 Form W-4. Regardless of the method used for calculating federal income taxes, the reduction for pre-tax items will remain the same. Publication 15-T contains tax tables to match the new criteria. The following examples reflect how tax deductions affect employee pay.

Federal Income Pre-Tax Computation Examples

EXAMPLE: GROSS PAY LESS 401(K) AND INSURANCE

Amanda Brady's gross wages are $950, she has subscribed to the company's cafeteria plan, and she has agreed to a 10 percent investment of her gross wages in a qualified 401(k) plan. Her portion of the health insurance is $56.90 per pay period. To calculate her taxable pay, we must first determine the 401(k) deduction: $950 × 10% = $95. Therefore, her taxable pay is

$950.00	gross pay
−95.00	401(k) deduction
−56.90	health insurance
$798.10	taxable income

EXAMPLE: EFFECT OF FIXED AMOUNT VS. PERCENTAGE DEDUCTION FOR 401(K) CONTRIBUTION ON TAXABLE WAGES

Daniel Cain has gross wages of $1,125, participates in the company's 401(k) program at $100 per pay period, and has health insurance and AFLAC (all pre-tax) totaling $113.80. The calculation of Daniel's taxable income is

$1,125.00	gross pay
−100.00	401(k) deduction
−113.80	health insurance and AFLAC
$ 911.20	taxable income

Had Daniel participated in the company's 401(k) as a percentage instead of a fixed dollar, the percent would be calculated before other deductions. For instance, if he elected to invest 3 percent of his gross pay, his taxable income would be

$1,125.00	
× 0.03	
33.75	401(k) contribution
$1,125.00	gross pay
−33.75	401(k) contribution
−113.80	health insurance and AFLAC
$ 977.45	taxable income

Note: Gross Pay − qualified medical = taxable wages for FICA. $1,125 − 113.80 = $1,011.20 would be the taxable amount for Social Security and Medicare because retirement contributions are not exempt from FICA taxes.

Starting in 2020, Form W-4 was very different in appearance than in years prior. The criteria for amounts withheld from employee payroll focused more on annual taxes than the employee's marital status and the number of dependents. The employee federal income tax criteria used starting in 2020 included the following:

- ▶ Filing status (Single, Married Filing Jointly, Married Filing Separately, and Head of Household)
- ▶ Multiple jobs or spouse's employment
- ▶ Dependents under the age of 17
- ▶ Other dependents

In prior years, the marital status and number of dependents served as the determinants for how much tax should be withheld. This method resulted in too little tax being withheld each pay period. The newer Form W-4 focuses on marital status, annual income, and dependents. The filing status was expanded to match the categories used on the annual tax return. The reality of an employee supporting other nonchild dependents was included as part of the form.

IF THE EMPLOYEE (AND SPOUSE, WHEN APPLICABLE) HAS MORE THAN ONE JOB, THEY SHOULD CHECK THE BOX AT STEP 2(C) ON FORM W-4 AND

- Complete page 3 of Form W-4 **OR**
- Use the IRS tax estimator at www.irs.gov/w4app

The following examples show how to compute the federal withholding tax using the manual method in Publication 15-T and Form W-4. In the example, the employee is married to a spouse who also has a job. No pre-tax deductions are contained in the first example.

Note: If an employee has more than one job or is married to a spouse who is also employed, they should complete step four of Form W-4 to have the appropriate amount of federal income tax withheld. Step 4(c) specifically addresses the amount of withholding when the employee has a multiple jobs situation.

EXAMPLE: MANUAL PAYROLL TAX COMPUTATION USING FORM W-4, NO PRE-TAX DEDUCTIONS

Tania Breckheim works for Tru-Deal Homebuilders and earns $48,550, paid semi-monthly. She has no other deductions. She is married, filing jointly with two dependents under 17 years of age. Her spouse earns $42,675 annually, paid biweekly, so she has checked the box on Step 2(c).

Steps 2 through 4 of her W-4 would appear as follows:

Step 2: Multiple Jobs or Spouse Works	Complete this step if you (1) hold more than one job at a time, or (2) are married filing jointly and your spouse also works. The correct amount of withholding depends on income earned from all of these jobs.
	Do **only one** of the following.
	(a) Use the estimator at *www.irs.gov/W4App* for most accurate withholding for this step (and Steps 3–4); **or**
	(b) Use the Multiple Jobs Worksheet on page 3 and enter the result in Step 4(c) below for roughly accurate withholding; **or**
	(c) If there are only two jobs total, you may check this box. Do the same on Form W-4 for the other job. This option is accurate for jobs with similar pay; otherwise, more tax than necessary may be withheld . . . . . ▶ ☒
	TIP: To be accurate, submit a 2021 Form W-4 for all other jobs. If you (or your spouse) have self-employment income, including as an independent contractor, use the estimator.

Complete Steps 3–4(b) on Form W-4 for only ONE of these jobs. Leave those steps blank for the other jobs. (Your withholding will be most accurate if you complete Steps 3–4(b) on the Form W-4 for the highest paying job.)

Step 3: Claim Dependents	If your total income will be $200,000 or less ($400,000 or less if married filing jointly):		
	Multiply the number of qualifying children under age 17 by $2,000 ▶ $ 4,000		
	Multiply the number of other dependents by $500 . . . . ▶ $		
	Add the amounts above and enter the total here	3	$ 4,000
Step 4 (optional): Other Adjustments	**(a) Other income (not from jobs).** If you want tax withheld for other income you expect this year that won't have withholding, enter the amount of other income here. This may include interest, dividends, and retirement income	4(a)	$
	(b) Deductions. If you expect to claim deductions other than the standard deduction and want to reduce your withholding, use the Deductions Worksheet on page 3 and enter the result here	4(b)	$
	(c) Extra withholding. Enter any additional tax you want withheld each **pay period** .	4(c)	$ 131.15

To determine the amount in Step 4(c), Tania should use either the online IRS app or pages 3 and 4 of Form W-4. Page 3 of Form W-4 would appear as follows:

Step 2(b)—Multiple Jobs Worksheet *(Keep for your records.)*

If you choose the option in Step 2(b) on Form W-4, complete this worksheet (which calculates the total extra tax for all jobs) on **only ONE** Form W-4. Withholding will be most accurate if you complete the worksheet and enter the result on the Form W-4 for the highest paying job.

Note: If more than one job has annual wages of more than $120,000 or there are more than three jobs, see Pub. 505 for additional tables; or, you can use the online withholding estimator at *www.irs.gov/W4App.*

1 **Two jobs.** If you have two jobs or you're married filing jointly and you and your spouse each have one job, find the amount from the appropriate table on page 4. Using the "Higher Paying Job" row and the "Lower Paying Job" column, find the value at the intersection of the two household salaries and enter that value on line 1. Then, **skip** to line 3 . . . . **1** $ 3410

2 **Three jobs.** If you and/or your spouse have three jobs at the same time, complete lines 2a, 2b, and 2c below. Otherwise, skip to line 3.

  a Find the amount from the appropriate table on page 4 using the annual wages from the highest paying job in the "Higher Paying Job" row and the annual wages for your next highest paying job in the "Lower Paying Job" column. Find the value at the intersection of the two household salaries and enter that value on line 2a . . . . **2a** $

  b Add the annual wages of the two highest paying jobs from line 2a together and use the total as the wages in the "Higher Paying Job" row and use the annual wages for your third job in the "Lower Paying Job" column to find the amount from the appropriate table on page 4 and enter this amount on line 2b . . . . **2b** $

  c Add the amounts from lines 2a and 2b and enter the result on line 2c . . . . **2c** $

3 Enter the number of pay periods per year for the highest paying job. For example, if that job pays weekly, enter 52; if it pays every other week, enter 26; if it pays monthly, enter 12, etc. **3** 26

4 **Divide** the annual amount on line 1 or line 2c by the number of pay periods on line 3. Enter this amount here and in **Step 4(c)** of Form W-4 for the highest paying job (along with any other additional amount you want withheld) . . . . **4** $ 131.15

Page 4 of Form W-4 gives us the amount to deduct for Tania and her spouse's jobs. Following is an excerpt from page 4 as it pertains to Tania.

Form W-4 (2021) Page **4**

Higher Paying Job Annual Taxable Wage & Salary	Married Filing Jointly or Qualifying Widow(er)											
	Lower Paying Job Annual Taxable Wage & Salary											
	$0 - 9,999	$10,000 - 19,999	$20,000 - 29,999	$30,000 - 39,999	$40,000 - 49,999	$50,000 - 59,999	$60,000 - 69,999	$70,000 - 79,999	$80,000 - 89,999	$90,000 - 99,999	$100,000 - 109,999	$110,000 - 120,000
$0 - 9,999	$0	$190	$850	$890	$1,020	$1,020	$1,020	$1,020	$1,020	$1,100	$1,870	$1,870
$10,000 - 19,999	190	1,190	1,890	2,090	2,220	2,220	2,220	2,220	2,300	3,300	4,070	4,070
$20,000 - 29,999	850	1,890	2,750	2,950	3,080	3,080	3,080	3,160	4,160	5,160	5,930	5,930
$30,000 - 39,999	890	2,090	2,950	3,150	3,280	3,280	3,360	4,360	5,360	6,360	7,130	7,130
$40,000 - 49,999	1,020	2,220	3,080	3,280	3,410	3,490	4,490	5,490	6,490	7,490	8,260	8,260
$50,000 - 59,999	1,020	2,220	3,080	3,280	3,490	4,490	5,490	6,490	7,490	8,490	9,260	9,260

Notice that the circled result, $3,410, appears on Step 2, line 1 of the multiple jobs worksheet.

Note that the Extra withholding from line 4(c) is rounded to the nearest dollar. Based on Publication 15-T, her withholding amount is $173 per pay period. However, the extra withholding of $131.15 must be added to the amount shown in the wage-bracket tables or the result of the percentage method. The federal income tax withheld from Tania's pay would be $173 + $131.15, or **$304.15,** per pay period.

This next example shows the manual federal tax computation for a married employee with dependents and pre-tax deductions. Form W-4 should be completed first to obtain the IRS Withholding Tax Assistant's data to work properly.

EXAMPLE: MANUAL PAYROLL TAX COMPUTATION USING FORM W-4 AND THE IRS INCOME TAX WITHHOLDING ASSISTANT <u>WITH</u> PRE-TAX DEDUCTIONS

Chen Bai is an employee at Benson Architects who earns $75,500 annually, paid biweekly. He is married, and his spouse is employed, earning $54,000 annually, paid semimonthly, so box 2(c) is checked. They have three dependents under the age of 17 and one other dependent. Chen has elected to contribute 5 percent of his gross pay to a 401(k) plan and has pre-tax medical insurance of $250 per pay period.

Steps 2 through 4 of Chen's W-4 would appear as follows:

Step 2: **Multiple Jobs** **or Spouse** **Works**	Complete this step if you (1) hold more than one job at a time, or (2) are married filing jointly and your spouse also works. The correct amount of withholding depends on income earned from all of these jobs. Do **only one** of the following. **(a)** Use the estimator at *www.irs.gov/W4App* for most accurate withholding for this step (and Steps 3–4); **or** **(b)** Use the Multiple Jobs Worksheet on page 3 and enter the result in Step 4(c) below for roughly accurate withholding; **or** **(c)** If there are only two jobs total, you may check this box. Do the same on Form W-4 for the other job. This option is accurate for jobs with similar pay; otherwise, more tax than necessary may be withheld . . . . . . ▶ ☑ **TIP:** To be accurate, submit a 2021 Form W-4 for all other jobs. If you (or your spouse) have self-employment income, including as an independent contractor, use the estimator.

Complete Steps 3–4(b) on Form W-4 for only ONE of these jobs. Leave those steps blank for the other jobs. (Your withholding will be most accurate if you complete Steps 3–4(b) on the Form W-4 for the highest paying job.)

Step 3: **Claim** **Dependents**	If your total income will be $200,000 or less ($400,000 or less if married filing jointly): Multiply the number of qualifying children under age 17 by $2,000 ▶ $ 6,000 Multiply the number of other dependents by $500 . . . . ▶ $ 500 Add the amounts above and enter the total here	**3**	$ 6,500
Step 4 **(optional):** **Other** **Adjustments**	**(a) Other income (not from jobs).** If you want tax withheld for other income you expect this year that won't have withholding, enter the amount of other income here. This may include interest, dividends, and retirement income	**4(a)**	$
	(b) Deductions. If you expect to claim deductions other than the standard deduction and want to reduce your withholding, use the Deductions Worksheet on page 3 and enter the result here	**4(b)**	$
	(c) Extra withholding. Enter any additional tax you want withheld each **pay period** .	**4(c)**	$ 249.61

To determine the amount for Step 4(c), Chen would need to complete the Multiple jobs worksheet on page 3 of Form W-4 as follows:

Form W-4 (2021)   Page **3**

Step 2(b)—Multiple Jobs Worksheet *(Keep for your records.)*

If you choose the option in Step 2(b) on Form W-4, complete this worksheet (which calculates the total extra tax for all jobs) on **only ONE** Form W-4. Withholding will be most accurate if you complete the worksheet and enter the result on the Form W-4 for the highest paying job.

Note: If more than one job has annual wages of more than $120,000 or there are more than three jobs, see Pub. 505 for additional tables; or, you can use the online withholding estimator at *www.irs.gov/W4App*.

1	**Two jobs.** If you have two jobs or you're married filing jointly and you and your spouse each have one job, find the amount from the appropriate table on page 4. Using the "Higher Paying Job" row and the "Lower Paying Job" column, find the value at the intersection of the two household salaries and enter that value on line 1. Then, **skip** to line 3	**1**	$ 6,500
2	**Three jobs.** If you and/or your spouse have three jobs at the same time, complete lines 2a, 2b, and 2c below. Otherwise, skip to line 3.		
a	Find the amount from the appropriate table on page 4 using the annual wages from the highest paying job in the "Higher Paying Job" row and the annual wages for your next highest paying job in the "Lower Paying Job" column. Find the value at the intersection of the two household salaries and enter that value on line 2a	**2a**	$
b	Add the annual wages of the two highest paying jobs from line 2a together and use the total as the wages in the "Higher Paying Job" row and use the annual wages for your third job in the "Lower Paying Job" column to find the amount from the appropriate table on page 4 and enter this amount on line 2b	**2b**	$
c	Add the amounts from lines 2a and 2b and enter the result on line 2c	**2c**	$

3 Enter the number of pay periods per year for the highest paying job. For example, if that job pays weekly, enter 52; if it pays every other week, enter 26; if it pays monthly, enter 12, etc. **3** 26

4 **Divide** the annual amount on line 1 or line 2c by the number of pay periods on line 3. Enter this amount here and in **Step 4(c)** of Form W-4 for the highest paying job (along with any other additional amount you want withheld) . . . .   **4** $ 249,61

To determine the amount on line 1 of the Multiple jobs worksheet, Chen would use page 4 of Form W-4 as follows:

Form W-4 (2021)   Page **4**

					Married Filing Jointly or Qualifying Widow(er)						
Higher Paying Job					**Lower Paying Job Annual Taxable Wage & Salary**						
Annual Taxable Wage & Salary	$0 - 9,999	$10,000 - 19,999	$20,000 - 29,999	$30,000 - 39,999	$40,000 - 49,999	$50,000 - 59,999	$60,000 - 69,999	$70,000 - 79,999	$80,000 - 89,999	$90,000 - 99,999	$100,000 - 109,999	$110,000 - 120,000
$0 - 9,999	$0	$190	$850	$890	$1,020	$1,020	$1,020	$1,020	$1,020	$1,100	$1,870	$1,870
$10,000 - 19,999	190	1,190	1,890	2,090	2,220	2,220	2,220	2,220	2,300	3,300	4,070	4,070
$20,000 - 29,999	850	1,890	2,750	2,950	3,080	3,080	3,080	3,160	4,160	5,160	5,930	5,930
$30,000 - 39,999	890	2,090	2,950	3,150	3,280	3,280	3,360	4,360	5,360	6,360	7,130	7,130
$40,000 - 49,999	1,020	2,220	3,080	3,280	3,410	3,490	4,490	5,490	6,490	7,490	8,260	8,260
$50,000 - 59,999	1,020	2,220	3,080	3,280	3,490	4,490	5,490	6,490	7,490	8,490	9,260	9,260
$60,000 - 69,999	1,020	2,220	3,080	3,360	4,490	5,490	6,490	7,490	8,490	9,490	10,260	10,260
$70,000 - 79,999	1,020	2,220	3,160	4,360	5,490	6,490	7,490	8,490	9,490	10,490	11,260	11,260

Notice that the circled result, $6,490, appears on Step 2, line 1 of the multiple jobs worksheet.

Before we compute the federal withholding tax per period, we need to apply the pre-tax deductions:

Period Salary: $75,500/26	$ 2,903.85
Less: 401(k) at 5% of salary	145.19
Less: Pre-tax Medical Insurance	250.00
Taxable Income	$ 2,508.66*
Federal tax per Publication 15-T	$ 371.00
Additional withholding (Box 4(c) is checked)	249.62
Total federal income tax	$ 620.62

Wage-Bracket Method

Using the *wage-bracket method*, the payroll clerk identifies the individual's marital status, number of exemptions, and taxable income level and then follows the chart in Publication 15-T for the amount to be withheld. If manually calculating the wage-bracket method, it is important to apply the appropriate number of withholding variables before calculating the tax amounts. The wage-bracket method is useful for manual payroll preparation because the process of federal tax withholding is an estimate for the year-end amount of taxes due. To determine taxes to withhold using Appendix C, the payroll clerk may use Publication 15-T. If the payroll clerk uses an automated system, periodic checking and ensuring that year-end updates do not run before the last payroll are important to ensuring the system's validity.

EXAMPLE: WAGE-BRACKET COMPUTATION OF FEDERAL INCOME TAX, SINGLE, BIWEEKLY

Steve Bishop is an employee at Vosgienne Farms. He is single with no dependents and earns $48,000 annually, paid biweekly. Using the Wage Bracket tables in Appendix C, we will determine Steve's federal income tax in different situations.

1. NO PRE-TAX DEDUCTIONS

Period pay ($48,000/26)	$1,846.15
Taxable income	1,846.15
Federal income tax	156.00*

(continued)

(concluded)

2. PRE-TAX HEALTH INSURANCE, $75, PRE-TAX SUPPLEMENTAL HEALTH INSURANCE, $55

Period pay ($48,000/26)	$1,846.15
Less: health insurance	75.00
Less: supplemental health insurance	55.00
Taxable income	$ 1,716.15
Federal income tax	$ 0.00

3. PRE-TAX HEALTH INSURANCE, $75, PRE-TAX SUPPLEMENTAL HEALTH INSURANCE, $55, 401(K) CONTRIBUTION, $100

Period pay ($48,000/26)	$1,846.15
Less: health insurance	75.00
Less: supplemental health insurance	55.00
Less: 401(k) contribution	100.00
Taxable income	$1,616.15
Federal income tax*	$ 128.00

***Note:** The taxable income for Social Security and Medicare tax is $1,846.15 − 75 − 55 = $1,716.15

When using the wage-bracket tables, it should be noted that many wage amounts are the same number as the beginning and the end of a range. If the number is the exact number of the range in these events, the next bracket should be used. For example, refer to the below image. It is important to notice the language at the top of the column: "And the wages are— At least. . . But less than." If the wages were $3,324.99, then the top row would be used. If the wages were precisely $3,325, then the second row would be used.

EXAMPLE: WAGE-BRACKET COMPUTATION OF FEDERAL INCOME TAX, MARRIED FILING JOINT, SEMIMONTHLY PAY PERIOD

Regina Smith is an employee of Centerspot Photo Designs. She earns $36,000 per year and is paid semimonthly. She is single with no dependents. Using the 2021 wage-bracket tables in Appendix C, we will determine Regina's federal income tax in different situations.

1. NO VOLUNTARY PRE-TAX DEDUCTIONS

Period pay ($36,000/24)	$1,500.00
Taxable income	1,500.00
Federal income tax	110.00

2. PRE-TAX HEALTH INSURANCE DEDUCTION, $150

Period pay ($36,000/24)	$1,500.00
Less: health insurance	150.00
Taxable income	$1,350.00
Federal income tax	$ 91.00

3. PRE-TAX HEALTH INSURANCE DEDUCTION, $150, AND 401(K) CONTRIBUTION, 4%

Period pay ($36,000/24)	$1,500.00
Less: health insurance	150.00
Less: 401(k) contribution	80.00
Taxable income*	$1,270.00
Federal income tax	$ 81.00

***Note:** The taxable income for Social Security and Medicare tax is $2,000 − 150 = $1,850

Percentage Method

There are many tables in IRS Publication 15-T to assist employers with the correct amount of withholding. The *percentage method* for calculating employee withholding is tiered, with each layer building upon the previous layer. In 2021, the change to tax credits drastically altered the computation method, focusing on consistency between the annual tax filing and the federal income tax per pay period. We will go through an example in which we complete the percentage method using a manual system.

Note that the wage-bracket and percentage methods will yield similar results as to income tax withholding. The percentage method shown in Figure 5-1 allows more flexibility for calculations involving high-wage earners or uncommon pay periods, but the wage-bracket method is simpler for manual payroll computations.

FIGURE 5-1
2021 Percentage Method Tables for Income Tax

2021 Percentage Method Tables for Manual Payroll Systems With Forms W-4 from 2020 or Later

WEEKLY Payroll Period

STANDARD Withholding Rate Schedules (Use these if the box in Step 2 of Form W-4 is **NOT** checked)					Form W-4, Step 2, Checkbox, Withholding Rate Schedules (Use these if the box in Step 2 of Form W-4 **IS** checked)				
If the Adjusted Wage Amount (line 1h) is:		The tentative amount to withhold is:	Plus this percentage—	of the amount that the Adjusted Wage exceeds—	If the Adjusted Wage Amount (line 1h) Is:		The tentative amount to withhold is:	Plus this percentage—	of the amount that the Adjusted Wage exceeds—
At least—	But less than—				At least—	But less than—			
A	B	C	D	E	A	B	C	D	E
Married Filing Jointly					**Married Filing Jointly**				
$0	$483	$0.00	0%	$0	$0	$241	$0.00	0%	$0
$483	$865	$0.00	10%	$483	$241	$433	$0.00	10%	$241
$865	$2,041	$38.20	12%	$865	$433	$1,021	$19.20	12%	$433
$2,041	$3,805	$179.32	22%	$2,041	$1,021	$1,902	$89.76	22%	$1,021
$3,805	$6,826	$567.40	24%	$3,805	$1,902	$3,413	$283.58	24%	$1,902
$6,826	$8,538	$1,292.44	32%	$6,826	$3,413	$4,269	$646.22	32%	$3,413
$8,538	$12,565	$1,840.28	35%	$8,538	$4,269	$6,283	$920.14	35%	$4,269
$12,565		$3,249.73	37%	$12,565	$6,283		$1,625.04	37%	$6,283
Single or Married Filing Separately					**Single or Married Filing Separately**				
$0	$241	$0.00	0%	$0	$0	$121	$0.00	0%	$0
$241	$433	$0.00	10%	$241	$121	$216	$0.00	10%	$121
$433	$1,021	$19.20	12%	$433	$216	$510	$9.50	12%	$216
$1,021	$1,902	$89.76	22%	$1,021	$510	$951	$44.78	22%	$510
$1,902	$3,413	$283.58	24%	$1,902	$951	$1,706	$141.80	24%	$951
$3,413	$4,269	$646.22	32%	$3,413	$1,706	$2,134	$323.00	32%	$1,706
$4,269	$10,311	$920.14	35%	$4,269	$2,134	$5,155	$459.96	35%	$2,134
$10,311		$3,034.84	37%	$10,311	$5,155		$1,517.31	37%	$5,155
Head of Household					**Head of Household**				
$0	$362	$0.00	0%	$0	$0	$181	$0.00	0%	$0
$362	$635	$0.00	10%	$362	$181	$317	$0.00	10%	$181
$635	$1,404	$27.30	12%	$635	$317	$702	$13.60	12%	$317
$1,404	$2,022	$119.58	22%	$1,404	$702	$1,011	$59.80	22%	$702
$2,022	$3,533	$255.54	24%	$2,022	$1,011	$1,766	$127.78	24%	$1,011
$3,533	$4,388	$618.18	32%	$3,533	$1,766	$2,194	$308.98	32%	$1,766
$4,388	$10,431	$891.78	35%	$4,388	$2,194	$5,215	$445.94	35%	$2,194
$10,431		$3,006.83	37%	$10,431	$5,215		$1,503.29	37%	$5,215

(continued)

2021 Percentage Method Tables for Manual Payroll Systems With Forms W-4 from 2020 or Later

BIWEEKLY Payroll Period

STANDARD Withholding Rate Schedules (Use these if the box in Step 2 of Form W-4 is **NOT** checked)					Form W-4, Step 2, Checkbox, Withholding Rate Schedules (Use these if the box in Step 2 of Form W-4 **IS** checked)				
If the Adjusted Wage Amount (line 1h) is:		The tentative amount to withhold is:	Plus this percentage—	of the amount that the Adjusted Wage exceeds—	If the Adjusted Wage Amount (line 1h) is:		The tentative amount to withhold is:	Plus this percentage—	of the amount that the Adjusted Wage exceeds—
At least—	But less than—				At least—	But less than—			
A	B	C	D	E	A	B	C	D	E
Married Filing Jointly					**Married Filing Jointly**				
$0	$965	$0.00	0%	$0	$0	$483	$0.00	0%	$0
$965	$1,731	$0.00	10%	$965	$483	$865	$0.00	10%	$483
$1,731	$4,083	$76.60	12%	$1,731	$865	$2,041	$38.20	12%	$865
$4,083	$7,610	$358.84	22%	$4,083	$2,041	$3,805	$179.32	22%	$2,041
$7,610	$13,652	$1,134.78	24%	$7,610	$3,805	$6,826	$567.40	24%	$3,805
$13,652	$17,075	$2,584.86	32%	$13,652	$6,826	$8,538	$1,292.44	32%	$6,826
$17,075	$25,131	$3,680.22	35%	$17,075	$8,538	$12,565	$1,840.28	35%	$8,538
$25,131		$6,499.82	37%	$25,131	$12,565		$3,249.73	37%	$12,565
Single or Married Filing Separately					**Single or Married Filing Separately**				
$0	$483	$0.00	0%	$0	$0	$241	$0.00	0%	$0
$483	$865	$0.00	10%	$483	$241	$433	$0.00	10%	$241
$865	$2,041	$38.20	12%	$865	$433	$1,021	$19.20	12%	$433
$2,041	$3,805	$179.32	22%	$2,041	$1,021	$1,902	$89.76	22%	$1,021
$3,805	$6,826	$567.40	24%	$3,805	$1,902	$3,413	$283.58	24%	$1,902
$6,826	$8,538	$1,292.44	32%	$6,826	$3,413	$4,269	$646.22	32%	$3,413
$8,538	$20,621	$1,840.28	35%	$8,538	$4,269	$10,311	$920.14	35%	$4,269
$20,621		$6,069.33	37%	$20,621	$10,311		$3,034.84	37%	$10,311
Head of Household					**Head of Household**				
$0	$723	$0.00	0%	$0	$0	$362	$0.00	0%	$0
$723	$1,269	$0.00	10%	$723	$362	$635	$0.00	10%	$362
$1,269	$2,808	$54.60	12%	$1,269	$635	$1,404	$27.30	12%	$635
$2,808	$4,044	$239.28	22%	$2,808	$1,404	$2,022	$119.58	22%	$1,404
$4,044	$7,065	$511.20	24%	$4,044	$2,022	$3,533	$255.54	24%	$2,022
$7,065	$8,777	$1,236.24	32%	$7,065	$3,533	$4,388	$618.18	32%	$3,533
$8,777	$20,862	$1,784.08	35%	$8,777	$4,388	$10,431	$891.78	35%	$4,388
$20,862		$6,013.83	37%	$20,862	$10,431		$3,006.83	37%	$10,431

2021 Percentage Method Tables for Manual Payroll Systems With Forms W-4 from 2020 or Later

MONTHLY Payroll Period

STANDARD Withholding Rate Schedules (Use these if the box in Step 2 of Form W-4 is **NOT** checked)					Form W-4, Step 2, Checkbox, Withholding Rate Schedules (Use these if the box in Step 2 of Form W-4 **IS** checked)				
If the Adjusted Wage Amount (line 1h) is:		The tentative amount to withhold is:	Plus this percentage—	of the amount that the Adjusted Wage exceeds—	If the Adjusted Wage Amount (line 1h) is:		The tentative amount to withhold is:	Plus this percentage—	of the amount that the Adjusted Wage exceeds—
At least—	But less than—				At least—	But less than—			
A	B	C	D	E	A	B	C	D	E
Married Filing Jointly					**Married Filing Jointly**				
$0	$2,092	$0.00	0%	$0	$0	$1,046	$0.00	0%	$0
$2,092	$3,750	$0.00	10%	$2,092	$1,046	$1,875	$0.00	10%	$1,046
$3,750	$8,846	$165.80	12%	$3,750	$1,875	$4,423	$82.90	12%	$1,875
$8,846	$16,488	$777.32	22%	$8,846	$4,423	$8,244	$388.66	22%	$4,423
$16,488	$29,579	$2,458.56	24%	$16,488	$8,244	$14,790	$1,229.28	24%	$8,244
$29,579	$36,996	$5,600.40	32%	$29,579	$14,790	$18,498	$2,800.32	32%	$14,790
$36,996	$54,450	$7,973.84	35%	$36,996	$18,498	$27,225	$3,986.88	35%	$18,498
$54,450		$14,082.74	37%	$54,450	$27,225		$7,041.33	37%	$27,225
Single or Married Filing Separately					**Single or Married Filing Separately**				
$0	$1,046	$0.00	0%	$0	$0	$523	$0.00	0%	$0
$1,046	$1,875	$0.00	10%	$1,046	$523	$938	$0.00	10%	$523
$1,875	$4,423	$82.90	12%	$1,875	$938	$2,211	$41.50	12%	$938
$4,423	$8,244	$388.66	22%	$4,423	$2,211	$4,122	$194.26	22%	$2,211
$8,244	$14,790	$1,229.28	24%	$8,244	$4,122	$7,395	$614.68	24%	$4,122
$14,790	$18,498	$2,800.32	32%	$14,790	$7,395	$9,249	$1,400.20	32%	$7,395
$18,498	$44,679	$3,986.88	35%	$18,498	$9,249	$22,340	$1,993.48	35%	$9,249
$44,679		$13,150.23	37%	$44,679	$22,340		$6,575.33	37%	$22,340

Head of Household						Head of Household			
$0	$1,567	$0.00	0%	$0	$0	$783	$0.00	0%	$0
$1,567	$2,750	$0.00	10%	$1,567	$783	$1,375	$0.00	10%	$783
$2,750	$6,083	$118.30	12%	$2,750	$1,375	$3,042	$59.20	12%	$1,375
$6,083	$8,763	$518.26	22%	$6,083	$3,042	$4,381	$259.24	22%	$3,042
$8,763	$15,308	$1,107.86	24%	$8,763	$4,381	$7,654	$553.82	24%	$4,381
$15,308	$19,017	$2,678.66	32%	$15,308	$7,654	$9,508	$1,339.34	32%	$7,654
$19,017	$45,200	$3,865.54	35%	$19,017	$9,508	$22,600	$1,932.62	35%	$9,508
$45,200		$13,029.59	37%	$45,200	$22,600		$6,514.82	37%	$22,600

2021 Percentage Method Tables for Manual Payroll Systems With Forms W-4 from 2020 or Later

SEMIMONTHLY Payroll Period

STANDARD Withholding Rate Schedules (Use these if the box in Step 2 of Form W-4 is **NOT** checked)					Form W-4, Step 2, Checkbox, Withholding Rate Schedules (Use these if the box in Step 2 of Form W-4 **IS** checked)				
If the Adjusted Wage Amount (line 1h) is:		The tentative amount to withhold is:	Plus this percentage—	of the amount that the Adjusted Wage exceeds—	If the Adjusted Wage Amount (line 1h) is:		The tentative amount to withhold is:	Plus this percentage—	of the amount that the Adjusted Wage exceeds—
At least—	But less than—				At least—	But less than—			
A	B	C	D	E	A	B	C	D	E
Married Filing Jointly					**Married Filing Jointly**				
$0	$1,046	$0.00	0%	$0	$0	$523	$0.00	0%	$0
$1,046	$1,875	$0.00	10%	$1,046	$523	$938	$0.00	10%	$523
$1,875	$4,423	$82.90	12%	$1,875	$938	$2,211	$41.50	12%	$938
$4,423	$8,244	$388.66	22%	$4,423	$2,211	$4,122	$194.26	22%	$2,211
$8,244	$14,790	$1,229.28	24%	$8,244	$4,122	$7,395	$614.68	24%	$4,122
$14,790	$18,498	$2,800.32	32%	$14,790	$7,395	$9,249	$1,400.20	32%	$7,395
$18,498	$27,225	$3,986.88	35%	$18,498	$9,249	$13,613	$1,993.48	35%	$9,249
$27,225		$7,041.33	37%	$27,225	$13,613		$3,520.88	37%	$13,613
Single or Married Filing Separately					**Single or Married Filing Separately**				
$0	$523	$0.00	0%	$0	$0	$261	$0.00	0%	$0
$523	$938	$0.00	10%	$523	$261	$469	$0.00	10%	$261
$938	$2,211	$41.50	12%	$938	$469	$1,106	$20.80	12%	$469
$2,211	$4,122	$194.26	22%	$2,211	$1,106	$2,061	$97.24	22%	$1,106
$4,122	$7,395	$614.68	24%	$4,122	$2,061	$3,697	$307.34	24%	$2,061
$7,395	$9,249	$1,400.20	32%	$7,395	$3,697	$4,624	$699.98	32%	$3,697
$9,249	$22,340	$1,993.48	35%	$9,249	$4,624	$11,170	$996.62	35%	$4,624
$22,340		$6,575.33	37%	$22,340	$11,170		$3,287.72	37%	$11,170
Head of Household					**Head of Household**				
$0	$783	$0.00	0%	$0	$0	$392	$0.00	0%	$0
$783	$1,375	$0.00	10%	$783	$392	$688	$0.00	10%	$392
$1,375	$3,042	$59.20	12%	$1,375	$688	$1,521	$29.60	12%	$688
$3,042	$4,381	$259.24	22%	$3,042	$1,521	$2,191	$129.56	22%	$1,521
$4,381	$7,654	$553.82	24%	$4,381	$2,191	$3,827	$276.96	24%	$2,191
$7,654	$9,508	$1,339.34	32%	$7,654	$3,827	$4,754	$669.60	32%	$3,827
$9,508	$22,600	$1,932.62	35%	$9,508	$4,754	$11,300	$966.24	35%	$4,754
$22,600		$6,514.82	37%	$22,600	$11,300		$3,257.34	37%	$11,300

2021 Percentage Method Tables for Manual Payroll Systems With Forms W-4 from 2020 or Later

DAILY Payroll Period

STANDARD Withholding Rate Schedules (Use these if the box in Step 2 of Form W-4 is **NOT** checked)					Form W-4, Step 2, Checkbox, Withholding Rate Schedules (Use these if the box in Step 2 of Form W-4 **IS** checked)				
If the Adjusted Wage Amount (line 1h) is:		The tentative amount to withhold is:	Plus this percentage—	of the amount that the Adjusted Wage exceeds—	If the Adjusted Wage Amount (line 1h) is:		The tentative amount to withhold is:	Plus this percentage—	of the amount that the Adjusted Wage exceeds—
At least—	But less than—				At least—	But less than—			
A	B	C	D	E	A	B	C	D	E
Married Filing Jointly					**Married Filing Jointly**				
$0.00	$96.50	$0.00	0%	$0.00	$0.00	$48.30	$0.00	0%	$0.00
$96.50	$173.10	$0.00	10%	$96.50	$48.30	$86.50	$0.00	10%	$48.30
$173.10	$408.30	$7.66	12%	$173.10	$86.50	$204.10	$3.82	12%	$86.50
$408.30	$761.00	$35.88	22%	$408.30	$204.10	$380.50	$17.93	22%	$204.10
$761.00	$1,365.20	$113.48	24%	$761.00	$380.50	$682.60	$56.74	24%	$380.50
$1,365.20	$1,707.50	$258.49	32%	$1,365.20	$682.60	$853.80	$129.24	32%	$682.60
$1,707.50	$2,513.10	$368.02	35%	$1,707.50	$853.80	$1,256.50	$184.03	35%	$853.80
$2,513.10		$649.98	37%	$2,513.10	$1,256.50		$324.97	37%	$1,256.50

(continued)

Single or Married Filing Separately					Single or Married Filing Separately				
$0.00	$48.30	$0.00	0%	$0.00	$0.00	$24.10	$0.00	0%	$0.00
$48.30	$86.50	$0.00	10%	$48.30	$24.10	$43.30	$0.00	10%	$24.10
$86.50	$204.10	$3.82	12%	$86.50	$43.30	$102.10	$1.92	12%	$43.30
$204.10	$380.50	$17.93	22%	$204.10	$102.10	$190.20	$8.98	22%	$102.10
$380.50	$682.60	$56.74	24%	$380.50	$190.20	$341.30	$28.36	24%	$190.20
$682.60	$853.80	$129.24	32%	$682.60	$341.30	$426.90	$64.62	32%	$341.30
$853.80	$2,062.10	$184.03	35%	$853.80	$426.90	$1,031.10	$92.01	35%	$426.90
$2,062.10		$606.93	37%	$2,062.10	$1,031.10		$303.48	37%	$1,031.10

Head of Household					Head of Household				
$0.00	$72.30	$0.00	0%	$0.00	$0.00	$36.20	$0.00	0%	$0.00
$72.30	$126.90	$0.00	10%	$72.30	$36.20	$63.50	$0.00	10%	$36.20
$126.90	$280.80	$5.46	12%	$126.90	$63.50	$140.40	$2.73	12%	$63.50
$280.80	$404.40	$23.93	22%	$280.80	$140.40	$202.20	$11.96	22%	$140.40
$404.40	$706.50	$51.12	24%	$404.40	$202.20	$353.30	$25.55	24%	$202.20
$706.50	$877.70	$123.62	32%	$706.50	$353.30	$438.80	$61.82	32%	$353.30
$877.70	$2,086.20	$178.41	35%	$877.70	$438.80	$1,043.10	$89.18	35%	$438.80
$2,086.20		$601.38	37%	$2,086.20	$1,043.10		$300.68	37%	$1,043.10

Source: Internal Revenue Service

The IRS has published guidance for using the percentage method tables manually. The process published in 2021 differs significantly from previous years because of the changes to Form W-4.

FIGURE 5-2
2021 Percentage Method Tables Directions

4. Percentage Method Tables for Manual Payroll Systems With Forms W-4 From 2020 or Later

If you compute payroll manually, your employee has submitted a Form W-4 for 2020 or later, and you prefer to use the Percentage Method or you can't use the Wage Bracket Method tables because the employee's annual wages exceed $100,000, use the worksheet below and the Percentage Method tables that follow to figure federal income tax withholding. This method works for any amount of wages.

Worksheet 4. Employer's Withholding Worksheet for Percentage Method Tables for Manual Payroll Systems With Forms W-4 From 2020 or Later

Keep for Your Records

Table 5	Monthly	Semimonthly	Biweekly	Weekly	Daily
	12	24	26	52	260

Step 1.   Adjust the employee's wage amount

1a   Enter the employee's total taxable wages this payroll period . . . .   1a $ _____

1b   Enter the number of pay periods you have per year (see Table 5) . . . .   1b   _____

1c   Enter the amount from Step 4(a) of the employee's Form W-4 . . . .   1c $ _____

1d   Divide line 1c by the number on line 1b . . . .   1d $ _____

1e   Add lines 1a and 1d . . . .   1e $ _____

1f   Enter the amount from Step 4(b) of the employee's Form W-4 . . . .   1f $ _____

1g   Divide line 1f by the number on line 1b . . . .   1g $ _____

1h   Subtract line 1g from line 1e. If zero or less, enter -0-. This is the **Adjusted Wage Amount** . . . . . .   1h $ _____

Step 2.   Figure the Tentative Withholding Amount

based on your pay frequency, the employee's Adjusted Wage Amount, filing status (Step 1(c) of Form W-4), and whether the box in Step 2 of Form W-4 is checked.

2a   Find the row in the *STANDARD Withholding Rate Schedules* (if the box in Step 2 of Form W-4 is NOT checked) or the *Form W-4, Step 2, Checkbox, Withholding Rate Schedules* (if it HAS been checked) of the Percentage Method tables in this section in which the amount on line 1h is at least the amount in column A but less than the amount in column B, then enter here the amount from column A of that row . . . .   2a $ _____

2b   Enter the amount from column C of that row ....   2b $ _____

2c   Enter the percentage from column D of that row ....   2c   _____ %

2d   Subtract line 2a from line 1h ....   2d $ _____

2e   Multiply the amount on line 2d by the percentage on line 2c ....   2e $ _____

2f   Add lines 2b and 2e. This is the **Tentative Withholding Amount** ....   2f $ _____

Step 3.   **Account for tax credits**

3a   Enter the amount from Step 3 of the employee's Form W-4 ....   3a $ _____

3b   Divide the amount on line 3a by the number of pay periods on line 1b ....   3b $ _____

3c   Subtract line 3b from line 2f. If zero or less, enter -0- ....   3c $ _____

Step 4.   **Figure the final amount to withhold**

4a   Enter the additional amount to withhold from Step 4(c) of the employee's Form W-4 ....   4a $ _____

4b   Add lines 3c and 4a. **This is the amount to withhold from the employee's wages this pay period** ....   4b $ _____

Using the percentage method can be confusing, so let's look at a step-by-step example. This first example uses data from the employee's Form W-4 and prior year income tax filing information.

EXAMPLE: MARRIED EMPLOYEE, PERCENTAGE METHOD

Caroline Smart is single and has two dependents under the age of 17 reported on her Form W-4 from 2021. She is paid semimonthly and earns $48,000 per year. She does not receive any other income and does not itemize her deductions. Form W-4, Step 2 box has not been checked. Caroline has no pre-tax deductions.

The following image is an excerpt from the percentage method tables with an outline around the row to be used for Step 2.

2021 Percentage Method Tables for Manual Payroll Systems With Forms W-4 from 2020 or Later

SEMIMONTHLY Payroll Period

STANDARD Withholding Rate Schedules (Use these if the box in Step 2 of Form W-4 is NOT checked)					Form W-4, Step 2, Checkbox, Withholding Rate Schedules (Use these if the box in Step 2 of Form W-4 IS checked)				
Single or Married Filing Separately					Single or Married Filing Separately				
$0	$523	$0.00	0%	$0	$0	$261	$0.00	0%	$0
$523	$938	$0.00	10%	$523	$261	$469	$0.00	10%	$261
$938	$2,211	$41.50	12%	$938	$469	$1,106	$20.80	12%	$469

Step 1: Adjust the employee's wage amount	**1a**	Total taxable wages for the period (Note: This is the amount after pre-tax deductions for insurance, etc.)	$48,000/24 = $2,000
	1b	Number of pay periods per year	24
	1c	Amount from Step 4(a) of Caroline's W-4 (other income not from jobs)	$0
	1d	Divide amount on 1c by the number on 1b	0
	1e	Add lines 1a and 1d	$2,000
	1f	Enter the amount from Step 4(b) of Caroline's W-4	$0
	1g	Divide line 1f by the number on line 1b	0
	1h	Subtract 1g from 1e. This is the adjusted wage amount.	$2,000
Step 2: Figure the tentative withholding amount	**2a**	Since Box 2 on Caroline's Form W-4 was not checked, use the left-hand tables on the Percentage Method Tables for the semimonthly pay period. For Caroline, this is row three in the section labeled "Single or Married Filing Separately." Enter the amount from Column A of that row	Column A: $938
	2b	Enter the amount of Column C of that row	$41.50

(continued)

(concluded)

	2c	Enter the percentage from Column D of that row	12%
	2d	Subtract line 2a from 1h	$2,000 − 938 = $1,062
	2e	Multiply the amount on 2d by the percentage on 2c	$1,062 × 12% = $127.44
	2f	Add lines 2b and 2e. This is the tentative withholding amount.	$41.50 + $127.44 = $168.94
Step 3: Account for tax credits	**3a**	Enter the amount from Step 3 of Caroline's Form W-4. Since Caroline has two dependents under the age of 17, the amount would be	$2,000 × 2 = $4,000
	3b	Divide the amount on line 3a by the number of pay periods on line 1b	$4,000/24 = $166.67
	3c	Subtract line 3b from line 2f. If zero or less, enter -0-	$168.94 − $166.67 = $2.27
Step 4: Figure the final amount to withhold	**4a**	Enter the additional amount to withhold from Step 4(c) of Caroline's Form W-4. Caroline has entered no additional amounts	0
	4b	Add lines 3c and 4a. This is the amount to withhold from the employee's wages this pay period	$2.27

(Source: Internal Revenue Service)

The amount of federal income tax withholding may differ slightly between the wage-bracket and percentage methods. However, the computation method is similar. Let's revisit the tax computation for Caroline's tax using the wage-bracket method and compare the two amounts side by side. Only the totals from each step are included because the other information remains the same in both methods.

EXAMPLE: MARRIED EMPLOYEE, PERCENTAGE METHOD VS. WAGE-BRACKET TABLE

Caroline Smart is single and has two dependents under the age of 17 reported on her Form W-4 from 2021. She is paid semimonthly and earns $48,000 per year. She does not receive any other income and does not itemize her deductions. Form W-4, Step 2 box has not been checked.

The following image is an excerpt from the wage-bracket method tables with an outline around the amount to be used for Step 2.

2021 Wage Bracket Method Tables for Manual Payroll Systems with Forms W-4 From 2020 or Later
SEMIMONTHLY Payroll Period

If the Adjusted Wage Amount (line 1h) is		Married Filing Jointly		Head of Household		Single or Married Filing Separately	
At least	But less than	Standard withholding	Form W-4, Step 2, Checkbox withholding	Standard withholding	Form W-4, Step 2, Checkbox withholding	Standard withholding	Form W-4, Step 2, Checkbox withholding
				The Tentative Withholding Amount is:			
$1,920	$1,940	$90	$161	$126	$220	$161	$279
$1,940	$1,960	$92	$163	$128	$224	$163	$283
$1,960	$1,980	$94	$165	$131	$228	$165	$287
$1,980	$2,000	$97	$168	$133	$233	$168	$292
$2,000	$2,020	$99	$170	$135	$237	$170	$296

Comparison of Percentage and Wage Bracket Methods

	Percentage method	Wage-Bracket method
Step 1: Adjusted wage amount	$2,000	$2,000
Step 2: Tentative withholding amount	$168.94	$170.00
Step 3: Account for tax credits	$166.67	$166.67
Step 4: Figure the final amount to withhold	$168.94 − 166.67 = $2.27	$170.00 − 166.67 = $3.33

(Source: Internal Revenue Service)

Note that the amount to withhold differs slightly between the percentage method and wage-bracket method. The cause for this discrepancy is rounding inherent to the wage-bracket method.

If using a manual payroll tax system, the wage-bracket method will be simpler to compute federal income tax amounts. However, note that the percentage method will yield more accurate results. If the company uses a software package to complete its payroll, the percentage method will be used by default.

How Much Tax to Withhold?

Stop & Check

1. Jennifer Parsons earns $52,000 annually. She is married filing jointly with two dependents not under 17, her spouse does work (box 2 is checked), and she is paid semimonthly. Her W-4 is from 2021. Calculate the amount to be withheld using (a) the wage-bracket method and (b) the percentage method.

2. If Jennifer elected to deduct $100 per pay period for her 401(k), how much would that change the tax withheld from her paycheck? (Use the wage-bracket method.)

3. How much would Jennifer's federal income tax be if her $75 health insurance and $55 AFLAC premiums were deducted each pay period pre-tax? (Use the wage-bracket method, independent of question 2.)

LO 5-3 Compute Social Security and Medicare Tax Withholding

zimmytws/iStockphoto/Getty Images

The Social Security Act of 1935 mandated the withholding of certain taxes in addition to federal income tax. Two different taxes were part of the Social Security Act legislation: Social Security tax and Medicare tax. Employers collect only federal income taxes on employees without making a corresponding contribution. Social Security and Medicare, collectively known as *FICA (Federal Insurance Contribution Act) taxes*, contain both the employer's and the employee's portion. When the employer deposits the federal withholding tax, it deposits the Social Security and Medicare amounts simultaneously. The deposits are usually done online but may be made by standard mail in certain circumstances. The report provided to the IRS does not provide a breakdown of tax amounts for individual employees. Specific questions about Social Security or Medicare tax situations should be directed to the Social Security Administration at www.ssa .gov or via telephone at 800-772-1213.

Social Security Tax

Social Security tax, formerly known as OASDI, was designed to cover people for illness, retirement, disability, and old age. As a social insurance method by which communities will help provide for people who are unable to work, Social Security has evolved into a tax that is levied upon all employees until their annual income reaches a specified level. The maximum income, known as the *wage base*, for the Social Security tax changes annually. In 2021, the wage base is $142,800. This means only the first $142,800 of wages earned are subject to the 6.2 percent tax. Every dollar earned above $142,800 will not be subject to Social Security tax. The tax rate on employee pay is 6.2 percent of eligible wages. Remember that eligible wages can be different from gross pay because of pre-tax deductions and the wage base maximum.

An important part of determining Social Security tax when an employee is close to the wage base is to compute the amount of year-to-date (YTD) pay. In programs such as QuickBooks, this computation occurs automatically. The following is a guide to computing Social Security Taxable pay.

You will need the following information to complete this computation:

- Period pay.
- Pay Frequency.
- The number of prior pay period periods in the calendar year.

The computation aims to ensure that the employee does not over-pay tax as they approach the annual wage base.

	Period Pay	Pay Frequency	Number of Prior Pay periods	YTD Pay (Period Pay × # of prior pay periods)	Social Security Taxable Pay for Next Pay Period
Employee 1	$3,500	Weekly	40	$3,500 × 40 = $140,000	$142,800 − 140,000 = $2,800
Employee 2	$5,850	Biweekly	24	$5,850 × 24 = $140,400	$142,800 − 140,400 = $2,400
Employee 3	$6,800	Semimonthly	21	$6,800 × 21 = $142,800	-0-

Note that these computations are used primarily in two instances:

- Highly paid employees.
- Pay periods near the end of the calendar year.

Examples of Social Security Tax Computations

Employee	Period Wages	YTD Salary at End of Previous Pay Period	Social Security Tax Computation	Social Security Tax Amount to Be Withheld
1	$ 1,700	$ 55,600	$1,700 × 6.2%	$105.40
2	2,850	90,000	2,850 × 6.2%	176.70
3	7,200	136,800	6,000 × 6.2%*	372.00
4	6,200	142,600	200 × 6.2%[†]	12.40
5	10,500	195,000	0[‡]	0

*The employee's wage base reaches the maximum during this pay period; thus, only the amount under the $142,800 cap is taxed for Social Security: $142,800 − $136,800 = $6,000, so only the $6,000 is taxed.
[†]The employee's wage base reaches the maximum during this pay period; thus, only the amount under the $142,800 cap is taxed for Social Security: $142,800 − $142,600 = $200, so only the $200 is taxed.
[‡]The employee's wage base maximum was met before the current pay period, so no Social Security taxes are withheld.

The employee earnings record is vital in computing and tracking the Social Security taxes due for each employee. Current records allow payroll accountants to keep track of annual salaries for each employee to avoid exceeding the maximum wage base, preventing excess deductions from employees' pay.

The employer and employee pay the same amount for the Social Security tax. Remember, the Social Security tax has a maximum annual wage amount, known as the wage base, for which taxes may be withheld. After reaching that maximum annual wage, neither the employee nor the employer pays any more Social Security tax for the remainder of the year.

In August 2020, the president issued an Executive Order (EO) that gave employers the option to defer the withholding of Social Security tax from employees who earned less than $4,000 biweekly. This EO was not mandatory and was only effective between September 1 and December 31, 2020. The deferred taxes had to be withheld from employee pay and remitted between January 1 and April 30, 2021, to avoid tax penalties. It is notable that the deferral was not mandatory. The Social Security tax deferral did not apply to the employer's share of the tax.

(Sources: Greater Baltimore Committee, DMJ & Co.)

Medicare Tax

Medicare taxes differ from Social Security taxes in a couple of significant ways. *Medicare taxes* were levied on employers and employees to help provide basic health coverage for all individuals qualified to enroll in Medicare benefits. The Medicare tax amount for employee wages is 1.45 percent on all wages earned; there is **no maximum wage base** for Medicare taxes. The Affordable Care Act of 2010 levied an *additional Medicare tax* of 0.9 percent on certain workers, known as highly compensated employees.

Highly compensated employees are subject to an additional 0.9 percent of Medicare tax due to the Affordable Care Act. The employee only pays this additional tax, and no employer match is required. The wage base for this additional Medicare tax depends on the marital and tax filing statuses reported on the employee's Form W-4 as follows:

- $200,000 for employees who report that they are single.
- $250,000 for employees who report that they are married and file taxes jointly.
- $125,000 for employees who report that they are married and file taxes separately.

This made the simple computations and tracking for Medicare taxes a little more challenging for payroll accountants and increased the employee earnings report's need for accuracy. Note the additional Medicare tax is levied *only* on the employees, so there is no employer match.

Examples of Medicare Tax Computations

Employee	Period Wages	YTD Salary at the end of Previous Pay Period	Medicare Tax Computation	Total Medicare Tax Liability (Employee and Employer)
1	$1,700	$ 55,600	$ 1,700 × 1.45%	$24.65 × 2 = $ 49.30
2	2,850	90,000	2,850 × 1.45%	41.33 × 2 = 82.66
3	7,200	112,600	7,200 × 1.45%	104.40 × 2 = 208.80
4	6,200	118,000	6,200 × 1.45%	89.90 × 2 = 179.80
5	10,500	195,000	Employee: (10,500 × 0.0145*) + (5,500[†] × 0.009) = $201.75	Employee: $201.75 + Employer: $152.25[‡] Total = $354.00

*10,500 * 0.0145 = 152.25
[†]195,000 + 10,500 = 205,500. 205,500 − 200,000 = 5,500
[‡]The employer does not pay the additional Medicare tax.

Remember the applicable wages may have pre-tax deductions. Social Security and Medicare taxes apply to the employee's gross pay if an employee elects to have a 401(k) deduction. However, qualified Section 125 (cafeteria) plans are exempt from FICA taxes. When computing employee taxes, understanding the pre-tax deductions' tax effect is important in computing accurate FICA deductions.

EXAMPLE: COMPUTATION OF SOCIAL SECURITY AND MEDICARE TAXES WITH PRE-TAX DEDUCTIONS

Chris McBride is an employee who earns an annual salary of $58,000, paid biweekly. He is single with no dependents. Chris has pre-tax deductions, including $155 for health insurance and a contribution of 5 percent of his gross pay to a 401(k) plan. Let's compute Chris's net pay using Publication 15-T to determine federal income tax, using the information for a 2021 Form W-4.

Gross pay per period (58,000/26)	$2,230.77
Less: health insurance	155.00
Less: 401(k) (2,230.77 × 0.05)	111.54
Taxable income*	$1,964.23
Federal income tax	170.00
Social Security tax[†]	128.70
Medicare tax[†]	30.10
Net pay	$1,635.43

*This taxable income is for federal income tax only.
[†]Social Security and Medicare taxes are computed on taxable income of $2,230.77 − $155.00 = $2,075.77, then $2,075.77 × 0.062 (Social Security) and $2,075.77 × 0.0145 (Medicare).

EXAMPLE: COMPUTATION OF NET PAY, HIGHLY COMPENSATED EMPLOYEE

Morris Malone is the CEO and president of Martens Flooring. His annual salary is $320,000, and he is paid semimonthly. He is married with three dependents under 17, files taxes jointly, and has pre-tax deductions for health insurance of $250 and 401(k) of $1,000. His spouse is not employed.

He will exceed the Social Security wage base in May 2021 and incur the additional Medicare tax in September. Let's look at his net pay computations on January 15, June 18, and August 27.

FEDERAL INCOME TAX COMPUTATION

Federal income tax is computed as follows, using the percentage tables in Publication 15-T:

Gross pay per period	$12,307.69
Less: health insurance	250.00
Less: 401(k)	1,000.00
Taxable income	$11,057.69
Total federal income tax	$ 62.63*

*Using the percentage method in Publication 15-T for a 2021 Form W-4: $11,057.69 − 7,610 = $3,447.69 × 24% = $827.45 (rounded) + 1,134.78 = $1,962.63.

JANUARY 15 PAY PERIOD

Gross pay per period	$12,307.69
Less: health insurance	250.00
Less: 401(k)	1,000.00
Taxable income*	$11,057.69
Federal income tax	1,962.63
Social Security tax[†]	747.58
Medicare tax[†]	174.84
Net pay	$ 8,172.64

*This taxable income is for federal income tax only.
[†]Social Security and Medicare taxes are computed using a base of $12,307.69 − 250 = $12,057.69.

JUNE 18 PAY PERIOD

As of June 4, Morris has earned year-to-date gross pay of $135,384.59 ($12,307.69 × 11 pay periods). This means that he will exceed the Social Security wage base during the next pay period, which ends June 18. Morris's salary is only taxable for Social Security wages up to the wage base of $142,800 (2021 amount), so the amount that may be taxed is $142,800 − $135,384.59 = $7,415.41. After the June 18 pay period, Morris will have no more Social Security tax deducted from his pay. His net pay for June 18 will be as follows:

Gross pay per period	$12,307.69
Less: health Insurance	250.00
Less: 401(k)	1,000.00
Taxable income*	$11,057.69
Federal income tax	1,962.63
Social Security tax†	459.76
Medicare tax‡	174.84
Net pay	$ 8,460.46

*This taxable income is for federal income tax only.
†Social Security tax is computed as $7,415.41 × 0.062 = $459.76.
‡Medicare tax is computed using a base of $12,057.69 * 0.0145 = $174.84.

OCTOBER 18 PAY PERIOD

As of October 4, Morris has earned year-to-date pay of $246,153.80 (12,307.69 × 20 pay periods). His next paycheck will be subject to the additional Medicare tax of 0.9 percent, levied only on employees (i.e., no employer match). Since he is married, he pays additional Medicare tax once his pay reaches $250,000. His net pay for October 18 will be computed as follows:

Gross pay per period	$12,307.69
Less: health insurance	250.00
Less: 401(k)	1,000.00
Taxable income*	$11,057.69
Federal income tax	1,962.63
Social Security tax	-0-
Medicare tax†	283.36
Net pay	$ 8,811.70

*This taxable income is for federal income tax only.
†Medicare taxes are computed as: $12,307.69 − $250.00 = $12,057.69 * (0.0145 + 0.009) = $283.36.

Maintaining accurate records of taxes withheld through payroll registers and employee earnings records is a critical part of calculating proper FICA tax deductions. Whether a company uses a manual system, an automated system, or outsources the payroll duties, it remains responsible for the accuracy of the deductions and maintenance of associated records.

Stop & Check

FICA Taxes

1. Trent Powell is an employee whose annual salary before the current pay period is $63,500. His gross pay for the current pay period is $5,280. What amount must be withheld for Social Security tax? For Medicare tax?

(continued)

(concluded)

2. For Trent's FICA taxes, what is the total tax liability, including employee and employer share?

3. Sarah Erickson is the CEO of a company, and she earns $250,000 per year. Her year-to-date salary for the 19th pay period of the year was $197,916.67. She is single and contributes 5 percent of her pay to her 401(k) and has a qualified Section 125 deduction of $75 per semi-monthly pay period.

    a. For the 20th pay period, what is her Social Security tax liability? Medicare tax liability?

    b. For the 21st pay period, what is her Medicare tax liability?

LO 5-4   Calculate State and Local Income Taxes

Many states and localities apply taxes in addition to the federal income tax, Social Security, and Medicare. According to the IRS, all but nine states withhold income taxes. As budgets become tighter and the unfunded pension liabilities come due, these states may look to income tax as a means for covering budget or pension shortfalls. The nine states are:

Alaska	New Hampshire*	Tennessee*
Florida	South Dakota	Washington
Nevada	Texas	Wyoming

*New Hampshire and Tennessee do not charge a payroll tax but obtain revenue from individual taxpayers through taxes on dividends and investments.

> Mississippi Governor Tate Reeves proposed the elimination of the state income tax in January 2021. He reasoned that eliminating income taxes would relieve the tax burden on people who work in Mississippi and invite economic development and business investments in the state. Governor Reeves stated that eliminating the income tax would be phased in over several years if approved by the state legislature.
>
> (Source: WCBI)

State-Specific Taxes

All states except for the nine just mentioned withhold income tax from their employees, and many apply other taxes as well. For instance, employees in the state of California pay State Disability Insurance (SDI) of 1.0 percent of gross pay (up to a maximum wage of $128,298 in 2021) in addition to the personal income tax (PIT) that the state levies. Like federal income tax, California's PIT amounts vary by income level, pay frequency, and marital status. Like many other states, California offers both the wage-bracket and the percentage method of determining the PIT amount due. In contrast, Pennsylvania charges a flat rate of 3.07 percent on all employees for its state withholding tax. (See Appendix D for state income tax information.)

If a firm operates only in one state, deciphering state income tax requirements is reasonably simple but becomes increasingly complex as it does business in more locations. During the COVID pandemic, some firms have employees working in states different from their previous locations, and it is important to file the appropriate state and local taxes for the employee's work locations.

State income tax information is readily available through each state's revenue department and most computerized payroll software programs. (See Appendix E for a state revenue department list.)

New York ranks as the highest state in *per capita* state and local income tax. The marginal tax rate in 2021 ranged from 4.0 percent–8.82 percent, depending on income, and many localities charge income taxes. Workers who reside or earn income in New York City pay a tax that ranges from approximately 3.078 percent to 3.876 percent in addition to any federal and state income taxes.

Steve Prezant/Image Source

(Source: SmartAsset, TaxFoundation)

Some states require the collection and remittance of income taxes based upon all wages earned within their state. This could result in the company having several state employer identification numbers, even if it does not have a physical presence in the state. For example, if a Floridian paper mill worker is stationed at its St. Marys, Georgia, location, the employer could be required to remit the employee's income taxes in Georgia. Other types of payroll taxes can include Oregon's public transportation payroll tax for any services performed within the state, regardless of residency status.

EXAMPLE: NET PAY WITH STATE INCOME TAX

Jeremy Underwood receives a salary of $850 per week at his job in Joliet, Illinois. He is married, filing jointly (box 2 is not checked) with one dependent under 17, and is paid weekly. We will use the Wage Bracket table in Appendix C to determine federal income tax. He has pre-tax deductions of $50 for insurance and $50 for 401(k). Using the Illinois state tax rate of 4.95 percent,

Taxable income ($850 − 50 − 50)	$750.00
State income tax ($750 × 0.0495)	$ 37.13

His net pay would be computed as follows:

Name	Marital Status	Dependents	Hourly Rate or Period Wage	No. of Regular Hours	No. of Overtime Hours	No. of Holiday Hours	Gross Earnings	401(k)	Insurance	Cafeteria Plan	Taxable Wages for Federal W/H	Taxable Wages for FICA
Jeremy Underwood	MJ	1 < 17	850.00				850.00	50.00	50.00		750.00	800.00

Name	Gross Earnings	Taxable Wages for Federal W/H	Taxable Wages for FICA	Federal W/H	Social Security Tax	Medicare W/H Tax	State W/H Tax	Charitable Contribution	Union Dues	Garnishment	Net Pay
Jeremy Underwood	850.00	750.00	800.00	0.00	49.60*	11.60†	37.13				651.67

*Social Security Tax: $800 × 0.062.
†Medicare Tax = $800 × 0.0145.

Local Income Taxes

Another mandatory tax is *local income tax* levied by certain municipalities and counties. Payroll accountants need to be aware of any local taxes that apply to their business. Information about applicable local taxes may be found through city and county governments, often through their Internet sites.

Denver, Colorado, has a local tax called the Occupational Privilege Tax (OPT), also known as the "head tax." The OPT is $5.75 per month for employees and $4 for employers of any business with any activity in Denver, even if the employee or business does not exist or reside in Denver itself, on wages exceeding $500. The local income tax is applied after any pre-tax deductions.

(Source: City and County of Denver)

EXAMPLE: NET PAY WITH LOCAL INCOME TAX

Shalie Rice is an employee at Keiser and Sons in Denver, Colorado. She earns $39,000 annually and is paid biweekly. She is a married filing joint with no dependents and box 2(c) is not checked. She has pre-tax deductions, including $100 for health insurance and a contribution of 6 percent of her gross pay to a 401(k) plan. We will use the Wage-Bracket table in Appendix C to compute Shalie's federal income tax. Colorado's state income tax is 4.63 percent. Her net pay would be as follows:

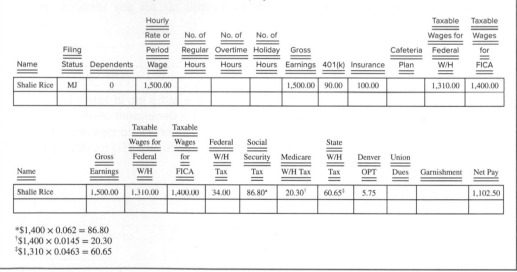

Name	Filing Status	Dependents	Hourly Rate or Period Wage	No. of Regular Hours	No. of Overtime Hours	No. of Holiday Hours	Gross Earnings	401(k)	Insurance	Cafeteria Plan	Taxable Wages for Federal W/H	Taxable Wages for FICA
Shalie Rice	MJ	0	1,500.00				1,500.00	90.00	100.00		1,310.00	1,400.00

Name	Gross Earnings	Taxable Wages for Federal W/H	Taxable Wages for FICA	Federal W/H Tax	Social Security Tax	Medicare W/H Tax	State W/H Tax	Denver OPT	Union Dues	Garnishment	Net Pay
Shalie Rice	1,500.00	1,310.00	1,400.00	34.00	86.80*	20.30[†]	60.65[‡]	5.75			1,102.50

*$1,400 × 0.062 = 86.80
[†]$1,400 × 0.0145 = 20.30
[‡]$1,310 × 0.0463 = 60.65

State and Local Income Taxes

Stop & Check

1. April Griffith works as a research scientist in Amasa, Michigan. She earns $62,500 annually, is married, filing jointly with no dependents (box 2 is not checked), paid biweekly. She has a pre-tax deduction of $150 for her 401(k) and $80 for qualified health insurance. Using the state tax listed in Appendix D, what is her state income tax?

2. Rick Barker works as an accountant in Denver, Colorado. Colorado has a state income tax of a flat 4.55 percent. Colorado's OPT is $5.75 per month per employee. If Rick is paid monthly and earns $2,850 after pre-tax deductions, what are his state and local taxes?

LO 5-5 Apply Post-Tax Deductions

Once the payroll clerk determines each employee's gross pay, pre-tax deductions, and taxes withheld, the post-tax deductions are applied to the remaining amount. All deductions, both voluntary and mandatory, should be listed on an attachment to the paycheck, in both pay-period and year-to-date amounts.

Post-tax deductions may include court-mandated or governmental debts as well as employee repayments of advances or overpayments. This section will explore examples of post-tax deductions and how they are included in net pay computations.

Markus Mainka/Shutterstock

Charitable Contributions

Employees may choose to contribute part of their pay to charitable organizations as an automatic deduction. This deduction is taken on a post-tax basis because the employee may deduct it from gross income on the annual tax return.

EXAMPLE: CHARITABLE CONTRIBUTION

Perry Wallace is an employee at Working Environments in Winchester, New Hampshire. He earns $29,000 annually and is paid weekly. He is single with no dependents. He has a pre-tax health insurance premium of $25 and a charitable contribution to the United Way of $10 per pay period. His net pay would be as follows:

Name	Filing Status	Dependents	Hourly Rate or Period Wage	No. of Regular Hours	No. of Overtime Hours	No. of Holiday Hours	Gross Earnings	401(k)	Insurance	Cafeteria Plan	Taxable Wages for Federal W/H	Taxable Wages for FICA
Perry Wallace	S	0	557.69				557.69		25.00		532.69	532.69

Name	Gross Earnings	Taxable Wages for Federal W/H	Taxable Wages for FICA	Federal W/H	Social Security Tax	Medicare W/H	State W/H Tax	Charitable Contribution	Union Dues	Garnishment	Net Pay
Perry Wallace	557.69	532.69	532.69	31.00	33.03	7.72		10.00			450.94

Garnishments

Remember garnishments are for court-mandated deductions such as child support obligations, liens, and consumer credit repayment. Title III of the CCPA limits the amount or percentage of pay deductions for garnishments. These deductions are taken on a post-tax basis because they are viewed as an obligation of the employee that must be paid out of post-tax income.

Table 5-1 reflects the maximum that may be garnished based on disposable income and pay frequency under Title III.

TABLE 5-1

Garnishment Maximum Based on Pay Frequency at the Federal Minimum Wage*

Weekly	Biweekly	Semimonthly	Monthly
Less than $217.50: $0	Less than $435.00: $0	Less than $471.25: $0	Less than $942.50: $0
$217.50 > $290.00: Only the amount over $217.50 may be garnished	$435.00 > $580.00: Only the amount over $435.00 may be garnished	$471.25 > $628.33: Only the amount over $471.25 may be garnished	$942.50 > $1,256.66: Only the amount over $942.50 may be garnished
Over $290.00: 25%	Over $580.00: 25%	Over $628.33: 25%	Over $1,256.66: 25%

Source: U.S. DOL

*In the case of bankruptcy, government tax liens, and child support, these maximums do not apply.

TABLE 5-2
Garnishments Maximum Percentage by Type

Garnishment Type	Maximum Percentage
Child Support or Alimony	50% if the employee is supporting a spouse or child 60% is the employee is not supporting a spouse or child 5% additional if child support is in arrears
Federal Student Loan	15%
Credit Card Debt	Up to 25%
Medical Debt	Up to 25%
Other Court-related Judgments	Up to 25%

Source: Nolo

Garnishments are subject to a maximum of 25 percent of disposable income for many situations. However, child support garnishment may be up to 60 percent, depending on how many people support financially. Table 5-2 contains an explanation of the type of garnishment and maximum allowed.

Federal student loan garnishment was suspended during the COVID pandemic until September 30, 2021. Before the garnishment suspension, student loan debt could constitute up to 15 percent of an employee's discretionary income. Although the suspension applied to federal student loan garnishments, private student loans were not covered by the suspension mandate.

(Source: NerdWallet)

EXAMPLE: CHILD SUPPORT

Andrew Malowitz is an employee of Kennesaw Mills. He earns $49,500 annually, paid semimonthly. He is single with one dependent under 17. He has a pre-tax health insurance deduction of $100 and contributes 3 percent of his gross pay to his 401(k) per pay period. The state income tax rate is 6 percent. He has a court-ordered garnishment of $300 per pay period for child support. His net pay would appear as follows (amounts rounded to the nearest dollar). Specific computations used in the payroll register follow immediately below the register.

Name	Filing Status	Dependents	Hourly Rate or Period Wage	No. of Regular Hours	No. of Overtime Hours	No. of Holiday Hours	Gross Earnings	401(k)	Insurance	Cafeteria Plan	Taxable Wages for Federal W/H	Taxable Wages for FICA
Andrew Malowitz	S	1 < 17	2,062.50				2,062.50	61.88	100.00		1,900.63	1,962.50

Name	Gross Earnings	Taxable Wages for Federal W/H	Taxable Wages for FICA	Federal W/H	Social Security Tax	Medicare W/H	State W/H Tax	Charitable Contribution	Union Dues	Garnishment	Net Pay
Andrew Malowitz	2,062.50	1,900.63	1,962.50	158.00	121.68	28.46	114.04			300.00	1,178.44

Payroll Register Computations

Payroll Register Column	Computation
Period wage	$49,500/24 = $2,062.50
401(k)	$2,062.50 × 0.03 = $61.88
Taxable wages for federal and state	$2,062.50 − 61.88 −100 = $1,900.63
Taxable wages for FICA	$2,062.50 −100 = $1,962.50
Social Security tax	$1,962.50 × 0.062 = $121.68
Medicare tax	$1,962.50 × 0.0145 = $24.68
State tax	$1,900.63 × 0.06 = $114.04
Net pay	$2,062.50 − 61.88 − 100 − 158 − 121.68 − 28.46 − 114.04 − 300 = $1,178.44

DISPOSABLE INCOME: CHILD SUPPORT

It is important to consider Andrew's disposable income to ensure the garnishment does not exceed legal maximums. His disposable income is computed as follows:

Gross pay	$2,062.50
Less: federal income tax	158.00
Less: state income tax	114.04
Less: Social Security tax	121.68
Less: Medicare tax	28.46
Total disposable income	$1,640.36
Percent of garnishment to disposable income	18.3%*

*$300 / 1,640.36 = 0.174 = 18.3% (rounded)

Andrey_Kuzmin/Shutterstock

Consumer Credit

Like other post-tax deductions such as student loans, consumer credit is considered an obligation to be paid out of a person's after-tax earnings. The next example shows the effect of a consumer credit garnishment on an employee's wages. In this case, the 25 percent maximum garnishment rule applies.

EXAMPLE: CONSUMER CREDIT

Mona Todd is an employee of Level Two Gallery in Ogden, Utah. She earns $38,500 annually, paid biweekly. She is single with no dependents. The state income tax rate is 4.95 percent. She has pre-tax deductions of $50 for health insurance and $30 for her contribution to a 401(k) plan, and she contributes $15 to the United Way. She has a court-ordered consumer credit garnishment of $100 per pay period. Her net pay would appear as follows:

Name	Filing Status	Dependents	Hourly Rate or Period Wage	No. of Regular Hours	No. of Overtime Hours	Gross Earnings	401(k)	Section 125	Taxable Wages for Federal W/H	Taxable Wages for FICA
Mona Todd	S	0	$1,480.77			$1,480.77	$30.00	$50.00	$1,400.77	$1,430.77

(continued)

(concluded)

Name	Gross Earnings	Taxable Wages for Federal/State W/H	Taxable Wages for FICA	Federal W/H	Social Security Tax	Medicare W/H Tax	State W/H Tax	Charitable Contribution	Garnishment	Net Pay
Mona Todd	$1,480.77	$1,400.77	$1,430.77	$106.00	$88.71	$20.75	$69.34	$15.00	$100.00	$1,000.97

DISPOSABLE INCOME: CONSUMER CREDIT

Let's ensure Mona's consumer credit garnishment is within legal guidelines:

Gross pay	$1,480.77
Less: federal income tax	104.00
Less: state income tax	69.34
Less: Social Security tax	88.71
Less: Medicare tax	20.75
Total disposable income	$1,197.97
Percent of garnishment to disposable income	8.4%*

*$100 / $1,197.97 = 0.0835 = 8.4\% \text{ (rounded)}$

A discussion topic between the American Payroll Association and the Wage and Hour Division of the Department of Labor has been the treatment of lump-sum distributions when a garnishment is imposed on an employee. The general guideline for considering a distribution as subject to garnishment is the concept of "personal service." If the distribution was for services rendered by the employee, then the amount may be garnished. Specific examples of lump-sum distributions that are subject to garnishment include the following:

- Sign-on bonuses
- Any performance or productivity bonus
- Commissions
- Holiday pay
- Retroactive pay
- Termination pay
- Any other bonuses or incentive payments

(Source: American Payroll Association)

Union Dues

Employees who belong to a collective bargaining unit usually pay dues to the unit for their representation. The CCPA disposable income limits do not pertain to union dues because those dues are not court-mandated. The following example shows how union dues affect employee pay. It should be noted the employee's deduction for union dues is voluntary.

EXAMPLE: UNION DUES

Forester Greer is an employee of Pacific High School in Washington state. He is a collective bargaining unit (i.e., union) that negotiates his salary, benefits, and working conditions and has dues of $50 per pay period. He earns $67,500 annually and is paid biweekly. He is married, filing jointly with 2 dependents under 17 (box 2 is not checked). He has pre-tax deductions of $150 for a 401(k) plan and $100 for a qualified Section 125 cafeteria plan. His net pay would appear as follows:

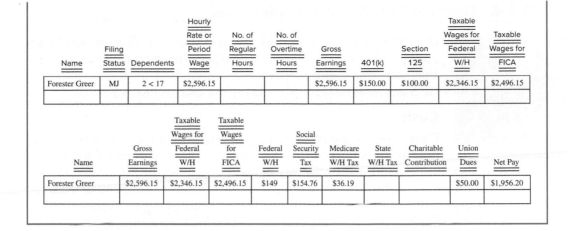

Name	Filing Status	Dependents	Hourly Rate or Period Wage	No. of Regular Hours	No. of Overtime Hours	Gross Earnings	401(k)	Section 125	Taxable Wages for Federal W/H	Taxable Wages for FICA
Forester Greer	MJ	2 < 17	$2,596.15			$2,596.15	$150.00	$100.00	$2,346.15	$2,496.15

Name	Gross Earnings	Taxable Wages for Federal W/H	Taxable Wages for FICA	Federal W/H	Social Security Tax	Medicare W/H Tax	State W/H Tax	Charitable Contribution	Union Dues	Net Pay
Forester Greer	$2,596.15	$2,346.15	$2,496.15	$149	$154.76	$36.19			$50.00	$1,956.20

Employee Advances and Overpayments

Employees may have an opportunity for an advance of money in anticipation of their pay. The timing of the repayment of advances depends on the agreement between the employee and employer. When the advance becomes due for repayment, it is treated as a post-tax deduction. The same concept applies to situations in which the employee is overpaid due to an error in computation or reporting.

> At Maricopa County Community College, a payroll system upgrade caused employees to be under- or overpaid, sometimes by thousands of dollars. The new payroll system's rollout caused issues with understanding the differences between the new and old systems. Accountants worked with managers and employees to ensure that all discrepancies were addressed promptly.
>
> Another underpayment issue that arose during the COVID pandemic was the omission of hazard pay to essential workers. Although they remained at work, they often did not receive additional pay for working in hazardous conditions.
>
> (Source: AZCentral, Brookings)

Post-tax deductions

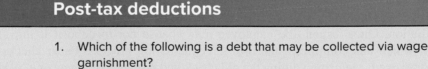

Stop & Check

1. Which of the following is a debt that may be collected via wage garnishment?
   a. Student loans
   b. Child support
   c. Debt to family members
   d. Tax liens
   e. Union dues
   f. Charitable contributions

2. Camden Crosby is an electrician who is a member of the IBEW union. He asks you, the payroll accountant, if he may pay his union dues by using a personal check instead of a post-tax deduction. The IBEW requires that the employer remit collected dues. What advice would you offer him?

LO 5-6   Discuss Employee Pay Methods

Romariolen/Shutterstock

Once the net pay is computed, the next step is to give the employees access to their money. Four common types of payment methods are available: cash, check, direct deposit, and paycard. Each method has its advantages and disadvantages. We will explore each method separately.

Cash

Cash is one of the oldest forms of paying employees but is not widely used as a contemporary payroll practice. The most common use of cash as a payment method involves paying for day laborers, temporary helpers, and odd jobs. Cash is one of the most difficult payroll forms to manage because it is difficult to track and control. Payments for wages in cash should involve a written receipt signed by the employee. Companies paying by cash must physically have the cash on hand for payroll, which increases the risk of theft from both internal and external sources. Payroll taxes must be withheld, which requires prior preparation so that the appropriate amount of cash is available to pay precisely what is due for each employee. For employees, cash is a very convenient payment method because of its inherent liquidity.

Comstock Images/Getty Images

Cash wage payment challenges the security of the funds for both the employer and the employee. For the employer, ensuring the employee receives and acknowledges the appropriate payment amount is the key. When using cash as a payment method for employees, a receipt that contains information about the gross pay, deductions, and net pay is important. The critical piece is to have the employee sign and date a copy acknowledging the receipt of the correct amount of cash on the specific date. Obtaining the employee's signature and date received can prevent future problems with perceived problems involving timely employee compensation payments.

Check

Paper checks are a common method of remitting employee compensation. For the employer, a paper check offers traceability and simplicity of accounting records. The use of checks instead of cash means the employer does not have to maintain large amounts of cash, reducing the vulnerability of keeping currency on hand. QuickBooks and Sage100 Cloud allow employers to print paychecks directly from the program on specifically designed, preprinted forms. Checks offer a security level that cash does not because they are issued to a specific employee, and they are the only person who can legally convert the check into cash.

The disadvantage of using paper checks for payroll purposes involves bank account reconciliation. Once issued, the employee may choose not to deposit it into their bank account, which can complicate the firm's reconciliation process. Paper checks could be lost or destroyed, requiring voiding the old check and issuance of a new one. Additionally, employees may not have a bank account, which makes cashing paychecks challenging and potentially costly. Paper checks may soon be phased out of current practice as other employee pay methods grow in popularity because of the convenience for both the employer and the employee.

> According to the Pew Internet and American Life Project in 2014, more than 53 million consumers in the United States use online banking. As of 2017, that number grew to more than two-thirds of Americans. The practice of payroll disbursement using paper checks is declining as people shift from traditional banking methods to a culture of electronic money management.
>
> (Source: Pew Research Center)

For employers who use paper checks as a compensation method, two significant best practices exist: (1) The use of a payroll-only checking account and (2) a procedure for the handling of the payroll checks themselves. A separate payroll-dedicated checking account prevents problems that could occur if the company has difficulties (such as insufficient funds) in the business's main account.

For the checks themselves, the payroll accountant needs to maintain a record that notes the use of each and every check, especially for checks that are voided, lost, or never cashed. If a company issues checks, it needs to maintain an unclaimed property account for payroll checks that the employee has never cashed. The process of leaving a check uncashed, especially if it is a payroll check, results in the *escheatment* of the payroll check because the payee of the check has never claimed the property (i.e., the payroll money) and is subject to state laws about the handling and distribution of such unclaimed money. Compliance with state escheatment laws is mandatory but not largely enforced—but that does not relieve the employer of the obligation to pay its employees. The use of a record in which the payroll accountant annotates each check's use (i.e., cashed, voided, or lost) is imperative.

> According to the State Comptroller of New York's office, the policy for escheatment is that uncashed payroll checks are escheated as of predetermined dates. As of 2021, over $16 billion in escheated funds remained in the custody of the state.
>
> (Source: Office of New York State Comptroller)

When a company pays employees by check, the check's numerical amount must also be represented in specific words for the bank to accept the check for payment to the payee. It is important to note banks pay the check based on the amount written in words on the check. The highlighted area in the image in Figure 5-3 shows how the information should appear on the check's face, specifically the written-out amount of the check. Figure 5-3 contains a sample of a paycheck.

A relevant concept in using checks for payroll is the potential for fraud by manipulating the checks' information. The check issuer (i.e., the employer) may be liable for the funds until the fraudulent activity is proven. Some red flags that may indicate check fraud include the following:

- Changes in font type between the company's address and the employee's name.
- Low check numbers (e.g., 1,001–1,500) because payroll fraud often involves new accounts.

FIGURE 5-3
Sample Paycheck

Wings of the North		
121 Nicholas Street		
North Pole, AK 99705		Check No. 23445
Petra Smith	Date	1/3/20XX
One Thousand One Hundred Twenty-four and 13/100	dollars	1,124.13
Payee: Petra Smith Address: 426 Candy Cane Lane City/State Zip: North Pole, AK 99705	Signed:	*Rudolph Donner*

- Evidence of typewriter use on the check (most payroll checks are generated via computerized programs).
- Stains or discolorations on the check.
- Notations in the memo line that contain the word "payroll" or "load."
- Handwritten additions to the check, such as the recipient's phone number.
- Absence of the bank's or the recipient's address.
- Check number is either absent or is the same on all checks.

(Source: National Check Fraud Center)

Paper checks are more vulnerable to fraud than electronic transfers because of the ease of obtaining preprinted checks. Many employers are transitioning to either direct deposits or paycards to protect company assets.

Direct Deposit

Direct deposit of employee compensation into the individual's bank account offers employers some of the same advantages as checks. Like checks, employee compensation is traceable through both the employer's bank and the optional paper pay advice issued to the employee. Employees often prefer direct deposit because their pay is immediately available in their bank account, eliminating the need to travel to the bank to deposit the paper check. However, for employees to receive their pay through direct deposit, they must have a bank account.

An advantage of direct deposit is that it prevents paper waste, promoting "green" business practices. According to the Association for Financial Professionals, the savings per employee per pay period is approximately $5.91. Although this may seem like a small

Comstock/PunchStock

amount, when multiplied by the number of employees and pay periods annually, it creates a potentially large saving for employers. These savings came from lower waste collection, paper usage, and recycling costs. Not only does direct deposit save a company money, but it also reduces the time needed for payroll processing, which frees payroll accountants to complete other tasks.

When using a direct deposit as an employee compensation method, a suggested best practice is to grant the employees access to a website or online portal by which they can securely view their *pay advice* and pay history, as this may substitute for paper payroll advice. Because direct deposit involves electronic data transmittal, the posting of the pay advice on a secure site could be linked with the human resources data, allowing the employee an element of self-maintenance in payroll records. The potential pitfall in using a website for these susceptible records is the vulnerability of the information to computer hacking. If an employer chooses to use a website in this manner, they must take steps to prevent hacking through data encryption, identity verification, and site security.

> The Federal Communications Commission (FCC) published guidelines for employer data security procedures, especially as it pertains to employee information on websites and the use of paycards. The FCC guidelines include advice about selecting data to be included on employee-accessible websites, password strength guidelines, update intervals, and data archiving.
>
> (Source: FCC)

Paycards

Paycards have been growing in popularity since the beginning of the 21st century. These cards are debit cards onto which an employer electronically transmits the employee's pay. The use of payroll cards started in the 1990s as a convenient way to compensate over-the-road truck

Tarik Kizilkaya/Getty Images

drivers who could not be in a predictable place on each payday. Comerica started issuing the paycards that could be used anywhere a conventional MasterCard was accepted, which is nearly everywhere. Unlike the use of paper checks or direct deposit, the paycard does not require an employee to maintain a bank account to access their pay. The convenience and ease of use for employees make the paycard an option that millions of workers in the United States have opted to use.

Paycards have grown in popularity because of their inherent flexibility for sending and receiving money. The paycard may be used as a debit card by people without bank accounts, which also grants them the ability to participate in online purchases even if they cannot qualify for a credit card. For the 13 million unbanked households in the United States, paycards grant the financial freedom and accessibility they may otherwise not have and allow unbanked employees to avoid check-cashing fees.

(Source: American Payroll Association)

What is the disadvantage of paycard use? Unlike the limits to access that a bank has for its account holders, a paycard can be lost or stolen. Some employees may encounter challenges such as withdrawal limits or cash back at point-of-sale (POS) purchases. Like paper checks, paycards may be subject to state escheatment laws that govern unclaimed funds.

An issue that haunted the early use of paycards was *Regulation E* of the Federal Deposit Insurance Corporation (FDIC), which protects consumers from loss of the availability of their funds on deposit in the event of bank losses. Until 2006, Regulation E applied to funds on deposit in an FDIC-insured institution. Regulation E was extended to cover payroll funds transferred to paycards, according to 12 CFR Part 205. As a payment method growing in popularity among employers and employees, paycards offer more compensation options for employers.

Paycards require different security types than the other types of employee compensation, but most elements remain the same. In addition to tracking hours and accurately com-

Nito/Shutterstock

pensating employees based on their marital status and withholdings, the employer must keep the employee's paycard number in a secure file. Software such as QuickBooks offers password encryption abilities for the files of employees who have paycards. Like any other debit card, the funds are electronically coded to the account number. The card issuer (not the employer) must remain compliant with Regulation E as far as card loss or theft is concerned. Still, the employer is responsible for ensuring this extra step of payroll security.

Visa Inc. introduced an improvement to its Visa Advanced Authorization technology, making compensation via paycards more secure and reliable. This new technology improved real-time fraud detection and was projected to prevent nearly $200 million in fraud within a five-year period. Since its inception, technology has evolved to include predictive analytics that detects unusual card usage.

(Source: Visa)

Zapp2Photo/Shutterstock

Cryptocurrency

An emerging wage payment method involves *cryptocurrency*, such as Bitcoin or Ethereum, and *blockchain* technology. Cryptocurrency uses Internet technology to transmit money securely from one "wallet," or account, to a recipient. The cryptocurrency itself is not a physical currency, as it exists only in electronic form. Transmission of wages is thought to be secure because blockchain technology makes it very difficult for wages to be diverted from the intended recipient. After all, the blockchain involves the transmission of packets of data through many computers, making a single transaction difficult to isolate.

The advantage of using cryptocurrency is it is not subject to international exchange rates, and it is transferred nearly instantaneously. The disadvantage of using cryptocurrency is that no centralized authority oversees the value of the currency, making it extremely volatile in value, which could lead to employees' underpayment if the currency loses value. As cryptocurrency becomes more accepted as a payroll payment form, additional governmental guidance will likely emerge.

> The company BitPay, which started in 2013, offered payroll via cryptocurrency in 2020. The service allowed employers to disburse payments without having to have a Bitcoin account. Using BitPay, employers transmit payroll directly to the employees' cryptocurrency wallets and charges each party a 1 percent fee for the service.
>
> (Source: CoinDesk)

Pay Methods

Stop & Check

1. What are the different employee pay methods?
2. What regulation governs paycard loss or theft?
3. For which pay method(s) must an employee have a bank account?

Trends to Watch

TAXES AND PAYMENT METHODS

Employee net pay changes each year because of legal developments regarding deductions and payment methods. Developments in employee withholdings since 2015 include the following:

- Changes to employee net pay because of the Affordable Care Act health insurance requirements for employers.
- Changes to sick-leave compensation at the state and local levels.
- Changes in the amounts that employees may contribute on a tax-deferred basis to pension plans.
- Increased public awareness of the effect of pay raises, especially for the cost of living, on net pay.
- Expanded regulatory guidance regarding data privacy and security, similar to the General Data Protection Regulation (GDPR) mandated in the European Union, to protect electronic employee payroll transmission.
- A continued trend of digital payroll disbursement in response to employees' demands for quick payroll access.
- Separation of payroll computations and disbursements, allowing companies to offer a single platform to access payroll amounts.
- On-demand pay through which employees can access earned payroll amounts at their discretion.
- Increasing regulation on digital payroll in response to online security and accessibility needs.

Summary of Employee Net Pay and Pay Methods

Employee pay is subject to various deductions that can be mandatory, mandated by a court or other authority, or voluntary. In 2020, the introduction of the new Form W-4 changed the factors by which federal income tax withholding was determined. The IRS provided an Excel-based tool to aid payroll accountants with the preparation of payroll. Deductions such as federal income tax and Medicare tax are virtually inescapable. Other taxes such as Social Security, state taxes, and local taxes are not applicable in every employee's situation and depend on various factors such as year-to-date pay and state of residence. Of the other deductions, some can be withheld from an employee's pay before taxes are deducted, which benefits an employee by reducing their payroll tax liability. Other deductions must be taken after taxes are withheld. Understanding the difference between gross pay and net pay is vital for payroll accountants because the net pay, not the gross, is the pay that the employee actually receives.

The question of employee pay methods is complex. Which payment method is the best? It is not an easy answer. An employer should consider the employees' needs and the business to decide if one method will suit everyone. Sometimes a combination of payment methods is the best solution, although it adds complexity for the payroll accountant. The most appropriate method for the organization will depend on many different factors. Attention to these factors, including payroll frequency, employee types, and the nature of the business itself, helps inform employer decisions about employee pay methods.

Key Points

- Net pay is gross pay less all deductions.
- Federal income tax applies to all workers, and the changes in federal income tax deductions changed because of the implementation of provisions of the Tax Cuts and Jobs Act.
- Employees hired after January 1, 2020, are subject to different factors as part of federal income tax computation. Employees hired in 2019 and prior years may continue to use their existing tax methods.
- Social Security tax has a maximum wage base that can change each year.
- Medicare tax has no maximum wage base, and an additional Medicare tax is levied on highly compensated employees.
- Employees subject to mandated deductions such as garnishments for child support and consumer credit liens have certain protections as to the percent of disposable income that may be withheld.
- Employees' pay may be disbursed in cash, by check, by paycard, or via direct deposit.
- Uncashed employee paychecks are turned over to state authorities as escheatments and become unclaimed property.
- Electronic means of transmitting pay, such as paycards, grow in popularity because of employee access and transmittal ease.
- Cryptocurrency is becoming a growing way for employers to transmit funds to employees and state agencies, although the standardization of cryptocurrency rules does not yet exist.

Vocabulary

Additional Medicare tax	Local income tax	Regulation E
Blockchain	Mandatory deductions	Social Security tax
Cryptocurrency	Medicare tax	State income taxes
Direct deposit	Net pay	Wage base
Escheatment	Pay advice	Wage-bracket method
Federal income tax	Paycard	
Federal Insurance	Percentage method	
Contribution Act (FICA)	Publication 15-T	

Review Questions

1. What factors affect how much federal income tax is withheld from an employee's pay using Form W-4?

2. How should employees complete their Form W-4 if they have multiple jobs or have a spouse who works?

3. How is Social Security tax computed? What is the maximum wage base?

4. How is Medicare tax computed? What is the maximum wage base?

5. Name four states that do not have an employee income tax.

6. How is an employee's net income computed?

7. Why is the difference between gross pay and taxable income important?

8. What are two of the five different payment methods?

9. What are the advantages and disadvantages of paycards?

10. What are an advantage and disadvantage of direct deposit?

11. How does the percentage method work using Form W-4 information?

12. When should the percentage method be used instead of the wage-bracket method?

13. What are two examples of garnishments?

14. Why are garnishments deducted on a post-tax basis?

15. Why are union dues not considered a garnishment?

16. How does cryptocurrency function as a payroll payment method?

Exercises Set A

E5-1A.
LO 5-1
Lyle Ingram, the payroll accountant, needs to compute net pay for the employees for Hay Industries. Place the following steps in the proper order.
a. Compute income taxes.
b. Subtract pre-tax deductions from gross pay.
c. Compute Social Security and Medicare taxes.
d. Subtract taxes and all other deductions from gross pay.
e. Determine gross pay.
Order: _____

E5-2A.
LO 5-1
Daryl Simpson is the owner of Padua Products. During the holiday season, he wants to reward his employees for their work during the year, and he has asked you to gross up their bonuses so that they receive the full amount as net pay. What amount(s) should you consider when computing the grossed-up pay? (Select all that apply.)
a. Desired bonus amount
b. Garnishments
c. Mandated deductions
d. Income tax(es)

E5-3A.

LO 5-2

Maria Koslov is a new employee at Financial Technologies, Ltd. She is married with children and her spouse works. What are items she needs to consider for her Form W-4 completion? (Select all that apply.)
a. Children's ages
b. Tax filing status
c. Spouse's income
d. Her birthdate

E5-4A.

LO 5-3

Under which circumstances could the percentage method be used to determine federal income tax withholding amounts? (Select all that apply.)
a. When the employee's taxable income exceeds the maximum amount on the appropriate wage-bracket table.
b. When using a computerized accounting system to compute payroll deductions.
c. When using a manual accounting system for a small number of low-pay employees.
d. When computational accuracy is critical.

E5-5A.

LO 5-3

Which of the following is true about Social Security and Medicare taxes as they pertain to earnings limits?
a. Social Security tax applies only to earnings greater than the wage base.
b. Highly compensated employees are subject to additional Medicare tax withholding.
c. Employers must match all Medicare contributions for highly-compensated employees.
d. Employees contribute the same percentage of gross pay to Medicare no matter what their YTD gross pay is.

E5-6A.

LO 5-3

What is the Social Security wage base for 2021?
a. $128,400
b. $132,900
c. $137,700
d. $142,800

E5-7A.

LO 5-4

Which of the following statements are true about state and local income taxes? (Select all that apply.)
a. All states tax employee earnings.
b. State tax rates on employee earnings vary among states.
c. Certain states have no personal income tax deduction.
d. Some localities levy income tax on employees.

E5-8A.

LO 5-6

Jeremiah Seafort of All Grains Bakery is considering offering additional payroll disbursal methods for his employees. Which of the following would be the safest for employees without a bank account?
a. Check
b. Paycard
c. Cash
d. Direct deposit

E5-9A.

LO 5-2

What are the two methods payroll accountants use to determine federal income tax withholding amounts? (Select all that apply.)
a. Percentage method
b. Salary-bracket method
c. Wage-salary method
d. Wage-bracket method

E5-10A.

LO 5-3

At what income level do many employees contribute an additional percentage to their Medicare tax deduction?
a. $128,400
b. $150,000
c. $175,000
d. $200,000

Problems Set A

P5-1A.

LO 5-1, 5-2, 5-3

Compute the net pay for Evelyn Khan and Margaret Rheinhart. Assume that they are paid a $2,500 salary biweekly, subject to federal income tax (use the wage-bracket method) in Appendix C and FICA taxes, and have no other deductions from their pay. They have a state tax rate of 3 percent. If they choose to participate in the cafeteria plan, the deduction for the pay period is $100; otherwise, there is no deduction for the cafeteria plan. The cafeteria plan qualifies under Section 125. You do not need to complete the number of hours. Additional information for Evelyn: Box 2 is not checked, and the dependents are under 17.

Name	Filing Status	Dependents	Hourly Rate or Period Wage	No. of Regular Hours	No. of Overtime Hours	No. of Holiday Hours	Commissions	Gross Earnings	Cafeteria Plan	Taxable Wages for Federal / State W/H	Taxable Wages for FICA
Evelyn Khan—no cafeteria plan	MJ	2 < 17	2,500.00								
Evelyn Khan— cafeteria plan	MJ	2 < 17	2,500.00								
Margaret Rheinhart—no cafeteria plan	S	0	2,500.00								
Margaret Rheinhart— cafeteria plan	S	0	2,500.00								

Name	Gross Earnings	Taxable Wages for Federal/ State W/H	Taxable Wages for FICA	Federal W/H	Social Security Tax	Medicare W/H Tax	State W/H Tax	Net Pay
Evelyn Khan—no cafeteria plan								
Evelyn Khan—cafeteria plan								
Margaret Rheinhart—no cafeteria plan								
Margaret Rheinhart—cafeteria plan								

P5-2A.

LO 5-1, 5-2, 5-3, 5-5

Enlightened Eats in Anchorage, Alaska, has six employees who are paid semimonthly. Calculate the net pay from the information provided below for the November 15 pay date. Assume that all wages are subject to Social Security and Medicare taxes. All 401(k) and Section 125 amounts are pre-tax deductions. Use the percentage method for manual payroll systems with Forms W-4 from 2020 or later in Appendix C to compute federal income taxes. You do not need to complete the number of hours.

a. W. Packer
   Married/Joint, two dependents <17, Box 2 checked
   Annual pay: $35,500
   401(k) deduction: $125 per pay period

b. K. Ela
   Married/Separate, two dependents <17, Box 2 checked
   Annual pay: $53,400
   401(k) deduction: $250 per pay period

c. G. Laureano
   Single, no dependents, Box 2 not checked
   Annual pay: $50,400
   Section 125 deduction: $75 per pay period
   401(k) deduction: $50 per pay period

d. T. Spraggins
Married/Joint, one dependent <17, Box 2 not checked
Annual pay: $45,000
United Way deduction: $50 per pay period
Garnishment: $50 per pay period

e. M. Christman
Single, two dependents <17, one other dependent, Box 2 checked
Annual pay: $58,800
Section 125 deduction: $50 per pay period
401(k) deduction: 6 percent of gross pay per pay period

f. J. Cherry
Married/Joint, one other dependent, Box 2 checked
Annual pay: $48,400
401(k) deduction: $75 per pay period

Name	Filing Status	Dependents	Hourly Rate or Period Wage	No. of Regular Hours	No. of Overtime Hours	No. of Holiday Hours	Commiss-ions	Gross Earnings	401(k)	Section 125	Taxable Wages for Federal / State W/H	Taxable Wages for FICA

Name	Gross Earnings	Taxable Wages for Federal/ State W/H	Taxable Wages for FICA	Federal W/H	Social Security Tax	Medicare W/H Tax	State W/H Tax	Garnish-ments	United Way	Net Pay

P5-3A.

LO 5-1, 5-2, 5-3, 5-4, 5-5

The following salaried employees of Mountain Stone Brewery in Fort Collins, Colorado, are paid semimonthly. Some employees have union dues or garnishments deducted from their pay. Calculate their net pay using the percentage method for manual payroll systems with Forms W-4 from 2020 or later in Appendix C to determine federal income tax. Assume box 2 is *not* checked for any employee. Include Colorado income tax of 4.55 percent of taxable pay. No employee has exceeded the maximum FICA limit. You do not need to complete the number of hours.

Employee	Filing Status, Dependents	Pay	Union Dues per Period	Garnishment per Period
S. Bergstrom	MJ-0	$1,700		$ 50
C. Pare	MJ-2 (<17)	3,500	$120	
L. Van der Hooven	S-1 (Other)	3,225	240	75
S. Lightfoot	MJ-0	2,850		100

Name	Filing Status	Dependents	Hourly Rate or Period Wage	No. of Regular Hours	No. of Overtime Hours	No. of Holiday Hours	Commiss-ions	Gross Earnings	401(k)	Section 125	Taxable Wages for Federal / State W/H	Taxable Wages for FICA

Name	Gross Earnings	Taxable Wages for Federal/State W/H	Taxable Wages for FICA	Federal W/H	Social Security Tax	Medicare W/H Tax	State W/H Tax	Union Dues	Garnish-ment	Net Pay

P5-4A.

LO 5-1, 5-2, 5-3, 5-4, 5-5

James Marbury is the payroll accountant at All's Fair Gifts. The employees of All's Fair Gifts are paid semimonthly. Lauren Stenn comes to him on April 2 and requests a pay advance of $1,000, which Lauren will pay back in equal parts on the April 15 and May 15 paychecks. Lauren is single (box 2 is checked) with one dependent under 17 and is paid $50,000 per year. Lauren contributes 3 percent of gross pay to a 401(k) and has $125 per paycheck deducted for a Section 125 plan. Compute the net pay on Lauren's April 15 paycheck. The applicable state income tax rate is 5.25 percent. Use the percentage method for manual payroll systems with Forms W-4 from 2020 or later in Appendix C to determine the federal income tax. Assume box 2 is *not* checked.

Name	Filing Status,	Dependents	Hourly Rate or Period Wage	No. of Regular Hours	No. of Overtime Hours	No. of Holiday Hours	Commiss-ions	Gross Earnings	401(k)	Section 125	Taxable Wages for Federal/ State W/H	Taxable Wages for FICA
L. Stenn												

Name	Gross Earnings	Taxable Wages for Federal/State W/H	Taxable Wages for FICA	Federal W/H	Social Security Tax	Medicare W/H Tax	State W/H Tax	Advance	Net Pay
Lauren Stenn									

P5-5A.

LO 5-1, 5-2

Milligan's Millworks pays its employees weekly. Use the wage-bracket tables from Appendix C to compute the federal income tax withholdings for the following employees of Milligan's Millworks. Assume that no pre-tax deductions exist for any employee and box 2 is not checked for all employees and manual payroll system is used.

Employee	Filing Status	Dependents	Weekly Pay	Federal Tax
D. Balestreri	Single	2 < 17	$ 845	
Y. Milligan	Single	One Other	1,233	
H. Curran	Married/Joint	2 < 17, One Other	682	
D. Liberti	Head of Household	1 < 17	755	

P5-6A.

LO 5-2

Moravanti Italian Imports has four employees and pays biweekly. Complete the W-4 multi-jobs worksheet (when applicable) Section 2(b), for all employees, each will use the standard deduction, and calculate the federal income tax withholding using the wage-bracket tables in Appendix C. Assume that box 2 is not checked for L. Torabi and R. Beninati and is checked for G. Fisher and J. Tillman.

Employee	Filing Status	Dependents	Annual Salary	Spouse Annual Salary/Pay Frequency	Federal Income Tax per period
L. Torabi	S	None	$39,500	n/a	
R. Beninati	S	One Other	48,500	n/a	
G. Fisher	MJ	3 < 17	45,300	$75,600/biweekly	
J. Tillman	MJ	2 < 17	42,000	$27,500/weekly	

Form **W-4**	**Employee's Withholding Certificate**	OMB No. 1545-0074
(Rev. December 2020) Department of the Treasury Internal Revenue Service	▶ Complete Form W-4 so that your employer can withhold the correct federal income tax from your pay. ▶ Give Form W-4 to your employer. ▶ Your withholding is subject to review by the IRS.	20**21**

Step 1:

Enter Personal Information

(a) First name and middle initial	Last name	(b) Social security number
Address		▶ Does your name match the name on your social security card? If not, to ensure you get credit for your earnings, contact SSA at 800-772-1213 or go to www.ssa.gov.
City or town, state, and ZIP code		

(c) ☐ Single or Married filing separately
☐ Married filing jointly or Qualifying widow(er)
☐ Head of household (Check only if you're unmarried and pay more than half the costs of keeping up a home for yourself and a qualifying individual.)

Complete Steps 2–4 ONLY if they apply to you; otherwise, skip to Step 5. See page 2 for more information on each step, who can claim exemption from withholding, when to use the estimator at *www.irs.gov/W4App*, and privacy.

Step 2:

Multiple Jobs or Spouse Works

Complete this step if you (1) hold more than one job at a time, or (2) are married filing jointly and your spouse also works. The correct amount of withholding depends on income earned from all of these jobs.

Do **only one** of the following.

(a) Use the estimator at *www.irs.gov/W4App* for most accurate withholding for this step (and Steps 3–4); **or**

(b) Use the Multiple Jobs Worksheet on page 3 and enter the result in Step 4(c) below for roughly accurate withholding; **or**

(c) If there are only two jobs total, you may check this box. Do the same on Form W-4 for the other job. This option is accurate for jobs with similar pay; otherwise, more tax than necessary may be withheld . . . . . ▶ ☐

TIP: To be accurate, submit a 2021 Form W-4 for all other jobs. If you (or your spouse) have self-employment income, including as an independent contractor, use the estimator.

Complete Steps 3–4(b) on Form W-4 for only ONE of these jobs. Leave those steps blank for the other jobs. (Your withholding will be most accurate if you complete Steps 3–4(b) on the Form W-4 for the highest paying job.)

Step 3:

Claim Dependents

If your total income will be $200,000 or less ($400,000 or less if married filing jointly):

Multiply the number of qualifying children under age 17 by $2,000 ▶ $ _____

Multiply the number of other dependents by $500 . . . . ▶ $ _____

| Add the amounts above and enter the total here . . . . | **3** | $ |

Step 4
(optional):
Other
Adjustments

(a) Other income (not from jobs). If you want tax withheld for other income you expect this year that won't have withholding, enter the amount of other income here. This may include interest, dividends, and retirement income . . . .   **4(a)** $

(b) Deductions. If you expect to claim deductions other than the standard deduction and want to reduce your withholding, use the Deductions Worksheet on page 3 and enter the result here . . . .   **4(b)** $

(c) Extra withholding. Enter any additional tax you want withheld each **pay period** .   **4(c)** $

Step 5:
Sign
Here

Under penalties of perjury, I declare that this certificate, to the best of my knowledge and belief, is true, correct, and complete.

▶ _____   ▶
Employee's signature (This form is not valid unless you sign it.)   **Date**

Employers
Only

Employer's name and address | First date of employment | Employer identification number (EIN)

For Privacy Act and Paperwork Reduction Act Notice, see page 3.   Cat. No. 10220Q   Form **W-4** (2021)

Form W-4 (2021)   Page **3**

Step 2(b)—Multiple Jobs Worksheet *(Keep for your records.)*

If you choose the option in Step 2(b) on Form W-4, complete this worksheet (which calculates the total extra tax for all jobs) on **only ONE** Form W-4. Withholding will be most accurate if you complete the worksheet and enter the result on the Form W-4 for the highest paying job.

Note: If more than one job has annual wages of more than $120,000 or there are more than three jobs, see Pub. 505 for additional tables; or, you can use the online withholding estimator at *www.irs.gov/W4App.*

1 **Two jobs.** If you have two jobs or you're married filing jointly and you and your spouse each have one job, find the amount from the appropriate table on page 4. Using the "Higher Paying Job" row and the "Lower Paying Job" column, find the value at the intersection of the two household salaries and enter that value on line 1. Then, **skip** to line 3 . . . .   **1** $

2 **Three jobs.** If you and/or your spouse have three jobs at the same time, complete lines 2a, 2b, and 2c below. Otherwise, skip to line 3.

    a Find the amount from the appropriate table on page 4 using the annual wages from the highest paying job in the "Higher Paying Job" row and the annual wages for your next highest paying job in the "Lower Paying Job" column. Find the value at the intersection of the two household salaries and enter that value on line 2a . . . .   **2a** $

    b Add the annual wages of the two highest paying jobs from line 2a together and use the total as the wages in the "Higher Paying Job" row and use the annual wages for your third job in the "Lower Paying Job" column to find the amount from the appropriate table on page 4 and enter this amount on line 2b . . . .   **2b** $

    c Add the amounts from lines 2a and 2b and enter the result on line 2c . . . .   **2c** $

3 Enter the number of pay periods per year for the highest paying job. For example, if that job pays weekly, enter 52; if it pays every other week, enter 26; if it pays monthly, enter 12, etc. . . . . .   **3** _____

4 **Divide** the annual amount on line 1 or line 2c by the number of pay periods on line 3. Enter this amount here and in **Step 4(c)** of Form W-4 for the highest paying job (along with any other additional amount you want withheld) . . . .   **4** $

Step 4(b)—Deductions Worksheet *(Keep for your records.)*

1 Enter an estimate of your 2021 itemized deductions (from Schedule A (Form 1040)). Such deductions may include qualifying home mortgage interest, charitable contributions, state and local taxes (up to $10,000), and medical expenses in excess of 7.5% of your income . . . .   **1** $

2 Enter: { • $25,100 if you're married filing jointly or qualifying widow(er)
            • $18,800 if you're head of household
            • $12,550 if you're single or married filing separately } . . . .   **2** $

3 If line 1 is greater than line 2, subtract line 2 from line 1 and enter the result here. If line 2 is greater than line 1, enter "-0-" . . . .   **3** $

4 Enter an estimate of your student loan interest, deductible IRA contributions, and certain other adjustments (from Part II of Schedule 1 (Form 1040)). See Pub. 505 for more information . . . .   **4** $

5 **Add** lines 3 and 4. Enter the result here and in **Step 4(b)** of Form W-4 . . . .   **5** $

Form W-4 (2021)   Page **4**

Married Filing Jointly or Qualifying Widow(er)

Higher Paying Job Annual Taxable Wage & Salary	Lower Paying Job Annual Taxable Wage & Salary											
	$0 - 9,999	$10,000 - 19,999	$20,000 - 29,999	$30,000 - 39,999	$40,000 - 49,999	$50,000 - 59,999	$60,000 - 69,999	$70,000 - 79,999	$80,000 - 89,999	$90,000 - 99,999	$100,000 - 109,999	$110,000 - 120,000
$0 - 9,999	$0	$190	$850	$890	$1,020	$1,020	$1,020	$1,020	$1,020	$1,100	$1,870	$1,870
$10,000 - 19,999	190	1,190	1,890	2,090	2,220	2,220	2,220	2,220	2,300	3,300	4,070	4,070
$20,000 - 29,999	850	1,890	2,750	2,950	3,080	3,080	3,080	3,160	4,160	5,160	5,930	5,930
$30,000 - 39,999	890	2,090	2,950	3,150	3,280	3,280	3,360	4,360	5,360	6,360	7,130	7,130
$40,000 - 49,999	1,020	2,220	3,080	3,280	3,410	3,490	4,490	5,490	6,490	7,490	8,260	8,260
$50,000 - 59,999	1,020	2,220	3,080	3,280	3,490	4,490	5,490	6,490	7,490	8,490	9,260	9,260
$60,000 - 69,999	1,020	2,220	3,080	3,360	4,490	5,490	6,490	7,490	8,490	9,490	10,260	10,260
$70,000 - 79,999	1,020	2,220	3,160	4,360	5,490	6,490	7,490	8,490	9,490	10,490	11,260	11,260
$80,000 - 99,999	1,020	3,150	5,010	6,210	7,340	8,340	9,340	10,340	11,340	12,340	13,260	13,460
$100,000 - 149,999	1,870	4,070	5,930	7,130	8,260	9,320	10,520	11,720	12,920	14,120	15,000	15,290
$150,000 - 239,999	2,040	4,440	6,500	7,900	9,230	10,430	11,630	12,830	14,030	15,230	16,190	16,400
$240,000 - 259,999	2,040	4,440	6,500	7,900	9,230	10,430	11,630	12,830	14,030	15,270	17,040	18,040
$260,000 - 279,999	2,040	4,440	6,500	7,900	9,230	10,430	11,630	12,870	14,870	16,870	18,640	19,640
$280,000 - 299,999	2,040	4,440	6,500	7,900	9,230	10,470	12,470	14,470	16,470	18,470	20,240	21,240
$300,000 - 319,999	2,040	4,440	6,500	7,940	10,070	12,070	14,070	16,070	18,070	20,070	21,840	22,840
$320,000 - 364,999	2,720	5,920	8,780	10,980	13,110	15,110	17,110	19,110	21,190	23,490	25,560	26,860
$365,000 - 524,999	2,970	6,470	9,630	12,130	14,560	16,860	19,100	21,460	23,760	26,060	28,130	29,430
$525,000 and over	3,140	6,840	10,200	12,900	15,530	18,030	20,530	23,030	25,530	28,030	30,300	31,800

Single or Married Filing Separately

Higher Paying Job Annual Taxable Wage & Salary	Lower Paying Job Annual Taxable Wage & Salary											
	$0 - 9,999	$10,000 - 19,999	$20,000 - 29,999	$30,000 - 39,999	$40,000 - 49,999	$50,000 - 59,999	$60,000 - 69,999	$70,000 - 79,999	$80,000 - 89,999	$90,000 - 99,999	$100,000 - 109,999	$110,000 - 120,000
$0 - 9,999	$440	$940	$1,020	$1,020	$1,410	$1,870	$1,870	$1,870	$1,870	$2,030	$2,040	$2,040
$10,000 - 19,999	940	1,540	1,620	2,020	3,020	3,470	3,470	3,470	3,640	3,840	3,840	3,840
$20,000 - 29,999	1,020	1,620	2,100	3,100	4,100	4,550	4,550	4,720	4,920	5,120	5,120	5,120
$30,000 - 39,999	1,020	2,020	3,100	4,100	5,100	5,550	5,720	5,920	6,120	6,320	6,320	6,320
$40,000 - 59,999	1,870	3,470	4,550	5,550	6,690	7,340	7,540	7,740	7,940	8,140	8,150	8,150
$60,000 - 79,999	1,870	3,470	4,690	5,890	7,090	7,740	7,940	8,140	8,340	8,540	9,190	9,990
$80,000 - 99,999	2,000	3,810	5,090	6,290	7,490	8,140	8,340	8,540	9,390	10,390	11,190	11,990
$100,000 - 124,999	2,040	3,840	5,120	6,320	7,520	8,360	9,360	10,360	11,360	12,360	13,410	14,510
$125,000 - 149,999	2,040	3,840	5,120	6,910	8,910	10,360	11,360	12,450	13,750	15,050	16,160	17,260
$150,000 - 174,999	2,220	4,830	6,910	8,910	10,910	12,600	13,900	15,200	16,500	17,800	18,910	20,010
$175,000 - 199,999	2,720	5,320	7,490	9,790	12,090	13,850	15,150	16,450	17,750	19,050	20,150	21,250
$200,000 - 249,999	2,970	5,880	8,260	10,560	12,860	14,620	15,920	17,220	18,520	19,820	20,930	22,030
$250,000 - 399,999	2,970	5,880	8,260	10,560	12,860	14,620	15,920	17,220	18,520	19,820	20,930	22,030
$400,000 - 449,999	2,970	5,880	8,260	10,560	12,860	14,620	15,920	17,220	18,520	19,910	21,220	22,520
$450,000 and over	3,140	6,250	8,830	11,330	13,830	15,790	17,290	18,790	20,290	21,790	23,100	24,400

Head of Household

Higher Paying Job Annual Taxable Wage & Salary	Lower Paying Job Annual Taxable Wage & Salary											
	$0 - 9,999	$10,000 - 19,999	$20,000 - 29,999	$30,000 - 39,999	$40,000 - 49,999	$50,000 - 59,999	$60,000 - 69,999	$70,000 - 79,999	$80,000 - 89,999	$90,000 - 99,999	$100,000 - 109,999	$110,000 - 120,000
$0 - 9,999	$0	$820	$930	$1,020	$1,020	$1,020	$1,420	$1,870	$1,870	$1,910	$2,040	$2,040
$10,000 - 19,999	820	1,900	2,130	2,220	2,220	2,620	3,620	4,070	4,110	4,310	4,440	4,440
$20,000 - 29,999	930	2,130	2,360	2,450	2,850	3,850	4,850	5,340	5,540	5,740	5,870	5,870
$30,000 - 39,999	1,020	2,220	2,450	2,940	3,940	4,940	5,980	6,630	6,830	7,030	7,160	7,160
$40,000 - 59,999	1,020	2,470	3,700	4,790	5,800	7,000	8,200	8,850	9,050	9,250	9,380	9,380
$60,000 - 79,999	1,870	4,070	5,310	6,600	7,800	9,000	10,200	10,850	11,050	11,250	11,520	12,320
$80,000 - 99,999	1,880	4,280	5,710	7,000	8,200	9,400	10,600	11,250	11,590	12,590	13,520	14,320
$100,000 - 124,999	2,040	4,440	5,870	7,160	8,360	9,560	11,240	12,690	13,690	14,690	15,670	16,770
$125,000 - 149,999	2,040	4,440	5,870	7,240	9,240	11,240	13,240	14,690	15,890	17,190	18,420	19,520
$150,000 - 174,999	2,040	4,920	7,150	9,240	11,240	13,290	15,590	17,340	18,640	19,940	21,170	22,270
$175,000 - 199,999	2,720	5,920	8,150	10,440	12,740	15,040	17,340	19,090	20,390	21,690	22,920	24,020
$200,000 - 249,999	2,970	6,470	9,000	11,390	13,690	15,990	18,290	20,040	21,340	22,640	23,880	24,980
$250,000 - 349,999	2,970	6,470	9,000	11,390	13,690	15,990	18,290	20,040	21,340	22,640	23,880	24,980
$350,000 - 449,999	2,970	6,470	9,000	11,390	13,690	15,990	18,290	20,040	21,340	22,640	23,900	25,200
$450,000 and over	3,140	6,840	9,570	12,160	14,660	17,160	19,660	21,610	23,110	24,610	26,050	27,350

P5-7A.

LO 5-3

The employees of Ethereal Bank are paid on a semimonthly basis. Compute the FICA taxes for the employees for the November 30 payroll. All employees have been employed for the entire calendar year. All employees are single.

Employee	Semimonthly Pay	YTD Pay for Nov 15 Pay Date	Social Security Tax for Nov. 30 Pay Date	Medicare Tax for Nov. 30 Pay Date
R. Bellagio	$ 9,500			
B. Khumalo	6,700			
S. Schriver	6,800			
K. Saetang	7,250			
T. Ahmad	9,750			
M. Petrova	8,100			

P5-8A.

LO 5-4

Fannon's Chocolate Factory operates in North Carolina. Calculate the state income tax for each employee using the state income tax rate of 4.75 percent. Assume that no pre-tax deductions exist for any employee.

Employee	Amount per Pay Period	North Carolina Income Tax
K. Jamieson	$ 550	
D. Macranie	4,895	
G. Lockhart	3,225	
K. McIntyre	1,795	

P5-9A.

LO 5-2

Using the percentage method for manual payroll with W-4s from 2020 or later in Appendix C calculate the federal withholding amounts for the following employees. No information was included in Step 4 of the W-4, and no box was checked in Step 2.

Employee	Filing Status	Dependents	Pay Frequency	Amount per Pay Period	Federal Income Tax
S. Calder	MJ	3 < 17	Monthly	$10,000	
P. Singh	HH	1 < 17	Biweekly	3,300	
B. Nelson	MJ	None	Daily	500	

P5-10A.

LO 5-6

Margaret Wilson is the new accountant for a start-up company, Peaceful Skunk Builders. The company has cross-country drivers, warehouse personnel, and office staff at the main location. The company is looking at options that allow its employees flexibility with receiving their pay. Margaret has been asked to present the advantages and disadvantages of the various payment methods for senior management. Which would be the best option for each class of workers?

Exercises Set B

E5-1B.

LO 5-1

Chastity Santos is in the process of computing net pay for the employees of Happy Crab Marketing. Place the following steps in order after Chastity has determined the amount of gross pay:

a. Compute Social Security and Medicare tax withholding
b. Compute income tax withholding(s)
c. Compute pre-tax deductions
d. Compute post-tax deductions

E5-2B.

LO 5-1

Chloe Ayers has received a court order for garnishment for her student loan payments. What must be considered in computing the garnishment? (Select all that apply.)
a. Year-to-date pay
b. Hourly wage
c. Disposable income
d. Pay frequency

E5-3B.

LO 5-2

Annika Nkosi of Trade Secrets Importing is preparing payroll taxes manually. As she prepares to use the wage-bracket tables to determine federal income tax withholdings for each employee, which information should she have available? (Select all that apply.)
a. Filing status
b. Job title
c. Year-to-date earnings
d. Age, type, and number of dependents

E5-4B.

LO 5-2

Which of the following are steps in computing federal income tax withholding using the percentage method? (Select all that apply.)
a. Compute and deduct withholding allowance.
b. Apply the tax rate to the taxable portion of the earnings.
c. Determine if the employee is exempt or nonexempt.
d. Add the marginal tax.

E5-5B.

LO 5-3

Which of the following is true about Social Security and Medicare tax deductions?
a. They are applied to the gross pay.
b. Contributions to a 401(k) plan are exempt from these taxes.
c. Medicare taxes apply to all earnings at the same rate.
d. Certain pre-tax deductions are exempt from Social Security and Medicare tax computations.

E5-6B.

LO 5-3

Scout Freeman is the vice president for marketing at Sun Field Industries. She earns $160,000 annually and is paid on a semimonthly basis. As of November 15, Scout has year-to-date earnings of $140,000. The Social Security wage base is $142,800. What is the maximum amount of her taxable earnings that may be subject to Social Security tax for the November 30 pay period?
a. $5,833
b. $1,833
c. $2,800
d. $0

E5-7B.

LO 5-4

Which of the following is true about state and local income tax? (Select all that apply.)
a. Pre-tax deduction rules for federal income tax are generally the same for state and local income taxes.
b. Nine states do not have a personal income tax on earnings.
c. All localities levy income taxes on employees.
d. State income tax computations vary among states.

E5-8B.

LO 5-6

Which of the following is true about employee pay methods? (Select all that apply.)
a. Employees must be able to access the full amount of their net pay on the pay date.
b. Employers must keep a record of all pay disbursements.
c. Employees do not need to own a bank account to receive their pay via direct deposit.
d. Employees must request the transfer of payroll earnings to their paycard each period.

E5-9B.   Which of the following is true about child support garnishments? (Select all
LO 5-4   that apply.)
    a. They are based on gross pay.
    b. The garnishment may be as high as 65 percent.
    c. Only the minimum wage amount of an employee's pay is subject to
       garnishment.
    d. Title III of the CCPA protects employees.

E5-10B.   Margarita Sutton is preparing a training session for her colleagues about
LO 5-6   payroll check fraud. Which of the following may be indicators of check
          fraud? (Select all that apply.)
    a. Changes in font type between company address and employee name.
    b. Company logo on the face of the check.
    c. The check number is missing from the check.
    d. Only one signature is required from the company.

Problems Set B

P5-1B.   Compute the net pay for Mehdi Gamal and Deion Green. Assume that they
LO 5-1,   are paid biweekly, subject to federal income tax (use wage bracket method)
5-2, 5-3   and FICA taxes, and have no other deductions from their pay. Mehdi's
           deduction if he chooses to participate in the cafeteria plan is $75; Deion's
           is $250. There is no deduction if they do not participate in the cafeteria
           plan. The cafeteria plan qualifies for Section 125. There are no state income
           taxes, and you do not need to complete the number of hours. All W-4s were
           received in 2021, and there is no information for Step 4. Deion did check
           the box in Step 2.

Name	Filing Status	Dependents	Hourly Rate or Period Wage	No. of Regular Hours	No. of Overtime Hours	No. of Holiday Hours	Commiss-ions	Gross Earnings	Cafeteria Plan	Taxable Wages for Federal / State W/H	Taxable Wages for FICA
Mehdi Gamal—no cafeteria plan	S	None	1,600.00								
Mehdi Gamal—cafeteria plan	S	None	1,600.00								
Deion Green—no cafeteria plan	MJ	2 < 17 One Other	1,875.00								
Deion Green—cafeteria plan	MJ	2 < 17 One Other	1,875.00								

Name	Gross Earnings	Taxable Wages for Federal / State W/H	Taxable Wages for FICA	Federal W/H	Social Security Tax	Medicare W/H	Net Pay
Mehdi Gamal—no cafeteria plan							
Mehdi Gamal—cafeteria plan							
Deion Green—no cafeteria plan							
Deion Green—cafeteria plan							

P5-2B.

LO 5-1, 5-2, 5-3, 5-5, 5-6

Teton Tours in Evanston, Wyoming, has six employees who are paid on a biweekly basis. Calculate the net pay from the information provided for the July 23 pay date. Assume that all wages are subject to Social Security and Medicare taxes. Use the wage-bracket tables in Appendix C to determine the federal income tax withholding. You do not need to complete the number of hours. No one has checked the box in Step 2, there is no additional information in Step 4.

a. A. Bowman
Married/Joint, Two dependents <17
Annual pay $36,320
401(k) deduction: 2 percent of gross pay per pay period

b. J. Raz
Single, No dependents
Annual pay: $46,350
401(k) deduction: $220 per pay period

c. G. Koskoris
Single, One dependent <17, One Other dependent
Annual pay: $55,120
Section 125 deduction: $25 per pay period
401(k) deduction: $150 per pay period

d. S. Hays-Smith
Married/Joint, Three dependents <17
Annual pay: $40,820
United Way deduction: $25 per pay period
Garnishment: $75 per period

e. H. Inhofe
Married/Joint, No dependents
Annual pay: $55,000
Section 125 deduction: $100 per period
401(k) deduction: 4 percent of gross pay

f. D. Wong
Single, One Other dependent
Annual pay: $38,600
401(k) deduction: $120 per period

Name	Filing Status	Dependents	Hourly Rate or Period Wage	No. of Regular Hours	No. of Overtime Hours	No. of Holiday Hours	Gross Earnings	401(k)	Section 125	Taxable Wages for Federal / State W/H	Taxable Wages for FICA

Name	Gross Earnings	Taxable Wages for Federal/ State W/H	Taxable Wages for FICA	Federal W/H Tax	Social Security Tax	Medicare Tax	State Tax	United Way	Garnishment	Net Pay

P5-3B.

LO 5-1, 5-2, 5-3, 5-4, 5-5

The following employees of Concordian Construction of Walla Walla, Washington, are paid biweekly. Some employees have union dues or garnishments deducted from their pay. Calculate their net pay. Use the percentage method for manual payrolls with Forms W-4 from 2020 or later in Appendix C to determine federal income tax. No employee has exceeded the maximum FICA limits. You do not need to complete the number of hours. No one checked the box in Step 2 and there is no additional information in Step 4.

Employee	Filing Status	Dependents	Annual Pay	Union Dues per Period	Garnishment per Period
J. Johnson	Married/Joint	1 < 17	$45,000	$102	
V. Roberson	Single	None	33,800		$70
T. Major	Married/Joint	None	65,650	110	90
M. Reice	Head of Household	1 < 17	76,600		45

Name	Filing Status	Dependents	Hourly Rate or Period Wage	No. of Regular Hours	No. of Overtime Hours	No. of Holiday Hours	Commiss-ions	Gross Earnings	401(k)	Section 125	Taxable Wages for Federal/ State W/H	Taxable Wages for FICA

Name	Gross Earnings	Taxable Wages for Federal/ State W/H	Taxable Wages for FICA	Federal W/H	Social Security Tax	Medicare W/H Tax	State W/H	Union Dues	Garnishment	Net Pay

P5-4B.
LO 5-1, 5-2, 5-3, 5-4, 5-5

Christine Erickson is the payroll accountant for Multi Winds Energy of Lincoln, Nebraska. The employees of Multi Winds Energy are paid biweekly. An employee, Linda Larson, comes to her on September 9 and requests a pay advance of $1,000, which she will pay back in equal parts on the September 24 and October 22 paychecks. Linda is single with no dependents and is paid $52,500 per year. She contributes 5 percent of her pay to a 401(k) plan and has $250 per paycheck deducted for a court-ordered garnishment. Compute her net pay for her September 24 paycheck. Her state income tax rate is 6.84 percent. Use the wage-bracket tables in Appendix C to determine the federal income tax withholding amount. You do not need to complete the number of hours. Assume that no pre-tax deductions exist for any employee and box 2 is not checked.

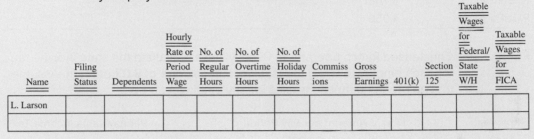

P5-5B.
LO 5-2

Wolfe Industries pays its employees on a semimonthly basis. Using the wage-bracket tables in Appendix C, compute the federal income tax deductions for the following employees of Wolfe Industries. No information was included in Step 4 of any W-4; McCollum checked the box in Step 2c. Assume that no pre-tax deductions exist for any employee and box 2 is not checked for all other employees. Do not round intermediate calculations. Round your final answers to nearest whole dollar.

Employee	Marital Status	Dependents	Semimonthly Pay	Federal Income Tax
T. Canter	Married/Joint	None	$1,050	
M. McCollum	Married/Joint	2 < 17	1,390	
C. Hammond	Head of Household	1 < 17	1,295	
T. Elliott	Single	2 < 17	1,165	

P5-6B.
LO 5-2

Country Pet Industries has employees with pay schedules that vary based on job classification. Compute the federal income tax liability for each employee using the percentage method for Manual Payroll Systems in Appendix C. All Forms W-4 were received in 2021. No one checked the box in Step 2 and there was no additional information in Step 4.

Employee	Filing Status	Dependents	Pay Frequency	Pay Amount	Federal Income Tax
X. Gander	Married/Joint	1 < 17	Biweekly	$1,825	
M. Stanley	Married/Separately	None	Weekly	750	
N. Heim	Single	1 < 17	Weekly	875	
D. Young	Married/Joint	1 Other	Semimonthly	2,025	

P5-7B.

LO 5-3

The employees of Lillian's Interiors are paid on a semimonthly basis. Compute the FICA taxes for the employees for December 31, 2021, pay period. All employees have been employed for the entire calendar year.

Employee	Semimonthly Pay	YTD Pay for 12-15-2021	Social Security Tax for 12-31-2021 Pay	Medicare Tax for 12-31-2021 Pay
W. Babish	$8,325			
G. Hanoush	6,275			
R. Fezzeti	9,250			
T. Gomez	4,550			
N. Bertraud	5,705			
R. LaPonte	4,950			

P5-8B.

LO 5-4

Christensen Ranch operates in Pennsylvania. Calculate the state income tax for each employee using the state income tax rate of 3.07 percent. Assume that no pre-tax deductions exist for any employee.

Employee	Amount per Pay Period	Pennsylvania Income Tax
G. Zonis	$1,325	
V. Sizemore	1,710	
R. Dawson	925	
C. Couture	2,550	

P5-9B.

LO 5-2

Using the percentage method for manual payroll systems with Forms W-4 from 2020 or later in Appendix C, calculate the federal withholding amounts for the following employees. No box was checked in Step 2, and no additional information was included in Step 4.

Employee	Filing Status	Dependents	Pay Frequency	Amount per Pay Period	Federal Income Tax
L. Abbey	Head of Household	2 < 17	Semimonthly	$3,500	
G. Narleski	Married/Joint	None	Weekly	1,000	
T. Leider	Single	None	Monthly	2,400	

P5-10B

LO 5-6

David Adams has been retained as a consultant for Marionet Industries. The company has had difficulty with its cross-country drivers receiving their pay in a timely manner because they are often away from their home banks. The company is looking at options that allow its employees flexibility with receiving their pay. Prepare a presentation for senior management depicting the advantages and disadvantages of the various payment methods.

Critical Thinking

For the Critical Thinking problems, use the following steps to compute the gross-up amount:

1. Compute tax rate: The tax rate on bonuses is 22 percent. Social Security (6.2 percent) and Medicare taxes (1.45 percent) must be added to this rate. For bonuses, the total tax rate equals 22% + 6.2% + 1.45%, or 29.65%.

2. Subtract 100 percent − tax rate percentage to get the net tax rate. For bonuses, it is 100% − 29.65%, or 70.35%.

3. Gross-up amount = net pay / net tax rate. For example, if you want the employee to receive a $150 bonus, the equation is $150/70.35% = $213.22.
   (Note: Typically voluntary pre-tax and post-tax deductions are not withheld from bonus checks.)

5-1. Vicky Le, an employee of Sweet Shoppe Industries, receives a bonus of $5,000 for her stellar work. Her boss wants Vicky to receive $5,000 on the check. She contributes 3 percent of her pay in a pre-tax deduction to her 401(k). Calculate the gross pay amount that would result in $5,000 paid to Vicky.

5-2. Your boss approaches you in mid-December and requests that you pay certain employees their gross pay amount as if there were no deductions as their year-end bonuses. None of the employees have reached the Social Security wage base for the year. What is the gross-up amount for each of the following employees? (Use the tax rate for bonuses and no state taxes.)

Employee	Regular Gross Pay per Period	Grossed-Up Amount
Yves St. John	$2,500	
Kim Johnson	3,380	
Michael Hale	3,178	

In the Real World: Scenario for Discussion

The state of Kansas passed legislation that allowed employers to select their employee pay method. The legislation was known as the "paperless payroll law," and many employers opted to give their employees paycards instead of cash, check, or direct deposit. This practice spread to many other states, including New York. In 2017, the law was revoked because it made employers into *de facto* financial institutions.

What are the issues with this practice? What are the benefits?

Internet Activities

5-1. Did you know that you can use an online calculator to see how your voluntary deductions will affect your paycheck? Many different payroll calculators exist. Go to one or more of the following sites and use the payroll calculator:

www.paycheckcity.com/

www.surepayroll.com/resources/calculator

www.adp.com/tools-and-resources/calculators-and-tools/payroll-calculators.aspx

5-2. Want to know more about the concepts in this chapter? Check out these sites:

https://www.irs.gov/pub/irs-pdf/p15t.pdf

https://www.irs.gov/businesses/small-businesses-self-employed/income-tax-withholding-assistant-for-employers

www.americanpayroll.org/Visa-Paycard-Portal/

5-3. Would you like to preview employee apps used to enter time and to calculate payroll disbursements? Check out these links:

DOL Timesheet: https://itunes.apple.com/us/app/dol-timesheet/id433638193?mt=8

Intuit payroll: https://payroll.intuit.com/additional-services/mobile-payroll-apps/

Sure payroll: https://www.surepayroll.com/payroll/mobile

Continuing Payroll Project: Prevosti Farms and Sugarhouse

For the February 5, 2021, pay period, use the gross pay totals from the end of Chapter 3 to compute each employee's net pay. Once you have computed the net pay (using the wage-bracket tables in Appendix C), state withholding tax for Vermont is computed at 3.35 percent of taxable wages (i.e., gross pay less pre-tax deductions). Note that the first pay period comprises only one week of work during the February 5 pay period. The federal income tax should be determined using the biweekly tables in Appendix C.

Initial pre-tax deductions for each employee are as follows:

Name	Deduction
Millen	Insurance: $155/paycheck/401(k): 3% of gross pay
Towle	Insurance: $100/paycheck/401(k): 5% of gross pay
Long	Insurance: $155/paycheck/401(k): 2% of gross pay
Shangraw	Insurance: $100/paycheck/401(k): 3% of gross pay
Lewis	Insurance: $155/paycheck/401(k): 4% of gross pay
Schwartz	Insurance: $100/paycheck/401(k): 5% of gross pay
Prevosti	Insurance: $155/paycheck/401(k): 6% of gross pay
You	Insurance: $100/paycheck/401(k): 2% of gross pay

February 5 is the end of the first pay period and includes work completed during the week of February 1–5. Compute the net pay for the February 5 pay period using the payroll register. All insurance and 401(k) deductions are pre-tax for federal and state. Update the Employee Earnings Records as of February 5, 2021.

Name	Filing Status	Dependents	Hourly Rate or Period Wage	No. of Regular Hours	No. of Overtime Hours	No. of Holiday Hours	Commission	Gross Earnings	401(k)	Sec 125	Taxable Wages for Federal / State W/H	Taxable Wages for FICA

Name	Gross Earnings	Taxable Wages for Federal/State W/H	Taxable Wages for FICA	Federal W/H Tax	Social Security Tax	Medicare W/H Tax	State W/H Tax	Total Deduc	Net Pay	Check No.

Compute the net pay for the February 19 pay period using the payroll register. All insurance and 401(k) deductions are pre-tax for federal and state. Update the Employee Earnings Records as of February 19, 2021.

Name	Filing Status	Dependents	Hourly Rate or Period Wage	No. of Regular Hours	No. of Overtime Hours	No. of Holiday Hours	Commission	Gross Earnings	401(k)	Sec 125	Taxable Wages for Federal W/H	Taxable Wages for FICA
Thomas Millen				70								
Avery Towle				70	10							
Charlie Long				70								
Mary Shangraw				40	2							
Kristen Lewis				70								
Joe Schwartz				70			225.00					
Toni Prevosti				70								
Student Success				70	1							

Name	Gross Earnings	Taxable Wages for Federal/ State W/H	Taxable Wages for FICA	Federal W/H Tax	Social Security Tax	Medicare W/H Tax	State W/H Tax	Total Deduc	Net Pay	Check No.
Thomas Millen										
Avery Towle										
Charlie Long										
Mary Shangraw										
Kristen Lewis										
Joe Schwartz										
Toni Prevosti										
Student Success										

EMPLOYEE EARNING RECORD

Name	Thomas Millen	Hire date	2/1/2021
Address	1022 Forest School Rd	Date of birth	12/16/1992
City/State/Zip	Woodstock, VT 05001	Exempt/Nonexempt	Exempt
Telephone	802-478-5055	Filing Status	Married/Joint
Social Security number	031-11-3456	No. of Dependents	3 < 17; 1 Other
Position	Production manager	Pay rate	$35,000/Year

Flex-Time	Child Care	FSA Amount	Educ. Assist.	Life Ins.	Long-Term Care	Gym

Period Ended	Hrs Worked	Reg Pay	OT Pay	Holiday	Comm	Gross Pay	401(k)	Sec 125	Taxable Wages for Federal W/H	Taxable Wages for FICA

Taxable Wages for Federal	Taxable Wages for FICA	Federal W/H	Social Security Tax	Medicare Tax	State W/H	Total Deduc	Net Pay	YTD Net Pay	YTD Gross Pay	Benefits Election

EMPLOYEE EARNING RECORD

Name	Avery Towle	Hire date	2/1/2021
Address	4011 Route 100	Date of birth	7/14/2001
City/State/Zip	Plymouth, VT 05102	Exempt/Nonexempt	Nonexempt
Telephone	802-967-5873	Filing Status	Single
Social Security number	089-74-0974	No. of Dependents	None
Position	Production Worker	Pay rate	$12.00/hour

Flex-Time	Child Care	FSA Amount	Educ. Assist.	Life Ins.	Long-Term Care	Gym	Total Benefit

Period Ended	Hrs Worked	Reg Pay	OT Pay	Holiday	Comm	Gross Pay	401(k)	Sec 125	Taxable Wages for Federal W/H	Taxable Wages for FICA

Taxable Wages for Federal	Taxable Wages for FICA	Federal W/H	Social Security Tax	Medicare Tax	State W/H	Total Deduc	Net Pay	YTD Net Pay	YTD Gross Pay	Benefits Election

EMPLOYEE EARNING RECORD

Name	Charlie Long	Hire date	2/1/2021
Address	242 Benedict Rd	Date of birth	3/16/1997
City/State/Zip	S. Woodstock, VT 05002	Exempt/Nonexempt	Nonexempt
Telephone	802-429-3846	Filing Status	Married/Joint
Social Security number	056-23-4593	No. of Dependents	2 < 17
Position	Production Worker	Pay rate	$12.50/hour

Flex-Time	Child Care	FSA Amount	Educ. Assist.	Life Ins.	Long-Term Care	Gym	Total Benefit

Period Ended	Hrs Worked	Reg Pay	OT Pay	Holiday	Comm	Gross Pay	401(k)	Sec 125	Taxable Wages for Federal W/H	Taxable Wages for FICA

Taxable Wages for Federal	Taxable Wages for FICA	Federal W/H	Social Security Tax	Medicare Tax	State W/H	Total Deduc	Net Pay	YTD Net Pay	YTD Gross Pay	Benefits Election

EMPLOYEE EARNING RECORD

Name	Mary Shangraw	Hire date	2/1/2021
Address	1901 Main St #2	Date of birth	8/20/1999
City/State/Zip	Bridgewater, VT 05520	Exempt/Nonexempt	Exempt
Telephone	802-575-5423	Filing Status	Single
Social Security number	075-28-8945	No. of Dependents	1 Other
Position	Administrative Assistant	Pay rate	$10.50/hour

Flex-Time	Child Care	FSA Amount	Educ. Assist.	Life Ins.	Long-Term Care	Gym	Total Benefit

Period Ended	Hrs Worked	Reg Pay	OT Pay	Holiday	Comm	Gross Pay	401(k)	Sec 125	Taxable Wages for Federal W/H	Taxable Wages for FICA

Taxable Wages for Federal	Taxable Wages for FICA	Federal W/H	Social Security Tax	Medicare Tax	State W/H	Total Deduc	Net Pay	YTD Net Pay	YTD Gross Pay	Benefits Election

EMPLOYEE EARNING RECORD

Name	Kristen Lewis	Hire date	2/1/2021
Address	840 Daily Hollow Rd	Date of birth	4/6/1985
City/State/Zip	Bridgewater, VT 05523	Exempt/Nonexempt	Exempt
Telephone	802-390-5572	Filing Status	Married/Joint
Social Security number	076-39-5673	No. of Dependents	2 < 17; 1 Other
Position	Office Manager	Pay rate	$32,000/year

Flex-Time	Child Care	FSA Amount	Educ. Assist.	Life Ins.	Long-Term Care	Gym	Total Benefit

Period Ended	Hrs Worked	Reg Pay	OT Pay	Holiday	Comm	Gross Pay	401(k)	Sec 125	Taxable Wages for Federal W/H	Taxable Wages for FICA

Taxable Wages for Federal	Taxable Wages for FICA	Federal W/H	Social Security Tax	Medicare Tax	State W/H	Total Deduc	Net Pay	YTD Net Pay	YTD Gross Pay	Benefits Election

EMPLOYEE EARNING RECORD

Name	Joel Schwartz	Hire date	2/1/2021
Address	55 Maple Farm Wy	Date of birth	5/23/1993
City/State/Zip	Woodstock, VT 05534	Exempt/Nonexempt	Exempt
Telephone	802-463-9985	Filing Status	Married/Joint
Social Security number	021-34-9876	No. of Dependents	2 < 17
Position	Sales	Pay rate	$24,000/year + commission

Flex-Time	Child Care	FSA Amount	Educ. Assist.	Life Ins.	Long-Term Care	Gym	Total Benefit

Period Ended	Hrs Worked	Reg Pay	OT Pay	Holiday	Comm	Gross Pay	401(k)	Sec 125	Taxable Wages for Federal W/H	Taxable Wages for FICA

Taxable Wages for Federal	Taxable Wages for FICA	Federal W/H	Social Security Tax	Medicare Tax	State W/H	Total Deduc	Net Pay	YTD Net Pay	YTD Gross Pay	Benefits Election

EMPLOYEE EARNING RECORD

Name	Toni Prevosti	Hire date	2/1/2021
Address	10520 Cox Hill Rd	Date of birth	9/18/1987
City/State/Zip	Bridgewater, VT 05521	Exempt/Nonexempt	Exempt
Telephone	802-673-2636	Filing Status	Married/Joint
Social Security number	055-22-0443	No. of Dependents	3 < 17; 2 Other
Position	Owner/President	Pay rate	$45,000/year

Flex-Time	Child Care	FSA Amount	Educ. Assist.	Life Ins.	Long-Term Care	Gym	Total Benefit

Period Ended	Hrs Worked	Reg Pay	OT Pay	Holiday	Comm	Gross Pay	401(k)	Sec 125	Taxable Wages for Federal W/H	Taxable Wages for FICA

Taxable Wages for Federal	Taxable Wages for FICA	Federal W/H	Social Security Tax	Medicare Tax	State W/H	Total Deduc	Net Pay	YTD Net Pay	YTD Gross Pay	Benefits Election

EMPLOYEE EARNING RECORD

Name	Student Success	Hire date	2/1/2021
Address	1644 Smitten Rd	Date of birth	1/1/2001
City/State/Zip	Woodstock, VT 05001	Exempt/Nonexempt	Nonexempt
Telephone	(555) 555-5555	Filing Status	Single
Social Security number	555-55-5555	No. of Dependents	None
Position	Accounting Clerk	Pay rate	$34,000/year

Flex-Time	Child Care	FSA Amount	Educ. Assist.	Life Ins.	Long-Term Care	Gym	Total Benefit

Period Ended	Hrs Worked	Reg Pay	OT Pay	Holiday	Comm	Gross Pay	401(k)	Sec 125	Taxable Wages for Federal W/H	Taxable Wages for FICA

Taxable Wages for Federal	Taxable Wages for FICA	Federal W/H	Social Security Tax	Medicare Tax	State W/H	Total Deduc	Net Pay	YTD Net Pay	YTD Gross Pay	Benefits Election

Answers to Stop & Check Exercises

Differentiating between Gross and Net Pay

1. Gross pay consists of wages or commissions earned by the employee before deductions. Net pay is the amount of cash the employee receives after all deductions.
2. Student answers may vary but could include Qualifying medical or dental plans, Internal Revenue Code Section 125 plans, 401(k) retirement plans, federal income

tax, Medicare tax, Social Security tax, state income tax, garnishments, charitable contributions, and union dues.

3. To "gross up" a payroll amount is to calculate the amount of gross pay necessary to receive a net pay result. This is most often done for bonuses.

How Much Tax to Withhold?

1. $52,000 paid semimonthly would give per period of $2,166.67 $52,000/24 = $2,166.67 rounded to $2,167 less dependents of ($1,000 (2 × 500)/24 pay periods for $41.67. Taxable income of $2,125 (2,166.67 − 41.67)
   (a) $185; (b) $183.96
2. $2,166.67 gross pay − $100 for 401(k) deduction per pay period − $41.67 dependents = $2,025 taxable pay. This is the amount used in conjunction with the wage-bracket table to calculate the federal income tax withheld of $173. The difference in taxes with the 401(k) deduction is $12 = $185 − $173
3. $168 = $2,166.67 gross pay − $75 health insurance − $55 AFLAC − $41.67 dependents = $1,995 taxable pay.

FICA Taxes

1. Social Security = $327.36 = $5,280 × 0.062; Medicare = $76.56 = $5,280 × 0.0145.
2. Total liability = $807.84 = ($327.36 + $76.56) × 2.
3. (a.) $0 Social Security liability because the maximum amount of wages taxable for social security is $137,700 and she has exceeded that. Her semimonthly salary is $250,000/24 = $10,416.67. Medicare taxable earnings would be reduced by the qualified insurance deduction $10,416.67 − 75 = $10,341.67. Year-to-date gross wages of $197,916.67 less qualified deduction of $1,425 ($75 × 19) gives $196,491.67 of YTD Medicare taxable earnings. Medicare base for this payroll is $200,000 − 196,491.67 = $3,508.33 to reach the $200,000 cap and $6,833.34 ($10,416.67 − 3,508.33 − 75.00) that will be charged the surcharge. ($3,508.33 × 1.45%) + ($6,833.37 × 2.35%) = $50.87 + 160.58 = $211.45 Medicare tax.
   (b.) Medicare liability will be: ($10,416.67 −75.00) × (0.0145 + 0.009) = $243.03

State and Local Income Taxes

1. $92.39 ($62,500 annual salary/26 biweekly = $2,403.85 gross pay − $150 for 401(k) pre-tax deduction − $80 health insurance pre-tax deduction = $2,173.85 taxable pay × 4.25% = $92.39 From Appendix D.
2. $129.68 ($2,850 × 4.55%) state, $5.75 local.

Post-Tax Deductions

1. a, b, d
2. Because the IBEW union requires that employees' union dues be remitted by the employer, the amount due must be deducted on a post-tax basis from his period pay.

Pay Methods

1. Cash, check, direct deposit, paycard, and cryptocurrencies.
2. Regulation E.
3. Direct deposit.

Chapter Six

Employer Payroll Taxes and Labor Planning

All facets of payroll accounting are important because they affect the company's success and its employees. An essential piece of the payroll puzzle is the employer's payroll tax responsibility. The reporting and remittance of payroll taxes is a significant aspect that requires scrupulous attention to detail. Many different tax forms exist that must be filed at regular intervals and with varying governmental bodies. Tax filing requires organizational skills, time management, and continued accuracy. Tax reporting is a huge responsibility for the business and its payroll accountant because of governmental oversight. Additionally, employment tax revenue remittances represent 70 percent of all federal revenue. Therefore, employment tax remittances are a vital part of the U.S. economy.

Employers must also consider payroll responsibilities as part of labor planning. Besides taxes, other aspects of an employer's payroll responsibilities include maintaining workers' compensation insurance, forwarding amounts withheld through employees' voluntary and mandated deductions, and determining labor expenses and employee benefits. The Internal Revenue Service and state employment departments have websites that contain important information about filing requirements, due dates, guidelines, and penalties (see Appendix E for state employment department contact information). Insurance responsibilities are a vital consideration when determining labor expenses and employee benefits because they are a significant element in the cost of doing business.

LEARNING OBJECTIVES

After studying Chapter 6, you should be able to:

LO 6-1   List Employer-Paid and Employee-Paid Obligations

LO 6-2   Discuss Reporting Periods and Requirements for Employer Tax Deposits

LO 6-3   Prepare Mid-Year and Year-End Employer Tax Reporting and Deposits

LO 6-4   Describe Payroll within the Context of Business Expenses

LO 6-5   Relate Labor Expenses to Company Profitability

LO 6-6   Complete Benefit Analysis as a Function of Payroll

Kamrad71/Shutterstock

Construction Industry Sees Revenue Increase

The COVID pandemic wreaked havoc on many employers during 2020, small businesses saw their revenue decrease and disappear altogether in some cases. The economic precipice of 2020 affected many industries and was reflected in the Gross Domestic Product for the United States. This economic shift caused many business owners and employers to reconsider their business plans. Additionally, it sparked legislation to reduce employers' tax burdens by offering tax deferrals and other tools to allow businesses to remain in operation during the pandemic.

However, the construction industry did not suffer as greatly as other economic sectors. As an essential business, construction companies have recognized gains and provided steady employment. Projects started in early 2020 required completion, and the economic conditions made sourcing products easier for many construction companies. Changes in tax legislation allowed construction companies to use tax deferrals to their advantage and retain employees when unemployment soared.

(Source: Construction Dive)

Labor costs potentially constitute a significant portion of a company's expense. Employee benefits such as company contributions to retirement plans, temporary disability insurance, and educational reimbursements represent additional business expenses. Chapter 6 will examine employer payroll tax responsibilities and how payroll is a tool in labor planning.

LO 6-1   List Employer-Paid and Employee-Paid Obligations

Nora Carol Photography/Getty Images

Employers must pay some of the same taxes that the employees do. However, a firm has additional liabilities that employees do not, such as certain unemployment taxes and workers' compensation insurance. A comparison of employee-paid and employer-paid taxes is given in Table 6-1.

The taxes an employer must pay are often known as *statutory deductions*, meaning that governmental statutes have made the tax a mandatory, legally obligated deduction. An important element of employer tax responsibility is that it continues after disbursing the employees' pay, often extending well after leaving the firm. Employers must file mandatory reconciliation reports detailing the amounts they have withheld from employee pay, tracking the employees throughout the company's accounting system, and maintaining the personnel files for current and terminated employees per the firm's payroll practices and governmental regulations.

Social Security and Medicare Taxes

The *FICA* taxes, which include both the Social Security and Medicare taxes, are among the statutory withholdings employees and employers pay. Employees and employers must each contribute 6.2 percent (for a total of 12.4 percent) of the employee's pay up to the maximum withholding amount for Social Security. Employers must match the employees' payroll deductions for the Medicare tax in the amount of 1.45 percent (for a total of 2.9 percent) of the employees'

TABLE 6-1

Employee-Paid and Employer-Paid Taxes

Tax	Employee Pays	Employer Pays
Social Security	XX	XX
Medicare	XX	XX
Federal Income Tax	XX	
Federal Unemployment Tax (FUTA)		XX
State Income Tax (where applicable)	XX	
State Unemployment Tax (SUTA)	Sometimes both are responsible at different percentages; see your local taxation authority for specific details.	XX
Local Income Taxes	XX	
Local Occupational Taxes (where applicable)	XX	XX
Workers' Compensation Premiums		XX
401(k)/Pension (if matching policy exists)	XX	XX
Other Voluntary Deductions	XX	

gross pay less applicable deductions. Remember that the Affordable Care Act mandated an additional tax for highly compensated employees. The employer does not match this additional Medicare tax.

The CARES Act in 2020 offered employers relief from payroll-related income taxes. Employers had the option for tax deferrals and tax credit programs to help their businesses remain solvent during the COVID pandemic. Certain CARES programs allowed employers to defer full remittance of payroll taxes until December 2022.

(Source: RSM)

Let's look at an example of how the employee's and the employer's share of the FICA tax works.

EXAMPLE: EMPLOYEE AND EMPLOYER SHARE, SOCIAL SECURITY TAX

Courtney Russo works as an hourly worker who earns an annual salary of $36,000 and is paid biweekly. Her gross pay is $1,384.62 per pay period ($36,000 per year/26 pay periods).

Courtney's share of the Social Security tax:	$1,384.62 × 6.2% = $85.85
Her employer's share of the Social Security tax:	$1,384.62 × 6.2% = $85.85
Total Social Security tax liability for Courtney's pay this period:	$171.70

As shown in the example, the employer and employee contribute the same amounts for the Social Security tax. Remember, the Social Security tax has a maximum withholding per year based on the employee's salary, which is $142,800 for 2021. After reaching that maximum, neither the employee nor the employer contributes any more Social Security tax.

EXAMPLE: EMPLOYEE AND EMPLOYER SHARE SOCIAL SECURITY TAXES, HIGHLY COMPENSATED, EMPLOYEE

William Perry is the vice president of Sunny Glassworks. His annual salary is $243,000, which is paid semimonthly. His gross pay per period is $10,125.00 ($243,000/24 pay periods). For the 14th pay period of the year, the Social Security tax withholding is as follows:

William's share of the Social Security tax:	$10,125 × 6.2% = $ 627.75
Sunny Glasswork's share of William's Social Security tax:	$10,125 × 6.2% = 627.75
Total Social Security tax liability for William's pay this period:	$1,255.50

After the 14th pay period, William's year-to-date pay is $10,125 × 14 = $141,750. As of the 15th pay period, William's year-to-date pay will be $10,125 × 15 = $151,875, which exceeds the Social Security wage base. The amount subject to Social Security tax for the 15th pay period equals the wage base minus the 14th pay period YTD pay:

$142,800 − $141,750 = $1,050 of William's pay during the 15th pay period is included for Social Security tax. Neither William nor his employer will be taxed on the remaining $9,075.

William's share of the Social Security tax:	$1,050 × 6.2% = $ 65.10
Sunny Glasswork's share of William's Social Security tax:	$1,050 × 6.2% = 65.10
Total Social Security tax liability for William's pay this period that must be remitted by Sunny Glassworks:	$130.20

Medicare tax, the other piece of the FICA taxes, has no maximum but does have an additional tax for high-wage employees. Let's look at Courtney Russo's pay again to see how the Medicare tax works and the total FICA tax for the pay period.

EXAMPLE: EMPLOYEE AND EMPLOYER SHARE, MEDICARE TAXES

Courtney's share of the Medicare tax:	$1,384.62 × 1.45% = $ 20.08
Her employer's share of the Medicare tax:	$1,384.62 × 1.45% = 20.08
Total Medicare tax liability for Courtney's pay this period that must be remitted by Sunny Glassworks:	$ 40.16
Total FICA responsibility from Courtney's pay this period ($171.70 + $40.16):	$211.86

Now let's look at Medicare and total FICA taxes for William. Note the additional Medicare tax and how the employer does not match it.

EXAMPLE: EMPLOYEE AND EMPLOYER SHARE MEDICARE TAXES, HIGHLY COMPENSATED EMPLOYEE

As of the 20th pay period of the year, William's YTD pay is $202,500. Amount subject to the additional Medicare tax: $2,500.

Medicare tax amounts:	
William's standard Medicare tax liability:	$10,125 × 1.45% = $146.81
Sunny Glasswork's Medicare tax liability:	$10,125 × 1.45% = 146.81
William's additional Medicare tax liability:	$ 2,500 × 0.9% = 22.50
Total Medicare tax liability:	$316.12
Total FICA responsibility for William's pay this period:	$316.12

Remember, no Social Security tax applies because William has already exceeded the wage base.

Social Security and Medicare amounts may be listed separately when the company makes its tax deposit. The employer's tax deposit will also include the amount deducted from the employee for federal income tax.

Maintaining accurate records of taxes withheld through payroll registers and employee earnings records is critical in calculating proper FICA tax deductions. Whether a company uses a manual system, has an automated system, or outsources the payroll duties, it remains responsible for the accuracy of the deductions and maintenance of associated records.

Federal and State Unemployment Taxes

Vitalii Vodolazskyi/Shutterstock

Another set of employer-paid payroll taxes include those mandated by the Federal Unemployment Tax Act *(FUTA)* and State Unemployment Tax Act *(SUTA)*. FUTA and SUTA are unemployment compensation funds established to provide for workers who have lost their jobs. Generally, the FUTA tax rate is lower than that for SUTA tax because the states govern the disbursement of unemployment funds and because unemployment rates vary by region. FUTA taxes pay for the administrative expenses of the unemployment insurance fund. SUTA tax rates provide a localized and individual focus for employer taxes. The unemployment insurance fund pays for half of the extended unemployment benefits and provides a fund of additional benefits against which states may borrow as necessary to cover unemployment claims. An interesting note is that FUTA and SUTA are employer-only taxes in all *but* three states: Alaska, New Jersey, and Pennsylvania.

FUTA pertains only to U.S. citizens and workers employed by American companies. According to the IRS, to be classified as an American company, an employer must meet the following criteria:

- An individual who is a resident of the United States,
- A partnership, if two-thirds or more of the partners are residents of the United States,
- A trust, if all of the trustees are residents of the United States, or
- A corporation organized under the U.S. laws of any state or the District of Columbia.

American citizens who work for companies outside of the United States who are not classified as American employers are not subject to FUTA provisions. Certain resident aliens and professions are exempt from FUTA provisions, as stipulated by Income Tax Regulation §31.3301-1. The professions from which employee compensation is exempt from FUTA provisions are

- Compensation paid to agricultural workers.
- Compensation paid to household employees unless the compensation exceeds $1,000 during any calendar quarter of the current year or prior year.
- Compensation paid to employees of religious, charitable, educational, or certain other tax-exempt organizations.
- Compensation paid to employees of the U.S. government or any of its agencies.
- Compensation paid to employees of the government of any state of the U.S. or any of its political subdivisions.
- Compensation paid to employees of the government of the District of Columbia or any of its political subdivisions.

The FUTA tax's full 2021 tax is 6.0 percent of the first $7,000 of an employee's wages paid during a calendar year. The employer pays FUTA. Employees who move to a different company will have the new employer paying additional FUTA taxes. Therefore, if an employer has a high turnover rate among its employees (i.e., a large number of employees remain employed for only a short period before terminating employment), the firm will pay FUTA tax for all employees for the first $7,000 of earnings, including the ones who remained in their employ for only a short time. FUTA is subject to a 5.4 percent reduction, for which employers may qualify on two conditions:

1. Employers make SUTA deposits on time and in full.
2. The state is not a credit reduction state. In 2021, the only FUTA credit reduction in effect is for the U.S. Virgin Islands.

Due to the COVID-19 outbreak, employers were granted a refundable tax credit of 50 percent of wages paid between April 2, 2020, and December 31, 2020, by certain employers who met the following criteria:

- Operations were suspended, partially or in full, because of the outbreak.
- Gross sales declined 50 percent or more because of the outbreak.*
- Tax-exempt businesses were also eligible for this break.

Also, a payroll tax credit was extended for businesses that continued to pay wages (up to $10,000 of compensation per employee, including fringe health benefits paid), as follows:

- For businesses with more than 100 employees, compensation for services not provided due to COVID-19 reasons.
- For businesses with fewer than 100 employees, all employee wages qualified for the credit.

*The gross sales tax credit eligibility ceased once the business's sales receipts reached 80 percent of the same amount earned during the same quarter of the prior calendar year.

(Source: U.S. Congress)

With the credit, the employer's FUTA rate will be 0.6 percent on the first $7,000 of every employee's wage. The minimum FUTA tax rate is 0.6 percent, which means that a minimum of $42 ($7,000 × 0.006) may be paid per employee. Note that FUTA tax liability is always reported for the prior year, which means that the FUTA tax liability in 2021 will increase with the first payroll and reflect both 2020 and 2021 liability if the 940 has not been filed yet. If the employer makes quarterly deposits, then the full 2020 liability would not be part of the FUTA Tax Payable account in 2021.

FOR EXAMPLE, FUTA TAX COMPUTATION, ALL EMPLOYEES EARNING MORE THAN $7,000

Snowborn Inc. is a company based in Great Falls, Montana. In 2021, the company had 178 employees, all of whom earned more than $7,000 in wages and salaries. At the end of the year, only 145 employees remained with the company. The 2021 FUTA tax liability for Snowborn Inc. would be computed as follows:

Number of employees during 2021	Multiplied by the first $7,000 of wages	Multiplied by 0.6% tax rate	FUTA tax liability for 2021
178	$7,000	0.006	$7,476

Note Snowborn Inc. is liable for the FUTA tax on all employees who worked for the company, even if they left employment with the company. The FUTA tax filing is due on January 31, 2022.

What happens when the employees earn less than $7,000 during the calendar year? The employer is still responsible for the FUTA tax on the employees' earnings and the amount earned during the calendar year.

EXAMPLE: FUTA TAX, EMPLOYEES WITH EARNINGS LESS THAN $7,000 DURING THE YEAR

Baja Brothers Wines, based in Tucson, Arizona, has 62 employees and the following employee data for FUTA taxes:

Number of employees who earned more than $7,000 during 2021	Multiplied by the first $7,000 of wages	Multiplied by 0.6% tax rate	FUTA tax liability for 2021
59	$7,000	0.006	$2,478.00
Employees who earned less than $7,000 during 2021:	Multiplied by the amount of wages earned in 2021	Multiplied by 0.6% tax rate	
Employee A	$5,894.00	0.006	$ 35.36
Employee B	3,198.00	0.006	19.19
Employee C	975.00	0.006	5.85
		Total FUTA tax	**$2,538.40**

The establishment of the SUTA in each state provided states with the local authority to offer unemployment or jobless benefits. Designed as an unemployment insurance program after the Great Depression of the 1930s, SUTA payments' remittance follows many of the same procedures as other payroll taxes. As a state-run fund, each state can establish its own qualification requirements for individual claims and business payments, the wage base for employers in the state, and the tax rate. The SUTA wage base and rate fluctuates among states and can be an incentive for businesses to change operations from one state to another. Note that all states' wage bases exceed the minimum required by the law, but the tax rate is variable.

FUTA Credit Reduction

As we noted, the nominal FUTA tax is 6.0 percent, of which the employer remits 0.6 percent to the federal government. A caveat to this 0.6 percent employer rate involves Title XII advances issued from the federal government to assist with payments of unemployment liabilities. This can occur when a high period of unemployment happens due to layoffs or economic downturns.

If a state defaults on its repayment of these federal loans, the credit is taken against the 6.0 percent FUTA rate may be reduced. Each year, states have until November 10 to repay the prior year's loan. If the loan remains unpaid for more than one year, the FUTA credit will continue to be reduced in the third and fifth years after the loan is due. An example of the FUTA credit reduction follows.

EXAMPLE: FUTA CREDIT REDUCTION

State Z had a loan taken during 2020 to supplement amounts paid for unemployment insurance liabilities. The balance of that loan would be due on November 10, 2021. If the balance is not paid by that date, the credit against the FUTA rate for the next calendar year would be as follows:

FUTA rate	Standard FUTA rate after credit	FUTA rate after credit reduction
6.0%	0.6%	2.4%

The credit would be reduced further in future years if the loan remains unpaid. Employers report the credit reduction on Form 940. For 2021, the FUTA credit reductions only apply to the U.S. Virgin Islands (3.0 percent).

(**Source:** EY)

State Unemployment Taxes

SUTA is limited to wages collected, and the 5.4 percent rate is a guideline. State rates vary based on employee retention and other factors. States examine employee turnover during an established period and determine if employers qualify for a credit against the nominal SUTA rate. Depending upon the company's state, this limit may be equal to, higher, or lower than the SUTA rate. For example, Alaska's SUTA wage base was $43,600 in 2021. A chart containing the SUTA wage base and rates is shown in Table 6-2.

TABLE 6-2
SUTA Wage Base and Rates 2021

State	Wage Base	Min/Max Rate
Alabama	$ 8,000	0.65%–6.8%
Alaska	$ 43,600	1.0%–5.4%
Arizona	$ 7,000	0.08%–20.6%
Arkansas	$ 10,000	0.3%–14.2%
California	$ 7,000	1.5%–6.2%
Colorado	$ 13,600	0.91%–9.64%
Connecticut	$ 15,000	1.9%–6.8%
Delaware	$ 16,500	0.3%–8.2%
District of Columbia	$ 9,000	1.6%–7.0%

(continued)

TABLE 6-2

SUTA Wage Base and Rates 2021 *(concluded)*

State	Wage Base	Min/Max Rate
Florida	$ 7,000	0.29%–5.4%
Georgia	$ 9,500	0.04%–8.1%
Hawaii	$ 47,400	0.0%–6.6%
Idaho	$ 43,000	0.201%–5.4%
Illinois	$ 12,960	0.675%–6.875%
Indiana	$ 9,500	0.5%–7.4%
Iowa	$ 32,400	0.0%–7.5%
Kansas	$ 14,000	0.2%–7.6%
Kentucky	$ 11,100	1.0%–10.0%
Louisiana	$ 7,700	0.09%–6.2%
Maine	$ 12,000	0.49%–5.81%
Maryland	$ 8,500	2.2%–13.5%
Massachusetts	$ 15,000	0.83%–12.65%
Michigan	$ 9,500	0.06%–10.3%
Minnesota	$ 35,000	0.2%–9.1%
Mississippi	$ 14,000	0.2%–5.6%
Missouri	$ 11,000	0.0%–9.45%
Montana	$ 35,300	0.13%–6.25%
Nebraska	$ 9,000	0.0%–5.4%
Nevada	$ 33,400	0.3%–5.4%
New Hampshire	$ 14,000	0.1%–7.0%
New Jersey	$ 36,200	0.4%–5.4%
New Mexico	$ 27,000	0.33%–5.4%
New York	$ 11,800	0.9%–7.9%
North Carolina	$ 26,000	0.06%–5.76%
North Dakota	$ 38,500	0.08%–9.69%
Ohio	$ 9,000	0.3%–9.3%
Oklahoma	$ 24,000	0.3%–7.5%
Oregon	$ 43,800	1.2%–5.4%
Pennsylvania	$ 10,000	1.2905%–9.9333%
Rhode Island	$ 24,600	1.2%–9.8%
South Carolina	$ 14,000	0.06%–5.46%
South Dakota	$ 15,000	0.0%–9.35%
Tennessee	$ 7,000	0.01%–10.0%
Texas	$ 9,000	0.31%–6.31%
Utah	$ 38,900	0.2%–7.2%
Vermont	$ 14,100	0.4%–5.4%
Virginia	$ 8,000	0.33%–6.43%
Washington	$ 56,500	0.13%–7.73%
West Virginia	$ 12,000	1.5%–8.5%
Wisconsin	$ 14,000	0.0%–12.0%
Wyoming	$ 27,300	0.18%–8.72%

(Sources: American Payroll Association, ADP)

An employer's SUTA rate is determined by a mix of state unemployment rates and company experience ratings. The SUTA rate for company A may be different from the rate for company B. For example, a construction company may experience higher unemployment claims because of the seasonal nature and higher risk associated with the industry; therefore, its rate could be 4.54 percent, whereas a similar-sized company in a professional services industry may have an unemployment rate of 3.28 percent. States issue letters annually to companies with the individually determined SUTA rate for the following year.

The first example is a company with a SUTA rate of 5.4 percent, and all employees have earned more than $7,000 for the year.

EXAMPLE: FUTA AND SUTA LIABILITY; SUTA = 5.4 PERCENT

JayMac Communications, a California company, has 15 employees, all of whom have met the FUTA tax's $7,000 threshold. The state portion for which JayMac is liable is 5.4 percent. The unemployment tax obligations are

FUTA:	15 employees × $7,000 × 0.006 = $ 630
SUTA:	15 employees × $7,000 × 0.054 = 5,670
Total unemployment tax liability:	$6,300

The next example is a company in Georgia with a SUTA rate of 2.3 percent and some employees who have earned less than $7,000 during the year.

EXAMPLE: FUTA AND SUTA LIABILITY; SUTA = 2.3 PERCENT

Charmer Industries of Georgia has 20 employees: 18 employees have met the FUTA and SUTA thresholds, and 2 employees have not, earning $5,400 and $2,500, respectively. The state obligation for Charmer is 2.3 percent, owing to a favorable employer rating. Charmer's unemployment taxes would be computed as follows:

FUTA:	18 employees × $7,000 × 0.006 =	$ 756.00
	($5,400 + $2,500) × 0.006 =	47.40
	Total FUTA liability:	$ 803.40
SUTA:	18 employees × $9,500 × 0.023 =	$3,933.00
	($5,400 + $2,500) × 0.023 =	181.70
	Total SUTA liability:	$4,114.70
Total unemployment tax liability:		$4,918.10

Tips to Minimize SUTA Taxes

Experience-Rating System
• Know how your company compares to other similar companies in the same industry as far as hiring and retention of employees.
Experience Rate Charges
• The employer's account is charged each time a former employee files for unemployment. Be careful to avoid improper use of the account by dumping employees into other states to avoid SUTA taxation.
Review the SUTA Account Regularly
• Ensure that charges to the employer's account are accurate and promptly alert the state unemployment office if inaccuracies occur.

Carefully Select New Employees
• An employee should be assessed before hiring to ensure that they are an appropriate fit for the company culture and have the needed skills for their job requirements.
Time Temporary or Seasonal Layoffs to Avoid Partial Weeks
• Partial weeks of unemployment can lead to large amounts being charged to the employer's SUTA account.
Employee Separation Review and Documentation
• Maintain documentation about the employee's departure from the company to ensure that they do not improperly claim SUTA benefits.
Former Employees and Retirement
• The offer of retirement with the possibility of rehiring can reduce unemployment claims because a retired employee cannot claim unemployment insurance.
Use State-Issued Forms if Contesting an Unemployment Claim
• This will make the processing quicker and ensure accuracy and remediation of any disputes.
Pay SUTA Taxes on Time
• A record of timely SUTA payments adds to the company's experience rating and allows the employer to avoid penalties or other fees.
Use Historical SUTA Reports to Estimate Future Unemployment Charges
• Knowing what to expect ahead of time will help with budgeting, hiring, and estimating future labor costs.

Other State and Local Employer-Only Payroll Taxes

Some states have employer-only taxes unique to the area. Delaware, Colorado, Hawaii, and several other states have additional taxes remitted under different names. Some examples of these types of taxes include

- Georgia employers pay an administrative assessment of 0.06 percent for employers with an unemployment range between 0.04–8.1 percent.
- Maine has an employer-paid Competitive Skills Scholarship Program tax of 0.07 percent.
- In California, employers pay an Employment Training Tax (ETT) of 0.1 percent on all wages up to the first $7,000 of wages.

As a payroll accountant, it is essential to be familiar with each state's tax withholding and employer responsibilities. The company has employees residing, even if there is not a business office located there. It is also important to be aware of any required forms within the state where the company has employees.

Individual counties and cities can also impose occupational taxes on the businesses within their jurisdiction. The reporting periods for the local and city taxes are separate from federal or state taxes' filing requirements. The payroll accountant must review all tiers of taxes to ensure compliance in collection, submission, and reporting.

Workers' Compensation Insurance

Workers' compensation insurance is another type of employer payroll responsibility. Although it is not considered a tax, states enforce workers' compensation statutes; the Federal Employment Compensation Act protects federal employees. Workers' compensation statutes are designed to protect workers who are injured (temporarily or permanently) or killed during the performance of their job-related duties.

Because workers' compensation is an insurance policy maintained by employers, premiums vary based on employees' job classifications and the risk of injury they typically encounter in the normal course of work. Premium amounts are expressed as amounts per $100 of payroll for each job classification. Premium amounts are estimated based on expected payroll amounts for the coming year and then adjusted at the end of the year once the actual payroll amounts are finalized.

Elnur/Shutterstock

EXAMPLE: WORKERS' COMPENSATION PREMIUM COMPUTATION

Jesse Hildreth is the owner of Eastern Freight Lines. She has three categories of employees: drivers, loaders, and administrative staff. The workers' compensation premium rates are as follows:

- Drivers: $1.45/$100 of payroll
- Loaders: $2.50/$100 of payroll
- Administrative staff: $0.40/$100 of payroll

For 20XX, Eastern Freight Lines payroll is expected to be the following:

Job Classification	Premium per $100 of Payroll	Estimated Payroll	Premium Due Jan. 1
Driver	$1.45	$387,500	$ 5,618.75*
Loader	2.50	435,200	10,880.00†
Administrative Staff	0.40	320,000	1,280.00‡
Total Premium Due, Jan. 1			$ 17,778.75

*($387,500/$100) × $1.45 = $5,618.75
†($435,200/$100) × $2.50 = $10,880
‡($320,000/$100) × $0.40 = $1,280

The 20XX premium is adjusted based on actual payroll. The difference between the paid estimated premium and the premium based on actual payroll results must either be remitted to the insurance company or refunded to the employer. An analysis of the actual payroll as of December 31, 20XX, revealed the following results:

Job Classification	Premium per $100 of Payroll	Actual Payroll	Premium Due Dec. 31
Driver	$1.45	$410,563	$ 5,953.16*
Loader	2.50	478,290	11,957.25†
Administrative staff	0.40	338,945	1,355.78‡
Total actual premium due December 31			$19,266.19
Less: Premium paid on Jan. 1			17,778.75
Difference to be remitted to the insurance company			$ 1,487.44

*($410,563/$100) × $1.45 = $5,953.16
†($478,290/$100) × $2.50 = $11,957.25
‡($338,945/$100) × $0.40 = $1,355.78

Eastern Freight Lines must remit $1,487.44 to the insurance company due to the difference between the estimated and the actual payroll for 20XX.

Workers' compensation premium rates may also vary based on the employer's safety record. For example, a company with multiple job-related injuries would have a higher premium than another company with few or no injuries. Employer compliance with OSHA guidelines is important to control the cost of workers' compensation insurance.

The majority of workers' compensation insurance claims occur in five main categories of injuries:

1. Sprains and strains.
2. Punctures or cuts.
3. Bruises or other contusions.
4. Inflammation.
5. Fractured bones.

Most work-related injuries can be avoided through employee safety training, attention to the facility's walking and working conditions, and employer diligence.

(Source: Insurance Journal)

FUTA, SUTA, and Workers' compensation

Stop & Check

1. AMS Enterprises in New Mexico has 30 employees. Of these, 25 have exceeded the FUTA and SUTA wage bases. This is the first quarter of the year, and AMS Enterprises has not yet paid FUTA or SUTA taxes for the year. The other five employees' YTD wages are as follows: Employee A, $15,800; Employee B, $7,800; Employee C, $11,115; Employee D, $22,800; Employee E, $2,575. AMS Enterprises receives the full FUTA tax credit and pays a SUTA rate of 4.2 percent (see Table 6-2 for SUTA taxable wage maximum). How much are AMS Enterprises' FUTA and SUTA liabilities?

2. Noodle Noggins of Maine has 12 employees and is eligible for the full FUTA tax credit; the SUTA rate is 3.26 percent. Ten of the 12 employees have exceeded the FUTA wage base. Eight employees have exceeded the SUTA wage base (see Table 6-2 for the SUTA taxable wage maximum). The remaining employees have the following YTD wages: $5,500, $6,800, $11,100, and $9,850. The Competitive Skills Scholarship tax applies to all employees. Noodle's YTD total wages are $279,580. What are the FUTA, SUTA, and Competitive Skills Scholarship tax liabilities for Noodle Noggins?

3. High Flyers Jump School has two classifications of employees: clerical employees and jump instructors. The workers' compensation premium rates are $0.45/$100 for clerical employees and $3.75/$100 for jump instructors. During 20XX, the estimated payroll amounts were $104,550 for clerical employees and $215,690 for jump instructors. How much would the estimated workers' compensation insurance policy cost High Flyers Jump School during 20XX?

Warunya Pamee/EyeEm/Getty Images

LO 6-2   Discuss Reporting Periods and Requirements for Employer Tax Deposits

The frequency of depositing federal income tax and FICA taxes depends on the size of the company's payroll. The depositing schedules have nothing to do with a company's pay frequency, although some of the names are similar. The IRS stipulates five different schedules for an employer's deposit of payroll taxes:

1. Annually
2. Quarterly
3. Monthly
4. Semiweekly
5. Next business day

Of these, the most common deposit schedules are monthly and semiweekly. Electronic tax deposits are usually processed through the *Electronic Federal Tax Payment System (EFTPS)* **website**. However, the IRS allows employers to transmit payments through certain financial institutions via *Automated Clearing House (ACH)* or wire transfer. When using the EFTPS, the employer must register with the IRS to access the site. The EFTPS is used for Form 941 (federal income tax, Social Security tax, and Medicare tax) and the quarterly/annual Form 940 FUTA tax deposit.

Lookback Period

The frequency of each company's deposits is determined through a *lookback period*, which is the amount of payroll taxes an employer has reported in the 12-month period before June 30 of the previous year. For example, the lookback period that the IRS would use for 2021 tax deposit frequency would be the period from July 1, 2019, through June 30, 2020. Employers

TABLE 6-3
Lookback Periods

Lookback Period for 2021 Taxes			
July 1, 2019, through	October 1, 2019, through	January 1, 2020, through	April 1, 2020, through
September 30, 2019	December 31, 2019	March 31, 2020	June 30, 2020

Source: Internal Revenue Service

receive notification about their deposit requirements in writing from the IRS in October of each year. Table 6-3 shows the lookback period.

> Section 2302(a)(1) and (a)(2) of the **CARES Act** allowed employers to defer eligible amounts of Social Security tax remittances in response to cash needs during COVID as such:
>
> - 50 percent of the eligible deferred amount must be paid by December 31, 2021.
>
> - If 50 percent of the eligible deferred amount was paid by December 31, 2021, the employer could defer the remainder of the eligible amount until December 31, 2022.
>
> (Source: Internal Revenue Service)

Deposit Frequencies

The IRS informs businesses in writing if they need to deposit their payroll taxes annually, monthly, or semiweekly based on the deposits during the lookback period. All new companies are monthly schedule depositors unless they have a total payroll liability over $100,000 during any pay period. It is important to note that the tax deposit due date is based on the payroll disbursement date, not the pay period ending date. For example, if a company's pay period ended on June 28, but the payroll was not disbursed until July 1, the payroll tax deposit date would be based on the July 1 disbursement. Table 6-4 outlines the criteria for differences among deposit frequencies.

TABLE 6-4
Criteria for Deposit Frequencies

Frequency	Criteria	Due Date
Annually	$1,000 or less in employment taxes to be remitted annually with Form 944.	January 31 of the following year.
Quarterly	For any amounts not deposited during the quarter that may be due to rounding errors or other undeposited amounts.	15th of the month following the end of the quarter.
Monthly	$50,000 or less in payroll tax liability during the lookback period. The amount of total tax liability is also found on Form 941, line 10. All new businesses are monthly schedule depositors unless they accrue more than $100,000 in payroll taxes for any pay period. (See the Next Business Day rule frequency.)	15th of the month following the month during which the company accrued payroll tax deposits. For example, taxes on March payroll would be due on **April 15** or the next business day if April 15 falls on a weekend or a holiday.
Semiweekly	More than $50,000 in payroll tax liability during the lookback period. The amount of total tax liability is also found on Form 941, line 10. The exception to the semiweekly deposit schedule is the Next Business Day rule.	For payroll paid on a Wednesday, Thursday, or Friday, the payroll tax deposit is due by the following **Wednesday.** For payroll paid on a Saturday, Sunday, Monday, or Tuesday, the payroll tax is due by the following **Friday.**
Next business day	$100,000 or more in payroll tax liability for any payroll period.	The payroll tax deposit is due on the **next business day.**

> **EXAMPLE: MONTHLY SCHEDULE DEPOSITOR**
> Generational Coffee is a company based in Wenatchee, Washington. During the lookback period ending June 30, 2020, the company had **$36,549** in total payroll tax liability. Generational Coffee would be a *monthly* schedule depositor. Payroll tax deposits would be due on the 15th of the following month (e.g., June 15 for May payroll taxes).

Notice the amount of total payroll tax for Generational Coffee. Because the total amount was less than $50,000, it is classified as a monthly schedule payroll tax depositor, and due dates are the 15th of the following month.

EXAMPLE: SEMIWEEKLY SCHEDULE DEPOSITOR
Pollak Woolens is a company based in Sault Ste. Marie, Michigan. During the look-back period ending June 30, 2020, it had **$75,984** in total payroll tax liability. Pollak Woolens would be a semiweekly schedule depositor. Depending on the payroll date, tax deposits are due on either the Wednesday or the Friday following the payroll date.

Notice the total tax liability during the lookback period. For Pollak Woolens, the amount exceeded $50,000 but is less than $100,000; this makes it a semiweekly schedule depositor. Because payroll tax deposits for semiweekly depositors are driven by the day of the week upon which payroll was paid, deposits may be due either on Wednesday or on Friday. For companies with a biweekly payroll frequency, the tax deposit date may remain the same, with few exceptions due to holidays. For companies with semimonthly payroll frequencies, the day of the tax deposit will likely vary.

EXAMPLE: NEXT BUSINESS DAY DEPOSITOR
Cornell Companies, based In Ohio, is a semiweekly schedule payroll tax depositor because of the total payroll tax liability of $693,259 during the lookback period ending June 30, 2020. The company had a total payroll tax liability of **$110,290** during the August 20, 2021, payroll period. August 20 is a Friday, so the payroll deposit would be due on Monday, August 23, because it exceeds $100,000.

In this example, Cornell Companies is already a semiweekly schedule depositor because of its payroll tax liability during the lookback period. Because the company's tax liability exceeds $100,000 for the payroll period, Cornell Companies must deposit those payroll taxes by the next business day.

EXAMPLE: ANNUAL SCHEDULE DEPOSITOR
Wallflower Guitars is based in Ocean Springs, Mississippi. During the lookback period ending June 30, 2020, the company had a total payroll tax liability of $954. The payroll tax deposit schedule for Wallflower Guitars would be annual because of the small total tax liability. As long as the total payroll tax liability remains less than $1,000 during 2021, the company may deposit its payroll taxes with its annual payroll tax return using Form 944.

In this example, Wallflower Guitars has a minimal payroll tax liability. It should be noted *annual schedule depositors* are assumed to have a minimal tax liability. If the company's payroll tax liability grows during the calendar year, the schedule depositors should be mindful of the monthly schedule deposit rules. However, the company will not become a monthly schedule depositor until notified in writing by the IRS.

Reporting Periods

Stop & Check

1. Perry Plastics had $46,986 in payroll taxes during the lookback period. How often must the company deposit its payroll taxes?
2. For Perry Plastics, when is the deposit for June payroll taxes due?
3. Charlie's Kitchens has a payroll tax liability of $126,463 on its Friday payroll. When is the payroll tax deposit due?

LO 6-3 Prepare Mid-Year and Year-End Employer Tax Reporting and Deposits

Companies and payroll accountants are responsible for the timely filing of the various tax documents required by governmental authorities. Note the dates for depositing and reporting taxes are not always the same. For example, an employer may be required to file payroll tax deposits through the EFTPS daily, semiweekly, or monthly, depending upon their payroll tax liability during the lookback period. However, that same employer would not be required to file tax forms until after the quarter. Like personal tax reporting, business reporting of statutory tax obligations has specific forms that employers must use. The most common forms used to deposit federal income tax and FICA taxes are Forms 941 (quarterly) and 944 (annual). An additional form used by agricultural businesses is Form 943, which serves the same purpose as Form 941.

lovelyday12/Shutterstock

> Employer tax remittance forms changed significantly for the calendar year 2021 because of CARES Act provisions. Since employers had the option to defer certain payroll taxes, the accounting for those tax amounts needed to be documented for financial tracking purposes.

Form 941

Monthly, semiweekly, and next-business-day payroll tax depositors file *Form 941* (see Figure 6-1), the employer's quarterly report of taxes deposited and taxes due. The form is used to reconcile the firm's deposits with the tax liability derived through mathematical computations. It is common to encounter minor adjustments while completing the form due to rounding differences incurred during monthly tax deposits. Form 941 has specific instructions for its completion, as shown in Table 6-5. Note: The IRS changed Form 941 in July 2021 due to revisions in COVID-19 tax credits and changes that went into effect for COBRA premiums with the *American Rescue Plan Act (ARPA)*. This new form was mandatory for employer tax reporting for the second quarter of 2021 but not for previous reporting periods.

Schedule B

Semiweekly depositors must file Schedule B (Figure 6-2) in addition to Form 941. This form allows firms to enter the details of payroll tax liabilities that occur multiple times during a month. On *Schedule B*, the payroll tax liability is entered on the days of the month on which the payroll occurred. The total tax liability for each month is entered in the right column. The total tax liability for the quarter must equal line 10 of Form 941.

EXAMPLE: PAYROLL TAX LIABILITY

Jeremiah Katzenberg is the owner of a company that pays its employees on the 15th and the last day of the month. All employees are salaried, exempt workers. Pay dates that fall on the weekend are paid on the preceding Friday. According to the lookback period, the company is required to deposit payroll taxes on a semiweekly basis. Because Katzenberg is a semiweekly schedule depositor, he must file Schedule B in addition to Form 941. For the first quarter of 2021, Katzenberg's company had the following pay dates and payroll tax liabilities:

Pay Date	Payroll Tax Liability
January 15	$ 41,486.47
January 29	41,486.47
February 12	41,486.47
February 26	41,486.47
March 12	41,486.47
March 31	41,486.47
Total Tax Liability for the Quarter	$ 248,918.82

Note: The payroll tax liability is (a) listed on the payroll date and (b) includes the FICA taxes (employee and employer share) and the federal income tax withheld.

TABLE 6-5
Instructions for Completing Form 941

Part 1: Data for Chalmette Company
Susan Wagner is the President of Chalmette Company, EIN 67-3983240, located at 572 Rue Bon Temps, New Orleans, Louisiana, 70116. The company's phone number is 504-555-2039. The following Form 941 is for the second quarter of the year. Chalmette Company had 12 employees during the second quarter.

Name	Gross Earning	Taxable Wages for Federal W/H	Taxable Wages for FICA	Taxable Wages for FUTA	Total Federal W/H	Total Social Security Tax	Total Medicare W/H	FUTA Tax	SUTA Tax	Net Pay
YTD Totals	$128,356.74	$128,356.74	$94,569.00	$84,000.00	$18,432.50	$11,726.56	$2,742.50	$504.00	$5,106.73	
Line # on Form 941		2	5a & 5c		3	5a	5c			

Line 1: The number of employees during the quarter reported, as indicated in the box in the upper right-hand corner.
Line 2: Total wages subject to federal income tax (less pre-tax deductions) for the quarter.
Line 3: Federal income tax withheld from wages paid during the quarter.
Line 4: Check the box only if no wages paid during the quarter were subject to taxes. (This is uncommon.)
Lines 5a–5d: Column 1 is for the wages and tips subject to Social Security and Medicare taxes; column 2 is the number of wages multiplied by the tax percent specified on the form.
Line 5e: Total of column 2, lines 5a–5d.
Line 5f: Tax on unreported tips.
Line 6: Total taxes due before adjustments.
Lines 7–9: Quarterly tax adjustments.
Line 10: Total tax after adjustments: line 6 minus lines 7, 8, and 9.
Line 11a: Qualified business tax credit for research activities
Lines 11b – c: CARES Act non-refundable adjustments
Line 11e: Total non-refundable credits
Line 12: Total taxes due, after adjustments and credits
Line 13a: Total taxes deposited during the quarter.
Line 13b: Reserved for future use
Line 13c-d: CARES Act refundable adjustments
Line 13e: Total deposits and refundable credits
Line 13f: Total advances received from Form(s) 7200 per quarter
Line 13g: Total deposits and refundable credits less advances
Line 14: Balance due.
Line 15: Overpayment.

Part 2:
Check the first box if the tax liability for the quarter is less than $2,500.
OR
Check the second box if the tax liability is greater than $2,500 and enter the taxes deposited each month during the quarter.
The total deposits must equal the total liability in Part 1.
If the business is a semiweekly depositor, then Schedule B must be completed.

The IRS changed Form 941 in July 2021 due to revisions in COVID-19 tax credits and changes that went into effect for COBRA premiums with the ***American Rescue Plan Act (ARPA)***. This new form was mandatory for employer tax reporting for the second quarter of 2021 but not for previous reporting periods.

FIGURE 6-1
Form 941

Form **941 for 2021:** **Employer's QUARTERLY Federal Tax Return**
(Rev. June 2021)   Department of the Treasury — Internal Revenue Service

951121

OMB No. 1545-0029

Employer identification number (EIN) 6 7 – 3 9 8 3 2 4 0

Name *(not your trade name)* Susan Wagner

Trade name *(if any)* Chalmette Company

Address 572 Rue Bon Temps

Number   Street   Suite or room number

New Orleans   LA   70116
City   State   ZIP code

Foreign country name   Foreign province/county   Foreign postal code

Report for this Quarter of 2021
(Check one.)

☐ **1:** January, February, March

☒ **2:** April, May, June

☐ **3:** July, August, September

☐ **4:** October, November, December

Go to *www.irs.gov/Form941* for instructions and the latest information.

Read the separate instructions before you complete Form 941. Type or print within the boxes.

Part 1: Answer these questions for this quarter.

1 Number of employees who received wages, tips, or other compensation for the pay period including: *June 12* (Quarter 2), *Sept. 12* (Quarter 3), or *Dec. 12* (Quarter 4) . . . . **1** | 12

2 Wages, tips, and other compensation . . . . **2** | 128,356 . 74

3 Federal income tax withheld from wages, tips, and other compensation . . . . . . **3** | 18,432 . 50

4 If no wages, tips, and other compensation are subject to social security or Medicare tax ☐ Check and go to line 6.

	Column 1		Column 2	
5a Taxable social security wages* . .	94,569 . 00	× 0.124 =	11,726 . 56	
5a (i) Qualified sick leave wages* .	.	× 0.062 =	.	
5a (ii) Qualified family leave wages* .	.	× 0.062 =	.	
5b Taxable social security tips . . .	.	× 0.124 =	.	
5c Taxable Medicare wages & tips. .	94,569 . 00	× 0.029 =	2,742 . 50	
5d Taxable wages & tips subject to Additional Medicare Tax withholding	.	× 0.009 =	.	

*Include taxable qualified sick and family leave wages for leave taken after March 31, 2021, on line 5a. Use lines 5a(i) and 5a(ii) **only** for wages paid after March 31, 2020, for leave taken before April 1, 2021.

5e Total social security and Medicare taxes. Add Column 2 from lines 5a, 5a(i), 5a(ii), 5b, 5c, and 5d   **5e** | 14,469 . 06

5f Section 3121(q) Notice and Demand—Tax due on unreported tips (see instructions) . . **5f** | .

6 Total taxes before adjustments. Add lines 3, 5e, and 5f . . . . **6** | .

7 Current quarter's adjustment for fractions of cents . . . . **7** | 32,901 . 56

8 Current quarter's adjustment for sick pay . . . . **8** | . 01

9 Current quarter's adjustments for tips and group-term life insurance . . . . . . **9** | .

10 Total taxes after adjustments. Combine lines 6 through 9 . . . . **10** | 32,901 . 57

11a Qualified small business payroll tax credit for increasing research activities. Attach Form 8974 **11a** | .

11b Nonrefundable portion of credit for qualified sick and family leave wages for leave taken before April 1, 2021 . . . . **11b** | .

11c Nonrefundable portion of employee retention credit . . . . **11c** | .

▶ **You MUST complete all three pages of Form 941 and SIGN it.**

Next ▶

For Privacy Act and Paperwork Reduction Act Notice, see the back of the Payment Voucher.   Cat. No. 17001Z   Form **941** (Rev. 6-2021)

951221

Name *(not your trade name)*	Employer identification number (EIN)
Susan Wagner	67-3983240

Part 1:   Answer these questions for this quarter. *(continued)*

11d   Nonrefundable portion of credit for qualified sick and family leave wages for leave taken after March 31, 2021 . . . .   **11d** [_____ . ___]

11e   Nonrefundable portion of COBRA premium assistance credit (see instructions for applicable quarters) . . . .   **11e** [_____ . ___]

11f   Number of individuals provided COBRA premium assistance [_____]

11g   Total nonrefundable credits. Add lines 11a, 11b, 11c, 11d, and 11e . . . .   **11g** [_____ . ___]

12   Total taxes after adjustments and nonrefundable credits. Subtract line 11g from line 10 .   **12** [32,901 . 57]

13a   Total deposits for this quarter, including overpayment applied from a prior quarter and overpayments applied from Form 941-X, 941-X (PR), 944-X, or 944-X (SP) filed in the current quarter   13a [32,901 . 57]

13b   Reserved for future use . . . .   **13b** [▓▓▓▓▓ . ▓]

13c   Refundable portion of credit for qualified sick and family leave wages for leave taken before April 1, 2021 . . . .   **13c** [_____ . ___]

13d   Refundable portion of employee retention credit . . . .   **13d** [_____ . ___]

13e   Refundable portion of credit for qualified sick and family leave wages for leave taken after March 31, 2021 . . . .   **13e** [_____ . ___]

13f   Refundable portion of COBRA premium assistance credit (see instructions for applicable quarters) . . . .   **13f** [_____ . ___]

13g   Total deposits and refundable credits. Add lines 13a, 13c, 13d, 13e, and 13f . . . . .   **13g** [32,901 . 57]

13h   Total advances received from filing Form(s) 7200 for the quarter . . . .   **13h** [_____ . ___]

13i   Total deposits and refundable credits less advances. Subtract line 13h from line 13g . . . .   **13i** [32,901 . 57]

14   Balance due. If line 12 is more than line 13i, enter the difference and see instructions . . .   **14** [_____ . ___]

15   Overpayment. If line 13i is more than line 12, enter the difference [_____ . ___] Check one: ☐ Apply to next return.   ☐ Send a refund.

Part 2:   Tell us about your deposit schedule and tax liability for this quarter.

If you're unsure about whether you're a monthly schedule depositor or a semiweekly schedule depositor, see section 11 of Pub. 15.

16   Check one: ☐   Line 12 on this return is less than $2,500 or line 12 on the return for the prior quarter was less than $2,500, and you didn't incur a $100,000 next-day deposit obligation during the current quarter. If line 12 for the prior quarter was less than $2,500 but line 12 on this return is $100,000 or more, you must provide a record of your federal tax liability. If you're a monthly schedule depositor, complete the deposit schedule below; if you're a semiweekly schedule depositor, attach Schedule B (Form 941). Go to Part 3.

☒   **You were a monthly schedule depositor for the entire quarter.** Enter your tax liability for each month and total liability for the quarter, then go to Part 3.

Tax liability: **Month 1** [10,967 . 19]

Month 2 [10,967 . 19]

Month 3 [10,967 . 19]

Total liability for quarter [32,901 . 57]   **Total must equal line 12.**

☐   **You were a semiweekly schedule depositor for any part of this quarter.** Complete Schedule B (Form 941), Report of Tax Liability for Semiweekly Schedule Depositors, and attach it to Form 941. Go to Part 3.

▶ **You MUST complete all three pages of Form 941 and SIGN it.**   Next ▶

Form **941** (Rev. 6-2021)

951921

Name *(not your trade name)*	Employer identification number (EIN)
Susan Wagner	67-3983240

Part 3: Tell us about your business. If a question does NOT apply to your business, leave it blank.

17 If your business has closed or you stopped paying wages . . . . ☐ Check here, and

enter the final date you paid wages [/ /] ; also attach a statement to your return. See instructions.

18a If you're a seasonal employer and you don't have to file a return for every quarter of the year . . . ☐ Check here.

18b If you're eligible for the employee retention credit solely because your business is a recovery startup business ☐ Check here.

19 Qualified health plan expenses allocable to qualified sick leave wages for leave taken before April 1, 2021   **19** [.]

20 Qualified health plan expenses allocable to qualified family leave wages for leave taken before April 1, 2021   **20** [.]

21 Qualified wages for the employee retention credit . . . . **21** [.]

22 Qualified health plan expenses for the employee retention credit . . . . **22** [.]

23 Qualified sick leave wages for leave taken after March 31, 2021 . . . . **23** [.]

24 Qualified health plan expenses allocable to qualified sick leave wages reported on line 23   **24** [.]

25 Amounts under certain collectively bargained agreements allocable to qualified sick leave wages reported on line 23 . . . . **25** [.]

26 Qualified family leave wages for leave taken after March 31, 2021 . . . . . . **26** [.]

27 Qualified health plan expenses allocable to qualified family leave wages reported on line 26   **27** [.]

28 Amounts under certain collectively bargained agreements allocable to qualified family leave wages reported on line 26 . . . . **28** [.]

Part 4: May we speak with your third-party designee?

Do you want to allow an employee, a paid tax preparer, or another person to discuss this return with the IRS? See the instructions for details.

☐ Yes. Designee's name and phone number [   ] [   ]

Select a 5-digit personal identification number (PIN) to use when talking to the IRS. ☐ ☐ ☐ ☐ ☐

☒ No.

Part 5: Sign here. You MUST complete all three pages of Form 941 and SIGN it.

Under penalties of perjury, I declare that I have examined this return, including accompanying schedules and statements, and to the best of my knowledge and belief, it is true, correct, and complete. Declaration of preparer (other than taxpayer) is based on all information of which preparer has any knowledge.

X

Sign your name here   *Susan Wagner*

Print your name here	Susan Wagner
Print your title here	President

Date [07 / 07 / 2021]

Best daytime phone	504-555-2039

Paid Preparer Use Only

Check if you're self-employed . . . ☐

Preparer's name	[ ]	PTIN	[ ]
Preparer's signature	[ ]	Date	[/ /]
Firm's name (or yours if self-employed)	[ ]	EIN	[ ]
Address	[ ]	Phone	[ ]
City	[ ] State [ ]	ZIP code	[ ]

   Form **941** (Rev. 6-2021)

FIGURE 6-2
Schedule B for Form 941

Schedule B (Form 941):

Report of Tax Liability for Semiweekly Schedule Depositors

960311

(Rev. January 2017)

Department of the Treasury — Internal Revenue Service

OMB No. 1545-0029

Employer identification number (EIN) 9 8 – 7 6 5 4 3 2 1

Name *(not your trade name)* Jeremiah Katzenberg

Calendar year 2 0 2 1 (Also check quarter)

Report for this Quarter...
(Check one.)

[X] **1:** January, February, March

[ ] **2:** April, May, June

[ ] **3:** July, August, September

[ ] **4:** October, November, December

Use this schedule to show your **TAX LIABILITY** for the quarter; don't use it to show your deposits. When you file this form with Form 941 or Form 941-SS, don't change your tax liability by adjustments reported on any Forms 941-X or 944-X. You must fill out this form and attach it to Form 941 or Form 941-SS if you're a semiweekly schedule depositor or became one because your accumulated tax liability on any day was $100,000 or more. Write your daily tax liability on the numbered space that corresponds to the date wages were paid. See Section 11 in Pub. 15 for details.

Month 1

#		#		#		#		Tax liability for Month 1
1	.	9	.	17	.	25	.	
2	.	10	.	18	.	26	.	82972 . 94
3	.	11	.	19	.	27	.	
4	.	12	.	20	.	28	.	
5	.	13	.	21	.	29	.	
6	.	14	.	22	.	30	.	
7	.	15	41486 . 47	23	.	31	41486 . 47	
8	.	16	.	24	.			

Month 2

#		#		#		#		Tax liability for Month 2
1	.	9	.	17	.	25	.	
2	.	10	.	18	.	26	41486 . 47	82972 . 94
3	.	11	.	19	.	27	.	
4	.	12	.	20	.	28	.	
5	.	13	.	21	.	29	.	
6	.	14	.	22	.	30	.	
7	.	15	41486 . 47	23	.	31	.	
8	.	16	.	24	.			

Month 3

#		#		#		#		Tax liability for Month 3
1	.	9	.	17	.	25	.	
2	.	10	.	18	.	26	.	82972 . 94
3	.	11	.	19	.	27	.	
4	.	12	.	20	.	28	.	
5	.	13	.	21	.	29	.	
6	.	14	.	22	.	30	.	
7	.	15	41486 . 47	23	.	31	41486 . 47	
8	.	16	.	24	.			

Fill in your total liability for the quarter (Month 1 + Month 2 + Month 3) ▶
Total must equal line 12 on Form 941 or Form 941-SS.

Total liability for the quarter

248918 . 82

For Paperwork Reduction Act Notice, see separate instructions.   IRS.gov/form941   Cat. No. 11967Q   **Schedule B (Form 941)** (Rev. 1-2017)

Source: Internal Revenue Service

FIGURE 6-3

Example of Completed California Quarterly Contribution Return and Report of Wages

EDD Employment Development Department State of California

QUARTERLY CONTRIBUTION RETURN AND REPORT OF WAGES
REMINDER: File your DE 9 and DE 9C together.
PLEASE TYPE THIS FORM—DO NOT ALTER PREPRINTED INFORMATION

00090112

YR	QTR
21	3

QUARTER ENDED **09/30/2021**   DUE **10/15/2021**   DELINQUENT IF NOT POSTMARKED OR RECEIVED BY **10/15/2021**

EMPLOYER ACCOUNT NO.
392-1002-3

Four Mountains Inn
19283 Aracita Boulevard
Jackson, California 94453

DEPT. USE ONLY

DO NOT ALTER THIS AREA

P1 P2 C P U S A
T
EFFECTIVE DATE   Mo. Day Yr.

FEIN **58-3020493**   A. NO WAGES PAID THIS QUARTER ☐   B. OUT OF BUSINESS/NO EMPLOYEES ☐

B1. OUT OF BUSINESS DATE   M M D D Y Y Y Y

ADDITIONAL FEINS

C. TOTAL SUBJECT WAGES PAID THIS QUARTER **48,394.78**

D. UNEMPLOYMENT INSURANCE (UI) (Total Employee Wages up to $ per employee per calendar year)

(D1) UI Rate %		(D2) UI TAXABLE WAGES FOR THE QUARTER		(D3) UI CONTRIBUTIONS
3.8	TIMES	19,840.62	=	753.94

E. EMPLOYMENT TRAINING TAX (ETT)

(E1) ETT Rate %				(E2) ETT CONTRIBUTIONS
.1	TIMES	UI Taxable Wages for the Quarter (D2)	=	19.84

F. STATE DISABILITY INSURANCE (SDI) (Total Employee Wages up to $ per employee per calendar year)

(F1) SDI Rate %		(F2) SDI TAXABLE WAGES FOR THE QUARTER		(F3) SDI EMPLOYEE CONTRIBUTIONS WITHHELD
1.2	TIMES	19,840.62	=	238.09

G. CALIFORNIA PERSONAL INCOME TAX (PIT) WITHHELD **3,275.29**

H. **SUBTOTAL** (Add Items D3, E2, F3, and G) **4,287.16**

I. LESS: CONTRIBUTIONS AND WITHHOLDINGS PAID FOR THE QUARTER ....
(**DO NOT** INCLUDE PENALTY AND INTEREST PAYMENTS)

J. TOTAL TAXES DUE OR OVERPAID   (Item H minus Item I) **4,287.16**

If amount due, prepare a *Payroll Tax Deposit* (DE 88), include the correct payment quarter, and mail to: Employment Development Department, P.O. Box 826276, Sacramento, CA 94230-6276. **NOTE:** Do not mail payments along with the DE 9 and *Quarterly Contribution Return and Report of Wages (Continuation)* (DE 9C), as this may delay processing and result in erroneous penalty and interest charges. **Mandatory Electronic Funds Transfer (EFT)** filers must remit all SDI/PIT deposits by EFT to avoid a noncompliance penalty.

K. I declare that the above, to the best of my knowledge and belief, is true and correct. If a refund was claimed, a reasonable effort was made to refund any erroneous deductions to the affected employee(s).

Signature *Benjamin Blanco*   Title **Owner**   Phone (530) 2931004   Date 10/14/2021
(Owner, Accountant, Preparer, etc.)

SIGN AND MAIL TO: State of California / Employment Development Department / P.O. Box 989071 / West Sacramento CA 95798-9071

DE 9 Rev. 1 (1-12) **(INTERNET)**   Page 1 of 2   *e-Services* Fast, Easy, and Convenient! Visit EDD's Web site at **www.edd.ca.gov**

Source: Internal Revenue Service

State Tax Remittance

Each state that charges income tax has its own form for employee income *tax remittance* purposes. State tax forms are similar to federal forms as far as the information included is concerned and generally have similar due dates. An important note is that each state has its own unique taxes. For example, California has an employee-only State Disability Insurance (SDI) tax of 1.2 percent on earnings up to $128,298 per employee (2021 figure), as well as an employer-only Employment Training Tax (ETT) of 0.1 percent on the first $7,000 of each employee's earnings. These additional taxes are included on the state's payroll tax return. Figure 6-3 contains an example of a completed California quarterly tax return.

Additionally, employers are responsible for reporting any other local or regional taxes. Employers must abide by the filing requirements for each of the taxes or face fines or penalties depending upon state/local tax code. The purpose of these taxes can include the provision of social services and the funding of infrastructure costs. The Denver Head Tax was designed to fulfill both of these purposes in response to the increase of infrastructure and municipal programs' availability for residents. An example of the Denver Occupational Privilege Tax Return quarterly form is located in Figure 6-4.

Form 944

Firms with a total annual tax liability of less than $1,000 use *Form 944* (see Figure 6-5). Like Form 941, the firm enters the details of wages paid and computes the taxes due. The firm reports the monthly deposits and liabilities in Part 2. However, instead of entering a quarterly liability, the firm enters the annual liability, which is the sum of all the monthly liabilities. The IRS must notify a company in writing of the requirement to file Form 944 before its use.

EXAMPLE: FORM 944

Sophie Jennings owns Forest Dog Walkers. Forest Dog Walkers is a sole proprietorship with one part-time employee who works only five months of the year. The IRS has notified Ms. Jennings that Forest Dog Walkers must report federal payroll tax liabilities using Form 944. The total wages paid to the employee during 2020 were $952.20. The federal income tax liability was $274, and the total payroll tax liability for the year was $638.26. Because the total annual payroll tax liability is less than $1,000, Forest Dog Walkers must file an annual return. The due date for Form 944 is January 31 of the following year.

Unemployment Tax Reporting

Form 940 is the employer's annual report of federal unemployment taxes due, based on employee wages paid during the year. This report is for a calendar year and is due by January 31 of the following year.

According to *26 IRC Section 3306*, certain fringe benefits are not subject to federal unemployment taxes because they represent noncash compensation that is not intended to be used as disposable income. Specific examples of these fringe benefits are employer contributions to employee retirement plans, such as the 401(k) and 403(b), and payments for benefits excluded under qualified Section 125 cafeteria plans.

EXAMPLE: EMPLOYER CONTRIBUTIONS TO RETIREMENT PLANS

Winterguard Products offers its employees a matching 401(k) contribution of 0.5 percent for each 1 percent of the employee's salary. In 2021, Susanna Stark, an employee of Winterguard Products, contributed 4 percent of her $36,500 annual salary to her 401(k) plan.

Susanna's contribution	$36,500 × 0.04 =	$1,460.00
Winterguard's contribution match	Half of the employee's contribution =	730.00
Amount exempt from FUTA tax		$ 730.00

The $730 would be listed on line 4 of Form 940 as exempt from FUTA taxes.

FIGURE 6-4

Example of a Denver Occupational Privilege Tax Return

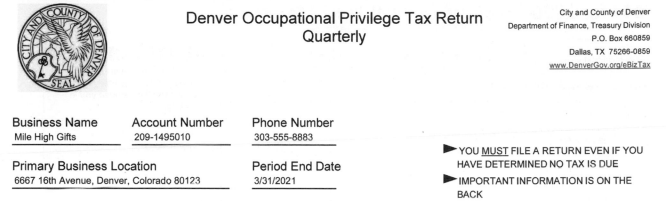

Denver Occupational Privilege Tax Return
Quarterly

City and County of Denver
Department of Finance, Treasury Division
P.O. Box 660859
Dallas, TX 75266-0859
www.DenverGov.org/eBizTax

Business Name	Account Number	Phone Number
Mile High Gifts	209-1495010	303-555-8883

Primary Business Location
6667 16th Avenue, Denver, Colorado 80123

Period End Date
3/31/2021

► YOU <u>MUST</u> FILE A RETURN EVEN IF YOU HAVE DETERMINED NO TAX IS DUE

► IMPORTANT INFORMATION IS ON THE BACK

If the number of employees for which the business is liable (Line 2) is different from the number of employees from whom the tax was withheld (Line 3) or if no tax is due, you must attach an explanation.

I. BUSINESS OCCUPATIONAL PRIVILEGE TAX

Line 1. Enter the number of self-employed individuals, owners, partners or managers. Multiply this number by $4.00 and enter the total.

NOTE: This line is for self-employed proprietors, partners, or managers of the business. There is no minimum level of monthly earnings required for self-employed proprietors, partners, or managers to be liable.

NOTE: All businesses located in Denver or performing work in Denver, regardless of the length or duration, are required to pay the minimum $4.00 Business Occupational Privilege Tax (OPT) for each month even when there are no taxable employees.

Line 2. Enter the number of employees for which the business is liable. Multiply this number by $4.00 and enter the total.

Liable employees are those who worked all or part of their time in Denver and received gross compensation of at least $500 for the month for services performed in Denver. Include all qualifying employees, even if some have another employer that is withholding this tax. The business is still liable for the business portion if the compensation was $500 or more. In the case of corporations for purposes of this tax, everyone, including all corporate officers, are considered employees.

II. EMPLOYEE OCCUPATIONAL PRIVILEGE TAX

Line 3. Enter the number of employees liable for this tax. Multiply this number by $5.75 and enter the total.

This line is for all employees who received gross compensation of at least $500 for the month for services performed in Denver. Corporations under the Business OPT ordinance are considered to only have employees, not owners. Therefore all corporate officers meeting the earnings requirement in Denver, should be included here. If any employee has another employer who is withholding this tax, Form TD-269 must be furnished to the secondary employer verifying the primary employer is withholding the tax.

Line 4a. If the return is filed or paid after the due date, enter 15% of Line 4, or $25.00, whichever is greater.

Line 4b. If the return is filed or paid after the due date enter 1% of Line 4 for each month or part of a month past due.

Line 5. Add Line 3, Line 4a, Line 4b. Enter the total. This is the total amount owed. Include a check or money order made payable to **Manager of Finance.**

RETURN LOWER PORTION - DETACH HERE

☐ CHECK HERE IF THIS IS AN AMENDED RETURN   **DENVER OCCUPATIONAL PRIVILEGE TAX RETURN**

ACCOUNT NUMBER	TaxType	Period End	Due Date	Media #	
209-1495010	Occupational Privilege Tax	3/31	4/15	000000000005	

NAME

PRIMARY BUSINESS LOCATION Mile High Gifts, 6667 16th Avenue, Denver, Colorado 80123   000000000005

I hereby certify, under penalty of perjury, that the statements made herein are to the best of my knowledge true and correct.

Signature (Required) *Kira Gardner*	Title	Owner	Date	4/14/2021

BUSINESS OCCUPATIONAL PRIVILEGE TAX

1 Enter the number of liable self-employed individuals, owners, partners or managers for each month, add across and enter the total.

Month 1	Month 2	Month 3	Total			
1	1	1	3	Multiply Total by $4.00	12	00

2 Enter the number of employees the business is liable for each month, add across and enter total.

Month 1	Month 2	Month 3	Total			
5	5	5	15	Multiply Total by $4.00	60	00

EMPLOYEE OCCUPATIONAL PRIVILEGE TAX

3 Enter the number of liable employees for each month, add across and enter total.

Month 1	Month 2	Month 3	Total			
5	5	5	15	Multiply Total by $5.75	86	25

4	**Total Tax: Add Lines 1, 2 and 3**	158	25

5	Late Filing - if return is filed after the due date - Add:	**a** Penalty: the greater of 15% of Line 4 or $25.00		
		b Interest: 1% of Line 4 for each month that the return is late		

6	TOTAL DUE AND PAYABLE: Add Line 4, 5a, 5b. This is the total due. Include a check or money order payable to **MANAGER OF FINANCE**	158	25

0000000000005000000000005

Source: Internal Revenue Service

FIGURE 6-5

Form 944 Note that a company that files Form 944 has the opportunity to remit payroll taxes using Form 944-V, a payment voucher.

Form **944 for 2020:** Employer's ANNUAL Federal Tax Return

Department of the Treasury — Internal Revenue Service

OMB No. 1545-2007

Employer identification number (EIN) `3  2 – 9  8  7  6  5  6  8`

Name *(not your trade name)*   Sophie Jennings

Trade name *(if any)*   Forest Dog Walkers

Address   403 Lake Road

Number   Street   Suite or room number

Rouse Point   NY   12809

City   State   ZIP code

Foreign country name   Foreign province/county   Foreign postal code

Who Must File Form 944

You must file annual Form 944 instead of filing quarterly Forms 941 **only if the IRS notified you in writing.**

Go to *www.irs.gov/Form944* for instructions and the latest information.

Read the separate instructions before you complete Form 944. Type or print within the boxes.

Part 1: Answer these questions for this year. Employers in American Samoa, Guam, the Commonwealth of the Northern Mariana Islands, the U.S. Virgin Islands, and Puerto Rico can skip lines 1 and 2, unless you have employees who are subject to U.S. income tax withholding.

1   Wages, tips, and other compensation . . . . **1**   `2380 . 78`

2   Federal income tax withheld from wages, tips, and other compensation . . . . **2**   `274 . 00`

3   If no wages, tips, and other compensation are subject to social security or Medicare tax   **3** ☐ Check and go to line 5.

4   Taxable social security and Medicare wages and tips:

	Column 1		Column 2	
4a Taxable social security wages	2380 . 78	× 0.124 =	295 . 22	
4a (i) Qualified sick leave wages	.	× 0.062 =	.	
4a (ii) Qualified family leave wages	.	× 0.062 =	.	
4b Taxable social security tips	.	× 0.124 =	.	
4c Taxable Medicare wages & tips	2380 . 78	× 0.029 =	69 . 04	
4d Taxable wages & tips subject to Additional Medicare Tax withholding	.	× 0.009 =	.	

4e Total social security and Medicare taxes. Add Column 2 from lines 4a, 4a(i), 4a(ii), 4b, 4c, and 4d   **4e**   `364 . 26`

5   Total taxes before adjustments. Add lines 2 and 4e . . . . **5**   `638 . 26`

6   Current year's adjustments (see instructions) . . . . **6**   `.`

7   Total taxes after adjustments. Combine lines 5 and 6 . . . . **7**   `638 . 26`

8a Qualified small business payroll tax credit for increasing research activities. Attach Form 8974   **8a**   `.`

8b Nonrefundable portion of credit for qualified sick and family leave wages from Worksheet 1   **8b**   `.`

8c Nonrefundable portion of employee retention credit from Worksheet 1 . . . . **8c**   `.`

8d Total nonrefundable credits. Add lines 8a, 8b, and 8c . . . . **8d**   `.`

▶ You MUST complete all three pages of Form 944 and SIGN it.   Next ▶

For Privacy Act and Paperwork Reduction Act Notice, see the back of the Payment Voucher.   Cat. No. 39316N   Form **944** (2020)

Source: Internal Revenue Service

Name *(not your trade name)* Sophie Jennings	Employer identification number (EIN) 32-9876568

Part 1:   Answer these questions for this year. *(continued)*

9	**Total taxes after adjustments and nonrefundable credits.** Subtract line 8d from line 7 . .	**9**	638 . 26	

10a **Total deposits for this year, including overpayment applied from a prior year and overpayments applied from Form 944-X, 944-X (SP), 941-X, or 941-X (PR)** . . . . . **10a** | 478 . 70

10b Deferred amount of the employer share of social security tax . . . . **10b** | .

10c Deferred amount of the employee share of social security tax . . . . **10c** | .

10d Refundable portion of credit for qualified sick and family leave wages from Worksheet 1 **10d** | .

10e Refundable portion of employee retention credit from Worksheet 1 . . . . **10e** | .

10f **Total deposits, deferrals, and refundable credits.** Add lines 10a, 10b, 10c, 10d, and 10e . **10f** | 478 . 70

10g Total advances received from filing Form(s) 7200 for the year . . . . **10g** | .

10h **Total deposits, deferrals, and refundable credits less advances.** Subtract line 10g from line 10f . . . . **10h** | .

11 **Balance due.** If line 9 is more than line 10h, enter the difference and see instructions . . . **11** | 159 . 56

12 **Overpayment.** If line 10h is more than line 9, enter the difference [.]   Check one: ☐ Apply to next return.   ☐ Send a refund.

Part 2:   Tell us about your deposit schedule and tax liability for this year.

13 **Check one:**   ☒ **Line 9 is less than $2,500. Go to Part 3.**

☐ Line 9 is $2,500 or more. Enter your tax liability for each month. If you're a semiweekly schedule depositor or you became one because you accumulated $100,000 or more of liability on any day during a deposit period, you must complete Form 945-A instead of the boxes below.

	Jan.		Apr.		July		Oct.
13a	.	**13d**	.	**13g**	.	**13j**	.
	Feb.		May		Aug.		Nov.
13b	.	**13e**	.	**13h**	.	**13k**	.
	Mar.		June		Sept.		Dec.
13c	.	**13f**	.	**13i**	.	**13l**	.

Total liability for year. Add lines 13a through 13l. Total must equal line 9.   **13m** | .

▶ **You MUST complete all three pages of Form 944 and SIGN it.**   Next ▶

Source: Internal Revenue Service

Name *(not your trade name)*	**Employer identification number (EIN)**
Sophie Jennings	32-9876568

Part 3: Tell us about your business. If any question does NOT apply to your business, leave it blank.

14 If your business has closed or you stopped paying wages . . . . ☐ Check here, and

enter the final date you paid wages [/ /] ; also attach a statement to your return. See instructions.

15	Qualified health plan expenses allocable to qualified sick leave wages	15	▢ .
16	Qualified health plan expenses allocable to qualified family leave wages	16	▢ .
17	Qualified wages for the employee retention credit	17	▢ .
18	Qualified health plan expenses allocable to wages reported on line 17	18	▢ .
19	Credit from Form 5884-C, line 11, for the year	19	▢ .

Part 4: May we speak with your third-party designee?

Do you want to allow an employee, a paid tax preparer, or another person to discuss this return with the IRS? See the instructions for details.

☐ **Yes.** Designee's name and phone number [   ] [   ]

Select a 5-digit personal identification number (PIN) to use when talking to the IRS. ▢ ▢ ▢ ▢ ▢

☒ **No.**

Part 5: Sign here. You MUST complete all three pages of Form 944 and SIGN it.

Under penalties of perjury, I declare that I have examined this return, including accompanying schedules and statements, and to the best of my knowledge and belief, it is true, correct, and complete. Declaration of preparer (other than taxpayer) is based on all information of which preparer has any knowledge.

X Sign your
name here

Sophie Jennings

Date 1/15/2021

Print your name here | Sophie Jennings
Print your title here | Owner
Best daytime phone | 518-555-4395

Paid Preparer Use Only Check if you're self-employed ☐

Preparer's name	[ ]	PTIN	[ ]
Preparer's signature	[ ]	Date	[ ]
Firm's name (or yours if self-employed)	[ ]	EIN	[ ]
Address	[ ]	Phone	[ ]
City	[ ]	State [ ]	ZIP code [ ]

Form **944** (2020)

Source: Internal Revenue Service

Form **944-V**	**Payment Voucher**	OMB No. 1545-2007
Department of the Treasury Internal Revenue Service	▶ **Don't staple this voucher or your payment to Form 944.**	20**20**

1	Enter your employer identification number (EIN). 32-9876568	2	**Enter the amount of your payment.** ▶ Make your check or money order payable to "**United States Treasury**"	Dollars	Cents
				159	56

3 Enter your business name (individual name if sole proprietor).

Forest Dog Walkers

Enter your address.

403 Lake Road

Enter your city, state, and ZIP code; or your city, foreign country name, foreign province/county, and foreign postal code.

Rouse Point, NY 12809

Source: Internal Revenue Service

Fringe benefits that may be exempt from FUTA taxes are those excluded from cafeteria plans, such as the ones in the following example:

EXAMPLE: EXCLUDED FRINGE BENEFITS NOT SUBJECT TO FUTA TAXES

Hutcheson Medical Products offers its employees the following fringe benefits:

Benefit	Annual Value	Amount Paid During the Calendar Year
Adoption assistance	$5,000 per employee	$15,000.00
Achievement awards	$250 per employee	10,000.00
Meals	$300 per employee	15,000.00
Total the annual value of excluded fringe benefits		$40,000.00

Hutcheson Medical Products would list $40,000 on Form 940 line 4, "Payments exempt from FUTA tax."

Other fringe benefits specifically exempt from FUTA tax and reported on line 4 include

- Dependent care (up to $2,500 per employee or $5,000 per married couple).
- Employer contributions to group term life insurance.
- Certain other noncash payments, as outlined in the **Instructions for Form 940**.

For tax reporting purposes, amounts contributed by employees to these exempt items must be treated in one of two ways on Form 940:

1. Deducted from Line 3 "Total payments to all employees."
2. Reported on Line 4 "Payments exempt from FUTA taxes."

EXAMPLE: ANNUAL FUTA TAX LIABILITY LESS THAN $500

Kimbro Painting has an annual FUTA liability of $392 during 2020. During the first three quarters of 2020, they would leave Part 5 blank because the tax liability is less than $500, and the liability would roll over to the next quarter. They would complete Part 5 to report the year-end FUTA deposit.

According to the IRS Tax Topic 759, they should deposit since it is year-end. "If your total FUTA tax liability for the year is $500 or less, you can either deposit the amount or pay the tax with your Form 940 by January 31." Because they have a total liability of $392 for the year, they should have an amount in Section 5 and make the payment with the year-end filing.

An example of Form 940 for Mustang Motorsports is found in Figure 6-6.

FIGURE 6-6

Form 940

Form **940 for 2020:** **Employer's Annual Federal Unemployment (FUTA) Tax Return**

850113

Department of the Treasury — Internal Revenue Service

OMB No. 1545-0028

Employer identification number (EIN) 7 9 – 5 3 1 2 2 4 9

Name *(not your trade name)* Kristina Hoff

Trade name *(if any)* Mustang Motorsports

Address 12298 El Toro Bouldevard

Number Street Suite or room number

Martinez CA 93778

City State ZIP code

Foreign country name Foreign province/county Foreign postal code

Type of Return
(Check all that apply.)

☐ **a.** Amended

☐ **b.** Successor employer

☐ **c.** No payments to employees in 2020

☐ **d.** Final: Business closed or stopped paying wages

Go to *www.irs.gov/Form940* for instructions and the latest information.

Read the separate instructions before you complete this form. Please type or print within the boxes.

Part 1: **Tell us about your return. If any line does NOT apply, leave it blank. See instructions before completing Part 1.**

1a	If you had to pay state unemployment tax in one state only, enter the state abbreviation .	1a C A
1b	If you had to pay state unemployment tax in more than one state, you are a multi-state employer	1b ☐ Check here. Complete Schedule A (Form 940).
2	If you paid wages in a state that is subject to CREDIT REDUCTION	2 ☐ Check here. Complete Schedule A (Form 940).

Part 2: **Determine your FUTA tax before adjustments. If any line does NOT apply, leave it blank.**

3	Total payments to all employees	3	364039 . 32
4	Payments exempt from FUTA tax	4 63364 . 00	

Check all that apply: **4a** ☒ Fringe benefits **4c** ☒ Retirement/Pension **4e** ☐ Other
4b ☐ Group-term life insurance **4d** ☐ Dependent care

5	Total of payments made to each employee in excess of $7,000	5 216675 . 32	
6	Subtotal (line 4 + line 5 = line 6)	6	280039 . 32
7	Total taxable FUTA wages (line 3 – line 6 = line 7). See instructions	7	84000 . 00
8	FUTA tax before adjustments (line 7 x 0.006 = line 8)	8	504 . 00

Part 3: **Determine your adjustments. If any line does NOT apply, leave it blank.**

9	If ALL of the taxable FUTA wages you paid were excluded from state unemployment tax, multiply line 7 by 0.054 (line 7 × 0.054 = line 9). Go to line 12	9 .
10	If SOME of the taxable FUTA wages you paid were excluded from state unemployment tax, OR you paid ANY state unemployment tax late (after the due date for filing Form 940), complete the worksheet in the instructions. Enter the amount from line 7 of the worksheet . .	10 .
11	If credit reduction applies, enter the total from Schedule A (Form 940)	11 .

Part 4: **Determine your FUTA tax and balance due or overpayment. If any line does NOT apply, leave it blank.**

12	Total FUTA tax after adjustments (lines 8 + 9 + 10 + 11 = line 12)	12 504 . 00
13	FUTA tax deposited for the year, including any overpayment applied from a prior year .	13 378 . 00
14	Balance due. If line 12 is more than line 13, enter the excess on line 14. • If line 14 is more than $500, you must deposit your tax. • If line 14 is $500 or less, you may pay with this return. See instructions	14 126 . 00
15	Overpayment. If line 13 is more than line 12, enter the excess on line 15 and check a box below	15 .

▶ You **MUST** complete both pages of this form and **SIGN** it. Check one: ☐ Apply to next return. ☐ Send a refund.

Next ▶

For Privacy Act and Paperwork Reduction Act Notice, see the back of the Payment Voucher. Cat. No. 11234O Form **940** (2020)

850212

Name *(not your trade name)*	Employer identification number (EIN)
Kristina Hoff	79-5312249

Part 5: Report your FUTA tax liability by quarter only if line 12 is more than $500. If not, go to Part 6.

16 Report the amount of your FUTA tax liability for each quarter; do NOT enter the amount you deposited. If you had no liability for a quarter, leave the line blank.

16a **1st quarter** (January 1 – March 31) **16a**	126 . 00
16b **2nd quarter** (April 1 – June 30) **16b**	126 . 00
16c **3rd quarter** (July 1 – September 30) **16c**	126 . 00
16d **4th quarter** (October 1 – December 31) **16d**	126 . 00

17 **Total tax liability for the year** (lines 16a + 16b + 16c + 16d = line 17) **17**   504 . 00   **Total must equal line 12.**

Part 6: May we speak with your third-party designee?

Do you want to allow an employee, a paid tax preparer, or another person to discuss this return with the IRS? See the instructions for details.

☐ **Yes.** Designee's name and phone number

Select a 5-digit personal identification number (PIN) to use when talking to the IRS.

☒ **No.**

Part 7: Sign here. You MUST complete both pages of this form and SIGN it.

Under penalties of perjury, I declare that I have examined this return, including accompanying schedules and statements, and to the best of my knowledge and belief, it is true, correct, and complete, and that no part of any payment made to a state unemployment fund claimed as a credit was, or is to be, deducted from the payments made to employees. Declaration of preparer (other than taxpayer) is based on all information of which preparer has any knowledge.

✗ **Sign your name here** *Kristina Hoff*

Print your name here Kristina Hoff

Print your title here Owner

Date 1/ 15 / 2021

Best daytime phone 831-564-6653

Paid Preparer Use Only

Check if you are self-employed ☐

Preparer's name		PTIN	
Preparer's signature		Date	/ /
Firm's name (or yours if self-employed)		EIN	
Address		Phone	
City		State		ZIP code	

Source: Internal Revenue Service

EXAMPLE: FORM 940

Kristina Hoff owns Mustang Motorsports, EIN 79-5312249. She filed the Annual FUTA Tax Return (Form 940) to report unemployment tax contributions during 2020. Mustang Motorsports has 12 employees, all of whom earned over the FUTA wage base. Lines 9 through 11 are adjustments to the FUTA deposited, rare, and do not apply in this scenario. (See pages 8–10 of Publication 15 for more details.)

Name	Gross Earnings (Including fringe benefits and retirement)	Fringe Benefits	Retirement/ Pension	Payments Exempt from FUTA	Payments over $7,000 per Employee	Taxable Wages for FUTA	FUTA Tax
YTD Totals	$364,039.32	$24,868.00	$38,496.00	$63,364.00	$216,675.32	$84,000.00	$504.00
The line on Form 940	3			4	5	7	8

Line 1a: If the company pays the unemployment tax in only one state, then the state abbreviation is entered here; otherwise, the company must check the box on line 1b and complete schedule A. Mustang Motorsports has only one location, which is in California.

Line 3: All wages paid during the calendar year are entered here ($364,039.32).

Line 4: Payments exempt from FUTA Tax. L&L has fringe benefits ($24,868.00) and retirement plan contributions ($38,496.00) that are exempt from FUTA.

Line 5: Wages for the year that are more than $7,000 per employee are entered here. The FUTA wage base is $7,000 per employee. In this example, all employees worked for the entire calendar year, so L&L is responsible for FUTA tax of $7,000 per employee. To compute Line 5:

Total wages	$364,039.32
Less: payments exempt from FUTA	(63,364.00)
Less: FUTA wage base ($7,000 × 12 employees)	(84,000.00)
Wages over $7,000	$216,675.32

Line 6: This is the sum of lines 4 and 5.

Line 7: FUTA Taxable wages, which are $84,000 for L&L Hay and Grain.

Line 8: FUTA Tax ($84,000 × 0.006) or $504.

Line 12: Total FUTA Tax of $504.

Line 13: Total FUTA Tax deposited during the year. This total must match Line 17 (side 2). Because all of Mustang Motorsports' employees exceeded their wage base by the end of the second quarter of 2020, all FUTA tax for the year has been deposited before completion of the tax return.

Lines 16a and 16b: Tax liability during each quarter. These boxes report the employer's FUTA tax liability based on wages paid or accrued during the quarter. In this case, Mustang Motorsports had a FUTA liability of $350 for the first quarter of 2020 and $104 for the second quarter of 2020. The sum of these liabilities (and any other quarterly liability, which does not exist in this example) is recorded on Line 17. The total on Line 17 must match the total on Line 13 (side 1).

Matching Final Annual Pay to Form W-2

One of the more common questions payroll accountants receive following the release of W-2s from the employees at the end of the year is, "why doesn't this match my final paycheck?" In short, it should—if you know how to calculate the income that belongs in each block of the W-2. The W-2 reflects all gross wages received by the employee, less any pre-tax deductions: health insurance, qualified retirement contributions, and other deductions adding any taxable fringe benefits. The total federal income taxes that the employer withheld from the employee and remitted as part of the 941 tax deposits also appear on the W-2 and acts as supporting documentation for the total wages reported on Forms 941 and 940.

As a result of the Affordable Care Act, the employer must report their contributions to employee health coverage on Form W-2. Amounts contributed by the employer should appear in Box 12 using code DD to designate the employer's share of the health care premium.

REPORTING OF EMPLOYER-SPONSORED HEALTH CARE COVERAGE

Type of Coverage	Form W-2, Box 12, Code DD		
	Must Report	Optional	Do Not Report
Major medical insurance	X		
Dental insurance, either as part of major medical or a separate, voluntary election		X	
Health FSA funded only by salary reduction (reported in Box 14)			X
Health FSA value over employee salary deduction for qualified benefits	X		
Health saving arrangement contribution (employer or employee funded)			X
Hospital indemnity or specified illness funded by employee pre-tax deduction or by employer	X		
Multi-employer plans		X	
Domestic partner coverage is included in gross income.	X		
The governmental plan provided for members of the military and their families			X
Federally recognized Indian tribal government plans			X
Accident or disability income			X
Long-term care			X
Workers' compensation			X
Excess reimbursement to highly compensated individual			X
Payment or reimbursement of premium to 2 percent shareholder-employee, included in gross income			X
Employers are required to file fewer than 250 W-2 forms in the preceding calendar year.		X	
Form W-2 furnished to the terminated employee before the end of the calendar year		X	
Form W-2 provided by the third-party sick-pay provider to employees of other employers		X	

Source: Internal Revenue Service

Similarly, Form W-2 contains the employee's Social Security and Medicare wages. These wages are not reduced by contributions by the employee to qualified pension accounts (401(k), 403(b), etc.), and therefore may be higher than box 1. The only difference between boxes 3 and 5 will come when employees earn more than the maximum Social Security wage in the given year, i.e., $142,800 for 2021. When this occurs, the Medicare wages reported in box 5 will be greater than the Social Security wages displayed in box 3. Boxes 4 and 6 contain the Social Security and Medicare taxes withheld from the employee and remitted through 941 deposits.

Tipped employees will have amounts represented in boxes 7 and 8 for their reported tips. Box 10 is used to report Dependent Care Benefits. Contributions to nonqualifying retirement plans will be represented in box 11. Employee contributions to qualifying plans are represented in box 12. An alphabetical code is assigned to the specific type of qualified retirement plan the contributions are made (A through EE). Box 13 denotes specific contributions to deferred compensation plans. Box 14 is used to report other information to employees, such as union dues, health insurance premiums (not pre-tax), educational assistance payments, and other similar items. State and local taxes and wages are represented in boxes 15 through 20.

The following is an explanation of each box and its contents for Form W-2.

Instructions for Completing Form W-2

Box	Explanation
a	Employee's Social Security number based on their Social Security card and/or Form W-4.
b	Employer Identification Number (EIN)
c	Employer address: This should match the address reported on other tax reports, such as Form 941 and Form 940.
d	Optional. This could be used for the company's employee number.
e–f	Employee's name and address as shown on the Social Security card and Form W-4.
1	Wages paid during the calendar year, including any additional amounts from • Bonuses • Cash value of prizes • Awards • Noncash value of fringe benefits • Educational assistance programs (over $5,250) • Group-term life insurance • Roth contributions made to certain retirement plans • Payments to statutory employees • HSA contributions • Nonqualified moving expenses and expense reimbursements • Any other compensation
2	Federal income tax withheld during the year.
3	Social Security wages: Wages paid subject to employees Social Security tax but not including Social Security and allocated tips. • Educational assistance programs (over $5,250)
4	Social Security tax withheld (employee share only)
5	Medicare wages and tips: This should be the same as the Social Security wages in box 3 unless employees reach the Social Security wage cap. • Educational assistance programs (over $5,250)
6	Medicare tax withheld (employee share only)
7	Social Security tips: Any tips reported to you by the employee go in this box.
8	Allocated tips: Use this box if the company allocates tips among employees.
9	Verification code: Used if the employer participates in the W-2 Verification Code pilot.
10	Dependent care benefits: Report all dependent care benefits paid during the calendar year under a dependent care benefit program.
11	Nonqualified plans: Used by the Social Security Administration.
12	Codes (see Figure 6-7)
13	Check the boxes for the following circumstances: • Statutory employee: Earnings are subject to Social Security and Medicare taxes but not federal income tax. • Retirement plan: If the employee was an active participant in a defined benefit or defined contribution plan. • Third-party sick pay: Used when reporting sick pay benefits.
14	Other: Used to report annual leave value of an employee's company car is the employer paid 100 percent.
15–20	Used for reporting state and local tax information. Deductions and inclusions would follow state laws.

Source: Internal Revenue Service

When completing *Form W-2*, you will have several copies of the same form. A sample Form W-2 is found in Figure 6-8. According to the order in which they print, the copies of Form W-2 are as follows:

Which Copy?	What Is It For?
Copy A	Social Security Administration
Copy 1	State, City, or Local Tax Department
Copy B	Filing with the Employee's Federal Tax Return
Copy C	Employee's Records
Copy 2	State, City, or Local Tax Department
Copy D	Employer

FIGURE 6-7

Box 12 Codes for Form W-2 and Retirement Plan checkbox Decisions Chart

Form W-2 Reference Guide for Box 12 Codes

A	Uncollected social security or RRTA tax on tips	L	Substantiated employee business expense reimbursements	Y	Deferrals under a section 409A nonqualified deferred compensation plan
B	Uncollected Medicare tax on tips (but not Additional Medicare Tax)	M	Uncollected social security or RRTA tax on taxable cost of group-term life insurance over $50,000 (former employees only)	Z	Income under a nonqualified deferred compensation plan that fails to satisfy section 409A
C	Taxable cost of group-term life insurance over $50,000	N	Uncollected Medicare tax on taxable cost of group-term life insurance over $50,000 (but not Additional Medicare Tax) (former employees only)	AA	Designated Roth contributions under a section 401(k) plan
D	Elective deferrals under a section 401(k) cash or deferred arrangement plan (including a SIMPLE 401(k) arrangement)	P	Excludable moving expense reimbursements paid directly to members of the Armed Forces	BB	Designated Roth contributions under a section 403(b) plan
E	Elective deferrals under a section 403(b) salary reduction agreement	Q	Nontaxable combat pay	DD	Cost of employer-sponsored health coverage
F	Elective deferrals under a section 408(k)(6) salary reduction SEP	R	Employer contributions to an Archer MSA	EE	Designated Roth contributions under a governmental section 457(b) plan
G	Elective deferrals and employer contributions (including nonelective deferrals) to a section 457(b) deferred compensation plan	S	Employee salary reduction contributions under a section 408(p) SIMPLE plan	FF	Permitted benefits under a qualified small employer health reimbursement arrangement
H	Elective deferrals to a section 501(c)(18)(D) tax-exempt organization plan	T	Adoption benefits	GG	Income from qualified equity grants under section 83(i)
J	Nontaxable sick pay	V	Income from exercise of nonstatutory stock option(s)	HH	Aggregate deferrals under section 83(i) elections as of the close of the calendar year
K	20% excise tax on excess golden parachute payments	W	Employer contributions (including employee contributions through a cafetaria plan) to an employee's health savings account (HSA)		

See *Box 12 Codes.*

Form W-2 Box 13 Retirement Plan Checkbox Decision Chart

Type of Plan	Conditions	Check Retirement Plan Box?
Defined benefit plan (for example, a traditional pension plan)	Employee qualifies for employer funding into the plan, due to age/years of service—even though the employee may not be vested or ever collect benefits	Yes
Defined contribution plan (for example, a 401(k) or 403(b) plan, a Roth 401(k) or 403(b) account, but not a 457 plan)	Employee is eligible to contribute but does not elect to contribute any money in this tax year	No
Defined contribution plan (for example, a 401(k) or 403(b) plan, a Roth 401(k) or 403(b) account, but not a 457 plan)	Employee is eligible to contribute and elects to contribute money in this tax year	Yes
Defined contribution plan (for example, a 401(k) or 403(b) plan, a Roth 401(k) or 403(b) account, but not a 457 plan)	Employee is eligible to contribute but does not elect to contribute any money in this tax year, but the employer does contribute funds	Yes
Defined contribution plan (for example, a 401(k) or 403(b) plan, a Roth 401(k) or 403(b) account, but not a 457 plan)	Employee contributed in past years but not during the current tax year under report	No (even if the account value grows due to gains in the investments)
Profit-sharing plan	Plan includes a grace period after the dose of the plan year when profit sharing can be added to the participant's account	Yes, unless the employer contribution is purely discretionary and no contribution is made by end of plan year

See *Box 13 Checkboxes.*

Source: Internal Revenue Service

FIGURE 6-8
Form W-2

22222	**a** Employee's social security number		

OMB No. 1545-0008

b Employer identification number (EIN) 46-5632149	**1** Wages, tips, other compensation 36,523.34	**2** Federal income tax withheld 3,671.04
c Employer's name, address, and ZIP code	**3** Social security wages 38,523.34	**4** Social security tax withheld 2,388.45
Daniel Christopherson 5978 Route 202 Pawtucket, RI 02862	**5** Medicare wages and tips 38,523.34	**6** Medicare tax withheld 588.89
	7 Social security tips	**8** Allocated tips
d Control number	**9**	**10** Dependent care benefits
e Employee's first name and initial Last name Suff.	**11** Nonqualified plans	**12a** D 2,000.00
Sunnystyles Senior Community 228 Maple Street Pawtucket, RI 02862	**13** Statutory employee ☐ Retirement plan ☐ Third-party sick pay ☐	**12b**
	14 Other	**12c**
		12d
f Employee's address and ZIP code		

15 State Employer's state ID number	**16** State wages, tips, etc.	**17** State income tax	**18** Local wages, tips, etc.	**19** Local income tax	**20** Locality name
RI 382948374	36,523.34	1,369.63			

Form **W-2** Wage and Tax Statement   **2021**   Department of the Treasury—Internal Revenue Service

Copy 1—For State, City, or Local Tax Department

Source: Internal Revenue Service

EXAMPLE: FORM W-2

Daniel Christopherson worked for Sunnystyles Senior Community during 2021. The following is on his W-2 for 2021:

Box 1 contains the wages, tips, and other compensation. Daniel earned $36,523.34 in 2021.

Box 2 contains the federal income tax withheld: Daniel had $3,671.04 withheld based on his W-4 information.

Boxes 3 and 5 contain the Social Security and Medicare wages. Note that these two boxes contain a higher amount than box 1. Daniel had a retirement plan into which he contributed $2,000 during 2021.

Boxes 4 and 6 contain the Social Security tax withheld ($2,388.45) and the Medicare tax withheld ($558.59).

Box 12 contains amounts for nontaxable items. Codes for box 12 are contained in Figure 6-7.

Boxes 15–17 contain the state tax information. Daniel had $1,369.63 withheld for state taxes based on the state withholding certificate he filed in January 2021.

Figure 6-8 is an example of a Form W-2 for Daniel Christopherson.

Form W-3 is the transmittal form that accompanies the submission of Copy A to the Social Security Administration. It contains the aggregate data for all W-2s issued by an employer. Form W-3 and all accompanying W-2s must be mailed or electronically transmitted by January 31 of the following year (i.e., W-2s and W-3s for 2020 are due on January 31, 2021). The total annual wages reported on the W-3 must match the annual wages reported on Forms 941 and 940. The following is an explanation of the boxes on Form W-3.

	Instructions for Completing Form W-3
Box	**Explanation**
a	Control number (optional)
b	Kind of payer: The employer indicates if one or more of the following applies: • Form 941 *and* no other category applies • Military • Form 943 (agricultural employers) • Form 944 *and* no other category applies • CT-1 (railroad employers) • Hshld. Emp. (Household employers) • Medicare govt. emp. (if the Forms W-2 are for employees subject only to Medicare tax) Kind of employer: Employers check the box that applies to them: • None, if none of the situations apply • 501c non-govt. (for tax-exempt non-governmental employers, such as private foundations, charities, social and recreational clubs, and veterans organizations) • State/local non-501c (for state/local governments or other entities with governmental authority) • State/local 501c (for state/local governments that have a tax-exempt designation) • Federal govt. (for federal government entities) Third-party sick pay: Employers who have indicated on the Form W-2 that they issue third-party sick pay must check this box.
c	Total number of Forms W-2 submitted with the W-3
d	Establishment number: Used to identify separate establishments within the same business.
e	Employer Identification Number (EIN)
f–g	Employer name and address
h	Any other EIN used during the year
	Employer contact information
1–8	Same as boxes 1–8 on Form W-2. The numbers in these boxes should reflect the total of each box for all forms submitted with Form W-3.
9	Leave blank.
10	Dependent care benefits: Report all dependent care benefits paid during the calendar year under a dependent care benefit program as a total of all Forms W-2.
11	The total reported in box 11 of Forms W-2.
12a	Deferred Compensation: Enter the total of all amounts reported with codes D-H, S, Y, AA, BB, and EE in Box 12 of Forms W-2. No code should be entered in Box 12a.
13	For third-party sick pay use only. Leave the box blank.
15	State/Employer's state ID number: Place the two-letter state abbreviation and the ID number. If the Forms W-2 are from more than one state, enter X in this box and omit the ID number.
16–19	Enter the state/local total wages and income tax withheld in the corresponding boxes.

The following example from Ferrigno Day Spa depicts the completion of Form W-3 for a company. (See Figure 6-9.)

EXAMPLE

Eva Longston is the owner of Longston Aesthetics, 2849 Water Street, Falls Church, Virginia, 22043, EIN 84-9943043, phone number 703-555-0904, fax number 703-555-0906. Her email address is elongston@longstonaesthetics.com.

Box b: Longston Aesthetics will file Form 941 to report quarterly tax liability, so box 941 is checked.

Box c: Longston Aesthetics had 25 employees who received W-2s.

Box 1: Wages and tips for 2019 were $654,087.35.

Box 2: The amount of federal income tax withheld from 2021 wages was $117,735.

Box 3: Social Security wages were $546,333.35.

Box 4: Social Security tax withheld was $33,872.67.

(continued)

(concluded)

Box 5: Medicare wages and tips were $546,666.25.

Box 6: Medicare tax withheld was $7,921.83.

Box 7: Social Security tips were $24,505.

Box 12a: Deferred compensation was $83,249.

Box 15: VA; Employer's State ID number: 66-2245538849A-238.

Box 16: State wages, tips, etc. were $654,087.35.

Box 17: State income tax withheld was $41,403.73.

Note: Taxable tips reported in Box 7 should be reported on IRS form 4070.

(Source: Internal Revenue Service)

Employers may occasionally need to correct filed tax forms. In this case, the employer should use the X version of the form (i.e., Form 941-X, Form 940-X, etc.). Note that any additional tax amounts owed that are discovered during the correction process should be remitted as soon as the employer completes the correction form. During the correction process, if an employer has withheld too much federal income tax or FICA from one or more employees, the employee has the option to recover these overages using **IRS Form** 843.

FIGURE 6-9
Form W-3

a Control number **33333**	For Official Use Only > OMB No. 1545-0008							sample not for official use

b **Kind of Payer** (Check one)	941 [X]	Military []	943 []	944 []		**Kind of Employer** (Check one)	None Apply [X] 501c non-govt []	Third-party sick pay (Check if applicable) []
	CT-1 []	Hshld Emp []	Medicare govt. empl. []				State/local non-501c [] State/local 501c [] Federal govt. []	

c Total number of Forms W-2 25	d Establishment number	1 Wages, tips, other compensation 654,087.35	2 Federal income tax withheld 117,735.00
e Employer identification number (EIN) 84-9943043		3 Social security wages 546,333.35	4 Social security tax withheld 33,872.67
f Employer's name Longston Aesthetics		5 Medicare wages and tips 546,333.35	6 Medicare tax withheld 7,921.83
2849 Water Street Falls Church, VA 22043		7 Social security tips	8 Allocated tips
g Employer's address and ZIP code		9	10 Dependent care benefits
h Other EIN used this year		11 Nonqualified plans	12a Deferred compensation 83,249.00

15 State VA	Employer's state ID number 66-2245538849A-238	14 Income tax withheld by payer of third-party sick pay	
16 State wages, tips, etc. 654,087.35	17 State income tax 41,403.73	18 Local wages, tips etc	19 Local income tax

Employer's contact person Eva Longston	Employer's telephone number 703-555-0904	For Official Use Only
Employer's fax number 703-555-0906	Employer's email address elongston@longstonaesthetics.com	

Under penalties of perjury, I declar that I have examined the return and accompanying documents and, to the best of my knowledge and belief, they are true, correct, and complete.

Signature> _____   Title> _____   Date> _____

Form **W-3** Transmittal of Wage and Tax Statements   **2021**   sample not for official use

Source: Internal Revenue Service

Tax Forms

Stop & Check

1. Jacobucci Enterprises is a monthly schedule depositor. According to the information it reported on Form 941, its quarterly tax liability is $8,462.96. During the quarter, it made deposits of $2,980.24 and $3,068.24. How much must it remit with its tax return?

2. Corrado's Corrals paid annual wages totaling $278,452.76 to 15 employees. Assuming that all employees were employed for the entire year, what is the amount of FUTA wages?

3. For Corrado's Corrals in the previous question, what is the FUTA tax liability?

4. Skyrockets Inc. had the following wage information reported in box 1 of its W-2s:

   Employee A: $25,650

   Employee B: $30,025

   Employee C: $28,550

   Employee D: $31,970

   What amount must it report as total wages on its Form W-3?

LO 6-4   Describe Payroll within the Context of Business Expenses

Jd8/Shutterstock

Taxes and Other Deductions Remittance

Understanding employer payroll expenses are important because of the wide range of mandatory activities and lesser-known expenses associated with maintaining employees. Compensation expenses and employer payroll-related liabilities must be accurately maintained in an accounting system. The scope of payroll-related employer responsibilities contributes to the need for knowledgeable payroll accountants.

> According to the Bureau of Labor Statistics, in 2020, employers' average hourly cost for employees was $38.26, of which wages were $26.25 and benefits totaled $12.01. For private-sector employers, the average hourly cost was $35.95; for governmental employers, the average hourly cost was $51.31.
>
> (Source: BLS)

The amounts withheld from employee pay and the employer liabilities must be deposited promptly with the appropriate authorities. The omission of any of the required filings, activities, or inaccuracy in the accounting system could lead to problems that could include governmental sanctions and penalties. No statute of limitations exists for unpaid taxes. If a company outsources its payroll processing, it is still liable for any late or unremitted payroll taxes.

> **The IRS will waive penalties under two conditions:**
>
> 1. The shortfall amount does not exceed the greater of $100 or 2 percent of the required tax deposit.
>
> 2. The amount of the shortfall is deposited either (a) by the due date of the period return (monthly and semiweekly depositors) or (b) the first Wednesday or Friday that falls after the 15th of the month (semiweekly depositors only).

Tax Penalties

Penalties fall into two classifications: (1) failure to deposit and (2) failure to file. The following penalties apply:

Failure to Deposit

2%	Deposits made 1 to 5 days late.
5%	Deposits made 6 to 15 days late.
10%	Deposits were made 16 or more days late. It also applies to amounts paid within 10 days of the date of the first notice the IRS sent asking for the tax due.
10%	Amounts (that should have been deposited) are paid directly to the IRS or paid with your tax return. See payment with the return, earlier in this section, for an exception.
15%	Amounts still unpaid more than 10 days after the date of the first notice the IRS sent asking for the tax due or the day on which you received notice and demand for immediate payment, whichever is earlier.

Source: Internal Revenue Service

EXAMPLE: FAILURE TO DEPOSIT PENALTY

Mane Street Hairstylists is a monthly schedule payroll tax depositor. The company owed $4,552 in payroll tax liabilities during July. The owner, Billy James, failed to deposit the July payroll taxes until August 27.

The failure to deposit penalty would be calculated as follows:

Tax Due	Number of Days Late	% Penalty	Total Penalty
$4,552.00	12	5%	$227.60

Failure to File

The failure to file penalty applies to amounts on Form 941 and is 5 percent of the unpaid tax due with the return. This penalty accrues for each month or partial month that the tax remains unpaid.

EXAMPLE: FAILURE TO FILE AND FAILURE TO DEPOSIT PENALTIES

Mary Warren, president of Great Meadows Farms, outsourced the payroll for the company during October 2021. On February 15, 2022, she received a notice that Form 941 for the fourth quarter of 2021 was not filed. After contacting the payroll service, she determined that $32,860 in payroll taxes due with Form 941 was never deposited. The penalties for this oversight would be as follows:

Failure to File Penalty

Tax Due	Number of Months Late	% Penalty per Month	Penalty
$32,860.00	2*	5%	$3,286

Failure to Deposit Penalty

Tax Due	Number of Days Late	% Penalty	Penalty
$32,860.00	30	10%	$3,286

		Total penalties due	$6,572

*The number of months is two because the failure to file penalty is based on both months and partial months. Because the notice was issued in February, the penalty would be for two months.

Notice how quickly the penalties can accrue for unfiled and undeposited taxes. The maximum penalty rate for failure to file is 25 percent, and the maximum for failure to deposit is 15 percent. Also, keep in mind that the penalties may be subject to interest charges.

A quick summary of general employer payroll expenses and responsibilities follows:

Employee Compensation	Tax Withholding	Tax Matching (FICA taxes only)
Tax remittance	Voluntary deductions from employee pay	Remittance of voluntary deductions
Tax reporting	Tax deposits	Accountability

It is important to understand the responsibility employers have for remitting the federal income tax and FICA tax amounts withheld from employees. According to IRS §6672, any responsible person within the company who *willfully* does not remit the withheld employee taxes—meaning they did not remit the taxes due to something as innocuous as a lack of funds—is subject to a 100 percent penalty for those nonremitted funds. It is important to note this penalty only applies to employee federal income tax and FICA taxes, not the employer's share of the FICA taxes or FUTA tax. The following diagram explains who is considered a responsible party for payroll tax deposits.

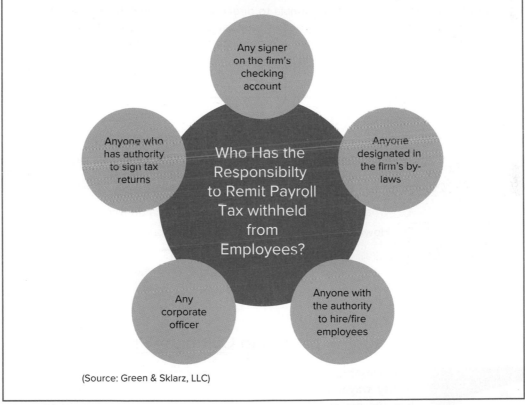

(Source: Green & Sklarz, LLC)

Employees and Company Framework

Singkham/Shutterstock

Beyond the payroll accounting system's expenses and responsibilities is understanding how the employees fit within the company's larger framework. Payroll is one part of the cost of employing people. Before the employee ever becomes productive for a company, employers will incur recruiting, hiring, and training costs that vary based on the company's location and minimum job requirements. Other costs include any tools, uniforms, and specific equipment that employees need to perform their jobs. Expenses associated with hiring and retaining well-qualified employees may comprise a significant amount of a company's overhead.

According to a study conducted by Hundred5, the cost to hire and train new employees averages 15 to 25 percent of the employee's salary. For a manager earning $36,000 per year, the cost to hire and train employees could total approximately $9,000.

While the employee is being hired and trained, the loss of productive time could range from 1 to 2.5 percent of company revenue. Although this may seem to be a minimal amount, companies with high turnover could realize a significant revenue loss because of training costs.

(Source: Hundred5)

Tracking employee payroll expenses is an important duty of payroll accountants. The use of payroll reports fosters cost analysis that informs accounting and human resource professionals of specific details needed for budget purposes. Companies need the information generated by payroll records to ensure profitability and competitiveness.

In February 2021, the Treasury Department permanently revised the Payroll Protection Program (PPP) loan computation formula to direct funding to small businesses. Under the new computation rules, independent contractors, such as realtors and driving services, had the chance to receive a greater amount of money as loans to retain employees.

(Source: Washington Post)

Payroll-Related Business Expenses

Stop & Check

1. What are the two types of penalties associated with payroll taxes?
2. How do payroll expenses relate to other business functions?

LO 6-5   Relate Labor Expenses to Company Profitability

ra2studio/Shutterstock

Compensating employees is far more complex than simply paying the hourly wage. The employer's expenses related to taxes, insurance, and benefits are an addition to the employee's annual salary. (See Figure 6-10.) Having employees affects the profitability of a company but is a vital part of doing business. Managers need to associate the proper amount of payroll costs with their department so they can make informed decisions about employee productivity and future budgets.

The Labor Distribution Report

The number of employees in a department is known as its *labor distribution*. Payroll accounting is a powerful tool in understanding the labor distribution of a company. Accounting records facilitate departmental identification of the number and type of employees, time worked, overtime used, and benefits paid. Integrating the department information into the employee earnings records facilitates labor distribution analysis.

FIGURE 6-10

Percent of Employee Compensation Component to Total Payroll Expense

Compensation Component	Civilian Workers	Private Industry	State and Local Government
Wages and salaries	68.6%	70.2%	61.8%
Benefits	31.4	29.8	38.2
Paid leave	7.4	7.3	7.5
Supplemental pay	3.0	3.0	1.0
Insurance	8.7	8.0	11.7
Health benefits	8.2	7.5	11.4
Retirement and savings	5.3	3.5	11.6
Legally required	7.2	7.6	5.5

(Source: Bureau of Labor Statistics)

For example, ABD Industries has three departments: administration, sales, and manufacturing. The employees are distributed as follows:

Administration: 15	Sales: 10	Manufacturing: 60

Without *departmental classification*, the payroll costs associated with the 85 employees at ABD would be allocated evenly among the departments. This allocation would result in the administration and sales departments absorbing an amount of the payroll costs that are disproportionate to the number of employees. The departmental classification yields an accurate picture of how the labor is distributed across a company.

EXAMPLE: LABOR DISTRIBUTION, NO DEPARTMENTAL CLASSIFICATION

Total payroll amount for ABD Industries = $500,000
Number of departments = 3
Payroll cost assigned to each department:
$500,000/3 = $166,666.67

Assigning payroll costs without departmental classification works when each department is composed of an equal number of employees with reasonably similar skills and job titles.

EXAMPLE: LABOR DISTRIBUTION WITH DEPARTMENTAL CLASSIFICATION

Total payroll for ABD: $500,000 or
Payroll cost per employee: $500,000/85 employees = $5,882.35 per employee (if allocated evenly per employee).

Departmental allocation:

Administration payroll costs = $5,882.35 × 15 = $88,235
Sales payroll costs = $5,882.35 × 10 = $58,824
Manufacturing payroll costs = $5,882.35 × 60 = $352,941

Allocating costs according to the number of employees in each department yields a more accurate amount than the equal distribution of the labor costs across the three departments at ABD. However, allocating by the number of departmental employees assumes that each employee has equal compensation, which is improbable. A payroll accounting system allows accurate allocation based on the precise amounts paid to each employee per payroll period. Labor distribution reports are among the tools that managers use to determine the productivity and costs specifically associated with their department.

Labor distribution reports may be used to reveal whatever information is important to a business. Funding sources, payroll accuracy, and budget projections are three common uses of labor distribution reports. Vanderbilt University uses a labor distribution report to ensure that payroll costs are linked to appropriate departments and to specific grant funding.

(Source: *Small Business Chronicle*)

Labor Distribution Report

Stop & Check

1. Pine Banks Tree Farms has 10 employees on staff: three office staff, five agricultural workers, and two drivers. The annual payroll expense is $300,000.

   a. What would be the labor distribution if Pine Banks Tree Farms uses departmental classification?

   b. What would be the labor distribution if Pine Banks Tree Farms does not use departmental classification?

2. Which method—departmental classification or nondepartmental classification—is most appropriate? Why?

LO 6-6 Complete Benefit Analysis as a Function of Payroll

Companies offer employee benefits to retain employees after the initial hire and remain competitive within their industry. The problem with offering benefits is the cost of the benefits directly affects a company's profitability. The challenge is to find ways to promote employee engagement, reduce employee turnover, and maintain company profitability. Payroll data plays an important role in completing an analysis of the benefits offered and their strategic advantage.

bleakstar/Shutterstock

Wages and salaries are often a company's largest employee expense. The second-largest expense to employers is employee benefits. According to Paychex, employee benefits potentially add 25-33 percent to an employee's base pay. Benefits may include paid time off, holiday pay, bonuses, and insurance. Many companies pay a percentage of the employee's insurance benefits, ranging from 70 percent to 100 percent in some cases. With the rising costs and mandatory nature of health insurance for certain employers, employee costs have become a major budget concern for many managers.

The COVID pandemic affected employer health insurance costs significantly. In New Jersey, healthcare costs increased by approximately $10 million. These additional costs led insurers to increase premium costs, which many employers passed along to their employees. These increases in healthcare costs affect small employers disproportionately because of the ratio of health care costs to company revenues.

(Source: Insider NJ)

Payroll-related employee costs need to be compared to the advantages of maintaining the employee, namely, the department's profitability and the company. To achieve the analysis required, a *benefit analysis* report needs to be compiled. Compiling a benefit analysis report is an important tool in maintaining a balance between employee retention and profitability. The payroll records of the company facilitate the compilation of the benefit analysis report.

IMPORTANCE OF THE BENEFIT ANALYSIS REPORT

The analysis of employee benefits considers all of the variables that comprise their compensation. Many managers are unaware of the full cost of having an employee added to or removed from their department, so the benefit analysis report serves the following purposes:

- Benefit analysis helps employers benchmark their employees' compensation to other companies with similar profiles or in certain geographic locations.

- The report helps employers with labor distribution and budgeting tasks by providing data for decision making.

- The benefit analysis facilitates managerial understanding of departmental impacts before hiring or dismissing employees.

Sebastiaan Blockmans/Alamy Stock Photo

Accurate reporting of the benefits costs to employers provides the management with guidance for budget analysis and employee compensation. A sample benefit analysis report is contained in Figure 6-11.

Note the differences between total employee benefit costs and total employer benefit costs. Mandatory and voluntary employee payroll deductions represent a significant monetary investment. When added to the employee's wages and the costs involved with recruitment and hiring, the amount of money dedicated to labor costs becomes a significant portion of a company's expenses.

Taking the information prepared above, the payroll accountant can determine each employee's cost to the company. This information can also determine the total cost of offering a particular benefit to the employees. The latter is used when the company is looking at annual renewals of health insurance benefits for comparison.

Annual Total Compensation Report

Some companies provide their employees with an *annual total compensation report*. The annual total compensation report is similar to the benefit analysis report because it contains a detailed analysis of employee costs. The difference between the two reports is the intended audience. The benefit analysis report is an internal report for the company's management, and the annual total compensation report is meant to be distributed to the employee. The work going into the total compensation report can come from either the human resources department or the accounting department, depending on its structure. Either way, the payroll accountant contributes vital information to the report.

> Despite the COVID pandemic, approximately 67 percent of employers planned to award bonuses in 2021. In a survey of over 700 U.S. companies, 35 percent of employers decided to lower employee compensation, and 50 percent planned no change in compensation. These changes in compensation were directly linked to revenue decreases in 2020. Compared to a 2.2 percent inflation rate, the result is decreased wages for most American workers.
>
> (Source: SHRM)

To prepare the information for the benefit analysis and total compensation reports, the payroll accountant will gather information from many sources: payroll registers, accounts payable invoices, *payroll tax reports*, and contributions to retirement programs (when employer matching is involved). The payroll accountant will start by printing the annual earnings report for the employee in question. A computerized earnings register can be configured to include taxes and

FIGURE 6-11
Sample Benefit Analysis Report

Statement for: Elizabeth M. Charette

Annual Gross Salary:		$44,137.60
Total Hours Worked Annually:		2,080 Hours

Health & Welfare Benefits:	Annual Employee Cost	Annual Employer Cost
Medical/Dental:	$ 600.00	$ 6,000.00
Life insurance:	0	1,200.00
AD&D coverage:	0	980.00
Dependent life insurance:	300.00	600.00
Disability insurance:	600.00	3,000.00
Total health & welfare:	$1,500.00	$ 1,780.00
Retirement Plan Benefits:	**Employee Cost**	**Employer Cost**
401(k) employee contribution:	$1,324.13	$ 662.07
Profit sharing:	0	3,000.00
Total retirement plan:	$1,324.13	$ 3,662.07
PTO & Holiday Pay	**Employee Cost**	**Employer Cost**
Paid time off:	$ 0	$ 1,697.60
Holiday pay:	0	1,867.36
Total PTO and holiday pay:	$ 0	$ 3,564.96
Additional Compensation:	**Employee Cost**	**Employer Cost**
Annual bonus:	$ 0	$ 2,500.00
Bereavement pay:	0	509.28
Production bonus:	0	500.00
Tuition reimbursement:	0	5,250.00
Total additional comp:	$ 0	$ 8,759.28
Government Mandated:	**Employee Cost**	**Employer Cost**
Social Security:	$2,736.53	$ 2,736.53
Medicare:	640.00	640.00
Federal unemployment:	0	253.28
State unemployment:	0	2,279.53
Workers' compensation:	0	353.10
Total government mandated:	$3,376.53	$ 6,262.44
Total cost of benefit provided by WLA Industries	$6,200.66	$34,028.75
Total cost of employing E. M. Charette*		$78,166.35

*44,137.60 + 34,028.75 = $78,166.35.

GaudiLab/Shutterstock

other deductions from the employee's pay. When the total compensation report covers periods greater than one year, it may be necessary for the payroll accountant to obtain Social Security and Medicare tax rates for the years in question. Employer portions of unemployment insurance, workers' compensation, and taxes are added to the employees' benefits in determining the total cost.

The payroll accountant will request copies of invoices for health insurance, life insurance, and any other benefits the employer provides, such as on-site meals and gym facilities/memberships, from the accounts payable accountant. Other items that may be added to the cost per employee for benefit analysis could be Company-provided awards, meals, clothing, or special facilities (break room, locker room, etc.). Once complete, the annual compensation report is distributed to employees to understand their annual compensation's total value. A sample total compensation report is in Figure 6-12.

FIGURE 6-12
Total Compensation Report

CASH COMPENSATION AND BENEFITS SUMMARY

The amount of your total compensation from ABC Company is much more than what is indicated in your yearly earnings statement. In addition to direct pay, it includes the value of your health care insurance, disability and life insurance, retirement benefits, and government mandated benefits. Below, we break out your total compensation.

CASH COMPENSATION	Amount
Base Salary	$52,000.00
Total:	**$52,000.00**

BENEFITS	Plan	Coverage	Your Contribution	Company Contribution
Medical Insurance	ABC One		$600.00	$5,400.00
Vision Insurance	ABC Vision		$0.00	$600.00
Dental Insurance	NL Dental		$120.00	$1,080.00
Total:			**$720.00**	**$7,080.00**

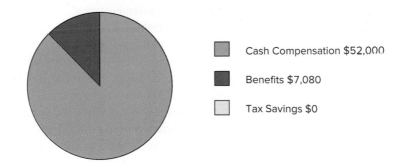

- Your Contribution 9.23%
- Company Contribution 90.77%

TOTAL COMPENSATION VALUE

The true value of your ABC Company total compensation includes your direct pay, the company's contribution to your benefits, and the consequent tax savings to you.

- Cash Compensation $52,000
- Benefits $7,080
- Tax Savings $0

Benefit Analysis Report

Stop & Check

1. What are the purposes of compiling a benefit analysis report?
2. What is the difference between a benefit analysis report and an annual total compensation report?

EMPLOYER TAXES AND BENEFIT ANALYSIS

Employers' tax rates and remittance methods tend to change annually based on federal, state, and local directives. Some developments in employer taxes that have changed since 2018 include the following:

- The EFTPS is a mandatory tax remittance method for new employers and the preferred method for existing employers.
- Additional guidance from the Financial Accounting Standards Board about the reporting of defined benefit and defined contribution plan accounting.
- Increased automation of employer taxes to improve and streamline remittance procedures.
- Continuing focus on employee wellness that includes health incentives as part of employees' total compensation package.
- Technology implementation that allows employees to access benefits on demand will become increasingly popular.
- Flexible scheduling will become the norm instead of the exception for many employees.
- Increased access to Employee Assistance Programs (EAPs) will acknowledge employee mental health needs.
- Employee development programs allowing employees to gain skills on demand will become an important part of the benefits package.

Summary of Employer Payroll Taxes and Labor Planning

Taxes are a part of conducting business. Whether taxes are income or employee-related, a business must abide by the regulations for timely submission and tax reporting. Employers have responsibilities for collecting federal income tax, Social Security, and Medicare taxes from their employees. The company is also responsible for setting aside federal unemployment taxes per employee based upon taxable wages. Apart from the federal taxes, employers may be liable for collecting, reporting, and submitting state and local income and unemployment taxes. Privilege taxes, such as the Denver Head Tax, may also be collected in specific districts. Employers who fail to meet the reporting, deposit, or submission requirements may be subject to fines and penalties.

Understanding the connection between the W-2 Form and the final paycheck of the year can save payroll accountants hours of work searching to find the answers to each employee's query. When the payroll accountant can explain the elements of the W-2 with confidence, fewer employees will come to ask why the difference, especially if the payroll accountant provides a written explanation with the final annual paycheck or W-2.

Although the human resources department could prepare the benefit analysis report, this duty can fall to the payroll accountant in smaller companies. Even in larger organizations, the human resources department will need specific information from the payroll accountant to feed into the benefit analysis report. Managers can examine the benefit analysis to understand how much their employees cost their department. Once receiving a total annual compensation report, the employee has a complete understanding of the compensation package, thereby feeding wage discussions and building a data-driven understanding of cost changes.

Key Points

- Employers share some of the same tax obligations as their employees. Some examples are Social Security, Medicare, and (in some states) SUTA taxes.
- FUTA taxes are paid only on the first $7,000 of each employee's annual taxable wage; SUTA tax wage base limits vary by state.

- Workers' compensation is a state-mandated insurance that employers carry to protect employees injured or killed while performing normal work duties.
- Workers' compensation insurance premium costs vary according to labor classifications.
- Payroll tax deposit frequency is determined by the amount of payroll taxes paid during a "lookback" period.
- All new employers are monthly schedule depositors until the next lookback period.
- Most employers file quarterly payroll tax returns on Form 941.
- Employers who deposit payroll taxes on a semiweekly basis must also file a Schedule B with their Form 941.
- Employers with less than $2,500 of annual tax liability file a Form 944 at the end of the calendar year.
- Employers report FUTA tax liability on an annual basis by using Form 940.
- Employers file an annual Form W-2 for each employee with the Social Security Administration.
- Form W-3 is the transmittal form used to report a company's aggregate annual wages and withholdings.
- Labor distribution affects company profitability, and benefit costs are a significant factor in managerial decisions.
- A total annual compensation report is used to communicate to employees the complete compensation package that they receive.
- Benefits packages are a strategic part of attracting high-quality candidates.

Vocabulary

American Rescue Plan Act (ARPA)	Form 940	Quarterly depositors
Annual schedule depositors	Form 941	Schedule B
Annual total compensation report	Form 944	Semiweekly schedule depositors
Automated Clearing House (ACH)	Form W-2	Statutory deductions
Benefit analysis	Form W-3	Tax remittance
Departmental classification	Labor distribution	
Electronic Federal Tax Payment System (EFTPS)	Lookback period	
	Monthly depositors	
	Next business day depositors	
	Payroll tax reports	

Review Questions

1. What taxes are paid only by the employer in most states?

2. What taxes are the shared responsibility of the employer and employee?

3. What taxes are paid by the employee only?

4. What determines the deposit requirements for employer taxes?

5. How often must a company report Form 941 earnings/withholdings?

6. How often must a company report Form 940 earnings/withholdings?

7. Which of the mandatory taxes have a maximum wage base?

8. How did the Affordable Care Act change Medicare tax withholding percentages?

9. What is the purpose of Form 941?

10. Which employers must use Schedule B?

11. How do employers know that they must use Form 944?

12. What is the purpose of Form 940?

13. What are three ways an employer could reduce their SUTA tax liability?

14. What is the difference between Form W-2 and Form W-3?

15. What are the employer's payroll responsibilities as far as taxes and other withholdings are concerned?

16. How does payroll relate to a company's costs of doing business?

17. What is meant by the term *labor distribution*?

18. How do payroll records inform managers about labor distribution?

19. What is a benefit analysis report?

20. How can a manager use the benefit analysis report in the decision-making process?

21. How do the payroll reports inform managers about department and company profitability?

Exercises Set A

E6-1A.
LO 6-1

Which of the following are *always* employer-only payroll obligations? (Select all that apply.)
a. Social Security tax
b. SUTA
c. Employee Income Tax
d. FUTA

E6-2A.
LO 6-1

As of 2021, which of the following accurately represents the full FUTA rate and wage base?
a. 0.6 percent, $142,800
b. Varies by state
c. 6.0 percent, $7,000
d. 0.6 percent, $7,000

E6-3A.
LO 6-1

Davis Reyes is the accountant for Heads Up Hat Corporation. As he prepares the payroll for the semimonthly pay period ending December 15, he notices that some of the year-to-date executives' salaries have exceeded $200,000. What payroll tax responsibilities does Heads Up Hat Corporation have, especially regarding FICA taxes? (Select all that apply.)
a. Social Security tax must be deducted from the executives' pay for those under the cap and matched by the corporation.
b. An additional 0.9 percent Medicare tax must be deducted from the employees' pay for those over the base and matched by the corporation.
c. An additional 0.9 percent Medicare tax must be deducted from the employee pay for those over the base, but no corporate match is required.
d. Medicare taxes should be deducted from all employees' pay and matched by the corporation.

E6-4A.
LO 6-2

Deshawn Booker is a payroll clerk at Elemental Exports. The company receives written notice from the IRS that the company is a monthly schedule depositor. How is the deposit schedule determined?
a. The age of the company.
b. The owner's choice or remittance frequency.
c. The payroll tax liability during the lookback period.
d. The total SUTA tax for the previous year

E6-5A.
LO 6-2

Match the amount of payroll tax liabilities from the lookback period with the appropriate tax deposit schedule.

a. $205,684 payroll tax for one pay period.

b. $2,490 annual payroll taxes.

c. $165,450 annual payroll taxes.

d. $48,350 annual payroll taxes.

1. Quarterly

2. Monthly

3. Semiweekly

4. Next business day

E6-6A.
LO 6-3

Which form(s) should be prepared and filed by companies with employees and payroll tax liabilities exceeding $50,000 as of December 31, 20XX? (Select all that apply.)

a. Form 940

b. Form W-4

c. Form 941

d. Form W-2

E6-7A.
LO 6-4

Gold Star Printing made its required tax deposits. However, it filed its third-quarter Form 941 on December 10, after receiving notice from the missing form's IRS. What is the failure to file penalty for Gold Star Printing?

a. 2 percent

b. 5 percent

c. 10 percent

d. 15 percent

E6-8A.
LO 6-4, 6-5

Which of the following is true about the cost of employees within a business context? (Select all that apply.)

a. Employees constitute a high cost of conducting business.

b. Hiring employees involves a significant overhead cost.

c. Costs associated with employees include only salary and limited hiring expenses.

d. The cost of providing employee benefits is minimal and of little importance.

E6-9A.
LO 6-6

Which of the following represents the purpose(s) of the benefit analysis report? (Select all that apply.)

a. Benchmarking with other companies.

b. Understanding of employer and employee benefits costs.

c. Billing employees for benefits costs.

d. Identification of opportunities for increasing profitability.

E6-10A.
LO 6-6

Why is it important to prepare the benefit analysis report or the total compensation report? (Select all that apply.)

a. The reports promote employee education about the total value of their salary and benefits.

b. The reports inform labor planning and employer cost strategies.

c. The reports may be used as employee contracts.

d. The reports may be used to accompany benefits billing.

E6-11A.
LO 6-1, 6-4

Which of the following is a characteristic of workers' compensation? (Select all that apply.)

a. Workers' compensation is an insurance policy.

b. Private employers are federally mandated to provide workers' compensation.

c. The cost of workers' compensation represents a labor expense to the business.

d. Workers' compensation is provided to cover employees who are injured or killed while performing work duties.

Problems Set A

P6-1A.
LO 6-1

Renee Signorini works for New & Old Apparel, which pays employees on a semimonthly basis. Renee's annual salary is $184,000. Calculate the following:

Pay Date	Prior YTD Earnings	Social Security Taxable Wages	Medicare Taxable Wages	Employer Share Social Security Tax	Employer Share Medicare Tax
October 15					
December 31					

P6-2A.
LO 6-1 6-3

White Lemon Cameras has the following employees:

Employee Name	Annual Taxable Wages
Mia Haskell	$26,000
Viktor Papadopoulos	35,000
Puja Anderson	32,000
Cady Billingmeier	29,000
Carl Johnson	46,000

White Lemon Cameras' SUTA tax rate is 5.4 percent and applies to the first $8,000 of employee wages. What is the annual amount due for each employee?

Employee	FUTA Due	SUTA Due
Mia Haskell		
Viktor Papadopoulos		
Puja Anderson		
Cady Billingmeier		
Carl Johnson		

P6-3A.
LO 6-1, 6-2, 6-3

El Arroyo North has 22 employees within Denver City and County. All the employees worked a predominant number of hours within the city. The employees earned $17.50 per hour and worked 160 hours each during the month. The employer must remit $4.00 per month per employee who earns more than $500 per month. Additionally, employees who earn more than $500 per month must have $5.75 withheld from their pay. What are the employee and company Occupational Privilege Tax for the employees of El Arroyo North?
Employee: _____
Employer: _____

P6-4A.
LO 6-1, 6-3

Gerald Utsey earned $47,500 in 2021 for a company in Kentucky. He is single with one dependent under 17 and is paid weekly. Compute the following employee share of the taxes using the percentage method in Appendix C and the state information in Appendix D. The box in Step 2 was not checked.
Federal income tax withholding: _____
Social Security tax: _____
Medicare tax: _____
State income tax withholding: _____

P6-5A.
LO 6-3

Using the information from P6-4A, compute the employer's share of the taxes. The FUTA rate in Kentucky for 2021 is 0.6 percent on the first $7,000 of employee wages, and the SUTA rate is 5.4 percent with a wage base of $11,100.

Federal income tax withholding: _____

Social Security tax: _____

Medicare tax: _____

FUTA tax: _____

SUTA tax: _____

State income tax withholding: _____

P6-6A.
LO 6-2

Veryclear Glassware is a new business owned by Samantha Peoples, the company president. Her first year of operation commenced on April 1, 2021. What schedule depositor would she be for the first year of operations?

P6-7A.
LO 6-3

Using the information from P6-6A, complete the following Form 941 for the second quarter of 2021. The report was signed on July 15, 2021

EIN: 78-7654398

Address: 23051 Old Redwood Highway, Sebastopol, California 95482, phone 707-555-5555

Number of employees: 7

Wages, tips, and other compensation paid during the second quarter of 2021: $244,798

Income tax withheld from employees: $48,000

Social Security tax withheld from employees: $15,177.48

Medicare tax withheld from employees: $3,549.57

Monthly tax liability:

April	$28,484.69
May	28,484.69
June	28,484.70

P6-8A.
LO 6-3

Using the information from P6-6A and P6-7A for Veryclear Glassware (California Employer Account Number 999-9999-9), complete the following State of California Form DE-9, Quarterly Contribution, and Report of Wages Report. Use 5.4 percent as the UI rate with a cap of $7,000 per employee, 0.1 percent as the ETT rate with a cap of $7,000 per employee, and 1.2 percent as the SDI rate with a cap of $128,298 per employee. All employees have worked the full quarter with the company, and all wages are subject to UI, ETT, and SDI. The California PIT taxes withheld for the quarter are $4,068. The company has deposited $6,656.18 for the quarter. Samantha Peoples submitted the form on 7/15/2021.

P6-9A.
LO 6-3

The Content Rabbit Graphics Company paid its 25 employees a total of $863,428.49 during 2020. Of these wages, $9,850 is exempt from retirement benefits (employer contributions to 401(k) plans). All employees have worked there for the full calendar year and reached the FUTA wage base during the first quarter; taxes were deposited then. The Content Rabbit Graphics Company is located at 3874 Palm Avenue, Sebring, Florida 20394. The owner is Eula Parks, EIN is 99-2039485, and the phone number is 461-555-9485. Complete Form 940, submitting it on January 13, 2021.

P6-10A.
LO 6-3

Leda Inc. is located at 433 Augusta Road, Caribou, Maine 04736, phone number 207-555-1212. The Federal EIN is 54-3910394, and it has a Maine Revenue Services number of 3884019. Owner Amanda Leda has asked you to prepare Form W-2 for each of the following employees of Leda Inc. as of December 31, 2021.

Form **941 for 2021:** **Employer's QUARTERLY Federal Tax Return**
(Rev. June 2021)
Department of the Treasury — Internal Revenue Service

951121

OMB No. 1545-0029

Employer identification number (EIN)

Name *(not your trade name)*

Trade name *(if any)*

Address

Number   Street   Suite or room number

City   State   ZIP code

Foreign country name   Foreign province/county   Foreign postal code

Report for this Quarter of 2021
(Check one.)

☐ **1:** January, February, March

☐ **2:** April, May, June

☐ **3:** July, August, September

☐ **4:** October, November, December

Go to *www.irs.gov/Form941* for instructions and the latest information.

Read the separate instructions before you complete Form 941. Type or print within the boxes.

Part 1:   **Answer these questions for this quarter.**

1 Number of employees who received wages, tips, or other compensation for the pay period including: *June 12* (Quarter 2), *Sept. 12* (Quarter 3), or *Dec. 12* (Quarter 4) **1**

2 Wages, tips, and other compensation **2**

3 Federal income tax withheld from wages, tips, and other compensation **3**

4 If no wages, tips, and other compensation are subject to social security or Medicare tax   ☐ Check and go to line 6.

	Column 1		Column 2
5a Taxable social security wages* . .		× 0.124 =	
5a (i) Qualified sick leave wages* . .		× 0.062 =	
5a (ii) Qualified family leave wages* .		× 0.062 =	
5b Taxable social security tips . . .		× 0.124 =	
5c Taxable Medicare wages & tips. . .		× 0.029 =	
5d Taxable wages & tips subject to Additional Medicare Tax withholding		× 0.009 =	

*Include taxable qualified sick and family leave wages for leave taken after March 31, 2021, on line 5a. Use lines 5a(i) and 5a(ii) **only** for wages paid after March 31, 2020, for leave taken before April 1, 2021.*

5e Total social security and Medicare taxes. Add Column 2 from lines 5a, 5a(i), 5a(ii), 5b, 5c, and 5d   **5e**

5f Section 3121(q) Notice and Demand—Tax due on unreported tips (see instructions) . .   **5f**

6 Total taxes before adjustments. Add lines 3, 5e, and 5f **6**

7 Current quarter's adjustment for fractions of cents **7**

8 Current quarter's adjustment for sick pay **8**

9 Current quarter's adjustments for tips and group-term life insurance **9**

10 Total taxes after adjustments. Combine lines 6 through 9 . . . .   **10**

11a Qualified small business payroll tax credit for increasing research activities. Attach Form 8974   **11a**

11b Nonrefundable portion of credit for qualified sick and family leave wages for leave taken before April 1, 2021 . . . .   **11b**

11c Nonrefundable portion of employee retention credit **11c**

▶ **You MUST complete all three pages of Form 941 and SIGN it.**   Next ▶

For Privacy Act and Paperwork Reduction Act Notice, see the back of the Payment Voucher.   Cat. No. 17001Z   Form **941** (Rev. 6-2021)

951221

Name *(not your trade name)*	Employer identification number (EIN)

Part 1: **Answer these questions for this quarter.** *(continued)*

11d Nonrefundable portion of credit for qualified sick and family leave wages for leave taken after March 31, 2021 . . . . **11d** [_____] .

11e Nonrefundable portion of COBRA premium assistance credit (see instructions for applicable quarters) . . . . **11e** [_____] .

11f Number of individuals provided COBRA premium assistance [_____]

11g Total nonrefundable credits. Add lines 11a, 11b, 11c, 11d, and 11e . . . . . . **11g** [_____] .

12 Total taxes after adjustments and nonrefundable credits. Subtract line 11g from line 10 . **12** [_____] .

13a Total deposits for this quarter, including overpayment applied from a prior quarter and overpayments applied from Form 941-X, 941-X (PR), 944-X, or 944-X (SP) filed in the current quarter **13a** [_____] .

13b Reserved for future use . . . . **13b** [████████] .

13c Refundable portion of credit for qualified sick and family leave wages for leave taken before April 1, 2021 . . . . **13c** [_____] .

13d Refundable portion of employee retention credit . . . . **13d** [_____] .

13e Refundable portion of credit for qualified sick and family leave wages for leave taken after March 31, 2021 . . . . **13e** [_____] .

13f Refundable portion of COBRA premium assistance credit (see instructions for applicable quarters) . . . . **13f** [_____] .

13g Total deposits and refundable credits. Add lines 13a, 13c, 13d, 13e, and 13f . . . . **13g** [_____] .

13h Total advances received from filing Form(s) 7200 for the quarter . . . . **13h** [_____] .

13i Total deposits and refundable credits less advances. Subtract line 13h from line 13g . . . **13i** [_____] .

14 Balance due. If line 12 is more than line 13i, enter the difference and see instructions . . . **14** [_____] .

15 Overpayment. If line 13i is more than line 12, enter the difference [_____] . Check one: ☐ Apply to next return. ☐ Send a refund.

Part 2: **Tell us about your deposit schedule and tax liability for this quarter.**

If you're unsure about whether you're a monthly schedule depositor or a semiweekly schedule depositor, see section 11 of Pub. 15.

16 Check one: ☐ **Line 12 on this return is less than $2,500 or line 12 on the return for the prior quarter was less than $2,500,** and you didn't incur a $100,000 next-day deposit obligation during the current quarter. If line 12 for the prior quarter was less than $2,500 but line 12 on this return is $100,000 or more, you must provide a record of your federal tax liability. If you're a monthly schedule depositor, complete the deposit schedule below; if you're a semiweekly schedule depositor, attach Schedule B (Form 941). Go to Part 3.

☐ **You were a monthly schedule depositor for the entire quarter.** Enter your tax liability for each month and total liability for the quarter, then go to Part 3.

Tax liability: Month 1 [_____] .

Month 2 [_____] .

Month 3 [_____] .

Total liability for quarter [_____] . **Total must equal line 12.**

☐ **You were a semiweekly schedule depositor for any part of this quarter.** Complete Schedule B (Form 941), Report of Tax Liability for Semiweekly Schedule Depositors, and attach it to Form 941. Go to Part 3.

▶ **You MUST complete all three pages of Form 941 and SIGN it.** Next ▶

951921

Name (not your trade name)	Employer identification number (EIN)

Part 3:   **Tell us about your business. If a question does NOT apply to your business, leave it blank.**

17   If your business has closed or you stopped paying wages . . . . ☐ Check here, and

enter the final date you paid wages   [/   /   ] ; also attach a statement to your return. See instructions.

18a   If you're a seasonal employer and you don't have to file a return for every quarter of the year . . . ☐ Check here.

18b   If you're eligible for the employee retention credit solely because your business is a recovery startup business ☐ Check here.

19	Qualified health plan expenses allocable to qualified sick leave wages for leave taken before April 1, 2021	19	▪
20	Qualified health plan expenses allocable to qualified family leave wages for leave taken before April 1, 2021	20	▪
21	Qualified wages for the employee retention credit	21	▪
22	Qualified health plan expenses for the employee retention credit	22	▪
23	Qualified sick leave wages for leave taken after March 31, 2021	23	▪
24	Qualified health plan expenses allocable to qualified sick leave wages reported on line 23	24	▪
25	Amounts under certain collectively bargained agreements allocable to qualified sick leave wages reported on line 23	25	▪
26	Qualified family leave wages for leave taken after March 31, 2021	26	▪
27	Qualified health plan expenses allocable to qualified family leave wages reported on line 26	27	▪
28	Amounts under certain collectively bargained agreements allocable to qualified family leave wages reported on line 26	28	▪

Part 4:   **May we speak with your third-party designee?**

Do you want to allow an employee, a paid tax preparer, or another person to discuss this return with the IRS? See the instructions for details.

☐ Yes. Designee's name and phone number   [   ]   [   ]

Select a 5-digit personal identification number (PIN) to use when talking to the IRS.   ☐ ☐ ☐ ☐ ☐

☐ No.

Part 5:   **Sign here. You MUST complete all three pages of Form 941 and SIGN it.**

Under penalties of perjury, I declare that I have examined this return, including accompanying schedules and statements, and to the best of my knowledge and belief, it is true, correct, and complete. Declaration of preparer (other than taxpayer) is based on all information of which preparer has any knowledge.

X   **Sign your name here**   [   ]   Print your name here   [   ]

Print your title here   [   ]

Date   [/   /   ]   Best daytime phone   [   ]

Paid Preparer Use Only   Check if you're self-employed . . . ☐

Preparer's name		PTIN	
Preparer's signature		Date	/ /
Firm's name (or yours if self-employed)		EIN	
Address		Phone	
City	State	ZIP code	

(Source: Internal Revenue Service)

EDD Employment Development Department State of California

QUARTERLY CONTRIBUTION RETURN AND REPORT OF WAGES
REMINDER: File your DE 9 and DE 9C together.

PLEASE TYPE THIS FORM—DO NOT ALTER PREPRINTED INFORMATION

00090112

YR QTR

QUARTER ENDED

DUE

DELINQUENT IF NOT POSTMARKED OR RECEIVED BY

EMPLOYER ACCOUNT NO.

DEPT. USE ONLY

DO NOT ALTER THIS AREA

P1 P2 C P U S A

T

Mo. Day Yr.

EFFECTIVE DATE

FEIN

A. NO WAGES PAID THIS QUARTER ☐

B. OUT OF BUSINESS/NO EMPLOYEES ☐

ADDITIONAL FEINS

B1. OUT OF BUSINESS DATE
M M D D Y Y Y Y

C. TOTAL SUBJECT WAGES PAID THIS QUARTER ....

D. UNEMPLOYMENT INSURANCE (UI) (Total Employee Wages up to $ _____ per employee per calendar year)

(D1) UI Rate %	(D2) UI TAXABLE WAGES FOR THE QUARTER	(D3) UI CONTRIBUTIONS
TIMES	=	0:00

E. EMPLOYMENT TRAINING TAX (ETT)

(E1) ETT Rate %	(E2) ETT CONTRIBUTIONS
TIMES UI Taxable Wages for the Quarter (D2) ...... =	0:00

F. STATE DISABILITY INSURANCE (SDI) (Total Employee Wages up to $ _____ per employee per calendar year)

(F1) SDI Rate %	(F2) SDI TAXABLE WAGES FOR THE QUARTER	(F3) SDI EMPLOYEE CONTRIBUTIONS WITHHELD
TIMES	=	0:00

G. CALIFORNIA PERSONAL INCOME TAX (PIT) WITHHELD ....

H. **SUBTOTAL** (Add Items D3, E2, F3, and G) 0:00

I. LESS: CONTRIBUTIONS AND WITHHOLDINGS PAID FOR THE QUARTER ....
(**DO NOT** INCLUDE PENALTY AND INTEREST PAYMENTS)

J. TOTAL TAXES DUE OR OVERPAID (Item H minus Item I) 0:00

If amount due, prepare a *Payroll Tax Deposit* (DE 88), include the correct payment quarter, and mail to: Employment Development Department, P.O. Box 826276, Sacramento, CA 94230-6276. **NOTE:** Do not mail payments along with the DE 9 and *Quarterly Contribution Return and Report of Wages (Continuation)* (DE 9C), as this may delay processing and result in erroneous penalty and interest charges. **Mandatory Electronic Funds Transfer (EFT)** filers must remit all SDI/PIT deposits by EFT to avoid a noncompliance penalty.

K. I declare that the above, to the best of my knowledge and belief, is true and correct. If a refund was claimed, a reasonable effort was made to refund any erroneous deductions to the affected employee(s).

Signature *Required* _____ Title _____ Phone (___) _____ Date _____
(Owner, Accountant, Preparer, etc.)

SIGN AND MAIL TO: State of California / Employment Development Department / P.O. Box 989071 / West Sacramento CA 95798-9071

DE 9 Rev. 1 (1-12) **(INTERNET)**   Page 1 of 2

Services Fast, Easy, and Convenient! Visit EDD's Web site at **www.edd.ca.gov**

(Source: Employment Development Department)

Form **940** for 2020: **Employer's Annual Federal Unemployment (FUTA) Tax Return**

Department of the Treasury — Internal Revenue Service

850113

OMB No. 1545-0028

Employer identification number (EIN)

Name *(not your trade name)*

Trade name *(if any)*

Address

Number   Street   Suite or room number

City   State   ZIP code

Foreign country name   Foreign province/county   Foreign postal code

Type of Return
(Check all that apply.)

☐ **a.** Amended

☐ **b.** Successor employer

☐ **c.** No payments to employees in 2020

☐ **d.** Final: Business closed or stopped paying wages

Go to *www.irs.gov/Form940* for instructions and the latest information.

Read the separate instructions before you complete this form. Please type or print within the boxes.

Part 1:	**Tell us about your return. If any line does NOT apply, leave it blank. See instructions before completing Part 1.**

1a If you had to pay state unemployment tax in one state only, enter the state abbreviation .   1a

1b If you had to pay state unemployment tax in more than one state, you are a multi-state employer . . . .   1b ☐ Check here. Complete Schedule A (Form 940).

2 If you paid wages in a state that is subject to **CREDIT REDUCTION** . . . .   2 ☐ Check here. Complete Schedule A (Form 940).

Part 2:	**Determine your FUTA tax before adjustments. If any line does NOT apply, leave it blank.**

3 Total payments to all employees . . . .   3 ____.

4 Payments exempt from FUTA tax . . . .   4 ____.

Check all that apply: **4a** ☐ Fringe benefits   **4c** ☐ Retirement/Pension   **4e** ☐ Other
                    4b ☐ Group-term life insurance   **4d** ☐ Dependent care

5 Total of payments made to each employee in excess of $7,000 . . . .   5 ____.

6 Subtotal (line 4 + line 5 = line 6) . . . .   6 ____.

7 Total taxable FUTA wages (line 3 – line 6 = line 7). See instructions . . . . . .   7 ____.

8 FUTA tax before adjustments (line 7 x 0.006 = line 8) . . . . . .   8 ____.

Part 3:	**Determine your adjustments. If any line does NOT apply, leave it blank.**

9 If ALL of the taxable FUTA wages you paid were excluded from state unemployment tax, multiply line 7 by 0.054 (line 7 × 0.054 = line 9). Go to line 12 . . . .   9 ____.

10 If SOME of the taxable FUTA wages you paid were excluded from state unemployment tax, OR you paid ANY state unemployment tax late (after the due date for filing Form 940), complete the worksheet in the instructions. Enter the amount from line 7 of the worksheet . .   10 ____.

11 If credit reduction applies, enter the total from Schedule A (Form 940) . . . . . .   11 ____.

Part 4:	**Determine your FUTA tax and balance due or overpayment. If any line does NOT apply, leave it blank.**

12 Total FUTA tax after adjustments (lines 8 + 9 + 10 + 11 = line 12) . . . . . .   12 ____.

13 FUTA tax deposited for the year, including any overpayment applied from a prior year   .   13 ____.

14 Balance due. If line 12 is more than line 13, enter the excess on line 14.
 • If line 14 is more than $500, you must deposit your tax.
 • If line 14 is $500 or less, you may pay with this return. See instructions . . . . . .   14 ____.

15 Overpayment. If line 13 is more than line 12, enter the excess on line 15 and check a box below   15 ____.

▶ You **MUST** complete both pages of this form and **SIGN** it.   Check one: ☐ Apply to next return.   ☐ Send a refund.

Next ➡

For Privacy Act and Paperwork Reduction Act Notice, see the back of the Payment Voucher.   Cat. No. 11234O   Form **940** (2020)

850212

Name (not your trade name)	Employer identification number (EIN)

Part 5: Report your FUTA tax liability by quarter only if line 12 is more than $500. If not, go to Part 6.

16 Report the amount of your FUTA tax liability for each quarter; do NOT enter the amount you deposited. If you had no liability for a quarter, leave the line blank.

16a **1st quarter** (January 1 – March 31) . . . . 16a [.   ]

16b **2nd quarter** (April 1 – June 30) . . . . 16b [.   ]

16c **3rd quarter** (July 1 – September 30) . . . . 16c [.   ]

16d **4th quarter** (October 1 – December 31) . . . . . . 16d [.   ]

17 **Total tax liability for the year** (lines 16a + 16b + 16c + 16d = line 17) **17** [.   ] **Total must equal line 12.**

Part 6: May we speak with your third-party designee?

Do you want to allow an employee, a paid tax preparer, or another person to discuss this return with the IRS? See the instructions for details.

☐ **Yes.** Designee's name and phone number [   ] [   ]

Select a 5-digit personal identification number (PIN) to use when talking to the IRS. ☐ ☐ ☐ ☐ ☐

☐ **No.**

Part 7: Sign here. You MUST complete both pages of this form and SIGN it.

Under penalties of perjury, I declare that I have examined this return, including accompanying schedules and statements, and to the best of my knowledge and belief, it is true, correct, and complete, and that no part of any payment made to a state unemployment fund claimed as a credit was, or is to be, deducted from the payments made to employees. Declaration of preparer (other than taxpayer) is based on all information of which preparer has any knowledge.

✗ **Sign your name here** [   ]

Print your name here [   ]

Print your title here [   ]

Date [/   /   ]

Best daytime phone [   ]

Paid Preparer Use Only Check if you are self-employed ☐

Preparer's name	[ ]	PTIN	[ ]
Preparer's signature	[ ]	Date	[/ /]
Firm's name (or yours if self-employed)	[ ]	EIN	[ ]
Address	[ ]	Phone	[ ]
City	[ ]	State [ ]	ZIP code	[ ]

Page **2**   Form **940** (2020)

(Source: Internal Revenue Service)

a Employee's social security number		
22222		

OMB No. 1545-0008

b Employer identification number (EIN)	**1** Wages, tips, other compensation	**2** Federal income tax withheld
c Employer's name, address, and ZIP code	**3** Social security wages	**4** Social security tax withheld
	5 Medicare wages and tips	**6** Medicare tax withheld
	7 Social security tips	**8** Allocated tips
d Control number	**9**	**10** Dependent care benefits
e Employee's first name and initial Last name Suff.	**11** Nonqualified plans	**12a** C o d e
	13 Statutory employee ☐ Retirement plan ☐ Third-party sick pay ☐	**12b** C o d e
	14 Other	**12c** C o d e
		12d C o d e
f Employee's address and ZIP code		

15 State Employer's state ID number	16 State wages, tips, etc.	17 State income tax	18 Local wages, tips, etc.	19 Local income tax	20 Locality name

Form **W-2** **Wage and Tax Statement**   **2021**   Department of the Treasury—Internal Revenue Service

Copy 1—For State, City, or Local Tax Department

(Source: Internal Revenue Service)

Sarah C. Niehaus
122 Main Street, #3
Caribou, ME 04736
SSN: 477-30-2234
Dependent Care Benefit: $1,800.00

Total 2021 wages: $34,768.53
401(k) contribution: $1,043.06
Section 125 contribution: $1,500.00
Federal income tax withheld: $2,028.00
Social Security tax withheld: $2,062.65
Medicare tax withheld: $482.39
State income tax withheld $1,869.08

Maxwell S. Law
1503 22nd Street
New Sweden, ME 04762
SSN: 493-55-2049

Total 2021 wages: $36,729.37
401(k) contribution: $1,469.18
Section 125 contribution: $1,675.00
Federal income tax withheld: none
Social Security tax withheld: $2,173.37
Medicare tax withheld: $508.29
State income tax withheld $1,947.94

Siobhan E. Manning
1394 West Highway 59
Woodland, ME 04694
SSN: 390-39-1002
Tuition in excess of $5,250: $1,575.00
(Include in boxes 1, 3, 5, 16)

Total 2021 wages: $30,034.87
401(k) contribution: $712.75
Section 125 contribution: $1,000.00
Federal income tax withheld: none
Social Security tax withheld: $1,897.81
Medicare tax withheld: $443.84
State income tax withheld $1,734.03

Donald A. Hendrix
1387 Rimbaud Avenue
Caribou, ME 04736
SSN: 288-30-5940

Total 2021 wages: $22,578.89
401(k) contribution: $1,354.73
Section 125 contribution: $2,250.00
Federal income tax withheld: $648.00
Social Security tax withheld: $1,260.39
Medicare tax withheld: $294.77
State income tax withheld $1,100.50

Alison K. Sutter
3664 Fairfield Street
Washburn, ME 04786
SSN: 490-55-0293

Total 2021 wages: $45,908.34
401(k) contribution: $2,754.50
Section 125 contribution: $1,750.00
Federal income tax withheld: $3,288.00
Social Security tax withheld: $2,737.82
Medicare tax withheld: $640.30
State income tax withheld $2,401.42

P6-11A.
LO 6-3

Using the information from P6-10A for Leda Inc., complete Form W-3 must accompany the company's W-2 Forms. Leda Inc. is a 941-SS payer and is a private, for-profit company. Amanda Leda is the owner; the phone number is 207-555-1212; no e-mail address to disclose; the fax number is 207-555-9898. No third-party sick pay was applied for 2020. The form was signed on January 20, 2022.

DO NOT STAPLE

33333	a Control number	For Official Use Only ▶ OMB No. 1545-0008		

b Kind of Payer (Check one)	941 ☐ CT-1 ☐ Military ☐ Hshld. emp. ☐ 943 ☐ Medicare govt. emp. ☐ 944 ☐	Kind of Employer (Check one)	None apply ☐ State/local non-501c ☐ 501c non-govt. ☐ State/local 501c ☐ Federal govt. ☐	Third-party sick pay (Check if applicable) ☐

c Total number of Forms W-2	d Establishment number	1 Wages, tips, other compensation	2 Federal income tax withheld
e Employer identification number (EIN)		3 Social security wages	4 Social security tax withheld
f Employer's name		5 Medicare wages and tips	6 Medicare tax withheld
		7 Social security tips	8 Allocated tips
		9	10 Dependent care benefits
		11 Nonqualified plans	12a Deferred compensation
g Employer's address and ZIP code			
h Other EIN used this year		13 For third-party sick pay use only	12b
15 State Employer's state ID number		14 Income tax withheld by payer of third-party sick pay	
16 State wages, tips, etc.	17 State income tax	18 Local wages, tips, etc.	19 Local income tax
Employer's contact person		Employer's telephone number	For Official Use Only
Employer's fax number		Employer's email address	

Under penalties of perjury, I declare that I have examined this return and accompanying documents, and, to the best of my knowledge and belief, they are true, correct, and complete.

Signature ▶ ___ Title ▶ ___ Date ▶ ___

Form **W-3** **Transmittal of Wage and Tax Statements**   **2021**   Department of the Treasury Internal Revenue Service

(Source: Internal Revenue Service)

P6-12A.
LO 6-4, 6-6

Park Mischner owns Old Times Buttons, which employs 20 people. Park wants to perform a benefits analysis report for one of the employees, Arnold Bower, for the year. Arnold's benefits package is as follows:

Annual salary: $35,650

401(k) contribution: 6 percent of annual salary. The company match is 75 percent of employee contribution up to 4 percent employee contribution.

Medical insurance deduction: $230 per month

Dental insurance: $15 per month

Complete the following Benefits Analysis Report for Arnold Bower for the year. Do not include FUTA and SUTA taxes. (Round your final answers to two decimal places.)

Yearly Benefit Costs	Company Cost	Arnold's Cost
Medical insurance	$7,200	$
Dental insurance	1,000	$
Life insurance	200	-0-
AD&D	50	-0-
Short-term disability	500	-0-
Long-term disability	250	-0-
401(k)	$	$
Social Security	$	$
Medicare	$	$
Tuition reimbursement	5,200	-0-
Total yearly benefit costs	$	$
Arnold's annual salary	$	
Total yearly benefit costs	$	
Total value of Arnold's compensation	$	

P6-13A.
LO 6-4, 6-5

Snow Mountain Equipment has 24 employees distributed among the following departments:

Sales: 5	Factory: 12	Administration: 7

The total annual payroll for Snow Mountain Equipment is $846,000. Compute the labor distribution based on an equal distribution among the departments.

Sales: _____

Factory: _____

Administration: _____

P6-14A.
LO 6-4, 6-5

For Snow Mountain Equipment in P6-13A, compute the labor distribution based on the number of employees per department:

Sales: _____

Factory: _____

Administration: _____

P6-15A.
LO 6-1, 6-4

Small Orange Fine Foods is a specialty grocery store. The employees are classified according to job titles for workers' compensation insurance premium computation purposes.

a. Based on the payroll estimates as of January 1, what is the total estimated workers' compensation premium for 20XX?

Employee Classification	Rate per $100 of Payroll	Estimated Payroll for 20XX	Workers' Compensation Premium
Grocery Clerk	$0.75	$192,500	
Shelf Stocker	1.90	212,160	
Stock Handler	2.40	237,120	
		Total Premium =	

b. The actual payroll for 20XX is listed below. What is the workers' compensation premium based on the actual payroll?

Employee Classification	Rate per $100 of Payroll	Actual Payroll for 20XX	Workers' Compensation Premium
Grocery Clerk	$0.75	$196,588	
Shelf Stocker	1.90	215,220	
Stock Handler	2.40	242,574	
		Total Premium =	

c. What is the difference between the actual and the estimated premiums?

_____

Exercises Set B

E6-1B.
LO 6-1
Of the following taxes, which one(s) is/are examples of mandatory and voluntary employee deductions? (Select all that apply.)
a. Social Security tax
b. Employee federal income tax
c. FUTA
d. 401(k) contributions

E6-2B.
LO 6-1
Which of the following is/are true about FUTA obligations? (Select all that apply.)
a. FUTA is an employer-only tax.
b. FUTA is subject to a 5.4 percent reduction based on employer and state factors.
c. FUTA is subject to a $20,000 wage base per employee.
d. FUTA applies to all companies.

E6-3B.
LO 6-1
Of the IRS-stipulated lookback periods, which one(s) is/are the most commonly used? (Select all that apply.)
a. Monthly
b. Semiweekly
c. Next Business Day
d. Annually

E6-4B.
LO 6-2
The Putney Youth Theater has annual payroll taxes of $3,564 during the most recent lookback period. Which payroll deposit frequency will the company have, based on that lookback period?
a. Quarterly
b. Monthly
c. Semiweekly
d. Annually

E6-5B.
LO 6-3
Ramesh Krishpoorthi is the new payroll accountant with Sal's Diamond Mart, Inc. in New York, NY. The company had a payroll tax liability of $49,580 during the most recent lookback period. For the quarter ending September 30, 2021, which federal form should he file to remit payroll taxes? (Select all that apply.)
a. Form 940
b. Form W-2
c. Form SS-8
d. Form 941

E6-6B.
LO 6-3
Which of the following is a form that must accompany all Forms W-2 submitted to the Social Security Administration?
a. Form 941
b. Form 940
c. Form W-3
d. Form W-4

E6-7B.
LO 6-4
What are the penalties associated with the lack of reporting and remitting payroll taxes? (Select all that apply.)
a. Failure to report
b. Failure to file
c. Failure to deposit
d. Failure to remit

E6-8B.
LO 6-4
Winston Briggs is the accounting supervisor for Cheeky Cat Furnishings, which has chosen to maintain its payroll on an in-house basis. For this purpose and has hired new accounting clerks. Which of the following are payroll responsibilities of Cheeky Cat Furnishings? (Select all that apply.)
a. Timely remittance of payroll taxes.
b. Remittance of voluntary deductions.
c. Accountability to employees and governmental agencies.
d. Publication of salary data in company-wide publications.

E6-9B.
LO 6-5

Which of the following represents the difference between the benefit analysis report and the annual total compensation report? (Select all that apply.)
a. The benefit analysis report is designed for review by company managers.
b. The annual total compensation report's intended audience is employees.
c. The benefit analysis report reflects actual benefit costs, and the annual total compensation report includes salary data.
d. The reports are maintained as public records.

E6-10B.
LO 6-5

Which of the following represent(s) the purpose(s) of the labor distribution report? (Select all that apply.)
a. Accurate payroll cost allocation among departments.
b. Explanation of individual employee costs.
c. Evaluation of labor planning efforts.
d. Determination of departmental performance.

E6-11B.
LO 6-1, 6-4

Sunny Day Flooring has employees in its manufacturing, sales, and administrative departments. Which department will have the highest rate for its workers' compensation insurance?
a. Manufacturing
b. Sales
c. Administrative
d. All departments will have the same rate.

Problems Set B

P6-1B.
LO 6-1

Brianna Whitman works for Schaum, Whitney, & Matte, LLP, in Washington, D.C., which pays employees on a biweekly basis. Brianna's annual salary is $160,000. The company started in 2021. Calculate the following:

Pay Period End	Prior YTD Earnings	Social Security Taxable Wages	Medicare Taxable Wages	Employer Share Social Security Tax	Employer Share Medicare Tax
September 24					
December 31					

P6-2B.
LO 6-1, 6-3

Mi Casa Restaurants of Las Cruces, New Mexico, has the following employees as of December 31:

Employee Name	Annual Taxable Wages
Arianna Shelby	$48,120
Mark Gomez	35,975
Cedric Wardly	22,350
Eric Burgess	40,950
Shionna Black	32,295

The company's SUTA tax rate is 4.25 percent and the wage base is $27,000. What is the annual amount of FUTA and SUTA taxes due for each employee?

Employee	FUTA Due	SUTA Due
Arianna Shelby		
Mark Gomez		
Cedric Wardly		
Eric Burgess		
Shionna Black		

P6-3B.
LO 6-1, 6-2, 6-3

Deep Mouse Designs has 22 employees within Denver City and County. The employees earned $12.50 per hour and worked 160 hours each during the month. The employer must remit $4.00 per month per employee who earns more than $500 per month. Additionally, employees who earn more than $500 per month must have $5.75 withheld from their pay. What is the employee and company Occupational Privilege Tax for these employees?

Employee: _____

Employer: _____

P6-4B.
LO 6-1, 6-2, 6-3

Fred Clark earned $55,875 in 2021 for Weather Gurus in Concord, New Hampshire. Weather Gurus' SUTA rate is 2.3 percent and has a wage base of $14,000 during 2021. Compute Weather Gurus' share of Fred's annual salary. The FUTA rate is 0.6 percent.

Social Security tax:_____

Medicare tax:_____

FUTA tax:_____

SUTA tax:_____

P6-5B.
LO 6-2, 6-3

Howard Murphy is the owner of Stormy Banana Films in West Hollywood, California. Stormy Banana Films had 15 employees with total annual wages of $214,750 (no one exceeded the Medicare tax surcharge or Social Security cap). The FUTA rate for California in 2021 is 2.2 percent because it is a credit reduction state. Stormy Banana Films has a SUTA rate of 3.2 percent for 2021 with a wage base of $7,000. Compute the following employer taxes:

Social Security tax:_____

Medicare tax:_____

FUTA tax:_____

SUTA tax:_____

P6-6B.
LO 6-1

Peaceful Cat Pet Foods is a new business owned by Sylvester Hammond. His first year of operations commenced on July 1, 2021. What schedule depositor would his company be for the first year of operations? Why?

P6-7B.
LO 6-3

Using the information from P6-6B, complete the following Form 941 for the third quarter of 2021. The form was signed by the owner on October 11, 2021.

EIN: 98-0050036

Address: 1021 Old Plainfield Road, Salina, California 95670

Phone: 707-555-0303

Number of employees: 8

Wages, tips, and other compensation paid during the third quarter of 2021: $302,374

Income tax withheld: $51,000

Monthly tax liability:

July	$32,421.08
August	32,421.08
September	32,421.07

Form **941 for 2021:** **Employer's QUARTERLY Federal Tax Return**

(Rev. June 2021)   Department of the Treasury — Internal Revenue Service

951121

OMB No. 1545-0029

Employer identification number (EIN) ☐☐ — ☐☐☐☐☐☐☐

Name *(not your trade name)* _____

Trade name *(if any)* _____

Address

Number	Street		Suite or room number
City		State	ZIP code
Foreign country name		Foreign province/county	Foreign postal code

Report for this Quarter of 2021
(Check one.)

☐ **1:** January, February, March

☐ **2:** April, May, June

☐ **3:** July, August, September

☐ **4:** October, November, December

Go to *www.irs.gov/Form941* for instructions and the latest information.

Read the separate instructions before you complete Form 941. Type or print within the boxes.

Part 1:   Answer these questions for this quarter.

1   Number of employees who received wages, tips, or other compensation for the pay period including: *June 12* (Quarter 2), *Sept. 12* (Quarter 3), or *Dec. 12* (Quarter 4) . . . . . .   **1** _____

2   Wages, tips, and other compensation . . . .   **2** _____

3   Federal income tax withheld from wages, tips, and other compensation . . . . . .   **3** _____

4   If no wages, tips, and other compensation are subject to social security or Medicare tax   ☐ **Check and go to line 6.**

	Column 1		**Column 2**	
5a Taxable social security wages* . .	_____ . _	× 0.124 =	_____ . _	
5a (i) Qualified sick leave wages* .	_____ . _	× 0.062 =	_____ . _	
5a (ii) Qualified family leave wages* .	_____ . _	× 0.062 =	_____ . _	
5b Taxable social security tips . . .	_____ . _	× 0.124 =	_____ . _	
5c Taxable Medicare wages & tips. .	_____ . _	× 0.029 =	_____ . _	
5d Taxable wages & tips subject to Additional Medicare Tax withholding	_____ . _	× 0.009 =	_____ . _	

*Include taxable qualified sick and family leave wages for leave taken after March 31, 2021, on line 5a. Use lines 5a(i) and 5a(ii) **only** for wages paid after March 31, 2020, for leave taken before April 1, 2021.*

5e   Total social security and Medicare taxes. Add Column 2 from lines 5a, 5a(i), 5a(ii), 5b, 5c, and 5d   **5e** _____

5f   Section 3121(q) Notice and Demand—Tax due on unreported tips (see instructions) . .   **5f** _____

6   Total taxes before adjustments. Add lines 3, 5e, and 5f . . . .   **6** _____

7   Current quarter's adjustment for fractions of cents . . . .   **7** _____

8   Current quarter's adjustment for sick pay . . . .   **8** _____

9   Current quarter's adjustments for tips and group-term life insurance . . . . . .   **9** _____

10   Total taxes after adjustments. Combine lines 6 through 9 . . . .   **10** _____

11a   Qualified small business payroll tax credit for increasing research activities. Attach Form 8974   **11a** _____

11b   Nonrefundable portion of credit for qualified sick and family leave wages for leave taken before April 1, 2021 . . . .   **11b** _____

11c   Nonrefundable portion of employee retention credit . . . .   **11c** _____

▶ **You MUST complete all three pages of Form 941 and SIGN it.**   Next ▶

For Privacy Act and Paperwork Reduction Act Notice, see the back of the Payment Voucher.   Cat. No. 17001Z   Form **941** (Rev. 6-2021)

951221

Name *(not your trade name)*	Employer identification number (EIN)

Part 1:   Answer these questions for this quarter. *(continued)*

11d Nonrefundable portion of credit for qualified sick and family leave wages for leave taken after March 31, 2021 . . . . **11d** [.]

11e Nonrefundable portion of COBRA premium assistance credit (see instructions for applicable quarters) . . . . **11e** [.]

11f Number of individuals provided COBRA premium assistance [ ]

11g Total nonrefundable credits. Add lines 11a, 11b, 11c, 11d, and 11e . . . . . **11g** [.]

12 Total taxes after adjustments and nonrefundable credits. Subtract line 11g from line 10 . **12** [.]

13a Total deposits for this quarter, including overpayment applied from a prior quarter and overpayments applied from Form 941-X, 941-X (PR), 944-X, or 944-X (SP) filed in the current quarter **13a** [.]

13b Reserved for future use . . . . **13b** [.]

13c Refundable portion of credit for qualified sick and family leave wages for leave taken before April 1, 2021 . . . . **13c** [.]

13d Refundable portion of employee retention credit . . . . **13d** [.]

13e Refundable portion of credit for qualified sick and family leave wages for leave taken after March 31, 2021 . . . . **13e** [.]

13f Refundable portion of COBRA premium assistance credit (see instructions for applicable quarters) . . . . **13f** [.]

13g Total deposits and refundable credits. Add lines 13a, 13c, 13d, 13e, and 13f . . . . . **13g** [.]

13h Total advances received from filing Form(s) 7200 for the quarter . . . . **13h** [.]

13i Total deposits and refundable credits less advances. Subtract line 13h from line 13g . . . **13i** [.]

14 Balance due. If line 12 is more than line 13i, enter the difference and see instructions . . . **14** [.]

15 Overpayment. If line 13i is more than line 12, enter the difference [.] Check one: ☐ Apply to next return. ☐ Send a refund.

Part 2:   Tell us about your deposit schedule and tax liability for this quarter.

If you're unsure about whether you're a monthly schedule depositor or a semiweekly schedule depositor, see section 11 of Pub. 15.

16 Check one: ☐   **Line 12 on this return is less than $2,500 or line 12 on the return for the prior quarter was less than $2,500, and you didn't incur a $100,000 next-day deposit obligation during the current quarter.** If line 12 for the prior quarter was less than $2,500 but line 12 on this return is $100,000 or more, you must provide a record of your federal tax liability. If you're a monthly schedule depositor, complete the deposit schedule below; if you're a semiweekly schedule depositor, attach Schedule B (Form 941). Go to Part 3.

☐   **You were a monthly schedule depositor for the entire quarter.** Enter your tax liability for each month and total liability for the quarter, then go to Part 3.

Tax liability: Month 1 [.]

Month 2 [.]

Month 3 [.]

Total liability for quarter [.]   Total must equal line 12.

☐   **You were a semiweekly schedule depositor for any part of this quarter.** Complete Schedule B (Form 941), Report of Tax Liability for Semiweekly Schedule Depositors, and attach it to Form 941. Go to Part 3.

▶ **You MUST complete all three pages of Form 941 and SIGN it.**   Next ▶

Form **941** (Rev. 6-2021)

951921

Name (not your trade name)	Employer identification number (EIN)

Part 3: Tell us about your business. If a question does NOT apply to your business, leave it blank.

17 If your business has closed or you stopped paying wages . . . . ☐ Check here, and

enter the final date you paid wages [/ /] ; also attach a statement to your return. See instructions.

18a If you're a seasonal employer and you don't have to file a return for every quarter of the year . . . ☐ Check here.

18b If you're eligible for the employee retention credit solely because your business is a recovery startup business ☐ Check here.

19 Qualified health plan expenses allocable to qualified sick leave wages for leave taken before April 1, 2021   **19** [.]

20 Qualified health plan expenses allocable to qualified family leave wages for leave taken before April 1, 2021   **20** [.]

21 Qualified wages for the employee retention credit . . . . **21** [.]

22 Qualified health plan expenses for the employee retention credit . . . . **22** [.]

23 Qualified sick leave wages for leave taken after March 31, 2021 . . . . **23** [.]

24 Qualified health plan expenses allocable to qualified sick leave wages reported on line 23   **24** [.]

25 Amounts under certain collectively bargained agreements allocable to qualified sick leave wages reported on line 23 . . . . **25** [.]

26 Qualified family leave wages for leave taken after March 31, 2021 . . . . **26** [.]

27 Qualified health plan expenses allocable to qualified family leave wages reported on line 26   **27** [.]

28 Amounts under certain collectively bargained agreements allocable to qualified family leave wages reported on line 26 . . . . **28** [.]

Part 4: May we speak with your third-party designee?

Do you want to allow an employee, a paid tax preparer, or another person to discuss this return with the IRS? See the instructions for details.

☐ Yes. Designee's name and phone number [ ] [ ]

    Select a 5-digit personal identification number (PIN) to use when talking to the IRS. ☐ ☐ ☐ ☐ ☐

☐ No.

Part 5: Sign here. You MUST complete all three pages of Form 941 and SIGN it.

Under penalties of perjury, I declare that I have examined this return, including accompanying schedules and statements, and to the best of my knowledge and belief, it is true, correct, and complete. Declaration of preparer (other than taxpayer) is based on all information of which preparer has any knowledge.

X Sign your name here [ ]

Print your name here [ ]

Print your title here [ ]

Date [/ /]

Best daytime phone [ ]

Paid Preparer Use Only   Check if you're self-employed . . . ☐

Preparer's name	[ ]	PTIN	[ ]
Preparer's signature	[ ]	Date	[/ /]
Firm's name (or yours if self-employed)	[ ]	EIN	[ ]
Address	[ ]	Phone	[ ]
City	[ ] State [ ]	ZIP code	[ ]

Form **941** (Rev. 6-2021)

(Source: Internal Revenue Service)

P6-8B.
LO 6-3

Using the information from P6-6B and P6-7B for Peaceful Cat Pet Foods, complete the following State of California Form DE-9, Quarterly Contribution Return and Report of Wages. The California employer account number is 989-8877-1. Use 5.4 percent as the UI rate, 0.1 percent as the ETT rate, and 1.2 percent as the SDI rate. California UI and ETT wage cap is $7,000 while SDI cap is $128,298 per employee. No employee has reached the SDI limit. All employees have worked with the company since July 1. The California PIT taxes withheld for the quarter are $40,000. The company has deposited no taxes for the quarter. Form DE-9 was completed and signed on October 11, 2021, with a due date of October 15, 2021.

P6-9B.
LO 6-3

Jealous Frog Toys paid its nine employees a total of $432,586.40 during 2020. All employees have worked there for the full calendar year and reached the FUTA wage base during the first quarter. Taxes were deposited on time. The employer contributed $12,470 to retirement plans during the year. Jealous Frog Toys is located at 783 Morehead Street, Fargo, ND 68383, phone number 701-555-3432. The owner is Noah Jackson, and the EIN is 73-4029848. Complete Form 940. The form was signed and submitted on January 8, 2021.

P6-10B.
LO 6-3

Philip Castor, owner of Castor Corporation, is located at 1310 Garrick Way, Sun Valley, Arizona, 86029, phone number 928-555-8842. The federal EIN is 20-1948348, and the state employer identification number is 9040-2038-1. Prepare Form W-2 (below) for each of the following employees of Castor Corporation as of December 31, 2021. The same deductions are allowed for state income tax as for federal.

Paul M. Parsons 5834 Moon Drive Sun Valley, AZ 86029 SSN: 578-33-3049	Total 2021 wages: $47,203.78 401(k) contribution: $2,832.23 Section 125 contribution: $1,400.00 Federal income tax withheld: $1,794.00 Social Security tax withheld: $2,839.83 Medicare tax withheld: $664.15 State income tax withheld: $1,435.25
Rachel Y. Maddox 32 Second Street Holbrook, AZ 86025 SSN: 734-00-1938 Tuition in excess of $5,250: $750 (Include in boxes 1, 3, 5, 16)	Total 2021 wages: $37,499.02 401(k) contribution: $1,124.97 Section 125 contribution: $500.00 Federal income tax withheld: $1,612.00 Social Security tax withheld: $2,340.44 Medicare tax withheld: $547.36 State income tax withheld: $1,223.24
Ari J. Featherstone 7784 Painted Desert Road Sun Valley, AZ 86029 SSN: 290-03-4992	Total 2021 wages: $41,904.29 401(k) contribution: $1,885.69 Federal income tax withheld: $3,146.00 Social Security tax withheld: $2,598.07 Medicare tax withheld: $607.61 State income tax withheld: $1,336.62
Connor L. Clearwater 7384 Ridge Road Woodruff, AZ 85942 SSN: 994-20-4837	Total 2021 wages: $29,874.37 401(k) contribution: $597.49 Section 125 contribution: $250.00 Federal income tax withheld: $390.00 Social Security tax withheld: $1,836.71 Medicare tax withheld: $429.55 State income tax withheld: $969.50
Tabitha L. Millen 229 Second Street #4A Holbrook, AZ 86025 SSN: 477-30-2234	Total 2021 wages: $15,889.04 Federal income tax withheld: $494.00 Social Security tax withheld: $985.12 Medicare tax withheld: $230.39 State income tax withheld: $411.53

P6-11B.
LO 6-3

Using the information from P6-10B for Castor Corporation, complete Form W3 (above) that must accompany the company's Form W2s. Castor Corporation is a 941-SS payer and is a private, for-profit company. No third-party sick pay was applied for 2021. The W-3 was signed and submitted on January 12, 2022.

EDD Employment Development Department
State of California

QUARTERLY CONTRIBUTION RETURN AND REPORT OF WAGES
REMINDER: File your DE 9 and DE 9C together.
PLEASE TYPE THIS FORM—DO NOT ALTER PREPRINTED INFORMATION

00090112

	YR	QTR

QUARTER ENDED

DUE

DELINQUENT IF NOT POSTMARKED OR RECEIVED BY

EMPLOYER ACCOUNT NO.

DEPT. USE ONLY

DO NOT ALTER THIS AREA

P1 P2 C P U S A

T

| | Mo. | Day | Yr. |
EFFECTIVE DATE

FEIN

A. NO WAGES PAID THIS QUARTER ☐   **B.** OUT OF BUSINESS/NO EMPLOYEES ☐

ADDITIONAL FEINS

B1. OUT OF BUSINESS DATE
M M D D Y Y Y Y

C. TOTAL SUBJECT WAGES PAID THIS QUARTER ....

D. UNEMPLOYMENT INSURANCE (UI) (Total Employee Wages up to $_____ per employee per calendar year)

(D1) UI Rate %   TIMES   (D2) UI TAXABLE WAGES FOR THE QUARTER   =   (D3) UI CONTRIBUTIONS   0:00

E. EMPLOYMENT TRAINING TAX (ETT)

(E1) ETT Rate %   TIMES   UI Taxable Wages for the Quarter (D2) ......   =   (E2) ETT CONTRIBUTIONS   0:00

F. STATE DISABILITY INSURANCE (SDI) (Total Employee Wages up to $_____ per employee per calendar year)

(F1) SDI Rate %   TIMES   (F2) SDI TAXABLE WAGES FOR THE QUARTER   =   (F3) SDI EMPLOYEE CONTRIBUTIONS WITHHELD   0:00

G. CALIFORNIA PERSONAL INCOME TAX (PIT) WITHHELD ....

H. SUBTOTAL (Add Items D3, E2, F3, and G) 0:00

I. LESS: CONTRIBUTIONS AND WITHHOLDINGS PAID FOR THE QUARTER ....
(**DO NOT** INCLUDE PENALTY AND INTEREST PAYMENTS)

J. TOTAL TAXES DUE OR OVERPAID (Item H minus Item I) 0:00

If amount due, prepare a *Payroll Tax Deposit* (DE 88), include the correct payment quarter, and mail to: Employment Development Department, P.O. Box 826276, Sacramento, CA 94230-6276. **NOTE:** Do not mail payments along with the DE 9 and *Quarterly Contribution Return and Report of Wages (Continuation)* (DE 9C), as this may delay processing and result in erroneous penalty and interest charges. **Mandatory Electronic Funds Transfer (EFT)** filers must remit all SDI/PIT deposits by EFT to avoid a noncompliance penalty.

K. I declare that the above, to the best of my knowledge and belief, is true and correct. If a refund was claimed, a reasonable effort was made to refund any erroneous deductions to the affected employee(s).

Signature *Required* _____ Title _____ Phone (___) _____ Date_____
(Owner, Accountant, Preparer, etc.)

SIGN AND MAIL TO: State of California / Employment Development Department / P.O. Box 989071 / West Sacramento CA 95798-9071

DE 9 Rev. 1 (1-12) **(INTERNET)**   Page 1 of 2

e-Services   Fast, Easy, and Convenient!
Visit EDD's Web site at www.edd.ca.gov

(Source: State of California)

Form **940 for 2020:** **Employer's Annual Federal Unemployment (FUTA) Tax Return**   850113

Department of the Treasury — Internal Revenue Service

OMB No. 1545-0028

Employer identification number (EIN) ☐☐ – ☐☐☐☐☐☐☐

Name *(not your trade name)*

Trade name *(if any)*

Address

Number   Street   Suite or room number

City   State   ZIP code

Foreign country name   Foreign province/county   Foreign postal code

Type of Return
(Check all that apply.)

☐ **a.** Amended

☐ **b.** Successor employer

☐ **c.** No payments to employees in 2020

☐ **d.** Final: Business closed or stopped paying wages

Go to *www.irs.gov/Form940* for instructions and the latest information.

Read the separate instructions before you complete this form. Please type or print within the boxes.

Part 1: **Tell us about your return. If any line does NOT apply, leave it blank. See instructions before completing Part 1.**

1a If you had to pay state unemployment tax in one state only, enter the state abbreviation . **1a** ☐ ☐

1b If you had to pay state unemployment tax in more than one state, you are a multi-state employer . **1b** ☐ Check here. Complete Schedule A (Form 940).

2 If you paid wages in a state that is subject to CREDIT REDUCTION . **2** ☐ Check here. Complete Schedule A (Form 940).

Part 2: **Determine your FUTA tax before adjustments. If any line does NOT apply, leave it blank.**

3 Total payments to all employees . **3** ☐

4 Payments exempt from FUTA tax . **4** ☐

Check all that apply: **4a** ☐ Fringe benefits   **4c** ☐ Retirement/Pension   **4e** ☐ Other
4b ☐ Group-term life insurance   **4d** ☐ Dependent care

5 Total of payments made to each employee in excess of $7,000 . **5** ☐

6 Subtotal (line 4 + line 5 = line 6) . **6** ☐

7 Total taxable FUTA wages (line 3 – line 6 = line 7). See instructions . **7** ☐

8 FUTA tax before adjustments (line 7 x 0.006 = line 8) . **8** ☐

Part 3: **Determine your adjustments. If any line does NOT apply, leave it blank.**

9 If ALL of the taxable FUTA wages you paid were excluded from state unemployment tax, multiply line 7 by 0.054 (line 7 × 0.054 = line 9). Go to line 12 . **9** ☐

10 If SOME of the taxable FUTA wages you paid were excluded from state unemployment tax, OR you paid ANY state unemployment tax late (after the due date for filing Form 940), complete the worksheet in the instructions. Enter the amount from line 7 of the worksheet . **10** ☐

11 If credit reduction applies, enter the total from Schedule A (Form 940) . **11** ☐

Part 4: **Determine your FUTA tax and balance due or overpayment. If any line does NOT apply, leave it blank.**

12 Total FUTA tax after adjustments (lines 8 + 9 + 10 + 11 = line 12) . **12** ☐

13 FUTA tax deposited for the year, including any overpayment applied from a prior year . **13** ☐

14 Balance due. If line 12 is more than line 13, enter the excess on line 14.
- If line 14 is more than $500, you must deposit your tax.
- If line 14 is $500 or less, you may pay with this return. See instructions . **14** ☐

15 Overpayment. If line 13 is more than line 12, enter the excess on line 15 and check a box below **15** ☐

▶ You **MUST** complete both pages of this form and **SIGN** it.   Check one: ☐ Apply to next return. ☐ Send a refund.

Next ▶

For Privacy Act and Paperwork Reduction Act Notice, see the back of the Payment Voucher.   Cat. No. 11234O   Form **940** (2020)

850212

Name *(not your trade name)*	**Employer identification number (EIN)**

Part 5:   Report your FUTA tax liability by quarter only if line 12 is more than $500. If not, go to Part 6.

16   Report the amount of your FUTA tax liability for each quarter; do NOT enter the amount you deposited. If you had no liability for a quarter, leave the line blank.

   16a   1st quarter (January 1 – March 31) . . . .   **16a** [▪   ]

   16b   2nd quarter (April 1 – June 30) . . . .   **16b** [▪   ]

   16c   3rd quarter (July 1 – September 30) . . . .   **16c** [▪   ]

   16d   4th quarter (October 1 – December 31) . . . .   **16d** [▪   ]

17   Total tax liability for the year (lines 16a + 16b + 16c + 16d = line 17)   **17** [▪   ]   **Total must equal line 12.**

Part 6:   May we speak with your third-party designee?

Do you want to allow an employee, a paid tax preparer, or another person to discuss this return with the IRS? See the instructions for details.

☐ **Yes.**   Designee's name and phone number   [   ]   [   ]

Select a 5-digit personal identification number (PIN) to use when talking to the IRS. [   ] [   ] [   ] [   ] [   ]

☐ **No.**

Part 7:   Sign here. You MUST complete both pages of this form and SIGN it.

Under penalties of perjury, I declare that I have examined this return, including accompanying schedules and statements, and to the best of my knowledge and belief, it is true, correct, and complete, and that no part of any payment made to a state unemployment fund claimed as a credit was, or is to be, deducted from the payments made to employees. Declaration of preparer (other than taxpayer) is based on all information of which preparer has any knowledge.

✗ **Sign your name here**   [   ]   Print your name here   [   ]

                                                                        Print your title here   [   ]

   Date   [/   /   ]   Best daytime phone   [   ]

Paid Preparer Use Only   Check if you are self-employed ☐

Preparer's name	[ ]	PTIN	[ ]
Preparer's signature	[ ]	Date	[/ /]
Firm's name (or yours if self-employed)	[ ]	EIN	[ ]
Address	[ ]	Phone	[ ]
City	[ ] State [ ]	ZIP code	[ ]

(Source: Internal Revenue Service)

22222	**a** Employee's social security number	OMB No. 1545-0008	
b Employer identification number (EIN)		**1** Wages, tips, other compensation	**2** Federal income tax withheld
c Employer's name, address, and ZIP code		**3** Social security wages	**4** Social security tax withheld
		5 Medicare wages and tips	**6** Medicare tax withheld
		7 Social security tips	**8** Allocated tips
d Control number		**9**	**10** Dependent care benefits
e Employee's first name and initial Last name Suff.		**11** Nonqualified plans	**12a** Code
		13 Statutory employee ☐ Retirement plan ☐ Third-party sick pay ☐	**12b** Code
		14 Other	**12c** Code
			12d Code
f Employee's address and ZIP code			

15 State Employer's state ID number	**16** State wages, tips, etc.	**17** State income tax	**18** Local wages, tips, etc.	**19** Local income tax	**20** Locality name

Form **W-2** Wage and Tax Statement   **2021**   Department of the Treasury—Internal Revenue Service

Copy 1—For State, City, or Local Tax Department

(Source: Internal Revenue Service)

DO NOT STAPLE

33333	**a** Control number	For Official Use Only ▶ OMB No. 1545-0008	
b **Kind of Payer** (Check one) ▶	941 ☐ CT-1 ☐ Military ☐ Hshld. emp. ☐ 943 ☐ Medicare govt. emp. ☐ 944 ☐	**Kind of Employer** (Check one) ▶ None apply ☐ State/local non-501c ☐ 501c non-govt. ☐ State/local 501c ☐ Federal govt. ☐	Third-party sick pay (Check if applicable) ☐
c Total number of Forms W-2	**d** Establishment number	**1** Wages, tips, other compensation	**2** Federal income tax withheld
e Employer identification number (EIN)		**3** Social security wages	**4** Social security tax withheld
f Employer's name		**5** Medicare wages and tips	**6** Medicare tax withheld
		7 Social security tips	**8** Allocated tips
		9	**10** Dependent care benefits
g Employer's address and ZIP code		**11** Nonqualified plans	**12a** Deferred compensation
h Other EIN used this year		**13** For third-party sick pay use only	**12b**
15 State Employer's state ID number		**14** Income tax withheld by payer of third-party sick pay	
16 State wages, tips, etc.	**17** State income tax	**18** Local wages, tips, etc.	**19** Local income tax
Employer's contact person		Employer's telephone number	For Official Use Only
Employer's fax number		Employer's email address	

Under penalties of perjury, I declare that I have examined this return and accompanying documents, and, to the best of my knowledge and belief, they are true, correct, and complete.

Signature ▶   Title ▶   Date ▶

Form **W-3** Transmittal of Wage and Tax Statements   **2021**   Department of the Treasury Internal Revenue Service

(Source: Internal Revenue Service)

P6-12B.
LO 6-5, 6-6

Oak Cove Resorts has 8 employees. The owner wants to perform a benefits analysis report for the year for one of its employees, Jerrika Cassidy. Jerrika's benefits package is as follows:

Annual Salary: $42,950

401(k) contribution: 8 percent of annual salary, the company match is half of the employee's contribution, up to 5 percent of the employee's annual salary.

Medical insurance deduction: $340 per month

Dental insurance: $21 per month

Complete the following Benefits Analysis Report for Jerrika Cassidy for 2021.

Yearly Benefit Costs	Company Cost	Jerrika's Cost
Medical insurance	$9,600	$
Dental insurance	800	$
Life insurance	1,200	-0-
AD&D	125	-0-
Short-term disability	500	-0-
Long-term disability	250	-0-
401(k)	$	$
Social Security	$	$
Medicare	$	$
Tuition reimbursement	2,500	-0-
Total yearly benefit costs	$	
Jerrika's annual salary	$	
Total value of Jerrika's compensation	$	

P6-13B.
LO 6-4, 6-5

Superfan Sportsgear has 30 employees distributed among the following departments:

Sales: 7   Factory: 13   Administration: 10

The total annual payroll for Superfan Sportsgear is $975,580.
Compute the labor distribution based on the equal distribution among the departments.

Sales: _____
Factory: _____
Administration: _____

P6-14B.
LO 6-4, 6-5

For Superfan Sportsgear in P6-13B, compute the labor distribution based on the number of employees per department:

Sales: _____
Factory: _____
Administration: _____

P6-15B.
LO 6-1, 6-4

At Fox Furniture, employees are classified according to the job title for workers' compensation insurance premium computation purposes.

a. Based on the following payroll estimates as of January 1, what is the estimated workers' compensation insurance premium for the year 2021?

Employee Classification	Rate per $100 of Payroll	Estimated Payroll for 2021	Workers' Compensation Premium
Sales Associate	$0.55	$213,680	
Loader	2.15	155,240	
Furniture Builder	2.95	102,590	
		Total Premium =	

b. The actual payroll for 2021 is listed below. What is the workers' compensation premium based on the actual payroll?

Employee Classification	Rate per $100 of Payroll	Actual Payroll for 2021	Workers' Compensation Premium
Sales Associate	$0.55	$228,944	
Loader	2.15	163,743	
Furniture Builder	2.95	105,389	
		Total Premium =	

c. What is the difference between the actual and the estimated premiums?

_____

Critical Thinking

6-1. Burton Book Memorabilia is a semiweekly depositor. Following a special project's success, Kelly Burton, the owner, pays each of the 250 employees a $2,000 bonus on August 13, 2021. Assume a 25 percent income tax rate. When will Kelly need to deposit the payroll taxes?

6-2. Claude Lopez is the president of Zebra Antiques. His employee, Dwight Francis, is due a raise. Dwight's current benefit analysis is as follows:

Yearly Benefit Costs	Company Cost (Current)	Employee Cost (Current)
Medical insurance	$ 8,000.00	$ 1,200
Dental insurance	120.00	120
Life insurance	300.00	-0-
AD&D	150.00	-0-
Short-term disability	60.00	-0-
Long-term disability	30.00	-0-
401(k)	750.00	1,500
Social Security	3,018.16	3,018.16
Medicare	705.86	705.86
Tuition reimbursement	2,000.00	-0-
Total yearly benefit costs (employer)	15,134.02	
Employee's annual salary	50,000.00	
Total value of employee's compensation	$65,134.02	

Compute the benefit analysis assuming:
- 3 percent increase in pay.
- Dwight will increase his 401(k) contribution to 8 percent with a company match of 50 percent up to 6 percent of the employee's annual salary.
- 15 percent increase in medical and dental insurance premiums.

Yearly Benefit Costs	Company Cost (New)	Employee Cost (New)
Medical insurance	$	$
Dental insurance	$	$
Life insurance	$300	-0-
AD&D	$150	-0-
Short-term disability	$60	-0-
Long-term disability	$30	-0-
401(k)	$	$
Social Security	$	$
Medicare	$	$
Tuition reimbursement	$2,000	-0-
Total yearly benefit costs (employer)	$	
Dwight's annual salary	$	
The total value of employee's compensation	$	

In the Real World: Scenario for Discussion

In Shavertown, Pennsylvania, the Wilkes-Barre Bookkeeping LLC owner was indicted for embezzling over $376,225 of his clients' payroll tax remittances between 2010 and 2016 and for lying to clients about his actions. Additionally, he embezzled nearly $70,000 from a nonprofit for which he was the treasurer. He was sentenced to 38 months in prison and ordered to pay restitution totaling nearly $500,000. Do you think this was a fair sentence? Why or why not?

Internet Activities

6-1. Would you like to know more about the Employment Cost Index? Check out the videos from the Bureau of Labor Statistics: www.bls.gov/eci/videos.htm

6-2. Go to www.bizfilings.com/toolkit/sbg/tax-info/payroll-taxes/unemployment.aspx and check out the unemployment tax laws for your state.

6-3. Want to know more about the concepts in this chapter? Go to one or more of the following sites. What are two or three things you notice about the information on the site?

www.smallbusiness.chron.com/example-employee-compensation-plan-10068.html

http://yourbusiness.azcentral.com/labor-cost-distribution-report-26061.html

www.irs.gov/publications/p80/ar02.html

6-4. Check out the employer payroll tax estimation tool at https://gusto.com/tools/employer-tax-calculator

6-5. Would you like to explore specific topics about being an employer in more depth? Check out https://www.employer.gov/

Continuing Payroll Project: Prevosti Farms and Sugarhouse

The first quarter tax return needs to be filed for Prevosti Farms and Sugarhouse by April 15, 2021. For the taxes, assume the second February payroll amounts were duplicated for the March 5 and March 19 payroll periods, and the new benefit elections went into effect as planned (see Chapter 4). The form was completed and signed on April 9, 2021.

	Exempt	
Benefit Information	**Federal**	**FICA**
Health Insurance	Yes	Yes
Life Insurance	Yes	Yes
Long-term care	Yes	Yes
FSA	Yes	Yes
401(k)	Yes	No
Gym	No	No

Number of employees	8
Gross quarterly wages (Exclusive of fringe benefits)	$32,086.87
Federal income tax withheld	360.00
401(k) contributions	1,259.90
Section 125 withheld	4,080.00
Gym membership	90.00
Month 1	-0-
Month 2	1,918.18
Month 3	2,726.72

Complete Form 941 for Prevosti Farms and Sugarhouse. Prevosti Farms and Sugarhouse was assigned EIN 22-6654454.

Form **941 for 2021:** Employer's QUARTERLY Federal Tax Return

(Rev. June 2021)

Department of the Treasury — Internal Revenue Service

951121

OMB No. 1545-0029

Employer identification number (EIN) ☐☐ – ☐☐☐☐☐☐☐

Name *(not your trade name)*

Trade name *(if any)*

Address

Number   Street   Suite or room number

City   State   ZIP code

Foreign country name   Foreign province/county   Foreign postal code

Report for this Quarter of 2021
(Check one.)

☐ **1:** January, February, March

☐ **2:** April, May, June

☐ **3:** July, August, September

☐ **4:** October, November, December

Go to *www.irs.gov/Form941* for instructions and the latest information.

Read the separate instructions before you complete Form 941. Type or print within the boxes.

Part 1: Answer these questions for this quarter.

1 Number of employees who received wages, tips, or other compensation for the pay period including: *June 12* (Quarter 2), *Sept. 12* (Quarter 3), or *Dec. 12* (Quarter 4) . . . . **1** ☐

2 Wages, tips, and other compensation . . . . **2** ☐

3 Federal income tax withheld from wages, tips, and other compensation . . . . **3** ☐

4 If no wages, tips, and other compensation are subject to social security or Medicare tax ☐ **Check and go to line 6.**

	Column 1		Column 2	
5a Taxable social security wages* . .	☐	× 0.124 =	☐	
5a (i) Qualified sick leave wages* .	☐	× 0.062 =	☐	
5a (ii) Qualified family leave wages* .	☐	× 0.062 =	☐	
5b Taxable social security tips . . .	☐	× 0.124 =	☐	
5c Taxable Medicare wages & tips . .	☐	× 0.029 =	☐	
5d Taxable wages & tips subject to Additional Medicare Tax withholding	☐	× 0.009 =	☐	

*Include taxable qualified sick and family leave wages for leave taken after March 31, 2021, on line 5a. Use lines 5a(i) and 5a(ii) **only** for wages paid after March 31, 2020, for leave taken before April 1, 2021.*

5e Total social security and Medicare taxes. Add Column 2 from lines 5a, 5a(i), 5a(ii), 5b, 5c, and 5d **5e** ☐

5f Section 3121(q) Notice and Demand—Tax due on unreported tips (see instructions) . . **5f** ☐

6 Total taxes before adjustments. Add lines 3, 5e, and 5f . . . . **6** ☐

7 Current quarter's adjustment for fractions of cents . . . . **7** ☐

8 Current quarter's adjustment for sick pay . . . . **8** ☐

9 Current quarter's adjustments for tips and group-term life insurance . . . . . **9** ☐

10 Total taxes after adjustments. Combine lines 6 through 9 . . . . **10** ☐

11a Qualified small business payroll tax credit for increasing research activities. Attach Form 8974 **11a** ☐

11b Nonrefundable portion of credit for qualified sick and family leave wages for leave taken before April 1, 2021 . . . . **11b** ☐

11c Nonrefundable portion of employee retention credit . . . . **11c** ☐

▶ **You MUST complete all three pages of Form 941 and SIGN it.**

Next ▶

For Privacy Act and Paperwork Reduction Act Notice, see the back of the Payment Voucher.   Cat. No. 17001Z   Form **941** (Rev. 6-2021)

951221

Name *(not your trade name)*	Employer identification number (EIN)

Part 1:   **Answer these questions for this quarter.** *(continued)*

11d   Nonrefundable portion of credit for qualified sick and family leave wages for leave taken after March 31, 2021 . . . . **11d** [.]

11e   Nonrefundable portion of COBRA premium assistance credit (see instructions for applicable quarters) . . . . **11e** [.]

11f   Number of individuals provided COBRA premium assistance   [   ]

11g   Total nonrefundable credits. Add lines 11a, 11b, 11c, 11d, and 11e . . . . **11g** [.]

12   Total taxes after adjustments and nonrefundable credits. Subtract line 11g from line 10 . **12** [.]

13a   Total deposits for this quarter, including overpayment applied from a prior quarter and overpayments applied from Form 941-X, 941-X (PR), 944-X, or 944-X (SP) filed in the current quarter   **13a** [.]

13b   Reserved for future use . . . . **13b** [.]

13c   Refundable portion of credit for qualified sick and family leave wages for leave taken before April 1, 2021 . . . . **13c** [.]

13d   Refundable portion of employee retention credit . . . . **13d** [.]

13e   Refundable portion of credit for qualified sick and family leave wages for leave taken after March 31, 2021 . . . . **13e** [.]

13f   Refundable portion of COBRA premium assistance credit (see instructions for applicable quarters) . . . . **13f** [.]

13g   Total deposits and refundable credits. Add lines 13a, 13c, 13d, 13e, and 13f . . . . . **13g** [.]

13h   Total advances received from filing Form(s) 7200 for the quarter . . . . **13h** [.]

13i   Total deposits and refundable credits less advances. Subtract line 13h from line 13g . . **13i** [.]

14   Balance due. If line 12 is more than line 13i, enter the difference and see instructions . . . **14** [.]

15   Overpayment. If line 13i is more than line 12, enter the difference   [.]   Check one: ☐ Apply to next return.   ☐ Send a refund.

Part 2:   **Tell us about your deposit schedule and tax liability for this quarter.**

If you're unsure about whether you're a monthly schedule depositor or a semiweekly schedule depositor, see section 11 of Pub. 15.

16   Check one: ☐   Line 12 on this return is less than $2,500 or line 12 on the return for the prior quarter was less than $2,500, and you didn't incur a $100,000 next-day deposit obligation during the current quarter. If line 12 for the prior quarter was less than $2,500 but line 12 on this return is $100,000 or more, you must provide a record of your federal tax liability. If you're a monthly schedule depositor, complete the deposit schedule below; if you're a semiweekly schedule depositor, attach Schedule B (Form 941). Go to Part 3.

☐   You were a monthly schedule depositor for the entire quarter. Enter your tax liability for each month and total liability for the quarter, then go to Part 3.

Tax liability: Month 1   [.]

Month 2   [.]

Month 3   [.]

Total liability for quarter   [.]   Total must equal line 12.

☐   You were a semiweekly schedule depositor for any part of this quarter. Complete Schedule B (Form 941), Report of Tax Liability for Semiweekly Schedule Depositors, and attach it to Form 941. Go to Part 3.

▶ **You MUST complete all three pages of Form 941 and SIGN it.**   Next ▶

951921

Name *(not your trade name)*	Employer identification number (EIN)

Part 3: **Tell us about your business. If a question does NOT apply to your business, leave it blank.**

17 If your business has closed or you stopped paying wages . . . . □ Check here, and

enter the final date you paid wages [/   /   ] ; also attach a statement to your return. See instructions.

18a **If you're a seasonal employer and you don't have to file a return for every quarter of the year** . . . □ Check here.

18b **If you're eligible for the employee retention credit solely because your business is a recovery startup business** □ Check here.

19 Qualified health plan expenses allocable to qualified sick leave wages for leave taken before April 1, 2021   19 [.]

20 Qualified health plan expenses allocable to qualified family leave wages for leave taken before April 1, 2021   20 [.]

21 Qualified wages for the employee retention credit   . . . .   21 [.]

22 Qualified health plan expenses for the employee retention credit   . . . .   22 [.]

23 Qualified sick leave wages for leave taken after March 31, 2021 . . . .   23 [.]

24 Qualified health plan expenses allocable to qualified sick leave wages reported on line 23   24 [.]

25 Amounts under certain collectively bargained agreements allocable to qualified sick
leave wages reported on line 23   . . . .   25 [.]

26 Qualified family leave wages for leave taken after March 31, 2021 . . . .   26 [.]

27 Qualified health plan expenses allocable to qualified family leave wages reported on line 26   27 [.]

28 Amounts under certain collectively bargained agreements allocable to qualified family
leave wages reported on line 26   . . . .   28 [.]

Part 4: **May we speak with your third-party designee?**

Do you want to allow an employee, a paid tax preparer, or another person to discuss this return with the IRS? See the instructions
for details.

□ Yes. Designee's name and phone number [   ] [   ]

Select a 5-digit personal identification number (PIN) to use when talking to the IRS. [ ] [ ] [ ] [ ] [ ]

□ No.

Part 5: **Sign here. You MUST complete all three pages of Form 941 and SIGN it.**

Under penalties of perjury, I declare that I have examined this return, including accompanying schedules and statements, and to the best of my knowledge
and belief, it is true, correct, and complete. Declaration of preparer (other than taxpayer) is based on all information of which preparer has any knowledge.

X **Sign your name here** [   ]

Print your name here [   ]

Print your title here [   ]

Date [/   /   ]

Best daytime phone [   ]

Paid Preparer Use Only   Check if you're self-employed . . . □

Preparer's name	[ ]	PTIN	[ ]
Preparer's signature	[ ]	Date	[/ /]
Firm's name (or yours if self-employed)	[ ]	EIN	[ ]
Address	[ ]	Phone	[ ]
City	[ ]	State [ ]	ZIP code	[ ]

Form **941** (Rev. 6-2021)

Form 941-V,
Payment Voucher

Purpose of Form

Complete Form 941-V if you're making a payment with Form 941. We will use the completed voucher to credit your payment more promptly and accurately, and to improve our service to you.

Making Payments With Form 941

To avoid a penalty, make your payment with Form 941 **only if:**

• Your total taxes after adjustments and nonrefundable credits (Form 941, line 12) for either the current quarter or the preceding quarter are less than $2,500, you didn't incur a $100,000 next-day deposit obligation during the current quarter, and you're paying in full with a timely filed return; or

• You're a monthly schedule depositor making a payment in accordance with the Accuracy of Deposits Rule. See section 11 of Pub. 15 for details. In this case, the amount of your payment may be $2,500 or more.

Otherwise, you must make deposits by electronic funds transfer. See section 11 of Pub. 15 for deposit instructions. Don't use Form 941-V to make federal tax deposits.

⚠️ **CAUTION** *Use Form 941-V when making any payment with Form 941. However, if you pay an amount with Form 941 that should've been deposited, you may be subject to a penalty. See* Deposit Penalties *in section 11 of Pub. 15.*

Specific Instructions

Box 1—Employer identification number (EIN). If you don't have an EIN, you may apply for one online by visiting the IRS website at *www.irs.gov/EIN*. You may also apply for an EIN by faxing or mailing Form SS-4 to the IRS. If you haven't received your EIN by the due date of Form 941, write "Applied For" and the date you applied in this entry space.

Box 2—Amount paid. Enter the amount paid with Form 941.

Box 3—Tax period. Darken the circle identifying the quarter for which the payment is made. Darken only one circle.

Box 4—Name and address. Enter your name and address as shown on Form 941.

• Enclose your check or money order made payable to "United States Treasury." Be sure to enter your EIN, "Form 941," and the tax period ("1st Quarter 2021," "2nd Quarter 2021," "3rd Quarter 2021," or "4th Quarter 2021") on your check or money order. Don't send cash. Don't staple Form 941-V or your payment to Form 941 (or to each other).

• Detach Form 941-V and send it with your payment and Form 941 to the address in the Instructions for Form 941.

Note: You must also complete the entity information above Part 1 on Form 941.

✂ ------------- ▼ **Detach Here and Mail With Your Payment and Form 941.** ▼ ------------- ✂

Form **941-V** Department of the Treasury Internal Revenue Service	**Payment Voucher** ▶ **Don't staple this voucher or your payment to Form 941.**	OMB No. 1545-0029 20**21**

1 Enter your employer identification number (EIN).	2 **Enter the amount of your payment.** ▶ Make your check or money order payable to **"United States Treasury"**	Dollars	Cents

3 Tax Period		4 Enter your business name (individual name if sole proprietor).

1st Quarter	○ 3rd Quarter	Enter your address.
○ 2nd Quarter	○ 4th Quarter	Enter your city, state, and ZIP code; or your city, foreign country name, foreign province/county, and foreign postal code.

(Source: Internal Revenue Service)

Answers to Stop & Check Exercises

FUTA, SUTA, and Workers' Compensation

1.	FUTA: $7,000 × 29 × 0.006 =	$ 1,218.00
	$2,575 × 0.006 =	15.45
	FUTA liability	$ 1,233.45
	SUTA: $27,000 × 25 × 0.042 =	$28,350.00
	$60,090 × 0.042 =	2,523.78
	(under the cap: 15,800 + 7,800 + 11,115 + 22,800 + 2,575)	
	SUTA liability	$30,873.78
	Total combined FUTA/SUTA liability	$32,107.23

2.	FUTA: $7,000 × 10 × 0.006 =	420.00
	($5,500 + 6,800) × 0.006 =	73.80
	Total FUTA liability	$ 493.80
	SUTA: $12,000 × 8 × 0.0326 =	$ 3,129.60
	$33,250 × 0.0326	
	(under the cap: 5,500 + 6,800 + 11,100 + 9,850) =	1,083.95
	Total SUTA liability	$ 4,213.55
	Competitive Skills Scholarship tax liability: $279,580 × 0.0007 =	195.71
	Total FUTA, SUTA, and Competitive Skills Scholarship =	$ 4,903.06

3.

Job Classification	Premium per $100 of Payroll	Estimated Payroll	Premium Due
Clerical Workers	$0.45	$104,550	$ 470.48
Jump Instructors	3.75	215,690	8,088.38
			$8,558.86

Reporting Periods

1. Monthly.
2. July 15.
3. Monday, the next business day.

Tax Forms

1. $2,414.48 = $8,462.96 − 2,980.24 − 3,068.24
2. $105,000 (15 employees × $7,000).
3. $630.00 ($105,000 (from problem 2) × 0.006 FUTA rate).
4. $116,195 = $25,650 + 30,025 + 28,550 + 31,970

Payroll-Related Business Expenses

1. Failure to file and failure to deposit penalties.
2. Payroll expenses relate to the company's profitability, worker productivity analyses, employee retention, and business competitiveness.

Labor Distribution Report

1. a. $300,000/10 employees = $30,000 per employee; Office, $90,000; agricultural, $150,000; drivers, $60,000.
   b. Each department would be allocated $100,000 of the payroll.
2. Student answers may vary but should include: Department classification is the most appropriate because it matches the costs more closely to each department.

Benefit Analysis Report

1. Student answers may vary but should include: One of the purposes of compiling a benefit analysis report is to represent graphically all of the variables that make up an employee's compensation package. The benefit analysis report provides managers and supervisors a budgetary tool to understand the full cost of hiring or dismissing employees. Additionally, the benefit analysis allows companies to compare benefits and employee costs to geographic or industry standards.

2. The benefit analysis report is an internal report for the company's management, and the annual total compensation report is meant to be distributed to the employee.

Chapter Seven

The Payroll Register, Employees' Earnings Records, and Accounting System Entries

This chapter will integrate the payroll register with the employees' earnings records and financial statements. In previous chapters, we have examined the effects of payroll on employees, employers, and governmental agencies. This chapter links *Generally Accepted Accounting Principles (GAAP)* with payroll elements we have explored in Chapters 1–6. We will discuss the debits and credits associated with payroll accrual and payment. For this chapter, we will use the accrual basis of accounting, which means that transactions are recognized when they take place.

Accounting entries are the transactions that place the payroll amounts into the correct ledger accounts. In automated systems, the software is designed to code each payroll item automatically to the correct General Ledger account. However, for the payroll accountant to record accurate expenses and period-end accruals in the correct month, manual entries are necessary. This is the final step of the payroll cycle for each pay period and is the most important piece of the process from an accounting perspective. The final piece of this chapter will include examining how payroll costs affect a company's financial reports.

LEARNING OBJECTIVES

After studying Chapter 7, you should be able to:

LO 7-1   Connect the Payroll Register to the Employees' Earnings Records

LO 7-2   Describe Financial Accounting Concepts

LO 7-3   Complete Payroll-Related General Journal Entries

LO 7-4   Generate Payroll-Related General Ledger Entries

LO 7-5   Describe Payroll Effects on the Accounting System

LO 7-6   Explain Payroll Entries in Accounting Reports

SFIO CRACHO/Shutterstock

Payroll Accounting: New Choices and Challenges

The COVID-19 pandemic ushered in challenges for payroll accountants. It also increased the need to recognize payroll as part of companywide strategic decisions. Businesses had to find ways to keep paying employees during a time of decreasing revenues. Many businesses re-evaluated expenses at every level, trying to find what could be reduced or must be eliminated. Cloud-based payroll technology allowed employees to perform their tasks from multiple locations. Governmental tax breaks, deferrals, and pandemic-related payroll loans helped some businesses to keep their people employed.

Common reductions businesses used included decreasing contributions to retirement plans, reducing or postponing charitable contributions, and transferring employees to remote-work locations. These measures allowed companies to access cash to maintain necessary operations. However, one hidden challenge for companies involved having to pay employees based on their work locations, which forced some firms to become multi-state employers and to navigate varying state tax rates. Unemployment rates increased as some employees were furloughed and able to return later, while others were terminated because of their employer's economic condition.

At the time of this publication, the future remains uncertain for businesses affected by pandemic-related economic challenges. One thing is certain: The pandemic will affect payroll accounting for the foreseeable future. Businesses will need to make new choices, and payroll accountants will be vital elements in company decision-making.

(Source: Accounting Today)

> **Accurate reporting of payroll costs in the financial statements is a key part of GAAP compliance and decision making. In Chapter 7, we will examine the accounting system entries for payroll costs, the effect on the company's financial reports, and how those reports influence managerial decisions.**

LO 7-1 Connect the Payroll Register to the Employees' Earnings Records

Oleksiy Mark/Shutterstock

In previous chapters, we have completed the payroll register, which is the primary tool used to compute payroll amounts. The payroll register has a related set of documents called the employee earnings records. Information from the payroll register is used to complete payroll entries in the General Journal.

Employee earnings records form the link between the accounting and the human resource departments and connect closely with the payroll register. The information contained within each row of the payroll register is transferred to the employee's earnings record, an example shown in Figure 7-1.

FIGURE 7-1
Employee Earnings Record

EMPLOYEE EARNING RECORD

NAME		Hire Date		Dependent child <17	
ADDRESS		Date of Birth		Dependent other	
CITY/STATE/ZIP		Position		Step 4a W-4 Info	
TELEPHONE		Filing Status		Step 4b W-4 Info	
SOCIAL SECURITY				Step 4c W-4 Info	
NUMBER		Pay Rate		Hr/Wk/Mo/Yr	

Period Ended	Hrs Worked	Reg Pay	OT Pay	Holiday	Comm	Gross Pay	Ins	401(k)	Taxable Pay for Federal	Taxable Pay for FICA

Taxable Pay for Federal	Taxable Pay for FICA	Fed Inc. Tax	Social Sec. Tax	Medicare	State Inc. Tax	Total Deduc	Net Pay	YTD Net Pay	YTD Gross Pay	YTD FUTA

The employee earnings record is the master document accountants use to track employees' marital status, deductions (mandatory, voluntary, and mandated), and year-to-date earnings. Remember, Social Security, FUTA, and SUTA taxes have annual earnings limits for each employee. Accountants update the employees' earnings records during each pay period to track all pay and tax deductions. Any employee changes, including pay rate, marital status, and the number of dependents, should be annotated in the earnings records as soon as possible to ensure the accuracy of the payroll.

EXAMPLE: EMPLOYEE EARNINGS RECORD, INDIVIDUAL EMPLOYEE

Using Lillian Quinn's example at Granite Hill Products, we will enter her data into her employee earnings record. She is paid semimonthly.

EMPLOYEE EARNING RECORD

Name	Lillian Quinn	Hire Date	3/1/20XX	Dependent child <17	2
Address	3450 Pine Street	Date of Birth	12/15/19XX	Dependent other	1
City/State/Zip	Laurel, DE 19956	Position	Manager	Step 4a W-4 Info	none
Telephone	302-555-3948	Filing Status	Married/Joint	Step 4b W-4 Info	none
Social Security Number	392-20-1030	Pay Rate	$2,500 semi monthly	Step 4c W-4 Info	none

Period Ended	Reg Hours Worked	OT Hours Worked	Regular Pay	OT Pay	Gross Pay	401(k)	Section 125	Taxable Pay for Federal	Taxable Pay for FICA
8/31/20xx			2,500.00		2,500.00	150.00	225.00	2,125.00	2,275.00

Taxable Pay for Federal	Taxable Pay for FICA	Fed Inc. Tax	Social Sec. Tax	Medicare	State Inc. Tax	Net Pay	YTD Net Pay	YTD Gross Pay	YTD FUTA
2,125.00	2,275.00	-	141.05	32.99	140.25	1,810.71	16,085.00	30,000.00	7,000.00

Note how the following employee information is reflected in the employee earnings record:

- Address.
- Telephone number.
- Social Security number.
- Amount paid per month.
- Filing status.
- Pay basis.
- Hire date.
- Birthdate.
- Position.
- Pay rate.
- Pay period date.

(continued)

(concluded)

- Year-to-date net pay.

- Year-to-date gross pay.

These items are common to most employee earnings records because of the connection between payroll and human resources. The information contained in the employee earnings record is used as the basis for the employee's Form W-2 and other company tax and benefits reporting.

The Employees' Earnings Records and Periodic Tax Reports

Period totals are also included in the earnings record. These totals facilitate the preparation of the quarterly and annual reports. Like any payroll record, the earnings records should be retained and destroyed simultaneously as other accounting records. Earnings records are typically included as supporting documents for internal copies of quarterly filings of Form 941 and state and local tax returns (where applicable). During a payroll audit, the documentation attached to the tax returns verifies the reports' information. A secondary use is that, in computer data failure, documents attached to payroll records can be used to re-create files.

In the village of Bellows Falls, Vermont, employees of the Windham Northeast Supervisory Union, the school district for the area, have experienced payroll problems for several months. These problems involved overpayment or underpayment of earnings, missing or delayed deposits of retirement deductions, and other anomalies. The Supervisory Union attributed the problem to new payroll software upon which employees were undertrained before use. The accuracy of employee payroll and remission of deductions is of paramount importance within a business of any type.

(Source: VTDigger)

Employees' Earnings Register

Stop & Check

1. How do the employees' earnings records relate to the payroll register?

2. Which of the following fields exist in both the payroll register and the employees' earnings records?

    a. Name

    b. Pay rate

    c. Job title

    d. Net pay

    e. Address

3. What reports and forms use information from the employees' earnings records?

tashatuvango/123RF

LO 7-2   Describe Financial Accounting Concepts

Now that we have explored computing and reporting payroll data principles, it is time to connect the information to financial accounting concepts. In financial accounting, the fundamental accounting equation is **Assets = Liabilities + Owners' Equity.**

EXAMPLE: FINANCIAL ACCOUNTING CATEGORIES

Assets: Cash or other items used in the business's operation and amounts owed to the business by customers.

Liabilities: Amounts owed by the business to other people or companies.

Owners' equity: The net investment that the owner has in the business, including earnings kept in the business.

Financial business transactions, such as the movement of cash used in paying employees and remitting amounts to third parties, are tracked using the accounting system. A fundamental concept in accounting involves the accounting equation, which must remain in balance at all times. As such, transactions will either increase an account (or multiple accounts), decrease an account (or multiple accounts), or a combination thereof. To understand the concept of equation balance, T-accounts are the first step in understanding the classification process that is part of transaction analysis.

EXAMPLE: TRANSACTION ANALYSIS USING T-ACCOUNTS

Phillip Rossman, the owner of Rossman Designs, paid an independent contractor $4,000 for work done during the course of business on August 1, 2021. Accountants classify the transaction into two accounts: assets and owners' equity. The cash account would decrease because the money was paid from the business. Barry's expenses would increase because he paid a contractor, which appears as an expense of the company and decreases the amount of equity Barry has in the business. Using the T-account approach, the transaction would look like this:

Contractor Expense	
Dr.	Cr.
4,000.00	

Cash	
Dr.	Cr.
	4,000.00

Debits and Credits

If accountants were to maintain T-accounts for all of a business's transactions, their work would be tedious and vulnerable to many errors. To simplify the addition and subtraction involved, accountants use the terms *debit* (abbreviated Dr.) and *credit* (abbreviated Cr.) to explain the transaction. In accounting parlance, *debit* means "the left side of the T-account," and *credit* means "the right side of the T-account." No connotation exists about good or bad with the use of these terms in accounting.

EXAMPLE: DEBIT AND CREDIT RULES

Debits Increase:	Credits Increase:
Expenses	Liabilities
Assets	Equity (Capital)
Dividends	Revenue

The General Journal

To simplify using T-accounts, accountants use a journal (called the *General Journal*) to record the daily financial transactions. The General Journal is maintained in chronological order. The General Journal is essentially one big T-account, has columns to record the debits and credits involved in each transaction, and contains a chronologically ordered list of transactions. Complementing the General Journal is the *General Ledger*, in which all journal transactions are recorded chronologically in their specific accounts.

In the transaction above, the transaction would appear in the General Journal as follows:

EXAMPLE: TRANSACTION IN THE GENERAL JOURNAL

Trans.	Date	Account Name & Description	Post Ref	Debit	Credit
1	8/1/2021	Contractor Expense	501	4,000.00	
		Cash	101		4,000.00
		Paid Contractor			

Note certain accounting conventions present in the journal entry:

- The date of the transaction is noted.
- The debit part of the transaction is on the first line and is flush left in the column.
- The credit part of the transaction is on the second line and is indented slightly.
- A brief description of the transaction is on line three.
- Account numbers are annotated in the Post Reference (Post Ref) column.
- The post reference in the General Journal is the General Ledger account number.

The General Ledger

Once the transaction has been recorded in the General Journal, the accountant posts the entry to corresponding General Ledger accounts. The following table notes that (1) the transaction itself is listed, and (2) the balance of each account is adjusted accordingly.

EXAMPLE: GENERAL LEDGER POSTING

			Account: 101 – Cash		
Date	Description	Post Ref.	Debit	Credit	Balance
8/1/2021	Paid Contractor	J1		4,000.00	4,000.00

			Account: 501 – Contractor Expense		
Date	Description	Post Ref.	Debit	Credit	Balance
8/1/2021	Paid Contractor	J1	4,000.00		4,000.00

The General Ledger account balances are used to generate the payroll reports discussed so far. The elements of the General Ledger and specific posting practices will appear later in this chapter.

Despite the increase in accounting software use, the need for payroll accountants is growing in importance. Accountants are needed to monitor accuracy in recorded transactions and adapt to industry changes, especially the integration of technology and the growing use of artificial intelligence. Payroll accountants are particularly in demand because of the specific skills involved and the increasing payroll accounting complexity.

(Source: Bloomberg BNA, In the Black)

Financial Accounting Concepts

Stop & Check

1. What is the fundamental accounting equation?
2. What increases the Wages and Salaries Payable account: a debit or a credit?
3. What increases the Wages and Salaries Expense account: a debit or a credit?

PointImages/Shutterstock

LO 7-3 Complete Payroll-Related General Journal Entries

Recording the specific General Journal entries that correspond to payroll activities is the next step in the process. General Journal entries are the original entry point for events to be recorded within the accounting system. A sample period payroll for L&L Grain follows.

EXAMPLE: L&L GRAIN PAYROLL DATA

L&L Grain pays its employees biweekly and operates on a calendar fiscal year (i.e., the year-end is December 31). The payroll accountant for L&L Grain has completed the payroll register for the January 24, 2021, payroll. Paychecks will be issued on January 30. Payroll totals are as follows:

Gross pay: $18,050.00
Federal income tax withheld: $1,500.00
Social Security tax withheld: $1,084.38
Medicare tax withheld: $253.61
State income tax withheld: $577.60
401(k) contributions withheld: $750.00
Health insurance premiums withheld: $560.00
United Way contributions withheld: $180.00
Net pay: $13,144.41

The totals row of the payroll register would appear as follows:

Name	Gross Earnings	401(k) Contributions	Insurance	Federal W/H	Social Security Tax	Medicare Tax	State W/H	United Way	Net Pay	Check No.
Totals	$18,050.00	$750.00	$560.00	$1,500.00	$1,084.38	$253.61	$577.60	$180.00	$13,144.41	

The payroll register is the tool used by payroll accountants to create pay-related journal entries. Here's how it works:

EXAMPLE: PAYROLL REGISTER TO GENERAL JOURNAL ENTRIES

Payroll Register Column	General Journal Account	L&L Grain Amount
Gross Earnings	Salaries and Wages Expense	$18,050.00
401(k) Contributions	401(k) Contributions Payable	750.00
Insurance	Health Insurance Premiums Payable	560.00
Federal W/H	FIT Payable	1,500.00
Social Security Tax	Social Security Tax Payable	1,084.38
Medicare Tax	Medicare Tax Payable	253.61
State W/H	State Income Tax Payable	577.60
United Way	United Way Contributions Payable	180.00
Net Pay	Salaries and Wages Payable	13,144.41

As the payroll data is transferred from the payroll register to the General Journal, notice the following accounting categories:

- Account names ending with the word "expense" are classified as Expense accounts (remember Debit increases).
- Account names ending with the word "payable" are classified as Liability accounts (remember Credit increases).

Employee Pay-Related Journal Entries

The General Journal entry to record the employee's portion of the payroll and the issuance of the checks to employees is in two parts:

EXAMPLE: L&L GRAIN GENERAL JOURNAL PAYROLL ENTRIES— EMPLOYEE PAYROLL TRANSACTION

Date	Description	Account	Debit	Credit
Jan. 24	Salaries and Wages Expense	511	$18,050.00	
	FIT Payable	221		$ 1,500.00
	Social Security Tax Payable	222		1,084.38
	Medicare Tax Payable	223		253.61
	State Income Tax Payable	224		577.60
	401(k) Contributions Payable	225		750.00
	Health Insurance Premiums Payable	226		560.00
	United Way Contributions Payable	227		180.00
	Salaries and Wages Payable	231		13,144.41
Jan. 30	Salaries and Wages Payable	231	13,144.41	
	Cash	101		13,144.41

Employer Payroll-Related Journal Entries

The employer's share of the payroll is similarly recorded. L&L Grain's share of the payroll expenses follows:

EXAMPLE: L&L GRAIN EMPLOYER PAYROLL TAX OBLIGATIONS DATA

Social Security tax: $1,084.38
Medicare tax: $253.61
FUTA tax: $104.94
SUTA tax: $944.46

The General Journal entry for the employer's share of the payroll taxes follows:

EXAMPLE: L&L GRAIN GENERAL JOURNAL PAYROLL ENTRIES—EMPLOYER PAYROLL TAX TRANSACTION

Date	Description	Account	Debit	Credit
Jan. 24	Payroll Taxes Expense	512	$2,387.39	
	Social Security Tax Payable	222		$1,084.38
	Medicare Tax Payable	223		253.61
	FUTA Tax Payable	228		104.94
	SUTA Tax Payable	229		944.46

Governmental audits in Louisiana found that although the number of employees decreased in 2020, payroll costs rose 5 percent. Auditors found the overall decrease in employees was due to employee resignation or retirement. The increase in payroll costs resulted from civil service wage and salary increases (averaging 16 percent from 2013 to 2020), additional overtime resulting from natural disasters during the same time period, and the increased use of independent contractors.

(Source: Hearst Communications)

Other Payroll-Related Journal Entries

What about the other deductions that L&L Grain withheld from its employees' pay? These other deductions, including federal and state income tax, 401(k) contributions, health insurance premiums, and United Way contributions, are liabilities of the company. These amounts will remain in the liability accounts until L&L Grain *remits* them, which means sending the collected money to the appropriate entity. Upon remittance, the General Journal entries will appear as a debit (decrease) to the Liability account and a credit (decrease) to Cash. An example for the January 24 payroll's voluntary deductions, paid to the appropriate companies on January 30, follows:

EXAMPLE: L&L GRAIN GENERAL JOURNAL PAYROLL ENTRIES— VOLUNTARY DEDUCTIONS REMITTANCE

Date	Description	Account	Debit	Credit
Jan. 30	401(k) Contributions Payable	225	$750.00	
	Health Insurance Payable	226	560.00	
	United Way Contribution Payable	227	180.00	
	Cash	101		$1,490.00

Remember, the remittance for governmental taxes has a specific schedule. The General Journal entry for the tax remittances would follow the same pattern as the voluntary deductions: debit the liability account(s) and credit Cash.

Payroll Accruals and Reversals

A common occurrence is a payroll period may be split between two months, as will be the case for L&L Grain. For example, most of the pay for the end of March will be paid on the March 27, 2021, pay date, but the payroll for March 30 and 31 will be paid in April. For accounting purposes, the accountant needs to record the *payroll's accrual* for March to represent the *expenses* and liabilities incurred during the period accurately, according to the matching principle of accounting. Some companies choose to record the period's expenses by *adjusting entries* and then reverse the entries after starting the next period to prevent confusion in the payroll accounting process.

Employee payroll data for L&L Grain is given below, followed by the related adjusting entry for the end of March:

EXAMPLE: L&L GRAIN ADJUSTING ENTRY—EMPLOYEE PAYROLL DATA

Gross pay: $16,245.00
Federal income tax withheld: $1,350.00
Social Security tax withheld: $1,007.19
Medicare tax withheld: $235.55
State income tax withheld: $519.84
Net pay: $13,132.42

The adjusting entry for March 31, 2021, would be as follows:

EXAMPLE: L&L GRAIN GENERAL JOURNAL—EMPLOYEE DATA ADJUSTING ENTRIES

Date	Description	Account	Debit	Credit
Mar. 31	Salaries and Wages Expense	511	$16,245.00	
	FIT Payable	221		$1,350.00
	Social Security Tax Payable	222		1,007.19
	Medicare Tax Payable	223		235.55
	State Income Tax Payable	224		519.84
	Salaries and Wages Payable	231		13,132.42

The amount for the employer's share would be as follows:

EXAMPLE: L&L GRAIN GENERAL JOURNAL—EMPLOYER PAYROLL TAX DATA ADJUSTING ENTRIES

Date	Description	Account	Debit	Credit
Mar. 31	Payroll Taxes Expense	512	$2,217.44	
	Social Security Tax Payable	222		$1,007.19
	Medicare Tax Payable	223		235.55
	FUTA Tax Payable (16,245 × 0.006)	228		97.47
	SUTA Tax Payable (16,245 × 0.054)	229		877.23

On April 1, 2021, the accountant could record a reversing entry as follows:

EXAMPLE: L&L GRAIN GENERAL JOURNAL—EMPLOYEE DATA REVERSING ENTRIES

Date	Description	Account	Debit	Credit
Apr. 1	FIT Payable	221	$1,350.00	
	Social Security Tax Payable	222	1,007.19	
	Medicare Tax Payable	223	235.55	
	State Income Tax Payable	224	519.84	
	Salaries and Wages Payable	231	13,132.42	
	Salaries and Wages Expense	511		$16,245.00

The *reversal* of the General Journal entries, used in accrual-based accounting to represent accrued employer payroll expenditures and liabilities at the end of the prior month, would be as follows:

EXAMPLE: L&L GRAIN GENERAL JOURNAL—EMPLOYER PAYROLL TAX DATA REVERSING ENTRIES

Date	Description	Account	Debit	Credit
Apr. 1	Social Security Tax Payable	222	$1,007.19	
	Medicare Tax Payable	223	235.55	
	FUTA Tax Payable	224	97.47	
	SUTA Tax Payable	229	877.23	
	Payroll Taxes Expense	512		$2,217.44

Note that not all companies and accountants use reversing entries. An advantage of using the reversing entry is that it simplifies the payroll process by avoiding calculating partial payroll periods due to the period's end. A disadvantage is a reversing entry becomes an additional entry that the accountant has to journalize and post. The use of reversing entries is at the company's discretion.

Payroll and the General Journal

Stop & Check

1. In the following General Journal entry, which account represents the employees' gross pay?

Description	Debit	Credit
Wages and Salaries Expense	$124,785.00	
Federal Income Tax Payable		$15,280.00
Social Security Tax Payable		7,736.67
Medicare Tax Payable		1,809.38
State Income Tax Payable		4,741.83
Wages and Salaries Payable		95,217.12

(continued)

(concluded)

2. Based on the preceding General Journal entry, what would be the entry for the employer's share of the payroll taxes? Omit FUTA/SUTA taxes.

3. Cecil's Craft Warehouse has created a journal entry to accrue the payroll to be paid out in the following period. The accrual amounts are as follows:

Wages and Salaries Expense	$42,795.00	
Federal Income Tax Payable		$6,234.00
Social Security Tax Payable		2,653.29
Medicare Tax Payable		620.53
State Income Tax Payable		1,626.21
Wages and Salaries Payable		31,660.97

What would be the reversing entry?

LO 7-4 Generate Payroll-Related General Ledger Entries

As mentioned before, the process of updating the General Ledger accounts with the transactions that the accountant records in the General Journal is called *posting*. Each account used in the General Journal has a corresponding General Ledger account used to track the individual balances.

For the January 24 payroll and January 30 remittances for L&L Grain that we discussed in the previous section, the General Ledger's postings would appear as depicted in Figure 7-2. Note that the entries shown reflect only the payroll entries for the end of January and February.

> Human input and payroll software have been a growing concern when facing computer security. Phishing attacks, where a computer hacker attempts to breach a company's software security, have been increasing in number and type, including situations in which a company's accounting data is compromised. These attacks have led to an increase in training costs for accounting personnel to educate them about the impacts of accounting breaches to ensure payroll accuracy.
>
> (Source: ADP)

General Ledger Posting Practices

Note the columns in the General Ledger are similar to those in the General Journal. Some specific practices in the General Ledger are worth noting:

*   Each line has a date. (In the General Journal, only the first line of each transaction is dated.)
*   The description is usually left blank, except for adjusting, closing, and reversing entries.

The post reference number is a combination of letters and numbers. The letters denote which journal the entry correlates. In this case, "J" means that the original entry may be found in the General Journal. The number in the Post Ref column reflects the journal's page on which the entry is recorded.

The first pair of Debit and Credit columns is used to record the General Journal entry. If the account had a debit in the General Journal transaction, then the amount would appear in the Debit column in the first pair of columns in the General Ledger. The same practice is used for credits.

The second pair of Debit and Credit columns is used to maintain a running balance of the account's total. These account balances are the

FIGURE 7-2
L&L Grain's General Ledger

					Account: 101 – Cash	
		Post			Balance	
Date		Description	Ref	Debit	Credit	Debit	Credit
Jan	30	Beginning Balance				122,367.43	
Jan	30		J1		13,144.91	109,222.52*	
Jan	30		J4		1,490.00	107,732.52	
Jan	30		J4		560.00	107,172.52	
Jan	30		J4		180.00	106,992.52	

*Cash has a normal debit balance. It will decrease when the account is credited. 122,367.43 – 13,144.91 = 109,222.52.

					Account: 221 – FIT Payable	
			Post			Balance	
Date		Description	Ref	Debit	Credit	Debit	Credit
Jan	24		J1		1,500.00		1,500.00
Mar	31	Accrue Payroll	J5		1,350.00		2,850.00*
Apr	1	Reverse Payroll	J7	1,350.00			1,500.00

*FIT Payable is a liability account. It will increase with a credit. 1,500 + 1,350 = 2,850.

					Account: 222 – Social Security Tax Payable	
			Post			Balance	
Date		Description	Ref	Debit	Credit	Debit	Credit
Jan	24		J1		1,084.38		1,084.38
Jan	24		J1		1,084.38		2,168.76
Mar	31	Accrue Payroll	J5		1,007.19		3,175.95
Mar	31	Accrue Payroll – Employer	J6		1,007.19		4,183.14
Apr	1	Reverse Payroll	J7	1,007.19			3,175.95
Apr	1	Reverse Payroll – Employer	J7	1,007.19			2,168.76

					Account: 223 – Medicare Tax Payable	
			Post			Balance	
Date		Description	Ref	Debit	Credit	Debit	Credit
Jan	24		J1		253.61		253.61
Jan	24		J1		253.61		507.22
Mar	31	Accrue Payroll	J5		235.55		742.77
Mar	31	Accrue Payroll – Employer	J6		235.55		978.32
Apr	1	Reverse Payroll	J7	235.55			742.77
Apr	1	Reverse Payroll – Employer	J8	235.55			507.22

					Account: 224 – State Income Tax Payable	
			Post			Balance	
Date		Description	Ref	Debit	Credit	Debit	Credit
Jan	24		J1		577.60		577.60
Mar	31	Accrue Payroll	J5		519.84		1,097.44
Apr	1	Reverse Payroll	J7	519.84			577.60

					Account: 225 – 401(k) Contributions Payable	
			Post			Balance	
Date		Description	Ref	Debit	Credit	Debit	Credit
Jan	24		J1		750.00		750.00
Jan	30		J4	750.00			—

(continued)

FIGURE 7-2
L&L Grain's General Ledger *(concluded)*

					Balance	
				Account: 226 – Health Insurance Payable		
Date		Description	Post Ref	Debit	Credit	Debit	Credit
Jan	24		J1		560.00		560.00
Jan	30		J4	560.00			—

					Balance	
				Account: 227 – United Way Contributions Payable		
Date		Description	Post Ref	Debit	Credit	Debit	Credit
Jan	24		J1		180.00		180.00
Jan	30		J4	180.00			—

					Balance	
				Account: 228 – FUTA Tax Payable		
Date		Description	Post Ref	Debit	Credit	Debit	Credit
Jan	24		J1		104.94		104.94
Mar	31	Accrue Payroll – Employer	J6		97.47		202.41
Apr	1	Reverse Payroll – Employer	J8	97.47			104.94

					Balance	
				Account: 229 – SUTA Tax Payable		
Date		Description	Post Ref	Debit	Credit	Debit	Credit
Jan	24		J1		944.46		944.46
Mar	31	Accrue Payroll – Employer	J6		877.23		1,821.69
Apr	1	Reverse Payroll – Employer	J8	877.23			944.46

					Balance	
				Account: 231 – Salaries and Wages Payable		
Date		Description	Post Ref	Debit	Credit	Debit	Credit
Jan	24		J1		13,144.41		13,144.41
Jan	30		J1	13,144.41			—
Mar	31	Accrue Payroll	J5		13,132.42		13,132.42
Apr	1	Reverse Payroll	J7	13,132.42			—

					Balance	
				Account: 512 – Payroll Taxes Expense		
Date		Description	Post Ref	Debit	Credit	Debit	Credit
Jan	24		J1	2,387.39		2,387.39	
Mar	31	Accrue Payroll	J6	2,217.17		4,604.56	
Apr	1	Reverse Payroll	J7		2,217.17	2,387.39	

					Balance	
				Account: 511 – Salaries and Wages Expense		
Date		Description	Post Ref	Debit	Credit	Debit	Credit
Jan	24		J1	18,050.00		18,050.00	
Mar	31	Accrue Payroll	J6	16,245.00		34,295.00	
Apr	1	Reverse Payroll	J7		16,245.00	18,050.00	

foundation for the accountant's financial reports and reviewed by managers, officers, customers, vendors, and governmental agencies.

Payroll Account Reconciliation

It is necessary for accountants to reconcile the payroll to ensure accuracy. If the payroll register has been completed correctly then the reconciliation process should be smooth. However, errors could occur and changes may need to be made after the payroll period ends. Since payroll accuracy is vital, the reconciliation process is strongly recommended. The following steps will help you reconcile your payroll:

Step	Actions
1. **Review hours worked and pay rate**	Check the accuracy of the employees' information, especially the hours worked and pay rate. If the firm has more than 20 employees, it may be best to check for new employees only.
2. **Review deductions**	Ensure that all deductions are accurate. It would be worthwhile to review the W-4s, especially for new employees, to make sure their tax deductions are correct. Check the computation of the deductions to ascertain the net pay figures.
3. **Verify the General Journal and General Ledger**	Make sure your payroll entries are correct in both the General Journal and the General Ledger. Remember that the pay disbursed is a debit and that all deductions from employee pay are credits.
4. **Check your pay period and deposit schedule tax amounts**	Run or create a report in which you check your payroll taxes for monthly, semiweekly, or next-business-day tax deposits. This involves reviewing the General Ledger entries and checking them against the employees' payroll deductions. This will help prevent tax reporting errors.
5. **At the end of the quarter, check your tax deposits again**	Double-check your deposited tax amounts in your General Ledger and verify that you are depositing the correct amount with the quarterly return (if applicable).
6. **Verify the accuracy of each employee's W-2**	You should check the W-2 against the previous year's form to check for any discrepancies. Run a payroll register for the entire year to make sure that all deductions match the W-2s. You can also verify this information against the quarterly tax deposits, when applicable. Once you have verified the accuracy of the W-2s, ensure that Form W-3 accurately reports all amounts by verifying totals against the year's payroll register.

(Source: Nowsta)

General Ledger Entries

Stop & Check

1. The Medicare Tax Payable account for Gulf Coast Shrimp had a credit balance on June 22 of $2,540. As of the June 30 payroll, credits totaling $220 were posted to the Medicare Tax Payable account. What is the balance in the account as of June 30?

2. The post reference for the June 30 journal entry is J34. What does this post reference mean?

mangostock/Age Fotostock

LO 7-5   Describe Payroll Effects on the Accounting System

Entries in the payroll system are posted into the General Ledger. When a company has an automated payroll system, the previously updated journal entries are automatically updated to the General Ledger. A payroll accountant needs to understand how the accounts should look after a payroll period is completed to ensure the automated system has performed correctly. Glitches within computer programs may cause the payroll entry to be one-sided, in which only the debit or credit entry will flow through to the General Ledger. When this occurs, the payroll accountant must discover what has not been posted to ensure the entire transaction posts correctly.

Payroll-Related Business Expenses

Payroll represents an expense to the business. As such, it reduces the company's profitability proportional to the wages earned and taxes paid. When the payroll accountant accrues the payroll expenses, the company's expenses will also increase. Companies that operate using a cash basis (i.e., recording activities only when cash is received or spent) will witness the payroll expenses reducing the income when wages and salaries are paid to the employees and when taxes are remitted to governmental agencies.

A study conducted in 2019 indicated that many accounting tasks, including payroll, will be automated by 2021. However, the need for educated accountants remains constant because of the rise in cybersecurity issues. Although artificial intelligence and computerized accounting will have replaced the need for manual entry of the majority of accounting transactions, the accounting professional must verify the accuracy of the transactions and the information's integrity. Automation in the accounting profession has been lower than predicted and has proven to be highly beneficial. It frees the accountant from certain basic functions and allows them to focus on higher-order tasks, such as analysis and strategy.

(Source: Untapped; AccountingToday)

Besides administering specific payroll tasks, the payroll accountant's responsibility is to allocate the employee expenses to specific accounts, departments, or business activities. Regardless of the employee's job description, some time can be allocable to jobs or customers. For example, a fabric manufacturing company will have sewing, accounting, and managerial staff. The bulk of the sewing staff's time will be allocable to specific jobs; however, some time will be considered overhead—cleaning or meetings, for example. The bulk of the accounting department's time will be considered overhead. However, if the accountant is working on analyzing a specific client's project, that time may be billed to the client. Managerial positions may also have specific times allocated to jobs depending upon the client's needs and the position.

Pavel Ignatov/Shutterstock

Payroll-Related Liabilities

Unpaid payroll obligations represent a liability to the company. These liabilities include amounts due to employees and money to be remitted for voluntary, mandatory, and mandated deductions. Until the money is remitted, the company holds it in its accounts. Specific examples of payroll liabilities include, but are certainly not limited to, the following:

- Federal income tax
- FICA taxes
- Health insurance premiums
- Retirement plan contributions
- Child support garnishments
- Union dues

Employers have a *fiduciary* responsibility to remit all amounts withheld from employee pay. Remember that the Current Tax Payment Act requires employers to remit taxes promptly, according to governmental guidelines. For the other deductions, according to **29 CFR 2510**, employers are subject to ERISA provisions to protect all amounts due to employees and other recipients.

The Employee Benefits Security Administration, a division of the Department of Labor, oversees employee contributions and estimated that approximately 68 million employees participated in employer-sponsored 401(k) plans and had invested over $425 trillion as of December 2017. The number of participants has historically increased at a rate of about 3 percent per year since 1975.

(Source: DOL)

The Business Effects of Payroll

Stop & Check

1. Does the payment of employee wages increase or decrease the profitability of a business?

2. Why is it important to allocate payroll-related expenses properly?

LO 7-6 Explain Payroll Entries in Accounting Reports

echoevg/Shutterstock

When examining the *income statement, balance sheet*, and post-closing *trial balance* (Figures 7-3, 7-4, and 7-5), payroll accountants must know what effect their work has on each statement. The financial statements are the key to integrating payroll accounting data and human resources information.

Let's start with the income statement, which reports all revenue and expenses for a specific time period. These periods are usually monthly, quarterly, and annually. The income statement's function is to correlate all money received during the course of business operations with the money spent to earn that income. Within the expense section of the income statement, you will see several accounts that relate to payroll. The Salaries and Wages Expense represents the gross pay from the period. Each of the taxes we have discussed is listed. Note the expenses related to the taxes are paid by the employer and forwarded to the taxing authority; thus, there is no accrued federal income tax expense. Expenses related to the employer portion of retirement fund matching, health benefits, or other benefits are also located within the income statement.

FIGURE 7-3
Income Statement Presentation (Partial)

L&L Grain Income Statement For the Quarter Ended March 31, 2021		
Revenue:		
Sales Revenue		$78,303.40
Expenses:		
Salaries and Wages Expense	$34,295.00	
Payroll Taxes Expense	4,638.16	
Utilities Expense	1,725.00	
Telephone Expense	884.00	
Rent Expense	5,175.00	
Total Expenses		46,717.16
Net Income for Quarter		$31,586.24

FIGURE 7-4
Balance Sheet Presentation (Partial)

L&L Grain Balance Sheet March 31, 2021		
Assets:		
Cash		$110,058.03
Accounts Receivable		39,723.67
Equipment		15,289.00
Inventory		225,960.00
Total Assets		$391,030.70
Liabilities:		
Accounts Payable		4,085.27
FIT Payable		2,850.00
Social Security Tax Payable		4,183.14
Medicare Tax Payable		978.32
State Income Tax Payable		1,097.44
Health Insurance Payable		560.00
FUTA Tax Payable		202.41
SUTA Tax Payable		1,821.69
Salaries and Wages Payable		13,132.42
Total Liabilities		28,910.69
Owners' Equity		
L. Wilson, Capital		330,500.74
Retained Earnings		31,619.27
Total Owners' Equity		362,120.01
Total Liabilities and Owners' Equity		$391,030.70

Moving on to the balance sheet, any unpaid liabilities to be paid during the next 12 months will be reported in the current liability section. In accrual accounting, there may also be end-of-period entries to accrue for payroll earned by the employees. Additional liability accounts for accrued salaries, accrued hourly wages, accrued holiday pay, and accrued paid time off could also appear, depending on the end of the period and the types of employees and benefits which the company operates. If employees have taken payroll advances, which are amounts to be repaid by the employee, these are reported in the current assets section as receivables.

The trial balance contains all accounts the company uses, spanning all of the financial statements. The accounts listed on the trial balance appear in the order of the chart of accounts. In the United States, these are typically listed assets first: short-term and then long-term. Following are the liabilities: short-term and then long-term. Equity accounts are listed next, followed by revenues and expenses. When examining the trial balance, the important thing to remember is that it should balance: Debits must equal credits. Should one side not balance with the other, the accountant must determine why and correct the error. A post-closing trial balance will have already closed the revenue, expense, and dividends accounts into the retained earnings account.

The purpose of all financial statements is to provide information to the stakeholders of a company. Stakeholders of a company include (but are certainly not limited to) company managers, governmental agencies, creditors, and employees who use the information to decide the business. Financial statements are prepared per GAAP guidelines to facilitate the presentation of the statements among various businesses. Managers of a company, in particular, use financial reports to make decisions about labor and benefits planning.

FIGURE 7-5
Post-Closing Trial Balance Presentation

L&L Grain Post-Closing Trial Balance March 31, 2021		
Account	**Debit**	**Credit**
Cash	$110,058.03	
Accounts Receivable	39,723.67	
Inventory	225,960.00	
Equipment	15,289.00	
Accounts Payable		$ 4,085.27
FIT Payable		2,850.00
Social Security Tax Payable		4,183.14
Medicare Tax Payable		978.32
State Income Tax Payable		1,097.44
Health Insurance Payable		560.00
FUTA Tax Payable		202.41
SUTA Tax Payable		1,821.69
Salaries and Wages Payable		13,132.42
L. Wilson, Capital		330,500.74
Retained Earnings		31,619.27
	$391,030.70	**$391,030.70**

> Companies are increasingly using application programming interfaces (API) to integrate financial data among their departments. The use of API fosters sharing information to improve company performance, employee access to their payroll and employment records, and transparency of financial data within the business. This software also allows payroll accountants to engage more fully in decision-making and other functions that involve critical thought and planning.
>
> (Source: What's Next Media)

Labor Reports

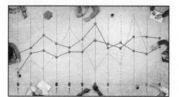
Rawpixel.com/Shutterstock

The payroll accountant may provide specific *labor reports* to management or department heads. These reports may have a variety of names and content depending on the needs of the business.

- The *labor usage* report designates where the labor is used within the company. When a company has several employees who work in different departments, the labor usage report can help determine overhead *allocations* by the department and the need for increased or decreased staff within a specific department.

- The *billable vs. nonbillable* report tracks the time employees have spent specifically on projects for which customers are paying. This report allows managers to determine if the time allocated to the job-costing process is accurate, the company is operating efficiently, or if the employee is taking too long on a specific job.

- *Overtime* reports allow managers to determine how much overtime has been paid to employees during a specified time period. This report allows managers to monitor labor distribution and scheduling to ensure adherence to budget guidelines.

- Employers can also make use of *trend* reports for payroll staffing needs. Trend reports of income over the period of the year or two can reveal seasonal increases or decreases in business. An informed business manager will know if the company needs to have seasonal or temporary workers for short-term increases. If the trend reflects a steady increase in business, the manager may determine that hiring a new employee would be beneficial. Analyzing the company's staffing needs compared to income projections may also lead managers to know if they need to lay off personnel, reduce hours of existing employees, or restructure company operations.

As of 2020, over 157 million Americans were employed and worked at least 15 hours per week. According to the Bureau of Labor Statistics, the level of employment in the United States has grown since 2010 and is projected to continue doing so through 2029. Because the number and type of employees are increasing, payroll accounting will become more complex. Understanding payroll accounting is a vital skill needed by all industries, government employers, and private-sector companies. It is safe to state that payroll accounting is a profession that will continue to be needed for the foreseeable future.

(Source: BLS)

Labor Reports

Stop & Check

1. Which of the following reports are affected by the payroll of an organization?
   a. Trial balance
   b. Statement of owners' equity
   c. Interest statement
   d. Income statement
   e. Balance sheet
2. What is a specific type of report that the payroll accountant provides to managerial staff?
3. What are trend reports?

Trends to Watch

ECONOMIC EFFECTS OF PAYROLL

Although payroll accounting principles remain relatively stable, payroll plays in the broader context of a business are subject to change. Some developments in payroll accounting in the business context that have changed since 2018 include the following:

- Accountants seeking roles as consultants (as opposed to technicians) because of increases in automation and technology that foster lower-level work completion.
- Increases in labor costs for employers resulting from changes to the minimum wage.
- Expansion of the gig economy has led to judicial review of employment practices.
- Expanded integration of financial technology to improve the automation of accounting transactions.
- Changes to federal reporting requirements to streamline and standardize company submissions.
- Payroll outsourcing as a way to reduce internal company costs may increase.
- Companies will become more agile and flexible about employee duties and workplaces.
- The transition to increased automation will lead to added transparency and accountability among company personnel.
- Company payroll will more closely resemble business-to-customer relations by becoming more intuitive and user friendly.

Summary of the Payroll Register, Employees' Earnings Records, and Accounting System Entries

The payroll register and employees' earnings records are two tools that payroll accountants need to accurately maintain their work. Both records track employee compensation and contain information about company liabilities to governmental agencies and other organizations. These records also provide information for company decision-makers by yielding data about labor distribution and cost allocation. Payroll records provide information about benefits given to employees and how those benefits affect a business's profitability. Information

FIGURE 7-6
Payroll Process Flowchart

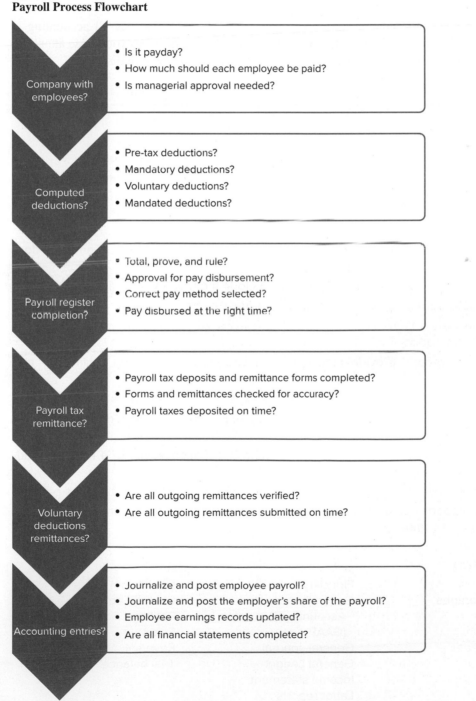

contained in these sources and tools used by payroll accountants provides integral insights for managerial functions.

The final piece of the payroll cycle is the creation of accounting system entries. Like other business transactions, recording, paying the payroll, and remitting money to governmental agencies and other firms requires General Journal and General Ledger entries. Business owners and departmental managers use this accounting information to measure business plans' effectiveness and plan both short- and long-term strategies. As an integral part of business operations, payroll-related expenses and liabilities represent an employer's financial duty, affect the financial reports, and influence its viability.

With this chapter's explanation of accounting system entries, we have now completed our journey through the payroll process. We have investigated the history of payroll, its many aspects and functions, and the importance of employee compensation within a business context.

We hope that after finishing this book, you will understand that payroll accounting is complex, involves many different decisions along the way, and deserves your close attention. Figures 7-6 depict the basic elements of the payroll process that we have discussed.

Key Points

- The payroll register connects directly to the employees' earnings records.
- The employees' earnings records link accounting and human resources and contain information from the payroll register.
- Accounting principles assist in the classification of payroll costs and organizational performance.
- Payroll transactions are recorded in the General Journal and posted to General Ledger accounts.
- The balances in the General Ledger accounts form the foundation of financial reports.
- Payroll costs represent an expense of the business.
- Employees are assigned to departments to foster accurate measurements of business segment profitability.
- Accounting reports provide managers with insights into company profitability and stability.
- Payroll-related transactions contain both the expenses and liabilities of a company.
- Employers have a fiduciary duty to ensure that all amounts deducted from employee pay are remitted to the appropriate entity.
- The increase in the automation of accounting information points to a need for educated, competent payroll professionals.
- Trend reports offer business leaders insight into changes in labor costs over a period.
- Financial reports contain the data that connects the payroll and human resources functions within a company.

Vocabulary

Accrual	Fiduciary	Liabilities
Adjusting entries	Generally Accepted	Owners' equity
Allocation	Accounting Principles	Posting
Assets	(GAAP)	Remit
Balance sheet	General Journal	Reversal
Credit	General Ledger	Trial balance
Debit	Income statement	
Expense	Labor reports	

Review Questions

1. What types of accounts does a debit increase?

2. What types of accounts does a credit increase?

3. Where are daily accounting entries recorded?

4. Once recorded, where are the entries posted?

5. What is the purpose of the payroll register?

6. What information is contained in employees' earnings records?

7. How are the payroll register and the employees' earnings records related?

8. What type of account is debited for the gross pay?

9. What are three of the accounts that may be credited for the employee payroll?

10. What two accounts are affected upon issuance of paychecks?

11. What accounts are debited and credited for the employer share of the payroll expenses?

12. How do payroll expenses affect the income statement and balance sheet?

13. How can companies use payroll information that is reported in the financial statements to determine labor distribution?

14. How can a company's payroll information contained in financial reports assist in corporate planning?

15. How do the payroll register and employees' earnings records help employers meet their responsibilities to different groups, such as the employees and governmental agencies?

16. What is the term for the responsibility that employers have for payroll deductions under ERISA?

Exercises Set A

E7-1A.
LO 7-1
Which column exists in the employees' earnings records but not in the payroll register?
   a. Gross pay
   b. Net pay
   c. YTD net pay
   d. 401(k) contributions

E7-2A.
LO 7-1
What is the connection between the employees' earnings records and payroll tax reporting? (Select all that apply.)
   a. Employees' earnings records do not connect with payroll tax reporting.
   b. Employees' earnings records may be used to ensure the accuracy of payroll tax reporting.
   c. Employees' earnings records contain details of payroll tax reporting and may be considered as source documents.
   d. Employees' earnings records contain year-to-date gross pay, which reflects when employees reach tax bases.

E7-3A.
LO 7-2
A credit increases which of the following types of accounts? (Select all that apply.)
   a. Liabilities
   b. Expenses
   c. Revenues
   d. Assets

E7-4A.

LO 7-3

Which amounts on the payroll register reduce Federal withholding tax but are *not* deducted for FICA tax computations? (Select all that apply.)
a. Charitable contributions
b. Nonqualified pre-tax insurance
c. Retirement plan (e.g., 401(k)) contributions
d. Garnishments

E7-5A.

LO 7-4

What is always true about the General Ledger? (Select all that apply.)
a. The process of transferring amounts from the General Journal to the General Ledger is called posting.
b. The General Ledger is a way to represent monthly groupings of entire General Journal entries.
c. The General Ledger contains information about the individual accounts used in General Journal transactions.
d. A debit to an account in a General Journal transaction is a debit to that account in the General Ledger.

E7-6A.

LO 7-4,
7-5, 7-6

How does a payroll accountant use the information in the General Ledger? (Select all that apply.)
a. The account balances form the basis for accounting reports.
b. The payroll accountant uses General Ledger balances to determine the effectiveness of individual employees.
c. General Ledger account balances aggregate data to determine payroll costs.
d. Payroll expenses contained in the General Ledger are not used to make personnel decisions.

E7-7A.

LO 7-6

Which of the following accounts would appear on the balance sheet? (Select all that apply.)
a. Payroll taxes expense
b. 401(k) contributions payable
c. 401(k) employer contributions expense
d. Social Security tax payable

E7-8A.

LO 7-6

What is always true about the income statement? (Select all that apply.)
a. Only accounts with balances at the end of the period are included.
b. All income and expense accounts are included in the report.
c. All liabilities are included in the report.
d. The report is prepared for a single date.

E7-9A.

LO 7-6

The purpose of a labor report is to do what? (Select all that apply.)
a. Report an individual employee's regular time and overtime.
b. Reflect all expenses of a firm.
c. Promote analysis of payroll expenses.
d. Update managers about payroll on a daily basis.

E7-10A.

LO 7-5,
7-6

Which law governs the fiduciary responsibility that employers have with regards to employees' payroll deductions?
a. FICA
b. FLSA
c. ERISA
d. ACA

Problems Set A

P7-1A.

LO 7-1

Alanis Morgan owns White Mountain Assessments in Laconia, New Hampshire. The standard workweek is 40 hours. For the weekly payroll ending September 10, 2021, checks dated September 15, 2021, complete the payroll register. Use the wage bracket method in the federal tax table from Appendix C. No employee has exceeded the Social Security tax wage base. All employees submitted a 2021 Form W-4, and no box was checked in Step 2. Total, prove, and rule the entries.

| P/R End Date | 9/10/2021 | Company Name | White Mountain Assessments |
| Check Date | 9/15/2021 | Check Date | |

Name	Filing Status	Dependents	Hourly Rate or Period Wage	No. of Regular Hours	No. of Overtime Hours	No. of Holiday Hours	Commissions	Gross Earnings	401(k)	Sect. 125	Taxable Wages for Federal W/H	Taxable Wages for FICA
Rosenberg, A.	Single	2 < 7	$16.25	40					$50.00			
Cintron, G.	Married/Joint	2 < 17; 1 Other	$18.20	39.25					$75.00			
Freeman, S.	Married/Joint	1 Other	$17.55	36								
Crosby, L.	Single	None	$19.25	40	4							
Kepes, T.	Single	2 Other	$16.75	37.5					$60.00	$20.00		
Hankard, J.	Married/Joint	2 < 7	$18.45	40					$75.00			
Nguyen, L.	Single	1 < 17	$15.75	40	7					$15.00		
Totals												

Name	Gross Earnings	Taxable Wages for Federal W/H	Taxable Wages for FICA	Federal W/H	Social Security Tax	Medicare Tax	State W/H	Garnishment	United Way	Net Pay	Check No.
Rosenberg, A.											
Cintron, G.									$10.00		
Freeman, S.								$100.00			
Crosby, L.									$25.00		
Kepes, T.											
Hankard, J.									$10.00		
Nguyen, L.											
Totals											

P7-2A.
LO 7-1

The employee earnings record for Lauren Crosby of White Mountain Assessments is listed below. Record her earnings from the September 10 weekly pay in P7-1A.

EMPLOYEE EARNING RECORD

NAME	Lauren Crosby	Hire Date	April 1, 2018	Dependent child <17	0
ADDRESS	1856 Henniker Road	Date of Birth	February 1, 1985	Dependent other	0
CITY/STATE/ZIP	Weare, NH 03558	Position	Assessor	Step 4a W-4 Info	none
TELEPHONE	603-555-7895	Filing Status	Single	Step 4b W-4 Info	none
SOCIAL SECURITY NUMBER	634-98-1463	Pay Rate	$19.25/hour	Step 4c W-4 Info	none

Period Ended	Regular Hours Worked	Overtime Hours Worked	Regular Pay	Overtime Pay	Gross Pay	401(k)	Section 125	Taxable Wages for Federal W/H	Taxable Wages for FICA
9/3/2021	40		$770.00		$770.00	—	—	$770.00	$770.00

Taxable Wages for Federal W/H	Taxable Wages for FICA W/H	Fed W/H	Social Sec. Tax	Medicare Tax	State W/H	Charitable Contrib.	Net Pay	YTD Net Pay	YTD Sec. Tax
$770.00	$770.00	$60.00	$47.74	$11.17	—	$25.00	$635.92	$24,490.00	$26,127.00

P7-3A.

LO 7-2, 7-3

Using the payroll register from P7-1A for White Mountain Assessments, complete the General Journal entry for the employees' pay for the September 10 pay date. Paychecks will be issued on September 15.

	Date	Description	Post Ref.	Debit	Credit	
1						1
2						2
3						3
4						4
5						5
6						6
7						7
8						8
9						9
10						10
11						11
12						12

P7-4A.

LO 7-2, 7-3

Using the payroll register from P7-1A for White Mountain Assessments, complete the General Journal entry for the employer's share of the payroll taxes for the September 10 payroll end date. Assume 5.4 percent SUTA and 0.6 percent FUTA tax rates and that $3,542.50 is subject to FUTA and SUTA taxes.

	Date	Description	Post Ref.	Debit	Credit	
1						1
2						2
3						3
4						4
5						5
6						6
7						7
8						8
9						9

P7-5A.

LO 7-2, 7-3

Using the employee payroll entry from P7-3A, post the September 10 employee pay for White Mountain Assessments to the selected General Ledger accounts shown next. This will have a Posting Reference of J4.

Account: Salaries and Wages Payable

	Date	Description	Post Ref.	Debit	Credit	Balance Debit	Balance Credit	
1								1
2								2
3								3
4								4
5								5
6								6

Account: Employee Federal Income Tax Payable

	Date	Description	Post Ref.	Debit	Credit	Balance Debit	Balance Credit	
1								1
2								2
3								3
4								4
5								5
6								6

Account: Social Security Tax Payable

	Date	Description	Post Ref.	Debit	Credit	Balance Debit	Balance Credit	
1								1
2								2
3								3
4								4
5								5
6								6

Account: Medicare Tax Payable

	Date	Description	Post Ref.	Debit	Credit	Balance Debit	Balance Credit	
1								1
2								2
3								3
4								4
5								5
6								6

Account: Salaries and Wages Expense

	Date	Description	Post Ref.	Debit	Credit	Balance Debit	Balance Credit	
1								1
2								2
3								3
4								4
5								5
6								6
7								7

P7-6A. Using the employee payroll entry from P7-3A, complete the General
LO 7-2, 7-3 Journal entry for the issuance of the pay for the September 10 payroll end date. The date of the checks is September 15, 2021.

	Date	Description	Post Ref.	Debit	Credit	
1						1
2						2
3						3
4						4
5						5

P7-7A.   Using the employer payroll entry from P7-4A, post the employer's share of
LO 7-2,   payroll taxes for the September 10 pay at White Mountain Assessments to
7-3, 7-4   the appropriate General Ledger accounts.

Account: Social Security Tax Payable

	Date	Description	Post Ref.	Debit	Credit	Balance Debit	Balance Credit	
1								1
2								2
3								3
4								4
5								5
6								6
7								7

Account: Medicare Tax Payable

	Date	Description	Post Ref.	Debit	Credit	Balance Debit	Balance Credit	
1								1
2								2
3								3
4								4
5								5
6								6
7								7

Account: Federal Unemployment Tax Payable

	Date	Description	Post Ref.	Debit	Credit	Balance Debit	Balance Credit	
1								1
2								2
3								3
4								4
5								5
6								6
7								7

Account: State Unemployment Tax Payable

	Date	Description	Post Ref.	Debit	Credit	Balance Debit	Balance Credit	
1								1
2								2
3								3
4								4
5								5
6								6
7								7

Account: Payroll Taxes Expense

	Date	Description	Post Ref.	Debit	Credit	Balance Debit	Balance Credit	
1								1
2								2
3								3
4								4
5								5
6								6
7								7

P7-8A.

LO 7-2, 7-3

KMH Industries is a monthly schedule depositor of payroll taxes. For the month of August 2021, the payroll taxes (employee and employer share combined) were as follows:

Social Security tax: $3,252.28

Medicare tax: $760.61

Employee federal income tax: $2,520.00

Create the General Journal entry for the remittance of the taxes. The entry should be dated September 15, 2021. Use check 2052 in the description.

	Date	Description	Post Ref.	Debit	Credit	
1						1
2						2
3						3
4						4
5						5
6						6
7						7
8						8

P7-9A.

LO 7-2, 7-3

Sophie Sue Breeders has the following voluntary withholdings to remit:

AFLAC payable: $560.00

401(k) payable: $1,280.00

Garnishments payable: $375.00

United Way contributions payable: $200.00

Create the General Journal entry on June 11, 2021, for the remittance of these withheld amounts.

	Date	Description	Post Ref.	Debit	Credit	
1						1
2						2
3						3
4						4
5						5
6						6
7						7

P7-10A.

LO 7-5, 7-6

Sheronda Rowe is the payroll accountant for Great Lake Lamps. The company's management has requested an analysis of the payroll effects on the expenses of the company. Explain which accounting report(s) you would use to construct your analysis. How would you explain the purpose of labor expenses as they affect company productivity?

P7-11A.

LO 7-6

The new vice president of marketing for your company has asked to meet with you regarding the purpose and location of payroll entries in accounting reports. What is your response to the vice president?

Exercises Set B

E7-1B.
LO 7-1
Which of the following information exists in both the employees' earnings records and the payroll register? (Select all that apply.)
a. Employee birthdate
b. Social Security number
c. Hourly rate or period wage
d. Employee name

E7-2B.
LO 7-1
How do the payroll register and employees' earnings records connect with payroll tax determination and remittance? (Select all that apply.)
a. Payroll register column totals contain information about pay period tax withholdings.
b. Employees' earnings records have pertinent information to determine individual taxable wage base attainment.
c. Payroll registers records reflect which employees have reached the Medicare additional tax.
d. Payroll registers contain specific information about each employee's raise history.

E7-3B.
LO 7-2
Which of the following are categories contained in the fundamental accounting equation? (Select all that apply.)
a. Liabilities
b. Revenues
c. Expenses
d. Owners' equity

E7-4B.
LO 7-2
Which of the following principles are always true about financial accounting? (Select all that apply.)
a. Transactions are posted first to the General Ledger.
b. Debits = Credits
c. Each transaction involves at least two accounts.
d. The balance sheet contains all accounts.

E7-5B.
LO 7-3
What is true about expenses and liabilities? (Select all that apply.)
a. Expenses usually have the word "expense" in the account title.
b. Expenses represent additional sums earned by the company.
c. Liabilities represent sums of money owed by third parties to the company.
d. Liabilities usually have the word "payable" in the account title.

E7-6B.
LO 7-3,
7-4, 7-5
How do payroll-related expenses affect financial statements? (Select all that apply.)
a. Payroll expenses may be allocable to work performed for a firm's vendors.
b. Payroll expense accounts are reported on the income statement.
c. The period's gross earnings are reported on the balance sheet.
d. Payroll expenses reduce the net income of a company.

E7-7B.
LO 7-6
Which of the following payroll-related accounts appear on the balance sheet? (Select all that apply.)
a. Wages and salaries payable
b. Medicare tax expense
c. Employee federal income tax payable
d. FUTA tax expense

E7-8B.
LO 7-2, 7-5
What is the purpose of payroll-related accrual and reversal entries on financial statements? (Select all that apply.)
a. Accrual entries represent payroll amounts incurred but not yet paid.
b. Reversing entries represent disbursement of accrued payroll prior to the end of the payroll period.
c. Accrual entries are used to improve the accuracy of the net income for a period.
d. Reversing entries are omitted from financial statements.

E7-9B.
LO 7-6

Managers use labor reports to do which of the following? (Select all that apply.)
a. Analyze labor trends
b. Determine staffing needs
c. Ensure FLSA wage and hour compliance
d. Formulate strategic plans for the company

E7-10B.
LO 7-5, 7-6

To which parties does an employer have a fiduciary duty when it incurs payroll liabilities? (Select all that apply.)
a. Customers
b. Employees
c. Government
d. Vendors

Problems Set B

P7-1B.
LO 7-1

Lucas Crossman owns Appalachian Limited Home Design in Versailles, Kentucky. Complete the payroll register for the weekly payroll dated March 12, 2021. Checks will be issued on March 17, 2021. Use the wage bracket method in the federal tax table in Appendix C. Assume 5 percent state income tax and the same deductions for federal tax apply for state. No employee has exceeded the Social Security wage base. Assume all employees submitted a 2021 Form W-4. If you have MS, use the single rate. Total, prove, and rule the entries.

| P/R End Date | 3/12/2021 | Company Name | Appalachian Limited Home Design |
| Check Date | 3/17/2021 | Check Date | |

Name	Filing Status	Dependents	Hourly Rate or Period Wage	No. of Regular Hours	No. of Overtime Hours	No. of Holiday Hours	Commissions	Gross Earnings	401(k)	Sect. 125	Taxable Wages for Federal W/H	Taxable Wages for FICA
Brooks, S.	Single	2 < 17	$15.25	40					$50.00			
Choi, L.	Married/Joint	3 < 17; 1 Other	$19.70	40	4					$20.00		
Hammersmith, R.	Married/Single	1 < 17; 2 Other	$17.25	38					$35.00	$10.00		
Agarwal, K.	Single	1 < 17	$18.20	36					$20.00			
Potter, D.	Married/Joint	1 Other	$15.50	40	7							
Ito, C.	Single	None	$16.85	40								
Crocker, T.	Married/Joint	2 < 17	$15.00	38.5					$45.00	$10.00		
Kollie, A.	Married/Joint	None	$18.10	40					$25.00			
Totals												

Name	Gross Earnings	Taxable Wages for Federal W/H	Taxable Wages for FICA	Federal W/H	Social Security Tax	Medicare Tax	State W/H	Garnishment	United Way	Net Pay	Check No.
Brooks, S.									$10.00		
Choi, L.											
Hammersmith, R.											
Agarwal, K.								$60.00			
Potter, D.								$50.00			
Ito, C.											
Crocker, T.											
Kollie, A.											
Totals											

P7-2B.
LO 7-1

What follows is the employee earnings record for Chikao Ito of Appalachian Limited Home Design. Record his earnings during the March 12, 2021, pay period from P7-1B.

EMPLOYEE EARNING RECORD

NAME	Chikao Ito	Hire Date	7/1/2018	Dependents <17	0
ADDRESS	150 Palomino Drive	Date of Birth	8/28/1994	Dependents other	0
CITY/STATE/ZIP	Versailles/KY/42235	Position	Graphic Designer	Step 4a W-4 Info	none
TELEPHONE	502-555-4395	Filing Status	Single	Step 4b W-4 Info	none
SOCIAL SECURITY NUMBER	789-25-6431	Pay Rate	$16.85/hour	Step 4c W-4 Info	none

Period Ended	Hrs Worked	Reg Pay	OT Pay	Holiday	Comm	Gross Pay	401(k)	Sec 125	Taxable Pay for Federal W/H	Taxable Pay for FICA
3/5/2021	40	$674.00				$674.00			$674.00	$674.00

Taxable Pay for Federal W/H	Taxable Pay for FICA	Fed Inc.	Social Sec. Tax	Medicare	State Inc. Tax	Garnishment	United Way	Net Pay	YTD Net Pay	YTD Gross Pay
$674.00	$674.00	$48.00	$41.79	$9.63	$33.70			$523.25	$4,597.92	$5,392.00

P7-3B.

LO 7-1, 7-2, 7-3

Using the payroll register from P7-1B for Appalachian Limited Home Design, complete the General Journal entry for the employees' pay for the March 12, 2021, payroll end date. Employees' paychecks will be issued on March 17.

	Date	Description	Post Ref.	Debit	Credit
1					
2					
3					
4					
5					
6					
7					
8					
9					

P7-4B.

LO 7-1, 7-2, 7-3

Using the payroll register from P7-1B for Appalachian Limited Home Design, complete the General Journal entry for the employer's share of the payroll taxes for the March 12, 2021, pay date. Assume a 5.4 percent SUTA rate and 0.6 percent FUTA rate, and assume that only $2,721.85 of the gross pay is subject to SUTA and FUTA taxes.

	Date	Description	Post Ref.	Debit	Credit
1					
2					
3					
4					
5					
6					
7					
8					
9					

P7-5B.

LO 7-3, 7-4

Using the employee payroll entry from P7-3B, post the March 12 employee payroll end date for Appalachian Limited Home Design to the selected General Ledger accounts. Posting reference will be J1.

Account: Salaries and Wages Payable

	Date	Description	Post Ref.	Debit	Credit	Balance Debit	Balance Credit
1							
2							
3							
4							
5							
6							

Account: Employee Federal Income Tax Payable

	Date	Description	Post Ref.	Debit	Credit	Balance Debit	Balance Credit
1							
2							
3							
4							
5							
6							

Account: Social Security Tax Payable

	Date	Description	Post Ref.	Debit	Credit	Balance Debit	Balance Credit
1							
2							
3							
4							
5							
6							

Account: Medicare Tax Payable

	Date	Description	Post Ref.	Debit	Credit	Balance Debit	Balance Credit
1							
2							
3							
4							
5							
6							

Account: Employee State Income Tax Payable

	Date	Description	Post Ref.	Debit	Credit	Balance Debit	Balance Credit
1							
2							
3							
4							
5							
6							

Account: Salaries and Wages Expense

	Date	Description	Post Ref.	Debit	Credit	Balance Debit	Balance Credit
1							
2							
3							
4							
5							
6							
7							

P7-6B.   Using the employee payroll entry from P7-3B, complete the General

LO 7-3, 7-4   Journal entry for the issuance of Appalachian Limited Home Design pay on March 17, 2021.

	Date	Description	Post Ref.	Debit	Credit	
1						1
2						2
3						3
4						4
5						5

P7-7B.   Using the employer payroll entry from P7-4B, post the employer's share

LO 7-3, 7-4   of payroll taxes for the March 12 pay period at Appalachian Limited Home Design to the appropriate General Ledger accounts. Employees are paid weekly. Assume a 5.4 percent SUTA rate and 0.6 percent FUTA rate, and assume that $954.05 of the gross pay is subject to SUTA and FUTA taxes. Note: FUTA and SUTA taxes are only employer share.

Account: Payroll Taxes Expense

	Date	Description	Post Ref.	Debit	Credit	Balance Debit	Balance Credit	
1								1
2								2
3								3
4								4
5								5
6								6
7								7

Account: Social Security Tax Payable

	Date	Description	Post Ref.	Debit	Credit	Balance Debit	Balance Credit	
1								1
2								2
3								3
4								4
5								5
6								6
7								7

Account: Medicare Tax Payable

	Date	Description	Post Ref.	Debit	Credit	Balance Debit	Balance Credit	
1								1
2								2
3								3
4								4
5								5
6								6
7								7

Account: Federal Unemployment Tax Payable

	Date	Description	Post Ref.	Debit	Credit	Balance Debit	Balance Credit	
1								1
2								2
3								3
4								4
5								5
6								6
7								7

Account: State Unemployment Tax Payable

	Date	Description	Post Ref.	Debit	Credit	Balance Debit	Balance Credit	
1								1
2								2
3								3
4								4
5								5
6								6
7								7

P7-8B.

LO 7-2, 7-3

Legends Leadworks is a monthly schedule depositor of payroll taxes. For the month of April 2021, the payroll taxes (employee and employer share) were as follows:

Social Security tax: $5,386.56

Medicare tax: $1,259.76

Employee federal income tax: $4,978.00

Create the General Journal entry for the remittance of the taxes on May 14, 2021. Use check 1320 in the description.

	Date	Description	Post Ref.	Debit	Credit	
1						1
2						2
3						3
4						4
5						5
6						6
7						7
8						8

P7-9B.

LO 7-2, 7-3

Candy Farms Incorporated has the following voluntary withholdings to remit as of September 30, 2021:

AFLAC payable: $687.00

Workers' compensation insurance payable: $1,042.00

401(k) contributions payable: $2,104.00

Garnishments payable: $450.00

U.S. savings bonds payable: $200.00

Create the General Journal entry for the remittance of these withheld amounts on October 15, 2021.

	Date	Description	Post Ref.	Debit	Credit	
1						1
2						2
3						3
4						4
5						5
6						6
7						7
8						8

P7-10B.

LO 7-5, 7-6

Pujah Srinivasan is the controller for HHT Industries. She has been asked to explain the payroll accounts on the financial statements for the preceding month. What information will she find about payroll on the financial statements?

P7-11B.

LO 7-5, 7-6

You are interviewing for a position with Limelight Photography. The president of the company, Emma Jankiewicz, asks you to explain how payroll is both an expense and a liability of the company. How will you answer her?

Critical Thinking

7-1. Your boss asks you for a five-year labor cost trend chart. The labor costs per year are as follows:

2017	$175,248
2018	165,225
2019	179,905
2020	151,250
2021	186,417

Construct a line chart to depict the data. What conclusions can you derive from the data about labor costs and trends over the past five years? Why?

7-2. Giblin's Goodies pays employees weekly on Fridays. However, the company notices that March 31 is a Wednesday, and the pay period will end on April 2. The payroll data for March 29–31 is as follows:

Gross pay: $4,500.00

Federal income tax: $520.00

Social Security tax: $279.00

Medicare tax: $65.25

State income tax: $90.00

Federal Unemployment Tax $27.00

State Unemployment Tax $243.00

Give the adjusting entry in the General Journal to recognize the employee and employer share of the payroll for March 29–31. The date of the entry is March 31. Then record the journal entry to reverse the adjustment on April 1, 2021.

	Date	Description	Post Ref.	Debit	Credit	
1						1
2						2
3						3
4						4
5						5
6						6
7						7
8						8
9						9
10						10
11						11
12						12
13						13
14						14
15						15
16						16
17						17
18						18
19						19
20						20
21						21
22						22
23						23
24						24
25						25
26						26
27						27
28						28
29						29
30						30

In the Real World: Scenario for Discussion

An ongoing discussion among business managers is the return on employee investment (ROEI). Employers want to maximize business profitability, and employees are a significant part of organizational success. Investments in employee training and professional development constitute a significant part of many companies' budgets. Measures including providing tablet computers for employees to pursue flexible learning opportunities and self-paced classes allow employers to reduce training and development costs. What are the pros and cons of this practice?

Internet Activities

7-1. Would you like to know about personal experiences as a payroll accountant? How about videos that detail the completion of payroll-related forms? Go to www.youtube. com and search the term *payroll accounting* to read personal perspectives about payroll practice, outsourcing, and tax form completion. What were three insights new to you?

7-2. Would you like to build your own favorites list of payroll accounting tools? Go to one or more of the following sites. What are three important items you noticed?

www.accountingtools.com

www.accountantsworld.com

www.americanpayroll.org

7-3. Join a conversation about payroll accounting with industry professionals. Go to www.linkedin.com and establish a profile (if you do not have one). Search groups for payroll accounting and follow the conversations. Which topics did you choose? Why?

7-4. Want to know more about the concepts in this chapter? Check out:

www.moneyinstructor.com/lesson/accountingconcepts.asp

https://www.accountingcoach.com/accounting-basics/outline

Continuing Payroll Project: Prevosti Farms and Sugarhouse

Complete the Payroll Register for the February and March biweekly pay periods, assuming benefits went into effect as anticipated.

Use the Wage Bracket Method Tables for Income Tax Withholding in Appendix C (or the IRS federal income tax withholding assistant). Complete the General Journal entries as follows:

February 5	Journalize the employee pay.
February 5	Journalize the employer payroll tax for the February 5 pay period. Use 5.4 percent SUTA and 0.6 percent FUTA. No employees will exceed the FUTA or SUTA wage base.
February 10	Issue the employee pay.
February 19	Journalize the employee pay.
February 19	Journalize the employer payroll tax for the February 19 pay period. Use 5.4 percent SUTA and 0.6 percent FUTA. No employee will exceed the FUTA or SUTA wage base.
February 24	Issue the employee pay.
February 24	Issue payment for the payroll liabilities.
March 5	Journalize the employee pay.
March 5	Journalize the employer payroll tax for the March 5 pay period. Use 5.4 percent SUTA and 0.6 percent FUTA. No employees will exceed the FUTA or SUTA wage base.
March 10	Issue the employee pay.
March 19	Journalize the employee pay.
March 19	Journalize the employer payroll tax for the March 19 pay period. Use 5.4 percent SUTA and 0.6 percent FUTA. No employees will exceed the FUTA or SUTA wage base.
March 24	Issue the employee pay.
March 24	Issue payment for the payroll liabilities.

	Date	Description	Post Ref.	Debit	Credit	
1						1
2						2
3						3
4						4
5						5
6						6
7						7
8						8
9						9
10						10
11						11
12						12
13						13
14						14
15						15
16						16
17						17
18						18
19						19
20						20
21						21
22						22
23						23
24						24
25						25
26						26
27						27
28						28
29						29
30						30
31						31
32						32
33						33
34						34
35						35

Post all journal entries to the appropriate General Ledger accounts.

Account: Cash   **101**

	Date	Description	Post Ref.	Debit	Credit	Balance Debit	Balance Credit	
1		Beg. Bal.				47 0 0 0 00		1
2								2
3								3
4								4
5								5
6								6

Account: Employee Federal Income Tax Payable   **203**

	Date	Description	Post Ref.	Debit	Credit	Balance Debit	Balance Credit	
1								1
2								2
3								3
4								4
5								5
6								6

Account: Social Security Tax Payable   **204**

	Date	Description	Post Ref.	Debit	Credit	Balance Debit	Balance Credit	
1								1
2								2
3								3
4								4
5								5
6								6

Account: Medicare Tax Payable   **205**

	Date	Description	Post Ref.	Debit	Credit	Balance Debit	Balance Credit	
1								1
2								2
3								3
4								4
5								5
6								6

Account: Employee State Income Tax Payable   **206**

	Date	Description	Post Ref.	Debit	Credit	Balance Debit	Balance Credit	
1								1
2								2
3								3
4								4
5								5
6								6

Account: 401(k) Contributions Payable   **208**

	Date	Description	Post Ref.	Debit	Credit	Balance Debit	Balance Credit	
1								1
2								2
3								3
4								4
5								5
6								6

Account: Health Insurance Payable   209

	Date	Description	Post Ref.	Debit	Credit	Balance Debit	Balance Credit	
1								1
2								2
3								3
4								4
5								5
6								6

Account: Salaries and Wages Payable   210

	Date	Description	Post Ref.	Debit	Credit	Balance Debit	Balance Credit	
1								1
2								2
3								3
4								4
5								5
6								6

Account: FUTA Tax Payable   211

	Date	Description	Post Ref.	Debit	Credit	Balance Debit	Balance Credit	
1								1
2								2
3								3
4								4
5								5
6								6

Account: SUTA Tax Payable   212

	Date	Description	Post Ref.	Debit	Credit	Balance Debit	Balance Credit	
1								1
2								2
3								3
4								4
5								5
6								6

Account: Payroll Taxes Expense   514

	Date	Description	Post Ref.	Debit	Credit	Balance Debit	Balance Credit	
1								1
2								2
3								3
4								4
5								5
6								6

Account: Salaries and Wages Expense   **515**

	Date	Description	Post Ref.	Debit	Credit	Balance Debit	Balance Credit	
1								1
2								2
3								3
4								4
5								5
6								6

Answers to Stop & Check Exercises

Employees' Earnings Records

1. The payroll register contains the period payroll information for all employees. The employees' earnings record lists all payroll data for a single employee.
2. a. Name
   b. Pay rate
   c. Net pay
3. Quarterly and annual tax reports use the totals from the employees' earnings records.

Financial Accounting Concepts

1. Assets = Liabilities + Owners' Equity
2. Credit
3. Debit

Payroll and the General Journal

1. Wages and Salaries Expense

2.
Account	Debit	Credit
Payroll Taxes Expense	$9,546.05	
Social Security Tax Payable		$7,736.67
Medicare Tax Payable		$1,809.38

3.
Account	Debit	Credit
Federal Income Tax Payable	$ 6,234.00	
Social Security Tax Payable	2,653.29	
Medicare Tax Payable	620.53	
State Income Tax Payable	1,626.21	
Wages and Salaries Payable	31,660.97	
Wages and Salaries Expense		$42,795.00

General Ledger Entries

1. $2,760 Cr.
2. The transaction may be found in the General Journal earlier in this section.

The Business Effects of Payroll

1. The payment of employee wages decreases profitability because it increases the expenses of a business.
2. Allocation of payroll expenses to specific jobs, clients, and so on allows the company to understand the costs associated with the activity.

Labor Reports

1. a. Trial balance
   b. Statement of owners' equity
   c. Income statement
   d. Balance sheet
2. Labor reports
3. Trend reports are used by managers to identify business patterns, needs, and opportunities.

Appendix A

Comprehensive Payroll Project: Wayland Custom Woodworking

Wayland Custom Woodworking is a firm that manufactures custom cabinets and woodwork for business and residential customers. Students will have the opportunity to establish payroll records and to complete a month of payroll information for Wayland.

Wayland Custom Woodworking is located at 12850 Old Highway 50, Glenbrook, Nevada, 89413, phone number 775-555-9877. The owner is Mark Wayland. Wayland's EIN is 91-7444533 and the Nevada Employer Account Number is E6462582020-6. Wayland has determined it will pay its employees on a semimonthly basis. Federal income tax should be computed using the *percentage* method.

Students will complete the payroll for the final quarter of 2021 and will file the fourth quarter and annual tax reports on the appropriate dates. At the instructor's discretion, students may complete a short version, which contains the payroll transactions beginning December 6. Directions for completion of the short version follow the November 30 transactions.

Rounding can create a challenge. For these exercises, the rate for the individuals is not rounded. Take the employee's salary and divide it by 2,080 (52 weeks at 40 hours per week) for full-time, nonexempt employees. Note: Leave the hourly rate rounded to 5 decimal places as shown in the next example. *After* the gross pay has been calculated, then round the result to two decimal points prior to calculating taxes or other withholdings.

EXAMPLE: ANNUAL SALARY TO HOURLY RATE, NONEXEMPT EMPLOYEE

Employee Cooper's annual salary is $62,000 and he is a nonexempt employee.

Hourly rate = $62,000/(52 × 40) = $62,000/2,080

Hourly rate = $29.80769 per hour

EXAMPLE: PERIOD GROSS PAY, SALARIED EMPLOYEE

Employee Chinson earns an annual salary of $48,000 and is paid semimonthly.

Period gross pay = $48,000/24 = $2,000 gross pay

For pay periods with holiday hours: determine the amount paid per day, multiply by the number of days applicable to each pay period.

Annual salary: $48,000/(52 × 5) = $48,000/260 = $184.61538 (rounded to 5 decimal points) per day. Once you have the holiday pay, subtract it from their salary for the period for regular time.

Employees are paid for the following holidays occurring during the final quarter:

- Thanksgiving day and the day after, Thursday and Friday, November 25–26.
- Christmas is on Saturday. Employees receive holiday pay for Friday, December 24.

For the completion of this project, students will use the percentage method for federal income tax. Employees' 401(k) and insurance are pre-tax for federal income tax located in Appendix C. The SUTA (UI) rate for Wayland Custom Woodworking is 3.25 percent on the first $33,400 of employee wages. There is an additional 0.05 percent for Career Enhancement Program (CEP). FUTA, SUTA, and CEP allow for a deduction for Section 125 contributions, not for 401(k) contributions. Employer contribution of Section 125 is 1.5 times the employee portion and should be added to the wages for the completion of FUTA and SUTA forms.

No employee has additional information in Step 4 of their W-4s, all W-4s were received in 2021, and no box 2c has been checked.

Semimonthly Federal Percentage Method for manual payrolls with Forms W-4 from 2020 or later Tax Table	Appendix C
Federal Unemployment Rate (employer only) (less Section 125)	0.6% on the first $7,000 of wages
State Unemployment Rate (employer only) (less Section 125)	3.25% on the first $33,400 of wages
Career Enhancement Program (employer only) (less Section 125)	0.05% on the first $33,400 of wages

October 1

Wayland Custom Woodworking (WCW) pays its employees according to their job classification. Wayland's staff comprises the following employees:

Employee Number	Name and Address	Payroll information
00-Chins	Anthony Chinson	Married/Joint; 2 < 17
	530 Chimney Rock Road	Exempt
	Stateline, NV 89449	$48,000/year + commission
	775-555-1212	Start Date: 10/1/2021
	Job title: Account Executive	SSN: 511-22-3333
00-Wayla	Mark Wayland	Married/Joint; 3 < 17, 1 Other
	1650 Power House Drive	Exempt
	Glenbrook, NV 89413	$85,000/year
	775-555-1110	Start Date: 10/1/2021
	Job title: President/Owner	SSN: 505-33-1775

Employee Number	Name and Address	Payroll information
01-Peppi	Sylvia Peppinico	Married/Joint; 1 < 17, 1 Other
	1575 Flowers Avenue	Exempt
	Glenbrook, NV 89413	$58,500/year
	775-555-2244	Start Date: 10/1/2021
	Job title: Craftsman	SSN: 047-55-9951
01-Coope	Stevon Cooper	Single; None
	2215 Lands End Drive	Nonexempt
	Glenbrook, NV 89413	$62,000/year
	775-555-9981	Start Date: 10/1/2021
	Job title: Craftsman	SSN: 022-66-1131
02-Hisso	Leonard Hissop	Single; 1 Other
	333 Engine House Circle	Nonexempt
	Glenbrook, NV 89413	$51,500/year
	775-555-5858	Start Date: 10/1/2021
	Job title: Purchasing/Shipping	SSN: 311-22-6698

Voluntary deductions for each employee are as follows:

Name	Deduction
Chinson	Insurance: $50/paycheck
	401(k): 3% of gross pay
Wayland	Insurance: $75/paycheck
	401(k): 6% of gross pay
Peppinico	Insurance: $75/paycheck
	401(k): $50 per paycheck
Cooper	Insurance: $50/paycheck
	401(k): 4% of gross pay
Hissop	Insurance: $75/paycheck
	401(k): 3% of gross pay
Success	Insurance: $50/paycheck
	401(k): 3% of gross pay

Complete the headers of the Employees' Earnings Register for all company employees. Enter the YTD earnings for each employee. The departments are as follows:

Department 00: Sales and Administration

Department 01: Factory Workers

Department 02: Delivery and Customer Service

1. You have been hired as of October 1 as the new accounting clerk. Your employee number is 00-SUCCE. Your name is STUDENT SUCCESS. Your address is 16 Kelly Circle #2, Glenbrook, NV 89413. Your phone number is 775-556-1211, you were born July 16, 1985, your Nevada driver's license number is 168575381944 expiring on your birthday in 2024, and your Social Security number is 555-55-5555. You are nonexempt and paid at a rate of $42,000 per year as an accounting clerk. Complete Form W-4 and, using the given information, complete the I-9 form to start your employee file. Complete it as if you are single with no dependents or other income, you contribute 3 percent to a 401(k), and health insurance is $50 per pay period.

The balance sheet for WCW as of September 30, 2021, is as follows:

Wayland Custom Woodworking
Balance Sheet
September 30, 2021

Assets		Liabilities & Equity	
Cash	$1,125,000.00	Accounts Payable	$ 112,490.00
Supplies	27,240.00	Salaries and Wages Payable	
Office Equipment	87,250.00	Federal Unemployment Tax Payable	
Inventory	123,000.00	Social Security Tax Payable	
Vehicle	25,000.00	Medicare Tax Payable	
Accumulated Depreciation, Vehicle		State Unemployment Tax Payable	
Building	164,000.00	Career Enhancement Program Payable	
Accumulated Depreciation, Building		Employee Federal Income Tax Payable	
Land	35,750.00	Employee State Income Tax Payable	
Total Assets	1,587,240.00	401(k) Contributions Payable	
		Employee Medical Premiums Payable	
		Notes Payable	224,750.00
		Total Liabilities	337,240.00
		Owners' Equity	1,250,000.00
		Retained Earnings	—
		Total Equity	1,250,000.00
		Total Liabilities and Equity	1,587,240.00

October 15

October 15 is the end of the first pay period for the month of October. Employee pay will be disbursed on October 19, 2021. Any time worked in excess of 88 hours during this pay period is considered overtime for nonexempt employees. Remember that the employees are paid on a semimonthly basis. The hours for the employees are as follows:

Name	Hourly Rate or Period Wage (round to 5 decimals)	Pay Period Hours 10/1–10/15	Regular (round to 2 decimals)	Overtime (round to 2 decimals)	Commission
Chinson		88 hours (exempt)			$1,500.00
Wayland		88 hours (exempt)			
Peppinico		88 hours (exempt)			
Cooper		88 hours			
Hissop		93.25 hours			
Success		90 hours			

October 2021

Sunday	Monday	Tuesday	Wednesday	Thursday	Friday	Saturday
					1	2
3	4	5	6	7	8	9
10	11	12	13	14	15	16
17	18	19	20	21	22	23
24	25	26	27	28	29	30
31						

Complete the Payroll Register for October 15. Round wages to five decimal points and all other final answers to two decimal points. Update the Employees' Earnings Records for the period's pay and update the YTD amounts. Insurance qualifies for Section 125 treatment. Use the percentage method for manual payroll systems with Forms W-4 From 2020 or later in Appendix C for the federal income tax. The starting check number is 4215.

Voluntary deductions for each employee are as follows:

Name	Deduction
Chinson	Insurance: $50/paycheck
	401(k): 3% of gross pay
Wayland	Insurance: $75/paycheck
	401(k): 6% of gross pay
Peppinico	Insurance: $75/paycheck
	401(k): $50 per paycheck
Cooper	Insurance: $50/paycheck
	401(k): 4% of gross pay
Hissop	Insurance: $75/paycheck
	401(k): 3% of gross pay
Success	Insurance: $50/paycheck
	101(k): 3% of gross pay

Complete the Payroll Register for October 15

P/R End Date _____　Company Name　Wayland Custom Woodworking

Check Date _____

Name	Filing Status	Dependents	Hourly Rate or Period wage	No. of Regular Hours	No. of Overtime Hours	No. of Holiday Hours	Commissions	Gross Earning	Sec 125	401(k)	Taxable Wages for Federal W/H	Taxable Wages for FICA
Anthony Chinson												
Mark Wayland												
Sylvia Peppinico												
Stevon Cooper												
Leonard Hissop												
Student Success												
Totals								–	–	–	–	–	–

Name	Gross Earning	Taxable Wages for Federal W/H	Taxable Wages for FICA	Federal W/H Tax	Social Security Tax	Medicare Tax	Total Deduc	Net Pay	Check No.
Anthony Chinson									4215
Mark Wayland									4216
Sylvia Peppinico									4217
Stevon Cooper									4218
Leonard Hissop									4219
Student Success									4220
Totals	–	–	–	–	–	–	–	–	

EMPLOYEE EARNING RECORD

NAME		Hire Date		Dependent child <17	
ADDRESS		Date of Birth		Dependent other	
CITY/STATE/ZIP		Position		Step 4a W-4 Info	
TELEPHONE		Filing Status		Step 4b W-4 Info	
SOCIAL SECURITY				Step 4c W-4 Info	
NUMBER		Pay Rate		Hr/Wk/Mo/Yr	

Period Ended	Hrs Worked	Reg Pay	OT Pay	Holiday	Comm	Gross Pay	Ins	401(k)	Taxable Pay for Federal	Taxable Pay for FICA

Taxable Pay for Federal	Taxable Pay for FICA	Fed Inc. Tax	Social Sec. Tax	Medicare	Total Deduc	Net Pay	YTD Net Pay	YTD Gross Pay	Current Taxable for FUTA	Current Taxable for SUTA

EMPLOYEE EARNING RECORD

NAME		Hire Date		Dependent child <17	
ADDRESS		Date of Birth		Dependent other	
CITY/STATE/ZIP		Position		Step 4a W-4 Info	
TELEPHONE		Filing Status		Step 4b W-4 Info	
SOCIAL SECURITY				Step 4c W-4 Info	
NUMBER		Pay Rate		Hr/Wk/Mo/Yr	

Period Ended	Hrs Worked	Reg Pay	OT Pay	Holiday	Comm	Gross Pay	Ins	401(k)	Taxable Pay for Federal	Taxable Pay for FICA

Taxable Pay for Federal	Taxable Pay for FICA	Fed Inc. Tax	Social Sec. Tax	Medicare	Total Deduc	Net Pay	YTD Net Pay	YTD Gross Pay	Current Taxable for FUTA	Current Taxable for SUTA

EMPLOYEE EARNING RECORD

NAME _____ Hire Date _____ Dependent child <17 _____
ADDRESS _____ Date of Birth _____ Dependent other _____
CITY/STATE/ZIP _____ Position _____ Step 4a W-4 Info _____
TELEPHONE _____ Filing Status _____ Step 4b W-4 Info _____
SOCIAL SECURITY _____ Step 4c W-4 Info _____
NUMBER _____ Pay Rate _____ Hr/Wk/Mo/Yr

Period Ended	Hrs Worked	Reg Pay	OT Pay	Holiday	Comm	Gross Pay	Ins	401(k)	Taxable Pay for Federal	Taxable Pay for FICA

Taxable Pay for Federal	Taxable Pay for FICA	Fed Inc. Tax	Social Sec. Tax	Medicare	Total Deduc	Net Pay	YTD Net Pay	YTD Gross Pay	Current Taxable for FUTA	Current Taxable for SUTA

EMPLOYEE EARNING RECORD

NAME _____ Hire Date _____ Dependent child <17 _____
ADDRESS _____ Date of Birth _____ Dependent other _____
CITY/STATE/ZIP _____ Position _____ Step 4a W-4 Info _____
TELEPHONE _____ Filing Status _____ Step 4b W-4 Info _____
SOCIAL SECURITY _____ Step 4c W-4 Info _____
NUMBER _____ Pay Rate _____ Hr/Wk/Mo/Yr

Period Ended	Hrs Worked	Reg Pay	OT Pay	Holiday	Comm	Gross Pay	Ins	401(k)	Taxable Pay for Federal	Taxable Pay for FICA

Taxable Pay for Federal	Taxable Pay for FICA	Fed Inc. Tax	Social Sec. Tax	Medicare	Total Deduc	Net Pay	YTD Net Pay	YTD Gross Pay	Current Taxable for FUTA	Current Taxable for SUTA

EMPLOYEE EARNING RECORD

NAME	_____	Hire Date	_____	Dependent child <17	_____
ADDRESS	_____	Date of Birth	_____	Dependent other	_____
CITY/STATE/ZIP	_____	Position	_____	Step 4a W-4 Info	_____
TELEPHONE	_____	Filing Status	_____	Step 4b W-4 Info	_____
SOCIAL SECURITY	_____			Step 4c W-4 Info	_____
NUMBER	_____	Pay Rate	_____	Hr/Wk/Mo/Yr	

Period Ended	Hrs Worked	Reg Pay	OT Pay	Holiday	Comm	Gross Pay	Ins	401(k)	Taxable Pay for Federal	Taxable Pay for FICA

Taxable Pay for Federal	Taxable Pay for FICA	Fed Inc. Tax	Social Sec. Tax	Medicare	Total Deduc	Net Pay	YTD Net Pay	YTD Gross Pay	Current Taxable for FUTA	Current Taxable for SUTA

EMPLOYEE EARNING RECORD

NAME	_____	Hire Date	_____	Dependent child <17	_____
ADDRESS	_____	Date of Birth	_____	Dependent other	_____
CITY/STATE/ZIP	_____	Position	_____	Step 4a W-4 Info	_____
TELEPHONE	_____	Filing Status	_____	Step 4b W-4 Info	_____
SOCIAL SECURITY	_____			Step 4c W-4 Info	_____
NUMBER	_____	Pay Rate	_____	Hr/Wk/Mo/Yr	

Period Ended	Hrs Worked	Reg Pay	OT Pay	Holiday	Comm	Gross Pay	Ins	401(k)	Taxable Pay for Federal	Taxable Pay for FICA

Taxable Pay for Federal	Taxable Pay for FICA	Fed Inc. Tax	Social Sec. Tax	Medicare	Total Deduc	Net Pay	YTD Net Pay	YTD Gross Pay	Current Taxable for FUTA	Current Taxable for SUTA

General Journal Entries

Complete the General Journal entries as follows:

15-Oct	Journalize employee pay.
15-Oct	Journalize employer payroll tax for the October 15 pay date.
19-Oct	Journalize the payment of payroll.

Post all journal entries to the appropriate General Ledger accounts.

Date		Description	Post Ref.	Debit	Credit

October 31

October 31 is the end of the final pay period for the month. Employee pay will be disbursed on November 4, 2021. Due to customer demand, all employees worked 10/23 in addition to normal weekdays. Any hours exceeding 80 during this pay period are considered overtime for nonexempt employees. Compute the employee pay. Update the Employees' Earnings Records for the period's pay and update the YTD amount.

Complete the Payroll Register for October 31. Round wages to five decimal points and all other final answers to two decimal points.

The hours for the employees are as follows:

Name	Hourly Rate or Period Wage (round to 5 decimals)	Hours Worked 10/16–10/31	Regular (round to 2 decimals)	Overtime (round to 2 decimals)	Commission
Chinson		80 hours (exempt)			$1,750.00
Wayland		80 hours (exempt)			
Peppinico		80 hours (exempt)			
Cooper		84 hours			
Hissop		87 hours			
Success		82 hours			

October 2021

Sunday	Monday	Tuesday	Wednesday	Thursday	Friday	Saturday
					1	2
3	4	5	6	7	8	9
10	11	12	13	14	15	16
17	18	19	20	21	22	23
24	25	26	27	28	29	30
31						

Complete the Payroll Register for October 31

P/R End Date _____   Company Name   Wayland Custom Woodworking

Check Date _____

Name	Filing Status	Dependents	Hourly Rate or Period wage	No. of Regular Hours	No. of Overtime Hours	No. of Holiday Hours	Commissions	Gross Earning	Sec 125	401(k)	Taxable Wages for Federal W/H	Taxable Wages for FICA
Anthony Chinson												
Mark Wayland												
Sylvia Peppinico												
Stevon Cooper												
Leonard Hissop												
Student Success												
Totals							–	–	–	–	–	–

Name	Gross Earning	Taxable Wages for Federal W/H	Taxable Wages for FICA	Federal W/H Tax	Social Security Tax	Medicare Tax	Total Deduc	Net Pay	Check No.
Anthony Chinson									4221
Mark Wayland									4222
Sylvia Peppinico									4223
Stevon Cooper									4224
Leonard Hissop									4225
Student Success									4226
Totals	–	–	–	–	–	–	–	–	

General Journal Entries

Complete the General Journal entries as follows:

31-Oct	Journalize employee pay.
31-Oct	Journalize employer payroll tax for the October 31 pay date.
04-Nov	Journalize the payment of payroll to employees. (Use one entry for all disbursements.)
04-Nov	Journalize remittance of 401(k) and Section 125 health insurance premiums deducted.
04-Nov	Journalize remittance of monthly payroll taxes.

Post all journal entries to the appropriate General Ledger accounts

Date		Description	Post Ref.	Debit	Credit

November 15

Compute the pay for each employee. Update the Employees' Earnings Record for the period's pay and the new YTD amount. Employee pay will be disbursed on November 19, 2021. Any hours exceeding 88 during this pay period are considered overtime for nonexempt employees. Remember that the employees are paid semimonthly.

Complete the Payroll Register for November 15. Round wages to five decimal points and all other final answers to two decimal points.

The hours for the employees are as follows:

Name	Hourly Rate or Period Wage (round to 5 decimals)	Pay Period Hours 11/01–11/15	Regular (round to 2 decimals)	Overtime (round to 2 decimals)	Commission
Chinson		88 hours (exempt)			$1,050.00
Wayland		88 hours (exempt)			
Peppinico		88 hours (exempt)			
Cooper		96 hours			
Hissop		91 hours			
Success		93 hours			

November 2021

Sunday	Monday	Tuesday	Wednesday	Thursday	Friday	Saturday
	1	2	3	4	5	6
7	8	9	10	11	12	13
14	15	16	17	18	19	20
21	22	23	24	25	26	27
28	29	30				

Complete the Payroll Register for November 15

P/R End Date _____   Company Name   Wayland Custom Woodworking

Check Date _____

Name	Filing Status	Dependents	Hourly Rate or Period wage	No. of Regular Hours	No. of Overtime Hours	No. of Holiday Hours	Commissions	Gross Earning	Sec 125	401(k)	Taxable Wages for Federal W/H	Taxable Wages for FICA
Anthony Chinson												
Mark Wayland												
Sylvia Peppinico												
Stevon Cooper												
Leonard Hissop												
Student Success												
Totals							–	–	–	–	–	–

Name	Gross Earning	Taxable Wages for Federal W/H	Taxable Wages for FICA	Federal W/H Tax	Social Security Tax	Medicare Tax	Total Deduc	Net Pay	Check No.
Anthony Chinson									4227
Mark Wayland									4228
Sylvia Peppinico									4229
Stevon Cooper									4230
Leonard Hissop									4231
Student Success									4232
Totals	–	–	–	–	–	–	–	–	

General Journal Entries

Complete the General Journal entries as follows:

15-Nov	Journalize employee pay.
15-Nov	Journalize employer payroll tax for the November 15 pay date.
19-Nov	Journalize payment of payroll to employees.

Post all journal entries to the appropriate General Ledger accounts.

Date		Description	Post Ref.	Debit	Credit

November 30

Compute the Net Pay for each employee. Employee pay will be disbursed on December 3, 2021. Update the Employees' Earnings Records with the November 30 pay and the new YTD amount.

The company is closed and pays for the Friday following Thanksgiving. The employees will receive holiday pay for Thanksgiving and the Friday following. All the hours over 88 are eligible for overtime for nonexempt employees as they were worked during the non-holiday week.

The hours for the employees are as follows:

Name	Hourly Rate or Period Wage (round to 5 decimals)	Pay Period Hours 11/16–11/30	Regular (round to 2 decimals)	Overtime (round to 2 decimals)	Holiday (round to 2 decimals)	Commission
Chinson		88 hours (exempt — 16 hours Holiday)				$2,325.00
Wayland		88 hours (exempt — 16 hours Holiday)				
Peppinico		88 hours (exempt — 16 hours Holiday)				
Cooper		90 hours (16 hours Holiday)				
Hissop		91 hours (16 hours Holiday)				
Success		89 hours (16 hours Holiday)				

November 2021						
Sunday	Monday	Tuesday	Wednesday	Thursday	Friday	Saturday
	1	2	3	4	5	6
7	8	9	10	11	12	13
14	15	16	17	18	19	20
21	22	23	24	25	26	27
28	29	30				

Complete the Payroll Register for November 30. Round wages to five decimal points and all other final answers to two decimal points.

Complete the Payroll Register for November 30

P/R End Date _____

Check Date _____

Company Name   Wayland Custom Woodworking

Name	Filing Status	Dependents	Hourly Rate or Period wage	No. of Regular Hours	No. of Overtime Hours	No. of Holiday Hours	Commissions	Gross Earning	Sec 125	401(k)	Taxable Wages for Federal W/H	Taxable Wages for FICA
Anthony Chinson												
Mark Wayland												
Sylvia Peppinico												
Stevon Cooper												
Leonard Hissop												
Student Success												
Totals								—	—	—	—	—	—

Name	Gross Earning	Taxable Wages for Federal W/H	Taxable Wages for FICA	Federal W/H Tax	Social Security Tax	Medicare Tax	Total Deduc	Net Pay	Check No.
Anthony Chinson									4233
Mark Wayland									4234
Sylvia Peppinico									4235
Stevon Cooper									4236
Leonard Hissop									4237
Student Success									4238
Totals	—	—	—	—	—	—	—	—	

General Journal Entries

Complete the General Journal entries as follows:

30-Nov	Journalize employee pay.
30-Nov	Journalize employer payroll tax for the November 30 pay date.
03-Dec	Journalize payment of payroll to employees.
03-Dec	Journalize remittance of 401(k) and health insurance premiums deducted.
03-Dec	Journalize remittance of monthly payroll taxes.

Post all journal entries to the appropriate General Ledger accounts.

Date		Description	Post Ref.	Debit	Credit

Short Version 1 Month option:

Wayland Custom Woodworking
Balance Sheet
November 30, 2021

Assets		Liabilities & Equity	
Cash	$ 1,076,814.02	Accounts Payable	$ 112,747.25
Supplies	42,240.11	Salaries and Wages Payable	12,682.32
Office Equipment	87,250.00	Federal Unemployment Tax Payable	58.86
Inventory	167,099.00	Social Security Tax Payable	4,041.50
Vehicle	25,000.00	Medicare Tax Payable	945.19
Accumulated Depreciation, Vehicle		State Unemployment Tax Payable	1,083.64
Building	164,000.00	Career Enhancement Program Payable	16.67
Accumulated Depreciation, Building		Employee Federal Income Tax Payable	4,227.54
Land	35,750.00	401(k) Contributions Payable	1,223.46
Total Assets	1,598,153.13	Employee Medical Premiums Payable	750.00
		Notes Payable	210,376.70
		Total Liabilities	348,153.13
		Owners' Equity	1,250,000.00
		Retained Earnings	-
		Total Equity	1,250,000.00
		Total Liabilities and Equity	1,598,153.13

Students will complete the payroll for the final month of 2021 and will file the fourth quarter and annual tax reports on the appropriate dates. Wayland Custom Woodworking is located at 12850 Old Highway 50, Glenbrook, Nevada, 89413, phone number 775-555-9877. The owner is Mark Wayland. Wayland's EIN is 91-7444533l. Wayland has determined it will pay its employees on a semimonthly basis. Federal income tax should be computed using the *percentage* method for manual payrolls with Forms W-4 from 2020 or later.

Rounding can create a challenge. For these exercises, the rate for the individuals is not rounded. For full-time, exempt employees take their salary and divide by 24 pay periods to get a period wage. So take their salary and divide by 2,080 (52 weeks at 40 hours per week) for full-time, nonexempt employees. Note: Leave the hourly rate rounded to 5 decimal places as shown in the example at the start of Appendix A. *After* the gross pay has been calculated, then round the result to two decimal points prior to calculating taxes or other withholdings.

December 15

Compute the net pay and update the Employees' Earnings Records with the December 15 pay and the new YTD information. Employee pay will be disbursed on December 20, 2021. Any hours worked in excess of 88 hours during this pay period are considered overtime for nonexempt employees.

The hours for the employees are as follows:

Name	Hourly Rate or Period Wage (round to 5 decimals)	Pay Period Hours 12/01–12/15	Regular (round to 2 decimals)	Overtime (round to 2 decimals)	Holiday (round to 2 decimals)	Commission
Chinson		88 hours (exempt)				$1,680.00
Wayland		88 hours (exempt)				
Peppinico		88 hours (exempt)				
Cooper		92 hours				
Hissop		88 hours				
Success		91 hours				

December 2021						
Sunday	Monday	Tuesday	Wednesday	Thursday	Friday	Saturday
			1	2	3	4
5	6	7	8	9	10	11
12	13	14	15	16	17	18
19	20	21	22	23	24	25
26	27	28	29	30	31	

Complete the Payroll Register for December 15. Round wages to five decimal points and all other final answers to two decimal points.

Complete the Payroll Register for December 15

P/R End Date [   ]   Company Name   Wayland Custom Woodworking

Check Date [   ]

Name	Filing Status	Dependents	Hourly Rate or Period wage	No. of Regular Hours	No. of Overtime Hours	No. of Holiday Hours	Commissions	Gross Earning	Sec 125	401(k)	Taxable Wages for Federal W/H	Taxable Wages for FICA
Anthony Chinson												
Mark Wayland												
Sylvia Peppinico												
Stevon Cooper												
Leonard Hissop												
Student Success												
Totals								–	–	–	–	–	–

Name	Gross Earning	Taxable Wages for Federal W/H	Taxable Wages for FICA	Federal W/H Tax	Social Security Tax	Medicare Tax	Total Deduc	Net Pay	Check No.
Anthony Chinson									4239
Mark Wayland									4240
Sylvia Peppinico									4241
Stevon Cooper									4242
Leonard Hissop									4243
Student Success									4244
Totals	–	–	–	–	–	–	–	–	

General Journal Entries

Complete the General Journal entries as follows:

15-Dec	Journalize employee pay.
20-Dec	Journalize employer payroll tax for the December 15 pay date.
20-Dec	Journalize payment of payroll to employees.

Post all journal entries to the appropriate General Ledger accounts.

Date		Description	Post Ref.	Debit	Credit

December 31

The final pay period of the year will not be paid to employees until January 4, 2022. The company will accrue the wages for the final pay period only. Since the pay period is complete, there will not be a reversing entry for the accrual.

The company pays for Christmas Eve and December 27 for 2021. Employees will be paid for both Friday and Monday as holiday pay.

Employee pay will be disbursed and reflected on the Employees' Earnings Register when paid. The remainder of the employer liability will be paid with the final filing for the year. Complete all state and federal tax forms for the year-end. Generate Forms W-2 and W-3 for employees, and recall that these forms only reflect wages actually paid during the calendar year. Employer amounts for health coverage should be reported as 1.5 times the employee's premium in Box 12, using Code DD. The forms will be signed on January 14, 2022.

The hours for the employees are as follows:

Name	Hourly Rate or Period Wage (round to 5 decimals)	Pay Period Hours 12/16–12/31	Regular (round to 2 decimals)	Overtime (round to 2 decimals)	Holiday (round to 2 decimals)	Commission
Chinson		96 hours (exempt — 16 hours Holiday)				$1,015.00
Wayland		96 hours (exempt — 16 hours Holiday)				
Peppinico		96 hours (exempt — 16 hours Holiday)				
Cooper		98 hours (16 Holiday)*				
Hissop		97 hours (16 Holiday)*				
Success		99 hours (16 Holiday)*				

*Employees worked extra hours on Wednesday, 12/29. Reminder, holidays and vacations are not included as hours *worked* for calculation of overtime.

December 2021						
Sunday	Monday	Tuesday	Wednesday	Thursday	Friday	Saturday
			1	2	3	4
5	6	7	8	9	10	11
12	13	14	15	16	17	18
19	20	21	22	23	24	25
26	27	28	29	30	31	

Complete the Payroll Register for December 31.

P/R End Date _____

Check Date _____

Company Name   Wayland Custom Woodworking

Name	Filing Status	Dependents	Hourly Rate or Period wage	No. of Regular Hours	No. of Overtime Hours	No. of Holiday Hours	Commissions	Gross Earning	Sec 125	401(k)	Taxable Wages for Federal W/H	Taxable Wages for FICA
Anthony Chinson												
Mark Wayland												
Sylvia Peppinico												
Stevon Cooper												
Leonard Hissop												
Student Success												
Totals							–	–	–	–	–	–

Name	Gross Earning	Taxable Wages for Federal W/H	Taxable Wages for FICA	Federal W/H Tax	Social Security Tax	Medicare Tax	Total Deduc	Net Pay	Check No.
Anthony Chinson									4245
Mark Wayland									4246
Sylvia Peppinico									4247
Stevon Cooper									4248
Leonard Hissop									4249
Student Success									4250
Totals	–	–	–	–	–	–	–	–	

General Journal Entries

Complete the General Journal entries as follows:

31-Dec	Accrue employee pay.
31-Dec	Accrue employer payroll tax for the December 31 pay date.

Post all journal entries to the appropriate General Ledger accounts.

Date		Description	Post Ref.	Debit	Credit

Employment Eligibility Verification
Department of Homeland Security
U.S. Citizenship and Immigration Services

USCIS
Form I-9
OMB No. 1615-0047
Expires 10/31/2022

▶**START HERE:** Read instructions carefully before completing this form. The instructions must be available, either in paper or electronically, during completion of this form. Employers are liable for errors in the completion of this form.

ANTI-DISCRIMINATION NOTICE: It is illegal to discriminate against work-authorized individuals. Employers **CANNOT** specify which document(s) an employee may present to establish employment authorization and identity. The refusal to hire or continue to employ an individual because the documentation presented has a future expiration date may also constitute illegal discrimination.

Section 1. Employee Information and Attestation *(Employees must complete and sign Section 1 of Form I-9 no later than the **first day of employment**, but not before accepting a job offer.)*

Last Name *(Family Name)*	First Name *(Given Name)*	Middle Initial	Other Last Names Used *(if any)*

Address *(Street Number and Name)*	Apt. Number	City or Town	State	ZIP Code

Date of Birth *(mm/dd/yyyy)*	U.S. Social Security Number	Employee's E-mail Address	Employee's Telephone Number
	☐☐☐-☐☐-☐☐☐☐		

I am aware that federal law provides for imprisonment and/or fines for false statements or use of false documents in connection with the completion of this form.

I attest, under penalty of perjury, that I am (check one of the following boxes):

☐ 1. A citizen of the United States

☐ 2. A noncitizen national of the United States *(See instructions)*

☐ 3. A lawful permanent resident   (Alien Registration Number/USCIS Number): _____

☐ 4. An alien authorized to work   until (expiration date, if applicable, mm/dd/yyyy): _____
Some aliens may write "N/A" in the expiration date field. *(See instructions)*

Aliens authorized to work must provide only one of the following document numbers to complete Form I-9:
An Alien Registration Number/USCIS Number OR Form I-94 Admission Number OR Foreign Passport Number.

QR Code - Section 1
Do Not Write In This Space

1. Alien Registration Number/USCIS Number: _____
OR
2. Form I-94 Admission Number: _____
OR
3. Foreign Passport Number: _____
Country of Issuance: _____

Signature of Employee	Today's Date *(mm/dd/yyyy)*

Preparer and/or Translator Certification (check one):

☐ I did not use a preparer or translator.   ☐ A preparer(s) and/or translator(s) assisted the employee in completing Section 1.

(Fields below must be completed and signed when preparers and/or translators assist an employee in completing Section 1.)

I attest, under penalty of perjury, that I have assisted in the completion of Section 1 of this form and that to the best of my knowledge the information is true and correct.

Signature of Preparer or Translator	Today's Date *(mm/dd/yyyy)*

Last Name *(Family Name)*	First Name *(Given Name)*

Address *(Street Number and Name)*	City or Town	State	ZIP Code

🛑 *Employer Completes Next Page* 🛑

Form I-9 10/21/2019

Page 1 of 3

United States Citizenship and Immigration Services

Employment Eligibility Verification
Department of Homeland Security
U.S. Citizenship and Immigration Services

USCIS
Form I-9
OMB No. 1615-0047
Expires 10/31/2022

Section 2. Employer or Authorized Representative Review and Verification

(Employers or their authorized representative must complete and sign Section 2 within 3 business days of the employee's first day of employment. You must physically examine one document from List A OR a combination of one document from List B and one document from List C as listed on the "Lists of Acceptable Documents.")

Employee Info from Section 1	Last Name *(Family Name)*	First Name *(Given Name)*	M.I.	Citizenship/Immigration Status

List A	OR	List B	AND	List C
Identity and Employment Authorization		**Identity**		**Employment Authorization**

List A — Identity and Employment Authorization	List B — Identity	List C — Employment Authorization
Document Title	Document Title	Document Title
Issuing Authority	Issuing Authority	Issuing Authority
Document Number	Document Number	Document Number
Expiration Date *(if any) (mm/dd/yyyy)*	Expiration Date *(if any) (mm/dd/yyyy)*	Expiration Date *(if any) (mm/dd/yyyy)*
Document Title		
Issuing Authority	Additional Information	QR Code - Sections 2 & 3 Do Not Write In This Space
Document Number		
Expiration Date *(if any) (mm/dd/yyyy)*		
Document Title		
Issuing Authority		
Document Number		
Expiration Date *(if any) (mm/dd/yyyy)*		

Certification: I attest, under penalty of perjury, that (1) I have examined the document(s) presented by the above-named employee, (2) the above-listed document(s) appear to be genuine and to relate to the employee named, and (3) to the best of my knowledge the employee is authorized to work in the United States.

The employee's first day of employment *(mm/dd/yyyy)*: _____   *(See instructions for exemptions)*

Signature of Employer or Authorized Representative	Today's Date *(mm/dd/yyyy)*	Title of Employer or Authorized Representative	
Last Name of Employer or Authorized Representative	First Name of Employer or Authorized Representative	Employer's Business or Organization Name	
Employer's Business or Organization Address *(Street Number and Name)*	City or Town	State	ZIP Code

Section 3. Reverification and Rehires *(To be completed and signed by employer or authorized representative.)*

A. New Name *(if applicable)*			B. Date of Rehire *(if applicable)*
Last Name *(Family Name)*	First Name *(Given Name)*	Middle Initial	Date *(mm/dd/yyyy)*

C. If the employee's previous grant of employment authorization has expired, provide the information for the document or receipt that establishes continuing employment authorization in the space provided below.

Document Title	Document Number	Expiration Date *(if any) (mm/dd/yyyy)*

I attest, under penalty of perjury, that to the best of my knowledge, this employee is authorized to work in the United States, and if the employee presented document(s), the document(s) I have examined appear to be genuine and to relate to the individual.

Signature of Employer or Authorized Representative	Today's Date *(mm/dd/yyyy)*	Name of Employer or Authorized Representative

Source: USCIS

LISTS OF ACCEPTABLE DOCUMENTS
All documents must be UNEXPIRED

Employees may present one selection from List A
or a combination of one selection from List B and one selection from List C.

LIST A Documents that Establish Both Identity and Employment Authorization		LIST B Documents that Establish Identity		LIST C Documents that Establish Employment Authorization
	OR		**AND**	
1. U.S. Passport or U.S. Passport Card		1. Driver's license or ID card issued by a State or outlying possession of the United States provided it contains a photograph or information such as name, date of birth, gender, height, eye color, and address		1. A Social Security Account Number card, unless the card includes one of the following restrictions: (1) NOT VALID FOR EMPLOYMENT (2) VALID FOR WORK ONLY WITH INS AUTHORIZATION (3) VALID FOR WORK ONLY WITH DHS AUTHORIZATION
2. Permanent Resident Card or Alien Registration Receipt Card (Form I-551)				
3. Foreign passport that contains a temporary I-551 stamp or temporary I-551 printed notation on a machine-readable immigrant visa		2. ID card issued by federal, state or local government agencies or entities, provided it contains a photograph or information such as name, date of birth, gender, height, eye color, and address		2. Certification of report of birth issued by the Department of State (Forms DS-1350, FS-545, FS-240)
4. Employment Authorization Document that contains a photograph (Form I-766)		3. School ID card with a photograph		3. Original or certified copy of birth certificate issued by a State, county, municipal authority, or territory of the United States bearing an official seal
5. For a nonimmigrant alien authorized to work for a specific employer because of his or her status: a. Foreign passport; and b. Form I-94 or Form I-94A that has the following: (1) The same name as the passport; and (2) An endorsement of the alien's nonimmigrant status as long as that period of endorsement has not yet expired and the proposed employment is not in conflict with any restrictions or limitations identified on the form.		4. Voter's registration card		
		5. U.S. Military card or draft record		
		6. Military dependent's ID card		4. Native American tribal document
		7. U.S. Coast Guard Merchant Mariner Card		5. U.S. Citizen ID Card (Form I-197)
		8. Native American tribal document		6. Identification Card for Use of Resident Citizen in the United States (Form I-179)
		9. Driver's license issued by a Canadian government authority		
		For persons under age 18 who are unable to present a document listed above:		7. Employment authorization document issued by the Department of Homeland Security
6. Passport from the Federated States of Micronesia (FSM) or the Republic of the Marshall Islands (RMI) with Form I-94 or Form I-94A indicating nonimmigrant admission under the Compact of Free Association Between the United States and the FSM or RMI		10. School record or report card		
		11. Clinic, doctor, or hospital record		
		12. Day-care or nursery school record		

Examples of many of these documents appear in the Handbook for Employers (M-274).

Refer to the instructions for more information about acceptable receipts.

Form **W-4**	**Employee's Withholding Certificate**	OMB No. 1545-0074
(Rev. December 2020) Department of the Treasury Internal Revenue Service	▶ Complete Form W-4 so that your employer can withhold the correct federal income tax from your pay. ▶ Give Form W-4 to your employer. ▶ Your withholding is subject to review by the IRS.	20**21**

Step 1: **Enter Personal Information**	(a) First name and middle initial	Last name	(b) **Social security number**
	Address		▶ **Does your name match the name on your social security card?** If not, to ensure you get credit for your earnings, contact SSA at 800-772-1213 or go to *www.ssa.gov.*
	City or town, state, and ZIP code		

(c) ☐ **Single** or **Married filing separately**

☐ **Married filing jointly** or **Qualifying widow(er)**

☐ **Head of household** (Check only if you're unmarried and pay more than half the costs of keeping up a home for yourself and a qualifying individual.)

Complete Steps 2–4 ONLY if they apply to you; otherwise, skip to Step 5. See page 2 for more information on each step, who can claim exemption from withholding, when to use the estimator at *www.irs.gov/W4App*, and privacy.

Step 2: **Multiple Jobs or Spouse Works**	Complete this step if you (1) hold more than one job at a time, or (2) are married filing jointly and your spouse also works. The correct amount of withholding depends on income earned from all of these jobs. Do **only one** of the following. (a) Use the estimator at *www.irs.gov/W4App* for most accurate withholding for this step (and Steps 3–4); **or** (b) Use the Multiple Jobs Worksheet on page 3 and enter the result in Step 4(c) below for roughly accurate withholding; **or** (c) If there are only two jobs total, you may check this box. Do the same on Form W-4 for the other job. This option is accurate for jobs with similar pay; otherwise, more tax than necessary may be withheld . . . . . ▶ ☐ **TIP:** To be accurate, submit a 2021 Form W-4 for all other jobs. If you (or your spouse) have self-employment income, including as an independent contractor, use the estimator.

Complete Steps 3–4(b) on Form W-4 for only ONE of these jobs. Leave those steps blank for the other jobs. (Your withholding will be most accurate if you complete Steps 3–4(b) on the Form W-4 for the highest paying job.)

Step 3: **Claim Dependents**	If your total income will be $200,000 or less ($400,000 or less if married filing jointly):		
	Multiply the number of qualifying children under age 17 by $2,000 ▶ $ _____		
	Multiply the number of other dependents by $500 . . . . ▶ $ _____		
	Add the amounts above and enter the total here	3	$
Step 4 (optional): **Other Adjustments**	(a) **Other income (not from jobs).** If you want tax withheld for other income you expect this year that won't have withholding, enter the amount of other income here. This may include interest, dividends, and retirement income	4(a)	$
	(b) **Deductions.** If you expect to claim deductions other than the standard deduction and want to reduce your withholding, use the Deductions Worksheet on page 3 and enter the result here	4(b)	$
	(c) **Extra withholding.** Enter any additional tax you want withheld each **pay period** .	4(c)	$

Step 5: **Sign Here**	Under penalties of perjury, I declare that this certificate, to the best of my knowledge and belief, is true, correct, and complete.
	▶ _____ ▶ _____ **Employee's signature** (This form is not valid unless you sign it.) Date

Employers Only	Employer's name and address	First date of employment	Employer identification number (EIN)

For Privacy Act and Paperwork Reduction Act Notice, see page 3.   Cat. No. 10220Q   Form **W-4** (2021)

Form W-4 (2021)   Page **3**

Step 2(b)—Multiple Jobs Worksheet *(Keep for your records.)*

If you choose the option in Step 2(b) on Form W-4, complete this worksheet (which calculates the total extra tax for all jobs) on **only ONE** Form W-4. Withholding will be most accurate if you complete the worksheet and enter the result on the Form W-4 for the highest paying job.

Note: If more than one job has annual wages of more than $120,000 or there are more than three jobs, see Pub. 505 for additional tables; or, you can use the online withholding estimator at *www.irs.gov/W4App*.

1   **Two jobs.** If you have two jobs or you're married filing jointly and you and your spouse each have one job, find the amount from the appropriate table on page 4. Using the "Higher Paying Job" row and the "Lower Paying Job" column, find the value at the intersection of the two household salaries and enter that value on line 1. Then, **skip** to line 3 . . . .   **1** $ _____

2   **Three jobs.** If you and/or your spouse have three jobs at the same time, complete lines 2a, 2b, and 2c below. Otherwise, skip to line 3.

    a   Find the amount from the appropriate table on page 4 using the annual wages from the highest paying job in the "Higher Paying Job" row and the annual wages for your next highest paying job in the "Lower Paying Job" column. Find the value at the intersection of the two household salaries and enter that value on line 2a . . . .   **2a** $ _____

    b   Add the annual wages of the two highest paying jobs from line 2a together and use the total as the wages in the "Higher Paying Job" row and use the annual wages for your third job in the "Lower Paying Job" column to find the amount from the appropriate table on page 4 and enter this amount on line 2b   . . . .   **2b** $ _____

    c   Add the amounts from lines 2a and 2b and enter the result on line 2c . . . .   **2c** $ _____

3   Enter the number of pay periods per year for the highest paying job. For example, if that job pays weekly, enter 52; if it pays every other week, enter 26; if it pays monthly, enter 12, etc. . . . . .   **3** _____

4   **Divide** the annual amount on line 1 or line 2c by the number of pay periods on line 3. Enter this amount here and in **Step 4(c)** of Form W-4 for the highest paying job (along with any other additional amount you want withheld) . . . .   **4** $ _____

Step 4(b)—Deductions Worksheet *(Keep for your records.)*

1   Enter an estimate of your 2021 itemized deductions (from Schedule A (Form 1040)). Such deductions may include qualifying home mortgage interest, charitable contributions, state and local taxes (up to $10,000), and medical expenses in excess of 7.5% of your income . . . .   **1** $ _____

2   Enter: { • $25,100 if you're married filing jointly or qualifying widow(er)
          • $18,800 if you're head of household
          • $12,550 if you're single or married filing separately }   . . . .   **2** $ _____

3   If line 1 is greater than line 2, subtract line 2 from line 1 and enter the result here. If line 2 is greater than line 1, enter "-0-"   . . . .   **3** $ _____

4   Enter an estimate of your student loan interest, deductible IRA contributions, and certain other adjustments (from Part II of Schedule 1 (Form 1040)). See Pub. 505 for more information   . . . .   **4** $ _____

5   **Add** lines 3 and 4. Enter the result here and in **Step 4(b)** of Form W-4 . . . .   **5** $ _____

Source: Internal Revenue Services

State of Nevada New Hire Report

All employers are required to report certain information on newly hired or rehired employees (those separated from your employment at least 60 consecutive days). Use of this form is not mandatory. It is provided for your convenience.

Federal Tax I.D. # _____
Company Name: _____
Company Address: _____
City, State, Zip: _____
Contact Person: _____
Phone Number: _____

☐

Social Security Number	First Name Middle Initial Last Name	Address, Street City, State, Zip	Date of Birth	Start Date	State of Hire
Required	Required	Required		Required	

Please return this form by fax to (775) 684-6379 or mail to:
Department of Employment, Training and Rehabilitation
Employment Security Division – New Hire Unit
500 East Third Street, Carson City, Nevada 89713-0033

Revised 02/12

Account: Cash   **101**

	Date	Description	Post Ref.	Debit	Credit	Balance Debit	Balance Credit	
Beg Bal								
1								1
2								2
3								3
4								4
5								5
6								6
7								7
8								8
9								9
10								10
11								11
12								12
13								13
14								14
15								15

Account: Employee Federal Income Tax Payable   **203**

	Date	Description	Post Ref.	Debit	Credit	Balance Debit	Balance Credit	
1								1
2								2
3								3
4								4
5								5
6								6
7								7
8								8
9								9

Account: Social Security Tax Payable   **204**

	Date	Description	Post Ref.	Debit	Credit	Balance Debit	Balance Credit	
1								1
2								2
3								3
4								4
5								5
6								6
7								7
8								8
9								9
10								10
11								11
12								12
13								13
14								14
15								15

Account: Medicare Tax Payable   **205**

	Date		Description	Post Ref.	Debit	Credit	Balance Debit	Balance Credit	
1									1
2									2
3									3
4									4
5									5
6									6
7									7
8									8
9									9
10									10
11									11
12									12
13									13
14									14
15									15

Account: 401(k) Contributions Payable   **208**

	Date		Description	Post Ref.	Debit	Credit	Balance Debit	Balance Credit	
1									1
2									2
3									3
4									4
5									5
6									6
7									7
8									8
9									9
10									10

Account: Employee Medical Premiums Payable   **209**

	Date		Description	Post Ref.	Debit	Credit	Balance Debit	Balance Credit	
1									1
2									2
3									3
4									4
5									5
6									6
7									7
8									8
9									9
10									10

Account: Salaries and Wages Payable   210

	Date		Description	Post Ref.	Debit	Credit	Balance Debit	Balance Credit	
1									1
2									2
3									3
4									4
5									5
6									6
7									7
8									8
9									9
10									10
11									11
12									12

Account: Federal Unemployment Tax Payable   211

	Date		Description	Post Ref.	Debit	Credit	Balance Debit	Balance Credit	
1									1
2									2
3									3
4									4
5									5
6									6
7									7
8									8
9									9
10									10

Account: State Unemployment Tax Payable   212

	Date		Description	Post Ref.	Debit	Credit	Balance Debit	Balance Credit	
1									1
2									2
3									3
4									4
5									5
6									6
7									7
8									8
9									9
10									10

Account: Career Enhancement Program Payable   213

	Date	Description	Post Ref.	Debit	Credit	Balance Debit	Balance Credit	
1								1
2								2
3								3
4								4
5								5
6								6
7								7
8								8
9								9
10								10

Account: Payroll Taxes Expense   514

	Date	Description	Post Ref.	Debit	Credit	Balance Debit	Balance Credit	
1								1
2								2
3								3
4								4
5								5
6								6
7								7
8								8
9								9
10								10

Account: Salaries and Wages Expense   515

	Date	Description	Post Ref.	Debit	Credit	Balance Debit	Balance Credit	
1								1
2								2
3								3
4								4
5								5
6								6
7								7
8								8
9								9
10								10

Form 941 for 2021: **Employer's QUARTERLY Federal Tax Return**

Form **941 for 2021:**
(Rev. June 2021)
Department of the Treasury — Internal Revenue Service

951121

OMB No. 1545-0029

Employer identification number (EIN) [ ][ ] — [ ][ ][ ][ ][ ][ ][ ]

Name *(not your trade name)*

Trade name *(if any)*

Address
Number   Street   Suite or room number

City   State   ZIP code

Foreign country name   Foreign province/county   Foreign postal code

Report for this Quarter of 2021
(Check one.)

☐ **1:** January, February, March

☐ **2:** April, May, June

☐ **3:** July, August, September

☐ **4:** October, November, December

Go to *www.irs.gov/Form941* for instructions and the latest information.

Read the separate instructions before you complete Form 941. Type or print within the boxes.

Part 1: **Answer these questions for this quarter.**

1   Number of employees who received wages, tips, or other compensation for the pay period including: *June 12* (Quarter 2), *Sept. 12* (Quarter 3), or *Dec. 12* (Quarter 4) **1**

2   Wages, tips, and other compensation **2**

3   Federal income tax withheld from wages, tips, and other compensation **3**

4   If no wages, tips, and other compensation are subject to social security or Medicare tax   ☐ **Check and go to line 6.**

		Column 1			Column 2	
5a	Taxable social security wages* . .		.	× 0.124 =		.
5a (i)	Qualified sick leave wages* .		.	× 0.062 =		.
5a (ii)	Qualified family leave wages* .		.	× 0.062 =		.
5b	Taxable social security tips . . .		.	× 0.124 =		.
5c	Taxable Medicare wages & tips. .		.	× 0.029 =		.
5d	Taxable wages & tips subject to Additional Medicare Tax withholding		.	× 0.009 =		.

*Include taxable qualified sick and family leave wages for leave taken after March 31, 2021, on line 5a. Use lines 5a(i) and 5a(ii) **only** for wages paid after March 31, 2020, for leave taken before April 1, 2021.

5e   Total social security and Medicare taxes. Add Column 2 from lines 5a, 5a(i), 5a(ii), 5b, 5c, and 5d   **5e**

5f   Section 3121(q) Notice and Demand—Tax due on unreported tips (see instructions) . . **5f**

6   Total taxes before adjustments. Add lines 3, 5e, and 5f **6**

7   Current quarter's adjustment for fractions of cents **7**

8   Current quarter's adjustment for sick pay **8**

9   Current quarter's adjustments for tips and group-term life insurance **9**

10   Total taxes after adjustments. Combine lines 6 through 9 . . . . **10**

11a   Qualified small business payroll tax credit for increasing research activities. Attach Form 8974   **11a**

11b   Nonrefundable portion of credit for qualified sick and family leave wages for leave taken before April 1, 2021 . . . . **11b**

11c   Nonrefundable portion of employee retention credit **11c**

▶ **You MUST complete all three pages of Form 941 and SIGN it.**   Next ▶

For Privacy Act and Paperwork Reduction Act Notice, see the back of the Payment Voucher.   Cat. No. 17001Z   Form **941** (Rev. 6-2021)

951221

Name *(not your trade name)*	Employer identification number (EIN)

Part 1:   Answer these questions for this quarter. *(continued)*

11d   Nonrefundable portion of credit for qualified sick and family leave wages for leave taken after March 31, 2021 . . . .   **11d** [_____ .]

11e   Nonrefundable portion of COBRA premium assistance credit (see instructions for applicable quarters) . . . .   **11e** [_____ .]

11f   Number of individuals provided COBRA premium assistance   [_____]

11g   **Total nonrefundable credits.** Add lines 11a, 11b, 11c, 11d, and 11e . . . .   **11g** [_____ .]

12   **Total taxes after adjustments and nonrefundable credits.** Subtract line 11g from line 10 .   **12** [_____ .]

13a   Total deposits for this quarter, including overpayment applied from a prior quarter and overpayments applied from Form 941-X, 941-X (PR), 944-X, or 944-X (SP) filed in the current quarter   **13a** [_____ .]

13b   Reserved for future use . . . .   **13b** [▓▓▓▓▓▓▓ .]

13c   Refundable portion of credit for qualified sick and family leave wages for leave taken before April 1, 2021 . . . .   **13c** [_____ .]

13d   Refundable portion of employee retention credit . . . .   **13d** [_____ .]

13e   Refundable portion of credit for qualified sick and family leave wages for leave taken after March 31, 2021 . . . .   **13e** [_____ .]

13f   Refundable portion of COBRA premium assistance credit (see instructions for applicable quarters) . . . .   **13f** [_____ .]

13g   **Total deposits and refundable credits.** Add lines 13a, 13c, 13d, 13e, and 13f . . . . .   **13g** [_____ .]

13h   Total advances received from filing Form(s) 7200 for the quarter . . . .   **13h** [_____ .]

13i   **Total deposits and refundable credits less advances.** Subtract line 13h from line 13g . . . .   **13i** [_____ .]

14   **Balance due.** If line 12 is more than line 13i, enter the difference and see instructions . . .   **14** [_____ .]

15   **Overpayment.** If line 13i is more than line 12, enter the difference   [_____ .]   Check one: ☐ Apply to next return.   ☐ Send a refund.

Part 2:   **Tell us about your deposit schedule and tax liability for this quarter.**

If you're unsure about whether you're a monthly schedule depositor or a semiweekly schedule depositor, see section 11 of Pub. 15.

16   Check one: ☐   **Line 12 on this return is less than $2,500 or line 12 on the return for the prior quarter was less than $2,500,** and you didn't incur a $100,000 next-day deposit obligation during the current quarter. If line 12 for the prior quarter was less than $2,500 but line 12 on this return is $100,000 or more, you must provide a record of your federal tax liability. If you're a monthly schedule depositor, complete the deposit schedule below; if you're a semiweekly schedule depositor, attach Schedule B (Form 941). Go to Part 3.

☐   **You were a monthly schedule depositor for the entire quarter.** Enter your tax liability for each month and total liability for the quarter, then go to Part 3.

	Tax liability: Month 1	[_____ .]
	Month 2	[_____ .]
	Month 3	[_____ .]
	Total liability for quarter	[_____ .] **Total must equal line 12.**

☐   **You were a semiweekly schedule depositor for any part of this quarter.** Complete Schedule B (Form 941), Report of Tax Liability for Semiweekly Schedule Depositors, and attach it to Form 941. Go to Part 3.

▶ **You MUST complete all three pages of Form 941 and SIGN it.**   Next ▶

951921

Name *(not your trade name)*   **Employer identification number (EIN)**

Part 3:   **Tell us about your business. If a question does NOT apply to your business, leave it blank.**

17   If your business has closed or you stopped paying wages . . . .   ☐ Check here, and

enter the final date you paid wages   [/   /   ]   ; also attach a statement to your return. See instructions.

18a   If you're a seasonal employer and you don't have to file a return for every quarter of the year . . .   ☐ Check here.

18b   If you're eligible for the employee retention credit solely because your business is a recovery startup business   ☐ Check here.

19   Qualified health plan expenses allocable to qualified sick leave wages for leave taken before April 1, 2021   19 [.]

20   Qualified health plan expenses allocable to qualified family leave wages for leave taken before April 1, 2021   20 [.]

21   Qualified wages for the employee retention credit . . . .   21 [.]

22   Qualified health plan expenses for the employee retention credit . . . .   22 [.]

23   Qualified sick leave wages for leave taken after March 31, 2021 . . . .   23 [.]

24   Qualified health plan expenses allocable to qualified sick leave wages reported on line 23   24 [.]

25   Amounts under certain collectively bargained agreements allocable to qualified sick leave wages reported on line 23 . . . .   25 [.]

26   Qualified family leave wages for leave taken after March 31, 2021 . . . .   26 [.]

27   Qualified health plan expenses allocable to qualified family leave wages reported on line 26   27 [.]

28   Amounts under certain collectively bargained agreements allocable to qualified family leave wages reported on line 26 . . . .   28 [.]

Part 4:   **May we speak with your third-party designee?**

Do you want to allow an employee, a paid tax preparer, or another person to discuss this return with the IRS? See the instructions for details.

☐ Yes. Designee's name and phone number   [   ]   [   ]

Select a 5-digit personal identification number (PIN) to use when talking to the IRS.   ☐ ☐ ☐ ☐ ☐

☐ No.

Part 5:   **Sign here. You MUST complete all three pages of Form 941 and SIGN it.**

Under penalties of perjury, I declare that I have examined this return, including accompanying schedules and statements, and to the best of my knowledge and belief, it is true, correct, and complete. Declaration of preparer (other than taxpayer) is based on all information of which preparer has any knowledge.

X   **Sign your name here**   [   ]

Print your name here   [   ]

Print your title here   [   ]

Date   [/   /   ]

Best daytime phone   [   ]

Paid Preparer Use Only   Check if you're self-employed . . . ☐

Preparer's name   [   ]   PTIN   [   ]

Preparer's signature   [   ]   Date   [/   /   ]

Firm's name (or yours if self-employed)   [   ]   EIN   [   ]

Address   [   ]   Phone   [   ]

City   [   ]   State [   ]   ZIP code   [   ]

Form 941-V,
Payment Voucher

Purpose of Form

Complete Form 941-V if you're making a payment with Form 941. We will use the completed voucher to credit your payment more promptly and accurately, and to improve our service to you.

Making Payments With Form 941

To avoid a penalty, make your payment with Form 941 **only if:**

• Your total taxes after adjustments and nonrefundable credits (Form 941, line 12) for either the current quarter or the preceding quarter are less than $2,500, you didn't incur a $100,000 next-day deposit obligation during the current quarter, and you're paying in full with a timely filed return; or

• You're a monthly schedule depositor making a payment in accordance with the Accuracy of Deposits Rule. See section 11 of Pub. 15 for details. In this case, the amount of your payment may be $2,500 or more.

Otherwise, you must make deposits by electronic funds transfer. See section 11 of Pub. 15 for deposit instructions. Don't use Form 941-V to make federal tax deposits.

⚠️ **CAUTION** *Use Form 941-V when making any payment with Form 941. However, if you pay an amount with Form 941 that should've been deposited, you may be subject to a penalty. See* Deposit Penalties *in section 11 of Pub. 15.*

Specific Instructions

Box 1—Employer identification number (EIN). If you don't have an EIN, you may apply for one online by visiting the IRS website at *www.irs.gov/EIN*. You may also apply for an EIN by faxing or mailing Form SS-4 to the IRS. If you haven't received your EIN by the due date of Form 941, write "Applied For" and the date you applied in this entry space.

Box 2—Amount paid. Enter the amount paid with Form 941.

Box 3—Tax period. Darken the circle identifying the quarter for which the payment is made. Darken only one circle.

Box 4—Name and address. Enter your name and address as shown on Form 941.

Enclose your check or money order made payable to "United States Treasury." Be sure to enter your EIN, "Form 941," and the tax period ("1st Quarter 2021," "2nd Quarter 2021," "3rd Quarter 2021," or "4th Quarter 2021") on your check or money order. Don't send cash. Don't staple Form 941-V or your payment to Form 941 (or to each other).

• Detach Form 941-V and send it with your payment and Form 941 to the address in the Instructions for Form 941.

Note: You must also complete the entity information above Part 1 on Form 941.

✂ ▼ **Detach Here and Mail With Your Payment and Form 941.** ▼ ✂

Form **941-V**	**Payment Voucher**	OMB No. 1545-0029
Department of the Treasury Internal Revenue Service	▶ Don't staple this voucher or your payment to Form 941.	20**21**

1 Enter your employer identification number (EIN).	2		Dollars	Cents
	Enter the amount of your payment. ▶ Make your check or money order payable to **"United States Treasury"**			

3 Tax Period		4 Enter your business name (individual name if sole proprietor).
○ 1st Quarter	○ 3rd Quarter	Enter your address.
○ 2nd Quarter	○ 4th Quarter	Enter your city, state, and ZIP code; or your city, foreign country name, foreign province/county, and foreign postal code.

Source: Internal Revenue Service

Form **940 for 2020:** **Employer's Annual Federal Unemployment (FUTA) Tax Return**   850113

Department of the Treasury — Internal Revenue Service

OMB No. 1545-0028

Employer identification number (EIN)

☐☐ – ☐☐☐☐☐☐☐

Name *(not your trade name)*

Trade name *(if any)*

Address

Number   Street   Suite or room number

City   State   ZIP code

Foreign country name   Foreign province/county   Foreign postal code

Type of Return
(Check all that apply.)

☐ **a.** Amended

☐ **b.** Successor employer

☐ **c.** No payments to employees in 2020

☐ **d.** Final: Business closed or stopped paying wages

Go to *www.irs.gov/Form940* for instructions and the latest information.

Read the separate instructions before you complete this form. Please type or print within the boxes.

Part 1: **Tell us about your return. If any line does NOT apply, leave it blank. See instructions before completing Part 1.**

1a If you had to pay state unemployment tax in one state only, enter the state abbreviation . **1a** ☐☐

1b If you had to pay state unemployment tax in more than one state, you are a multi-state employer . . . . **1b** ☐ Check here. Complete Schedule A (Form 940).

2 If you paid wages in a state that is subject to **CREDIT REDUCTION** . . . . **2** ☐ Check here. Complete Schedule A (Form 940).

Part 2: **Determine your FUTA tax before adjustments. If any line does NOT apply, leave it blank.**

3 Total payments to all employees . . . . **3** ☐ .

4 Payments exempt from FUTA tax . . . . **4** ☐ .

Check all that apply: **4a** ☐ Fringe benefits   **4c** ☐ Retirement/Pension   **4e** ☐ Other
4b ☐ Group-term life insurance   **4d** ☐ Dependent care

5 Total of payments made to each employee in excess of $7,000 . . . . **5** ☐ .

6 Subtotal (line 4 + line 5 = line 6) . . . . **6** ☐ .

7 Total taxable FUTA wages (line 3 – line 6 = line 7). See instructions . . . . . **7** ☐ .

8 FUTA tax before adjustments (line 7 × 0.006 = line 8) . . . . **8** ☐ .

Part 3: **Determine your adjustments. If any line does NOT apply, leave it blank.**

9 If ALL of the taxable FUTA wages you paid were excluded from state unemployment tax, multiply line 7 by 0.054 (line 7 × 0.054 = line 9). Go to line 12 . . . . . . **9** ☐ .

10 If SOME of the taxable FUTA wages you paid were excluded from state unemployment tax, OR you paid ANY state unemployment tax late (after the due date for filing Form 940), complete the worksheet in the instructions. Enter the amount from line 7 of the worksheet . . **10** ☐ .

11 If credit reduction applies, enter the total from Schedule A (Form 940) . . . . . **11** ☐ .

Part 4: **Determine your FUTA tax and balance due or overpayment. If any line does NOT apply, leave it blank.**

12 Total FUTA tax after adjustments (lines 8 + 9 + 10 + 11 = line 12) . . . . **12** ☐ .

13 FUTA tax deposited for the year, including any overpayment applied from a prior year . **13** ☐ .

14 Balance due. If line 12 is more than line 13, enter the excess on line 14.
   • If line 14 is more than $500, you must deposit your tax.
   • If line 14 is $500 or less, you may pay with this return. See instructions . . . . . **14** ☐ .

15 Overpayment. If line 13 is more than line 12, enter the excess on line 15 and check a box below **15** ☐ .

▶ You **MUST** complete both pages of this form and **SIGN** it.   Check one: ☐ Apply to next return.   ☐ Send a refund.

Next ▶

For Privacy Act and Paperwork Reduction Act Notice, see the back of the Payment Voucher.   Cat. No. 11234O   Form **940** (2020)

850212

Name *(not your trade name)*	Employer identification number (EIN)

Part 5:   Report your FUTA tax liability by quarter only if line 12 is more than $500. If not, go to Part 6.

16 Report the amount of your FUTA tax liability for each quarter; do NOT enter the amount you deposited. If you had no liability for a quarter, leave the line blank.

16a **1st quarter** (January 1 – March 31) . . . . **16a** ☐ .

16b **2nd quarter** (April 1 – June 30) . . . . **16b** ☐ .

16c **3rd quarter** (July 1 – September 30) . . . . **16c** ☐ .

16d **4th quarter** (October 1 – December 31) . . . . . . **16d** ☐ .

17 Total tax liability for the year (lines 16a + 16b + 16c + 16d = line 17) **17** ☐ .   **Total must equal line 12.**

Part 6:   May we speak with your third-party designee?

Do you want to allow an employee, a paid tax preparer, or another person to discuss this return with the IRS? See the instructions for details.

☐ **Yes.**   Designee's name and phone number   ☐   ☐

Select a 5-digit personal identification number (PIN) to use when talking to the IRS. ☐ ☐ ☐ ☐ ☐

☐ **No.**

Part 7:   Sign here. You MUST complete both pages of this form and SIGN it.

Under penalties of perjury, I declare that I have examined this return, including accompanying schedules and statements, and to the best of my knowledge and belief, it is true, correct, and complete, and that no part of any payment made to a state unemployment fund claimed as a credit was, or is to be, deducted from the payments made to employees. Declaration of preparer (other than taxpayer) is based on all information of which preparer has any knowledge.

**✗ Sign your
name here**   ☐

Print your name here   ☐

Print your title here   ☐

Date   /   /

Best daytime phone   ☐

Paid Preparer Use Only   Check if you are self-employed ☐

Preparer's name	☐	PTIN	☐
Preparer's signature	☐	Date	/ /
Firm's name (or yours if self-employed)	☐	EIN	☐
Address	☐	Phone	☐
City	☐	State ☐	ZIP code ☐

Form **940** (2020)

DO NOT STAPLE THIS FORM

Page 1

State of Nevada
Department of Employment, Training & Rehabilitation
EMPLOYMENT SECURITY DIVISION
500 E. Third St., Carson City, NV 89713-0030
Telephone (775) 687-4540

EMPLOYER'S QUARTERLY CONTRIBUTION AND WAGE REPORT

PLEASE CORRECT ANY NAME OR ADDRESS INFORMATION BELOW. 1a. EMPLOYER ACCOUNT NUMBER	1b. FOR QUARTER ENDING	1e. FEDERAL I.D. NO.
	1c. DELINQUENT AFTER	**IMPORTANT** FOR YOUR PROTECTION, VERIFY YOUR FEDERAL I.D. NO. ABOVE. IF IT IS IN ERROR, PLEASE ENTER THE CORRECT NUMBER HERE
	1d. YOUR RATES	

	Dollars : Cents	**A REPORT MUST BE FILED**
3. TOTAL GROSS WAGES (INCLUDING TIPS) PAID THIS QUARTER (If you paid no wages, write "NONE," sign report and return.) (See Instructions)		INSTRUCTIONS ENCLOSED
4. LESS WAGES IN EXCESS OF PER INDIVIDUAL (Cannot exceed amount in Item 3.) (See Instructions)		2. **REPORT OF CHANGES** If any of the following changes have occurred, please check the appropriate box and provide details on page 2.
5. TAXABLE WAGES PAID THIS QUARTER (Item 3 less Item 4.)		☐ Business Discontinued
6. UI AMOUNT DUE THIS QUARTER (Item 5 x your UI Rate shown in Item 1d.)		☐ Ownership Change
7. CEP AMOUNT DUE THIS QUARTER (Item 5 x the CEP Rate in Item 1d.) (Add) (Do not include the CEP amount on federal unemployment tax return Form 940.)		☐ Entire Business Sold ☐ Part of Business Sold
8. PRIOR CREDIT (Attach "Statement of Employer Account") (Subtract)		☐ Legal Ownership Change ☐ Business Added
9. CHARGE FOR LATE FILING OF THIS REPORT (Add) (One or more days late add $5.00 forfeit.)		(FOR DIVISION USE ONLY)
10. ADDITIONAL CHARGE FOR LATE FILING, AFTER 10 DAYS (Add) (Item 5 x 1/10% (.001) for each month or part of month delinquent.)		
11. INTEREST ON PAST DUE UI CONTRIBUTIONS (Add) (Item 6 x 1% (.01) for each month or part of month delinquent.) (See Instructions)		
12. TOTAL PAYMENT DUE (Total Items 6 through 11.) MAKE PAYABLE TO NEVADA EMPLOYMENT SECURITY DIVISION. Please enter Employer Account Number on check.		

13. SOCIAL SECURITY NUMBER	14. EMPLOYEE NAME Do not make adjustments to prior quarters.	15. TOTAL TIPS REPORTED Dollars : Cents	16. TOTAL GROSS WAGES INCLUDING TIPS Dollars : Cents	
				17. NUMBER OF WORKERS LISTED ON THIS REPORT
				18. FOR EACH MONTH, REPORT THE NUMBER OF WORKERS WHO WORKED DURING OR RECEIVED PAY FOR THE PAYROLL PERIOD WHICH INCLUDES THE 12TH OF THE MONTH.
				1 MO 2 MO 3 MO
19.TOTAL PAGES THIS REPORT	20. TOTAL TIPS AND TOTAL WAGES THIS PAGE ——→	$	$	

21. I certify that the information contained on this report and the attachments is true and correct.

Signed/Title _____   Name of Preparer if Other Than Employer _____

(____) _____ (____) _____ (____) _____ _____
Area Code Fax Number   Area Code Telephone Number   Area Code   Telephone Number   Date

NUCS-4072 (Rev.9-02)

Source: Internal Revenue Service

22222	**a** Employee's social security number		
	OMB No. 1545-0008		
b Employer identification number (EIN)		**1** Wages, tips, other compensation	**2** Federal income tax withheld
c Employer's name, address, and ZIP code		**3** Social security wages	**4** Social security tax withheld
		5 Medicare wages and tips	**6** Medicare tax withheld
		7 Social security tips	**8** Allocated tips
d Control number		**9**	**10** Dependent care benefits
e Employee's first name and initial Last name Suff.		**11** Nonqualified plans	**12a** C o d e
		13 Statutory employee ☐ Retirement plan ☐ Third-party sick pay ☐	**12b** C o d e
		14 Other	**12c** C o d e
			12d C o d e
f Employee's address and ZIP code			

15 State Employer's state ID number	16 State wages, tips, etc.	17 State income tax	18 Local wages, tips, etc.	19 Local income tax	20 Locality name

Form **W-2** **Wage and Tax Statement**   2021   Department of the Treasury—Internal Revenue Service

Copy 1—For State, City, or Local Tax Department

Source: Internal Revenue Service

DO NOT STAPLE

33333	**a** Control number	**For Official Use Only** ▶
		OMB No. 1545-0008

b **Kind of Payer** (Check one) ▶	941 ☐ Military ☐ 943 ☐ 944 ☐ CT-1 ☐ Hshld. emp. ☐ Medicare govt. emp. ☐	**Kind of Employer** (Check one) ▶	None apply ☐ 501c non-govt. ☐ State/local non-501c ☐ State/local 501c ☐ Federal govt. ☐	Third-party sick pay (Check if applicable) ☐

c Total number of Forms W-2	**d** Establishment number	**1** Wages, tips, other compensation	**2** Federal income tax withheld
e Employer identification number (EIN)		**3** Social security wages	**4** Social security tax withheld
f Employer's name		**5** Medicare wages and tips	**6** Medicare tax withheld
		7 Social security tips	**8** Allocated tips
		9	**10** Dependent care benefits
g Employer's address and ZIP code		**11** Nonqualified plans	**12a** Deferred compensation
h Other EIN used this year		**13** For third-party sick pay use only	**12b**
15 State Employer's state ID number		**14** Income tax withheld by payer of third-party sick pay	
16 State wages, tips, etc.	**17** State income tax	**18** Local wages, tips, etc.	**19** Local income tax
Employer's contact person		Employer's telephone number	For Official Use Only
Employer's fax number		Employer's email address	

Under penalties of perjury, I declare that I have examined this return and accompanying documents, and, to the best of my knowledge and belief, they are true, correct, and complete.

Signature ▶   Title ▶   Date ▶

Form **W-3** **Transmittal of Wage and Tax Statements**   2021   Department of the Treasury
Internal Revenue Service

Source: Internal Revenue Service

Appendix B

Special Classes of Federal Tax Withholding

Special Classes of Employment and Special Types of Payments	Treatment under Employment Taxes		
	Income Tax Withholding	Social Security and Medicare (Including Additional Medicare Tax When Wages Are Paid in Excess of $200,000)	FUTA
Aliens, Nonresident	See Publication 515, "Withholding of Tax on Nonresident Aliens and Foreign Entities," and Publication 519, "U.S. Tax Guide for Aliens."		
Aliens, Resident			
1. Service performed in the United States	Same as U.S. citizens.	Same as U.S. citizens. (Exempt if any part of service as a crew member of foreign vessel or aircraft is performed outside the United States.)	Same as U.S. citizens.
2. Service performed outside the United States	Withhold	Taxable if (1) working for an American employer or (2) an American employer by agreement covers U.S. citizens and residents employed by its foreign affiliates.	Exempt unless on or in connection with an American vessel or aircraft and performed under a contract made in the United States, or alien is employed on such vessel or aircraft when it touches U.S. port.
Cafeteria Plan Benefits under Section 125	If an employee chooses cash, subject to all employment taxes. If an employee chooses another benefit, the treatment is the same as if the benefit was provided outside the plan. See Publication 15-B for more information.		
Deceased Worker			
1. Wages paid to beneficiary or estate in the same calendar year as worker's death. See the "Instructions for Forms W-2 and W-3" for details.	Exempt	Taxable	Taxable
2. Wages paid to beneficiary or estate after calendar year of worker's death.	Exempt	Exempt	Exempt

Special Classes of Employment and Special Types of Payments	Treatment under Employment Taxes		
	Income Tax Withholding	Social Security and Medicare (Including Additional Medicare Tax When Wages Are Paid in Excess of $200,000)	FUTA
Dependent Care Assistance Programs	Exempt to the extent it is reasonable to believe amounts are excludable from gross income under Section 129.		
Disabled Worker's Wages paid after the year in which worker became entitled to disability insurance benefits under the Social Security Act.	Withhold	Exempt, if the worker did not perform service for the employer during the period for which payment is made.	Taxable
Employee Business Expense Reimbursement			
1. Accountable plan			
a. Amounts not exceeding specified government rate for per diem or standard mileage.	Exempt	Exempt	Exempt
b. Amounts in excess of specified government rate for per diem or standard mileage.	Withhold	Taxable	Taxable
2. Nonaccountable plan. See Section 5 of IRS Publication 15 for details.	Withhold	Taxable	Taxable
Family Employees			
1. A child employed by the parent (or partnership in which each partner is a parent of the child).	Withhold	Exempt until age 18; age 21 for domestic service.	Exempt until age 21.
2. Parent employed by a child	Withhold	Taxable if in course of the son's or daughter's business. For domestic services, see Section 3 of IRS Publication 15.	Exempt
3. Spouse employed by a spouse. See Section 3 of IRS Publication 15 for more information.	Withhold	Taxable if in course of a spouse's business.	Exempt
Fishing and Related Activities	See Publication 334, "Tax Guide for Small Business."		
Foreign Governments and International Organizations	Exempt	Exempt	Exempt
Foreign Service by U.S. Citizens			
1. As U.S. government employees	Withhold	Same as within the United States.	Exempt
2. For foreign affiliates of American employers and other private employers	Exempt if at the time of payment (1) it is reasonable to believe the employee is entitled to an exclusion from income under Section 911 or (2) the employer is required by the law of the foreign country to withhold income tax on such payment.	Exempt unless (1) an American employer by agreement covers U.S. citizens employed by its foreign affiliates or (2) U.S. citizen works for an American employer.	Exempt unless (1) on American vessel or aircraft and work is performed under contract made in United States or worker is employed on vessel when it touches U.S. port or (2) U.S. citizen works for American employer (except in a contiguous country with which the United States has an agreement for unemployment compensation) or in the U.S. Virgin Islands.

Special Classes of Employment and Special Types of Payments	Treatment under Employment Taxes		
	Income Tax Withholding	Social Security and Medicare (Including Additional Medicare Tax When Wages Are Paid in Excess of $200,000)	FUTA
Fringe Benefits	Taxable on the excess of the fair market value of the benefit over the sum of an amount paid for it by the employee and any amount excludable by law. However, special valuation rules may apply. Benefits provided under cafeteria plans may qualify for exclusion from wages for Social Security, Medicare, and FUTA taxes. See Publication 15-B for details.		
Government Employment State/local governments and political subdivisions, employees of			
1. Salaries and wages (includes payments to most elected and appointed officials)	Withhold	Generally taxable for (1) services performed by employees who are either (a) covered under a Section 218 agreement or (b) not covered under a Section 218 agreement and not a member of a public retirement system (mandatory Social Security and Medicare coverage), and (2) (Medicare tax only) services performed by employees hired or rehired after 3/31/86 who are not covered under a Section 218 agreement or the mandatory Social Security provisions, unless specifically excluded by law. See Publication 963.	Exempt
2. Election workers. Election workers are individuals who are employed to perform services for state or local governments at election booths in connection with national, state, or local elections. **Note:** File Form W-2 for payments of $600 or more even if no Social Security or Medicare taxes were withheld.	Exempt	Taxable if paid $2,000 or more in 2021 (lesser amount if specified by a Section 218 Social Security agreement). See Revenue Ruling 2000-6.	Exempt
3. Emergency workers. Emergency workers who were hired on a temporary basis in response to a specific unforeseen emergency and are not intended to become permanent employees.	Withhold	Exempt if serving on a temporary basis in case of fire, storm, snow, earthquake, flood, or similar emergency.	Exempt
U.S. federal government employees	Withhold	Taxable for Medicare. Taxable for Social Security unless hired before 1984. See Section 3121(b)(5).	Exempt
Homeworkers (Industrial, Cottage Industry)			
1. Common-law employees	Withhold	Taxable	Taxable
2. Statutory employees. See Section 2 of IRS Publication 15 for details.	Exempt	Taxable if paid $100 or more in cash in a year.	Exempt

Special Classes of Employment and Special Types of Payments	Treatment under Employment Taxes		
	Income Tax Withholding	Social Security and Medicare (Including Additional Medicare Tax When Wages Are Paid in Excess of $200,000)	FUTA
Hospital Employees			
1. Interns	Withhold	Taxable	Exempt
2. Patients	Withhold	Taxable (exempt for state or local government hospitals).	Exempt
Household Employees			
1. Domestic service in private homes. Farmers, see Publication 51 (Circular A).	Exempt (withhold if both employer and employee agree).	Taxable if paid $2,300 or more in cash in 2021. Exempt if performed by an individual younger than age 18 during any portion of the calendar year and is not the principal occupation of the employee.	Taxable if the employer paid total cash wages of $1,000 or more in any quarter in the current or preceding calendar year.
2. Domestic service in college clubs, fraternities, and sororities.	Exempt (withhold if both employer and employee agree).	Exempt if paid to regular students; also exempt if an employee is paid less than $100 in a year by an income-tax-exempt employer.	Taxable if the employer paid total cash wages of $1,000 or more in any quarter in the current or preceding calendar year.
Insurance for Employees			
1. Accident and health insurance premiums under a plan or system for employees and their dependents generally or for a class or classes of employees and their dependents.	Exempt (except 2 percent shareholder-employees of S corporations).	Exempt	Exempt
2. Group-term life insurance costs. See Publication 15-B for details.	Exempt	Exempt, except for the cost of group–term life insurance includible in the employee's gross income. Special rules apply to former employees.	Exempt
Insurance Agents or Solicitors			
1. Full-time life insurance salesperson	Withhold only if an employee under common law. See Section 2 of IRS Publication 15.	Taxable	Taxable if (1) employee under common law and (2) not paid solely by commissions.
2. Other salespeople of life, casualty, and so on, insurance	Withhold only if an employee under common law.	Taxable only if an employee under common law.	Taxable if (1) employee under common law and (2) not paid solely by commissions.
Interest on Loans with Below-Market Interest Rates (forgone interest and deemed original issue discount)	See Publication 15-A.		
Leave-Sharing Plans Amounts paid to an employee under a leave-sharing plan	Withhold	Taxable	Taxable

Special Classes of Employment and Special Types of Payments	Treatment under Employment Taxes		
	Income Tax Withholding	Social Security and Medicare (Including Additional Medicare Tax When Wages Are Paid in Excess of $200,000)	FUTA
Newspaper Carriers and Vendors Newspaper carriers younger than age 18; newspaper and magazine vendors buying at fixed prices and retaining receipts from sales to customers. See Publication 15-A for information on statutory nonemployee status.	Exempt (withhold if both employer and employee voluntarily agree).	Exempt	Exempt
Noncash Payments:			
1. For household work, agricultural labor, and service not in the course of the employer's trade or business	Exempt (withhold if both employer and employee voluntarily agree).	Exempt	Exempt
2. To certain retail commission salespersons ordinarily paid solely on a cash commission basis	Optional with the employer, except to the extent employee's supplemental wages during the year exceed $1 million.	Taxable	Taxable
Nonprofit Organizations	See Publication 15-A.		
Officers or Shareholders of an S-Corporation Distributions and other payments by an S-corporation to a corporate officer or shareholder must be treated as wages to the extent the amounts are reasonable compensation for services to the corporation by an employee. See the instructions for Form 1120-S.	Withhold	Taxable	Taxable
Partners: Payments to general or limited partners of a partnership. See Publication 541, "Partnerships," for partner reporting rules.	Exempt	Exempt	Exempt
Railroads: Payments subject to the Railroad Retirement Act. See Publication 915, Social Security and Equivalent Railroad Retirement Benefits, and the instructions for Form CT-1 for more details.	Withhold	Exempt	Exempt
Religious Exemptions	See Publication 15-A and Publication 517, "Social Security and Other Information for Members of the Clergy and Religious Workers."		

Special Classes of Employment and Special Types of Payments	Treatment under Employment Taxes		
	Income Tax Withholding	Social Security and Medicare (Including Additional Medicare Tax When Wages Are Paid in Excess of $200,000)	FUTA
Retirement and Pension Plans			
1. Employer contributions to a qualified plan	Exempt	Exempt	Exempt
2. Elective employee contributions and deferrals to a plan containing a qualified cash or deferred compensation arrangement (for example, 401(k))	Generally exempt, but see Section 402(g) for limitation.	Taxable	Taxable
3. Employer contributions to individual retirement accounts under a simplified employee pension plan (SEP)	Generally exempt, but see Section 402(g) for salary reduction SEP limitation.	Exempt, except for amounts contributed under a salary reduction SEP agreement.	
4. Employer contributions to Section 403(b) annuities	Generally exempt, but see Section 402(g) for limitation.	Taxable if paid through a salary reduction agreement (written or otherwise).	
5. Employee salary reduction contributions to a SIMPLE retirement account	Exempt	Taxable	Taxable
6. Distributions from qualified retirement and pension plans and Section 403(b) annuities. See Publication 15-A for information on pensions, annuities, and employer contributions to nonqualified deferred compensation arrangements	Withhold, but the recipient may elect exemption on Form W-4P in certain cases; mandatory 20 percent withholding applies to an eligible rollover distribution that is not a direct rollover; exempt for a direct rollover. See Publication 15-A.	Exempt	Exempt
7. Employer contributions to a Section 457(b) plan	Generally exempt, but see Section 402(g) limitation.	Taxable	Taxable
8. Employee salary reduction contributions to a Section 457(b) plan	Generally exempt, but see Section 402(g) salary reduction limitation.	Taxable	Taxable
Salespersons:			
1. Common-law employees	Withhold	Taxable	Taxable
2. Statutory employees	Exempt	Taxable	Taxable, except for full-time life insurance sales agents.
3. Statutory nonemployees (qualified real estate agents, direct sellers, and certain companion sitters). See Publication 15-A for details.	Exempt	Exempt	Exempt
Scholarships and Fellowship Grants (Includible in Income under Section 117(c))	Withhold	Taxability depends on the nature of employment and the status of the organization. See Students, scholars, trainees, teachers, etc., below	
Severance or Dismissal Pay	Withhold	Taxable	Taxable

Special Classes of Employment and Special Types of Payments	Treatment under Employment Taxes		
	Income Tax Withholding	Social Security and Medicare (Including Additional Medicare Tax When Wages Are Paid in Excess of $200,000)	FUTA
Service Not in the Course of the Employer's Trade or Business (Other Than on a Farm Operated for Profit or for Household Employment in Private Homes)	Withhold only if an employee earns $50 or more in cash in a quarter and works on 24 or more different days in that quarter or in the preceding quarter.	Taxable if an employee receives $100 or more in cash in a calendar year.	Taxable only if an employee earns $50 or more in cash in a quarter and works on 24 or more different days in that quarter or in the preceding quarter.
Sick Pay See Publication 15-A for more information.	Withhold	Exempt after the end of 6 calendar months after the calendar month employee last worked for the employer.	
Students, Scholars, Trainees, Teachers, etc. 1. A student enrolled and regularly attending classes, performing services for			
a. Private school, college, or university	Withhold	Exempt	Exempt
b. The auxiliary nonprofit organization operated for and controlled by the school, college, or university	Withhold	Exempt unless services are covered by a Section 218 (Social Security Act) agreement.	Exempt
c. Public school, college, or university	Withhold	Exempt unless services are covered by a Section 218 (Social Security Act) agreement.	Exempt
2. Full-time student performing service for academic credit, combining instruction with work experience as an integral part of the program	Withhold	Taxable	Exempt unless the program was established for or on behalf of an employer or group of employers.
3. Student nurses performing part-time services for nominal earnings at a hospital as an incidental part of the training	Withhold	Exempt	Exempt
4. A student employed by organized camps	Withhold	Taxable	Exempt
5. Student, scholar, trainee, teacher, and so on, as nonimmigrant alien under Section 101(a)(15)(F), (J), (M), or (Q) of Immigration and Nationality Act (that is, aliens holding F-1, J-1, M-1, or Q-1 visas)	Withhold unless excepted by regulations.	Exempt if service is performed for the purpose specified in Section 101(a)(15)(F), (J), (M), or (Q) of Immigration and Nationality Act. However, these taxes may apply if the employee becomes a resident alien. See the special residency tests for exempt individuals in Chapter 1 of Pub. 519, Tax Guide for Aliens.	
Supplemental Unemployment Compensation Plan Benefits	Withhold	Exempt under certain conditions. See Publication 15-A.	
Tips 1. If $20 or more in a month	Withhold	Taxable	Taxable for all tips reported in writing to the employer.
2. If less than $20 in a month. See Section 6 of IRS Publication 15 for more information	Exempt	Exempt	Exempt
Workers' Compensation	Exempt	Exempt	Exempt

(Source: Internal Revenue Service)

Appendix C

Federal Income Tax Tables*

The following is information about federal income tax withholding for 2021 using Publication 15-T. Specific questions about federal income taxes and business situations may be directed to the Internal Revenue Service via the IRS website at https://www.irs.gov/businesses.

*Note: Appendix C is derived from IRS Publication 15-T. A comment to refer to pages 44 and 47 exists at the section end for wage-bracket tables when the taxable wages exceed the table. These page references are for Publication 15-T itself and not to pages within this text.

1. Percentage Method Tables for Automated Payroll Systems

If you have an automated payroll system, use the worksheet below and the Percentage Method tables that follow to figure federal income tax withholding. This method works for Forms W-4 for all prior, current, and future years. This method also works for any amount of wages. If the Form W-4 is from 2019 or earlier, this method works for any number of withholding allowances claimed.

Worksheet 1. Employer's Withholding Worksheet for Percentage Method Tables for Automated Payroll Systems

Keep for Your Records

Table 3	Semiannually	Quarterly	Monthly	Semimonthly	Biweekly	Weekly	Daily
	2	4	12	24	26	52	260

Step 1.   Adjust the empolyee's payment amount

1a   Enter the employee's total taxable wages this payroll period . . . .   1a $ _____

1b   Enter the number of pay periods you have per year (see Table 3) . . . .   1b   _____

1c   Multiply the amount on line 1a by the number on line 1b . . . .   1c $ _____

If the employee **HAS** submitted a Form W-4 for 2020 or later, figure the Adjusted Annual Wage Amount as follows:

1d   Enter the amount from Step 4(a) of the employee's Form W-4 . . . .   1d $ _____

1e   Add lines 1c and 1d . . . .   1e $ _____

1f   Enter the amount from Step 4(b) of the employee's Form W-4 . . . .   1f $ _____

1g   If the box in Step 2 of Form W-4 is checked, enter -0-. If the box is not checked, enter $12,900 if the taxpayer is married filing jointly or $8,600 otherwise . . . .   1g $ _____

1h   Add lines 1f and 1g . . . .   1h $ _____

1i   Subtract line 1h from line 1e. If zero or less, enter -0-. This is the **Adjusted Annual Wage Amount** . . . .   1i $ _____

If the employee **HAS NOT** submitted a Form W-4 for 2020 or later, figure the Adjusted Annual Wage Amount as follows:

1j   Enter the number of allowances claimed on the employee's most recent Form W-4 . . . .   1j   _____

1k   Multiply line 1j by $4,300 . . . .   1k $ _____

1l   Subtract line 1k from line 1c. If zero or less, enter -0-. This is the **Adjusted Annual Wage Amount** . . . .   1l $ _____

Step 2.   Figure the Tentative Withholding Amount

based on the employee's Adjusted Annual Wage Amount; filing status (Step 1(c) of the 2020 or later Form W-4) or marital status (line 3 of Form W-4 from 2019 or earlier); and whether the box in Step 2 of 2020 or later Form W-4 is checked.
Note. Don't use the Head of Household table if the Form W-4 is from 2019 or earlier.

2a   Enter the employee's **Adjusted Annual Wage Amount** from line 1i or 1l above . . . .   2a $ _____

2b   Find the row in the appropriate **Annual** Percentage Method table in which the amount on line 2a is at least the amount in column A but less than the amount in column B, then enter here the amount from column A of that row . . . .   2b $ _____

2c   Enter the amount from column C of that row . . . .   2c $ _____

2d   Enter the percentage from column D of that row . . . .   2d   _____ %

2e   Subtract line 2b from line 2a . . . .   2e $ _____

2f   Multiply the amount on line 2e by the percentage on line 2d . . . .   2f $ _____

2g   Add lines 2c and 2f . . . .   2g $ _____

2h   Divide the amount on line 2g by the number of pay periods on line 1b. This is the **Tentative Withholding Amount** . . . .   2h $ _____

Step 3.   Account for tax credits

3a   If the employee's Form W-4 is from 2020 or later, enter the amount from Step 3 of that form; otherwise enter -0- . . . .   3a $ _____

3b   Divide the amount on line 3a by the number of pay periods on line 1b . . . .   3b $ _____

3c   Subtract line 3b from line 2h. If zero or less, enter -0- . . . .   3c $ _____

Step 4.   Figure the final amount to withhold

4a   Enter the additional amount to withhold from the employee's Form W-4 (Step 4(c) of the 2020 or later form or line 6 on earlier forms) . . . .   4a $ _____

4b   Add lines 3c and 4a. **This is the amount to withhold from the employee's wages this pay period** . . . .   4b $ _____

2021 Percentage Method Tables for Automated Payroll Systems

STANDARD Withholding Rate Schedules					Form W-4, Step 2, Checkbox, Withholding Rate Schedules				
(Use these if the Form W-4 is from 2019 or earlier, or if the Form W-4 is from 2020 or later and the box in Step 2 of Form W-4 is **NOT** checked)					(Use these if the Form W-4 is from 2020 or later and the box in Step 2 of Form W-4 **IS** checked)				
If the Adjusted Annual Wage Amount (line 2a) is:		The tentative amount to withhold is:	Plus this percentage—	of the amount that the Adjusted Annual Wage exceeds—	If the Adjusted Annual Wage Amount (line 2a) is:		The tentative amount to withhold is:	Plus this percentage—	of the amount that the Adjusted Annual Wage exceeds—
At least—	But less than—				At least—	But less than—			
A	B	C	D	E	A	B	C	D	E
Married Filing Jointly					**Married Filing Jointly**				
$0	$12,200	$0.00	0%	$0	$0	$12,550	$0.00	0%	$0
$12,200	$32,100	$0.00	10%	$12,200	$12,550	$22,500	$0.00	10%	$12,550
$32,100	$93,250	$1,990.00	12%	$32,100	$22,500	$53,075	$995.00	12%	$22,500
$93,250	$184,950	$9,328.00	22%	$93,250	$53,075	$98,925	$4,664.00	22%	$53,075
$184,950	$342,050	$29,502.00	24%	$184,950	$98,925	$177,475	$14,751.00	24%	$98,925
$342,050	$431,050	$67,206.00	32%	$342,050	$177,475	$221,975	$33,603.00	32%	$177,475
$431,050	$640,500	$95,686.00	35%	$431,050	$221,975	$326,700	$47,843.00	35%	$221,975
$640,500		$168,993.50	37%	$640,500	$326,700		$84,496.75	37%	$326,700
Single or Married Filing Separately					**Single or Married Filing Separately**				
$0	$3,950	$0.00	0%	$0	$0	$6,275	$0.00	0%	$0
$3,950	$13,900	$0.00	10%	$3,950	$6,275	$11,250	$0.00	10%	$6,275
$13,900	$44,475	$995.00	12%	$13,900	$11,250	$26,538	$497.50	12%	$11,250
$44,475	$90,325	$4,664.00	22%	$44,475	$26,538	$49,463	$2,332.00	22%	$26,538
$90,325	$168,875	$14,751.00	24%	$90,325	$49,463	$88,738	$7,375.50	24%	$49,463
$168,875	$213,375	$33,603.00	32%	$168,875	$88,738	$110,988	$16,801.50	32%	$88,738
$213,375	$527,550	$47,843.00	35%	$213,375	$110,988	$268,075	$23,921.50	35%	$110,988
$527,550		$157,804.25	37%	$527,550	$268,075		$78,902.13	37%	$268,075
Head of Household					**Head of Household**				
$0	$10,200	$0.00	0%	$0	$0	$9,400	$0.00	0%	$0
$10,200	$24,400	$0.00	10%	$10,200	$9,400	$16,500	$0.00	10%	$9,400
$24,400	$64,400	$1,420.00	12%	$24,400	$16,500	$36,500	$710.00	12%	$16,500
$64,400	$96,550	$6,220.00	22%	$64,400	$36,500	$52,575	$3,110.00	22%	$36,500
$96,550	$175,100	$13,293.00	24%	$96,550	$52,575	$91,850	$6,646.50	24%	$52,575
$175,100	$219,600	$32,145.00	32%	$175,100	$91,850	$114,100	$16,072.50	32%	$91,850
$219,600	$533,800	$46,385.00	35%	$219,600	$114,100	$271,200	$23,192.50	35%	$114,100
$533,800		$156,355.00	37%	$533,800	$271,200		$78,177.50	37%	$271,200

Source: Internal Revenue Service

2. Wage Bracket Method Tables for Manual Payroll Systems With Forms W-4 From 2020 or Later

If you compute payroll manually, your employee has submitted a Form W-4 for 2020 or later, and you prefer to use the Wage Bracket method, use the worksheet below and the Wage Bracket Method tables that follow to figure federal income tax withholding.

The Wage Bracket Method tables cover only up to approximately $100,000 in annual wages. If you can't use the Wage Bracket Method tables because taxable wages exceed the amount from the last bracket of the table (based on filing status and pay period), use the Percentage Method tables in section 4.

Worksheet 2. Employer's Withholding Worksheet for Wage Bracket Method Tables for Manual Payroll Systems With Forms W-4 From 2020 or Later

Keep for Your Records

Table 4	Monthly	Semimonthly	Biweekly	Weekly	Daily
	12	24	26	52	260

Step 1. **Adjust the employee's wage amount**

1a Enter the employee's total taxable wages this payroll period .... 1a $ _____

1b Enter the number of pay periods you have per year (see Table 4) .... 1b _____

1c Enter the amount from Step 4(a) of the employee's Form W-4 .... 1c $ _____

1d Divide the amount on line 1c by the number of pay periods on line 1b .... 1d $ _____

1e Add lines 1a and 1d .... 1e $ _____

1f Enter the amount from Step 4(b) of the employee's Form W-4 .... 1f $ _____

1g Divide the amount on line 1f by the number of pay periods on line 1b .... 1g $ _____

1h Subtract line 1g from line 1e. If zero or less, enter -0-. This is the **Adjusted Wage Amount** ...... 1h $ _____

Step 2. **Figure the Tentative Withholding Amount**

2a Use the amount on line 1h to look up the tentative amount to withhold in the appropriate Wage Bracket Table in this section for your pay frequency, given the employee's filing status and whether the employee has checked the box in Step 2 of Form W-4. This is the **Tentative Withholding Amount** .... 2a $ _____

Step 3. **Account for tax credits**

3a Enter the amount from Step 3 of the employee's Form W-4 .... 3a $ _____

3b Divide the amount on line 3a by the number of pay periods on line 1b .... 3b $ _____

3c Subtract line 3b from line 2a. If zero or less, enter -0- .... 3c $ _____

Step 4. **Figure the final amount to withhold**

4a Enter the additional amount to withhold from Step 4(c) of the employee's Form W-4 .... 4a $ _____

4b Add lines 3c and 4a. **This is the amount to withhold from the employee's wages this pay period** .... 4b $ _____

2021 Wage Bracket Method Tables for Manual Payroll Systems with Forms W-4 From 2020 or Later
WEEKLY Payroll Period

If the Adjusted Wage Amount (line 1h) is		Married Filing Jointly		Head of Household		Single or Married Filing Separately	
		Standard withholding	Form W-4, Step 2, Checkbox withholding	Standard withholding	Form W-4, Step 2, Checkbox withholding	Standard withholding	Form W-4, Step 2, Checkbox withholding
At least	But less than	The Tentative Withholding Amount is:					
$0	$125	$0	$0	$0	$0	$0	$0
$125	$135	$0	$0	$0	$0	$0	$1
$135	$145	$0	$0	$0	$0	$0	$2
$145	$155	$0	$0	$0	$0	$0	$3
$155	$165	$0	$0	$0	$0	$0	$4
$165	$175	$0	$0	$0	$0	$0	$5
$175	$185	$0	$0	$0	$0	$0	$6
$185	$195	$0	$0	$0	$1	$0	$7
$195	$205	$0	$0	$0	$2	$0	$8
$205	$215	$0	$0	$0	$3	$0	$9
$215	$225	$0	$0	$0	$4	$0	$10
$225	$235	$0	$0	$0	$5	$0	$11
$235	$245	$0	$0	$0	$6	$0	$12
$245	$255	$0	$1	$0	$7	$1	$14
$255	$265	$0	$2	$0	$8	$2	$15
$265	$275	$0	$3	$0	$9	$3	$16
$275	$285	$0	$4	$0	$10	$4	$17
$285	$295	$0	$5	$0	$11	$5	$18
$295	$305	$0	$6	$0	$12	$6	$20
$305	$315	$0	$7	$0	$13	$7	$21
$315	$325	$0	$8	$0	$14	$8	$22
$325	$335	$0	$9	$0	$15	$9	$23
$335	$345	$0	$10	$0	$16	$10	$24
$345	$355	$0	$11	$0	$18	$11	$26
$355	$365	$0	$12	$0	$19	$12	$27
$365	$375	$0	$13	$1	$20	$13	$28
$375	$385	$0	$14	$2	$21	$14	$29
$385	$395	$0	$15	$3	$22	$15	$30
$395	$405	$0	$16	$4	$24	$16	$32
$405	$415	$0	$17	$5	$25	$17	$33
$415	$425	$0	$18	$6	$26	$18	$34
$425	$435	$0	$19	$7	$27	$19	$35
$435	$445	$0	$20	$8	$28	$20	$36
$445	$455	$0	$21	$9	$30	$21	$38
$455	$465	$0	$22	$10	$31	$22	$39
$465	$475	$0	$24	$11	$32	$24	$40
$475	$485	$0	$25	$12	$33	$25	$41
$485	$495	$1	$26	$13	$34	$26	$42
$495	$505	$2	$27	$14	$36	$27	$44
$505	$515	$3	$28	$15	$37	$28	$45
$515	$525	$4	$30	$16	$38	$30	$47
$525	$535	$5	$31	$17	$39	$31	$49
$535	$545	$6	$32	$18	$40	$32	$51
$545	$555	$7	$33	$19	$42	$33	$54
$555	$565	$8	$34	$20	$43	$34	$56
$565	$575	$9	$36	$21	$44	$36	$58
$575	$585	$10	$37	$22	$45	$37	$60
$585	$595	$11	$38	$23	$46	$38	$62
$595	$605	$12	$39	$24	$48	$39	$65
$605	$615	$13	$40	$25	$49	$40	$67
$615	$625	$14	$42	$26	$50	$42	$69
$625	$635	$15	$43	$27	$51	$43	$71
$635	$645	$16	$44	$28	$52	$44	$73
$645	$655	$17	$45	$29	$54	$45	$76
$655	$665	$18	$46	$30	$55	$46	$78
$665	$675	$19	$48	$32	$56	$48	$80
$675	$685	$20	$49	$33	$57	$49	$82
$685	$695	$21	$50	$34	$58	$50	$84
$695	$705	$22	$51	$35	$60	$51	$87
$705	$715	$23	$52	$36	$62	$52	$89
$715	$725	$24	$54	$38	$64	$54	$91
$725	$735	$25	$55	$39	$66	$55	$93
$735	$745	$26	$56	$40	$68	$56	$95
$745	$755	$27	$57	$41	$70	$57	$98
$755	$765	$28	$58	$42	$73	$58	$100

2021 Wage Bracket Method Tables for Manual Payroll Systems with Forms W-4 From 2020 or Later
WEEKLY Payroll Period

If the **Adjusted Wage Amount** (line 1h) is		Married Filing Jointly		Head of Household		Single or Married Filing Separately	
		Standard withholding	Form W-4, Step 2, Checkbox withholding	Standard withholding	Form W-4, Step 2, Checkbox withholding	Standard withholding	Form W-4, Step 2, Checkbox withholding
At least	But less than			The Tentative Withholding Amount is:			
$765	$775	$29	$60	$44	$75	$60	$102
$775	$785	$30	$61	$45	$77	$61	$104
$785	$795	$31	$62	$46	$79	$62	$106
$795	$805	$32	$63	$47	$81	$63	$109
$805	$815	$33	$64	$48	$84	$64	$111
$815	$825	$34	$66	$50	$86	$66	$113
$825	$835	$35	$67	$51	$88	$67	$115
$835	$845	$36	$68	$52	$90	$68	$117
$845	$855	$37	$69	$53	$92	$69	$120
$855	$865	$38	$70	$54	$95	$70	$122
$865	$875	$39	$72	$56	$97	$72	$124
$875	$885	$40	$73	$57	$99	$73	$126
$885	$895	$41	$74	$58	$101	$74	$128
$895	$905	$42	$75	$59	$103	$75	$131
$905	$915	$44	$76	$60	$106	$76	$133
$915	$925	$45	$78	$62	$108	$78	$135
$925	$935	$46	$79	$63	$110	$79	$137
$935	$945	$47	$80	$64	$112	$80	$139
$945	$955	$48	$81	$65	$114	$81	$142
$955	$965	$50	$82	$66	$117	$82	$144
$965	$975	$51	$84	$68	$119	$84	$146
$975	$985	$52	$85	$69	$121	$85	$149
$985	$995	$53	$86	$70	$123	$86	$151
$995	$1,005	$54	$87	$71	$125	$87	$154
$1,005	$1,015	$56	$88	$72	$128	$88	$156
$1,015	$1,025	$57	$90	$74	$130	$90	$158
$1,025	$1,035	$58	$92	$75	$132	$92	$161
$1,035	$1,045	$59	$94	$76	$135	$94	$163
$1,045	$1,055	$60	$96	$77	$137	$96	$166
$1,055	$1,065	$62	$98	$78	$140	$98	$168
$1,065	$1,075	$63	$101	$80	$142	$101	$170
$1,075	$1,085	$64	$103	$81	$144	$103	$173
$1,085	$1,095	$65	$105	$82	$147	$105	$175
$1,095	$1,105	$66	$107	$83	$149	$107	$178
$1,105	$1,115	$68	$109	$84	$152	$109	$180
$1,115	$1,125	$69	$112	$86	$154	$112	$182
$1,125	$1,135	$70	$114	$87	$156	$114	$185
$1,135	$1,145	$71	$116	$88	$159	$116	$187
$1,145	$1,155	$72	$118	$89	$161	$118	$190
$1,155	$1,165	$74	$120	$90	$164	$120	$192
$1,165	$1,175	$75	$123	$92	$166	$123	$194
$1,175	$1,185	$76	$125	$93	$168	$125	$197
$1,185	$1,195	$77	$127	$94	$171	$127	$199
$1,195	$1,205	$78	$129	$95	$173	$129	$202
$1,205	$1,215	$80	$131	$96	$176	$131	$204
$1,215	$1,225	$81	$134	$98	$178	$134	$206
$1,225	$1,235	$82	$136	$99	$180	$136	$209
$1,235	$1,245	$83	$138	$100	$183	$138	$211
$1,245	$1,255	$84	$140	$101	$185	$140	$214
$1,255	$1,265	$86	$142	$102	$188	$142	$216
$1,265	$1,275	$87	$145	$104	$190	$145	$218
$1,275	$1,285	$88	$147	$105	$192	$147	$221
$1,285	$1,295	$89	$149	$106	$195	$149	$223
$1,295	$1,305	$90	$151	$107	$197	$151	$226
$1,305	$1,315	$92	$153	$108	$200	$153	$228
$1,315	$1,325	$93	$156	$110	$202	$156	$230
$1,325	$1,335	$94	$158	$111	$204	$158	$233
$1,335	$1,345	$95	$160	$112	$207	$160	$235
$1,345	$1,355	$96	$162	$113	$209	$162	$238
$1,355	$1,365	$98	$164	$114	$212	$164	$240
$1,365	$1,375	$99	$167	$116	$214	$167	$242
$1,375	$1,385	$100	$169	$117	$216	$169	$245
$1,385	$1,395	$101	$171	$118	$219	$171	$247
$1,395	$1,405	$102	$173	$119	$221	$173	$250
$1,405	$1,415	$104	$175	$121	$224	$175	$252

2021 Wage Bracket Method Tables for Manual Payroll Systems with Forms W-4 From 2020 or Later
WEEKLY Payroll Period

If the Adjusted Wage Amount (line 1h) is		Married Filing Jointly		Head of Household		Single or Married Filing Separately	
At least	But less than	Standard withholding	Form W-4, Step 2, Checkbox withholding	Standard withholding	Form W-4, Step 2, Checkbox withholding	Standard withholding	Form W-4, Step 2, Checkbox withholding
		The Tentative Withholding Amount is:					
$1,415	$1,425	$105	$178	$123	$226	$178	$254
$1,425	$1,435	$106	$180	$125	$228	$180	$257
$1,435	$1,445	$107	$182	$128	$231	$182	$259
$1,445	$1,455	$108	$184	$130	$233	$184	$262
$1,455	$1,465	$110	$186	$132	$236	$186	$264
$1,465	$1,475	$111	$189	$134	$238	$189	$266
$1,475	$1,485	$112	$191	$136	$240	$191	$269
$1,485	$1,495	$113	$193	$139	$243	$193	$271
$1,495	$1,505	$114	$195	$141	$245	$195	$274
$1,505	$1,515	$116	$197	$143	$248	$197	$276
$1,515	$1,525	$117	$200	$145	$250	$200	$278
$1,525	$1,535	$118	$202	$147	$252	$202	$281
$1,535	$1,545	$119	$204	$150	$255	$204	$283
$1,545	$1,555	$120	$206	$152	$257	$206	$286
$1,555	$1,565	$122	$208	$154	$260	$208	$288
$1,565	$1,575	$123	$211	$156	$262	$211	$290
$1,575	$1,585	$124	$213	$158	$264	$213	$293
$1,585	$1,595	$125	$215	$161	$267	$215	$295
$1,595	$1,605	$126	$217	$163	$269	$217	$298
$1,605	$1,615	$128	$219	$165	$272	$219	$300
$1,615	$1,625	$129	$222	$167	$274	$222	$302
$1,625	$1,635	$130	$224	$169	$276	$224	$305
$1,635	$1,645	$131	$226	$172	$279	$226	$307
$1,645	$1,655	$132	$228	$174	$281	$228	$310
$1,655	$1,665	$134	$230	$176	$284	$230	$312
$1,665	$1,675	$135	$233	$178	$286	$233	$314
$1,675	$1,685	$136	$235	$180	$288	$235	$317
$1,685	$1,695	$137	$237	$183	$291	$237	$319
$1,695	$1,705	$138	$239	$185	$293	$239	$322
$1,705	$1,715	$140	$241	$187	$296	$241	$324
$1,715	$1,725	$141	$244	$189	$298	$244	$327
$1,725	$1,735	$142	$246	$191	$300	$246	$331
$1,735	$1,745	$143	$248	$194	$303	$248	$334
$1,745	$1,755	$144	$250	$196	$305	$250	$337
$1,755	$1,765	$146	$252	$198	$308	$252	$340
$1,765	$1,775	$147	$255	$200	$310	$255	$343
$1,775	$1,785	$148	$257	$202	$313	$257	$347
$1,785	$1,795	$149	$259	$205	$317	$259	$350
$1,795	$1,805	$150	$261	$207	$320	$261	$353
$1,805	$1,815	$152	$263	$209	$323	$263	$356
$1,815	$1,825	$153	$266	$211	$326	$266	$359
$1,825	$1,835	$154	$268	$213	$329	$268	$363
$1,835	$1,845	$155	$270	$216	$333	$270	$366
$1,845	$1,855	$156	$272	$218	$336	$272	$369
$1,855	$1,865	$158	$274	$220	$339	$274	$372
$1,865	$1,875	$159	$277	$222	$342	$277	$375
$1,875	$1,885	$160	$279	$224	$345	$279	$379
$1,885	$1,895	$161	$281	$227	$349	$281	$382
$1,895	$1,905	$162	$283	$229	$352	$283	$385
$1,905	$1,915	$164	$285	$231	$355	$285	$388
$1,915	$1,925	$165	$288	$233	$358	$288	$391

2021 Wage Bracket Method Tables for Manual Payroll Systems with Forms W-4 From 2020 or Later
BIWEEKLY Payroll Period

| If the Adjusted Wage Amount (line 1h) is | | Married Filing Jointly | | Head of Household | | Single or Married Filing Separately | |
At least	But less than	Standard withholding	Form W-4, Step 2, Checkbox withholding	Standard withholding	Form W-4, Step 2, Checkbox withholding	Standard withholding	Form W-4, Step 2, Checkbox withholding
				The Tentative Withholding Amount is:			
$0	$245	$0	$0	$0	$0	$0	$0
$245	$255	$0	$0	$0	$0	$0	$1
$255	$265	$0	$0	$0	$0	$0	$2
$265	$275	$0	$0	$0	$0	$0	$3
$275	$285	$0	$0	$0	$0	$0	$4
$285	$295	$0	$0	$0	$0	$0	$5
$295	$305	$0	$0	$0	$0	$0	$6
$305	$315	$0	$0	$0	$0	$0	$7
$315	$325	$0	$0	$0	$0	$0	$8
$325	$335	$0	$0	$0	$0	$0	$9
$335	$345	$0	$0	$0	$0	$0	$10
$345	$355	$0	$0	$0	$0	$0	$11
$355	$365	$0	$0	$0	$0	$0	$12
$365	$375	$0	$0	$0	$1	$0	$13
$375	$385	$0	$0	$0	$2	$0	$14
$385	$395	$0	$0	$0	$3	$0	$15
$395	$405	$0	$0	$0	$4	$0	$16
$405	$415	$0	$0	$0	$5	$0	$17
$415	$425	$0	$0	$0	$6	$0	$18
$425	$435	$0	$0	$0	$7	$0	$19
$435	$450	$0	$0	$0	$8	$0	$20
$450	$465	$0	$0	$0	$10	$0	$22
$465	$480	$0	$0	$0	$11	$0	$24
$480	$495	$0	$0	$0	$13	$0	$26
$495	$510	$0	$2	$0	$14	$0	$28
$510	$525	$0	$3	$0	$16	$3	$29
$525	$540	$0	$5	$0	$17	$5	$31
$540	$555	$0	$6	$0	$19	$6	$33
$555	$570	$0	$8	$0	$20	$8	$35
$570	$585	$0	$9	$0	$22	$9	$37
$585	$600	$0	$11	$0	$23	$11	$38
$600	$615	$0	$12	$0	$25	$12	$40
$615	$630	$0	$14	$0	$26	$14	$42
$630	$645	$0	$15	$0	$28	$15	$44
$645	$660	$0	$17	$0	$29	$17	$46
$660	$675	$0	$18	$0	$31	$18	$47
$675	$690	$0	$20	$0	$33	$20	$49
$690	$705	$0	$21	$0	$35	$21	$51
$705	$720	$0	$23	$0	$37	$23	$53
$720	$735	$0	$24	$0	$38	$24	$55
$735	$750	$0	$26	$2	$40	$26	$56
$750	$765	$0	$27	$3	$42	$27	$58
$765	$780	$0	$29	$5	$44	$29	$60
$780	$795	$0	$30	$6	$46	$30	$62
$795	$810	$0	$32	$8	$47	$32	$64
$810	$825	$0	$33	$9	$49	$33	$65
$825	$840	$0	$35	$11	$51	$35	$67
$840	$855	$0	$36	$12	$53	$36	$69
$855	$870	$0	$38	$14	$55	$38	$71
$870	$885	$0	$40	$15	$56	$40	$73
$885	$900	$0	$42	$17	$58	$42	$74
$900	$915	$0	$43	$18	$60	$43	$76
$915	$930	$0	$45	$20	$62	$45	$78
$930	$945	$0	$47	$21	$64	$47	$80
$945	$960	$0	$49	$23	$65	$49	$82
$960	$975	$0	$51	$24	$67	$51	$83
$975	$990	$2	$52	$26	$69	$52	$85
$990	$1,005	$3	$54	$27	$71	$54	$87
$1,005	$1,020	$5	$56	$29	$73	$56	$89
$1,020	$1,040	$6	$58	$31	$75	$58	$92
$1,040	$1,060	$8	$60	$33	$77	$60	$96
$1,060	$1,080	$10	$63	$35	$80	$63	$101
$1,080	$1,100	$12	$65	$37	$82	$65	$105
$1,100	$1,120	$14	$68	$39	$84	$68	$109
$1,120	$1,140	$16	$70	$41	$87	$70	$114

2021 Wage Bracket Method Tables for Manual Payroll Systems with Forms W-4 From 2020 or Later
BIWEEKLY Payroll Period

If the Adjusted Wage Amount (line 1h) is		Married Filing Jointly		Head of Household		Single or Married Filing Separately	
At least	But less than	Standard withholding	Form W-4, Step 2, Checkbox withholding	Standard withholding	Form W-4, Step 2, Checkbox withholding	Standard withholding	Form W-4, Step 2, Checkbox withholding
		The Tentative Withholding Amount is:					
$1,140	$1,160	$18	$72	$43	$89	$72	$118
$1,160	$1,180	$20	$75	$45	$92	$75	$123
$1,180	$1,200	$22	$77	$47	$94	$77	$127
$1,200	$1,220	$24	$80	$49	$96	$80	$131
$1,220	$1,240	$26	$82	$51	$99	$82	$136
$1,240	$1,260	$28	$84	$53	$101	$84	$140
$1,260	$1,280	$30	$87	$55	$104	$87	$145
$1,280	$1,300	$32	$89	$57	$106	$89	$149
$1,300	$1,320	$34	$92	$60	$108	$92	$153
$1,320	$1,340	$36	$94	$62	$111	$94	$158
$1,340	$1,360	$38	$96	$64	$113	$96	$162
$1,360	$1,380	$40	$99	$67	$116	$99	$167
$1,380	$1,400	$42	$101	$69	$118	$101	$171
$1,400	$1,420	$44	$104	$72	$121	$104	$175
$1,420	$1,440	$46	$106	$74	$125	$106	$180
$1,440	$1,460	$48	$108	$76	$130	$108	$184
$1,460	$1,480	$50	$111	$79	$134	$111	$189
$1,480	$1,500	$52	$113	$81	$139	$113	$193
$1,500	$1,520	$54	$116	$84	$143	$116	$197
$1,520	$1,540	$56	$118	$86	$147	$118	$202
$1,540	$1,560	$58	$120	$88	$152	$120	$206
$1,560	$1,580	$60	$123	$91	$156	$123	$211
$1,580	$1,600	$62	$125	$93	$161	$125	$215
$1,600	$1,620	$64	$128	$96	$165	$128	$219
$1,620	$1,640	$66	$130	$98	$169	$130	$224
$1,640	$1,660	$68	$132	$100	$174	$132	$228
$1,660	$1,680	$70	$135	$103	$178	$135	$233
$1,680	$1,700	$72	$137	$105	$183	$137	$237
$1,700	$1,720	$74	$140	$108	$187	$140	$241
$1,720	$1,740	$76	$142	$110	$191	$142	$246
$1,740	$1,760	$79	$144	$112	$196	$144	$250
$1,760	$1,780	$81	$147	$115	$200	$147	$255
$1,780	$1,800	$84	$149	$117	$205	$149	$259
$1,800	$1,820	$86	$152	$120	$209	$152	$263
$1,820	$1,840	$88	$154	$122	$213	$154	$268
$1,840	$1,860	$91	$156	$124	$218	$156	$272
$1,860	$1,880	$93	$159	$127	$222	$159	$277
$1,880	$1,900	$96	$161	$129	$227	$161	$281
$1,900	$1,925	$98	$164	$132	$232	$164	$286
$1,925	$1,950	$101	$167	$135	$237	$167	$292
$1,950	$1,975	$104	$170	$138	$243	$170	$298
$1,975	$2,000	$107	$173	$141	$248	$173	$304
$2,000	$2,025	$110	$176	$144	$254	$176	$310
$2,025	$2,050	$113	$179	$147	$259	$179	$316
$2,050	$2,075	$116	$184	$150	$265	$184	$322
$2,075	$2,100	$119	$190	$153	$271	$190	$328
$2,100	$2,125	$122	$195	$156	$277	$195	$334
$2,125	$2,150	$125	$201	$159	$283	$201	$340
$2,150	$2,175	$128	$206	$162	$289	$206	$346
$2,175	$2,200	$131	$212	$165	$295	$212	$352
$2,200	$2,225	$134	$217	$168	$301	$217	$358
$2,225	$2,250	$137	$223	$171	$307	$223	$364
$2,250	$2,275	$140	$228	$174	$313	$228	$370
$2,275	$2,300	$143	$234	$177	$319	$234	$376
$2,300	$2,325	$146	$239	$180	$325	$239	$382
$2,325	$2,350	$149	$245	$183	$331	$245	$388
$2,350	$2,375	$152	$250	$186	$337	$250	$394
$2,375	$2,400	$155	$256	$189	$343	$256	$400
$2,400	$2,425	$158	$261	$192	$349	$261	$406
$2,425	$2,450	$161	$267	$195	$355	$267	$412
$2,450	$2,475	$164	$272	$198	$361	$272	$418
$2,475	$2,500	$167	$278	$201	$367	$278	$424
$2,500	$2,525	$170	$283	$204	$373	$283	$430
$2,525	$2,550	$173	$289	$207	$379	$289	$436
$2,550	$2,575	$176	$294	$210	$385	$294	$442

2021 Wage Bracket Method Tables for Manual Payroll Systems with Forms W-4 From 2020 or Later
BIWEEKLY Payroll Period

If the **Adjusted Wage Amount** (line 1h) is		Married Filing Jointly		Head of Household		Single or Married Filing Separately	
At least	But less than	Standard withholding	Form W-4, Step 2, Checkbox withholding	Standard withholding	Form W-4, Step 2, Checkbox withholding	Standard withholding	Form W-4, Step 2, Checkbox withholding
		The Tentative Withholding Amount is:					
$2,575	$2,600	$179	$300	$213	$391	$300	$448
$2,600	$2,625	$182	$305	$216	$397	$305	$454
$2,625	$2,650	$185	$311	$219	$403	$311	$460
$2,650	$2,675	$188	$316	$222	$409	$316	$466
$2,675	$2,700	$191	$322	$225	$415	$322	$472
$2,700	$2,725	$194	$327	$228	$421	$327	$478
$2,725	$2,750	$197	$333	$231	$427	$333	$484
$2,750	$2,775	$200	$338	$234	$433	$338	$490
$2,775	$2,800	$203	$344	$237	$439	$344	$496
$2,800	$2,825	$206	$349	$240	$445	$349	$502
$2,825	$2,850	$209	$355	$246	$451	$355	$508
$2,850	$2,875	$212	$360	$251	$457	$360	$514
$2,875	$2,900	$215	$366	$257	$463	$366	$520
$2,900	$2,925	$218	$371	$262	$469	$371	$526
$2,925	$2,950	$221	$377	$268	$475	$377	$532
$2,950	$2,975	$224	$382	$273	$481	$382	$538
$2,975	$3,000	$227	$388	$279	$487	$388	$544
$3,000	$3,025	$230	$393	$284	$493	$393	$550
$3,025	$3,050	$233	$399	$290	$499	$399	$556
$3,050	$3,075	$236	$404	$295	$505	$404	$562
$3,075	$3,100	$239	$410	$301	$511	$410	$568
$3,100	$3,125	$242	$415	$306	$517	$415	$574
$3,125	$3,150	$245	$421	$312	$523	$421	$580
$3,150	$3,175	$248	$426	$317	$529	$426	$586
$3,175	$3,200	$251	$432	$323	$535	$432	$592
$3,200	$3,225	$254	$437	$328	$541	$437	$598
$3,225	$3,250	$257	$443	$334	$547	$443	$604
$3,250	$3,275	$260	$448	$339	$553	$448	$610
$3,275	$3,300	$263	$454	$345	$559	$454	$616
$3,300	$3,325	$266	$459	$350	$565	$459	$622
$3,325	$3,350	$269	$465	$356	$571	$465	$628
$3,350	$3,375	$272	$470	$361	$577	$470	$634
$3,375	$3,400	$275	$476	$367	$583	$476	$640
$3,400	$3,425	$278	$481	$372	$589	$481	$646
$3,425	$3,450	$281	$487	$378	$595	$487	$654
$3,450	$3,475	$284	$492	$383	$601	$492	$662
$3,475	$3,500	$287	$498	$389	$607	$498	$670
$3,500	$3,525	$290	$503	$394	$613	$503	$678
$3,525	$3,550	$293	$509	$400	$620	$509	$686
$3,550	$3,575	$296	$514	$405	$628	$514	$694
$3,575	$3,600	$299	$520	$411	$636	$520	$702
$3,600	$3,625	$302	$525	$416	$644	$525	$710
$3,625	$3,650	$305	$531	$422	$652	$531	$718
$3,650	$3,675	$308	$536	$427	$660	$536	$726
$3,675	$3,700	$311	$542	$433	$668	$542	$734
$3,700	$3,725	$314	$547	$438	$676	$547	$742
$3,725	$3,750	$317	$553	$444	$684	$553	$750
$3,750	$3,775	$320	$558	$449	$692	$558	$758
$3,775	$3,800	$323	$564	$455	$700	$564	$766
$3,800	$3,825	$326	$569	$460	$708	$569	$774
$3,825	$3,850	$329	$575	$466	$716	$575	$782

2021 Wage Bracket Method Tables for Manual Payroll Systems with Forms W-4 From 2020 or Later
SEMIMONTHLY Payroll Period

If the Adjusted Wage Amount (line 1h) is		Married Filing Jointly		Head of Household		Single or Married Filing Separately	
At least	But less than	Standard withholding	Form W-4, Step 2, Checkbox withholding	Standard withholding	Form W-4, Step 2, Checkbox withholding	Standard withholding	Form W-4, Step 2, Checkbox withholding
		The Tentative Withholding Amount is:					
$0	$265	$0	$0	$0	$0	$0	$0
$265	$275	$0	$0	$0	$0	$0	$1
$275	$285	$0	$0	$0	$0	$0	$2
$285	$295	$0	$0	$0	$0	$0	$3
$295	$305	$0	$0	$0	$0	$0	$4
$305	$315	$0	$0	$0	$0	$0	$5
$315	$325	$0	$0	$0	$0	$0	$6
$325	$335	$0	$0	$0	$0	$0	$7
$335	$345	$0	$0	$0	$0	$0	$8
$345	$355	$0	$0	$0	$0	$0	$9
$355	$365	$0	$0	$0	$0	$0	$10
$365	$375	$0	$0	$0	$0	$0	$11
$375	$385	$0	$0	$0	$0	$0	$12
$385	$395	$0	$0	$0	$0	$0	$13
$395	$405	$0	$0	$0	$1	$0	$14
$405	$415	$0	$0	$0	$2	$0	$15
$415	$425	$0	$0	$0	$3	$0	$16
$425	$435	$0	$0	$0	$4	$0	$17
$435	$445	$0	$0	$0	$5	$0	$18
$445	$455	$0	$0	$0	$6	$0	$19
$455	$465	$0	$0	$0	$7	$0	$20
$465	$475	$0	$0	$0	$8	$0	$21
$475	$490	$0	$0	$0	$9	$0	$22
$490	$505	$0	$0	$0	$11	$0	$24
$505	$520	$0	$0	$0	$12	$0	$26
$520	$535	$0	$0	$0	$14	$0	$28
$535	$550	$0	$2	$0	$15	$2	$30
$550	$565	$0	$3	$0	$17	$3	$31
$565	$580	$0	$5	$0	$18	$5	$33
$580	$595	$0	$6	$0	$20	$6	$35
$595	$610	$0	$8	$0	$21	$8	$37
$610	$625	$0	$9	$0	$23	$9	$39
$625	$640	$0	$11	$0	$24	$11	$40
$640	$655	$0	$12	$0	$26	$12	$42
$655	$670	$0	$14	$0	$27	$14	$44
$670	$685	$0	$15	$0	$29	$15	$46
$685	$700	$0	$17	$0	$30	$17	$48
$700	$715	$0	$18	$0	$32	$18	$49
$715	$730	$0	$20	$0	$34	$20	$51
$730	$745	$0	$21	$0	$36	$21	$53
$745	$760	$0	$23	$0	$37	$23	$55
$760	$775	$0	$24	$0	$39	$24	$57
$775	$790	$0	$26	$0	$41	$26	$58
$790	$805	$0	$27	$1	$43	$27	$60
$805	$820	$0	$29	$3	$45	$29	$62
$820	$835	$0	$30	$4	$46	$30	$64
$835	$850	$0	$32	$6	$48	$32	$66
$850	$865	$0	$33	$7	$50	$33	$67
$865	$880	$0	$35	$9	$52	$35	$69
$880	$895	$0	$36	$10	$54	$36	$71
$895	$910	$0	$38	$12	$55	$38	$73
$910	$925	$0	$39	$13	$57	$39	$75
$925	$940	$0	$41	$15	$59	$41	$76
$940	$955	$0	$43	$16	$61	$43	$78
$955	$970	$0	$44	$18	$63	$44	$80
$970	$985	$0	$46	$19	$64	$46	$82
$985	$1,000	$0	$48	$21	$66	$48	$84
$1,000	$1,015	$0	$50	$22	$68	$50	$85
$1,015	$1,030	$0	$52	$24	$70	$52	$87
$1,030	$1,045	$0	$53	$25	$72	$53	$89
$1,045	$1,060	$1	$55	$27	$73	$55	$91
$1,060	$1,075	$2	$57	$28	$75	$57	$93
$1,075	$1,090	$4	$59	$30	$77	$59	$94
$1,090	$1,105	$5	$61	$31	$79	$61	$96
$1,105	$1,120	$7	$62	$33	$81	$62	$99

2021 Wage Bracket Method Tables for Manual Payroll Systems with Forms W-4 From 2020 or Later
SEMIMONTHLY Payroll Period

If the **Adjusted Wage Amount** (line 1h) is		Married Filing Jointly		Head of Household		Single or Married Filing Separately	
At least	But less than	Standard withholding	Form W-4, Step 2, Checkbox withholding	Standard withholding	Form W-4, Step 2, Checkbox withholding	Standard withholding	Form W-4, Step 2, Checkbox withholding
		The Tentative Withholding Amount is:					
$1,120	$1,140	$8	$65	$35	$83	$65	$103
$1,140	$1,160	$10	$67	$37	$85	$67	$107
$1,160	$1,180	$12	$69	$39	$87	$69	$111
$1,180	$1,200	$14	$72	$41	$90	$72	$116
$1,200	$1,220	$16	$74	$43	$92	$74	$120
$1,220	$1,240	$18	$77	$45	$95	$77	$125
$1,240	$1,260	$20	$79	$47	$97	$79	$129
$1,260	$1,280	$22	$81	$49	$99	$81	$133
$1,280	$1,300	$24	$84	$51	$102	$84	$138
$1,300	$1,320	$26	$86	$53	$104	$86	$142
$1,320	$1,340	$28	$89	$55	$107	$89	$147
$1,340	$1,360	$30	$91	$57	$109	$91	$151
$1,360	$1,380	$32	$93	$59	$111	$93	$155
$1,380	$1,400	$34	$96	$61	$114	$96	$160
$1,400	$1,420	$36	$98	$63	$116	$98	$164
$1,420	$1,440	$38	$101	$66	$119	$101	$169
$1,440	$1,460	$40	$103	$68	$121	$103	$173
$1,460	$1,480	$42	$105	$71	$123	$105	$177
$1,480	$1,500	$44	$108	$73	$126	$108	$182
$1,500	$1,520	$46	$110	$75	$128	$110	$186
$1,520	$1,540	$48	$113	$78	$132	$113	$191
$1,540	$1,560	$50	$115	$80	$136	$115	$195
$1,560	$1,580	$52	$117	$83	$140	$117	$199
$1,580	$1,600	$54	$120	$85	$145	$120	$204
$1,600	$1,620	$56	$122	$87	$149	$122	$208
$1,620	$1,640	$58	$125	$90	$154	$125	$213
$1,640	$1,660	$60	$127	$92	$158	$127	$217
$1,660	$1,680	$62	$129	$95	$162	$129	$221
$1,680	$1,700	$64	$132	$97	$167	$132	$226
$1,700	$1,720	$66	$134	$99	$171	$134	$230
$1,720	$1,740	$68	$137	$102	$176	$137	$235
$1,740	$1,760	$70	$139	$104	$180	$139	$239
$1,760	$1,780	$72	$141	$107	$184	$141	$243
$1,780	$1,800	$74	$144	$109	$189	$144	$248
$1,800	$1,820	$76	$146	$111	$193	$146	$252
$1,820	$1,840	$78	$149	$114	$198	$149	$257
$1,840	$1,860	$80	$151	$116	$202	$151	$261
$1,860	$1,880	$82	$153	$119	$206	$153	$265
$1,880	$1,900	$85	$156	$121	$211	$156	$270
$1,900	$1,920	$87	$158	$123	$215	$158	$274
$1,920	$1,940	$90	$161	$126	$220	$161	$279
$1,940	$1,960	$92	$163	$128	$224	$163	$283
$1,960	$1,980	$94	$165	$131	$228	$165	$287
$1,980	$2,000	$97	$168	$133	$233	$168	$292
$2,000	$2,020	$99	$170	$135	$237	$170	$296
$2,020	$2,040	$102	$173	$138	$242	$173	$301
$2,040	$2,060	$104	$175	$140	$246	$175	$305
$2,060	$2,090	$107	$178	$143	$252	$178	$311
$2,090	$2,120	$111	$182	$147	$258	$182	$318
$2,120	$2,150	$114	$185	$150	$265	$185	$325
$2,150	$2,180	$118	$189	$154	$271	$189	$332
$2,180	$2,210	$121	$192	$158	$278	$192	$339
$2,210	$2,240	$125	$197	$161	$285	$197	$347
$2,240	$2,270	$129	$204	$165	$292	$204	$354
$2,270	$2,300	$132	$211	$168	$300	$211	$361
$2,300	$2,330	$136	$217	$172	$307	$217	$368
$2,330	$2,360	$139	$224	$176	$314	$224	$375
$2,360	$2,390	$143	$230	$179	$321	$230	$383
$2,390	$2,420	$147	$237	$183	$328	$237	$390
$2,420	$2,450	$150	$244	$186	$336	$244	$397
$2,450	$2,480	$154	$250	$190	$343	$250	$404
$2,480	$2,510	$157	$257	$194	$350	$257	$411
$2,510	$2,540	$161	$263	$197	$357	$263	$419
$2,540	$2,570	$165	$270	$201	$364	$270	$426
$2,570	$2,600	$168	$277	$204	$372	$277	$433

2021 Wage Bracket Method Tables for Manual Payroll Systems with Forms W-4 From 2020 or Later
SEMIMONTHLY Payroll Period

If the Adjusted Wage Amount (line 1h) is		Married Filing Jointly		Head of Household		Single or Married Filing Separately	
At least	But less than	Standard withholding	Form W-4, Step 2, Checkbox withholding	Standard withholding	Form W-4, Step 2, Checkbox withholding	Standard withholding	Form W-4, Step 2, Checkbox withholding
		The Tentative Withholding Amount is:					
$2,600	$2,630	$172	$283	$208	$379	$283	$440
$2,630	$2,660	$175	$290	$212	$386	$290	$447
$2,660	$2,690	$179	$296	$215	$393	$296	$455
$2,690	$2,720	$183	$303	$219	$400	$303	$462
$2,720	$2,750	$186	$310	$222	$408	$310	$469
$2,750	$2,780	$190	$316	$226	$415	$316	$476
$2,780	$2,810	$193	$323	$230	$422	$323	$483
$2,810	$2,840	$197	$329	$233	$429	$329	$491
$2,840	$2,870	$201	$336	$237	$436	$336	$498
$2,870	$2,900	$204	$343	$240	$444	$343	$505
$2,900	$2,930	$208	$349	$244	$451	$349	$512
$2,930	$2,960	$211	$356	$248	$458	$356	$519
$2,960	$2,990	$215	$362	$251	$465	$362	$527
$2,990	$3,020	$219	$369	$255	$472	$369	$534
$3,020	$3,050	$222	$376	$258	$480	$376	$541
$3,050	$3,080	$226	$382	$264	$487	$382	$548
$3,080	$3,110	$229	$389	$271	$494	$389	$555
$3,110	$3,140	$233	$395	$278	$501	$395	$563
$3,140	$3,170	$237	$402	$284	$508	$402	$570
$3,170	$3,200	$240	$409	$291	$516	$409	$577
$3,200	$3,230	$244	$415	$297	$523	$415	$584
$3,230	$3,260	$247	$422	$304	$530	$422	$591
$3,260	$3,290	$251	$428	$311	$537	$428	$599
$3,290	$3,320	$255	$435	$317	$544	$435	$606
$3,320	$3,350	$258	$442	$324	$552	$442	$613
$3,350	$3,380	$262	$448	$330	$559	$448	$620
$3,380	$3,410	$265	$455	$337	$566	$455	$627
$3,410	$3,440	$269	$461	$344	$573	$461	$635
$3,440	$3,470	$273	$468	$350	$580	$468	$642
$3,470	$3,500	$276	$475	$357	$588	$475	$649
$3,500	$3,530	$280	$481	$363	$595	$481	$656
$3,530	$3,560	$283	$488	$370	$602	$488	$663
$3,560	$3,590	$287	$494	$377	$609	$494	$671
$3,590	$3,620	$291	$501	$383	$616	$501	$678
$3,620	$3,650	$294	$508	$390	$624	$508	$685
$3,650	$3,680	$298	$514	$396	$631	$514	$692
$3,680	$3,710	$301	$521	$403	$638	$521	$699
$3,710	$3,740	$305	$527	$410	$645	$527	$709
$3,740	$3,770	$309	$534	$416	$652	$534	$718
$3,770	$3,800	$312	$541	$423	$660	$541	$728
$3,800	$3,830	$316	$547	$429	$667	$547	$738
$3,830	$3,860	$319	$554	$436	$675	$554	$747
$3,860	$3,890	$323	$560	$443	$685	$560	$757
$3,890	$3,920	$327	$567	$449	$695	$567	$766
$3,920	$3,950	$330	$574	$456	$704	$574	$776
$3,950	$3,980	$334	$580	$462	$714	$580	$786
$3,980	$4,010	$337	$587	$469	$723	$587	$795
$4,010	$4,040	$341	$593	$476	$733	$593	$805
$4,040	$4,070	$345	$600	$482	$743	$600	$814
$4,070	$4,100	$348	$607	$489	$752	$607	$824
$4,100	$4,130	$352	$613	$495	$762	$613	$834
$4,130	$4,160	$355	$620	$502	$771	$620	$843

2021 Wage Bracket Method Tables for Manual Payroll Systems with Forms W-4 From 2020 or Later
MONTHLY Payroll Period

If the Adjusted Wage Amount (line 1h) is		Married Filing Jointly		Head of Household		Single or Married Filing Separately	
At least	But less than	Standard withholding	Form W-4, Step 2, Checkbox withholding	Standard withholding	Form W-4, Step 2, Checkbox withholding	Standard withholding	Form W-4, Step 2, Checkbox withholding
		The Tentative Withholding Amount is:					
$0	$525	$0	$0	$0	$0	$0	$0
$525	$545	$0	$0	$0	$0	$0	$1
$545	$565	$0	$0	$0	$0	$0	$3
$565	$585	$0	$0	$0	$0	$0	$5
$585	$605	$0	$0	$0	$0	$0	$7
$605	$625	$0	$0	$0	$0	$0	$9
$625	$645	$0	$0	$0	$0	$0	$11
$645	$665	$0	$0	$0	$0	$0	$13
$665	$685	$0	$0	$0	$0	$0	$15
$685	$705	$0	$0	$0	$0	$0	$17
$705	$725	$0	$0	$0	$0	$0	$19
$725	$745	$0	$0	$0	$0	$0	$21
$745	$765	$0	$0	$0	$0	$0	$23
$765	$785	$0	$0	$0	$0	$0	$25
$785	$805	$0	$0	$0	$1	$0	$27
$805	$825	$0	$0	$0	$3	$0	$29
$825	$845	$0	$0	$0	$5	$0	$31
$845	$865	$0	$0	$0	$7	$0	$33
$865	$885	$0	$0	$0	$9	$0	$35
$885	$905	$0	$0	$0	$11	$0	$37
$905	$925	$0	$0	$0	$13	$0	$39
$925	$945	$0	$0	$0	$15	$0	$41
$945	$975	$0	$0	$0	$18	$0	$44
$975	$1,005	$0	$0	$0	$21	$0	$48
$1,005	$1,035	$0	$0	$0	$24	$0	$51
$1,035	$1,065	$0	$0	$0	$27	$0	$55
$1,065	$1,095	$0	$3	$0	$30	$3	$59
$1,095	$1,125	$0	$6	$0	$33	$6	$62
$1,125	$1,155	$0	$9	$0	$36	$9	$66
$1,155	$1,185	$0	$12	$0	$39	$12	$69
$1,185	$1,215	$0	$15	$0	$42	$15	$73
$1,215	$1,245	$0	$18	$0	$45	$18	$77
$1,245	$1,275	$0	$21	$0	$48	$21	$80
$1,275	$1,305	$0	$24	$0	$51	$24	$84
$1,305	$1,335	$0	$27	$0	$54	$27	$87
$1,335	$1,365	$0	$30	$0	$57	$30	$91
$1,365	$1,395	$0	$33	$0	$60	$33	$95
$1,395	$1,425	$0	$36	$0	$63	$36	$98
$1,425	$1,455	$0	$39	$0	$67	$39	$102
$1,455	$1,485	$0	$42	$0	$71	$42	$105
$1,485	$1,515	$0	$45	$0	$74	$45	$109
$1,515	$1,545	$0	$48	$0	$78	$48	$113
$1,545	$1,575	$0	$51	$0	$81	$51	$116
$1,575	$1,605	$0	$54	$2	$85	$54	$120
$1,605	$1,635	$0	$57	$5	$89	$57	$123
$1,635	$1,665	$0	$60	$8	$92	$60	$127
$1,665	$1,695	$0	$63	$11	$96	$63	$131
$1,695	$1,725	$0	$66	$14	$99	$66	$134
$1,725	$1,755	$0	$69	$17	$103	$69	$138
$1,755	$1,785	$0	$72	$20	$107	$72	$141
$1,785	$1,815	$0	$75	$23	$110	$75	$145
$1,815	$1,845	$0	$78	$26	$114	$78	$149
$1,845	$1,875	$0	$81	$29	$117	$81	$152
$1,875	$1,905	$0	$85	$32	$121	$85	$156
$1,905	$1,935	$0	$88	$35	$125	$88	$159
$1,935	$1,965	$0	$92	$38	$128	$92	$163
$1,965	$1,995	$0	$96	$41	$132	$96	$167
$1,995	$2,025	$0	$99	$44	$135	$99	$170
$2,025	$2,055	$0	$103	$47	$139	$103	$174
$2,055	$2,085	$0	$106	$50	$143	$106	$177
$2,085	$2,115	$1	$110	$53	$146	$110	$181
$2,115	$2,145	$4	$114	$56	$150	$114	$185
$2,145	$2,175	$7	$117	$59	$153	$117	$188
$2,175	$2,205	$10	$121	$62	$157	$121	$192
$2,205	$2,235	$13	$124	$65	$161	$124	$196

2021 Wage Bracket Method Tables for Manual Payroll Systems with Forms W-4 From 2020 or Later
MONTHLY Payroll Period

If the Adjusted Wage Amount (line 1h) is		Married Filing Jointly		Head of Household		Single or Married Filing Separately	
At least	But less than	Standard withholding	Form W-4, Step 2, Checkbox withholding	Standard withholding	Form W-4, Step 2, Checkbox withholding	Standard withholding	Form W-4, Step 2, Checkbox withholding
		The Tentative Withholding Amount is:					
$2,235	$2,275	$16	$129	$69	$165	$129	$204
$2,275	$2,315	$20	$133	$73	$170	$133	$213
$2,315	$2,355	$24	$138	$77	$174	$138	$222
$2,355	$2,395	$28	$143	$81	$179	$143	$230
$2,395	$2,435	$32	$148	$85	$184	$148	$239
$2,435	$2,475	$36	$153	$89	$189	$153	$248
$2,475	$2,515	$40	$157	$93	$194	$157	$257
$2,515	$2,555	$44	$162	$97	$198	$162	$266
$2,555	$2,595	$48	$167	$101	$203	$167	$274
$2,595	$2,635	$52	$172	$105	$208	$172	$283
$2,635	$2,675	$56	$177	$109	$213	$177	$292
$2,675	$2,715	$60	$181	$113	$218	$181	$301
$2,715	$2,755	$64	$186	$117	$222	$186	$310
$2,755	$2,795	$68	$191	$121	$227	$191	$318
$2,795	$2,835	$72	$196	$126	$232	$196	$327
$2,835	$2,875	$76	$201	$131	$237	$201	$336
$2,875	$2,915	$80	$205	$136	$242	$205	$345
$2,915	$2,955	$84	$210	$141	$246	$210	$354
$2,955	$2,995	$88	$215	$145	$251	$215	$362
$2,995	$3,035	$92	$220	$150	$256	$220	$371
$3,035	$3,075	$96	$225	$155	$262	$225	$380
$3,075	$3,115	$100	$229	$160	$271	$229	$389
$3,115	$3,155	$104	$234	$165	$280	$234	$398
$3,155	$3,195	$108	$239	$169	$289	$239	$406
$3,195	$3,235	$112	$244	$174	$297	$244	$415
$3,235	$3,275	$116	$249	$179	$306	$249	$424
$3,275	$3,315	$120	$253	$184	$315	$253	$433
$3,315	$3,355	$124	$258	$189	$324	$258	$442
$3,355	$3,395	$128	$263	$193	$333	$263	$450
$3,395	$3,435	$132	$268	$198	$341	$268	$459
$3,435	$3,475	$136	$273	$203	$350	$273	$468
$3,475	$3,515	$140	$277	$208	$359	$277	$477
$3,515	$3,555	$144	$282	$213	$368	$282	$486
$3,555	$3,595	$148	$287	$217	$377	$287	$494
$3,595	$3,635	$152	$292	$222	$385	$292	$503
$3,635	$3,675	$156	$297	$227	$394	$297	$512
$3,675	$3,715	$160	$301	$232	$403	$301	$521
$3,715	$3,755	$164	$306	$237	$412	$306	$530
$3,755	$3,795	$169	$311	$241	$421	$311	$538
$3,795	$3,835	$174	$316	$246	$429	$316	$547
$3,835	$3,875	$178	$321	$251	$438	$321	$556
$3,875	$3,915	$183	$325	$256	$447	$325	$565
$3,915	$3,955	$188	$330	$261	$456	$330	$574
$3,955	$3,995	$193	$335	$265	$465	$335	$582
$3,995	$4,035	$198	$340	$270	$473	$340	$591
$4,035	$4,075	$202	$345	$275	$482	$345	$600
$4,075	$4,115	$207	$349	$280	$491	$349	$609
$4,115	$4,155	$212	$354	$285	$500	$354	$618
$4,155	$4,215	$218	$360	$291	$511	$360	$630
$4,215	$4,275	$225	$367	$298	$524	$367	$644
$4,275	$4,335	$232	$375	$305	$537	$375	$659
$4,335	$4,395	$240	$382	$312	$550	$382	$673
$4,395	$4,455	$247	$389	$319	$564	$389	$687
$4,455	$4,515	$254	$402	$327	$579	$402	$702
$4,515	$4,575	$261	$416	$334	$593	$416	$716
$4,575	$4,635	$268	$429	$341	$608	$429	$731
$4,635	$4,695	$276	$442	$348	$622	$442	$745
$4,695	$4,755	$283	$455	$355	$636	$455	$759
$4,755	$4,815	$290	$468	$363	$651	$468	$774
$4,815	$4,875	$297	$482	$370	$665	$482	$788
$4,875	$4,935	$304	$495	$377	$680	$495	$803
$4,935	$4,995	$312	$508	$384	$694	$508	$817
$4,995	$5,055	$319	$521	$391	$708	$521	$831
$5,055	$5,115	$326	$534	$399	$723	$534	$846
$5,115	$5,175	$333	$548	$406	$737	$548	$860

2021 Wage Bracket Method Tables for Manual Payroll Systems with Forms W-4 From 2020 or Later
MONTHLY Payroll Period

If the Adjusted Wage Amount (line 1h) is		Married Filing Jointly		Head of Household		Single or Married Filing Separately	
At least	But less than	Standard withholding	Form W-4, Step 2, Checkbox withholding	Standard withholding	Form W-4, Step 2, Checkbox withholding	Standard withholding	Form W-4, Step 2, Checkbox withholding
		The Tentative Withholding Amount is:					
$5,175	$5,235	$340	$561	$413	$752	$561	$875
$5,235	$5,295	$348	$574	$420	$766	$574	$889
$5,295	$5,355	$355	$587	$427	$780	$587	$903
$5,355	$5,415	$362	$600	$435	$795	$600	$918
$5,415	$5,475	$369	$614	$442	$809	$614	$932
$5,475	$5,535	$376	$627	$449	$824	$627	$947
$5,535	$5,595	$384	$640	$456	$838	$640	$961
$5,595	$5,655	$391	$653	$463	$852	$653	$975
$5,655	$5,715	$398	$666	$471	$867	$666	$990
$5,715	$5,775	$405	$680	$478	$881	$680	$1,004
$5,775	$5,835	$412	$693	$485	$896	$693	$1,019
$5,835	$5,895	$420	$706	$492	$910	$706	$1,033
$5,895	$5,955	$427	$719	$499	$924	$719	$1,047
$5,955	$6,015	$434	$732	$507	$939	$732	$1,062
$6,015	$6,075	$441	$746	$514	$953	$746	$1,076
$6,075	$6,135	$448	$759	$523	$968	$759	$1,091
$6,135	$6,195	$456	$772	$536	$982	$772	$1,105
$6,195	$6,255	$463	$785	$550	$996	$785	$1,119
$6,255	$6,315	$470	$798	$563	$1,011	$798	$1,134
$6,315	$6,375	$477	$812	$576	$1,025	$812	$1,148
$6,375	$6,435	$484	$825	$589	$1,040	$825	$1,163
$6,435	$6,495	$492	$838	$602	$1,054	$838	$1,177
$6,495	$6,555	$499	$851	$616	$1,068	$851	$1,191
$6,555	$6,615	$506	$864	$629	$1,083	$864	$1,206
$6,615	$6,675	$513	$878	$642	$1,097	$878	$1,220
$6,675	$6,735	$520	$891	$655	$1,112	$891	$1,235
$6,735	$6,795	$528	$904	$668	$1,126	$904	$1,249
$6,795	$6,855	$535	$917	$682	$1,140	$917	$1,263
$6,855	$6,915	$542	$930	$695	$1,155	$930	$1,278
$6,915	$6,975	$549	$944	$708	$1,169	$944	$1,292
$6,975	$7,035	$556	$957	$721	$1,184	$957	$1,307
$7,035	$7,095	$564	$970	$734	$1,198	$970	$1,321
$7,095	$7,155	$571	$983	$748	$1,212	$983	$1,335
$7,155	$7,215	$578	$996	$761	$1,227	$996	$1,350
$7,215	$7,275	$585	$1,010	$774	$1,241	$1,010	$1,364
$7,275	$7,335	$592	$1,023	$787	$1,256	$1,023	$1,379
$7,335	$7,395	$600	$1,036	$800	$1,270	$1,036	$1,393
$7,395	$7,455	$607	$1,049	$814	$1,284	$1,049	$1,410
$7,455	$7,515	$614	$1,062	$827	$1,299	$1,062	$1,429
$7,515	$7,575	$621	$1,076	$840	$1,313	$1,076	$1,448
$7,575	$7,635	$628	$1,089	$853	$1,328	$1,089	$1,467
$7,635	$7,695	$636	$1,102	$866	$1,343	$1,102	$1,487
$7,695	$7,755	$643	$1,115	$880	$1,362	$1,115	$1,506
$7,755	$7,815	$650	$1,128	$893	$1,381	$1,128	$1,525
$7,815	$7,875	$657	$1,142	$906	$1,400	$1,142	$1,544
$7,875	$7,935	$664	$1,155	$919	$1,420	$1,155	$1,563
$7,935	$7,995	$672	$1,168	$932	$1,439	$1,168	$1,583
$7,995	$8,055	$679	$1,181	$946	$1,458	$1,181	$1,602
$8,055	$8,115	$686	$1,194	$959	$1,477	$1,194	$1,621
$8,115	$8,175	$693	$1,208	$972	$1,496	$1,208	$1,640
$8,175	$8,235	$700	$1,221	$985	$1,516	$1,221	$1,659
$8,235	$8,295	$708	$1,234	$998	$1,535	$1,234	$1,679
$8,295	$8,355	$715	$1,249	$1,012	$1,554	$1,249	$1,698

2021 Wage Bracket Method Tables for Manual Payroll Systems with Forms W-4 From 2020 or Later
DAILY Payroll Period

If the **Adjusted Wage Amount** (line 1h) is		Married Filing Jointly		Head of Household		Single or Married Filing Separately	
		Standard withholding	Form W-4, Step 2, Checkbox withholding	Standard withholding	Form W-4, Step 2, Checkbox withholding	Standard withholding	Form W-4, Step 2, Checkbox withholding
At least	But less than			The Tentative Withholding Amount is:			
$0	$25	$0.00	$0.00	$0.00	$0.00	$0.00	$0.00
$25	$30	$0.00	$0.00	$0.00	$0.00	$0.00	$0.30
$30	$35	$0.00	$0.00	$0.00	$0.00	$0.00	$0.80
$35	$40	$0.00	$0.00	$0.00	$0.10	$0.00	$1.30
$40	$45	$0.00	$0.00	$0.00	$0.60	$0.00	$1.80
$45	$50	$0.00	$0.00	$0.00	$1.10	$0.00	$2.40
$50	$55	$0.00	$0.40	$0.00	$1.60	$0.40	$3.00
$55	$60	$0.00	$0.90	$0.00	$2.10	$0.90	$3.60
$60	$65	$0.00	$1.40	$0.00	$2.60	$1.40	$4.20
$65	$70	$0.00	$1.90	$0.00	$3.20	$1.90	$4.80
$70	$75	$0.00	$2.40	$0.00	$3.80	$2.40	$5.40
$75	$80	$0.00	$2.90	$0.50	$4.40	$2.90	$6.00
$80	$85	$0.00	$3.40	$1.00	$5.00	$3.40	$6.60
$85	$90	$0.00	$3.90	$1.50	$5.60	$3.90	$7.20
$90	$95	$0.00	$4.50	$2.00	$6.20	$4.50	$7.80
$95	$100	$0.10	$5.10	$2.50	$6.80	$5.10	$8.40
$100	$105	$0.60	$5.70	$3.00	$7.40	$5.70	$9.10
$105	$110	$1.10	$6.30	$3.50	$8.00	$6.30	$10.20
$110	$115	$1.60	$6.90	$4.00	$8.60	$6.90	$11.30
$115	$120	$2.10	$7.50	$4.50	$9.20	$7.50	$12.40
$120	$125	$2.60	$8.10	$5.00	$9.80	$8.10	$13.50
$125	$130	$3.10	$8.70	$5.50	$10.40	$8.70	$14.60
$130	$135	$3.60	$9.30	$6.10	$11.00	$9.30	$15.70
$135	$140	$4.10	$9.90	$6.70	$11.60	$9.90	$16.80
$140	$145	$4.60	$10.50	$7.30	$12.40	$10.50	$17.90
$145	$150	$5.10	$11.10	$7.90	$13.50	$11.10	$19.00
$150	$155	$5.60	$11.70	$8.50	$14.60	$11.70	$20.10
$155	$160	$6.10	$12.30	$9.10	$15.70	$12.30	$21.20
$160	$165	$6.60	$12.90	$9.70	$16.80	$12.90	$22.30
$165	$170	$7.10	$13.50	$10.30	$17.90	$13.50	$23.40
$170	$175	$7.60	$14.10	$10.90	$19.00	$14.10	$24.50
$175	$180	$8.20	$14.70	$11.50	$20.10	$14.70	$25.60
$180	$185	$8.80	$15.30	$12.10	$21.20	$15.30	$26.70
$185	$190	$9.40	$15.90	$12.70	$22.30	$15.90	$27.80
$190	$195	$10.00	$16.50	$13.30	$23.40	$16.50	$28.90
$195	$200	$10.60	$17.10	$13.90	$24.50	$17.10	$30.10
$200	$205	$11.20	$17.70	$14.50	$25.60	$17.70	$31.30
$205	$210	$11.80	$18.70	$15.10	$26.80	$18.70	$32.50
$210	$215	$12.40	$19.80	$15.70	$28.00	$19.80	$33.70
$215	$220	$13.00	$20.90	$16.30	$29.20	$20.90	$34.90
$220	$225	$13.60	$22.00	$16.90	$30.40	$22.00	$36.10
$225	$230	$14.20	$23.10	$17.50	$31.60	$23.10	$37.30
$230	$235	$14.80	$24.20	$18.10	$32.80	$24.20	$38.50
$235	$240	$15.40	$25.30	$18.70	$34.00	$25.30	$39.70
$240	$245	$16.00	$26.40	$19.30	$35.20	$26.40	$40.90
$245	$250	$16.60	$27.50	$19.90	$36.40	$27.50	$42.10
$250	$255	$17.20	$28.60	$20.50	$37.60	$28.60	$43.30
$255	$260	$17.80	$29.70	$21.10	$38.80	$29.70	$44.50
$260	$265	$18.40	$30.80	$21.70	$40.00	$30.80	$45.70
$265	$270	$19.00	$31.90	$22.30	$41.20	$31.90	$46.90
$270	$275	$19.60	$33.00	$22.90	$42.40	$33.00	$48.10
$275	$280	$20.20	$34.10	$23.50	$43.60	$34.10	$49.30
$280	$285	$20.80	$35.20	$24.30	$44.80	$35.20	$50.50
$285	$290	$21.40	$36.30	$25.40	$46.00	$36.30	$51.70
$290	$295	$22.00	$37.40	$26.50	$47.20	$37.40	$52.90
$295	$300	$22.60	$38.50	$27.60	$48.40	$38.50	$54.10
$300	$305	$23.20	$39.60	$28.70	$49.60	$39.60	$55.30
$305	$310	$23.80	$40.70	$29.80	$50.80	$40.70	$56.50
$310	$315	$24.40	$41.80	$30.90	$52.00	$41.80	$57.70
$315	$320	$25.00	$42.90	$32.00	$53.20	$42.90	$58.90
$320	$325	$25.60	$44.00	$33.10	$54.40	$44.00	$60.10
$325	$330	$26.20	$45.10	$34.20	$55.60	$45.10	$61.30
$330	$335	$26.80	$46.20	$35.30	$56.80	$46.20	$62.50
$335	$340	$27.40	$47.30	$36.40	$58.00	$47.30	$63.70
$340	$345	$28.00	$48.40	$37.50	$59.20	$48.40	$65.00

2021 Wage Bracket Method Tables for Manual Payroll Systems with Forms W-4 From 2020 or Later
DAILY Payroll Period

If the **Adjusted Wage Amount** (line 1h) is		Married Filing Jointly		Head of Household		Single or Married Filing Separately	
At least	But less than	Standard withholding	Form W-4, Step 2, Checkbox withholding	Standard withholding	Form W-4, Step 2, Checkbox withholding	Standard withholding	Form W-4, Step 2, Checkbox withholding
		The Tentative Withholding Amount is:					
$345	$350	$28.60	$49.50	$38.60	$60.40	$49.50	$66.60
$350	$355	$29.20	$50.60	$39.70	$61.60	$50.60	$68.20
$355	$360	$29.80	$51.70	$40.80	$63.20	$51.70	$69.80
$360	$365	$30.40	$52.80	$41.90	$64.80	$52.80	$71.40
$365	$370	$31.00	$53.90	$43.00	$66.40	$53.90	$73.00
$370	$375	$31.60	$55.00	$44.10	$68.00	$55.00	$74.60
$375	$380	$32.20	$56.10	$45.20	$69.60	$56.10	$76.20
$380	$385	$32.80	$57.20	$46.30	$71.20	$57.20	$77.80
$385	$390	$33.40	$58.40	$47.40	$72.80	$58.40	$79.40

Source: Internal Revenue Service

3. Wage Bracket Method Tables for Manual Payroll Systems With Forms W-4 From 2019 or Earlier

If you compute payroll manually and your employee **has not** submitted a Form W-4 for 2020 or later, use the worksheet below and the Wage Bracket Method tables that follow to figure federal income tax withholding.

The Wage Bracket Method tables cover only up to approximately $100,000 in annual wages and up to 10 allowances. If you can't use the Wage Bracket Method tables because taxable wages exceed the amount from the last bracket of the table (based on marital status and pay period) or the employee claimed more than 10 allowances, use the Percentage Method tables in section 5.

Worksheet 3. Employer's Withholding Worksheet for Wage Bracket Method Tables for Manual Payroll Systems With Forms W-4 From 2019 or Earlier

Keep for Your Records

Step 1.	**Figure the tentative withholding amount**	
	1a Enter the employee's total taxable wages this payroll period	1a $ _____
	1b Use the amount on line 1a to look up the tentative amount to withhold in the appropriate Wage Bracket Table in this section for your pay frequency, given the employee's marital status (line 3 of Form W-4) and number of allowances claimed. This is the **Tentative Withholding Amount**	1b $ _____
Step 2.	**Figure the final amount to withhold**	
	2a Enter the additional amount to withhold from line 6 of the employee's Form W-4	2a $ _____
	2b Add lines 1b and 2a. **This is the amount to withhold from the employee's wages this pay period**	2b $ _____

2021 Wage Bracket Method Tables for Manual Payroll Systems With Forms W-4 From 2019 or Earlier

WEEKLY Payroll Period

If the Wage Amount (line 1a) is		MARRIED Persons										
		And the number of allowances is:										
At least	But less than	0	1	2	3	4	5	6	7	8	9	10
		The Tentative Withholding Amount is:										
$0	$235	$0	$0	$0	$0	$0	$0	$0	$0	$0	$0	$0
$235	$245	$1	$0	$0	$0	$0	$0	$0	$0	$0	$0	$0
$245	$255	$2	$0	$0	$0	$0	$0	$0	$0	$0	$0	$0
$255	$265	$3	$0	$0	$0	$0	$0	$0	$0	$0	$0	$0
$265	$275	$4	$0	$0	$0	$0	$0	$0	$0	$0	$0	$0
$275	$285	$5	$0	$0	$0	$0	$0	$0	$0	$0	$0	$0
$285	$295	$6	$0	$0	$0	$0	$0	$0	$0	$0	$0	$0
$295	$305	$7	$0	$0	$0	$0	$0	$0	$0	$0	$0	$0
$305	$315	$8	$0	$0	$0	$0	$0	$0	$0	$0	$0	$0
$315	$325	$9	$0	$0	$0	$0	$0	$0	$0	$0	$0	$0
$325	$335	$10	$1	$0	$0	$0	$0	$0	$0	$0	$0	$0
$335	$345	$11	$2	$0	$0	$0	$0	$0	$0	$0	$0	$0
$345	$355	$12	$3	$0	$0	$0	$0	$0	$0	$0	$0	$0
$355	$365	$13	$4	$0	$0	$0	$0	$0	$0	$0	$0	$0
$365	$375	$14	$5	$0	$0	$0	$0	$0	$0	$0	$0	$0
$375	$385	$15	$6	$0	$0	$0	$0	$0	$0	$0	$0	$0
$385	$395	$16	$7	$0	$0	$0	$0	$0	$0	$0	$0	$0
$395	$405	$17	$8	$0	$0	$0	$0	$0	$0	$0	$0	$0
$405	$415	$18	$9	$1	$0	$0	$0	$0	$0	$0	$0	$0
$415	$425	$19	$10	$2	$0	$0	$0	$0	$0	$0	$0	$0
$425	$435	$20	$11	$3	$0	$0	$0	$0	$0	$0	$0	$0
$435	$445	$21	$12	$4	$0	$0	$0	$0	$0	$0	$0	$0
$445	$455	$22	$13	$5	$0	$0	$0	$0	$0	$0	$0	$0
$455	$465	$23	$14	$6	$0	$0	$0	$0	$0	$0	$0	$0
$465	$475	$24	$15	$7	$0	$0	$0	$0	$0	$0	$0	$0
$475	$485	$25	$16	$8	$0	$0	$0	$0	$0	$0	$0	$0
$485	$495	$26	$17	$9	$1	$0	$0	$0	$0	$0	$0	$0
$495	$505	$27	$18	$10	$2	$0	$0	$0	$0	$0	$0	$0
$505	$515	$28	$19	$11	$3	$0	$0	$0	$0	$0	$0	$0
$515	$525	$29	$20	$12	$4	$0	$0	$0	$0	$0	$0	$0
$525	$535	$30	$21	$13	$5	$0	$0	$0	$0	$0	$0	$0
$535	$545	$31	$22	$14	$6	$0	$0	$0	$0	$0	$0	$0
$545	$555	$32	$23	$15	$7	$0	$0	$0	$0	$0	$0	$0
$555	$565	$33	$24	$16	$8	$0	$0	$0	$0	$0	$0	$0
$565	$575	$34	$25	$17	$9	$0	$0	$0	$0	$0	$0	$0
$575	$585	$35	$26	$18	$10	$1	$0	$0	$0	$0	$0	$0
$585	$595	$36	$27	$19	$11	$2	$0	$0	$0	$0	$0	$0
$595	$605	$37	$28	$20	$12	$3	$0	$0	$0	$0	$0	$0
$605	$615	$38	$29	$21	$13	$4	$0	$0	$0	$0	$0	$0
$615	$625	$39	$30	$22	$14	$5	$0	$0	$0	$0	$0	$0
$625	$640	$40	$32	$23	$15	$7	$0	$0	$0	$0	$0	$0
$640	$655	$42	$33	$25	$16	$8	$0	$0	$0	$0	$0	$0
$655	$670	$44	$35	$26	$18	$10	$1	$0	$0	$0	$0	$0
$670	$685	$45	$36	$28	$19	$11	$3	$0	$0	$0	$0	$0
$685	$700	$47	$38	$29	$21	$13	$4	$0	$0	$0	$0	$0
$700	$715	$49	$39	$31	$22	$14	$6	$0	$0	$0	$0	$0
$715	$730	$51	$41	$32	$24	$16	$7	$0	$0	$0	$0	$0
$730	$745	$53	$43	$34	$25	$17	$9	$1	$0	$0	$0	$0
$745	$760	$54	$45	$35	$27	$19	$10	$2	$0	$0	$0	$0
$760	$775	$56	$46	$37	$28	$20	$12	$4	$0	$0	$0	$0
$775	$790	$58	$48	$38	$30	$22	$13	$5	$0	$0	$0	$0

2021 Wage Bracket Method Tables for Manual Payroll Systems With Forms W-4 From 2019 or Earlier

WEEKLY Payroll Period

If the Wage Amount (line 1a) is		MARRIED Persons										
		And the number of allowances is:										
At least	But less than	0	1	2	3	4	5	6	7	8	9	10
		The Tentative Withholding Amount is:										
$790	$805	$60	$50	$40	$31	$23	$15	$7	$0	$0	$0	$0
$805	$820	$62	$52	$42	$33	$25	$16	$8	$0	$0	$0	$0
$820	$835	$63	$54	$44	$34	$26	$18	$10	$1	$0	$0	$0
$835	$850	$65	$55	$45	$36	$28	$19	$11	$3	$0	$0	$0
$850	$865	$67	$57	$47	$37	$29	$21	$13	$4	$0	$0	$0
$865	$880	$69	$59	$49	$39	$31	$22	$14	$6	$0	$0	$0
$880	$895	$71	$61	$51	$41	$32	$24	$16	$7	$0	$0	$0
$895	$910	$72	$63	$53	$43	$34	$25	$17	$9	$1	$0	$0
$910	$925	$74	$64	$54	$45	$35	$27	$19	$10	$2	$0	$0
$925	$940	$76	$66	$56	$46	$37	$28	$20	$12	$4	$0	$0
$940	$955	$78	$68	$58	$48	$38	$30	$22	$13	$5	$0	$0
$955	$970	$80	$70	$60	$50	$40	$31	$23	$15	$7	$0	$0
$970	$985	$81	$72	$62	$52	$42	$33	$25	$16	$8	$0	$0
$985	$1,000	$83	$73	$63	$54	$44	$34	$26	$18	$10	$1	$0
$1,000	$1,015	$85	$75	$65	$55	$45	$36	$28	$19	$11	$3	$0
$1,015	$1,030	$87	$77	$67	$57	$47	$37	$29	$21	$13	$4	$0
$1,030	$1,045	$89	$79	$69	$59	$49	$39	$31	$22	$14	$6	$0
$1,045	$1,060	$90	$81	$71	$61	$51	$41	$32	$24	$16	$7	$0
$1,060	$1,075	$92	$82	$72	$63	$53	$43	$34	$25	$17	$9	$1
$1,075	$1,090	$94	$84	$74	$64	$54	$44	$35	$27	$19	$10	$2
$1,090	$1,105	$96	$86	$76	$66	$56	$46	$37	$28	$20	$12	$4
$1,105	$1,120	$98	$88	$78	$68	$58	$48	$38	$30	$22	$13	$5
$1,120	$1,135	$99	$90	$80	$70	$60	$50	$40	$31	$23	$15	$7
$1,135	$1,150	$101	$91	$81	$72	$62	$52	$42	$33	$25	$16	$8
$1,150	$1,165	$103	$93	$83	$73	$63	$53	$44	$34	$26	$18	$10
$1,165	$1,180	$105	$95	$85	$75	$65	$55	$45	$36	$28	$19	$11
$1,180	$1,195	$107	$97	$87	$77	$67	$57	$47	$37	$29	$21	$13
$1,195	$1,210	$108	$99	$89	$79	$69	$59	$49	$39	$31	$22	$14
$1,210	$1,225	$110	$100	$90	$81	$71	$61	$51	$41	$32	$24	$16
$1,225	$1,240	$112	$102	$92	$82	$72	$62	$53	$43	$34	$25	$17
$1,240	$1,255	$114	$104	$94	$84	$74	$64	$54	$44	$35	$27	$19
$1,255	$1,270	$116	$106	$96	$86	$76	$66	$56	$46	$37	$28	$20
$1,270	$1,285	$117	$108	$98	$88	$78	$68	$58	$48	$38	$30	$22
$1,285	$1,300	$119	$109	$99	$90	$80	$70	$60	$50	$40	$31	$23
$1,300	$1,315	$121	$111	$101	$91	$81	$71	$62	$52	$42	$33	$25
$1,315	$1,330	$123	$113	$103	$93	$83	$73	$63	$53	$44	$34	$26
$1,330	$1,345	$125	$115	$105	$95	$85	$75	$65	$55	$45	$36	$28
$1,345	$1,360	$126	$117	$107	$97	$87	$77	$67	$57	$47	$37	$29
$1,360	$1,375	$128	$118	$108	$99	$89	$79	$69	$59	$49	$39	$31
$1,375	$1,390	$130	$120	$110	$100	$90	$80	$71	$61	$51	$41	$32
$1,390	$1,405	$132	$122	$112	$102	$92	$82	$72	$62	$53	$43	$34
$1,405	$1,420	$134	$124	$114	$104	$94	$84	$74	$64	$54	$44	$35
$1,420	$1,435	$135	$126	$116	$106	$96	$86	$76	$66	$56	$46	$37
$1,435	$1,450	$137	$127	$117	$108	$98	$88	$78	$68	$58	$48	$38
$1,450	$1,465	$139	$129	$119	$109	$99	$89	$80	$70	$60	$50	$40
$1,465	$1,480	$141	$131	$121	$111	$101	$91	$81	$71	$62	$52	$42
$1,480	$1,495	$143	$133	$123	$113	$103	$93	$83	$73	$63	$53	$43
$1,495	$1,510	$144	$135	$125	$115	$105	$95	$85	$75	$65	$55	$45
$1,510	$1,525	$146	$136	$126	$117	$107	$97	$87	$77	$67	$57	$47
$1,525	$1,540	$148	$138	$128	$118	$108	$98	$89	$79	$69	$59	$49
$1,540	$1,555	$150	$140	$130	$120	$110	$100	$90	$80	$71	$61	$51

2021 Wage Bracket Method Tables for Manual Payroll Systems With Forms W-4 From 2019 or Earlier

WEEKLY Payroll Period

If the Wage Amount (line 1a) is		MARRIED Persons										
		And the number of allowances is:										
At least	But less than	0	1	2	3	4	5	6	7	8	9	10
		The Tentative Withholding Amount is:										
$1,555	$1,570	$152	$142	$132	$122	$112	$102	$92	$82	$72	$62	$52
$1,570	$1,585	$153	$144	$134	$124	$114	$104	$94	$84	$74	$64	$54
$1,585	$1,600	$155	$145	$135	$126	$116	$106	$96	$86	$76	$66	$56
$1,600	$1,615	$157	$147	$137	$127	$117	$107	$98	$88	$78	$68	$58
$1,615	$1,630	$159	$149	$139	$129	$119	$109	$99	$89	$80	$70	$60
$1,630	$1,645	$161	$151	$141	$131	$121	$111	$101	$91	$81	$71	$61
$1,645	$1,660	$162	$153	$143	$133	$123	$113	$103	$93	$83	$73	$63
$1,660	$1,675	$164	$154	$144	$135	$125	$115	$105	$95	$85	$75	$65
$1,675	$1,690	$166	$156	$146	$136	$126	$116	$107	$97	$87	$77	$67
$1,690	$1,705	$168	$158	$148	$138	$128	$118	$108	$98	$89	$79	$69
$1,705	$1,720	$170	$160	$150	$140	$130	$120	$110	$100	$90	$80	$70
$1,720	$1,735	$171	$162	$152	$142	$132	$122	$112	$102	$92	$82	$72
$1,735	$1,750	$173	$163	$153	$144	$134	$124	$114	$104	$94	$84	$74
$1,750	$1,765	$175	$165	$155	$145	$135	$125	$116	$106	$96	$86	$76
$1,765	$1,780	$177	$167	$157	$147	$137	$127	$117	$107	$98	$88	$78
$1,780	$1,795	$179	$169	$159	$149	$139	$129	$119	$109	$99	$89	$79
$1,795	$1,810	$181	$171	$161	$151	$141	$131	$121	$111	$101	$91	$81
$1,810	$1,825	$185	$172	$162	$153	$143	$133	$123	$113	$103	$93	$83
$1,825	$1,840	$188	$174	$164	$154	$144	$134	$125	$115	$105	$95	$85
$1,840	$1,855	$191	$176	$166	$156	$146	$136	$126	$116	$107	$97	$87
$1,855	$1,870	$195	$178	$168	$158	$148	$138	$128	$118	$108	$98	$88
$1,870	$1,885	$198	$180	$170	$160	$150	$140	$130	$120	$110	$100	$90
$1,885	$1,900	$201	$183	$171	$162	$152	$142	$132	$122	$112	$102	$92
$1,900	$1,915	$205	$186	$173	$163	$153	$143	$134	$124	$114	$104	$94
$1,915	$1,930	$208	$190	$175	$165	$155	$145	$135	$125	$116	$106	$96

2021 Wage Bracket Method Tables for Manual Payroll Systems With Forms W-4 From 2019 or Earlier

WEEKLY Payroll Period

If the Wage Amount (line 1a) is		SINGLE Persons										
		And the number of allowances is:										
At least	But less than	0	1	2	3	4	5	6	7	8	9	10
		The Tentative Withholding Amount is:										
$0	$80	$0	$0	$0	$0	$0	$0	$0	$0	$0	$0	$0
$80	$90	$1	$0	$0	$0	$0	$0	$0	$0	$0	$0	$0
$90	$100	$2	$0	$0	$0	$0	$0	$0	$0	$0	$0	$0
$100	$110	$3	$0	$0	$0	$0	$0	$0	$0	$0	$0	$0
$110	$120	$4	$0	$0	$0	$0	$0	$0	$0	$0	$0	$0
$120	$130	$5	$0	$0	$0	$0	$0	$0	$0	$0	$0	$0
$130	$140	$6	$0	$0	$0	$0	$0	$0	$0	$0	$0	$0
$140	$150	$7	$0	$0	$0	$0	$0	$0	$0	$0	$0	$0
$150	$160	$8	$0	$0	$0	$0	$0	$0	$0	$0	$0	$0
$160	$170	$9	$1	$0	$0	$0	$0	$0	$0	$0	$0	$0
$170	$180	$10	$2	$0	$0	$0	$0	$0	$0	$0	$0	$0
$180	$190	$11	$3	$0	$0	$0	$0	$0	$0	$0	$0	$0
$190	$200	$12	$4	$0	$0	$0	$0	$0	$0	$0	$0	$0
$200	$210	$13	$5	$0	$0	$0	$0	$0	$0	$0	$0	$0
$210	$220	$14	$6	$0	$0	$0	$0	$0	$0	$0	$0	$0
$220	$230	$15	$7	$0	$0	$0	$0	$0	$0	$0	$0	$0
$230	$240	$16	$8	$0	$0	$0	$0	$0	$0	$0	$0	$0
$240	$250	$17	$9	$0	$0	$0	$0	$0	$0	$0	$0	$0
$250	$260	$18	$10	$1	$0	$0	$0	$0	$0	$0	$0	$0
$260	$270	$19	$11	$2	$0	$0	$0	$0	$0	$0	$0	$0
$270	$285	$20	$12	$4	$0	$0	$0	$0	$0	$0	$0	$0
$285	$300	$22	$13	$5	$0	$0	$0	$0	$0	$0	$0	$0
$300	$315	$24	$15	$7	$0	$0	$0	$0	$0	$0	$0	$0
$315	$330	$26	$16	$8	$0	$0	$0	$0	$0	$0	$0	$0
$330	$345	$28	$18	$10	$1	$0	$0	$0	$0	$0	$0	$0
$345	$360	$29	$19	$11	$3	$0	$0	$0	$0	$0	$0	$0
$360	$375	$31	$21	$13	$4	$0	$0	$0	$0	$0	$0	$0
$375	$390	$33	$23	$14	$6	$0	$0	$0	$0	$0	$0	$0
$390	$405	$35	$25	$16	$7	$0	$0	$0	$0	$0	$0	$0
$405	$420	$37	$27	$17	$9	$1	$0	$0	$0	$0	$0	$0
$420	$435	$38	$28	$19	$10	$2	$0	$0	$0	$0	$0	$0
$435	$450	$40	$30	$20	$12	$4	$0	$0	$0	$0	$0	$0
$450	$465	$42	$32	$22	$13	$5	$0	$0	$0	$0	$0	$0
$465	$480	$44	$34	$24	$15	$7	$0	$0	$0	$0	$0	$0
$480	$495	$46	$36	$26	$16	$8	$0	$0	$0	$0	$0	$0
$495	$510	$47	$37	$28	$18	$10	$1	$0	$0	$0	$0	$0
$510	$525	$49	$39	$29	$19	$11	$3	$0	$0	$0	$0	$0
$525	$540	$51	$41	$31	$21	$13	$4	$0	$0	$0	$0	$0
$540	$555	$53	$43	$33	$23	$14	$6	$0	$0	$0	$0	$0
$555	$570	$55	$45	$35	$25	$16	$7	$0	$0	$0	$0	$0
$570	$585	$56	$46	$37	$27	$17	$9	$1	$0	$0	$0	$0
$585	$600	$58	$48	$38	$28	$19	$10	$2	$0	$0	$0	$0
$600	$615	$60	$50	$40	$30	$20	$12	$4	$0	$0	$0	$0
$615	$630	$62	$52	$42	$32	$22	$13	$5	$0	$0	$0	$0
$630	$645	$64	$54	$44	$34	$24	$15	$7	$0	$0	$0	$0
$645	$660	$65	$55	$46	$36	$26	$16	$8	$0	$0	$0	$0
$660	$675	$67	$57	$47	$37	$27	$18	$10	$1	$0	$0	$0
$675	$690	$69	$59	$49	$39	$29	$19	$11	$3	$0	$0	$0
$690	$705	$71	$61	$51	$41	$31	$21	$13	$4	$0	$0	$0
$705	$720	$73	$63	$53	$43	$33	$23	$14	$6	$0	$0	$0
$720	$735	$74	$64	$55	$45	$35	$25	$16	$7	$0	$0	$0

2021 Wage Bracket Method Tables for Manual Payroll Systems With Forms W-4 From 2019 or Earlier

WEEKLY Payroll Period

If the **Wage Amount** (line 1a) is		SINGLE Persons										
		And the number of allowances is:										
At least	But less than	0	1	2	3	4	5	6	7	8	9	10
		The Tentative Withholding Amount is:										
$735	$750	$76	$66	$56	$46	$36	$27	$17	$9	$1	$0	$0
$750	$765	$78	$68	$58	$48	$38	$28	$19	$10	$2	$0	$0
$765	$780	$80	$70	$60	$50	$40	$30	$20	$12	$4	$0	$0
$780	$795	$82	$72	$62	$52	$42	$32	$22	$13	$5	$0	$0
$795	$810	$83	$73	$64	$54	$44	$34	$24	$15	$7	$0	$0
$810	$825	$85	$75	$65	$55	$45	$36	$26	$16	$8	$0	$0
$825	$840	$87	$77	$67	$57	$47	$37	$27	$18	$10	$1	$0
$840	$855	$89	$79	$69	$59	$49	$39	$29	$19	$11	$3	$0
$855	$870	$91	$81	$71	$61	$51	$41	$31	$21	$13	$4	$0
$870	$885	$95	$82	$73	$63	$53	$43	$33	$23	$14	$6	$0
$885	$900	$98	$84	$74	$64	$54	$45	$35	$25	$16	$7	$0
$900	$915	$101	$86	$76	$66	$56	$46	$36	$26	$17	$9	$0
$915	$930	$104	$88	$78	$68	$58	$48	$38	$28	$19	$10	$2
$930	$945	$108	$90	$80	$70	$60	$50	$40	$30	$20	$12	$3
$945	$960	$111	$93	$82	$72	$62	$52	$42	$32	$22	$13	$5
$960	$975	$114	$96	$83	$73	$63	$54	$44	$34	$24	$15	$6
$975	$990	$118	$99	$85	$75	$65	$55	$45	$35	$26	$16	$8
$990	$1,005	$121	$103	$87	$77	$67	$57	$47	$37	$27	$18	$9
$1,005	$1,020	$124	$106	$89	$79	$69	$59	$49	$39	$29	$19	$11
$1,020	$1,035	$128	$109	$91	$81	$71	$61	$51	$41	$31	$21	$12
$1,035	$1,050	$131	$113	$94	$82	$72	$63	$53	$43	$33	$23	$14
$1,050	$1,065	$134	$116	$98	$84	$74	$64	$54	$44	$35	$25	$15
$1,065	$1,080	$137	$119	$101	$86	$76	$66	$56	$46	$36	$26	$17
$1,080	$1,095	$141	$123	$104	$88	$78	$68	$58	$48	$38	$28	$18
$1,095	$1,110	$144	$126	$108	$90	$80	$70	$60	$50	$40	$30	$20
$1,110	$1,125	$147	$129	$111	$93	$81	$72	$62	$52	$42	$32	$22
$1,125	$1,140	$151	$132	$114	$96	$83	$73	$63	$53	$44	$34	$24
$1,140	$1,155	$154	$136	$118	$99	$85	$75	$65	$55	$45	$35	$26
$1,155	$1,170	$157	$139	$121	$103	$87	$77	$67	$57	$47	$37	$27
$1,170	$1,185	$161	$142	$124	$106	$89	$79	$69	$59	$49	$39	$29
$1,185	$1,200	$164	$146	$127	$100	$91	$81	$71	$61	$51	$41	$31
$1,200	$1,215	$167	$149	$131	$113	$94	$82	$72	$62	$53	$43	$33
$1,215	$1,230	$170	$152	$134	$116	$98	$84	$74	$64	$54	$44	$35
$1,230	$1,245	$174	$156	$137	$119	$101	$86	$76	$66	$56	$46	$36
$1,245	$1,260	$177	$159	$141	$123	$104	$88	$78	$68	$58	$48	$38
$1,260	$1,275	$180	$162	$144	$126	$108	$90	$80	$70	$60	$50	$40
$1,275	$1,290	$184	$165	$147	$129	$111	$93	$81	$71	$62	$52	$42
$1,290	$1,305	$187	$169	$151	$132	$114	$96	$83	$73	$63	$53	$44
$1,305	$1,320	$190	$172	$154	$136	$118	$99	$85	$75	$65	$55	$45
$1,320	$1,335	$194	$175	$157	$139	$121	$103	$87	$77	$67	$57	$47
$1,335	$1,350	$197	$179	$160	$142	$124	$106	$89	$79	$69	$59	$49
$1,350	$1,365	$200	$182	$164	$146	$127	$109	$91	$80	$71	$61	$51
$1,365	$1,380	$203	$185	$167	$149	$131	$113	$94	$82	$72	$62	$53
$1,380	$1,395	$207	$189	$170	$152	$134	$116	$98	$84	$74	$64	$54
$1,395	$1,410	$210	$192	$174	$156	$137	$119	$101	$86	$76	$66	$56
$1,410	$1,425	$213	$195	$177	$159	$141	$122	$104	$88	$78	$68	$58
$1,425	$1,440	$217	$198	$180	$162	$144	$126	$108	$89	$80	$70	$60
$1,440	$1,455	$220	$202	$184	$165	$147	$129	$111	$93	$81	$71	$62
$1,455	$1,470	$223	$205	$187	$169	$151	$132	$114	$96	$83	$73	$63
$1,470	$1,485	$227	$208	$190	$172	$154	$136	$117	$99	$85	$75	$65
$1,485	$1,500	$230	$212	$193	$175	$157	$139	$121	$103	$87	$77	$67

2021 Wage Bracket Method Tables for Manual Payroll Systems With Forms W-4 From 2019 or Earlier

WEEKLY Payroll Period

If the **Wage Amount** (line 1a) is		SINGLE Persons										
		And the number of allowances is:										
At least	But less than	0	1	2	3	4	5	6	7	8	9	10
		The Tentative Withholding Amount is:										
$1,500	$1,515	$233	$215	$197	$179	$160	$142	$124	$106	$89	$79	$69
$1,515	$1,530	$236	$218	$200	$182	$164	$146	$127	$109	$91	$80	$71
$1,530	$1,545	$240	$222	$203	$185	$167	$149	$131	$112	$94	$82	$72
$1,545	$1,560	$243	$225	$207	$189	$170	$152	$134	$116	$98	$84	$74
$1,560	$1,575	$246	$228	$210	$192	$174	$155	$137	$119	$101	$86	$76
$1,575	$1,590	$250	$231	$213	$195	$177	$159	$141	$122	$104	$88	$78
$1,590	$1,605	$253	$235	$217	$198	$180	$162	$144	$126	$107	$89	$80
$1,605	$1,620	$256	$238	$220	$202	$184	$165	$147	$129	$111	$93	$81
$1,620	$1,635	$260	$241	$223	$205	$187	$169	$150	$132	$114	$96	$83
$1,635	$1,650	$263	$245	$226	$208	$190	$172	$154	$136	$117	$99	$85
$1,650	$1,665	$266	$248	$230	$212	$193	$175	$157	$139	$121	$102	$87
$1,665	$1,680	$269	$251	$233	$215	$197	$179	$160	$142	$124	$106	$89
$1,680	$1,695	$273	$255	$236	$218	$200	$182	$164	$145	$127	$109	$91
$1,695	$1,710	$276	$258	$240	$222	$203	$185	$167	$149	$131	$112	$94
$1,710	$1,725	$279	$261	$243	$225	$207	$188	$170	$152	$134	$116	$97
$1,725	$1,740	$283	$264	$246	$228	$210	$192	$174	$155	$137	$119	$101
$1,740	$1,755	$286	$268	$250	$231	$213	$195	$177	$159	$140	$122	$104
$1,755	$1,770	$290	$271	$253	$235	$217	$198	$180	$162	$144	$126	$107
$1,770	$1,785	$293	$274	$256	$238	$220	$202	$183	$165	$147	$129	$111
$1,785	$1,800	$297	$278	$259	$241	$223	$205	$187	$169	$150	$132	$114
$1,800	$1,815	$301	$281	$263	$245	$226	$208	$190	$172	$154	$135	$117

2021 Wage Bracket Method Tables for Manual Payroll Systems With Forms W-4 From 2019 or Earlier

BIWEEKLY Payroll Period

If the **Wage Amount** (line 1a) is		**MARRIED** Persons										
		And the number of allowances is:										
At least	But less than	0	1	2	3	4	5	6	7	8	9	10
		The Tentative Withholding Amount is:										
$0	$470	$0	$0	$0	$0	$0	$0	$0	$0	$0	$0	$0
$470	$480	$1	$0	$0	$0	$0	$0	$0	$0	$0	$0	$0
$480	$490	$2	$0	$0	$0	$0	$0	$0	$0	$0	$0	$0
$490	$500	$3	$0	$0	$0	$0	$0	$0	$0	$0	$0	$0
$500	$510	$4	$0	$0	$0	$0	$0	$0	$0	$0	$0	$0
$510	$520	$5	$0	$0	$0	$0	$0	$0	$0	$0	$0	$0
$520	$530	$6	$0	$0	$0	$0	$0	$0	$0	$0	$0	$0
$530	$540	$7	$0	$0	$0	$0	$0	$0	$0	$0	$0	$0
$540	$550	$8	$0	$0	$0	$0	$0	$0	$0	$0	$0	$0
$550	$560	$9	$0	$0	$0	$0	$0	$0	$0	$0	$0	$0
$560	$570	$10	$0	$0	$0	$0	$0	$0	$0	$0	$0	$0
$570	$580	$11	$0	$0	$0	$0	$0	$0	$0	$0	$0	$0
$580	$590	$12	$0	$0	$0	$0	$0	$0	$0	$0	$0	$0
$590	$600	$13	$0	$0	$0	$0	$0	$0	$0	$0	$0	$0
$600	$610	$14	$0	$0	$0	$0	$0	$0	$0	$0	$0	$0
$610	$620	$15	$0	$0	$0	$0	$0	$0	$0	$0	$0	$0
$620	$630	$16	$0	$0	$0	$0	$0	$0	$0	$0	$0	$0
$630	$640	$17	$0	$0	$0	$0	$0	$0	$0	$0	$0	$0
$640	$650	$18	$1	$0	$0	$0	$0	$0	$0	$0	$0	$0
$650	$660	$19	$2	$0	$0	$0	$0	$0	$0	$0	$0	$0
$660	$670	$20	$3	$0	$0	$0	$0	$0	$0	$0	$0	$0
$670	$680	$21	$4	$0	$0	$0	$0	$0	$0	$0	$0	$0
$680	$690	$22	$5	$0	$0	$0	$0	$0	$0	$0	$0	$0
$690	$700	$23	$6	$0	$0	$0	$0	$0	$0	$0	$0	$0
$700	$710	$24	$7	$0	$0	$0	$0	$0	$0	$0	$0	$0
$710	$720	$25	$8	$0	$0	$0	$0	$0	$0	$0	$0	$0
$720	$730	$26	$9	$0	$0	$0	$0	$0	$0	$0	$0	$0
$730	$740	$27	$10	$0	$0	$0	$0	$0	$0	$0	$0	$0
$740	$750	$28	$11	$0	$0	$0	$0	$0	$0	$0	$0	$0
$750	$760	$29	$12	$0	$0	$0	$0	$0	$0	$0	$0	$0
$760	$770	$30	$13	$0	$0	$0	$0	$0	$0	$0	$0	$0
$770	$780	$31	$14	$0	$0	$0	$0	$0	$0	$0	$0	$0
$780	$790	$32	$15	$0	$0	$0	$0	$0	$0	$0	$0	$0
$790	$800	$33	$16	$0	$0	$0	$0	$0	$0	$0	$0	$0
$800	$810	$34	$17	$1	$0	$0	$0	$0	$0	$0	$0	$0
$810	$820	$35	$18	$2	$0	$0	$0	$0	$0	$0	$0	$0
$820	$830	$36	$19	$3	$0	$0	$0	$0	$0	$0	$0	$0
$830	$840	$37	$20	$4	$0	$0	$0	$0	$0	$0	$0	$0
$840	$850	$38	$21	$5	$0	$0	$0	$0	$0	$0	$0	$0
$850	$860	$39	$22	$6	$0	$0	$0	$0	$0	$0	$0	$0
$860	$870	$40	$23	$7	$0	$0	$0	$0	$0	$0	$0	$0
$870	$880	$41	$24	$8	$0	$0	$0	$0	$0	$0	$0	$0
$880	$890	$42	$25	$9	$0	$0	$0	$0	$0	$0	$0	$0
$890	$900	$43	$26	$10	$0	$0	$0	$0	$0	$0	$0	$0
$900	$910	$44	$27	$11	$0	$0	$0	$0	$0	$0	$0	$0
$910	$920	$45	$28	$12	$0	$0	$0	$0	$0	$0	$0	$0
$920	$930	$46	$29	$13	$0	$0	$0	$0	$0	$0	$0	$0
$930	$940	$47	$30	$14	$0	$0	$0	$0	$0	$0	$0	$0
$940	$950	$48	$31	$15	$0	$0	$0	$0	$0	$0	$0	$0
$950	$960	$49	$32	$16	$0	$0	$0	$0	$0	$0	$0	$0
$960	$970	$50	$33	$17	$0	$0	$0	$0	$0	$0	$0	$0

2021 Wage Bracket Method Tables for Manual Payroll Systems With Forms W-4 From 2019 or Earlier

BIWEEKLY Payroll Period

If the **Wage Amount** (line 1a) is		MARRIED Persons										
		And the number of allowances is:										
At least	But less than	0	1	2	3	4	5	6	7	8	9	10
		The Tentative Withholding Amount is:										
$970	$980	$51	$34	$18	$1	$0	$0	$0	$0	$0	$0	$0
$980	$990	$52	$35	$19	$2	$0	$0	$0	$0	$0	$0	$0
$990	$1,000	$53	$36	$20	$3	$0	$0	$0	$0	$0	$0	$0
$1,000	$1,010	$54	$37	$21	$4	$0	$0	$0	$0	$0	$0	$0
$1,010	$1,020	$55	$38	$22	$5	$0	$0	$0	$0	$0	$0	$0
$1,020	$1,030	$56	$39	$23	$6	$0	$0	$0	$0	$0	$0	$0
$1,030	$1,040	$57	$40	$24	$7	$0	$0	$0	$0	$0	$0	$0
$1,040	$1,050	$58	$41	$25	$8	$0	$0	$0	$0	$0	$0	$0
$1,050	$1,060	$59	$42	$26	$9	$0	$0	$0	$0	$0	$0	$0
$1,060	$1,070	$60	$43	$27	$10	$0	$0	$0	$0	$0	$0	$0
$1,070	$1,080	$61	$44	$28	$11	$0	$0	$0	$0	$0	$0	$0
$1,080	$1,090	$62	$45	$29	$12	$0	$0	$0	$0	$0	$0	$0
$1,090	$1,100	$63	$46	$30	$13	$0	$0	$0	$0	$0	$0	$0
$1,100	$1,110	$64	$47	$31	$14	$0	$0	$0	$0	$0	$0	$0
$1,110	$1,120	$65	$48	$32	$15	$0	$0	$0	$0	$0	$0	$0
$1,120	$1,130	$66	$49	$33	$16	$0	$0	$0	$0	$0	$0	$0
$1,130	$1,140	$67	$50	$34	$17	$0	$0	$0	$0	$0	$0	$0
$1,140	$1,150	$68	$51	$35	$18	$1	$0	$0	$0	$0	$0	$0
$1,150	$1,160	$69	$52	$36	$19	$2	$0	$0	$0	$0	$0	$0
$1,160	$1,170	$70	$53	$37	$20	$3	$0	$0	$0	$0	$0	$0
$1,170	$1,180	$71	$54	$38	$21	$4	$0	$0	$0	$0	$0	$0
$1,180	$1,190	$72	$55	$39	$22	$5	$0	$0	$0	$0	$0	$0
$1,190	$1,200	$73	$56	$40	$23	$6	$0	$0	$0	$0	$0	$0
$1,200	$1,210	$74	$57	$41	$24	$7	$0	$0	$0	$0	$0	$0
$1,210	$1,220	$75	$58	$42	$25	$8	$0	$0	$0	$0	$0	$0
$1,220	$1,230	$76	$59	$43	$26	$9	$0	$0	$0	$0	$0	$0
$1,230	$1,270	$78	$62	$45	$28	$12	$0	$0	$0	$0	$0	$0
$1,270	$1,310	$83	$66	$49	$32	$16	$0	$0	$0	$0	$0	$0
$1,310	$1,350	$88	$70	$53	$36	$20	$3	$0	$0	$0	$0	$0
$1,350	$1,390	$93	$74	$57	$40	$24	$7	$0	$0	$0	$0	$0
$1,390	$1,430	$98	$78	$61	$44	$28	$11	$0	$0	$0	$0	$0
$1,430	$1,470	$102	$83	$65	$48	$32	$15	$0	$0	$0	$0	$0
$1,470	$1,510	$107	$87	$69	$52	$36	$19	$3	$0	$0	$0	$0
$1,510	$1,550	$112	$92	$73	$56	$40	$23	$7	$0	$0	$0	$0
$1,550	$1,590	$117	$97	$77	$60	$44	$27	$11	$0	$0	$0	$0
$1,590	$1,630	$122	$102	$82	$64	$48	$31	$15	$0	$0	$0	$0
$1,630	$1,670	$126	$107	$87	$68	$52	$35	$19	$2	$0	$0	$0
$1,670	$1,710	$131	$111	$91	$72	$56	$39	$23	$6	$0	$0	$0
$1,710	$1,750	$136	$116	$96	$76	$60	$43	$27	$10	$0	$0	$0
$1,750	$1,790	$141	$121	$101	$81	$64	$47	$31	$14	$0	$0	$0
$1,790	$1,830	$146	$126	$106	$86	$68	$51	$35	$18	$2	$0	$0
$1,830	$1,870	$150	$131	$111	$91	$72	$55	$39	$22	$6	$0	$0
$1,870	$1,910	$155	$135	$115	$96	$76	$59	$43	$26	$10	$0	$0
$1,910	$1,950	$160	$140	$120	$100	$81	$63	$47	$30	$14	$0	$0
$1,950	$1,990	$165	$145	$125	$105	$85	$67	$51	$34	$18	$1	$0
$1,990	$2,030	$170	$150	$130	$110	$90	$71	$55	$38	$22	$5	$0
$2,030	$2,070	$174	$155	$135	$115	$95	$75	$59	$42	$26	$9	$0
$2,070	$2,110	$179	$159	$139	$120	$100	$80	$63	$46	$30	$13	$0
$2,110	$2,150	$184	$164	$144	$124	$105	$85	$67	$50	$34	$17	$1
$2,150	$2,190	$189	$169	$149	$129	$109	$90	$71	$54	$38	$21	$5
$2,190	$2,230	$194	$174	$154	$134	$114	$94	$75	$58	$42	$25	$9

2021 Wage Bracket Method Tables for Manual Payroll Systems With Forms W-4 From 2019 or Earlier

BIWEEKLY Payroll Period

If the Wage Amount (line 1a) is		MARRIED Persons										
		And the number of allowances is:										
At least	But less than	0	1	2	3	4	5	6	7	8	9	10
		The Tentative Withholding Amount is:										
$2,230	$2,270	$198	$179	$159	$139	$119	$99	$79	$62	$46	$29	$13
$2,270	$2,310	$203	$183	$163	$144	$124	$104	$84	$66	$50	$33	$17
$2,310	$2,350	$208	$188	$168	$148	$129	$109	$89	$70	$54	$37	$21
$2,350	$2,390	$213	$193	$173	$153	$133	$114	$94	$74	$58	$41	$25
$2,390	$2,430	$218	$198	$178	$158	$138	$118	$99	$79	$62	$45	$29
$2,430	$2,470	$222	$203	$183	$163	$143	$123	$103	$83	$66	$49	$33
$2,470	$2,510	$227	$207	$187	$168	$148	$128	$108	$88	$70	$53	$37
$2,510	$2,550	$232	$212	$192	$172	$153	$133	$113	$93	$74	$57	$41
$2,550	$2,590	$237	$217	$197	$177	$157	$138	$118	$98	$78	$61	$45
$2,590	$2,630	$242	$222	$202	$182	$162	$142	$123	$103	$83	$65	$49
$2,630	$2,670	$246	$227	$207	$187	$167	$147	$127	$107	$88	$69	$53
$2,670	$2,710	$251	$231	$211	$192	$172	$152	$132	$112	$92	$73	$57
$2,710	$2,750	$256	$236	$216	$196	$177	$157	$137	$117	$97	$77	$61
$2,750	$2,790	$261	$241	$221	$201	$181	$162	$142	$122	$102	$82	$65
$2,790	$2,830	$266	$246	$226	$206	$186	$166	$147	$127	$107	$87	$69
$2,830	$2,870	$270	$251	$231	$211	$191	$171	$151	$131	$112	$92	$73
$2,870	$2,910	$275	$255	$235	$216	$196	$176	$156	$136	$116	$97	$77
$2,910	$2,950	$280	$260	$240	$220	$201	$181	$161	$141	$121	$101	$82
$2,950	$2,990	$285	$265	$245	$225	$205	$186	$166	$146	$126	$106	$86
$2,990	$3,030	$290	$270	$250	$230	$210	$190	$171	$151	$131	$111	$91
$3,030	$3,070	$294	$275	$255	$235	$215	$195	$175	$155	$136	$116	$96
$3,070	$3,110	$299	$279	$259	$240	$220	$200	$180	$160	$140	$121	$101
$3,110	$3,150	$304	$284	$264	$244	$225	$205	$185	$165	$145	$125	$106
$3,150	$3,190	$309	$289	$269	$249	$229	$210	$190	$170	$150	$130	$110
$3,190	$3,230	$314	$294	$274	$254	$234	$214	$195	$175	$155	$135	$115
$3,230	$3,270	$318	$299	$279	$259	$239	$219	$199	$179	$160	$140	$120
$3,270	$3,310	$323	$303	$283	$264	$244	$224	$204	$184	$164	$145	$125
$3,310	$3,350	$328	$308	$288	$268	$249	$229	$209	$189	$169	$149	$130
$3,350	$3,390	$333	$313	$293	$273	$253	$234	$214	$194	$174	$154	$134
$3,390	$3,430	$338	$318	$298	$278	$258	$238	$219	$199	$179	$159	$139
$3,430	$3,470	$342	$323	$303	$283	$263	$243	$223	$203	$184	$164	$144
$3,470	$3,510	$347	$327	$307	$288	$268	$248	$228	$208	$188	$169	$149

2021 Wage Bracket Method Tables for Manual Payroll Systems With Forms W-4 From 2019 or Earlier

BIWEEKLY Payroll Period

If the **Wage Amount** (line 1a) is		SINGLE Persons										
		And the number of allowances is:										
At least	But less than	0	1	2	3	4	5	6	7	8	9	10
		The Tentative Withholding Amount is:										
$0	$155	$0	$0	$0	$0	$0	$0	$0	$0	$0	$0	$0
$155	$165	$1	$0	$0	$0	$0	$0	$0	$0	$0	$0	$0
$165	$175	$2	$0	$0	$0	$0	$0	$0	$0	$0	$0	$0
$175	$185	$3	$0	$0	$0	$0	$0	$0	$0	$0	$0	$0
$185	$195	$4	$0	$0	$0	$0	$0	$0	$0	$0	$0	$0
$195	$205	$5	$0	$0	$0	$0	$0	$0	$0	$0	$0	$0
$205	$215	$6	$0	$0	$0	$0	$0	$0	$0	$0	$0	$0
$215	$225	$7	$0	$0	$0	$0	$0	$0	$0	$0	$0	$0
$225	$235	$8	$0	$0	$0	$0	$0	$0	$0	$0	$0	$0
$235	$245	$9	$0	$0	$0	$0	$0	$0	$0	$0	$0	$0
$245	$255	$10	$0	$0	$0	$0	$0	$0	$0	$0	$0	$0
$255	$265	$11	$0	$0	$0	$0	$0	$0	$0	$0	$0	$0
$265	$275	$12	$0	$0	$0	$0	$0	$0	$0	$0	$0	$0
$275	$285	$13	$0	$0	$0	$0	$0	$0	$0	$0	$0	$0
$285	$295	$14	$0	$0	$0	$0	$0	$0	$0	$0	$0	$0
$295	$305	$15	$0	$0	$0	$0	$0	$0	$0	$0	$0	$0
$305	$315	$16	$0	$0	$0	$0	$0	$0	$0	$0	$0	$0
$315	$325	$17	$0	$0	$0	$0	$0	$0	$0	$0	$0	$0
$325	$335	$18	$1	$0	$0	$0	$0	$0	$0	$0	$0	$0
$335	$345	$19	$2	$0	$0	$0	$0	$0	$0	$0	$0	$0
$345	$355	$20	$3	$0	$0	$0	$0	$0	$0	$0	$0	$0
$355	$365	$21	$4	$0	$0	$0	$0	$0	$0	$0	$0	$0
$365	$375	$22	$5	$0	$0	$0	$0	$0	$0	$0	$0	$0
$375	$385	$23	$6	$0	$0	$0	$0	$0	$0	$0	$0	$0
$385	$395	$24	$7	$0	$0	$0	$0	$0	$0	$0	$0	$0
$395	$405	$25	$8	$0	$0	$0	$0	$0	$0	$0	$0	$0
$405	$415	$26	$9	$0	$0	$0	$0	$0	$0	$0	$0	$0
$415	$425	$27	$10	$0	$0	$0	$0	$0	$0	$0	$0	$0
$425	$435	$28	$11	$0	$0	$0	$0	$0	$0	$0	$0	$0
$435	$445	$29	$12	$0	$0	$0	$0	$0	$0	$0	$0	$0
$445	$455	$30	$13	$0	$0	$0	$0	$0	$0	$0	$0	$0
$455	$465	$31	$14	$0	$0	$0	$0	$0	$0	$0	$0	$0
$465	$475	$32	$15	$0	$0	$0	$0	$0	$0	$0	$0	$0
$475	$485	$33	$16	$0	$0	$0	$0	$0	$0	$0	$0	$0
$485	$495	$34	$17	$1	$0	$0	$0	$0	$0	$0	$0	$0
$495	$505	$35	$18	$2	$0	$0	$0	$0	$0	$0	$0	$0
$505	$515	$36	$19	$3	$0	$0	$0	$0	$0	$0	$0	$0
$515	$525	$37	$20	$4	$0	$0	$0	$0	$0	$0	$0	$0
$525	$535	$38	$21	$5	$0	$0	$0	$0	$0	$0	$0	$0
$535	$565	$40	$23	$7	$0	$0	$0	$0	$0	$0	$0	$0
$565	$595	$44	$26	$10	$0	$0	$0	$0	$0	$0	$0	$0
$595	$625	$47	$29	$13	$0	$0	$0	$0	$0	$0	$0	$0
$625	$655	$51	$32	$16	$0	$0	$0	$0	$0	$0	$0	$0
$655	$685	$55	$35	$19	$2	$0	$0	$0	$0	$0	$0	$0
$685	$715	$58	$38	$22	$5	$0	$0	$0	$0	$0	$0	$0
$715	$745	$62	$42	$25	$8	$0	$0	$0	$0	$0	$0	$0
$745	$775	$65	$45	$28	$11	$0	$0	$0	$0	$0	$0	$0
$775	$805	$69	$49	$31	$14	$0	$0	$0	$0	$0	$0	$0
$805	$835	$73	$53	$34	$17	$1	$0	$0	$0	$0	$0	$0
$835	$865	$76	$56	$37	$20	$4	$0	$0	$0	$0	$0	$0
$865	$895	$80	$60	$40	$23	$7	$0	$0	$0	$0	$0	$0

2021 Wage Bracket Method Tables for Manual Payroll Systems With Forms W-4 From 2019 or Earlier
BIWEEKLY Payroll Period

If the **Wage Amount** (line 1a) is		SINGLE Persons										
		And the number of allowances is:										
At least	But less than	0	1	2	3	4	5	6	7	8	9	10
		The Tentative Withholding Amount is:										
$895	$925	$83	$63	$44	$26	$10	$0	$0	$0	$0	$0	$0
$925	$955	$87	$67	$47	$29	$13	$0	$0	$0	$0	$0	$0
$955	$985	$91	$71	$51	$32	$16	$0	$0	$0	$0	$0	$0
$985	$1,015	$94	$74	$54	$35	$19	$2	$0	$0	$0	$0	$0
$1,015	$1,045	$98	$78	$58	$38	$22	$5	$0	$0	$0	$0	$0
$1,045	$1,075	$101	$81	$62	$42	$25	$8	$0	$0	$0	$0	$0
$1,075	$1,105	$105	$85	$65	$45	$28	$11	$0	$0	$0	$0	$0
$1,105	$1,135	$109	$89	$69	$49	$31	$14	$0	$0	$0	$0	$0
$1,135	$1,165	$112	$92	$72	$53	$34	$17	$1	$0	$0	$0	$0
$1,165	$1,195	$116	$96	$76	$56	$37	$20	$4	$0	$0	$0	$0
$1,195	$1,225	$119	$99	$80	$60	$40	$23	$7	$0	$0	$0	$0
$1,225	$1,255	$123	$103	$83	$63	$44	$26	$10	$0	$0	$0	$0
$1,255	$1,285	$127	$107	$87	$67	$47	$29	$13	$0	$0	$0	$0
$1,285	$1,315	$130	$110	$90	$71	$51	$32	$16	$0	$0	$0	$0
$1,315	$1,345	$134	$114	$94	$74	$54	$35	$19	$2	$0	$0	$0
$1,345	$1,375	$137	$117	$98	$78	$58	$38	$22	$5	$0	$0	$0
$1,375	$1,405	$141	$121	$101	$81	$62	$42	$25	$8	$0	$0	$0
$1,405	$1,435	$145	$125	$105	$85	$65	$45	$28	$11	$0	$0	$0
$1,435	$1,465	$148	$128	$108	$89	$69	$49	$31	$14	$0	$0	$0
$1,465	$1,495	$152	$132	$112	$92	$72	$52	$34	$17	$1	$0	$0
$1,495	$1,525	$155	$135	$116	$96	$76	$56	$37	$20	$4	$0	$0
$1,525	$1,555	$159	$139	$119	$99	$80	$60	$40	$23	$7	$0	$0
$1,555	$1,585	$163	$143	$123	$103	$83	$63	$43	$26	$10	$0	$0
$1,585	$1,615	$166	$146	$126	$107	$87	$67	$47	$29	$13	$0	$0
$1,615	$1,645	$170	$150	$130	$110	$90	$70	$51	$32	$16	$0	$0
$1,645	$1,675	$173	$153	$134	$114	$94	$74	$54	$35	$19	$2	$0
$1,675	$1,705	$177	$157	$137	$117	$98	$78	$58	$38	$22	$5	$0
$1,705	$1,735	$181	$161	$141	$121	$101	$81	$61	$42	$25	$8	$0
$1,735	$1,775	$189	$165	$145	$125	$105	$85	$66	$46	$28	$11	$0
$1,775	$1,815	$198	$170	$150	$130	$110	$90	$70	$51	$32	$15	$0
$1,815	$1,855	$207	$174	$155	$135	$115	$95	$75	$55	$36	$19	$3
$1,855	$1,895	$216	$179	$159	$140	$120	$100	$80	$60	$40	$23	$7
$1,895	$1,935	$224	$188	$164	$144	$125	$105	$85	$65	$45	$27	$11
$1,935	$1,975	$233	$197	$169	$149	$129	$109	$90	$70	$50	$31	$15
$1,975	$2,015	$242	$206	$174	$154	$134	$114	$94	$75	$55	$35	$19
$2,015	$2,055	$251	$214	$179	$159	$139	$119	$99	$79	$60	$40	$23
$2,055	$2,095	$260	$223	$187	$164	$144	$124	$104	$84	$64	$45	$27
$2,095	$2,135	$268	$232	$196	$168	$149	$129	$109	$89	$69	$49	$31
$2,135	$2,175	$277	$241	$204	$173	$153	$133	$114	$94	$74	$54	$35
$2,175	$2,215	$286	$250	$213	$178	$158	$138	$118	$99	$79	$59	$39
$2,215	$2,255	$295	$258	$222	$186	$163	$143	$123	$103	$84	$64	$44
$2,255	$2,295	$304	$267	$231	$194	$168	$148	$128	$108	$88	$69	$49
$2,295	$2,335	$312	$276	$240	$203	$173	$153	$133	$113	$93	$73	$53
$2,335	$2,375	$321	$285	$248	$212	$177	$157	$138	$118	$98	$78	$58
$2,375	$2,415	$330	$294	$257	$221	$184	$162	$142	$123	$103	$83	$63
$2,415	$2,455	$339	$302	$266	$230	$193	$167	$147	$127	$108	$88	$68
$2,455	$2,495	$348	$311	$275	$238	$202	$172	$152	$132	$112	$93	$73
$2,495	$2,535	$356	$320	$284	$247	$211	$177	$157	$137	$117	$97	$77
$2,535	$2,575	$365	$329	$292	$256	$220	$183	$162	$142	$122	$102	$82
$2,575	$2,615	$374	$338	$301	$265	$228	$192	$166	$147	$127	$107	$87
$2,615	$2,655	$383	$346	$310	$274	$237	$201	$171	$151	$132	$112	$92

2021 Wage Bracket Method Tables for Manual Payroll Systems With Forms W-4 From 2019 or Earlier

BIWEEKLY Payroll Period

If the Wage Amount (line 1a) is		SINGLE Persons										
		And the number of allowances is:										
At least	But less than	0	1	2	3	4	5	6	7	8	9	10
		The Tentative Withholding Amount is:										
$2,655	$2,695	$392	$355	$319	$282	$246	$210	$176	$156	$136	$117	$97
$2,695	$2,735	$400	$364	$328	$291	$255	$218	$182	$161	$141	$121	$101
$2,735	$2,775	$409	$373	$336	$300	$264	$227	$191	$166	$146	$126	$106
$2,775	$2,815	$418	$382	$345	$309	$272	$236	$200	$171	$151	$131	$111
$2,815	$2,855	$427	$390	$354	$318	$281	$245	$208	$175	$156	$136	$116
$2,855	$2,895	$436	$399	$363	$326	$290	$254	$217	$181	$160	$141	$121
$2,895	$2,935	$444	$408	$372	$335	$299	$262	$226	$190	$165	$145	$125
$2,935	$2,975	$453	$417	$380	$344	$308	$271	$235	$198	$170	$150	$130
$2,975	$3,015	$462	$426	$389	$353	$316	$280	$244	$207	$175	$155	$135
$3,015	$3,055	$471	$434	$398	$362	$325	$289	$252	$216	$180	$160	$140
$3,055	$3,095	$480	$443	$407	$370	$334	$298	$261	$225	$188	$165	$145
$3,095	$3,135	$488	$452	$416	$379	$343	$306	$270	$234	$197	$169	$149
$3,135	$3,175	$497	$461	$424	$388	$352	$315	$279	$242	$206	$174	$154
$3,175	$3,215	$506	$470	$433	$397	$360	$324	$288	$251	$215	$179	$159
$3,215	$3,255	$515	$478	$442	$406	$369	$333	$296	$260	$224	$187	$164
$3,255	$3,295	$524	$487	$451	$414	$378	$342	$305	$269	$232	$196	$169
$3,295	$3,335	$532	$496	$460	$423	$387	$350	$314	$278	$241	$205	$173
$3,335	$3,375	$541	$505	$468	$432	$396	$359	$323	$286	$250	$214	$178
$3,375	$3,415	$550	$514	$477	$441	$404	$368	$332	$295	$259	$222	$186
$3,415	$3,455	$559	$522	$486	$450	$413	$377	$340	$304	$268	$231	$195
$3,455	$3,495	$568	$531	$495	$458	$422	$386	$349	$313	$276	$240	$204

2021 Wage Bracket Method Tables for Manual Payroll Systems With Forms W-4 From 2019 or Earlier

SEMIMONTHLY Payroll Period

If the **Wage Amount** (line 1a) is		MARRIED Persons										
		And the number of allowances is:										
At least	But less than	0	1	2	3	4	5	6	7	8	9	10
		The Tentative Withholding Amount is:										
$0	$510	$0	$0	$0	$0	$0	$0	$0	$0	$0	$0	$0
$510	$520	$1	$0	$0	$0	$0	$0	$0	$0	$0	$0	$0
$520	$530	$2	$0	$0	$0	$0	$0	$0	$0	$0	$0	$0
$530	$540	$3	$0	$0	$0	$0	$0	$0	$0	$0	$0	$0
$540	$550	$4	$0	$0	$0	$0	$0	$0	$0	$0	$0	$0
$550	$560	$5	$0	$0	$0	$0	$0	$0	$0	$0	$0	$0
$560	$570	$6	$0	$0	$0	$0	$0	$0	$0	$0	$0	$0
$570	$580	$7	$0	$0	$0	$0	$0	$0	$0	$0	$0	$0
$580	$590	$8	$0	$0	$0	$0	$0	$0	$0	$0	$0	$0
$590	$600	$9	$0	$0	$0	$0	$0	$0	$0	$0	$0	$0
$600	$610	$10	$0	$0	$0	$0	$0	$0	$0	$0	$0	$0
$610	$620	$11	$0	$0	$0	$0	$0	$0	$0	$0	$0	$0
$620	$630	$12	$0	$0	$0	$0	$0	$0	$0	$0	$0	$0
$630	$640	$13	$0	$0	$0	$0	$0	$0	$0	$0	$0	$0
$640	$650	$14	$0	$0	$0	$0	$0	$0	$0	$0	$0	$0
$650	$660	$15	$0	$0	$0	$0	$0	$0	$0	$0	$0	$0
$660	$670	$16	$0	$0	$0	$0	$0	$0	$0	$0	$0	$0
$670	$680	$17	$0	$0	$0	$0	$0	$0	$0	$0	$0	$0
$680	$690	$18	$0	$0	$0	$0	$0	$0	$0	$0	$0	$0
$690	$700	$19	$1	$0	$0	$0	$0	$0	$0	$0	$0	$0
$700	$710	$20	$2	$0	$0	$0	$0	$0	$0	$0	$0	$0
$710	$720	$21	$3	$0	$0	$0	$0	$0	$0	$0	$0	$0
$720	$730	$22	$4	$0	$0	$0	$0	$0	$0	$0	$0	$0
$730	$740	$23	$5	$0	$0	$0	$0	$0	$0	$0	$0	$0
$740	$750	$24	$6	$0	$0	$0	$0	$0	$0	$0	$0	$0
$750	$760	$25	$7	$0	$0	$0	$0	$0	$0	$0	$0	$0
$760	$770	$26	$8	$0	$0	$0	$0	$0	$0	$0	$0	$0
$770	$780	$27	$9	$0	$0	$0	$0	$0	$0	$0	$0	$0
$780	$790	$28	$10	$0	$0	$0	$0	$0	$0	$0	$0	$0
$790	$800	$29	$11	$0	$0	$0	$0	$0	$0	$0	$0	$0
$800	$810	$30	$12	$0	$0	$0	$0	$0	$0	$0	$0	$0
$810	$820	$31	$13	$0	$0	$0	$0	$0	$0	$0	$0	$0
$820	$830	$32	$14	$0	$0	$0	$0	$0	$0	$0	$0	$0
$830	$840	$33	$15	$0	$0	$0	$0	$0	$0	$0	$0	$0
$840	$850	$34	$16	$0	$0	$0	$0	$0	$0	$0	$0	$0
$850	$860	$35	$17	$0	$0	$0	$0	$0	$0	$0	$0	$0
$860	$870	$36	$18	$0	$0	$0	$0	$0	$0	$0	$0	$0
$870	$880	$37	$19	$1	$0	$0	$0	$0	$0	$0	$0	$0
$880	$890	$38	$20	$2	$0	$0	$0	$0	$0	$0	$0	$0
$890	$900	$39	$21	$3	$0	$0	$0	$0	$0	$0	$0	$0
$900	$910	$40	$22	$4	$0	$0	$0	$0	$0	$0	$0	$0
$910	$920	$41	$23	$5	$0	$0	$0	$0	$0	$0	$0	$0
$920	$930	$42	$24	$6	$0	$0	$0	$0	$0	$0	$0	$0
$930	$940	$43	$25	$7	$0	$0	$0	$0	$0	$0	$0	$0
$940	$950	$44	$26	$8	$0	$0	$0	$0	$0	$0	$0	$0
$950	$960	$45	$27	$9	$0	$0	$0	$0	$0	$0	$0	$0
$960	$970	$46	$28	$10	$0	$0	$0	$0	$0	$0	$0	$0
$970	$980	$47	$29	$11	$0	$0	$0	$0	$0	$0	$0	$0
$980	$990	$48	$30	$12	$0	$0	$0	$0	$0	$0	$0	$0
$990	$1,000	$49	$31	$13	$0	$0	$0	$0	$0	$0	$0	$0
$1,000	$1,010	$50	$32	$14	$0	$0	$0	$0	$0	$0	$0	$0

2021 Wage Bracket Method Tables for Manual Payroll Systems With Forms W-4 From 2019 or Earlier

SEMIMONTHLY Payroll Period

If the Wage Amount (line 1a) is		MARRIED Persons										
		And the number of allowances is:										
At least	But less than	0	1	2	3	4	5	6	7	8	9	10
		The Tentative Withholding Amount is:										
$1,010	$1,020	$51	$33	$15	$0	$0	$0	$0	$0	$0	$0	$0
$1,020	$1,030	$52	$34	$16	$0	$0	$0	$0	$0	$0	$0	$0
$1,030	$1,040	$53	$35	$17	$0	$0	$0	$0	$0	$0	$0	$0
$1,040	$1,050	$54	$36	$18	$0	$0	$0	$0	$0	$0	$0	$0
$1,050	$1,060	$55	$37	$19	$1	$0	$0	$0	$0	$0	$0	$0
$1,060	$1,070	$56	$38	$20	$2	$0	$0	$0	$0	$0	$0	$0
$1,070	$1,080	$57	$39	$21	$3	$0	$0	$0	$0	$0	$0	$0
$1,080	$1,090	$58	$40	$22	$4	$0	$0	$0	$0	$0	$0	$0
$1,090	$1,100	$59	$41	$23	$5	$0	$0	$0	$0	$0	$0	$0
$1,100	$1,110	$60	$42	$24	$6	$0	$0	$0	$0	$0	$0	$0
$1,110	$1,120	$61	$43	$25	$7	$0	$0	$0	$0	$0	$0	$0
$1,120	$1,130	$62	$44	$26	$8	$0	$0	$0	$0	$0	$0	$0
$1,130	$1,140	$63	$45	$27	$9	$0	$0	$0	$0	$0	$0	$0
$1,140	$1,150	$64	$46	$28	$10	$0	$0	$0	$0	$0	$0	$0
$1,150	$1,160	$65	$47	$29	$11	$0	$0	$0	$0	$0	$0	$0
$1,160	$1,170	$66	$48	$30	$12	$0	$0	$0	$0	$0	$0	$0
$1,170	$1,180	$67	$49	$31	$13	$0	$0	$0	$0	$0	$0	$0
$1,180	$1,190	$68	$50	$32	$14	$0	$0	$0	$0	$0	$0	$0
$1,190	$1,200	$69	$51	$33	$15	$0	$0	$0	$0	$0	$0	$0
$1,200	$1,210	$70	$52	$34	$16	$0	$0	$0	$0	$0	$0	$0
$1,210	$1,220	$71	$53	$35	$17	$0	$0	$0	$0	$0	$0	$0
$1,220	$1,230	$72	$54	$36	$18	$0	$0	$0	$0	$0	$0	$0
$1,230	$1,240	$73	$55	$37	$19	$1	$0	$0	$0	$0	$0	$0
$1,240	$1,250	$74	$56	$38	$20	$2	$0	$0	$0	$0	$0	$0
$1,250	$1,260	$75	$57	$39	$21	$3	$0	$0	$0	$0	$0	$0
$1,260	$1,270	$76	$58	$40	$22	$4	$0	$0	$0	$0	$0	$0
$1,270	$1,280	$77	$59	$41	$23	$5	$0	$0	$0	$0	$0	$0
$1,280	$1,290	$78	$60	$42	$24	$6	$0	$0	$0	$0	$0	$0
$1,290	$1,300	$79	$61	$43	$25	$7	$0	$0	$0	$0	$0	$0
$1,300	$1,310	$80	$62	$44	$26	$8	$0	$0	$0	$0	$0	$0
$1,310	$1,320	$81	$63	$45	$27	$9	$0	$0	$0	$0	$0	$0
$1,320	$1,330	$82	$64	$46	$28	$10	$0	$0	$0	$0	$0	$0
$1,330	$1,340	$83	$65	$47	$29	$11	$0	$0	$0	$0	$0	$0
$1,340	$1,380	$86	$67	$49	$31	$14	$0	$0	$0	$0	$0	$0
$1,380	$1,420	$90	$71	$53	$35	$18	$0	$0	$0	$0	$0	$0
$1,420	$1,460	$95	$75	$57	$39	$22	$4	$0	$0	$0	$0	$0
$1,460	$1,500	$100	$79	$61	$43	$26	$8	$0	$0	$0	$0	$0
$1,500	$1,540	$105	$83	$65	$47	$30	$12	$0	$0	$0	$0	$0
$1,540	$1,580	$110	$88	$69	$51	$34	$16	$0	$0	$0	$0	$0
$1,580	$1,620	$114	$93	$73	$55	$38	$20	$2	$0	$0	$0	$0
$1,620	$1,660	$119	$98	$77	$59	$42	$24	$6	$0	$0	$0	$0
$1,660	$1,700	$124	$103	$81	$63	$46	$28	$10	$0	$0	$0	$0
$1,700	$1,740	$129	$107	$86	$67	$50	$32	$14	$0	$0	$0	$0
$1,740	$1,780	$134	$112	$91	$71	$54	$36	$18	$0	$0	$0	$0
$1,780	$1,820	$138	$117	$95	$75	$58	$40	$22	$4	$0	$0	$0
$1,820	$1,860	$143	$122	$100	$79	$62	$44	$26	$8	$0	$0	$0
$1,860	$1,900	$148	$127	$105	$84	$66	$48	$30	$12	$0	$0	$0
$1,900	$1,940	$153	$131	$110	$88	$70	$52	$34	$16	$0	$0	$0
$1,940	$1,980	$158	$136	$115	$93	$74	$56	$38	$20	$2	$0	$0
$1,980	$2,020	$162	$141	$119	$98	$78	$60	$42	$24	$6	$0	$0
$2,020	$2,060	$167	$146	$124	$103	$82	$64	$46	$28	$10	$0	$0

2021 Wage Bracket Method Tables for Manual Payroll Systems With Forms W-4 From 2019 or Earlier
SEMIMONTHLY Payroll Period

If the **Wage Amount** (line 1a) is		**MARRIED** Persons										
		And the number of allowances is:										
At least	But less than	0	1	2	3	4	5	6	7	8	9	10
		The Tentative Withholding Amount is:										
$2,060	$2,100	$172	$151	$129	$108	$86	$68	$50	$32	$14	$0	$0
$2,100	$2,140	$177	$155	$134	$112	$91	$72	$54	$36	$18	$0	$0
$2,140	$2,180	$182	$160	$139	$117	$96	$76	$58	$40	$22	$4	$0
$2,180	$2,220	$186	$165	$143	$122	$100	$80	$62	$44	$26	$8	$0
$2,220	$2,260	$191	$170	$148	$127	$105	$84	$66	$48	$30	$12	$0
$2,260	$2,300	$196	$175	$153	$132	$110	$89	$70	$52	$34	$16	$0
$2,300	$2,340	$201	$179	$158	$136	$115	$93	$74	$56	$38	$20	$2
$2,340	$2,380	$206	$184	$163	$141	$120	$98	$78	$60	$42	$24	$6
$2,380	$2,420	$210	$189	$167	$146	$124	$103	$82	$64	$46	$28	$10
$2,420	$2,460	$215	$194	$172	$151	$129	$108	$86	$68	$50	$32	$14
$2,460	$2,500	$220	$199	$177	$156	$134	$113	$91	$72	$54	$36	$18
$2,500	$2,540	$225	$203	$182	$160	$139	$117	$96	$76	$58	$40	$22
$2,540	$2,580	$230	$208	$187	$165	$144	$122	$101	$80	$62	$44	$26
$2,580	$2,620	$234	$213	$191	$170	$148	$127	$105	$84	$66	$48	$30
$2,620	$2,660	$239	$218	$196	$175	$153	$132	$110	$89	$70	$52	$34
$2,660	$2,700	$244	$223	$201	$180	$158	$137	$115	$94	$74	$56	$38
$2,700	$2,740	$249	$227	$206	$184	$163	$141	$120	$98	$78	$60	$42
$2,740	$2,780	$254	$232	$211	$189	$168	$146	$125	$103	$82	$64	$46
$2,780	$2,820	$258	$237	$215	$194	$172	$151	$129	$108	$86	$68	$50
$2,820	$2,860	$263	$242	$220	$199	$177	$156	$134	$113	$91	$72	$54
$2,860	$2,900	$268	$247	$225	$204	$182	$161	$139	$118	$96	$76	$58
$2,900	$2,940	$273	$251	$230	$208	$187	$165	$144	$122	$101	$80	$62
$2,940	$2,980	$278	$256	$235	$213	$192	$170	$149	$127	$106	$84	$66
$2,980	$3,020	$282	$261	$239	$218	$196	$175	$153	$132	$110	$89	$70
$3,020	$3,060	$287	$266	$244	$223	$201	$180	$158	$137	$115	$94	$74
$3,060	$3,100	$292	$271	$249	$228	$206	$185	$163	$142	$120	$99	$78
$3,100	$3,140	$297	$275	$254	$232	$211	$189	$168	$146	$125	$103	$82
$3,140	$3,180	$302	$280	$259	$237	$216	$194	$173	$151	$130	$108	$87
$3,180	$3,220	$306	$285	$263	$242	$220	$199	$177	$156	$134	$113	$91
$3,220	$3,260	$311	$290	$268	$247	$225	$204	$182	$161	$139	$118	$96
$3,260	$3,300	$316	$295	$273	$252	$230	$209	$187	$166	$144	$123	$101
$3,300	$3,340	$321	$299	$278	$256	$235	$213	$192	$170	$149	$127	$106

2021 Wage Bracket Method Tables for Manual Payroll Systems With Forms W-4 From 2019 or Earlier

SEMIMONTHLY Payroll Period

If the **Wage Amount** (line 1a) is		SINGLE Persons										
		And the number of allowances is:										
At least	But less than	0	1	2	3	4	5	6	7	8	9	10
		The Tentative Withholding Amount is:										
$0	$165	$0	$0	$0	$0	$0	$0	$0	$0	$0	$0	$0
$165	$175	$1	$0	$0	$0	$0	$0	$0	$0	$0	$0	$0
$175	$185	$2	$0	$0	$0	$0	$0	$0	$0	$0	$0	$0
$185	$195	$3	$0	$0	$0	$0	$0	$0	$0	$0	$0	$0
$195	$205	$4	$0	$0	$0	$0	$0	$0	$0	$0	$0	$0
$205	$215	$5	$0	$0	$0	$0	$0	$0	$0	$0	$0	$0
$215	$225	$6	$0	$0	$0	$0	$0	$0	$0	$0	$0	$0
$225	$235	$7	$0	$0	$0	$0	$0	$0	$0	$0	$0	$0
$235	$245	$8	$0	$0	$0	$0	$0	$0	$0	$0	$0	$0
$245	$255	$9	$0	$0	$0	$0	$0	$0	$0	$0	$0	$0
$255	$265	$10	$0	$0	$0	$0	$0	$0	$0	$0	$0	$0
$265	$275	$11	$0	$0	$0	$0	$0	$0	$0	$0	$0	$0
$275	$285	$12	$0	$0	$0	$0	$0	$0	$0	$0	$0	$0
$285	$295	$13	$0	$0	$0	$0	$0	$0	$0	$0	$0	$0
$295	$305	$14	$0	$0	$0	$0	$0	$0	$0	$0	$0	$0
$305	$315	$15	$0	$0	$0	$0	$0	$0	$0	$0	$0	$0
$315	$325	$16	$0	$0	$0	$0	$0	$0	$0	$0	$0	$0
$325	$335	$17	$0	$0	$0	$0	$0	$0	$0	$0	$0	$0
$335	$345	$18	$0	$0	$0	$0	$0	$0	$0	$0	$0	$0
$345	$355	$19	$1	$0	$0	$0	$0	$0	$0	$0	$0	$0
$355	$365	$20	$2	$0	$0	$0	$0	$0	$0	$0	$0	$0
$365	$375	$21	$3	$0	$0	$0	$0	$0	$0	$0	$0	$0
$375	$385	$22	$4	$0	$0	$0	$0	$0	$0	$0	$0	$0
$385	$395	$23	$5	$0	$0	$0	$0	$0	$0	$0	$0	$0
$395	$405	$24	$6	$0	$0	$0	$0	$0	$0	$0	$0	$0
$405	$415	$25	$7	$0	$0	$0	$0	$0	$0	$0	$0	$0
$415	$425	$26	$8	$0	$0	$0	$0	$0	$0	$0	$0	$0
$425	$435	$27	$9	$0	$0	$0	$0	$0	$0	$0	$0	$0
$435	$445	$28	$10	$0	$0	$0	$0	$0	$0	$0	$0	$0
$445	$455	$29	$11	$0	$0	$0	$0	$0	$0	$0	$0	$0
$455	$465	$30	$12	$0	$0	$0	$0	$0	$0	$0	$0	$0
$465	$475	$31	$13	$0	$0	$0	$0	$0	$0	$0	$0	$0
$475	$485	$32	$14	$0	$0	$0	$0	$0	$0	$0	$0	$0
$485	$495	$33	$15	$0	$0	$0	$0	$0	$0	$0	$0	$0
$495	$505	$34	$16	$0	$0	$0	$0	$0	$0	$0	$0	$0
$505	$515	$35	$17	$0	$0	$0	$0	$0	$0	$0	$0	$0
$515	$525	$36	$18	$0	$0	$0	$0	$0	$0	$0	$0	$0
$525	$535	$37	$19	$1	$0	$0	$0	$0	$0	$0	$0	$0
$535	$545	$38	$20	$2	$0	$0	$0	$0	$0	$0	$0	$0
$545	$555	$39	$21	$3	$0	$0	$0	$0	$0	$0	$0	$0
$555	$565	$40	$22	$4	$0	$0	$0	$0	$0	$0	$0	$0
$565	$575	$41	$23	$5	$0	$0	$0	$0	$0	$0	$0	$0
$575	$585	$42	$24	$6	$0	$0	$0	$0	$0	$0	$0	$0
$585	$625	$45	$26	$8	$0	$0	$0	$0	$0	$0	$0	$0
$625	$665	$49	$30	$12	$0	$0	$0	$0	$0	$0	$0	$0
$665	$705	$54	$34	$16	$0	$0	$0	$0	$0	$0	$0	$0
$705	$745	$59	$38	$20	$2	$0	$0	$0	$0	$0	$0	$0
$745	$785	$64	$42	$24	$6	$0	$0	$0	$0	$0	$0	$0
$785	$825	$69	$47	$28	$10	$0	$0	$0	$0	$0	$0	$0
$825	$865	$73	$52	$32	$14	$0	$0	$0	$0	$0	$0	$0
$865	$905	$78	$57	$36	$18	$0	$0	$0	$0	$0	$0	$0

2021 Wage Bracket Method Tables for Manual Payroll Systems With Forms W-4 From 2019 or Earlier
SEMIMONTHLY Payroll Period

If the **Wage Amount** (line 1a) is		SINGLE Persons										
		And the number of allowances is:										
At least	But less than	0	1	2	3	4	5	6	7	8	9	10
		The Tentative Withholding Amount is:										
$905	$945	$83	$61	$40	$22	$4	$0	$0	$0	$0	$0	$0
$945	$985	$88	$66	$45	$26	$8	$0	$0	$0	$0	$0	$0
$985	$1,025	$93	$71	$50	$30	$12	$0	$0	$0	$0	$0	$0
$1,025	$1,065	$97	$76	$54	$34	$16	$0	$0	$0	$0	$0	$0
$1,065	$1,105	$102	$81	$59	$38	$20	$2	$0	$0	$0	$0	$0
$1,105	$1,145	$107	$85	$64	$42	$24	$6	$0	$0	$0	$0	$0
$1,145	$1,185	$112	$90	$69	$47	$28	$10	$0	$0	$0	$0	$0
$1,185	$1,225	$117	$95	$74	$52	$32	$14	$0	$0	$0	$0	$0
$1,225	$1,265	$121	$100	$78	$57	$36	$18	$1	$0	$0	$0	$0
$1,265	$1,305	$126	$105	$83	$62	$40	$22	$5	$0	$0	$0	$0
$1,305	$1,345	$131	$109	$88	$66	$45	$26	$9	$0	$0	$0	$0
$1,345	$1,385	$136	$114	$93	$71	$50	$30	$13	$0	$0	$0	$0
$1,385	$1,425	$141	$119	$98	$76	$55	$34	$17	$0	$0	$0	$0
$1,425	$1,465	$145	$124	$102	$81	$59	$38	$21	$3	$0	$0	$0
$1,465	$1,505	$150	$129	$107	$86	$64	$43	$25	$7	$0	$0	$0
$1,505	$1,545	$155	$133	$112	$90	$69	$47	$29	$11	$0	$0	$0
$1,545	$1,585	$160	$138	$117	$95	$74	$52	$33	$15	$0	$0	$0
$1,585	$1,625	$165	$143	$122	$100	$79	$57	$37	$19	$1	$0	$0
$1,625	$1,665	$169	$148	$126	$105	$83	$62	$41	$23	$5	$0	$0
$1,665	$1,705	$174	$153	$131	$110	$88	$67	$45	$27	$9	$0	$0
$1,705	$1,745	$179	$157	$136	$114	$93	$71	$50	$31	$13	$0	$0
$1,745	$1,785	$184	$162	$141	$119	$98	$76	$55	$35	$17	$0	$0
$1,785	$1,825	$189	$167	$146	$124	$103	$81	$60	$39	$21	$3	$0
$1,825	$1,865	$193	$172	$150	$129	$107	$86	$64	$43	$25	$7	$0
$1,865	$1,905	$201	$177	$155	$134	$112	$91	$69	$48	$29	$11	$0
$1,905	$1,945	$210	$181	$160	$138	$117	$95	$74	$52	$33	$15	$0
$1,945	$1,985	$219	$186	$165	$143	$122	$100	$79	$57	$37	$19	$1
$1,985	$2,025	$228	$191	$170	$148	$127	$105	$84	$62	$41	$23	$5
$2,025	$2,065	$237	$197	$174	$153	$131	$110	$88	$67	$45	$27	$9
$2,065	$2,105	$245	$206	$179	$158	$136	$115	$93	$72	$50	$31	$13
$2,105	$2,145	$254	$215	$184	$162	$141	$119	$98	$76	$55	$35	$17
$2,145	$2,185	$263	$224	$189	$167	$146	$124	$103	$81	$60	$39	$21
$2,185	$2,225	$272	$232	$194	$172	$151	$129	$108	$86	$65	$43	$25
$2,225	$2,265	$281	$241	$202	$177	$155	$134	$112	$91	$69	$48	$29
$2,265	$2,305	$289	$250	$211	$182	$160	$139	$117	$96	$74	$53	$33
$2,305	$2,345	$298	$259	$219	$186	$165	$143	$122	$100	$79	$57	$37
$2,345	$2,385	$307	$268	$228	$191	$170	$148	$127	$105	$84	$62	$41
$2,385	$2,425	$316	$276	$237	$197	$175	$153	$132	$110	$89	$67	$46
$2,425	$2,465	$325	$285	$246	$206	$179	$158	$136	$115	$93	$72	$50
$2,465	$2,505	$333	$294	$255	$215	$184	$163	$141	$120	$98	$77	$55
$2,505	$2,545	$342	$303	$263	$224	$189	$167	$146	$124	$103	$81	$60
$2,545	$2,585	$351	$312	$272	$233	$194	$172	$151	$129	$108	$86	$65
$2,585	$2,625	$360	$320	$281	$241	$202	$177	$156	$134	$113	$91	$70
$2,625	$2,665	$369	$329	$290	$250	$211	$182	$160	$139	$117	$96	$74
$2,665	$2,705	$377	$338	$299	$259	$220	$187	$165	$144	$122	$101	$79
$2,705	$2,745	$386	$347	$307	$268	$228	$191	$170	$148	$127	$105	$84
$2,745	$2,785	$395	$356	$316	$277	$237	$198	$175	$153	$132	$110	$89
$2,785	$2,825	$404	$364	$325	$285	$246	$207	$180	$158	$137	$115	$94
$2,825	$2,865	$413	$373	$334	$294	$255	$215	$184	$163	$141	$120	$98
$2,865	$2,905	$421	$382	$343	$303	$264	$224	$189	$168	$146	$125	$103
$2,905	$2,945	$430	$391	$351	$312	$272	$233	$194	$172	$151	$129	$108

2021 Wage Bracket Method Tables for Manual Payroll Systems With Forms W-4 From 2019 or Earlier
SEMIMONTHLY Payroll Period

If the **Wage Amount** (line 1a) is		SINGLE Persons										
		And the number of allowances is:										
At least	But less than	0	1	2	3	4	5	6	7	8	9	10
		The Tentative Withholding Amount is:										
$2,945	$2,985	$439	$400	$360	$321	$281	$242	$202	$177	$156	$134	$113
$2,985	$3,025	$448	$408	$369	$329	$290	$251	$211	$182	$161	$139	$118
$3,025	$3,065	$457	$417	$378	$338	$299	$259	$220	$187	$165	$144	$122
$3,065	$3,105	$465	$426	$387	$347	$308	$268	$229	$192	$170	$149	$127
$3,105	$3,145	$474	$435	$395	$356	$316	$277	$238	$198	$175	$153	$132
$3,145	$3,185	$483	$444	$404	$365	$325	$286	$246	$207	$180	$158	$137
$3,185	$3,225	$492	$452	$413	$373	$334	$295	$255	$216	$185	$163	$142
$3,225	$3,265	$501	$461	$422	$382	$343	$303	$264	$225	$189	$168	$146
$3,265	$3,305	$509	$470	$431	$391	$352	$312	$273	$233	$194	$173	$151
$3,305	$3,345	$518	$479	$439	$400	$360	$321	$282	$242	$203	$177	$156
$3,345	$3,385	$527	$488	$448	$409	$369	$330	$290	$251	$212	$182	$161
$3,385	$3,425	$536	$496	$457	$417	$378	$339	$299	$260	$220	$187	$166
$3,425	$3,465	$545	$505	$466	$426	$387	$347	$308	$269	$229	$192	$170
$3,465	$3,505	$553	$514	$475	$435	$396	$356	$317	$277	$238	$199	$175
$3,505	$3,545	$562	$523	$483	$444	$404	$365	$326	$286	$247	$207	$180
$3,545	$3,585	$571	$532	$492	$453	$413	$374	$334	$295	$256	$216	$185
$3,585	$3,625	$580	$540	$501	$461	$422	$383	$343	$304	$264	$225	$190
$3,625	$3,665	$589	$549	$510	$470	$431	$391	$352	$313	$273	$234	$194
$3,665	$3,705	$597	$558	$519	$479	$440	$400	$361	$321	$282	$243	$203
$3,705	$3,745	$606	$567	$527	$488	$448	$409	$370	$330	$291	$251	$212
$3,745	$3,785	$615	$576	$536	$497	$457	$418	$378	$339	$300	$260	$221
$3,785	$3,825	$625	$584	$545	$505	$466	$427	$387	$348	$308	$269	$230
$3,825	$3,865	$634	$593	$554	$514	$475	$435	$396	$357	$317	$278	$238
$3,865	$3,905	$644	$602	$563	$523	$484	$444	$405	$365	$326	$287	$247
$3,905	$3,945	$653	$611	$571	$532	$492	$453	$414	$374	$335	$295	$256
$3,945	$3,985	$663	$620	$580	$541	$501	$462	$422	$383	$344	$304	$265
$3,985	$4,025	$673	$630	$589	$549	$510	$471	$431	$392	$352	$313	$274
$4,025	$4,065	$682	$639	$598	$558	$519	$479	$440	$401	$361	$322	$282

2021 Wage Bracket Method Tables for Manual Payroll Systems With Forms W-4 From 2019 or Earlier

MONTHLY Payroll Period

If the Wage Amount (line 1a) is		MARRIED Persons										
		And the number of allowances is:										
At least	But less than	0	1	2	3	4	5	6	7	8	9	10
		The Tentative Withholding Amount is:										
$0	$1,020	$0	$0	$0	$0	$0	$0	$0	$0	$0	$0	$0
$1,020	$1,060	$2	$0	$0	$0	$0	$0	$0	$0	$0	$0	$0
$1,060	$1,100	$6	$0	$0	$0	$0	$0	$0	$0	$0	$0	$0
$1,100	$1,140	$10	$0	$0	$0	$0	$0	$0	$0	$0	$0	$0
$1,140	$1,180	$14	$0	$0	$0	$0	$0	$0	$0	$0	$0	$0
$1,180	$1,220	$18	$0	$0	$0	$0	$0	$0	$0	$0	$0	$0
$1,220	$1,260	$22	$0	$0	$0	$0	$0	$0	$0	$0	$0	$0
$1,260	$1,300	$26	$0	$0	$0	$0	$0	$0	$0	$0	$0	$0
$1,300	$1,340	$30	$0	$0	$0	$0	$0	$0	$0	$0	$0	$0
$1,340	$1,380	$34	$0	$0	$0	$0	$0	$0	$0	$0	$0	$0
$1,380	$1,420	$38	$3	$0	$0	$0	$0	$0	$0	$0	$0	$0
$1,420	$1,460	$42	$7	$0	$0	$0	$0	$0	$0	$0	$0	$0
$1,460	$1,500	$46	$11	$0	$0	$0	$0	$0	$0	$0	$0	$0
$1,500	$1,540	$50	$15	$0	$0	$0	$0	$0	$0	$0	$0	$0
$1,540	$1,580	$54	$19	$0	$0	$0	$0	$0	$0	$0	$0	$0
$1,580	$1,620	$58	$23	$0	$0	$0	$0	$0	$0	$0	$0	$0
$1,620	$1,660	$62	$27	$0	$0	$0	$0	$0	$0	$0	$0	$0
$1,660	$1,700	$66	$31	$0	$0	$0	$0	$0	$0	$0	$0	$0
$1,700	$1,740	$70	$35	$0	$0	$0	$0	$0	$0	$0	$0	$0
$1,740	$1,780	$74	$39	$3	$0	$0	$0	$0	$0	$0	$0	$0
$1,780	$1,820	$78	$43	$7	$0	$0	$0	$0	$0	$0	$0	$0
$1,820	$1,860	$82	$47	$11	$0	$0	$0	$0	$0	$0	$0	$0
$1,860	$1,900	$86	$51	$15	$0	$0	$0	$0	$0	$0	$0	$0
$1,900	$1,940	$90	$55	$19	$0	$0	$0	$0	$0	$0	$0	$0
$1,940	$1,980	$94	$59	$23	$0	$0	$0	$0	$0	$0	$0	$0
$1,980	$2,020	$98	$63	$27	$0	$0	$0	$0	$0	$0	$0	$0
$2,020	$2,060	$102	$67	$31	$0	$0	$0	$0	$0	$0	$0	$0
$2,060	$2,100	$106	$71	$35	$0	$0	$0	$0	$0	$0	$0	$0
$2,100	$2,140	$110	$75	$39	$3	$0	$0	$0	$0	$0	$0	$0
$2,140	$2,180	$114	$79	$43	$7	$0	$0	$0	$0	$0	$0	$0
$2,180	$2,220	$118	$83	$47	$11	$0	$0	$0	$0	$0	$0	$0
$2,220	$2,260	$122	$87	$51	$15	$0	$0	$0	$0	$0	$0	$0
$2,260	$2,300	$126	$91	$55	$19	$0	$0	$0	$0	$0	$0	$0
$2,300	$2,340	$130	$95	$59	$23	$0	$0	$0	$0	$0	$0	$0
$2,340	$2,380	$134	$99	$63	$27	$0	$0	$0	$0	$0	$0	$0
$2,380	$2,420	$138	$103	$67	$31	$0	$0	$0	$0	$0	$0	$0
$2,420	$2,460	$142	$107	$71	$35	$0	$0	$0	$0	$0	$0	$0
$2,460	$2,500	$146	$111	$75	$39	$3	$0	$0	$0	$0	$0	$0
$2,500	$2,540	$150	$115	$79	$43	$7	$0	$0	$0	$0	$0	$0
$2,540	$2,580	$154	$119	$83	$47	$11	$0	$0	$0	$0	$0	$0
$2,580	$2,620	$158	$123	$87	$51	$15	$0	$0	$0	$0	$0	$0
$2,620	$2,660	$162	$127	$91	$55	$19	$0	$0	$0	$0	$0	$0
$2,660	$2,700	$166	$131	$95	$59	$23	$0	$0	$0	$0	$0	$0
$2,700	$2,760	$172	$136	$100	$64	$28	$0	$0	$0	$0	$0	$0
$2,760	$2,820	$180	$142	$106	$70	$34	$0	$0	$0	$0	$0	$0
$2,820	$2,880	$187	$148	$112	$76	$40	$4	$0	$0	$0	$0	$0
$2,880	$2,940	$194	$154	$118	$82	$46	$10	$0	$0	$0	$0	$0
$2,940	$3,000	$201	$160	$124	$88	$52	$16	$0	$0	$0	$0	$0
$3,000	$3,060	$208	$166	$130	$94	$58	$22	$0	$0	$0	$0	$0
$3,060	$3,120	$216	$173	$136	$100	$64	$28	$0	$0	$0	$0	$0
$3,120	$3,180	$223	$180	$142	$106	$70	$34	$0	$0	$0	$0	$0

2021 Wage Bracket Method Tables for Manual Payroll Systems With Forms W-4 From 2019 or Earlier

MONTHLY Payroll Period

If the **Wage Amount** (line 1a) is		**MARRIED** Persons										
		And the number of allowances is:										
At least	But less than	0	1	2	3	4	5	6	7	8	9	10
		The Tentative Withholding Amount is:										
$3,180	$3,240	$230	$187	$148	$112	$76	$40	$4	$0	$0	$0	$0
$3,240	$3,300	$237	$194	$154	$118	$82	$46	$10	$0	$0	$0	$0
$3,300	$3,360	$244	$201	$160	$124	$88	$52	$16	$0	$0	$0	$0
$3,360	$3,420	$252	$209	$166	$130	$94	$58	$22	$0	$0	$0	$0
$3,420	$3,480	$259	$216	$173	$136	$100	$64	$28	$0	$0	$0	$0
$3,480	$3,540	$266	$223	$180	$142	$106	$70	$34	$0	$0	$0	$0
$3,540	$3,600	$273	$230	$187	$148	$112	$76	$40	$5	$0	$0	$0
$3,600	$3,660	$280	$237	$194	$154	$118	$82	$46	$11	$0	$0	$0
$3,660	$3,720	$288	$245	$202	$160	$124	$88	$52	$17	$0	$0	$0
$3,720	$3,780	$295	$252	$209	$166	$130	$94	$58	$23	$0	$0	$0
$3,780	$3,840	$302	$259	$216	$173	$136	$100	$64	$29	$0	$0	$0
$3,840	$3,900	$309	$266	$223	$180	$142	$106	$70	$35	$0	$0	$0
$3,900	$3,960	$316	$273	$230	$187	$148	$112	$76	$41	$5	$0	$0
$3,960	$4,020	$324	$281	$238	$195	$154	$118	$82	$47	$11	$0	$0
$4,020	$4,080	$331	$288	$245	$202	$160	$124	$88	$53	$17	$0	$0
$4,080	$4,140	$338	$295	$252	$209	$166	$130	$94	$59	$23	$0	$0
$4,140	$4,200	$345	$302	$259	$216	$173	$136	$100	$65	$29	$0	$0
$4,200	$4,260	$352	$309	$266	$223	$180	$142	$106	$71	$35	$0	$0
$4,260	$4,320	$360	$317	$274	$231	$188	$148	$112	$77	$41	$5	$0
$4,320	$4,380	$367	$324	$281	$238	$195	$154	$118	$83	$47	$11	$0
$4,380	$4,440	$374	$331	$288	$245	$202	$160	$124	$89	$53	$17	$0
$4,440	$4,500	$381	$338	$295	$252	$209	$166	$130	$95	$59	$23	$0
$4,500	$4,560	$388	$345	$302	$259	$216	$173	$136	$101	$65	$29	$0
$4,560	$4,620	$396	$353	$310	$267	$224	$181	$142	$107	$71	$35	$0
$4,620	$4,680	$403	$360	$317	$274	$231	$188	$148	$113	$77	$41	$5
$4,680	$4,740	$410	$367	$324	$281	$238	$195	$154	$119	$83	$47	$11
$4,740	$4,800	$417	$374	$331	$288	$245	$202	$160	$125	$89	$53	$17
$4,800	$4,860	$424	$381	$338	$295	$252	$209	$166	$131	$95	$59	$23
$4,860	$4,920	$432	$389	$346	$303	$260	$217	$174	$137	$101	$65	$29
$4,920	$4,980	$439	$396	$353	$310	$267	$224	$181	$143	$107	$71	$35
$4,980	$5,040	$446	$403	$360	$317	$274	$231	$188	$149	$113	$77	$41
$5,040	$5,100	$453	$410	$367	$324	$281	$238	$195	$155	$119	$83	$47
$5,100	$5,160	$460	$417	$374	$331	$288	$245	$202	$161	$125	$89	$53
$5,160	$5,220	$468	$425	$382	$339	$296	$253	$210	$167	$131	$95	$59
$5,220	$5,280	$475	$432	$389	$346	$303	$260	$217	$174	$137	$101	$65
$5,280	$5,340	$482	$439	$396	$353	$310	$267	$224	$181	$143	$107	$71
$5,340	$5,400	$489	$446	$403	$360	$317	$274	$231	$188	$149	$113	$77
$5,400	$5,460	$496	$453	$410	$367	$324	$281	$238	$195	$155	$119	$83
$5,460	$5,520	$504	$461	$418	$375	$332	$289	$246	$203	$161	$125	$89
$5,520	$5,580	$511	$468	$425	$382	$339	$296	$253	$210	$167	$131	$95
$5,580	$5,640	$518	$475	$432	$389	$346	$303	$260	$217	$174	$137	$101
$5,640	$5,700	$525	$482	$439	$396	$353	$310	$267	$224	$181	$143	$107
$5,700	$5,760	$532	$489	$446	$403	$360	$317	$274	$231	$188	$149	$113
$5,760	$5,820	$540	$497	$454	$411	$368	$325	$282	$239	$196	$155	$119
$5,820	$5,880	$547	$504	$461	$418	$375	$332	$289	$246	$203	$161	$125
$5,880	$5,940	$554	$511	$468	$425	$382	$339	$296	$253	$210	$167	$131
$5,940	$6,000	$561	$518	$475	$432	$389	$346	$303	$260	$217	$174	$137
$6,000	$6,060	$568	$525	$482	$439	$396	$353	$310	$267	$224	$181	$143
$6,060	$6,120	$576	$533	$490	$447	$404	$361	$318	$275	$232	$189	$149
$6,120	$6,180	$583	$540	$497	$454	$411	$368	$325	$282	$239	$196	$155
$6,180	$6,240	$590	$547	$504	$461	$418	$375	$332	$289	$246	$203	$161

2021 Wage Bracket Method Tables for Manual Payroll Systems With Forms W-4 From 2019 or Earlier

MONTHLY Payroll Period

If the **Wage Amount** (line 1a) is		**MARRIED** Persons										
		And the number of allowances is:										
At least	But less than	0	1	2	3	4	5	6	7	8	9	10
		The Tentative Withholding Amount is:										
$6,240	$6,300	$597	$554	$511	$468	$425	$382	$339	$296	$253	$210	$167
$6,300	$6,360	$604	$561	$518	$475	$432	$389	$346	$303	$260	$217	$174
$6,360	$6,420	$612	$569	$526	$483	$440	$397	$354	$311	$268	$225	$182
$6,420	$6,480	$619	$576	$533	$490	$447	$404	$361	$318	$275	$232	$189
$6,480	$6,540	$626	$583	$540	$497	$454	$411	$368	$325	$282	$239	$196
$6,540	$6,600	$633	$590	$547	$504	$461	$418	$375	$332	$289	$246	$203
$6,600	$6,660	$640	$597	$554	$511	$468	$425	$382	$339	$296	$253	$210
$6,660	$6,720	$648	$605	$562	$519	$476	$433	$390	$347	$304	$261	$218
$6,720	$6,780	$655	$612	$569	$526	$483	$440	$397	$354	$311	$268	$225
$6,780	$6,840	$662	$619	$576	$533	$490	$447	$404	$361	$318	$275	$232
$6,840	$6,900	$669	$626	$583	$540	$497	$454	$411	$368	$325	$282	$239
$6,900	$6,960	$676	$633	$590	$547	$504	$461	$418	$375	$332	$289	$246
$6,960	$7,020	$684	$641	$598	$555	$512	$469	$426	$383	$340	$297	$254
$7,020	$7,080	$691	$648	$605	$562	$519	$476	$433	$390	$347	$304	$261
$7,080	$7,140	$698	$655	$612	$569	$526	$483	$440	$397	$354	$311	$268
$7,140	$7,200	$705	$662	$619	$576	$533	$490	$447	$404	$361	$318	$275
$7,200	$7,260	$712	$669	$626	$583	$540	$497	$454	$411	$368	$325	$282
$7,260	$7,320	$720	$677	$634	$591	$548	$505	$462	$419	$376	$333	$290
$7,320	$7,380	$727	$684	$641	$598	$555	$512	$469	$426	$383	$340	$297
$7,380	$7,440	$734	$691	$648	$605	$562	$519	$476	$433	$390	$347	$304
$7,440	$7,500	$741	$698	$655	$612	$569	$526	$483	$440	$397	$354	$311
$7,500	$7,560	$748	$705	$662	$619	$576	$533	$490	$447	$404	$361	$318
$7,560	$7,620	$756	$713	$670	$627	$584	$541	$498	$455	$412	$369	$326
$7,620	$7,680	$763	$720	$677	$634	$591	$548	$505	$462	$419	$376	$333
$7,680	$7,740	$770	$727	$684	$641	$598	$555	$512	$469	$426	$383	$340
$7,740	$7,800	$777	$734	$691	$648	$605	$562	$519	$476	$433	$390	$347
$7,800	$7,870	$791	$742	$699	$656	$613	$570	$527	$484	$441	$398	$355
$7,870	$7,940	$807	$750	$707	$664	$621	$578	$535	$492	$449	$406	$363
$7,940	$8,010	$822	$759	$716	$673	$630	$587	$544	$501	$458	$415	$372
$8,010	$8,080	$838	$767	$724	$681	$638	$595	$552	$509	$466	$423	$380
$8,080	$8,150	$853	$776	$733	$690	$647	$604	$561	$518	$475	$432	$389
$8,150	$8,220	$868	$790	$741	$698	$655	$612	$569	$526	$483	$440	$397

2021 Wage Bracket Method Tables for Manual Payroll Systems With Forms W-4 From 2019 or Earlier

MONTHLY Payroll Period

If the Wage Amount (line 1a) is		SINGLE Persons										
		And the number of allowances is:										
At least	But less than	0	1	2	3	4	5	6	7	8	9	10
		The Tentative Withholding Amount is:										
$0	$330	$0	$0	$0	$0	$0	$0	$0	$0	$0	$0	$0
$330	$360	$2	$0	$0	$0	$0	$0	$0	$0	$0	$0	$0
$360	$390	$5	$0	$0	$0	$0	$0	$0	$0	$0	$0	$0
$390	$420	$8	$0	$0	$0	$0	$0	$0	$0	$0	$0	$0
$420	$450	$11	$0	$0	$0	$0	$0	$0	$0	$0	$0	$0
$450	$480	$14	$0	$0	$0	$0	$0	$0	$0	$0	$0	$0
$480	$510	$17	$0	$0	$0	$0	$0	$0	$0	$0	$0	$0
$510	$540	$20	$0	$0	$0	$0	$0	$0	$0	$0	$0	$0
$540	$570	$23	$0	$0	$0	$0	$0	$0	$0	$0	$0	$0
$570	$600	$26	$0	$0	$0	$0	$0	$0	$0	$0	$0	$0
$600	$630	$29	$0	$0	$0	$0	$0	$0	$0	$0	$0	$0
$630	$660	$32	$0	$0	$0	$0	$0	$0	$0	$0	$0	$0
$660	$690	$35	$0	$0	$0	$0	$0	$0	$0	$0	$0	$0
$690	$720	$38	$2	$0	$0	$0	$0	$0	$0	$0	$0	$0
$720	$750	$41	$5	$0	$0	$0	$0	$0	$0	$0	$0	$0
$750	$780	$44	$8	$0	$0	$0	$0	$0	$0	$0	$0	$0
$780	$810	$47	$11	$0	$0	$0	$0	$0	$0	$0	$0	$0
$810	$840	$50	$14	$0	$0	$0	$0	$0	$0	$0	$0	$0
$840	$870	$53	$17	$0	$0	$0	$0	$0	$0	$0	$0	$0
$870	$900	$56	$20	$0	$0	$0	$0	$0	$0	$0	$0	$0
$900	$930	$59	$23	$0	$0	$0	$0	$0	$0	$0	$0	$0
$930	$960	$62	$26	$0	$0	$0	$0	$0	$0	$0	$0	$0
$960	$990	$65	$29	$0	$0	$0	$0	$0	$0	$0	$0	$0
$990	$1,020	$68	$32	$0	$0	$0	$0	$0	$0	$0	$0	$0
$1,020	$1,050	$71	$35	$0	$0	$0	$0	$0	$0	$0	$0	$0
$1,050	$1,080	$74	$38	$2	$0	$0	$0	$0	$0	$0	$0	$0
$1,080	$1,110	$77	$41	$5	$0	$0	$0	$0	$0	$0	$0	$0
$1,110	$1,140	$80	$44	$8	$0	$0	$0	$0	$0	$0	$0	$0
$1,140	$1,170	$83	$47	$11	$0	$0	$0	$0	$0	$0	$0	$0
$1,170	$1,230	$88	$51	$15	$0	$0	$0	$0	$0	$0	$0	$0
$1,230	$1,290	$95	$57	$21	$0	$0	$0	$0	$0	$0	$0	$0
$1,290	$1,350	$102	$63	$27	$0	$0	$0	$0	$0	$0	$0	$0
$1,350	$1,410	$110	$69	$33	$0	$0	$0	$0	$0	$0	$0	$0
$1,410	$1,470	$117	$75	$39	$4	$0	$0	$0	$0	$0	$0	$0
$1,470	$1,530	$124	$81	$45	$10	$0	$0	$0	$0	$0	$0	$0
$1,530	$1,590	$131	$88	$51	$16	$0	$0	$0	$0	$0	$0	$0
$1,590	$1,650	$138	$95	$57	$22	$0	$0	$0	$0	$0	$0	$0
$1,650	$1,710	$146	$103	$63	$28	$0	$0	$0	$0	$0	$0	$0
$1,710	$1,770	$153	$110	$69	$34	$0	$0	$0	$0	$0	$0	$0
$1,770	$1,830	$160	$117	$75	$40	$4	$0	$0	$0	$0	$0	$0
$1,830	$1,890	$167	$124	$81	$46	$10	$0	$0	$0	$0	$0	$0
$1,890	$1,950	$174	$131	$88	$52	$16	$0	$0	$0	$0	$0	$0
$1,950	$2,010	$182	$139	$96	$58	$22	$0	$0	$0	$0	$0	$0
$2,010	$2,070	$189	$146	$103	$64	$28	$0	$0	$0	$0	$0	$0
$2,070	$2,130	$196	$153	$110	$70	$34	$0	$0	$0	$0	$0	$0
$2,130	$2,190	$203	$160	$117	$76	$40	$4	$0	$0	$0	$0	$0
$2,190	$2,250	$210	$167	$124	$82	$46	$10	$0	$0	$0	$0	$0
$2,250	$2,310	$218	$175	$132	$89	$52	$16	$0	$0	$0	$0	$0
$2,310	$2,370	$225	$182	$139	$96	$58	$22	$0	$0	$0	$0	$0
$2,370	$2,430	$232	$189	$146	$103	$64	$28	$0	$0	$0	$0	$0
$2,430	$2,490	$239	$196	$153	$110	$70	$34	$0	$0	$0	$0	$0

2021 Wage Bracket Method Tables for Manual Payroll Systems With Forms W-4 From 2019 or Earlier

MONTHLY Payroll Period

If the **Wage Amount** (line 1a) is		SINGLE Persons										
		And the number of allowances is:										
At least	But less than	0	1	2	3	4	5	6	7	8	9	10
		The Tentative Withholding Amount is:										
$2,490	$2,550	$246	$203	$160	$117	$76	$40	$4	$0	$0	$0	$0
$2,550	$2,610	$254	$211	$168	$125	$82	$46	$10	$0	$0	$0	$0
$2,610	$2,670	$261	$218	$175	$132	$89	$52	$16	$0	$0	$0	$0
$2,670	$2,730	$268	$225	$182	$139	$96	$58	$22	$0	$0	$0	$0
$2,730	$2,790	$275	$232	$189	$146	$103	$64	$28	$0	$0	$0	$0
$2,790	$2,850	$282	$239	$196	$153	$110	$70	$34	$0	$0	$0	$0
$2,850	$2,910	$290	$247	$204	$161	$118	$76	$40	$4	$0	$0	$0
$2,910	$2,970	$297	$254	$211	$168	$125	$82	$46	$10	$0	$0	$0
$2,970	$3,030	$304	$261	$218	$175	$132	$89	$52	$16	$0	$0	$0
$3,030	$3,090	$311	$268	$225	$182	$139	$96	$58	$22	$0	$0	$0
$3,090	$3,150	$318	$275	$232	$189	$146	$103	$64	$28	$0	$0	$0
$3,150	$3,210	$326	$283	$240	$197	$154	$111	$70	$34	$0	$0	$0
$3,210	$3,270	$333	$290	$247	$204	$161	$118	$76	$40	$4	$0	$0
$3,270	$3,330	$340	$297	$254	$211	$168	$125	$82	$46	$10	$0	$0
$3,330	$3,390	$347	$304	$261	$218	$175	$132	$89	$52	$16	$0	$0
$3,390	$3,450	$354	$311	$268	$225	$182	$139	$96	$58	$22	$0	$0
$3,450	$3,510	$362	$319	$276	$233	$190	$147	$104	$64	$28	$0	$0
$3,510	$3,570	$369	$326	$283	$240	$197	$154	$111	$70	$34	$0	$0
$3,570	$3,630	$376	$333	$290	$247	$204	$161	$118	$76	$40	$5	$0
$3,630	$3,690	$383	$340	$297	$254	$211	$168	$125	$82	$46	$11	$0
$3,690	$3,750	$392	$347	$304	$261	$218	$175	$132	$89	$52	$17	$0
$3,750	$3,820	$406	$355	$312	$269	$226	$183	$140	$97	$59	$23	$0
$3,820	$3,890	$421	$364	$321	$278	$235	$192	$149	$106	$66	$30	$0
$3,890	$3,960	$437	$372	$329	$286	$243	$200	$157	$114	$73	$37	$1
$3,960	$4,030	$452	$380	$337	$294	$251	$208	$165	$122	$80	$44	$8
$4,030	$4,100	$468	$389	$346	$303	$260	$217	$174	$131	$88	$51	$15
$4,100	$4,170	$483	$404	$354	$311	$268	$225	$182	$139	$96	$58	$22
$4,170	$4,240	$498	$420	$363	$320	$277	$234	$191	$148	$105	$65	$29
$4,240	$4,310	$514	$435	$371	$328	$285	$242	$199	$156	$113	$72	$36
$4,310	$4,380	$529	$450	$379	$336	$293	$250	$207	$164	$121	$79	$43
$4,380	$4,450	$545	$466	$388	$345	$302	$259	$216	$173	$130	$87	$50
$4,450	$4,520	$560	$481	$402	$353	$310	$267	$224	$181	$138	$95	$57
$4,520	$4,590	$575	$497	$418	$362	$319	$276	$233	$190	$147	$104	$64
$4,590	$4,660	$591	$512	$433	$370	$327	$284	$241	$198	$155	$112	$71
$4,660	$4,730	$606	$527	$449	$378	$335	$292	$249	$206	$163	$120	$78
$4,730	$4,800	$622	$543	$464	$387	$344	$301	$258	$215	$172	$129	$86
$4,800	$4,870	$637	$558	$479	$400	$352	$309	$266	$223	$180	$137	$94
$4,870	$4,940	$652	$574	$495	$416	$361	$318	$275	$232	$189	$146	$103
$4,940	$5,010	$668	$589	$510	$431	$369	$326	$283	$240	$197	$154	$111
$5,010	$5,080	$683	$604	$526	$447	$377	$334	$291	$248	$205	$162	$119
$5,080	$5,150	$699	$620	$541	$462	$386	$343	$300	$257	$214	$171	$128
$5,150	$5,220	$714	$635	$556	$477	$399	$351	$308	$265	$222	$179	$136
$5,220	$5,290	$729	$651	$572	$493	$414	$360	$317	$274	$231	$188	$145
$5,290	$5,360	$745	$666	$587	$508	$429	$368	$325	$282	$239	$196	$153
$5,360	$5,430	$760	$681	$603	$524	$445	$376	$333	$290	$247	$204	$161
$5,430	$5,500	$776	$697	$618	$539	$460	$385	$342	$299	$256	$213	$170
$5,500	$5,570	$791	$712	$633	$554	$476	$397	$350	$307	$264	$221	$178
$5,570	$5,640	$806	$728	$649	$570	$491	$412	$359	$316	$273	$230	$187
$5,640	$5,710	$822	$743	$664	$585	$506	$428	$367	$324	$281	$238	$195
$5,710	$5,780	$837	$758	$680	$601	$522	$443	$375	$332	$289	$246	$203
$5,780	$5,850	$853	$774	$695	$616	$537	$458	$384	$341	$298	$255	$212

2021 Wage Bracket Method Tables for Manual Payroll Systems With Forms W-4 From 2019 or Earlier

MONTHLY Payroll Period

If the **Wage Amount** (line 1a) is		SINGLE Persons										
		And the number of allowances is:										
At least	But less than	0	1	2	3	4	5	6	7	8	9	10
		The Tentative Withholding Amount is:										
$5,850	$5,920	$868	$789	$710	$631	$553	$474	$395	$349	$306	$263	$220
$5,920	$5,990	$883	$805	$726	$647	$568	$489	$410	$358	$315	$272	$229
$5,990	$6,060	$899	$820	$741	$662	$583	$505	$426	$366	$323	$280	$237
$6,060	$6,130	$914	$835	$757	$678	$599	$520	$441	$374	$331	$288	$245
$6,130	$6,200	$930	$851	$772	$693	$614	$535	$457	$383	$340	$297	$254
$6,200	$6,270	$945	$866	$787	$708	$630	$551	$472	$393	$348	$305	$262
$6,270	$6,340	$960	$882	$803	$724	$645	$566	$487	$409	$357	$314	$271
$6,340	$6,410	$976	$897	$818	$739	$660	$582	$503	$424	$365	$322	$279
$6,410	$6,480	$991	$912	$834	$755	$676	$597	$518	$439	$373	$330	$287
$6,480	$6,550	$1,007	$928	$849	$770	$691	$612	$534	$455	$382	$339	$296
$6,550	$6,620	$1,022	$943	$864	$785	$707	$628	$549	$470	$391	$347	$304
$6,620	$6,690	$1,037	$959	$880	$801	$722	$643	$564	$486	$407	$356	$313
$6,690	$6,760	$1,053	$974	$895	$816	$737	$659	$580	$501	$422	$364	$321
$6,760	$6,830	$1,068	$989	$911	$832	$753	$674	$595	$516	$438	$372	$329
$6,830	$6,900	$1,084	$1,005	$926	$847	$768	$689	$611	$532	$453	$381	$338
$6,900	$6,970	$1,099	$1,020	$941	$862	$784	$705	$626	$547	$468	$389	$346
$6,970	$7,040	$1,114	$1,036	$957	$878	$799	$720	$641	$563	$484	$405	$355
$7,040	$7,110	$1,130	$1,051	$972	$893	$814	$736	$657	$578	$499	$420	$363
$7,110	$7,180	$1,145	$1,066	$988	$909	$830	$751	$672	$593	$515	$436	$371
$7,180	$7,250	$1,161	$1,082	$1,003	$924	$845	$766	$688	$609	$530	$451	$380
$7,250	$7,320	$1,176	$1,097	$1,018	$939	$861	$782	$703	$624	$545	$466	$388
$7,320	$7,390	$1,191	$1,113	$1,034	$955	$876	$797	$718	$640	$561	$482	$403
$7,390	$7,460	$1,207	$1,128	$1,049	$970	$891	$813	$734	$655	$576	$497	$418
$7,460	$7,530	$1,222	$1,143	$1,065	$986	$907	$828	$749	$670	$592	$513	$434
$7,530	$7,600	$1,238	$1,159	$1,080	$1,001	$922	$843	$765	$686	$607	$528	$449
$7,600	$7,670	$1,255	$1,174	$1,095	$1,016	$938	$859	$780	$701	$622	$543	$465
$7,670	$7,740	$1,272	$1,190	$1,111	$1,032	$953	$874	$795	$717	$638	$559	$480
$7,740	$7,810	$1,289	$1,205	$1,126	$1,047	$968	$890	$811	$732	$653	$574	$495

2021 Wage Bracket Method Tables for Manual Payroll Systems With Forms W-4 From 2019 or Earlier

DAILY Payroll Period

If the **Wage Amount** (line 1a) is		**MARRIED** Persons										
		And the number of allowances is:										
At least	But less than	0	1	2	3	4	5	6	7	8	9	10
		The Tentative Withholding Amount is:										
$0	$50	$0.00	$0.00	$0.00	$0.00	$0.00	$0.00	$0.00	$0.00	$0.00	$0.00	$0.00
$50	$55	$0.60	$0.00	$0.00	$0.00	$0.00	$0.00	$0.00	$0.00	$0.00	$0.00	$0.00
$55	$60	$1.10	$0.00	$0.00	$0.00	$0.00	$0.00	$0.00	$0.00	$0.00	$0.00	$0.00
$60	$65	$1.60	$0.00	$0.00	$0.00	$0.00	$0.00	$0.00	$0.00	$0.00	$0.00	$0.00
$65	$70	$2.10	$0.40	$0.00	$0.00	$0.00	$0.00	$0.00	$0.00	$0.00	$0.00	$0.00
$70	$75	$2.60	$0.90	$0.00	$0.00	$0.00	$0.00	$0.00	$0.00	$0.00	$0.00	$0.00
$75	$80	$3.10	$1.40	$0.00	$0.00	$0.00	$0.00	$0.00	$0.00	$0.00	$0.00	$0.00
$80	$85	$3.60	$1.90	$0.30	$0.00	$0.00	$0.00	$0.00	$0.00	$0.00	$0.00	$0.00
$85	$90	$4.10	$2.40	$0.80	$0.00	$0.00	$0.00	$0.00	$0.00	$0.00	$0.00	$0.00
$90	$95	$4.60	$2.90	$1.30	$0.00	$0.00	$0.00	$0.00	$0.00	$0.00	$0.00	$0.00
$95	$100	$5.10	$3.40	$1.80	$0.10	$0.00	$0.00	$0.00	$0.00	$0.00	$0.00	$0.00
$100	$105	$5.60	$3.90	$2.30	$0.60	$0.00	$0.00	$0.00	$0.00	$0.00	$0.00	$0.00
$105	$110	$6.10	$4.40	$2.80	$1.10	$0.00	$0.00	$0.00	$0.00	$0.00	$0.00	$0.00
$110	$115	$6.60	$4.90	$3.30	$1.60	$0.00	$0.00	$0.00	$0.00	$0.00	$0.00	$0.00
$115	$120	$7.10	$5.40	$3.80	$2.10	$0.40	$0.00	$0.00	$0.00	$0.00	$0.00	$0.00
$120	$125	$7.60	$5.90	$4.30	$2.60	$0.90	$0.00	$0.00	$0.00	$0.00	$0.00	$0.00
$125	$130	$8.10	$6.40	$4.80	$3.10	$1.40	$0.00	$0.00	$0.00	$0.00	$0.00	$0.00
$130	$135	$8.70	$6.90	$5.30	$3.60	$1.90	$0.30	$0.00	$0.00	$0.00	$0.00	$0.00
$135	$140	$9.30	$7.40	$5.80	$4.10	$2.40	$0.80	$0.00	$0.00	$0.00	$0.00	$0.00
$140	$145	$9.90	$8.00	$6.30	$4.60	$2.90	$1.30	$0.00	$0.00	$0.00	$0.00	$0.00
$145	$150	$10.50	$8.60	$6.80	$5.10	$3.40	$1.80	$0.10	$0.00	$0.00	$0.00	$0.00
$150	$155	$11.10	$9.20	$7.30	$5.60	$3.90	$2.30	$0.60	$0.00	$0.00	$0.00	$0.00
$155	$160	$11.70	$9.80	$7.80	$6.10	$4.40	$2.80	$1.10	$0.00	$0.00	$0.00	$0.00
$160	$165	$12.30	$10.40	$8.40	$6.60	$4.90	$3.30	$1.60	$0.00	$0.00	$0.00	$0.00
$165	$170	$12.90	$11.00	$9.00	$7.10	$5.40	$3.80	$2.10	$0.50	$0.00	$0.00	$0.00
$170	$175	$13.50	$11.60	$9.60	$7.60	$5.90	$4.30	$2.60	$1.00	$0.00	$0.00	$0.00
$175	$180	$14.10	$12.20	$10.20	$8.20	$6.40	$4.80	$3.10	$1.50	$0.00	$0.00	$0.00
$180	$185	$14.70	$12.80	$10.80	$8.80	$6.90	$5.30	$3.60	$2.00	$0.30	$0.00	$0.00
$185	$190	$15.30	$13.40	$11.40	$9.40	$7.40	$5.80	$4.10	$2.50	$0.80	$0.00	$0.00
$190	$195	$15.90	$14.00	$12.00	$10.00	$8.00	$6.30	$4.60	$3.00	$1.30	$0.00	$0.00
$195	$200	$16.50	$14.60	$12.60	$10.60	$8.60	$6.80	$5.10	$3.50	$1.80	$0.20	$0.00
$200	$205	$17.10	$15.20	$13.20	$11.20	$9.20	$7.30	$5.60	$4.00	$2.30	$0.70	$0.00
$205	$210	$17.70	$15.80	$13.80	$11.80	$9.80	$7.80	$6.10	$4.50	$2.80	$1.20	$0.00
$210	$215	$18.30	$16.40	$14.40	$12.40	$10.40	$8.40	$6.60	$5.00	$3.30	$1.70	$0.00
$215	$220	$18.90	$17.00	$15.00	$13.00	$11.00	$9.00	$7.10	$5.50	$3.80	$2.20	$0.50
$220	$225	$19.50	$17.60	$15.60	$13.60	$11.60	$9.60	$7.60	$6.00	$4.30	$2.70	$1.00
$225	$230	$20.10	$18.20	$16.20	$14.20	$12.20	$10.20	$8.20	$6.50	$4.80	$3.20	$1.50
$230	$235	$20.70	$18.80	$16.80	$14.80	$12.80	$10.80	$8.80	$7.00	$5.30	$3.70	$2.00
$235	$240	$21.30	$19.40	$17.40	$15.40	$13.40	$11.40	$9.40	$7.50	$5.80	$4.20	$2.50
$240	$245	$21.90	$20.00	$18.00	$16.00	$14.00	$12.00	$10.00	$8.00	$6.30	$4.70	$3.00
$245	$250	$22.50	$20.60	$18.60	$16.60	$14.60	$12.60	$10.60	$8.60	$6.80	$5.20	$3.50
$250	$255	$23.10	$21.20	$19.20	$17.20	$15.20	$13.20	$11.20	$9.20	$7.30	$5.70	$4.00
$255	$260	$23.70	$21.80	$19.80	$17.80	$15.80	$13.80	$11.80	$9.80	$7.90	$6.20	$4.50
$260	$265	$24.30	$22.40	$20.40	$18.40	$16.40	$14.40	$12.40	$10.40	$8.50	$6.70	$5.00
$265	$270	$24.90	$23.00	$21.00	$19.00	$17.00	$15.00	$13.00	$11.00	$9.10	$7.20	$5.50
$270	$275	$25.50	$23.60	$21.60	$19.60	$17.60	$15.60	$13.60	$11.60	$9.70	$7.70	$6.00
$275	$280	$26.10	$24.20	$22.20	$20.20	$18.20	$16.20	$14.20	$12.20	$10.30	$8.30	$6.50
$280	$285	$26.70	$24.80	$22.80	$20.80	$18.80	$16.80	$14.80	$12.80	$10.90	$8.90	$7.00
$285	$290	$27.30	$25.40	$23.40	$21.40	$19.40	$17.40	$15.40	$13.40	$11.50	$9.50	$7.50
$290	$295	$27.90	$26.00	$24.00	$22.00	$20.00	$18.00	$16.00	$14.00	$12.10	$10.10	$8.10
$295	$300	$28.50	$26.60	$24.60	$22.60	$20.60	$18.60	$16.60	$14.60	$12.70	$10.70	$8.70

2021 Wage Bracket Method Tables for Manual Payroll Systems With Forms W-4 From 2019 or Earlier

DAILY Payroll Period

If the **Wage Amount** (line 1a) is		MARRIED Persons										
		And the number of allowances is:										
At least	But less than	0	1	2	3	4	5	6	7	8	9	10
		The Tentative Withholding Amount is:										
$300	$305	$29.10	$27.20	$25.20	$23.20	$21.20	$19.20	$17.20	$15.20	$13.30	$11.30	$9.30
$305	$310	$29.70	$27.80	$25.80	$23.80	$21.80	$19.80	$17.80	$15.80	$13.90	$11.90	$9.90
$310	$315	$30.30	$28.40	$26.40	$24.40	$22.40	$20.40	$18.40	$16.40	$14.50	$12.50	$10.50
$315	$320	$30.90	$29.00	$27.00	$25.00	$23.00	$21.00	$19.00	$17.00	$15.10	$13.10	$11.10
$320	$325	$31.50	$29.60	$27.60	$25.60	$23.60	$21.60	$19.60	$17.60	$15.70	$13.70	$11.70
$325	$330	$32.10	$30.20	$28.20	$26.20	$24.20	$22.20	$20.20	$18.20	$16.30	$14.30	$12.30
$330	$335	$32.70	$30.80	$28.80	$26.80	$24.80	$22.80	$20.80	$18.80	$16.90	$14.90	$12.90
$335	$340	$33.30	$31.40	$29.40	$27.40	$25.40	$23.40	$21.40	$19.40	$17.50	$15.50	$13.50
$340	$345	$33.90	$32.00	$30.00	$28.00	$26.00	$24.00	$22.00	$20.00	$18.10	$16.10	$14.10
$345	$350	$34.50	$32.60	$30.60	$28.60	$26.60	$24.60	$22.60	$20.60	$18.70	$16.70	$14.70
$350	$355	$35.10	$33.20	$31.20	$29.20	$27.20	$25.20	$23.20	$21.20	$19.30	$17.30	$15.30
$355	$360	$35.70	$33.80	$31.80	$29.80	$27.80	$25.80	$23.80	$21.80	$19.90	$17.90	$15.90
$360	$365	$36.70	$34.40	$32.40	$30.40	$28.40	$26.40	$24.40	$22.40	$20.50	$18.50	$16.50
$365	$370	$37.80	$35.00	$33.00	$31.00	$29.00	$27.00	$25.00	$23.00	$21.10	$19.10	$17.10
$370	$375	$38.90	$35.60	$33.60	$31.60	$29.60	$27.60	$25.60	$23.60	$21.70	$19.70	$17.70
$375	$380	$40.00	$36.40	$34.20	$32.20	$30.20	$28.20	$26.20	$24.20	$22.30	$20.30	$18.30
$380	$385	$41.10	$37.50	$34.80	$32.80	$30.80	$28.80	$26.80	$24.80	$22.90	$20.90	$18.90
$385	$390	$42.20	$38.60	$35.40	$33.40	$31.40	$29.40	$27.40	$25.40	$23.50	$21.50	$19.50
$390	$395	$43.30	$39.70	$36.00	$34.00	$32.00	$30.00	$28.00	$26.00	$24.10	$22.10	$20.10
$395	$400	$44.40	$40.80	$37.10	$34.60	$32.60	$30.60	$28.60	$26.60	$24.70	$22.70	$20.70
$400	$405	$45.50	$41.90	$38.20	$35.20	$33.20	$31.20	$29.20	$27.20	$25.30	$23.30	$21.30
$405	$410	$46.60	$43.00	$39.30	$35.80	$33.80	$31.80	$29.80	$27.80	$25.90	$23.90	$21.90
$410	$415	$47.70	$44.10	$40.40	$36.80	$34.40	$32.40	$30.40	$28.40	$26.50	$24.50	$22.50

2021 Wage Bracket Method Tables for Manual Payroll Systems With Forms W-4 From 2019 or Earlier

DAILY Payroll Period

If the **Wage Amount** (line 1a) is		SINGLE Persons										
		And the number of allowances is:										
At least	But less than	0	1	2	3	4	5	6	7	8	9	10
		The Tentative Withholding Amount is:										
$0	$20	$0.00	$0.00	$0.00	$0.00	$0.00	$0.00	$0.00	$0.00	$0.00	$0.00	$0.00
$20	$25	$0.70	$0.00	$0.00	$0.00	$0.00	$0.00	$0.00	$0.00	$0.00	$0.00	$0.00
$25	$30	$1.20	$0.00	$0.00	$0.00	$0.00	$0.00	$0.00	$0.00	$0.00	$0.00	$0.00
$30	$35	$1.70	$0.10	$0.00	$0.00	$0.00	$0.00	$0.00	$0.00	$0.00	$0.00	$0.00
$35	$40	$2.20	$0.60	$0.00	$0.00	$0.00	$0.00	$0.00	$0.00	$0.00	$0.00	$0.00
$40	$45	$2.70	$1.10	$0.00	$0.00	$0.00	$0.00	$0.00	$0.00	$0.00	$0.00	$0.00
$45	$50	$3.20	$1.60	$0.00	$0.00	$0.00	$0.00	$0.00	$0.00	$0.00	$0.00	$0.00
$50	$55	$3.70	$2.10	$0.40	$0.00	$0.00	$0.00	$0.00	$0.00	$0.00	$0.00	$0.00
$55	$60	$4.30	$2.60	$0.90	$0.00	$0.00	$0.00	$0.00	$0.00	$0.00	$0.00	$0.00
$60	$65	$4.90	$3.10	$1.40	$0.00	$0.00	$0.00	$0.00	$0.00	$0.00	$0.00	$0.00
$65	$70	$5.50	$3.60	$1.90	$0.30	$0.00	$0.00	$0.00	$0.00	$0.00	$0.00	$0.00
$70	$75	$6.10	$4.10	$2.40	$0.80	$0.00	$0.00	$0.00	$0.00	$0.00	$0.00	$0.00
$75	$80	$6.70	$4.70	$2.90	$1.30	$0.00	$0.00	$0.00	$0.00	$0.00	$0.00	$0.00
$80	$85	$7.30	$5.30	$3.40	$1.80	$0.10	$0.00	$0.00	$0.00	$0.00	$0.00	$0.00
$85	$90	$7.90	$5.90	$3.90	$2.30	$0.60	$0.00	$0.00	$0.00	$0.00	$0.00	$0.00
$90	$95	$8.50	$6.50	$4.50	$2.80	$1.10	$0.00	$0.00	$0.00	$0.00	$0.00	$0.00
$95	$100	$9.10	$7.10	$5.10	$3.30	$1.60	$0.00	$0.00	$0.00	$0.00	$0.00	$0.00
$100	$105	$9.70	$7.70	$5.70	$3.80	$2.10	$0.50	$0.00	$0.00	$0.00	$0.00	$0.00
$105	$110	$10.30	$8.30	$6.30	$4.40	$2.60	$1.00	$0.00	$0.00	$0.00	$0.00	$0.00
$110	$115	$10.90	$8.90	$6.90	$5.00	$3.10	$1.50	$0.00	$0.00	$0.00	$0.00	$0.00
$115	$120	$11.50	$9.50	$7.50	$5.60	$3.60	$2.00	$0.30	$0.00	$0.00	$0.00	$0.00
$120	$125	$12.10	$10.10	$8.10	$6.20	$4.20	$2.50	$0.80	$0.00	$0.00	$0.00	$0.00
$125	$130	$12.70	$10.70	$8.70	$6.80	$4.80	$3.00	$1.30	$0.00	$0.00	$0.00	$0.00
$130	$135	$13.30	$11.30	$9.30	$7.40	$5.40	$3.50	$1.80	$0.20	$0.00	$0.00	$0.00
$135	$140	$13.90	$11.90	$9.90	$8.00	$6.00	$4.00	$2.30	$0.70	$0.00	$0.00	$0.00
$140	$145	$14.50	$12.50	$10.50	$8.60	$6.60	$4.60	$2.80	$1.20	$0.00	$0.00	$0.00
$145	$150	$15.10	$13.10	$11.10	$9.20	$7.20	$5.20	$3.30	$1.70	$0.00	$0.00	$0.00
$150	$155	$15.70	$13.70	$11.70	$9.80	$7.80	$5.80	$3.80	$2.20	$0.50	$0.00	$0.00
$155	$160	$16.30	$14.30	$12.30	$10.40	$8.40	$6.40	$4.40	$2.70	$1.00	$0.00	$0.00
$160	$165	$16.90	$14.90	$12.90	$11.00	$9.00	$7.00	$5.00	$3.20	$1.50	$0.00	$0.00
$165	$170	$17.50	$15.50	$13.50	$11.60	$9.60	$7.60	$5.60	$3.70	$2.00	$0.30	$0.00
$170	$175	$18.30	$16.10	$14.10	$12.20	$10.20	$8.20	$6.20	$4.20	$2.50	$0.80	$0.00
$175	$180	$19.40	$16.70	$14.70	$12.80	$10.80	$8.80	$6.80	$4.80	$3.00	$1.30	$0.00
$180	$185	$20.50	$17.30	$15.30	$13.40	$11.40	$9.40	$7.40	$5.40	$3.50	$1.80	$0.20
$185	$190	$21.60	$17.90	$15.90	$14.00	$12.00	$10.00	$8.00	$6.00	$4.00	$2.30	$0.70
$190	$195	$22.70	$19.00	$16.50	$14.60	$12.60	$10.60	$8.60	$6.60	$4.60	$2.80	$1.20
$195	$200	$23.80	$20.10	$17.10	$15.20	$13.20	$11.20	$9.20	$7.20	$5.20	$3.30	$1.70
$200	$205	$24.90	$21.20	$17.70	$15.80	$13.80	$11.80	$9.80	$7.80	$5.80	$3.90	$2.20
$205	$210	$26.00	$22.30	$18.70	$16.40	$14.40	$12.40	$10.40	$8.40	$6.40	$4.50	$2.70
$210	$215	$27.10	$23.40	$19.80	$17.00	$15.00	$13.00	$11.00	$9.00	$7.00	$5.10	$3.20
$215	$220	$28.20	$24.50	$20.90	$17.60	$15.60	$13.60	$11.60	$9.60	$7.60	$5.70	$3.70
$220	$225	$29.30	$25.60	$22.00	$18.30	$16.20	$14.20	$12.20	$10.20	$8.20	$6.30	$4.30
$225	$230	$30.40	$26.70	$23.10	$19.40	$16.80	$14.80	$12.80	$10.80	$8.80	$6.90	$4.90
$230	$235	$31.50	$27.80	$24.20	$20.50	$17.40	$15.40	$13.40	$11.40	$9.40	$7.50	$5.50
$235	$240	$32.60	$28.90	$25.30	$21.60	$18.00	$16.00	$14.00	$12.00	$10.00	$8.10	$6.10
$240	$245	$33.70	$30.00	$26.40	$22.70	$19.10	$16.60	$14.60	$12.60	$10.60	$8.70	$6.70
$245	$250	$34.80	$31.10	$27.50	$23.80	$20.20	$17.20	$15.20	$13.20	$11.20	$9.30	$7.30
$250	$255	$35.90	$32.20	$28.60	$24.90	$21.30	$17.80	$15.80	$13.80	$11.80	$9.90	$7.90
$255	$260	$37.00	$33.30	$29.70	$26.00	$22.40	$18.80	$16.40	$14.40	$12.40	$10.50	$8.50

2021 Wage Bracket Method Tables for Manual Payroll Systems With Forms W-4 From 2019 or Earlier

DAILY Payroll Period

If the **Wage Amount** (line 1a) is		SINGLE Persons										
		And the number of allowances is:										
At least	But less than	0	1	2	3	4	5	6	7	8	9	10
		The Tentative Withholding Amount is:										
$260	$265	$38.10	$34.40	$30.80	$27.10	$23.50	$19.90	$17.00	$15.00	$13.00	$11.10	$9.10
$265	$270	$39.20	$35.50	$31.90	$28.20	$24.60	$21.00	$17.60	$15.60	$13.60	$11.70	$9.70
$270	$275	$40.30	$36.60	$33.00	$29.30	$25.70	$22.10	$18.40	$16.20	$14.20	$12.30	$10.30
$275	$280	$41.40	$37.70	$34.10	$30.40	$26.80	$23.20	$19.50	$16.80	$14.80	$12.90	$10.90
$280	$285	$42.50	$38.80	$35.20	$31.50	$27.90	$24.30	$20.60	$17.40	$15.40	$13.50	$11.50
$285	$290	$43.60	$39.90	$36.30	$32.60	$29.00	$25.40	$21.70	$18.10	$16.00	$14.10	$12.10
$290	$295	$44.70	$41.00	$37.40	$33.70	$30.10	$26.50	$22.80	$19.20	$16.60	$14.70	$12.70
$295	$300	$45.80	$42.10	$38.50	$34.80	$31.20	$27.60	$23.90	$20.30	$17.20	$15.30	$13.30
$300	$305	$46.90	$43.20	$39.60	$35.90	$32.30	$28.70	$25.00	$21.40	$17.80	$15.90	$13.90
$305	$310	$48.00	$44.30	$40.70	$37.00	$33.40	$29.80	$26.10	$22.50	$18.80	$16.50	$14.50
$310	$315	$49.10	$45.40	$41.80	$38.10	$34.50	$30.90	$27.20	$23.60	$19.90	$17.10	$15.10
$315	$320	$50.20	$46.50	$42.90	$39.20	$35.60	$32.00	$28.30	$24.70	$21.00	$17.70	$15.70
$320	$325	$51.30	$47.60	$44.00	$40.30	$36.70	$33.10	$29.40	$25.80	$22.10	$18.50	$16.30
$325	$330	$52.40	$48.70	$45.10	$41.40	$37.80	$34.20	$30.50	$26.90	$23.20	$19.60	$16.90
$330	$335	$53.50	$49.80	$46.20	$42.50	$38.90	$35.30	$31.60	$28.00	$24.30	$20.70	$17.50
$335	$340	$54.60	$50.90	$47.30	$43.60	$40.00	$36.40	$32.70	$29.10	$25.40	$21.80	$18.20
$340	$345	$55.70	$52.00	$48.40	$44.70	$41.10	$37.50	$33.80	$30.20	$26.50	$22.90	$19.30
$345	$350	$56.80	$53.10	$49.50	$45.80	$42.20	$38.60	$34.90	$31.30	$27.60	$24.00	$20.40
$350	$355	$58.00	$54.20	$50.60	$46.90	$43.30	$39.70	$36.00	$32.40	$28.70	$25.10	$21.50
$355	$360	$59.20	$55.30	$51.70	$48.00	$44.40	$40.80	$37.10	$33.50	$29.80	$26.20	$22.60
$360	$365	$60.40	$56.40	$52.80	$49.10	$45.50	$41.90	$38.20	$34.60	$30.90	$27.30	$23.70
$365	$370	$61.60	$57.60	$53.90	$50.20	$46.60	$43.00	$39.30	$35.70	$32.00	$28.40	$24.80
$370	$375	$62.80	$58.80	$55.00	$51.30	$47.70	$44.10	$40.40	$36.80	$33.10	$29.50	$25.90
$375	$380	$64.00	$60.00	$56.10	$52.40	$48.80	$45.20	$41.50	$37.90	$34.20	$30.60	$27.00
$380	$385	$65.20	$61.20	$57.20	$53.50	$49.90	$46.30	$42.60	$39.00	$35.30	$31.70	$28.10
$385	$390	$66.40	$62.40	$58.40	$54.60	$51.00	$47.40	$43.70	$40.10	$36.40	$32.80	$29.20
$390	$395	$67.60	$63.60	$59.60	$55.70	$52.10	$48.50	$44.80	$41.20	$37.50	$33.90	$30.30

Source: Internal Revenue Service

4. Percentage Method Tables for Manual Payroll Systems With Forms W-4 From 2020 or Later

If you compute payroll manually, your employee has submitted a Form W-4 for 2020 or later, and you prefer to use the Percentage Method or you can't use the Wage Bracket Method tables because the employee's annual wages exceed $100,000, use the worksheet below and the Percentage Method tables that follow to figure federal income tax withholding. This method works for any amount of wages.

Worksheet 4. Employer's Withholding Worksheet for Percentage Method Tables for Manual Payroll Systems With Forms W-4 From 2020 or Later

Keep for Your Records

Table 5	Monthly	Semimonthly	Biweekly	Weekly	Daily
	12	24	26	52	260

Step 1.   Adjust the employee's wage amount

1a Enter the employee's total taxable wages this payroll period .... 1a $ _____

1b Enter the number of pay periods you have per year (see Table 5) .... 1b _____

1c Enter the amount from Step 4(a) of the employee's Form W-4 .... 1c $ _____

1d Divide line 1c by the number on line 1b .... 1d $ _____

1e Add lines 1a and 1d .... 1e $ _____

1f Enter the amount from Step 4(b) of the employee's Form W-4 .... 1f $ _____

1g Divide line 1f by the number on line 1b .... 1g $ _____

1h Subtract line 1g from line 1e. If zero or less, enter -0-. This is the **Adjusted Wage Amount** ...... 1h $ _____

Step 2.   Figure the Tentative Withholding Amount

based on your pay frequency, the employee's Adjusted Wage Amount, filing status (Step 1(c) of Form W-4), and whether the box in Step 2 of Form W-4 is checked.

2a Find the row in the *STANDARD Withholding Rate Schedules* (if the box in Step 2 of Form W-4 is NOT checked) or the *Form W-4, Step 2, Checkbox, Withholding Rate Schedules* (if it HAS been checked) of the Percentage Method tables in this section in which the amount on line 1h is at least the amount in column A but less than the amount in column B, then enter here the amount from column A of that row .... 2a $ _____

2b Enter the amount from column C of that row .... 2b $ _____

2c Enter the percentage from column D of that row .... 2c _____ %

2d Subtract line 2a from line 1h .... 2d $ _____

2e Multiply the amount on line 2d by the percentage on line 2c .... 2e $ _____

2f Add lines 2b and 2e. This is the **Tentative Withholding Amount** .... 2f $ _____

Step 3.   Account for tax credits

3a Enter the amount from Step 3 of the employee's Form W-4 .... 3a $ _____

3b Divide the amount on line 3a by the number of pay periods on line 1b .... 3b $ _____

3c Subtract line 3b from line 2f. If zero or less, enter -0- .... 3c $ _____

Step 4.   Figure the final amount to withhold

4a Enter the additional amount to withhold from Step 4(c) of the employee's Form W-4 .... 4a $ _____

4b Add lines 3c and 4a. **This is the amount to withhold from the employee's wages this pay period** .... 4b $ _____

2021 Percentage Method Tables for Manual Payroll Systems With Forms W-4 from 2020 or Later
WEEKLY Payroll Period

STANDARD Withholding Rate Schedules (Use these if the box in Step 2 of Form W-4 is **NOT** checked)					Form W-4, Step 2, Checkbox, Withholding Rate Schedules (Use these if the box in Step 2 of Form W-4 **IS** checked)				
If the Adjusted Wage Amount (line 1h) is:		The tentative amount to withhold is:	Plus this percentage—	of the amount that the Adjusted Wage exceeds—	If the Adjusted Wage Amount (line 1h) is:		The tentative amount to withhold is:	Plus this percentage—	of the amount that the Adjusted Wage exceeds—
At least—	But less than—				At least—	But less than—			
A	B	C	D	E	A	B	C	D	E
Married Filing Jointly					**Married Filing Jointly**				
$0	$483	$0.00	0%	$0	$0	$241	$0.00	0%	$0
$483	$865	$0.00	10%	$483	$241	$433	$0.00	10%	$241
$865	$2,041	$38.20	12%	$865	$433	$1,021	$19.20	12%	$433
$2,041	$3,805	$179.32	22%	$2,041	$1,021	$1,902	$89.76	22%	$1,021
$3,805	$6,826	$567.40	24%	$3,805	$1,902	$3,413	$283.58	24%	$1,902
$6,826	$8,538	$1,292.44	32%	$6,826	$3,413	$4,269	$646.22	32%	$3,413
$8,538	$12,565	$1,840.28	35%	$8,538	$4,269	$6,283	$920.14	35%	$4,269
$12,565		$3,249.73	37%	$12,565	$6,283		$1,625.04	37%	$6,283
Single or Married Filing Separately					**Single or Married Filing Separately**				
$0	$241	$0.00	0%	$0	$0	$121	$0.00	0%	$0
$241	$433	$0.00	10%	$241	$121	$216	$0.00	10%	$121
$433	$1,021	$19.20	12%	$433	$216	$510	$9.50	12%	$216
$1,021	$1,902	$89.76	22%	$1,021	$510	$951	$44.78	22%	$510
$1,902	$3,413	$283.58	24%	$1,902	$951	$1,706	$141.80	24%	$951
$3,413	$4,269	$646.22	32%	$3,413	$1,706	$2,134	$323.00	32%	$1,706
$4,269	$10,311	$920.14	35%	$4,269	$2,134	$5,155	$459.96	35%	$2,134
$10,311		$3,034.84	37%	$10,311	$5,155		$1,517.31	37%	$5,155
Head of Household					**Head of Household**				
$0	$362	$0.00	0%	$0	$0	$181	$0.00	0%	$0
$362	$635	$0.00	10%	$362	$181	$317	$0.00	10%	$181
$635	$1,404	$27.30	12%	$635	$317	$702	$13.60	12%	$317
$1,404	$2,022	$119.58	22%	$1,404	$702	$1,011	$59.80	22%	$702
$2,022	$3,533	$255.54	24%	$2,022	$1,011	$1,766	$127.78	24%	$1,011
$3,533	$4,388	$618.18	32%	$3,533	$1,766	$2,194	$308.98	32%	$1,766
$4,388	$10,431	$891.78	35%	$4,388	$2,194	$5,215	$445.94	35%	$2,194
$10,431		$3,006.83	37%	$10,431	$5,215		$1,503.29	37%	$5,215

2021 Percentage Method Tables for Manual Payroll Systems With Forms W-4 from 2020 or Later

BIWEEKLY Payroll Period

STANDARD Withholding Rate Schedules (Use these if the box in Step 2 of Form W-4 is **NOT** checked)					Form W-4, Step 2, Checkbox, Withholding Rate Schedules (Use these if the box in Step 2 of Form W-4 **IS** checked)				
If the Adjusted Wage Amount (line 1h) is:		The tentative amount to withhold is:	Plus this percentage—	of the amount that the Adjusted Wage exceeds—	If the Adjusted Wage Amount (line 1h) is:		The tentative amount to withhold is:	Plus this percentage—	of the amount that the Adjusted Wage exceeds—
At least—	But less than—				At least—	But less than—			
A	B	C	D	E	A	B	C	D	E
Married Filing Jointly					**Married Filing Jointly**				
$0	$965	$0.00	0%	$0	$0	$483	$0.00	0%	$0
$965	$1,731	$0.00	10%	$965	$483	$865	$0.00	10%	$483
$1,731	$4,083	$76.60	12%	$1,731	$865	$2,041	$38.20	12%	$865
$4,083	$7,610	$358.84	22%	$4,083	$2,041	$3,805	$179.32	22%	$2,041
$7,610	$13,652	$1,134.78	24%	$7,610	$3,805	$6,826	$567.40	24%	$3,805
$13,652	$17,075	$2,584.86	32%	$13,652	$6,826	$8,538	$1,292.44	32%	$6,826
$17,075	$25,131	$3,680.22	35%	$17,075	$8,538	$12,565	$1,840.28	35%	$8,538
$25,131		$6,499.82	37%	$25,131	$12,565		$3,249.73	37%	$12,565
Single or Married Filing Separately					**Single or Married Filing Separately**				
$0	$483	$0.00	0%	$0	$0	$241	$0.00	0%	$0
$483	$865	$0.00	10%	$483	$241	$433	$0.00	10%	$241
$865	$2,041	$38.20	12%	$865	$433	$1,021	$19.20	12%	$433
$2,041	$3,805	$179.32	22%	$2,041	$1,021	$1,902	$89.76	22%	$1,021
$3,805	$6,826	$567.40	24%	$3,805	$1,902	$3,413	$283.58	24%	$1,902
$6,826	$8,538	$1,292.44	32%	$6,826	$3,413	$4,269	$646.22	32%	$3,413
$8,538	$20,621	$1,840.28	35%	$8,538	$4,269	$10,311	$920.14	35%	$4,269
$20,621		$6,069.33	37%	$20,621	$10,311		$3,034.84	37%	$10,311
Head of Household					**Head of Household**				
$0	$723	$0.00	0%	$0	$0	$362	$0.00	0%	$0
$723	$1,269	$0.00	10%	$723	$362	$635	$0.00	10%	$362
$1,269	$2,808	$54.60	12%	$1,269	$635	$1,404	$27.30	12%	$635
$2,808	$4,044	$239.28	22%	$2,808	$1,404	$2,022	$119.58	22%	$1,404
$4,044	$7,065	$511.20	24%	$4,044	$2,022	$3,533	$255.54	24%	$2,022
$7,065	$8,777	$1,236.24	32%	$7,065	$3,533	$4,388	$618.18	32%	$3,533
$8,777	$20,862	$1,784.08	35%	$8,777	$4,388	$10,431	$891.78	35%	$4,388
$20,862		$6,013.83	37%	$20,862	$10,431		$3,006.83	37%	$10,431

2021 Percentage Method Tables for Manual Payroll Systems With Forms W-4 from 2020 or Later

SEMIMONTHLY Payroll Period

STANDARD Withholding Rate Schedules (Use these if the box in Step 2 of Form W-4 is **NOT** checked)					Form W-4, Step 2, Checkbox, Withholding Rate Schedules (Use these if the box in Step 2 of Form W-4 **IS** checked)				
If the Adjusted Wage Amount (line 1h) is:		The tentative amount to withhold is:	Plus this percentage—	of the amount that the Adjusted Wage exceeds—	If the Adjusted Wage Amount (line 1h) is:		The tentative amount to withhold is:	Plus this percentage—	of the amount that the Adjusted Wage exceeds—
At least—	But less than—				At least—	But less than—			
A	B	C	D	E	A	B	C	D	E
Married Filing Jointly					**Married Filing Jointly**				
$0	$1,046	$0.00	0%	$0	$0	$523	$0.00	0%	$0
$1,046	$1,875	$0.00	10%	$1,046	$523	$938	$0.00	10%	$523
$1,875	$4,423	$82.90	12%	$1,875	$938	$2,211	$41.50	12%	$938
$4,423	$8,244	$388.66	22%	$4,423	$2,211	$4,122	$194.26	22%	$2,211
$8,244	$14,790	$1,229.28	24%	$8,244	$4,122	$7,395	$614.68	24%	$4,122
$14,790	$18,498	$2,800.32	32%	$14,790	$7,395	$9,249	$1,400.20	32%	$7,395
$18,498	$27,225	$3,986.88	35%	$18,498	$9,249	$13,613	$1,993.48	35%	$9,249
$27,225		$7,041.33	37%	$27,225	$13,613		$3,520.88	37%	$13,613
Single or Married Filing Separately					**Single or Married Filing Separately**				
$0	$523	$0.00	0%	$0	$0	$261	$0.00	0%	$0
$523	$938	$0.00	10%	$523	$261	$469	$0.00	10%	$261
$938	$2,211	$41.50	12%	$938	$469	$1,106	$20.80	12%	$469
$2,211	$4,122	$194.26	22%	$2,211	$1,106	$2,061	$97.24	22%	$1,106
$4,122	$7,395	$614.68	24%	$4,122	$2,061	$3,697	$307.34	24%	$2,061
$7,395	$9,249	$1,400.20	32%	$7,395	$3,697	$4,624	$699.98	32%	$3,697
$9,249	$22,340	$1,993.48	35%	$9,249	$4,624	$11,170	$996.62	35%	$4,624
$22,340		$6,575.33	37%	$22,340	$11,170		$3,287.72	37%	$11,170
Head of Household					**Head of Household**				
$0	$783	$0.00	0%	$0	$0	$392	$0.00	0%	$0
$783	$1,375	$0.00	10%	$783	$392	$688	$0.00	10%	$392
$1,375	$3,042	$59.20	12%	$1,375	$688	$1,521	$29.60	12%	$688
$3,042	$4,381	$259.24	22%	$3,042	$1,521	$2,191	$129.56	22%	$1,521
$4,381	$7,654	$553.82	24%	$4,381	$2,191	$3,827	$276.96	24%	$2,191
$7,654	$9,508	$1,339.34	32%	$7,654	$3,827	$4,754	$669.60	32%	$3,827
$9,508	$22,600	$1,932.62	35%	$9,508	$4,754	$11,300	$966.24	35%	$4,754
$22,600		$6,514.82	37%	$22,600	$11,300		$3,257.34	37%	$11,300

2021 Percentage Method Tables for Manual Payroll Systems With Forms W-4 from 2020 or Later

MONTHLY Payroll Period

STANDARD Withholding Rate Schedules (Use these if the box in Step 2 of Form W-4 is **NOT** checked)					Form W-4, Step 2, Checkbox, Withholding Rate Schedules (Use these if the box in Step 2 of Form W-4 **IS** checked)				
If the Adjusted Wage Amount (line 1h) is:		The tentative amount to withhold is:	Plus this percentage—	of the amount that the Adjusted Wage exceeds—	If the Adjusted Wage Amount (line 1h) is:		The tentative amount to withhold is:	Plus this percentage—	of the amount that the Adjusted Wage exceeds—
At least—	But less than—				At least—	But less than—			
A	B	C	D	E	A	B	C	D	E
Married Filing Jointly					**Married Filing Jointly**				
$0	$2,092	$0.00	0%	$0	$0	$1,046	$0.00	0%	$0
$2,092	$3,750	$0.00	10%	$2,092	$1,046	$1,875	$0.00	10%	$1,046
$3,750	$8,846	$165.80	12%	$3,750	$1,875	$4,423	$82.90	12%	$1,875
$8,846	$16,488	$777.32	22%	$8,846	$4,423	$8,244	$388.66	22%	$4,423
$16,488	$29,579	$2,458.56	24%	$16,488	$8,244	$14,790	$1,229.28	24%	$8,244
$29,579	$36,996	$5,600.40	32%	$29,579	$14,790	$18,498	$2,800.32	32%	$14,790
$36,996	$54,450	$7,973.84	35%	$36,996	$18,498	$27,225	$3,986.88	35%	$18,498
$54,450		$14,082.74	37%	$54,450	$27,225		$7,041.33	37%	$27,225
Single or Married Filing Separately					**Single or Married Filing Separately**				
$0	$1,046	$0.00	0%	$0	$0	$523	$0.00	0%	$0
$1,046	$1,875	$0.00	10%	$1,046	$523	$938	$0.00	10%	$523
$1,875	$4,423	$82.90	12%	$1,875	$938	$2,211	$41.50	12%	$938
$4,423	$8,244	$388.66	22%	$4,423	$2,211	$4,122	$194.26	22%	$2,211
$8,244	$14,790	$1,229.28	24%	$8,244	$4,122	$7,395	$614.68	24%	$4,122
$14,790	$18,498	$2,800.32	32%	$14,790	$7,395	$9,249	$1,400.20	32%	$7,395
$18,498	$44,679	$3,986.88	35%	$18,498	$9,249	$22,340	$1,993.48	35%	$9,249
$44,679		$13,150.23	37%	$44,679	$22,340		$6,575.33	37%	$22,340
Head of Household					**Head of Household**				
$0	$1,567	$0.00	0%	$0	$0	$783	$0.00	0%	$0
$1,567	$2,750	$0.00	10%	$1,567	$783	$1,375	$0.00	10%	$783
$2,750	$6,083	$118.30	12%	$2,750	$1,375	$3,042	$59.20	12%	$1,375
$6,083	$8,763	$510.26	22%	$6,083	$3,042	$4,381	$259.24	22%	$3,042
$8,763	$15,308	$1,107.86	24%	$8,763	$4,381	$7,654	$553.82	24%	$4,381
$15,308	$19,017	$2,678.66	32%	$15,308	$7,654	$9,508	$1,339.34	32%	$7,654
$19,017	$45,200	$3,865.54	35%	$19,017	$9,508	$22,600	$1,932.62	35%	$9,508
$45,200		$13,029.59	37%	$45,200	$22,600		$6,514.82	37%	$22,600

2021 Percentage Method Tables for Manual Payroll Systems With Forms W-4 from 2020 or Later

DAILY Payroll Period

STANDARD Withholding Rate Schedules (Use these if the box in Step 2 of Form W-4 is **NOT** checked)					Form W-4, Step 2, Checkbox, Withholding Rate Schedules (Use these if the box in Step 2 of Form W-4 **IS** checked)				
If the Adjusted Wage Amount (line 1h) is:		The tentative amount to withhold is:	Plus this percentage—	of the amount that the Adjusted Wage exceeds—	If the Adjusted Wage Amount (line 1h) is:		The tentative amount to withhold is:	Plus this percentage—	of the amount that the Adjusted Wage exceeds—
At least—	But less than—				At least—	But less than—			
A	B	C	D	E	A	B	C	D	E
Married Filing Jointly					**Married Filing Jointly**				
$0.00	$96.50	$0.00	0%	$0.00	$0.00	$48.30	$0.00	0%	$0.00
$96.50	$173.10	$0.00	10%	$96.50	$48.30	$86.50	$0.00	10%	$48.30
$173.10	$408.30	$7.66	12%	$173.10	$86.50	$204.10	$3.82	12%	$86.50
$408.30	$761.00	$35.88	22%	$408.30	$204.10	$380.50	$17.93	22%	$204.10
$761.00	$1,365.20	$113.48	24%	$761.00	$380.50	$682.60	$56.74	24%	$380.50
$1,365.20	$1,707.50	$258.49	32%	$1,365.20	$682.60	$853.80	$129.24	32%	$682.60
$1,707.50	$2,513.10	$368.02	35%	$1,707.50	$853.80	$1,256.50	$184.03	35%	$853.80
$2,513.10		$649.98	37%	$2,513.10	$1,256.50		$324.97	37%	$1,256.50
Single or Married Filing Separately					**Single or Married Filing Separately**				
$0.00	$48.30	$0.00	0%	$0.00	$0.00	$24.10	$0.00	0%	$0.00
$48.30	$86.50	$0.00	10%	$48.30	$24.10	$43.30	$0.00	10%	$24.10
$86.50	$204.10	$3.82	12%	$86.50	$43.30	$102.10	$1.92	12%	$43.30
$204.10	$380.50	$17.93	22%	$204.10	$102.10	$190.20	$8.98	22%	$102.10
$380.50	$682.60	$56.74	24%	$380.50	$190.20	$341.30	$28.36	24%	$190.20
$682.60	$853.80	$129.24	32%	$682.60	$341.30	$426.90	$64.62	32%	$341.30
$853.80	$2,062.10	$184.03	35%	$853.80	$426.90	$1,031.10	$92.01	35%	$426.90
$2,062.10		$606.93	37%	$2,062.10	$1,031.10		$303.48	37%	$1,031.10
Head of Household					**Head of Household**				
$0.00	$72.30	$0.00	0%	$0.00	$0.00	$36.20	$0.00	0%	$0.00
$72.30	$126.90	$0.00	10%	$72.30	$36.20	$63.50	$0.00	10%	$36.20
$126.90	$280.80	$5.46	12%	$126.90	$63.50	$140.40	$2.73	12%	$63.50
$280.80	$404.40	$23.93	22%	$280.80	$140.40	$202.20	$11.96	22%	$140.40
$404.40	$706.50	$51.12	24%	$404.40	$202.20	$353.30	$25.55	24%	$202.20
$706.50	$877.70	$123.62	32%	$706.50	$353.30	$438.80	$61.82	32%	$353.30
$877.70	$2,086.20	$178.41	35%	$877.70	$438.80	$1,043.10	$89.18	35%	$438.80
$2,086.20		$601.38	37%	$2,086.20	$1,043.10		$300.68	37%	$1,043.10

Source: Internal Revenue Service

5. Percentage Method Tables for Manual Payroll Systems With Forms W-4 From 2019 or Earlier

If you compute payroll manually and your employee **has not** submitted a Form W-4 for 2020 or later, and you prefer to use the Percentage Method or you can't use the Wage Bracket Method tables because the employee's annual wages exceed $100,000 or the employee claimed more than 10 allowances, use the worksheet below and the Percentage Method tables that follow to figure federal income tax withholding. This method works for any number of withholding allowances claimed and any amount of wages.

Periodic payments of pensions or annuities. Periodic payments are those made in installments at regular intervals over a period of more than 1 year. They may be paid annually, quarterly, monthly, etc. Withholding from periodic payments of a pension or annuity is figured in the same manner as withholding from wages, except it doesn't matter if the Form W-4P is from 2019 or earlier or a 2020 or later Form W-4P. Use Worksheet 5 and the Percentage Method tables in this section to figure federal income tax withholding on periodic payments of pensions or annuities. However, if you prefer to use the Wage Bracket Method of withholding, you may use Worksheet 3 and the Wage Bracket Method tables in section 3 to figure federal income tax withholding on periodic payments of pensions or annuities. If the recipient doesn't submit Form W-4P, you must withhold on periodic payments as if the recipient were married claiming three withholding allowances.

Worksheet 5. Employer's Withholding Worksheet for Percentage Method Tables for Manual Payroll Systems With Forms W-4 From 2019 or Earlier

Keep for Your Records

Table 6	Annually	Semiannually	Quarterly	Monthly	Semimonthly	Biweekly	Weekly	Daily
	$4,300	$2,150	$1,075	$358	$179	$165	$83	$17

Step 1. Adjust the employee's wage amount

1a Enter the employee's total taxable wages this payroll period . . . . 1a $ _____

1b Enter the number of allowances claimed on the employee's most recent Form W-4 . . . . 1b _____

1c Multiply line 1b by the amount in Table 6 for your pay frequency . . . . 1c $ _____

1d Subtract line 1c from line 1a. If zero or less, enter -0-. This is the **Adjusted Wage Amount** . . . . 1d $ _____

Step 2. Figure the Tentative Withholding Amount

based on your pay frequency, the employee's Adjusted Wage Amount, and marital status (line 3 of Form W-4).

2a Find the row in the Percentage Method table in this section in which the amount on line 1d is at least the amount in column A but less than the amount in column B, then enter here the amount from column A of that row . . . . 2a $ _____

2b Enter the amount from column C of that row . . . . 2b $ _____

2c Enter the percentage from column D of that row . . . . 2c _____ %

2d Subtract line 2a from line 1d . . . . 2d $ _____

2e Multiply the amount on line 2d by the percentage on line 2c . . . . 2e $ _____

2f Add lines 2b and 2e. This is the **Tentative Withholding Amount** . . . . 2f $ _____

Step 3. Figure the final amount to withhold

3a Enter the additional amount to withhold from line 6 of the employee's Form W-4 . . . . 3a $ _____

3b Add lines 2f and 3a. **This is the amount to withhold from the employee's wages this pay period** . . . . . . 3b $ _____

2021 Percentage Method Tables for Manual Payroll Systems With Forms W-4 From 2019 or Earlier

WEEKLY Payroll Period

MARRIED Persons					SINGLE Persons				
If the Adjusted Wage Amount (line 1d) is		The tentative amount to withhold is...	Plus this percentage ...	of the amount that the wage exceeds...	If the Adjusted Wage Amount (line 1d) is		The tentative amount to withhold is...	Plus this percentage ...	of the amount that the wage exceeds...
at least...	But less than...				at least...	But less than...			
A	B	C	D	E	A	B	C	D	E
$0	$235	$0.00	0%	$0	$0	$76	$0.00	0%	$0
$235	$617	$0.00	10%	$235	$76	$267	$0.00	10%	$76
$617	$1,793	$38.20	12%	$617	$267	$855	$19.10	12%	$267
$1,793	$3,557	$179.32	22%	$1,793	$855	$1,737	$89.66	22%	$855
$3,557	$6,578	$567.40	24%	$3,557	$1,737	$3,248	$283.70	24%	$1,737
$6,578	$8,289	$1,292.44	32%	$6,578	$3,248	$4,103	$646.34	32%	$3,248
$8,289	$12,317	$1,839.96	35%	$8,289	$4,103	$10,145	$919.94	35%	$4,103
$12,317		$3,249.76	37%	$12,317	$10,145		$3,034.64	37%	$10,145

BIWEEKLY Payroll Period

MARRIED Persons					SINGLE Persons				
If the Adjusted Wage Amount (line 1d) is		The tentative amount to withhold is...	Plus this percentage ...	of the amount that the wage exceeds...	If the Adjusted Wage Amount (line 1d) is		The tentative amount to withhold is...	Plus this percentage ...	of the amount that the wage exceeds...
at least...	But less than...				at least...	But less than...			
A	B	C	D	E	A	B	C	D	E
$0	$469	$0.00	0%	$0	$0	$152	$0.00	0%	$0
$469	$1,235	$0.00	10%	$469	$152	$535	$0.00	10%	$152
$1,235	$3,587	$76.60	12%	$1,235	$535	$1,711	$38.30	12%	$535
$3,587	$7,113	$358.84	22%	$3,587	$1,711	$3,474	$179.42	22%	$1,711
$7,113	$13,156	$1,134.56	24%	$7,113	$3,474	$6,495	$567.28	24%	$3,474
$13,156	$16,579	$2,584.88	32%	$13,156	$6,495	$8,207	$1,292.32	32%	$6,495
$16,579	$24,635	$3,680.24	35%	$16,579	$8,207	$20,290	$1,840.16	35%	$8,207
$24,635		$6,499.84	37%	$24,635	$20,290		$6,069.21	37%	$20,290

SEMIMONTHLY Payroll Period

MARRIED Persons					SINGLE Persons				
If the Adjusted Wage Amount (line 1d) is		The tentative amount to withhold is...	Plus this percentage ...	of the amount that the wage exceeds...	If the Adjusted Wage Amount (line 1d) is		The tentative amount to withhold is...	Plus this percentage ...	of the amount that the wage exceeds...
at least...	But less than...				at least...	But less than...			
A	B	C	D	E	A	B	C	D	E
$0	$508	$0.00	0%	$0	$0	$165	$0.00	0%	$0
$508	$1,338	$0.00	10%	$508	$165	$579	$0.00	10%	$165
$1,338	$3,885	$83.00	12%	$1,338	$579	$1,853	$41.40	12%	$579
$3,885	$7,706	$388.64	22%	$3,885	$1,853	$3,764	$194.28	22%	$1,853
$7,706	$14,252	$1,229.26	24%	$7,706	$3,764	$7,036	$614.70	24%	$3,764
$14,252	$17,960	$2,800.30	32%	$14,252	$7,036	$8,891	$1,399.98	32%	$7,036
$17,960	$26,688	$3,986.86	35%	$17,960	$8,891	$21,981	$1,993.58	35%	$8,891
$26,688		$7,041.66	37%	$26,688	$21,981		$6,575.08	37%	$21,981

2021 Percentage Method Tables for Manual Payroll Systems With Forms W-4 From 2019 or Earlier

MONTHLY Payroll Period

MARRIED Persons					SINGLE Persons				
If the Adjusted Wage Amount (line 1d) is		The tentative amount to withhold is...	Plus this percentage ...	of the amount that the wage exceeds...	If the Adjusted Wage Amount (line 1d) is		The tentative amount to withhold is...	Plus this percentage ...	of the amount that the wage exceeds...
at least...	But less than...				at least...	But less than...			
A	B	C	D	E	A	B	C	D	E
$0	$1,017	$0.00	0%	$0	$0	$329	$0.00	0%	$0
$1,017	$2,675	$0.00	10%	$1,017	$329	$1,158	$0.00	10%	$329
$2,675	$7,771	$165.80	12%	$2,675	$1,158	$3,706	$82.90	12%	$1,158
$7,771	$15,413	$777.32	22%	$7,771	$3,706	$7,527	$388.66	22%	$3,706
$15,413	$28,504	$2,458.56	24%	$15,413	$7,527	$14,073	$1,229.28	24%	$7,527
$28,504	$35,921	$5,600.40	32%	$28,504	$14,073	$17,781	$2,800.32	32%	$14,073
$35,921	$53,375	$7,973.84	35%	$35,921	$17,781	$43,963	$3,986.88	35%	$17,781
$53,375		$14,082.74	37%	$53,375	$43,963		$13,150.58	37%	$43,963

QUARTERLY Payroll Period

MARRIED Persons					SINGLE Persons				
If the Adjusted Wage Amount (line 1d) is		The tentative amount to withhold is...	Plus this percentage ...	of the amount that the wage exceeds...	If the Adjusted Wage Amount (line 1d) is		The tentative amount to withhold is...	Plus this percentage ...	of the amount that the wage exceeds...
at least...	But less than...				at least...	But less than...			
A	B	C	D	E	A	B	C	D	E
$0	$3,050	$0.00	0%	$0	$0	$988	$0.00	0%	$0
$3,050	$8,025	$0.00	10%	$3,050	$988	$3,475	$0.00	10%	$988
$8,025	$23,313	$497.50	12%	$8,025	$3,475	$11,119	$248.70	12%	$3,475
$23,313	$46,238	$2,332.06	22%	$23,313	$11,119	$22,581	$1,165.98	22%	$11,119
$46,238	$85,513	$7,375.56	24%	$46,238	$22,581	$42,219	$3,687.62	24%	$22,581
$85,513	$107,763	$16,801.56	32%	$85,513	$42,219	$53,344	$8,400.74	32%	$42,219
$107,763	$160,125	$23,921.56	35%	$107,763	$53,344	$131,888	$11,960.74	35%	$53,344
$160,125		$42,248.26	37%	$160,125	$131,888		$39,451.14	37%	$131,888

SEMIANNUAL Payroll Period

MARRIED Persons					SINGLE Persons				
If the Adjusted Wage Amount (line 1d) is		The tentative amount to withhold is...	Plus this percentage ...	of the amount that the wage exceeds...	If the Adjusted Wage Amount (line 1d) is		The tentative amount to withhold is...	Plus this percentage ...	of the amount that the wage exceeds...
at least...	But less than...				at least...	But less than...			
A	B	C	D	E	A	B	C	D	E
$0	$6,100	$0.00	0%	$0	$0	$1,975	$0.00	0%	$0
$6,100	$16,050	$0.00	10%	$6,100	$1,975	$6,950	$0.00	10%	$1,975
$16,050	$46,625	$995.00	12%	$16,050	$6,950	$22,238	$497.50	12%	$6,950
$46,625	$92,475	$4,664.00	22%	$46,625	$22,238	$45,163	$2,332.06	22%	$22,238
$92,475	$171,025	$14,751.00	24%	$92,475	$45,163	$84,438	$7,375.56	24%	$45,163
$171,025	$215,525	$33,603.00	32%	$171,025	$84,438	$106,688	$16,801.56	32%	$84,438
$215,525	$320,250	$47,843.00	35%	$215,525	$106,688	$263,775	$23,921.56	35%	$106,688
$320,250		$84,496.75	37%	$320,250	$263,775		$78,902.01	37%	$263,775

2021 Percentage Method Tables for Manual Payroll Systems With Forms W-4 From 2019 or Earlier

ANNUAL Payroll Period

MARRIED Persons					SINGLE Persons				
If the Adjusted Wage Amount (line 1d) is		The tentative amount to withhold is...	Plus this percentage ...	of the amount that the wage exceeds...	If the Adjusted Wage Amount (line 1d) is		The tentative amount to withhold is...	Plus this percentage ...	of the amount that the wage exceeds...
at least...	But less than...				at least...	But less than...			
A	B	C	D	E	A	B	C	D	E
$0	$12,200	$0.00	0%	$0	$0	$3,950	$0.00	0%	$0
$12,200	$32,100	$0.00	10%	$12,200	$3,950	$13,900	$0.00	10%	$3,950
$32,100	$93,250	$1,990.00	12%	$32,100	$13,900	$44,475	$995.00	12%	$13,900
$93,250	$184,950	$9,328.00	22%	$93,250	$44,475	$90,325	$4,664.00	22%	$44,475
$184,950	$342,050	$29,502.00	24%	$184,950	$90,325	$168,875	$14,751.00	24%	$90,325
$342,050	$431,050	$67,206.00	32%	$342,050	$168,875	$213,375	$33,603.00	32%	$168,875
$431,050	$640,500	$95,686.00	35%	$431,050	$213,375	$527,550	$47,843.00	35%	$213,375
$640,500		$168,993.50	37%	$640,500	$527,550		$157,804.25	37%	$527,550

DAILY Payroll Period

MARRIED Persons					SINGLE Persons				
If the Adjusted Wage Amount (line 1d) is		The tentative amount to withhold is...	Plus this percentage ...	of the amount that the wage exceeds...	If the Adjusted Wage Amount (line 1d) is		The tentative amount to withhold Is...	Plus this percentage ...	of the amount that the wage exceeds...
at least...	But less than...				at least...	But less than...			
A	B	C	D	E	A	B	C	D	E
$0.00	$46.90	$0.00	0%	$0.00	$0.00	$15.20	$0.00	0%	$0.00
$46.90	$123.50	$0.00	10%	$46.90	$15.20	$53.50	$0.00	10%	$15.20
$123.50	$358.70	$7.66	12%	$123.50	$53.50	$171.10	$3.83	12%	$53.50
$358.70	$711.30	$35.88	22%	$358.70	$171.10	$347.40	$17.94	22%	$171.10
$711.30	$1,315.60	$113.46	24%	$711.30	$347.40	$649.50	$56.73	24%	$347.40
$1,315.60	$1,657.90	$258.49	32%	$1,315.60	$649.50	$820.70	$129.23	32%	$649.50
$1,657.90	$2,463.50	$368.02	35%	$1,657.90	$820.70	$2,029.00	$184.02	35%	$820.70
$2,463.50		$649.98	37%	$2,463.50	$2,029.00		$606.92	37%	$2,029.00

Source: Internal Revenue Service

6. Alternative Methods for Figuring Withholding

You may use various methods of figuring federal income tax withholding. The methods described next may be used instead of the Percentage Method and Wage Bracket Method discussed earlier in this publication. Use the method that best suits your payroll system and employees.

⚠️ **CAUTION** *Employers must use a modified procedure to figure the amount of federal income tax withholding on the wages of nonresident alien employees. Before you use any of the alternative methods to figure the federal income tax withholding on the wages of nonresident alien employees, see* Withholding Adjustment for Nonresident Alien Employees, *earlier.*

Annualized wages. The Percentage Method Tables for Automated Payroll Systems in section 1 and Worksheet 1 allow you to figure federal income tax withholding based on annualized wages.

Average estimated wages. You may withhold the tax for a payroll period based on estimated average wages, with necessary adjustments, for any quarter. For details, see Regulations section 31.3402(h)(1)-1.

Cumulative wages. An employee may ask you, in writing, to withhold tax on cumulative wages. If you agree to do so, and you've paid the employee for the same kind of payroll period (weekly, biweekly, etc.) since the beginning of the year, you may figure the tax as follows.

Add the wages you've paid the employee for the current calendar year to the current payroll period amount. Divide this amount by the number of payroll periods so far this year, including the current period. Figure the withholding on this amount, and multiply the withholding by the number of payroll periods so far this year, including the current period. Subtract the total tax already deducted and withheld during the calendar year from the total amount of tax calculated. The excess is the amount to withhold for the current payroll period. See Revenue Procedure 78-8, 1978-1 C.B. 562, for an example of the cumulative method.

Part-year employment. A part-year employee who figures income tax on a calendar-year basis may ask you to withhold tax by the part-year employment method. The request must be in writing, under penalties of perjury, and must contain the following information.

- The last day of any employment during the calendar year with any prior employer.
- A statement that the employee uses the calendar year accounting period.
- A statement that the employee reasonably anticipates that he or she will be employed by all employers for a total of no more than 245 days in all terms of continuous employment (defined below in this section) during the current calendar year.

Complete the following steps to figure withholding tax by the part-year method.

1. Add the wages to be paid to the employee for the current payroll period to any wages that you've already paid to the employee in the current term of continuous employment. See definition for "term of continuous employment," later.

2. Add the number of payroll periods used in step 1 to the number of payroll periods between the employee's last employment and current employment. To find the number of periods between the last employment and current employment, divide the number of calendar days between the employee's last day of earlier employment (or the previous December 31, if later) and the first day of current employment by the number of calendar days in the current payroll period.

3. Divide the step 1 amount by the total number of payroll periods from step 2.

4. Find the tax in the withholding tax tables on the step 3 amount. Be sure to use the correct payroll period table and to take into account the employee's withholding allowances if their Form W-4 is from 2019 or earlier; or take into account other information provided on the employee's 2020 or later Form W-4.

5. Multiply the total number of payroll periods from step 2 by the step 4 amount.

6. Subtract from the step 5 amount the total tax already withheld during the current term of continuous employment. Any excess is the amount to withhold for the current payroll period.

See Regulations section 31.3402(h)(4)-1(c) for more information about the part-year method.

Term of continuous employment. A term of continuous employment may be a single term or two or more following terms of employment with the same employer. A term of continuous employment includes holidays, regular days off, and days off for illness or vacation. A term of continuous employment begins on the first day that an employee works for you and earns pay. It ends on the earlier of the employee's last day of work for you or, if the employee performs no services for you for more than 30 calendar days, the last workday before the 30-day period. If an employment relationship is ended, the term of continuous employment is ended even if a new employment relationship is established with the same employer within 30 days.

Other methods. You may use other methods and tables for withholding taxes, as long as the amount of tax withheld is consistently about the same as it would be under the Percentage Method, as discussed in section 1. If you develop an alternative method or table, you should test the full range of wage and allowance situations to be sure that they meet the tolerances contained in Regulations section 31.3402(h)(4)-1(a) as shown in the chart below.

Appendix D

State Income Tax Information

The employee income tax rates for each state for 2021 are presented below. *Tax Bracket* refers to the year-to-date earnings of the individual. *Marginal Tax Rate* refers to the amount of tax actually collected on each dollar the employee earns and is subject to change as the employee's earnings increase during the year. Note that the tax bracket, although generally pertaining to payroll-related income, also applies to other sources of personal revenue such as interest and dividends.

State	Tax Bracket (Single)	Tax Bracket (Married)	Marginal Tax Rate
Alabama	$0+	$0+	2.0%
	$501+	$1,001+	4.0%
	$3,000+	$6,000+	5.0%
Alaska	$0+	$0+	0%
Arizona	$0+	$0+	2.59%
	$27,272+	$54,544+	3.34%
	$54,544+	$109,088+	4.17%
	$163,632+	$327,263+	4.50%
Arkansas	$0+	$0+	2.0%
	$4,001+	$4,001+	4.0%
	$8,001+	$8,001+	5.9%
California	$0+	$0+	1.0%
	$8,933+	$17,865+	2.0%
	$21,176+	$42,351+	4.0%
	$33,422+	$66,843+	6.0%
	$46,395+	$92,789+	8.0%
	$58,635+	$117,269+	9.3%
	$299,909+	$599,017+	10.3%
	$359,408+	$718,815+	11.3%
	$599,012+	$1,198,024+	12.3%
Colorado	$0+	$0+	4.55%

State	Tax Bracket (Single)	Tax Bracket (Married)	Marginal Tax Rate
Connecticut	$0+	$0+	3.0%
	$10,001+	$20,001+	5.0%
	$50,001+	$100,001+	5.50%
	$100,001+	$200,001+	6.0%
	$200,001+	$400,001+	6.50%
	$250,001+	$500,001+	6.90%
	$500,000+	$1,000,000+	6.99%
Delaware	$2,001+	$2,001+	2.20%
	$5,001+	$5,001+	3.90%
	$10,001+	$10,001+	4.80%
	$20,001+	$20,001+	5.20%
	$25,001+	$25,001+	5.50%
	$60,000+	$60,000+	6.60%
District of Columbia	$0+	$0+	4.0%
	$10,001+	$10,001+	6.0%
	$40,001+	$40,001+	6.50%
	$60,001+	$60,001+	8.50%
	$350,001+	$350,001+	8.75%
	$1,000,000+	$1,000,000+	8.95%
Florida	$0+	$0+	0%
Georgia	$0	$0+	1.0%
	$751+	$1,001+	2.0%
	$2,251+	$3,001+	3.0%
	$3,751+	$5,001+	4.0%
	$5,251+	$7,001+	5.0%
	$7,000+	$10,000+	5.5%
Hawaii	$0+	$0+	1.40%
	$2,401	$4,801+	3.20%
	$4,801+	$9,601+	5.50%
	$9,601+	$19,201+	6.40%
	$14,401+	$28,801+	6.80%
	$19,201+	$38,401+	7.20%
	$24,001+	$48,001+	7.60%
	$36,001+	$72,001+	7.90%
	$48,001+	$96,001+	8.25%
	$150,001+	$300,001+	9.00%
	$175,001+	$350,001+	10.00%
	$200,000+	$400,000+	11.00%
Idaho	$0+	$0+	1.125%
	$1,568+	$3,136+	3.125%
	$3,136+	$6,272+	3.625%
	$4,704+	$9,408+	4.625%
	$6,272+	$12,544+	5.625%
	$7,840+	$15,680+	6.625%
	$11,760+	$23,520+	6.925%
Illinois	$0+	$0+	4.95%
Indiana	$0+	$0+	3.23%

State	Tax Bracket (Single)	Tax Bracket (Married)	Marginal Tax Rate
Iowa	$0+	$0+	0.33%
	$1,676+	$1,676+	0.67%
	$3,352+	$3,352+	2.25%
	$6,704+	$6,704+	4.14%
	$15,084+	$15,084+	5.63%
	$25,140+	$25,140+	5.96%
	$33,520+	$33,520+	6.25%
	$50,280+	$50,280+	7.44%
	$75,420+	$75,420+	8.53%
Kansas	$0+	$0+	3.10%
	$15,001+	$30,001+	5.25%
	$30,000+	$60,000+	5.70%
Kentucky	$0+	$0+	5.0%
Louisiana	$0+	$0+	2.0%
	$12,501+	$25,001+	4.0%
	$50,000+	$100,000+	6.0%
Maine	$0+	$0+	5.80%
	$22,450+	$44,950+	6.75%
	$53,150+	$106,350+	7.15%
Maryland	$0+	$0+	2.00%
	$1,001+	$1,001+	3.00%
	$2,001+	$2,001+	4.00%
	$3,001+	$3,001+	4.75%
	$100,001+	$150,001+	5.00%
	$125,001+	$175,001+	5.25%
	$150,001+	$225,001+	5.50%
	$250,000+	$300,000+	5.75%
Massachusetts	$0+	$0+	5.0%
Michigan	$0+	$0+	4.25%
Minnesota	$0+	$0+	5.35%
	$27,230+	$39,810+	7.05%
	$89,440+	$158,140+	7.85%
	$166,040+	$276,200+	9.85%
Mississippi	$4,000+	$4,000+	3.0%
	$5,001+	$5,001+	4.0%
	$10,000+	$10,000+	5.0%
Missouri	$107+	$107+	1.5%
	$1,073+	$1,073+	2.0%
	$2,146+	$2,146+	2.5%
	$3,219+	$3,219+	3.0%
	$4,292+	$4,292+	3.5%
	$5,365+	$5,365+	4.0%
	$6,438+	$6,438+	4.5%
	$7,511+	$7,511+	5.0%
	$8,584+	$8,584+	5.4%

State	Tax Bracket (Single)	Tax Bracket (Married)	Marginal Tax Rate
Montana	$0+	$0+	1.0%
	$3,100+	$3,100+	2.0%
	$5,500+	$5,500+	3.0%
	$8,400+	$8,400+	4.0%
	$11,300+	$11,300+	5.0%
	$14,500+	$14,500+	6.0%
	$18,700+	$18,700+	6.9%
Nebraska	$0+	$0+	2.46%
	$3,340+	$6,660+	3.51%
	$19,990+	$39,990+	5.01%
	$32,210+	$64,430+	6.84%
Nevada	$0+	$0+	0%
New Hampshire	$0+	$0+	0%
New Jersey	$0+	$0+	1.40%
	$20,001+	$20,001+	1.75%
	$35,001+	$50,001+	3.50%s/2.45%m
	$40,001+	$70,001+	5.525%s/3.50%m
	$75,001+	$80,001+	6.37%s/5.525%m
	$500,001+	$150,001+	8.97%s/6.37%m
	$1,000,001+	$500,001+	10.75%s/8.97%m
		$5,000,000+	10.75%
New Mexico	$0+	$0+	1.70%
	$5,501+	$8,001+	3.20%
	$11,001+	$16,001+	4.70%
	$16,000+	$24,000+	4.90%
New York	$0+	$0+	4.00%
	$8,501+	$17,151+	4.50%
	$11,701+	$23,601+	5.25%
	$13,901+	$27,901+	5.90%
	$21,401+	$43,001+	6.09%
	$80,651+	$161,551+	6.41%
	$215,401+	$323,201+	6.85%
	$1,077,550+	$2,155,350+	8.82%
North Carolina	$0+	$0+	5.25%
North Dakota	$0+	$0+	1.10%
	$40,125+	$67,050+	2.04%
	$97,150+	$161,950+	2.27%
	$202,650+	$246,700+	2.64%
	$440,600+	$440,600+	2.90%
Ohio	$22,151+	$22,151+	2.850%
	$44,251+	$44,251+	3.326%
	$88,451+	$88,451+	3.802%
	$110,651+	$110,651+	4.413%
	$221,300+	$221,300+	4.797%

State	Tax Bracket (Single)	Tax Bracket (Married)	Marginal Tax Rate
Oklahoma	$0+	$0+	0.5%
	$1,001+	$2,001+	1.0%
	$2,501+	$5,001+	2.0%
	$3,751+	$7,501+	3.0%
	$4,901+	$9,801+	4.0%
	$7,200+	$12,200+	5.0%
Oregon	$0+	$0+	4.75%
	$3,650+	$7,300+	6.75%
	$9,200+	$18,400+	8.75%
	$125,000+	$250,000+	9.9%
Pennsylvania	$0+	$0+	3.07%
Rhode Island	$0+	$0+	3.75%
	$66,200+	$66,200+	4.75%
	$150,550+	$150,550+	5.99%
South Carolina	$0+	$0+	0%
	$3,070+	$3,070+	3.0%
	$6,150+	$6,150+	4.0%
	$9,230+	$9,230+	5.0%
	$12,310+	$12,310+	6.0%
	$15,400+	$15,400+	7.0%
South Dakota	$0+	$0+	0%
Tennessee	$0+	$0+	0%
Texas	$0+	$0+	0%
Utah	$0+	$0+	4.95%
Vermont	$0+	$0+	3.35%
	$40,351+	$67,451+	6.60%
	$97,801+	$163,001+	7.60%
	$204,000+	$248,350+	8.75%
Virginia	$0+	$0+	2.0%
	$3,001+	$3,001+	3.0%
	$5,001+	$5,001+	5.0%
	$17,000+	$17,000+	5.75%
Washington	$0+	$0+	0%
West Virginia	$0+	$0+	3.0%
	$10,000+	$10,000+	4.0%
	$25,000+	$25,000+	4.5%
	$40,000+	$40,000+	6.0%
	$60,000+	$60,000+	6.5%
Wisconsin	$0+	$0+	3.54%
	$12,120+	$16,160+	4.65%
	$24,250+	$32,330+	6.27%
	$266,930+	$355,910+	7.65%
Wyoming	$0+	$0+	0%

(Source: Tax Foundation.org with a URL of https://files.taxfoundation.org/20210722161949/State-Individual-Income-Tax-Rates-and-Brackets-for-2021..pdf)

Appendix E

State Revenue or Labor Department Information

The following are state revenue or labor offices. Where possible, the email address is included. Many states have an Internet email submission form or live chat availability to answer questions.

Alabama

Alabama Department of Labor
50 North Ripley Street
P.O. Box 303500
Montgomery, AL 36104
334-223-7450
www.labor.alabama.gov

Alaska

Department of Labor and Workforce Development
P.O. Box 110400
Juneau, AK 99811-1149
907-465-4842
www.labor.alaska.gov

Arizona

Department of Labor, Industrial Commission
800 West Washington Street
Phoenix, AZ 85007
602-542-4515
www.azica.gov/divisions/labor-department

Arkansas

Department of Labor, Wage and Hour Section
10421 West Markham
Little Rock, AR 72205
501-682-4500
www.portal.arkansas.gov/agency/department-of-labor-and-licensing/arkansas-department-of-labor/labor-standards-division/service/wage-hour-division/

California

Labor and Workforce Development Agency
1515 Clay Street, Room 401
Oakland, CA 94612
510-285-2118
www.labor.ca.gov/

Colorado

Department of Labor and Employment
633 17th Street
Suite 600
Denver, CO 80202-3660
303-318-8441
www.cdle.colorado.gov/

Connecticut

Division of Wage and Workplace
Standards

200 Folly Brook Road

Wethersfield, CT 06109

860-263-6790

www.ctdol.state.ct.us/wgwkstnd/

Delaware

Division of Industrial Affairs

4425 North Market Street, 4th Floor

Wilmington, DE 19802

302-761-8200

www.labor.delaware.gov/divisions/
industrial-affairs/

District of Columbia

Department of Employment
Services

4058 Minnesota Avenue, N.E.

Washington, DC 20019

202-671-1880

www.does.dc.gov/

Florida

Department of Economic
Opportunity

107 East Madison St.

Caldwell Building

Tallahassee, FL 32399-4120

850-245-7105

www.floridajobs.org

Georgia

Department of Labor

148 Andrew Young International
Blvd., N.E.

Suite 600

Atlanta, GA 30303-1751

404-232-3515

www.dol.georgia.gov

Hawaii

Department of Labor and Industrial
Relations

830 Punchbowl Street, Room 340

Honolulu, HI 96813

808-586-8777

www.labor.hawaii.gov

Idaho

Wage and Hour Bureau

317 West Main Street

Boise, ID 83735

208-332-3579

www.labor.idaho.gov

Illinois

Department of Labor Fair Labor
Standards Division

160 North La Salle, Suite C-1300

Chicago, IL 60601-3150

312-793-2800

www2.illinois.gov/idol/Laws-Rules/
FLS

Indiana

Department of Labor Wage and
Hour Division

402 West Washington Street, Room
W195

Indianapolis, IN 46204

317-232-2655

www.in.gov/dol/wagehour.htm

Iowa

Iowa Workforce Development

150 Des Moines Street

Des Moines, IA 50309-1836

515-725-5619

www.iowaworkforcedevelopment.
gov/

Kansas

Department of Labor Office of
Employment Standards

401 SW Topeka Boulevard

Topeka, KS 66603-3182

785-296-5000, ext. 1068

www.dol.ks.gov/

Kentucky

Labor Cabinet Department of
Workplace Standards

1047 U.S. Highway 127 South,
Suite 4

Frankfort, KY 40601-4381

502-564-3534

www.labor.ky.gov/standards

Louisiana

Workforce Commission

1001 North 23rd Street

P.O. Box 94094

Baton Rouge, LA 70802-3338

225-342-3111

www.laworks.net/

Maine

Department of Labor Bureau of Labor Standards

45 State House Station

Augusta, ME 04333-0045

207-623-7900

www.maine.gov/labor/bls/

Maryland

Department of Labor, Licensing and Regulation

1100 North Eutaw Street, Room 607

Baltimore, MD 21201

410-767-2357

www.dllr.state.md.us/

Massachusetts

Executive Office of Labor and Workforce

19 Staniford Street, 2nd Floor

Boston, MA 02114-2502

617-727-3465

www.mass.gov/orgs/executive-office-of-labor-and-workforce-development

Michigan

Department of Labor and Economic Opportunity

P.O. Box 30476

Lansing, MI 48909-7976

517-284-5070

www.michigan.gov/leo/

Minnesota

Department of Labor and Industry

443 Lafayette Road, North

St. Paul, MN 55155-4306

651-284-5070

www.dli.mn.gov/

Mississippi

Department of Employment Security

1235 Echelon Parkway

P.O. Box 1699

Jackson, MS 39215-1699

601-321-6000

www.mdes.ms.gov

Missouri

Department of Labor and Industrial Relations

Beck Building

1805 Prospect Avenue, Room 205

P.O. Box 449

Jefferson City, MO 65102-0449

573-751-3403

www.labor.mo.gov

Montana

Department of Labor and Industry

1805 Prospect Avenue

P.O. Box 201503

Helena, MT 59620-1503

406-444-6543

www.dli.mt.gov/

Nebraska

Nebraska Workforce Development

301 Centennial Mall South

PO Box 95024

Lincoln, NE 68509-5024

402-471-2239

www.neworks.nebraska.gov

Nevada

Department of Business and Industry

3300 West Sahara Avenue, Suite 225

Las Vegas, NV 89102

775-486-2650

business.nv.gov/

New Hampshire

Department of Labor Inspection Division

P.O. Box 2076

Concord, NH 03302-2076

603-271-3176

www.nh.gov/labor/inspection

New Jersey

Department of Labor and
Workforce Development
P.O. Box 389
Trenton, NJ 08625-0389
609-292-2305
www.nj.gov/labor

New Mexico

Department of Workforce Solutions
Labor Relations Division
401 Broadway Boulevard NE
P.O. Box 1928
Albuquerque, NM 87102
505-841-4400
www.dws.state.nm.us/en-us/Labor-
Relations/Labor-Information/
Wage-and-Hour

New York

Department of Labor Division of
Labor Standards
State Office Campus, Building 12,
Room 266B
Albany, NY 12240
518-457-9000
www.labor.ny.gov/
workerprotection/laborstandards

North Carolina

Department of Labor Wage and
Hour Bureau
1101 Mail Service Center
Raleigh, NC 27699-1101
919-807-2796
www.labor.nc.gov/

North Dakota

Department of Labor and Human
Rights
600 East Boulevard Avenue,
Department 406
Bismarck, ND 58505-0340
701-328-2660
www.nd.gov/labor

Ohio

Ohio Department of
Commerce
6606 Tussing Road
P.O. Box 4009
Reynoldsburg, OH 43068-9009
614-644-2239
www.com.ohio.gov/

Oklahoma

Department of Labor Employment
Standards Division
3017 N. Stiles, suite 100
Oklahoma City, OK 73105
405-521-6598
www.ok.gov/odol/
Employment_Issues/
Wage_and_Hour

Oregon

Bureau of Labor and Industries
800 NE Oregon Street
Portland, OR 97232
971-673-0761
www.oregon.gov/BOLI

Pennsylvania

Department of Labor
and Industry
Labor and Industry Building,
room 1700
651 Boas Street
Harrisburg, PA 17120
717-787-1064
www.dli.pa.gov/

Rhode Island

Department of Labor
and Training
Central General Complex
1511 Pontiac Avenue
Cranston, RI 02920
401-462-8550
www.dlt.ri.gov/

South Carolina

Department of Labor, Licensing and Regulation
110 Centerview Drive
Columbia, SC 29210
803-896-7756
www.llr.sc.gov/

South Dakota

Department of Labor and Regulation
123 West Missouri Avenue
Pierre, SD 57501-4505
605-773-3681
www.dlr.sd.gov

Tennessee

Tennessee Department of Labor and Workforce Development
220 French Landing Drive
Nashville, TN 37243
844-224-5818
www.tn.gov/workforce

Texas

Texas Workforce Commission Labor Law Department
111 East 15th Street, Room 514
Austin, TX 78778-0001
512-475-2670
www.twc.texas.gov

Utah

Labor Commission
160 East 300 South, 3rd Floor
P.O. Box 146640
Salt Lake City, UT 84114-6640
801-530-6801
www.laborcommission.utah.gov

Vermont

Department of Labor Wage and Hour Program
63 Pearl Street
Burlington, VT 05401-4331
802-951-4083
www.labor.vermont.gov

Virginia

Department of Labor and Industry
Main Street Centre
600 East Main Street, Suite 207
Richmond, VA 23219-4101
804-371-2327
www.virginia.gov/agencies/department-of-labor-and-industry

Washington

Department of Labor and Industries
P.O. Box 44400
Olympia, WA 98504-4000
360-902-5316
www.lni.wa.gov/

West Virginia

Division of Labor Wage and Hour Section
1900 Kanawha Boulevard East
State Capitol Complex Building 3, Room 200
Charleston, WV 25305
304-558-7890
www.labor.wv.gov/Wage-Hour

Wisconsin

Department of Workforce Development
201 East Washington Avenue, Room A100
P.O. Box 8928
Madison, WI 53707-8928
608-266-6860
www.dwd.wisconsin.gov/

Wyoming

Department of Workforce Services
5221 Yellowstone Blvd.
Cheyenne, WY 82002
307-777-7261
www.wyomingworkforce.org

Appendix F

Payroll Certification Information

Payroll certification examinations are available to document mastery of payroll accounting topics. The National Association of Certified Professional Bookkeepers (NACPB), the American Institute of Professional Bookkeepers (AIPB), and the American Payroll Association (APA) each offer certification exams. Contact details for each examination are at the end of this appendix.

Correlation of Certification Exam Topics and Specific Learning Objectives

The following table contains information about the topics covered by each payroll certification and the location of that information in this text.

Payroll Certification Exam Topics	Learning Objective
401(k) plans	4-2, 4-5
Account classification	7-2, 7-3
Accounting terminology	7-2
Additional Medicare tax—highly compensated employees	1-2, 5-3
Advances and overpayments	5-5
Affordable Care Act Form 1095	1-2
Benefits costs and benchmarking	6-6, 7-6
Bonuses and commissions	3-2, 3-6
Cafeteria (Section 125) plans	4-2
Calculation of FICA taxes (Social Security and Medicare): Employee	5-3
Calculation of FICA taxes (Social Security and Medicare): Employer	6-1, 6-3
Calculation of involuntary (mandated) deductions	4-5, 5-5
Communication with IRS and SSA	2-2, 4-6
Data privacy	1-4
Data retention	2-5
Deceased employee pay	3-7
De minimis fringe benefits	4-1, 4-3
Deferred compensation	3-6
Docking exempt employee pay	3-2
Employee benefits	4-1, 4-2

Payroll Certification Exam Topics	Learning Objective
Employee classification	1-6
Employee vs. independent contractor	1-2, 1-6, 2-2
Employer-provided benefits: Cafeteria plan, awards, personal use of company vehicle, group-term life insurance	4-2, 4-3, 4-4
Employment forms	2-2
Enterprise test	3-1
Exempt vs. nonexempt	1-6
Expatriate taxation	2-2
Fair Labor Standards Act	1-2
Federal forms	1-4, 6-3
Federal income tax calculation: Taxable wages, tax computation	5-2
Fiduciary responsibility	7-5
FLSA provisions	1-2
Form W-4: Additional withholding, employee changes	2-2
Form 843 treatment	6-3
Fringe benefits	4-1, 4-3, 4-4
FUTA, including credit reduction states	5-3
General Journal entries	7-3
General Ledger entries	7-4
Global payroll	2-2
Gross pay calculation	3-2, 3-3, 3-4, 3-5, 3-6
Gross-up of compensation	5-1
Identifying payroll job requirements	3-2, 3-4, 6-1, 6-2, 7-2
Internal controls	2-4
IRS regulations	5-2, 6-1, 6-2
Jury duty	3-7
Leased employees	2-3
Legislation affecting payroll, contract acts	1-1, 1-2
Multiple worksite reporting	1-4, 1-5, 2-2
Net pay calculations	5-1, 5-2, 5-3, 5-4, 5-5
New hire documentation	2-2
Nonproductive time	3-7
Nonqualified deferred compensation	3-7
Nonqualified plans	4-2, 4-3
Nontaxable benefits	4-3
On-premises benefits: Athletic facilities, child care, etc.	4-3
Overtime premium calculation: FLSA, weighted average, commission, salary, piece-rate	3-4
Pay calculation: Regular, tipped, time worked, other pay situations	3-2, 3-3, 3-5, 3-6
Payment methods: Cash, check, direct deposit, paycard	5-6
Payroll account reconciliation	7-4, 7-6
Payroll audit	2-5, 7-6
Payroll in the United States: Employee documentation	2-2
Payroll practices, confidentiality	1-4, 1-5, 2-3
Payroll systems	1-4, 1-5, 7-5
Payroll: Process and challenges	1-4, 1-5, 7-5, 7-6
Payroll technology	1-4, 1-5, 5-6
Payroll trending	7-6
Penalties	6-4
Pension payments and withholding	4-1, 4-6
Planning and organizing payroll operations	1-4, 1-5, 2-1

Payroll Certification Exam Topics	Learning Objective
Qualified employee discounts	4-3, 4-4
Qualified moving expenses	4-3, 4-4
Reconciling wages and taxes	6-3
Recording accruals and reversals	7-4, 7-5
Recordkeeping requirements, including retention	2-3, 2-4, 2-5
Repaying employer loans	5-5
Resident nonalien	2-2
Retirement plans: Qualified	4-2
Retroactive pay	3-7
State wage and hour laws	3-1
State withholding certificates	2-2
Stock compensation	3-2, 3-6
Tax deposits: Requirements, lookback period, deposits	6-2, 6-3
Taxable tips	6-3
Temporary employees	2-3
Time management	1-4, 1-5
Trends: Technology	1-4, 1-5
Unemployment and disability taxes	6-1, 6-3
Voluntary deductions/other deductions calculations computation	4-5, 4-6
Withholding taxes, FICA taxes	5-2, 5-3, 5-4

Contact Information for Payroll Certifications

National Association of Certified Professional Bookkeepers

844-249-3551

info@certifiedpublicbookkeeper.org

http://certifiedpublicbookkeeper.org/certification.cfm

Requirement

- Successful completion of the NACPB Payroll Certification Exam.

American Institute of Professional Bookkeepers

800-622-0121

info@aipb.org

https://aipb.org/certification-program/

Requirements

- A minimum of two years' professional full-time (or part-time equivalent) experience, which may be obtained either before or after the exam.
- Successful completion of a two-part exam.
- Signed acknowledgment of the AIPB's Code of Ethics.

American Payroll Association

(210) 224-6406

http://www.americanpayroll.org/certification

Two levels of payroll certification are available from the American Payroll Association: Certified Payroll Professional (CPP) and Fundamental Payroll Certification (FPC). The following are the criteria for eligibility for each certification available from the APA.

Certified Payroll Professional

The Certification Board of the American Payroll Association (APA) requires that payroll professionals fulfill **ONE** of the following criteria before they take the Certified Payroll Professional Examination.

Criteria 1

The payroll professional has been practicing a total of three (3) years out of the five (5) years preceding the date of the examination. The practice of payroll is defined as direct or related involvement in at least one of the following:

- Payroll production, payroll reporting, and payroll accounting.
- Payroll systems and payroll taxation.
- Payroll administration.
- Payroll education/consulting.

Criteria 2

Before a candidate takes the examination, the payroll professional has been employed in the practice of payroll as defined in Criteria 1 for at least the past 24 months *and* has completed within the last 24 months ALL of the following courses within **ONE** of the following three options offered by the APA:

Option 1

- Payroll Practice Essentials (three-day course: live or virtual) and
- Intermediate Payroll Concepts (two-day course: live or virtual) and
- Advanced Payroll Concepts (two-day course: live or virtual) and
- Strategic Payroll Practices (two-day course: live or virtual)

Option 2

- Payroll 101: Foundations of Payroll Certificate Program and
- Payroll 201: The Payroll Administration Certificate Program

Option 3
- Certified Payroll Professional Boot Camp

Criteria 3

Before a candidate takes the examination, the payroll professional has been employed in the practice of payroll as defined in Criteria 1 for at least the past 18 months, has **obtained** the **Fundamental Payroll Certification (FPC),** *and* has completed within the past 18 months ALL of the following courses within **ONE** of the following two options offered by the APA:

Option 1

- Intermediate Payroll Concepts (two-day course: live or virtual) and
- Advanced Payroll Concepts (two-day course: live or virtual) and
- Strategic Payroll Practices (two-day course: live or virtual)

Option 2
- Payroll 201: The Payroll Administration Certificate Program

Fundamental Payroll Certification (FPC)   The Fundamental Payroll Certification (FPC) is open to all those who wish to demonstrate a baseline of payroll competency. The FPC is designed for all of the following:

- Entry-level payroll professionals.
- Sales professionals/consultants serving the payroll industry.
- Systems analysts/engineers writing payroll programs.
- Payroll Service Bureau client representatives.

APA membership and payroll experience are not required to take the FPC examination.

Glossary

401(k): A defined contribution plan in which employees may contribute either a specific amount or a percentage of their gross pay on a pre-tax or post-tax basis through payroll deductions.

403(b): A retirement plan designed for employees of certain nonprofit organizations.

457: A retirement plan offered by governmental and certain nongovernmental employers in which contributions are deducted on a pre-tax basis.

A

Accrual: An accounting method in which revenues and expenses are recorded when they occur, not necessarily when any cash is exchanged.

Additional Medicare tax: An additional 0.9% Medicare tax levied upon employees who earn in excess of a certain amount per year, as mandated by the Affordable Care Act.

Adjusting entries: Journal entries created at the end of an accounting period to allocate income and expenses to the proper accounts.

Affordable Care Act of 2010 (ACA): Mandated health care coverage for all Americans regardless of employment status.

Age Discrimination in Employment Act (ADEA): The Age Discrimination in Employment Act of 1967 that protects workers over age 40 from age-based discrimination.

Allocation: The storing of costs in one account and then dividing the costs based on a quantifiable activity.

American Recovery and Reinvestment Act of 2009 (ARRA): Legislation designed to stimulate the economy by creating jobs and prescribing transparency by employers.

American Rescue Plan Act (ARPA): Legislation that prevented the expiration of tax cuts that would have affected employees.

American Taxpayer Relief Act of 2012 (ATRA): Legislation that prevented the expirations of tax cuts that would have affected employees.

Americans with Disabilities Act Amendments Act of 2008 (ADAAA): Legislation that extended the definition of disabilities to protect workers from discrimination in the workplace.

Annual depositor: Employers who have an annual payroll tax liability of less than $1,000 during the look back period and are notified in writing by the IRS that they submit Form 944 and remit taxes on an annual basis.

Annual schedule depositors: Employers who have an annual payroll tax liability of less than $1,000 during the lookback period and are notified in writing by the IRS that they submit Form 944 and remit taxes on an annual basis.

Annual total compensation report: A list of all compensation that an employee earns per year, including (but not limited to) salary, commissions, bonuses, and all fringe benefits; examples include health insurance, employer contributions to the employee's retirement plan, life insurance, and tuition reimbursement.

Asset: An item of value that a business uses in the course of its operations and from which it expects future economic benefit.

Automated Clearing House (ACH): The electronic network of financial institutions in the United States through which monetary transactions are transmitted in batches.

B

Balance sheet: A financial statement that lists the totals in the assets, liabilities, and owners' equity accounts of a firm for a specific date.

Benefit analysis: A calculation of the costs and benefits of a company, department, project, or employee.

Biweekly payroll: A pay frequency in which employees are paid 26 times per year.

Blockchain: A digital means of transferring electronic currency using small amounts of data transmitted via multiple computers.

C

Cafeteria plan: A benefit plan pursuant to Section 125 of the Internal Revenue Code that allows employees to designate specific amounts to be deducted from their payroll to pay for health and child care expenses on a pre-tax basis.

Cents-per-mile rule: A method used to determine the value of a company car fringe benefit based on a fixed amount times the number of miles driven for personal purposes.

Certified payroll: A report mandated for certain federal government contracts that verifies the accuracy of labor expenses incurred during completion of contract-related activities.

Charitable contribution: A payroll deduction in which an employee designates a specific amount of gross pay to be paid to community, religious, educational, or another IRS-designated charitable organization.

Circular E: See *Publication 15.*

Civil Rights Act of 1964: Federal legislation that protects employees from discrimination based on race, color, religion, sex, or national origin.

Civil Rights Act of 1991: Federal law that instituted monetary penalties for companies found guilty of discrimination as described under the Civil Rights Act of 1964.

COBRA: The Consolidated Omnibus Budget Reconciliation Act of 1985, which provided continuance of employee medical benefits after separation from the company.

Combination pay: Employee compensation that reflects two or more discrete pay bases during the same pay period.

Commission: Employee compensation paid upon completion of a task, often pertaining to sales-based activities.

Commuting rule: A valuation method used to determine the personal use of a company vehicle based on the number of miles driven for commuting to and from work.

Compensation: The total amount of cash and noncash salary/wages and benefits that an employee receives in return for working for a company.

Compensatory (comp) time: Paid time off granted to employees instead of paid overtime.

Consolidated Appropriations Act of 2018: Signed into law in March 2018, this act increased the funding for the E-Verify program, which is an Internet-based system that offers employers instant verification of an employee's eligibility to work in the United States. It is important to note that the E-Verify program does not replace the need for the completion of Form I-9 upon employee hire because it is a voluntary service.

Consumer Credit Protection Act (CCPA): Federal law that pertains to the percentage of wage garnishment that may be withheld from employee pay to satisfy legal obligations.

Copeland Anti-Kickback Act: Federal legislation enacted in 1934 that prohibits a federal contractor or subcontractor from inducing an employee to forgo a portion of the wages guaranteed by the contract.

Coronavirus Aid, Relief and Economic Stimulus (CARES) Act of 2020: Provided economic support and payroll tax relief during the Sars Cov-2 (COVID-19) pandemic to encourage employers to retain their employees and tax relief for businesses.

Credit: The right side of the T-account.

Cryptocurrency: A form of currency that is digitally encrypted and transmitted.

Current Tax Payment Act (CTPA) of 1943: Federal law enacted in 1943 that required employers to submit a timely remittance to the government of any taxes withheld from employee pay.

D

Daily payroll: A pay frequency in which employees are paid each business day.

Davis–Bacon Act of 1931: Federal legislation enacted in 1931 that requires federal contractors to pay employees an amount commensurate with the prevailing local wage.

De minimis: A benefit with a very small monetary value that is deemed impractical in terms of tracking using an accounting system.

Debit: The left side of the T-account.

Defense of Marriage Act of 1996 (DOMA): Legislation, which was repealed in 2013, that prevented same-sex marriages and related employment benefits.

Defined benefit: A company-sponsored pension plan that uses the employee's salary and length of service to compute the amount of the benefit.

Defined contribution: A retirement plan to which the employee, and sometimes the employer, makes a regular contribution.

Departmental classification: The division of payroll-related costs by employee function or organizational department.

Direct deposit: The electronic transmission of employee wages from the employer to the employee's account at a financial institution.

Disposable income: The amount of employee wages remaining after withholding federal, state, and local taxes.

Document destruction: The act of destroying documents that contain sensitive payroll and employee information.

Draw: A loan against future earnings that employees will repay from commissions.

Due care: The caution that a reasonable person would exercise to avoid being charged with negligence.

E

E-verify: An internet-based system that allows employers to verify an employee's legal eligibility to work inside the United States by checking Social Security and Department of Homeland Security databases electronically. It does not replace the legal requirement to file the I-9.

Eight and Eighty (8 and 80): A two-week, 80-hour pay period used to determine overtime for employees who work for hospitals and emergency providers.

Electronic Federal Tax Payment System (EFTPS): The Electronic Federal Tax Payment System, a free tax payment service provided for use for employers in the United States.

Employee Retirement Income Security Act (ERISA): Legislation provided protection for employees' retirement savings, preventing employers from using employee savings to satisfy business expenses.

Employer Identification Number (EIN): A number assigned to employers by the IRS for tax reporting.

Enterprise Coverage: Firms explicitly covered under FLSA.

Equal Employment Opportunity Commission (EEOC): An entity of the federal government created as part of the Civil Rights Act of 1984, the EEOC enforces civil rights provisions in the workplace.

Equal Pay Act of 1963: Federal legislation mandating that males and females receive equal compensation for comparable work.

Escheatment: The transfer of personal property to the employee's state of residence when no legal owner claims the property.

ESOP: Employee Stock Ownership Plan.

Ethics: An individual's definition of right and wrong.

Exempt: An employee who is not subject to the overtime provisions of the Fair Labor Standards Act.

Expense: The cost of doing business, which may contain both cash and noncash amounts.

F

Fair Labor Standards Act (FLSA): The law established the idea of minimum hourly wage and maximum weekly hours for hourly employees, among other employee-centered items.

Fair market value (FMV): The amount of money that a person would spend to obtain a good or service in an arm's-length transaction.

Family and Medical Leave Act of 1993 (FMLA): Legislation provided protection for employees to take unpaid leave with employer-provided benefits and still retain their original job or a similar one with the same pay rate upon return to work.

Federal income tax: A tax levied by the federal government on individuals.

Federal Insurance Contributions Act of 1935 (FICA): Legislation that provided funding for social welfare benefits including Social Security and Medicare.

Federal Unemployment Tax Act of 1939 (FUTA): Legislation that pays for the federal administration of unemployment laws, which are managed by each state.

FICA tax: The collective term for the combination of Social Security and Medicare taxes.

Fiduciary: A relationship, specifically financial, built on trust between a trustee and a beneficiary.

File maintenance: The application of all transactions, including any necessary modifications, to an employee's file.

File security: The protection of sensitive payroll information by restricting access and securely storing files.

Flexible spending arrangement (FSA): A tax-advantaged employee spending account as designated by the Internal Revenue Code.

Foreign Account Tax Compliance Act (FATCA): Federal law that regulates the income tax withholdings of foreign employees.

Form 940: The Employer's Annual Federal Unemployment Tax Return.

Form 941: The Employer's Quarterly Federal Tax Return.

Form 944: The Employer's Annual Federal Tax Return.

Form SS-8: The form used by the IRS to determine if a worker is an employee or an independent contractor.

Form W-2: Wage and Tax Statement.

Form W-3: Transmittal of Wage and Tax Statements.

Fringe benefit: A company-sponsored benefit that supplements an employee's salary, usually on a noncash basis.

G

Garnishments: A legal procedure for the collection of money owed to a plaintiff through payroll deductions.

General Journal: A chronological record of a firm's financial transactions.

General Ledger: A record of a firm's financial transactions, grouped by account.

General valuation rule (GVR): The method used to determine the value of most fringe benefits using fair market value.

Generally Accepted Accounting Principles (GAAP): A framework relating to accounting practice including rules, procedures, and standards defined by industry professionals and used by U.S. companies.

Gross pay: The amount of wages paid to an employee based on work performed, prior to any deductions for mandatory or voluntary deductions.

H

H-1B visa: A program that allows employers to temporarily hire foreign workers who possess specialized expertise and have earned a bachelor's degree or higher.

Health Insurance Portability and Accountability Act of 1996 (HIPAA): Legislation that protects confidential personal medical records.

Health savings account (HSA): A savings account that provides tax advantages for individuals with health plans that have high deductions via pre-tax payroll deductions.

High-deductible health plan (HDHP): A health care plan with an annual deductible that is at least $1,400 for self-coverage and $2,800 for family coverage; annual out-of-pocket limits are $6,900 for self-coverage and $13,800 for family coverage.

Hiring packet: A package of forms that a firm issues to new employees; examples are Form W-4, Form I-9, and health insurance enrollment.

Hourly: Wage determination based on the number of complete and partial hours during which an employee performs work-related tasks.

Hundredth-hour system: The division of an hour into 100 increments used to compute employee wages as accurately as possible.

I

I-9: The Employment Eligibility Verification form issued by U.S. Citizenship and Immigration Services.

Immigration Reform and Control Act of 1986 (IRCA): Legislation requiring employers to verify the employee's eligibility to work in the United States or to sponsor their ability to work.

Incentive stock options (ISOs): A type of employee compensation in which the employee receives a firm's stock on a tax-advantaged basis.

Income statement: A financial report used to determine a firm's net income by computing the difference between revenues and expenses for a period; also known as the profit and loss statement.

Independence: The ability of an accountant to act professionally without external pressures that would cause a third party to question the integrity of actions and decisions.

Independent contractor: An individual who contracts to do work for a firm using his or her own tools and processes without being subject to direction by a firm's management.

Individual Coverage: FLSA coverage for employees whose firms do not meet the requirements for enterprise coverage.

Integrity: Possessing honesty and high moral principles.

Internal control: A firm's process of maintaining efficiency and effectiveness, work quality, accurate and reliable financial reports, and legal compliance.

IRA: Individual Retirement Account.

L

Labor distribution: The classification of a firm's labor by internally designated classifications.

Labor reports: Reports that contain details about the number of hours worked and the wages paid to employees.

Lease value rule: A method of determining the value of a company car as a fringe benefit using the fair market value and the annual lease as the basis.

Leased employee: A person who provides services for a company subject to the provisions of IRS code section 414(n).

Liability: A financial obligation of the firm arising from revenues received in advance of services or sales or expenses incurred but not paid.

Lilly Ledbetter Fair Pay Act of 2009: Federal law that removed the 180-day statute of limitations in allegations of unfair pay practices.

Living Wage: The minimum amount that a family would need to live comfortably for a normal standard of living.

Local income taxes: Payroll taxes levied by a city or county government.

Lookback period: The time frame used by the IRS to determine the payroll tax deposit schedule for a firm.

M

Mandated deductions: Post-tax payroll deductions ordered by a court of law or otherwise nonvoluntary in nature.

Mandatory deductions: Payroll deductions over which the employee has no control; examples include taxes, garnishments, and certain retirement contributions.

Marketplace: A service provided through the Affordable Care Act of 2010 in which people may shop for and select health care plans.

Medicare tax: A payroll tax mandated to be paid by all employees of a firm to fund the Medicare program.

Minimum wage: The minimum hourly amount that employers may legally pay to employees.

Monthly depositor: A firm that must deposit its Federal Income Tax and FICA payroll withholdings and contributions on a monthly basis, based on the lookback period.

Monthly payroll: A pay frequency in which employees are paid 12 times per year.

N

Net pay: An employee's wages or salary less all mandatory and voluntary deductions.

New hire reporting: A process by which a firm notifies governmental authorities of any new hires shortly after the hire date.

Next business day depositor: A semiweekly schedule depositor whose payroll tax liabilities exceed $100,000 for any pay period.

Nonexempt: An employee who is subject to all overtime provisions of the Fair Labor Standards Act; generally, an hourly employee.

O

Objectivity: Making decisions that are free from bias or subjectivity.

Occupational Safety and Health Act (OSHA): The legislation that provided guidance for safe workplace conditions.

Old-Age, Survivors, and Disability Insurance (OASDI): Synonymous with Social Security, this is the original name for the social welfare structure.

On-call time: The nonwork time that an employee is expected to be available for workplace-related emergencies.

Outsourced vendor: A party external to a firm that provides goods or services.

Overtime: Time that an employee works beyond his or her normal working hours.

Owners' equity: The financial investment and any accumulated profits or losses of the owner of a firm.

P

Pay advice: A document detailing employee pay and deductions that either accompanies the paycheck or notifies the employee of the direct deposit of net pay.

Pay period: The recurring period during which a firm collects employee labor data and pays employees in accordance with wage or salary agreements.

Paycard: A debit card, issued to employees, that contains electronically transmitted wages.

Payroll audit: An examination of a firm's payroll records to determine legal compliance.

Payroll register: A payroll register is the payroll accountant's internal tool that helps ensure the accuracy of employee compensation and includes each employee's earnings information for a pay period.

Payroll review: Verification of payroll accuracy for a period.

Payroll tax reports: Reports offering details of the period's tax liability that an employer must file with governmental authorities.

Percentage method: A method used to compute an employee's income tax liability that involves computations based on the employee's wages, marital status, pay frequency, and number of withholdings claimed on Form W-4.

Personal Responsibility and Work Opportunity Reconciliation Act of 1996 (PRWOR): Legislation that provided social welfare relief for a limited time.

Personal Responsibility, Work and Family Promotion Act of 2002: Act that reauthorized PRWOR when it expired.

Piece rate: Employee compensation based on production of unit or completion of an action during a specified time period.

Post-tax deductions: Amounts deducted from employee pay after all income and FICA taxes have been deducted; amounts may be voluntary or court mandated.

Posting: Transferring the details of General Journal entries to the General Ledger accounts.

Premium only plan (POP): A form of cafeteria plan in which employee portions of employer-provided insurance plans may be deducted on a pre-tax basis.

Privacy Act of 1974: Protecting employees by removing personal identifiers from payroll records and restricting access to personnel records.

Professional competence: The continuing capability to perform professional duties with an agreed-upon standard of quality.

Professionalism: A process reflecting the transparency and public accountability of accounting records.

Protecting Americans from Tax Hikes (PATH) Act: An act to prevent tax fraud that extended the Work Opportunity Tax Credit.

Prove: Ensuring that the sum of the rows of the payroll register equals the sum of the columns.

Publication 15: The Employer's Tax Guide published by the Internal Revenue Service; also known as *Circular E*.

Publication 15-B: The IRS Employer's Guide to Fringe Benefits.

Publication 15-T: The Federal Income Tax Withholding Methods.

Q

Qualified plan: A written plan for the issuance of employee achievement awards that does not favor highly compensated employees.

Quarter-hour system: The division of an hour into 15-minute increments as a means of computing hourly work.

Quarterly depositors: Monthly schedule depositors who have a payroll tax liability of less than $2,500 during the preceding or current quarter may remit the payroll tax liability when filing Form 941.

R

Regulation E: Federal legislation protecting consumers who use electronic funds transfer to access their net pay.

Remit: To send money in payment of an obligation.

Resignation: Voluntary termination of employment, usually initiated by the employee.

Reversal: A general journal entry recorded at the start of the following month to undo the accruals recorded in the prior month.

Review process: Examination and analysis of accounting records to ensure accuracy and completeness.

Rule: The accounting practice in which the final totals of financial reports are double-underlined.

S

Salary: A fixed amount paid to an employee on a regular basis, often expressed in annual terms.

Sarbanes–Oxley Act of 2002 (SOX): Public law 107-204, concerning publicly owned companies and auditing firms to ensure appropriate internal controls and the integrity of financial statements.

Schedule B: The report of tax liability for semiweekly depositors.

Semimonthly payroll: The payroll frequency in which employees are paid 24 times per year.

Semiweekly schedule depositor: A firm that must deposit its federal income tax and FICA payroll withholdings and contributions within three days of the pay date, based on the lookback period.

SEP: A Simplified Employee Pension individual retirement account.

Separation of duties: An internal control method in which payroll duties are spread among two or more employees.

Setting Every Community Up for Retirement Enhancement (SECURE) Act: An Act that incentivizes small employers to offer retirement plans, either alone or collectively with other small employers, to improve retirement security for U.S. workers.

SIMPLE 401(k): A retirement plan for employees of companies that employ 100 or fewer workers. An annual investment limit of $11,500 exists for this type of retirement plan.

SIMPLE: The Savings Incentive Match Plan for Employees.

Sixteenth Amendment to the U.S. Constitution: Allowed the United States government to levy and collect income taxes on individuals.

Sleep time: Employees who are required to be on duty for 24 hours or more may be allowed up to 5 hours of sleep without a reduction in pay.

Social Security Act (SSA): An act that was passed to promote social welfare for old-age workers and surviving families of workers who had been disabled or deceased in the course of their employment.

Social Security tax: A tax paid by both employers and employees that is used to fund the Social Security program.

SOX: The Sarbanes–Oxley Act of 2002. Public law 107-204, concerning publicly owned companies and auditing firms to ensure appropriate internal controls and the integrity of financial statements.

Special accounting rule: Employers may elect to treat employee amounts for noncash fringe benefits used during November and December as not being paid until January of the following year; employees must be notified in writing by January 31 of the following year if the special accounting rule was used.

State income taxes: Income taxes levied by a state government on employee payroll.

State Unemployment Tax Act of 1939 (SUTA): Employment tax requiring employers to provide monetary benefits for workers who are displaced through no fault of their own.

Statutory deductions: Payroll deductions mandated by law.

Statutory employee: A special class of employees who run their own business but must be treated as employees for tax reasons.

T

Tax Cuts and Jobs Act: An act to provide a budget resolution that represented changes to individual and business tax rates.

Tax remittance: The payment of a firm's payroll tax liability.

Temporary employee: A worker who is employed by a temporary staffing agency and works under the direction of the agency on a temporary basis for different companies.

Termination: Cessation of employment with a firm initiated by the employer

The Americans with Disabilities Act of 1990 (ADA): Legislation protecting the anti-discrimination rights of American workers with disabilities as an extension of the Civil Rights Act of 1964.

Time cards: A record of the time worked during a period for an individual employee.

Tip credit: The difference between the tipped employee minimum wage and the federal minimum wage.

Tipped employee: An employee who engages in an occupation in which he or she customarily and regularly receives more than $30 per month in tips.

Tipped wage: The base wage paid to employees who earn the majority of their income through customer tips.

Total: Computing the sum of each row and each column of the payroll register.

Travel time: Time that an employee spends traveling for the employer's benefit.

Trial balance: An internal accounting statement in which the accountant determines that the debits equal the credits for the amounts in the General Ledger.

U

Uniformed Services Employment and Reemployment Rights Act of 1994 (USERRA): Legislation protecting the job rights of employees called to full-time service by the U.S. military.

Union dues: Amounts paid on a regular basis by employees who are required to be part of a union as a condition of their employment.

V

Virtual private network (VPN): A method to provide employees with secured internet connections when working from remote locations.

Voluntary deductions: Amounts that an employee elects to have deducted from his or her paycheck and remitted to a third party; examples include charitable contributions, savings bond purchases, and health club fees.

W

W-4: The Employee Withholding Allowance Certificate.

Wage base: The maximum annual salary that is subject to tax liability, commonly used for Social Security, FUTA, and SUTA taxes.

Wage-bracket method: The use of tax tables located in federal and state publications that facilitate the determination of employee income tax deductions for payroll.

Wait time: The time that an employee is paid to wait on the employer's premises for the benefit of the employer.

Walsh–Healey Public Contracts Act: Legislation enacted in 1936 that required employers working on federal contracts in excess of $10,000 to pay employees the federal minimum wage and follow the overtime provisions of the Fair Labor Standards Act.

Weekly payroll: The payroll frequency in which employees are paid 52 times per year.

Workers' compensation: A mandatory insurance policy paid by employers that provides wage replacement and medical benefits to employees who are injured in the course of their employment.

Index